PARENTAL LOSS OF A CHILD

EDITED BY

THERESE A. RANDO

RESEARCH PRESS COMPANY

2612 NORTH MATTIS AVENUE
CHAMPAIGN, ILLINOIS 61821

Advisory Editor, Frederick H. Kanfer

Copies of this book may be ordered from the publisher at the address given on the title page.

Cover design by Jack W. Davis
Composition by Omegatype

ISBN 0-87822-281-2
Library of Congress Catalog Card Number 86-61549

To my best friend,

Anthony

Contents

Acknowledgments

This book has been an extraordinarily difficult one to complete. Even those individuals with long experience in contributing to the thanatological literature found their respective tasks more painful to accomplish than usual. It was not uncommon for me, as editor, to hear about the great resistance with which numerous authors had to contend. Clearly, this phenomenon echoed the general societal anxiety over confronting the possible loss of one's child.

First, I want to thank each of the contributors for sharing in the commitment to develop this resource, overcoming personal feelings and working diligently to make the dream of this book a reality. The contributors, whether writing specifically as bereaved parents, experts in thanatology, or a combination of the two, have produced a work that will help to provide innumerable bereaved parents with appropriate support in the future. For those who shared their personal experiences of the pain of parental loss of a child, I respectfully offer my heartfelt admiration along with my gratitude.

I must publicly acknowledge my indebtedness to the 54 parents who participated in my original study of bereaved parents in Cleveland, Ohio in 1979. Their willingness to open up their hearts and minds and share the agony of their parental bereavements provided me with the information and experiences that engendered my deep personal commitment to this traditionally misunderstood, ostracized, and underserved population of individuals.

I have been fortunate enough to have received special insight into the experience of child loss through my work with individuals in various self-help groups of bereaved parents. I especially want to recognize Jim and Priscilla Norton from the Greater Providence Chapter of The Compassionate Friends and Art and Ronnie Peterson from the national office of The Compassionate Friends. Through their concerned contributions to others, their children, Linda and Tony, will forever be remembered. In addition, there are countless anonymous others whom I have encountered through psychotherapeutic relationships, education or consulting contacts, or informal channels who also receive my deepest appreciation for teaching me about and sensitizing me to the parental loss of a child. I will always consider myself privileged to have worked with these special individuals who teach so much about life as they struggle with the impact of death.

Particular mention must be made of Ann Wendel of Research Press for her endorsement of this project. She had the faith to take a chance on this attempt to minister to the needs of a unique group of mourners. Those bereaved parents who benefit from this work will owe no small amount of thanks to this exceptional woman. Also, warm appreciation necessarily must go to Patricia Sammann, formerly of Research Press, who continued her superb work of editing this book even after her professional relocation. Her continued interest in and commitment to this work makes her an exception in this field, where too many authors have been detrimentally affected by the comings and goings of their editors. I offer to her my sincere gratitude for all she has done, and to those who will have her as their editor in the future goes my envy of their good fortune to be working with such a professional. In addition, for their conscientious efforts in the marketing of my work, I wish to thank Gail Salyards and Russell Pence of the Research Press marketing department. Mary Wolf deserves mention for her assistance in the latter portions of the book's production.

Ms. Jodi Pollack provided important assistance during part of the preparation of this book, and I am most grateful for her help.

Again, as always, I must specifically underscore the crucial contributions of my administrative assistant, Barbara A. Tremaine-Vargas, in all dimensions of this project. Barbara became the mother of a son, Matthew, during the preparation of this book. There is no doubt in my mind that her unique professional and personal support of me has been a major factor influencing the successful completion of this long-dreamt-of book.

Finally, in classic understatement, the most special acknowledgment of all goes both to my parents, Thomas A. and Letitia G. Rando, for teaching me through their example about what good parents are and to Anthony Viscione, Jr., to whom this book is dedicated, for keeping my parents and their daughter "alive."

Introduction

Parental loss of a child is unlike any other loss. The grief of parents is particularly severe, complicated, and long lasting, with major and unparalleled symptom fluctuations over time. *Parental Loss of a Child* investigates this specific and quite unique case of bereavement.

The field of thanatology has progressed from a general understanding of bereavement to a more specific understanding of the uniqueness of different types of losses and how they are experienced. Early investigations concentrated on describing general reactions to death, usually the death of a male spouse since widows were the easiest population to reach among the bereaved. From this data, plus scattered research on other types of bereavement, those in the field of thanatology identified key issues, general responses, and resulting tasks of mourning that commonly follow the death of a loved one. All of us in the field are indebted to the work of these pioneering researchers and clinicians, who contributed significantly to the current understanding of the processes of grief and mourning and who helped establish the criteria for unresolved grief. However, today significant sociocultural and technological changes along with changing medical realities have created new concerns related to illness, loss, and death. Such changes have affected areas ranging from the individual's psychological, social, physiological, and practical needs to society's economic, legal, and governmental demands, and even to ethical and spiritual considerations. These changes have influenced the direction of the study of bereavement. Instead of primarily investigating the general description of reactions to loss in the first year of bereavement, researchers have turned to examining individual and idiosyncratic responses to loss over time. The focus has shifted from the collective to the individual perspective, already apparent in the increased concerns with issues such as the quality of life and the ethics of health care, in the emphasis on primary prevention, in the greater interest in the grief processes of children and caregivers, in the increased concern about the needs of suicide survivors, and in the heightened attention paid to the negative consequences of bereavement.

At this point in the development of the study of bereavement, we must critically evaluate what we know about general responses to loss in light of the realities of specific bereavements. To revise and hone the general concepts, we will need to make some fine discriminations within the experience of bereavement, recognizing several points. First, no two bereavements are exactly alike. Even if two persons each lose a brother, or if two parents lose the same daughter, the grief responses of these individuals will be unique. Their responses will be based on the complex interaction of a number of psychological factors, such as the personality and roles of the deceased, the nature and meaning of the relationship lost, the personal characteristics of the mourner, and the circumstances of the death, as well as a host of specific social and physiological factors. Without an understanding of and appreciation for these variables and how they affect a particular individual's grief experience, *no* judgments can ever legitimately be made about that person's grief response.

The second major point, which is actually a corollary of the first, is that different types of bereavement experiences will receive different types of treatment interventions. No less an authority than John Bowlby (1980) has asserted that losses are experienced differently depending on the mourner's relationship to the deceased person. For example, just as the affectional bonds of a child to a parent will differ greatly from those of a spouse to a spouse, so will the loss of a child be experienced much differently than the loss of a spouse. For this reason, it is unrealistic to hold similar expectations for bereavements arising from different losses. Since most of our understanding of grief and mourning stems from the analysis of conjugal loss, we must now recognize the need for new clinical and empirical data on other types of bereavement. In addition, we must realize that even those who sustain similar losses will have different grief experiences, depending on the individual variables influencing their idiosyncratic responses. A failure to recognize the differences among bereavement experiences can result in a misapplication of treatment intervention. Research has indicated that treatment approaches must be matched to the types of grief reactions to be treated, with some forms of intervention that are appropriate for one type of bereavement being useless or even harmful to others.

Finally, while it is always dangerous to compare the intensity of different losses (for example, "My loss is worse than yours"), it is equally dangerous *not* to look at the unique dilemmas posed by specific types of losses. We can no longer afford to ignore the distinct needs of different types of bereavement. What a bereaved parent needs to cope with the death of a child will necessarily differ from what a young father of three children whose wife dies will need, which again will be different from what an aged widow will need.

This book encompasses all three points in its investigation of the parental loss of a child—a specific and quite unique case of bereavement. The book includes descriptions of the experiences, needs, issues, and conflicts confronted by parents whose children die and the particular types of treatment interventions appropriate to this type of loss. There is both implicit and explicit recognition that just as all bereavements are not alike, neither are all losses experienced by bereaved parents. The crucial awareness of particular issues in parental bereavement and how they affect a given individual is reflected in those chapters in which different parental bereavement variables are analyzed. These variables include the different effects of a child's death on self, marriage, family, and society; the age of the child; the specific type of death; the particular role of the bereaved; the sex of the bereaved parent; the types of treatment intervention available; and the kinds of professional and psychosocial support required.

The main premise of the book is that the parental loss of a child is unlike any other loss. A number of factors inherent in the experience predispose parents to have difficulty handling their grief, making them likely to be diagnosed as having unresolved grief. This occurs, as is made clear in the book, because general models of mourning actually describe a process that is specifically impeded by the dynamics of the parental loss of a child. The traditional criteria commonly used for identifying and classifying pathological grief are themselves normal components of parental bereavement, and so cannot be used to detect abnormality within this special type of bereavement. Consequently, it is argued that there is a need for a new model of parental mourning that will take into consideration the particular difficulties inherent in mourning the loss of one's child. There also is a need for new criteria to identify pathological bereavement in parental grief.

The purpose of this book is to acquaint professionals in all disciplines with the experience of parental loss of a child. Its goal is to promote more appropriate clinical interventions and therapeutic support for bereaved parents, while at the same time establishing more realistic expectations for coping with this particular loss. It has been written to provide practical information for anyone dealing with any aspect of child loss. The authors are a group of experts who have provided readable and insightful chapters that integrate personal stories with didactic material, resulting in rich clinical information and illustration. They represent professionals, bereaved parents, and those who are both. In recognition of the fact that not all losses are acknowledged, and in order to create as comprehensive a resource as possible for all types of parental loss, some chapters in this book also have been addressed to the special cases of unacknowledged bereavement. Too often the grief resulting from these symbolic, unacknowledged, or unconfirmed deaths fails to be legitimized in our society. As a result, critically needed support and understanding is missing for these particular bereaved parents. This section of the book, it is hoped, will sensitize caregivers to this issue.

The first section of the book deals with overall perspectives on the unique issues of parental loss of a child and the argument that these issues make current conceptualizations of grief and mourning less applicable to parental bereavement. Specific types of child death are addressed in section two, where it becomes clear that different types of child death will leave parents with different treatment needs. Section three covers socially unacknowledged parental bereavements. In section four, the subjective experiences of survivors in different role relationships with the deceased child are addressed. Section five contains specific advice to professionals on treatment for bereaved parents and family members. The final section, section six, consists of descriptions of various organizations and self-help groups that aid bereaved parents.

References

Bowlby, J. (1980). *Attachment and loss: Vol. 3. Loss, sadness and depression.* New York: Basic Books.

Each substance of a grief hath twenty shadows.

—Shakespeare

Section 1

Perspectives on the Parental Loss of a Child

Chapter 1

The Unique Issues and Impact of the Death of a Child

Therese A. Rando

Therese A. Rando, Ph.D., is a clinical psychologist in private practice in North Scituate, Rhode Island. She received her doctorate in Clinical Psychology from the University of Rhode Island and has participated in advanced training in psychotherapy and medical consultation-liaison psychiatry at Case Western Reserve University Medical School and University Hospitals of Cleveland. Presently she is the Clinical Director of Therese A. Rando Associates, Ltd., a multidisciplinary team providing psychotherapy, training, and consultation in the area of mental health, specializing in loss and grief and the psychosocial care of the chronically and terminally ill.

As a consultant to the U.S. Department of Health and Human Services' Hospice Education Program for Nurses, Dr. Rando developed their program for training hospice nurses to cope with loss, grief, and terminal illness. Her research interests focus on mourning, the experience of bereaved parents, and the emotional reactions of rescue workers. She is the Co-investigator in The National Bereavement Study, a longitudinal multidisciplinary research project investigating the processes and effects of grief.

Dr. Rando has lectured nationally and written about grief and death since 1970. She has numerous articles and chapters in print on the clinical aspects of thanatology, and is the author of *Grief, Dying, and Death: Clinical Interventions for Caregivers* and the editor of *Loss and Anticipatory Grief*.

Some of the material in this chapter has been adapted from *Grief, Dying, and Death: Clinical Interventions for Caregivers* by T. A. Rando. Published by Research Press, Champaign, Illinois, 1984. Reprinted by permission.

This chapter is lovingly dedicated to the
memory of Philip Maini, Jr., who profoundly
influenced the life of this author, both ·
personally and professionally.

The loss of a child through death is quite unlike any other loss known. Ask adults what loss they dread most and the majority will state that, while they may worry about the loss of a parent, spouse, sibling, or friend, the loss they fear they could never cope with is the death of their child. Studies have shown that in comparison with other types of bereavement the grief of parents is particularly severe (Clayton, 1980; Clayton, Desmarais, & Winokur, 1968; Sanders, 1979–80; Schwab, Chalmers, Conroy, Farris, & Markush, 1975; Shanfield & Swain, 1984; Singh & Raphael, 1981), complicated and long lasting (Osterweis, Solomon, & Green, 1984), with major and unparalleled symptom fluctuations occurring over time (Fish & Whitty, 1983; Levav, 1982; Rando, 1983). This dubious honor has been accorded parental bereavement because the loss of one's child involves unique issues. It impacts on four different dimensions: the individual parent, the marital dyad, the family system, and society. After a brief discussion of the age of the deceased child as a factor in parental grief, the impact on each of these dimensions will be described.

AGE OF THE DECEASED CHILD

There has been much discussion in the literature of the child's age at death as a determinant of parental grief. Evidence can be provided supporting claims that it is the loss of the young child, the loss of the adolescent child, or the loss of the adult child that is the most difficult bereavement for the parent to experience. Although researchers may argue about it, the clinical evidence suggests that the question is academic and meaningless to bereaved parents. No matter what the age of their child, parents have lost their hopes, dreams, expectations, fantasies, and wishes for that child. They have lost parts of themselves, each other, their family, and their future. This is often forgotten when the child who dies is at one end or the other of the age spectrum, that is, when the death is a miscarriage, stillbirth, or infant death, or the death of an adult child. There exists a curious social phenomenon of denying the significance of child loss unless it lies somewhere between these age points. When the child who dies is an infant, parents are told that they are lucky they did not have a longer time to become attached to it or are reminded that they can have other children. Parental bereavement is often overlooked entirely when the child who dies is an adult. The bereaved parents are usually pushed aside in favor of the spouse and children of the deceased adult. Nevertheless, no matter what the age of the deceased, the parents have still lost their "child" and the loss is just as unnatural as losing a school-age child.

It is true that the age of the child will define some of the specific issues that must be addressed in the parents' grief. This is because the parent-child relationship is colored by the particular developmentally related issues that prevail at a given stage in a child's life. For example, when a child dies during the tumultuous stage of adolescence, and has been actively involved in normal adolescent rebellion and conflict with his parents, his death may be relatively more difficult for the parents to resolve because of the normal ambivalence in the parent-child relationship at that time. This does not mean it is necessarily harder or easier to lose a child of one age as opposed to another; it is merely a different kind of pain (Macon, 1979).

THE INDIVIDUAL PARENT

It is on the individual, personal dimension that the death of the child is experienced initially. This dimension shall be examined first.

The Parent-Child Relationship

From the moment of knowledge of conception, whether a child is desired or not, there are feelings attached to the fantasized image of the child-to-be. These feelings, both positive and negative, expand in number and intensify during the pregnancy. The emotional bonding between parents and child, therefore, occurs well in advance of actual birth. Frequently mothers are more quickly able to form this bond because they carry the child and feel it develop within them. However, many fathers begin to cathect to the image of their fantasized child from the time the news of the pregnancy is delivered. As the fetus develops within the woman, and body changes occur and movements are felt, the father may participate more actively in his bonding with the unborn child.

All relationships may be multiply determined, that is, be heavily influenced by a number of conscious and unconscious factors and conflicts. No relationship has the potential for being as multiply determined as that between parent and child. This is because the child stems from the parents, and their feelings about him are an admixture of feelings about themselves and their significant others, as well as about the individual child himself. These feelings come from the past and present, and extend out into the future.

The child is not only an extension of the parents biologically; he is also an extension of them psychologically. Freud (1914/1957) points out that parental love for a child is actually the parents' own long-since abandoned childish narcissism born again. Unwittingly, parents are in love with themselves as children. This accounts for the parental investment in the child, with its attendant overestimation, positive bias, and determination that he will have things better than his parents. It also means that the child is expected to fulfill the unmet dreams and wishes of his parents, meet their needs, and provide them with security in the face of mortality. This attitude feeds the parental drive to provide the child with more than the parents had. However, it can turn unhealthy and cause the child to feel compelled to perform those tasks that the parents never completed, fulfill those wishes that the parents could never gratify, or heighten the parental self-esteem that could not be heightened by the parents.

As the child is a product of the parents themselves, parents often project feelings about themselves and others onto the child. To them, the child can be a narcissistic delight, a veritable pleasure, or a symbol of the best or worst parts of themselves and others. In terms of the past, the child may be a symbolic extension of another person, and the interaction in the parent-child relationship may represent attempts to repair earlier losses or disappointments. Or the relationship itself may resurrect old sibling rivalries or the parents' own parent-child conflicts. The child is a product of generations past, a link with ancestors, a recipient of and contributor to the family heritage.

In the present, the child may signify many things to the parents (Raphael, 1983). He may represent hopes for resolution of an intrapsychic conflict. For each parent there may be conscious or unconscious fantasies that he will replace someone who has been lost, provide someone who will need and love the parent, or compensate the parent for his own deprived childhood. The child may serve as proof that the parent is mature, sexual, or attractive, or be a source of power or a weapon in a relationship with someone else. Children also provide their parents with a sense of purpose and meaning. For some, the child is the only thing in their lives that is truly their own. In a world of powerlessness, deprivation, and decreasing personal control, the birth of a child is a personal accomplishment that can render a sense of competence, distinction, productivity, and hope for the future.

In terms of the future, children represent promise. A new life, a baby represents aspirations, dreams, fantasies, and new beginnings. A baby signifies the potential for fulfilling dreams, starting over, rectifying past mistakes, and putting new insights into practice. He provides his parents with opportunities for growth and engagement with life. For most people a baby, indeed, any child, is the very antithesis of death. The child concretely represents the parents' continuity and immortality, allowing the parents to be undefeated by the death that shall claim their bodies but not the carrier of their genes. But if the child serves as a type of denial of death for parents, his death foreshadows their own. If the death of a parent removes the barrier between an adult and mortality, what then does the death of a child do?

Each child has a particular specificity of meaning for his parents. There are no truly unselfish reasons for desiring a child, so as a result there are always parental needs and hopes that are represented in each child from the moment of news of the pregnancy. Yet, whatever the child represents, he is also a unique person, connected to his parents in fundamental and lasting ways, yet separate as well. The relationship to the child will be determined by the particular and distinctly original person that he is, his personality, characteristics, abilities, and roles, in addition to the meanings, needs, and hopes that have been placed upon him by his parents.

After the birth of a baby, the parents, family, and society begin to accommodate to the reality of the child's presence. The image that began in the shadows of the parents' minds now starts to solidify. Parents begin to define themselves by the parental role. The relationship between the parents and child—a relationship having no equal in its intimate closeness and long-term bodily and mental interdependence—is a mutual and nonstatic one, in which, hopefully, the child grows and thrives and the parents gain confidence. The child becomes an integral part of the parents' lives, an extension of them, internalizing their feelings, thoughts, behaviors, and attitudes. This close identification, under optimal conditions, breeds a type of empathy in which many times the parents are able to "feel" what the child feels and "understand" him in ways that do not require words. The child sees the parents as omnipotent, a role that they embrace despite insight into its realistic limitations (Benedek, 1970).

In no other role except that of the parent are there so many inherently assumed and socially assigned responsibilities. Parents are to be all-loving, all-good, all-concerned, totally selfless, and motivated only by the child and his welfare. In no other relationship is the individual subject to such unrealistic expectations that can never be fulfilled (one reason why resolution of parental grief is such a difficult task). Nevertheless, parents internalize these expectations, measuring themselves against impossible standards. Consequently, even when struggling with issues less traumatic than death, parents are burdened by unachievable ideals that fail to allow for the normal feelings of ambivalence, frustration, and anger that are part of any close relationship. Lacking legitimization of normal parental ambivalence, and believing that they should be able to unequivocally love, nurture, and protect the child in all situations, parents are haunted with guilt whenever these expectations are unmet. Parents take on the roles of protector, provider, and problem solver. They become accustomed to being self-sufficient and in control of what happens to and for the child. Parents become used to being able to "fix" things so they will work out to the child's advantage. The broken bicycle is repaired, the upset feelings after a friend's rejection are soothed. These daily interactions in successfully caring for the child serve to define the parents' senses of self, role, and reality. They cement the unparalleled closeness of the parent-child relationship.

The Loss of a Child

When a child dies, the factors that accounted for the intimacy and uniqueness of the parent-child relationship are the very factors that intensify the bereavement experience. Psychologically, the process of mourning for one's child involves not only dealing with the loss of that specific child, but with the loss of parts of oneself, since parental attachment consists both of love for the child and self-love (Furman, 1976). The unique dynamics of the parent-child relationship intensify the losses to self usually sustained subsequent to the death of a loved one. There is an assault on the self and one's sense of immortality:

> With the death of a child in the family the blow is felt narcissistically and as a threat to the sense of our immortality. . . . The bereavement for the child is intimately connected with, and related to, the libidinal investments. The child serves as a tie with the traditional past, but also, and perhaps more importantly, with the future and with our sense of immortality. (Schwartz, 1977, p. 196)

The incomparable closeness of the relationship causes the parent to be particularly vulnerable to the loss, which constitutes a failure to sustain the basic function of parenthood:

> Physiologically, psychologically, and socially, the relationship that exists between parents and their children may well be the most intense that life can generate. Obviously, then, vulnerability to loss through death is most acute when one's child dies. . . . Not only is the death of a child inappropriate in the context of living, but its tragic and untimely nature is a basic threat to the function of parenthood—to preserve some dimension of the self, the family, and the social group. (Jackson, 1977, p. 187)

There are numerous other losses that result from this initial loss of the child through death:

> Parents who lose a child are multiply victimized. We are victimized by the realistic loss of the child we love, we are victimized by the loss of the dreams and hopes we had invested in that child, and we are victimized by the loss of our own self-esteem. Not unlike the survivors of the concentration camps, we cannot comprehend why we did not die instead. (Kliman, 1977, p. 191)

Parents feel cheated and robbed. They experience an aching sense of incompletion. In addition to grieving for the loss of their child, parents are confronted with the need to relinquish all of the hopes, dreams, and expectations that they had for and with that child. These exemplify some of the many secondary losses that parents must experience, losses that develop as a consequence of the death (Rando, 1984).

Other secondary losses stem from the parents' experiencing "an overwhelming assault on their parental identities as protectors and providers" (Wallace, 1967, p. 151), of feeling "mutilated" and "disabled" (Stephens, 1974). This mutilation stems not only from the loss of the child, who had been such an extension of themselves, or from the loss of the self that had existed in the relationship with the child, but also from the ripping asunder of the adult identity that centers around providing and doing for children, one of the basic functions of the adult. The parents, who had been in control of the child's life and who had successfully assumed the roles of provider, problem solver, and protector, must now confront the interruption of these roles and the involuntary severing of the relationship with the child. They are robbed of the ability to carry out their functional roles and left with an oppressive sense of failure, a loss of power and ability, and a deep sense of being violated. They must then contend with the resulting secondary losses of disillusionment, emptiness, and insecurity that derive from a diminished sense of self. Their old identities, as well as their former assumptions and beliefs about themselves and their capabilities, have to be given up, mourned, and eventually reformed to reflect the reality of the death and its specific affects on them.

In addition to all of these losses, parents have also lost the family as they have known it. Although the family will continue after the death, it will forever be changed by the irretrievable loss of the presence and role-fulfilling behaviors and functions of the deceased child. This additional secondary loss will need to be recognized, mourned, and accommodated. For the parents, as well as each individual member of the family, there is grief for the loss of that part of the self that had existed both in relationship to the deceased child and to the family unit that is changing. For example, a mother loses that special part of herself that was a mother to the deceased child. Even though she may still be a mother to other surviving children, that interactive relationship that was unique to her and the deceased child is now gone. The relationship between the two of them that constituted a subsystem in the family is also now gone. Consequently, both mother and family are changed. This leaves bereaved parents and all other family members in a position of being forced to cope with multiple grief experiences occurring simultaneously, a situation that in other contexts would be seen as bereavement overload.

The natural cycle of life is such that the old die first and are replaced by the young. Given that a basic function of the parent is to preserve the family and protect the child, there is an implicit expectation that the parent will die before the child. The orderliness of the universe seems to be undermined when this expectation is unmet (Gorer, 1965).

> Bereaved parents come in all ages. It does not appear to make a difference whether one's child is three, thirteen, or thirty if he dies. The emotion in each of us is the same. How could it be that a parent outlives a child? (Schiff, 1977, p. 4)

The unnaturalness is not determined by the age of the child, but by the fact that the child dies out of turn with the parent. The strangeness of the event becomes a major stumbling block for the bereaved parents, who cannot comprehend why it happened and can take no solace in the idea that the loss was inevitable. Survival guilt appears to be fostered by the uncommon nature of this loss. Because this is an age where infant and child mortality are at the lowest rates ever, parents are more unprepared to deal with the loss of their children than they were in centuries past. At a time when babies begin life in test tubes, it seems inconceivable that a child's death cannot be prevented by medical intervention.

Another factor contributing to the unnaturalness of a child's death is that, especially with children and adolescents, death is often sudden, dramatic, unexpected, and untimely—the result of accidents. Such deaths are more likely to produce traumatic effects and poor bereavement outcomes because of their unanticipated nature (Parkes, 1975; Parkes & Weiss, 1983). They also are more likely to involve violence, mutilation, and destruction, leaving the survivors with a greater sense of helplessness and threat. This type of death prompts enormous efforts by the parents to find meaning in the death, determine who is to blame, and regain a sense of control.

In those situations where the death results from genetic or unex-plained medical factors, parents often take on additional burdens of grief. They try to explain why their child died prematurely and violated the laws of nature. Parents hold themselves responsible for not produc-ing a healthy child that could survive longer, and often feel deficient and worthless as a result. Often, when answers about the cause of death are not forthcoming, parents tend to search all the way back to the earliest prenatal experiences in attempts to identify the reason for the medical condition: "Perhaps it was because I took the aspirin when I was pregnant that she developed the beginnings of the illness that took her life at 11."

A final issue, one that may be uncomfortable for some parents to admit, is that in losing their child parents lose someone who could care for them later in life. This may be particularly salient for those parents who are already older and may have been receiving emotional, physical, or financial assistance from the adult child who died. For the parents who wished to live to see their grown children and their children's children, the broken expectation only serves to underscore the unnat-uralness of the loss and make it more difficult to contend with.

The Grief Reactions of Bereaved Parents

A number of reactions comprise the normal grief experience. These are delineated next, with special issues pertinent to bereaved parents highlighted. The schema is taken from Rando (1984).

The Avoidance Phase

In the avoidance phase, that period of time in which the news of the death is initially received, there is a desire to avoid the terrible acknowledgment that the child who is loved is now lost. The world is shaken and the parent overwhelmed by the impact. Just as the human body goes into shock after a large enough insult, so too does the psyche go into shock when confronted with such an important loss. It is the natural reaction to the impact of such a blow. During this period the parents may be confused and dazed, unable to comprehend what has happened. A feeling of bewilderment and numbness is quite common. In cases of sudden death this is intensified, since there has been no cognitive preparation for the death and the news of it is so overwhelm-ing that the parents cannot make any sense out of it. The reactions to death described next may be greatly exacerbated in sudden loss.

As recognition starts to seep in and shock slowly starts to wear off, denial immediately crops up. It is only natural that parents would want or need to deny that such a terrible event has occurred. At this juncture denial is therapeutic. It functions as a buffer by allowing the parents to absorb the reality of the loss a little at a time, preventing them from being completely overwhelmed. Disbelief and a need to know why the death occurred usually appear at this time. Depending on the nature of the parent's personality, there may be an explosion of anger or hysteria, quiet withdrawal, mechanical action, or depersonalization. Confusion and disorganization are common. Occasionally the initial response will be an intellectualized acceptance of the death, followed by initiation of seemingly appropriate activities such as comforting others or making funeral arrangements. In such a case the loss is recognized, but the emotional response to it is denied. Often fathers respond in this manner, as they seek to be stoic and productive in the face of their loss, attempting to live out their traditional sex role.

The Confrontation Phase

The confrontation phase is the highly emotional time during which the grief is most intense and the reactions to the loss are most acute. The loss has been recognized and the shock has worn off to a great degree. Denial and disbelief may occur intermittently; however, a whole host of new reactions springs from the parents' confrontation with the child's death and its implications.

This phase has been described as a time of "angry sadness." Extremes of emotions are felt, sometimes within very short intervals of time. Some parents will allow these feelings to be readily expressed; others will be conflicted about giving vent to them; and still others will want to express them but find they are unable to do so.

Fear and anxiety. The perception of new reactions so different from the parents' usual feelings and modes of behavior may prompt fear and anxiety. The variety and intensity of the feelings are usually enough to make parents wonder if they are losing their minds. These reactions are so different, uncontrollable, unexpected, and severe that a majority of parents believe that they have actually lost touch with reality. Individuals are scarcely ever adequately prepared for the type and strength of grief reactions they sustain. This is one of the reasons why providing normative data about parental bereavement, and finding validation for one's feelings in such self-help groups as The Compassionate Friends, is such a critical therapeutic intervention. Since there are few models or culturally prescribed roles for mourners in our society, it is difficult for bereaved parents to know how they should act or feel. The ambiguity fostered in the absence of such guidelines increases stress and anxiety in a situation already overburdened by it.

This further contributes to the parents' feelings of losing control and "going crazy." Actually such feelings are normal for grievers at this point, despite the fact that if they were occurring in an individual who was not grieving a major loss they would be considered pathological. Although grief is a "craziness," grievers are not usually crazy.

A sense of panic or generalized anxiety is frequent during this phase, either intermittently or chronically. This stems partially from the apprehension of the unknown and unfamiliar. It is frequently experienced by the parent when she awakens in the morning and remembers she must face another day without her child. Concerns about being able to deal with the separation pain, fear about what the absence of the child will mean to the parents' existence, upset over the recognition that they are markedly different from before, worry over the family, fright arising from the sense of vulnerability caused by the loss, distress associated with memories of earlier losses and separations, heightened emotional and physical arousal—all serve to intensify the parents' grief experience. High anxiety in bereaved parents is also attributable to the feelings of loss of control over their life and their world that result from the unnaturalness of the loss and the violation of expectations.

Anger and guilt. The two emotions in grief that cause tremendous problems because of society's attitudes toward them are anger and guilt. Both of these feelings are intensified when a parent loses a child. Anger is always to be expected to some degree following a significant loss. It is a natural consequence of being deprived of something valued. Many times the anger is displaced onto other people, frequently without the griever's conscious knowledge or intent. This anger may be vented at God, the doctors, others who have not sustained the loss, and even the bereaved parents themselves in such forms as self-hatred, guilt, feelings of worthlessness, and self-punishment. Especially in cases where children have been killed as a result of accidents, parents have profound anger that is not easily channeled. Anger at the deceased for dying and "abandoning" the parents is not uncommon. Yet this is often very difficult for the parents to admit, since it is not socially appropriate to speak ill of the dead or, except in cases of suicide, blame the deceased for the death. Parents can become very bitter, easily hurt, and oversensitive to real or imagined slights. They may feel an intense anger toward those unaffected by death. Anger may also be the result of a loss of faith in God or a loss of faith in a philosophy of life that can no longer be maintained after the child's death.

Guilt is a normal and expectable aspect of any grief experience. The emotion appears to be the single most pervasive parental response to the death of a child. Guilt is a natural reaction whenever an individual perceives herself to be falling short of her self-image or violating a conscious or unconscious personal standard. Parents are particularly susceptible to guilt because of the inappropriate social expectations they have in their roles as parents and the unrealistic standards by which they judge themselves. It is not humanly possible to meet these ideals consistently, and after a child's death the parent inevitably confronts intense feelings of guilt because of this inability. Miles and Demi (in Chapter 4 of this book) suggest six specific sources of parental guilt: death causation guilt; illness-related guilt; parental role guilt; moral guilt; survival guilt; and grief guilt. In addition to these forms of guilt, parents must contend with all the normal guilt reactions of grief. Because human relationships always contain some measure of ambivalence (despite societal beliefs about parent-child relationships to the contrary), and because our relationships, as ourselves, are not perfect, guilt will always be a natural concomitant to the loss of an important loved one. In the early phases of experiencing a loss, people usually tend to recall everything that was negative in their relationship with the deceased, while failing to remember the positives equally well. Parents are no exception. They are often found contemplating their relationship with the child and focusing on acts of omission and commission, dwelling on the "if onlys," "could haves," and "should haves," and obsessing over guilt-producing thoughts and feelings. No matter how wonderful the relationship may have been in reality, the parent will remember the one time it was less than ideal.

The many diverse emotions of grief themselves may prompt guilt. For example, a parent may feel guilty for having felt normal anger at the child for dying and leaving her or for feeling dependent and regressed. Crying over the loss or experiencing other normal emotions of grief may be sufficient to cause guilt for some parents if they interpret such reactions as unacceptable losses of control. Some other responses associated with guilt, and often seen in bereaved parents, are self-reproach and a sense of worthlessness. The unique nature of child loss exacerbates these feelings. These may serve not only as a form of self-punishment to expiate guilt, but also may constitute expressions of anger directed inward or reactions to the loss of a primary support figure.

Sometimes there is a sense of relief experienced by parents after a death. It is a feeling about which most feel quite guilty. Parents may be relieved when the end finally comes, especially when the child has been suffering or there has been a long drawn-out illness. It is not necessarily a statement about the feelings or lack of feelings for the child, but more often a reflection of the parents' response to the alleviation of suffering and the termination of responsibilities. Although parents may be reluctant to admit it, some may also feel relief simply because they themselves did not die or because their relationship with the child had been marked by a great deal of conflict or oppression and they are happy it has ended. In most cases, the former is not readily admitted to, while the consequences of the latter become evident in increased feelings of guilt and difficulty with mourning.

Separation and longing. Other grief reactions at this time typically include acute feelings of separation, deprivation, anguish, sadness, yearning, and longing. The intensity of these reactions usually surprises and shocks parents. Many parents feel that they will be overwhelmed by this mental suffering. Mothers may feel the physical emptiness that characterizes their inability to embrace their child. Parents may express their loss in physical terms, saying they feel "mutilated." This not only reflects their sense of separation from the child, but reveals their own awareness of the loss of the parts of their identities that have been validated by the relationship with the child. In this sense, part of the parent herself dies, making some of the grief for the parent, as well as for the child. The yearning, aching, and pining that accompany the separation from one's offspring are unparalleled in magnitude and urgency. Sometimes these feelings are experienced physically, as well as psychologically—a gut-wrenching, gnawing emptiness that needs to be filled, or sharp, intense pangs of grief that cut deeply into the heart.

A natural response to this is preoccupation with the child. This occurs both as a wish to undo the loss and a reflection of the internal grief work being done. The preoccupation is often manifested in the parent's obsessive rumination about the child, dreaming about him, thinking she has seen him, or actively "searching" for the child and trying to recover him. A significant proportion of mourners actually experiences some type of visual or auditory hallucination of the child, or feels an intuitive, overwhelming sense of his presence.

Depression. Depression and despair are common reactions to important losses. Numerous symptoms of depression are also among the usual manifestations of grief, as shown in Table 1.1.

This table illustrates the differentially experienced impact of depression which, like grief in general, does not always mirror the stereotypical expectation. (The stereotypical expectation in this case is classic melancholic depression in which the mourner becomes significantly debilitated emotionally and physically and can no longer function.)

The grieving parent's inability to concentrate or process information must not be underestimated. She often feels she is losing control because she feels so confused and lacks the decision-making abilities

Table 1.1. Manifestations of Depression in Grief

VEGETATIVE SYMPTOMS
 Anhedonia
 Anorexia
 Apathy
 Decreased energy
 Decreased initiative
 Decreased motivation
 Decreased sexual desire
  or hypersexuality
 Psychomotor retardation
  or agitation
 Sleep difficulties
 Social withdrawal
 Somatic problems
 Tearfulness and crying
 Tension and anxiety
 Weight loss or gain
 Withdrawal

COGNITIVE DISRUPTION
 Concerns about going crazy
  or losing control
 Confusion
 Decreased effectiveness
  or productivity
 Depersonalization
 Disorganization
 Feeling out of control
 Feeling overwhelmed
 Feeling tentative or unsure
 Lack of clarity
 Lack of concentration
 Obsessive thinking
 Problems with decision making

COMBINATION OF ANGER
 AND DEPRESSION
 Aggression
 Agitation
 Anxiety
 Belligerence
 Disillusionment
 Emotional lability
 Feeling as if something is
  about to happen
 Feeling bombarded or
  overwhelmed

Frustration
Heightened psychological
 and physiological arousal
Hyperactivity
Intolerance
Irritability
Nervousness
Obstinacy
Overreactivity
Oversensitivity
Restlessness
Rigidity
Searching behavior
Tension

SUBJECTIVE FEELINGS
 Abandonment
 Ambivalence
 Anguish
 Anxiety
 Dependency
 Deprivation
 Despair
 Fear
 Guilt
 Helplessness
 Hopelessness
 Inadequacy
 Insecurity
 Lack of concern for self
 Loneliness
 Meaninglessness
 Pessimism
 Pining, yearning, and
  longing
 Powerlessness
 Regression
 Sadness
 Self-reproach
 Separation
 Shame
 Timidity and
  nonassertiveness
 Unreality
 Vulnerability
 Worry
 Worthlessness

and incisiveness she once had. She may be nonassertive and lack clarity and certainty. This only heightens the anxiety and unreality of the situation for her. These types of changes resulting from grief's depression and diminution of normal capabilities often cause the parent to feel childlike, helpless, and dependent on others.

Accompanying depression may be a lack of concern for the self. When moderate, it appears as a disregard for personal matters due to preoccupation with the child. Self-care may be permitted only as it benefits others; for example, "If it weren't for the other children, I would have ended it all myself." When taken to an extreme, this lack of concern is manifested in self-destructive behaviors, even suicide. While many bereaved parents have fleeting thoughts of suicide as a means of reuniting with their child and escaping the pains of grief, most do not act on them. However, suicide threats should be taken seriously and must be evaluated, especially with the following high-risk groups: those who have previously attempted suicide; those with past or present psychological disorders, especially problems with impulse control or acting-out personalities; those who have difficulty dealing with anger; those who feel hopeless; those who are overly dependent; those who feel they lack the resources they need to cope or who lack social support; those who are deeply depressed; and those who have made concrete plans for suicide.

Several important reactions are a combination of both depression and anger. These include irritability, anxiety, tension, and frustration. There is heightened psychological arousal. This predisposes bereaved parents to oversensitivity, overreaction, and feelings of being bombarded and overwhelmed. It interferes with their ability to relax because there is a sense of being "geared up." It is common for the bereaved parents to be very restless, to wander anxiously, or to feel a sense that something is going to happen. This is part of the searching behavior that normally occurs in grief in which the parents are preoccupied with thoughts and images of the child in the attempt to locate and retrieve her (Bowlby, 1961; Parkes, 1970/1974). This searching, which is consistently unrewarded since the child cannot be brought back, ultimately helps the parents realize the finality of the loss.

Obsession. In an effort to gain some control and understanding over what appears to be a meaningless, unmanageable event, bereaved parents often engage in an obsessional review of the circumstances of the death. They also attempt to cognitively restructure the situation so that it seems that they had had some inkling that it could happen. This provides them with a sense of control and predictability in the midst of what appears to be chaos. Because the loss of a child is such an unnatural and difficult event to understand, bereaved parents can be expected to engage in this type of obsessional review quite frequently as they try to comprehend the event and its implications. When it is combined with the circumstances of a sudden death, this process is to be expected even more often.

Search for meaning. The search for the causes and meaning of a death is critically important to parents who have lost a child. Because of the unnaturalness of losing a child, and the sense of guilt and failure it produces, it is an essential component of the parental grief process. Bereaved parents can be expected to be left with overwhelming questions which they may ruminate about for a long time, if not forever. Some of these questions will be capable of being answered. For example, questions about causes, about how the death occurred, can be answered medically or seen as a direct consequence of a given action. However, questions pertaining to the reason it happened, the understanding of how it fits into the scheme of life, are more difficult to answer. Why children must suffer and die is a question that few can answer satisfactorily. Reasons that cannot be understood may have to be assimilated as that, something that cannot be comprehended, but must be accepted or at least tolerated. For parents, accepting the fact that there is a reason, although unknown, is often a therapeutic step that frequently helps them cope just a little better with the unfathomable event of losing a child.

This quest to answer the questions and make sense out of the death may result in a profound sense of injustice and disillusionment if values and beliefs that once were comforting and promised security become viewed as meaningless and useless. Some parents will alienate others with their bitterness when their value systems fail them. In time some of them may be able to put the loss into a perspective that lends it some meaning; however, some never recover their trust and are chronically angry toward religion, authority figures, or life.

Grief attacks. One relatively common type of experience that causes great concern to bereaved parents is the grief attack. This is an acute upsurge of grief that occurs suddenly and often when least expected, interrupting ongoing activities and temporarily leaving the parent out of control. At times such feelings may not be experienced as an attack, but as waves or pangs that produce painful emotional and physical sensations. While normal for quite some time after the death, parents must stop their activities and deal with their feelings until they are in control again, or else risk possible injury to themselves or others.

Such grief attacks have contributed to automobile accidents, occupational injuries, and countless other types of mishaps. A grief attack is an extreme example of distractability and confusion. For example, the griever may find himself lost in a fog, stopping at green lights, or arriving at a destination and not recalling how he got there. Small or surprising things can trigger these off, for example, moving the refrigerator a year after the child has died and unexpectedly finding a tiny toy that had become stuck behind it.

Identification. Parents will usually have some amount of identification with their deceased child. In appropriate amounts this is not harmful and serves as a way of holding on to portions of the child. For example, a father may pick up his dead son's hobby of stamp collecting or become a fan of his favorite football team. A mother may continue her son's commitment to animals by volunteering at the animal shelter. However, if identification occurs too intensely (e.g., the parent loses a sense of personal identity), is inappropriate to adult functioning (e.g., the parent starts to act immaturely or takes on the symptoms of the child's illness), or occurs in areas where the parent lacks competence (e.g., the physically limited parent tries to become the star athlete the child was), the process has become unhealthy. If it is employed to avoid appropriate decathexis it is equally nontherapeutic.

Social manifestations. Some of the social manifestations of grief are seen in the bereaved parent's restlessness and inability to sit still, her painful lack of ability to initiate and maintain organized patterns of activity, and her social withdrawal behavior (Lindemann, 1944). The grieving parent is solely interested in her attempts to find and reunite with her deceased child. As a result she tends to devalue all help offered, often driving away potential supporters. The focus on the lost relationship causes the parent to neglect other relationships, and the pain of seeing others with their loved ones encourages further withdrawal.

Physiological manifestations. A number of physiological reactions accompany the bereaved parent's psychological and social reactions to the death of the child. These include anorexia and other gastrointestinal disturbances, loss of weight, inability to sleep, crying, the tendency to sigh, a lack of strength, physical exhaustion, feelings of emptiness and heaviness, feelings of something stuck in the throat, heart palpitations and other indications of anxiety, nervousness and tension, loss of sexual desire or hypersexuality, lack of energy and psychomotor retardation, restlessness and searching for something to do, and shortness of breath (Lindemann, 1944; Parkes, 1964, 1970, 1972). Taken together, the studies of mortality and morbidity reviewed by Raphael (1983) and Rando (1984) corroborate clinical observations that bereavement is a state of great risk physically, as well as emotionally and socially. For this reason, the importance of adequate resolution of grief work cannot be stressed too much.

The Reestablishment Phase

In the reestablishment phase, there is a gradual decline of grief and the beginning of an emotional and social reentry back into the everyday world. The loss is not forgotten, but put in a special place which, while allowing it to be remembered, also frees the mourner to go on to new attachments without being pathologically tied to old ones. The parent knows now that he will survive, but will never be quite the same. He recognizes the changes in himself and learns to live with the loss, as his emotional energy is reinvested in new relationships, objects, activities, ideas, and goals. This phase is not an all-or-nothing phase. Rather, it waxes and wanes during the latter part of the confrontation phase and continues slowly thereafter. It never arrives all at once and for some time it coexists with many of the previous reactions. Guilt often accompanies the beginning efforts at reestablishment as the parent copes with the fact that he continues to live and experience life despite the death of the child. This is a particularly thorny issue for parents, as they may erroneously feel that they are betraying the child if they start to enjoy life again without him.

It is often unrecognized that parents must "grow up with the loss" in a grieving process spanning the years. For example, the times at which the child would have graduated, gotten married, or had children are often marked by upsurges in grief. Since parents are rarely prepared for these occurrences, and are frequently unaware of their source, they may feel that they are acting abnormally or that they have not adequately addressed their grief. For this reason, parents need to have this phenomenon explained to them in advance. The phenomenon must be differentiated from chronic grief, in which there is a continual process of grieving. This is a series of acute grief reactions that occur at what would have been significant points in the child's life and are similar to anniversary reactions except that they mark events that never actually occurred.

Factors Influencing the Parental Grief Response

Each parent's bereavement experience will be colored by a unique constellation of specific and idiosyncratic factors. It is a mistake to lump all bereaved parents together, an error to assume that all bereaved parents are alike merely because they all have lost a child. In fact, they are more like themselves before the loss than they necessarily are like other bereaved parents. While the objective experience of the loss of a child is similar, the relationship that is lost in each case, and the factors influencing both the griever and the loss situation, will be different. The following psychological, social, and physiological factors must always be taken into account when attempting to evaluate or understand a bereaved parent's response. (See Chapter 22, "Individual and Couples Treatment Following the Death of a Child," for elaboration on the particular influence of each of these factors.)

The psychological factors influencing the bereaved parent's response to the death of the child include the following:

Characteristics and meaning of the loss sustained and the relationship severed

- The unique nature and meaning of the relationship severed
- The individual qualities of the relationship lost
- The roles that the child occupied in the family
- The characteristics of the deceased child
- The amount of unfinished business between the parent and the child
- The parent's perception of the child's fulfillment in life
- The number, type, and quality of secondary losses for the parent

Characteristics of the grieving parent

- The parent's coping behaviors, personality, and mental health
- The parent's level of maturity and intelligence
- The parent's past experiences with loss and death
- The parent's social, cultural, ethnic, and religious/philosophical background
- The parent's sex-role conditioning
- The parent's age
- The presence of concurrent stresses or crises in the parent's life

Characteristics of the death

- The death surround
- The timeliness of the death
- The parent's perception of the preventability of the death
- Whether the death was sudden or expected
- The length of the illness prior to death

- The amount of the parent's anticipatory grief and involvement with the dying child

The social factors influencing the bereaved parent's response to the death of the child include the following:

- The parent's social support system and the acceptance and assistance of its members
- The parent's sociocultural, ethnic, and religious/philosophical background
- The parent's educational, economic, and occupational status
- The funerary rituals utilized

The physiological factors influencing the bereaved parent's response to the death of the child include the following:

- The parent's use of drugs and sedatives
- The parent's nutrition
- The amount of rest and sleep the parent receives
- The parent's physical health
- The amount of exercise the parent gets

Without an understanding of and appreciation for these variables and how they affect a particular parent's grief experience, *no* judgments can ever legitimately be made about that person's grief response.

When assessing bereaved parents, it should be remembered that their grief has been clinically and empirically documented as being more intense and long lasting than that resulting from other losses. They are also more susceptible to those factors found to impede the successful resolution of grief. In light of this, general bereavement models and commonly accepted criteria for unresolved grief should be used judiciously with bereaved parents. This is not to dismiss their relevance, but to point out their limitations when it comes to this particular loss. (Refer to Chapter 2 for a full discussion of this issue.)

THE MARITAL DYAD

The marital relationship is the second main dimension on which the death of a child is intensely experienced. It is also the sphere in which many secondary losses occur. The characteristics of the relationship will obviously determine how grief over the death of a child is experienced by the couple. For purposes of discussion, in this chapter the marital relationship is assumed to be an ideal one. Departures from this ideal in real-life circumstances would be expected to alter the dynamics described herein accordingly.

Effects on the Emotional Relationship

One of the most difficult aspects of parental bereavement is that the death of the child strikes both partners in the marital dyad simultaneously and confronts them with the same overwhelming loss. Consequently, each partner's most therapeutic resource is taken away, as the person to whom each would normally turn for support is also deeply involved in grief. The parents experience loss upon loss. Then the closeness that characterizes the marital relationship and usually provides its greatest strength can be a disadvantage in this case, as it makes partners particularly vulnerable to the feelings of blame and anger grievers often displace onto those nearest to them.

In the ideal relationship, the parents work together, presenting a united front to their children. The warm and stable relationship between the partners fosters love and responsible behavior toward the child. The marital relationship is positive, strong, and healthy: a growing, vibrant relationship in which both mutual and complementary needs are worked out sufficiently in an atmosphere of respect and understanding of each other. There is open discussion of what is best for the child and consistent and reliable behavior in agreed-upon roles and functions. Parents feel good about themselves and their spouse. The relationship replenishes each partner and offers a refuge from other stresses of the world. Problems that are encountered in the relationship can be successfully negotiated based upon prevailing family norms and rules.

Unsurprisingly, the ideal situation often drastically changes when a child dies. In this case, the closeness of the ideal marital relationship just described poses additional burdens. Whereas previously parents may have had the time, energy, ability, and interest to relate to and take care of the spouse, now these resources are in short supply, if they are there at all. Additionally, parents must deal with the grief of their spouse as well as themselves. Because of the tight bond there is little opportunity to get away from the grief psychologically or physically. Secondary losses increase as one can see the grief and pain in the face of one's loved one. Because of the intimacy of the marital dyad, although one spouse may desperately need a respite from the other, it is often hard to request and even harder to take. Guilt abounds. Consequently, feelings of incompetence may develop in the marital role, as well as in the parental role. This generalized feeling of incompetence only over-whelms the parent and makes her doubtful of her capacity to recover. Such severe grief is not conducive to maintaining a good relationship. It attacks feelings of assertiveness, strength, independence, security, and health.

Difficulties can arise in the best of marriages when normal patterns of relating are disrupted by grief. For example, communication dys-function often develops when one partner asks the other unanswerable questions, such as why the death occurred, or avoids communicating with the other spouse for fear it will precipitate a mutual downward spiral. Irrational demands may be made, as when one spouse expects the other to take away the pain. Rational but unrealistic demands, such as requests for one to assume all the duties of the other, breed stress. Day-to-day problems may not be confronted because of preoccupation with the loss of the child, because one spouse seeks to protect the other, or because of the lack of available strength. Such problems tend to accumulate until there is an explosion, often resulting in greater misunderstandings and feelings of helplessness in an already over-wrought couple. Often parents fear they will lose their marriages and their families, in addition to having lost their deceased child.

Problems Arising from Differing Grief Experiences

Problems frequently occur when partners assume that they both will experience the same grief because they have suffered the loss of the same child or make assumptions about their partner's grief based on their own. This is sometimes difficult for partners to remember. They may clearly understand that other people will have their own idiosyn-cratic ways of grieving, yet still be unable to accept that the two of them will grieve differently as well. In many respects each parent is confront-ing quite a different loss, despite the fact that they have both lost the same child. This is because each has sustained a unique relationship with the child. Variables such as the personal attributes of the parent and child and their specific roles in the family combine with the parent's premorbid personality, coping abilities, previous loss history, and other psychosocial characteristics to create the idiosyncratic grief response of each parent. For example, the different social roles assumed by mother and father influenced the relationship and interactions each one had with that child. This helps determine the type of grief experience that occurs after the death. For the mother, who is often accustomed to more intimate contact with the child on a daily basis, there may be more of an acute sense of loss over the lack of presence of the child: not being able to touch him, feed him, smell him, see him, or hear his voice. For the father, whose contact is usually different because of responsibilities centered outside of the home, the inability to interact with the child through roughhousing, playing sports, or building things may be more painful. He may especially miss the child on weekends, when they had shared time together. In contrast, his wife may find the time after school most difficult to bear, since that had been a special time for her and her child. Since each parent had a separate and individual relationship with the child, different things will constitute losses to each parent. Bereaved parents must recognize this and not expect their mate to be grieving the exact same losses as they are.

The often differing grief experiences of parents are also indicated in the ways that a spouse takes to the division of labor following the death of the child. For example, in traditional families, despite frustration at not being able to function as well as usual, the husband may find that his usual role at work affords him some respite from his grief; his wife may not find the same consolation in her usual role of being at home. Conducting some of her typical maternal duties may only serve to illustrate the loss even more poignantly, as she travels through the supermarket and sees the child's favorite brand of cereal or cleans the room he had occupied. While couples often comprehend that their responses to the loss of a child differ from those of other bereaved parents, they typically forget that this is equally true when looking at the responses of their mate.

Another of the major factors contributing to differences in parental grief is sex-role socialization. Traditionally the male has been conditioned to be self-sufficient and to exert emotional control. He prides himself on the roles of provider, protector, and problem solver. However, with the death of his child he fails in each of these roles; he cannot provide, protect, or solve the problem that is his child's death. These additional feelings of failure exacerbate his grief. There are further difficulties when it becomes apparent that precisely what is demanded in grief work is that which is precluded by his social role: expressing feelings, being preoccupied with memories, requiring support and validation from others. Conversely, women have traditionally been socialized to accept assistance from others and to express their emotions, although they appear to have more difficulty accepting and ventilating their anger than do their husbands. Most of the tasks of grief work are compatible with their social roles and conditioning.

The situation between bereaved parents will be ripe for conflict if one spouse interprets the other's grief response as indicating that the mate did not love the deceased child enough. It is imperative that parents grant one another a very wide latitude for differences in their individual grief expression and that they attempt to understand these in the psychosocial context of their spouse's past. There is no one correct way to grieve. Parents cannot expect their spouse to be just like them in grief, any more than they can expect such similarity in other areas of life. Grief is an individual process. Despite certain universal feelings and issues, each parent must complete the grief work in his own way. If parents fail to recognize that each of them has personal ways of grieving and of coping with the grief and the implications of the death, they will set themselves up for additional problems.

Not only are couples always somewhat dissimilar in their grief processes; they also typically lack synchronicity in their grief experiences. It is not unusual for one spouse to be up emotionally while the other is down. This asymmetry may occur in four grief work areas: expressing feelings; working and doing daily activities (one may find comfort in work, while the other is overwhelmed by it); relating to things that trigger memories of the deceased child (one may desire all photographs to be removed from the house, while the other will cling to them); and searching for the meaning of what has happened (one may find solace in religion, while the other may relinquish his former faith) (Montgomery, 1979/1980). As individual needs change over time there are corresponding changes in the approaches to each of these four areas.

Couples may have widely divergent styles of grief expression or avoidance that fluctuate over time, which may bring them together or push them apart. Any of these differences may cause spouses to erroneously conclude that their mate has rejected them, especially when depression and lack of communication are manifested. Although partners may have pulled together to meet crises in the past, they will have to recognize that they will seldom be at the same place at the same time in their grief process and that this does not mean that they do not still love one another. They will need to convey to each other that this sentiment still exists, despite apparent differences.

Accompanying this must be the recognition that the grief experience will change each of them. They cannot expect their mate to be exactly the same person as before. Predictably this will create a change in the marital relationship that also must be recognized and accommodated. This is another example of a typical secondary loss.

Overuse of coping behaviors and diversions that continually direct attention away from the grief process and the marital relationship will seriously compromise the marriage. For example, inappropriate consumption of alcohol, overinvolvement at work, or too much time spent with others outside of the family all can contribute to further marital strain.

Another sensitive issue that spouses must confront is that their physical presence and mannerisms can remind one another of the deceased child. Part of the couple has been lost irretrievably, both in terms of the past they have shared and the future of which they had dreamt. To be constantly reminded of this by the sight of each other is a very painful experience.

Sexual Problems

One of the primary areas in which a partner's response to grief can dramatically alter the couple's relationship is in the sexual realm. A classic and quite frequent problem is the inhibition of sexual response and intimacy in bereaved parents. This constitutes a major secondary loss for most parents affected. The problem may be the result of fear of having and losing other children or guilt over experiencing pleasure, or may be a symptom of grief or depression experienced by one or both of the partners. While the intimacy of sexual contact may be comforting to one spouse, it may be precisely what the other cannot endure at that moment. If the barriers to feelings are let down in order to experience the closeness of sexual intimacy, then the spouse may also be vulnerable to other, less positive feelings, such as pain, loss, and grief. Since sexual intimacy and orgasm can put the spouse in touch with feelings at a deep level, she may seek to avoid it for fear of tapping into painful emotions. Unless each member of the couple understands the differences between each other's differing grieving styles, and can appreciate the fact that the sexual relationship as well as other aspects of the relationship can be intensely affected by grief, there will be further problems. It is not unusual for the sexual relationship to be compromised by disinterest, depression, avoidance, or other grief-related responses for 2 years after the death.

Divorce and Other Changes

All of these secondary losses place additional burdens of grief, loss, and adaptation on couples already overwrought with responsibilities and demands. These problems contribute to the assertion that there may be higher divorce rates in bereaved couples. However, it is invalid to assume that the loss of a child must lead to parental divorce. The assumption that it invariably destroys the marital relationship is an erroneous interpretation of the facts. This belief has unfortunately been fostered by early research that failed to take into account normal divorce rates and longitudinal designs. In these studies (conducted on families with a child with cancer) family disruption was thought to be relatively higher than in more recent studies. In these, although it is clear that parents suffer more distress than a normal group, they appear to experience less than marriage counselees (Cairns & Lansky, 1980) and may actually even have divorce rates lower than average in the states covered by the study (Lansky, Cairns, Hassanein, Wehr, & Lowman, 1978).

There is related evidence suggesting that parents are not inevitably headed for divorce court. This has been provided by information from parents who experienced the long-term survival of their child with cancer (Foster, O'Malley, & Koocher, 1981). In this study parents reported that the extreme stress of cancer did not affect their marriage. Although a few couples reported a negative effect, most felt that the impact was generally positive over the long run, as they became sensitive to both positive and negative aspects of the marital relationship. Those couples who had been in the process of separating or divorcing at the time of diagnosis did not alter their decision; but many couples were able to share their feelings from the beginning of the experience and felt their marriages became stronger through reliance on each other's strengths and increasing respect for each other. For these people family relationships became a conscious priority and they were no longer taken for granted. They reported a deeper sense of unity than they had been aware of prior to the experience with cancer. Although this information pertains to individuals whose children did not ultimately die, it is important because it illustrates that while the stress of childhood illness is exceptionally high, it does not automatically have to disrupt family relationships. Each family's strengths and weaknesses must be evaluated individually.

A final source of evidence disproving the notion that divorce inevitably befalls bereaved parents is the information provided by those who study the positive responses to bereavement. It is well known clinically that such an experience can open up the eyes of the bereaved to new experiences and priorities that were formerly overlooked. Becoming more compassionate and caring toward others was a growth response reported by Miles and Crandall (1983) in their research on responses to parental bereavement. Shanfield, Benjamin, and Swain (1984) found that over half of the bereaved parents they studied reported they had felt a sense of personal growth, had become more expressive of feelings, were able to talk more about sensitive emotional issues, and felt more productive. Nearly half felt more content and had become more religious, and nearly two-thirds experienced an increased sense of spirituality. It is not uncommon for parents to report a heightened sensitivity to others, closer relationships, and a commitment to living life more fully and meaningfully because of their child's death.

Major contributions have been made by parents who were determined that some good should evolve from their loss. Self-help groups such as The Compassionate Friends and political action-oriented groups such as Mothers Against Drunk Driving or Parents of Murdered Children have arisen out of the anguish of bereaved parents and have had inestimable positive personal and social impacts. The increased awareness of life's preciousness, fragility, and brevity have stimulated changes that, while they did not take away the deep and long-lasting pain of grief, did channel the pain and rage into meaningful endeavors, assisting both the parent and society as well.

This is clearly the type of hopeful message that one wants to give bereaved parents. The notion that the stress of childhood illness and/or death automatically leads to divorce only exacerbates the pressure already felt by parents in such situations. Clinicians and researchers in this area need to clarify earlier research findings that present such an unrealistic picture of "the way it has to be" for bereaved parents.

Special Circumstances

Before moving on to family considerations, it would be inexcusable not to mention the instances of the bereaved single parent, the unmarried parent, and the loss of the only child. Clearly not all bereaved parents are in pairs with the child's other biological parent. A bereaved parent may be single or remarried to someone who is not the child's natural parent. In these cases there will inevitably be additional factors that impinge on the parent's grief experience. Some of these will be negative, as seen in the demands placed on the single parent to make critical funeral decisions or care for surviving children and herself with little support from others. Sometimes these factors will be positive. Not all biological parents of a child relate well to one another. A new spouse may offer infinitely more support than did the natural parent of the child. As with all other issues, the unique factors of a particular bereaved parent and her particular loss must be carefully identified before any evaluation or treatment intervention is made.

Parents who lose only children are faced with a confusing question: "Are we still parents?" Those with other children have no difficulty in answering this question, although they may encounter some conflict in deciding how many children they should say they have. Some feel they should include their deceased child in with the surviving ones when counting the number of offspring; others do not. However, parents who lose only children, who experience a complete cessation of parental responsibilities, as well as gratifications, are forced to contend with a total lack of experiences reinforcing their former parental identities. This can be a tremendously disorganizing, confusing, and demoralizingly painful loss. These parents also must face never being grandparents. There will be no biological continuation of self at all. This situation presents such parents with special issues to be addressed. (See Chapter 20, "A Single Parent Confronting the Loss of an Only Child.") This does not mean that parents with surviving children grieve less, but that bereaved parents in different circumstances will encounter different issues and experiences.

THE FAMILY SYSTEM

The family constellation is a system in which the sum is more than the total of its parts. It operates under the same conditions as does any system: anything that affects the system as a whole will affect the individual members, while anything that affects the individual members will necessarily affect the system as a whole. Like all systems, the family system struggles to maintain its homeostatic balance and equilibrium. To do this families develop specific roles, rules, communication patterns, expectations, and patterns of behavior that reflect their beliefs, coping strategies, system alliances, and coalitions. These work to keep the system consistent and stable.

Family Reorganization

When a child dies there is a dramatic shift in the homeostatic balance of the family. One element has been changed, throwing the entire family system into disequilibrium with a resulting demand for adaptation. The degree of disruption to the family system is affected most significantly by (1) the timing of the death in the family life cycle, (2) the nature of the death, (3) the openness of the family system, and (4) the family position of the deceased family member (Herz, 1980). The emotional energy of the family will be directed toward reestablishing the balance in the system. This will affect not only the system as a whole and its individual members, but also the various subsystem dyads and coalitions that exist within the family. Power, responsibilities, and roles will be reassigned as the family system struggles to reestablish stability in the face of a changed situation.

The degree of role reorganization that will be necessary in the family system following a death will be a function of two variables: the number of roles held by the individual and the types of roles the individual fulfilled (Vollman, Ganzert, Picher, & Williams, 1971). Necessary role shifts put additional burdens on family members, who are already quite vulnerable and overtaxed because of the loss. Role reassignments can be potentially harmful, as when a child is expected to assume parental responsibilities because of the dysfunction of a parent following a sibling's death, or is assigned the identity of a deceased sibling. All role reassignments must be made with consideration of such issues as the appropriateness of a given role responsibility for a specific family member, the member's preparation for and probable rewards in assuming the role, and the congruence of the new responsibilities with existing roles (Arndt & Gruber, 1977). New role assignments may constitute either secondary losses or secondary gains for individual family members. It is not uncommon for siblings to be robbed of some of their identity by being expected to assume the preferences of a sibling who died (as discussed later). In some cases, however, the reassignment of roles allows individuals to receive recognition and/or responsibilities that may have been withheld and adds meaningful functions to their lives. In families where role reorganization does not occur, a malignant process of scapegoating may develop in the family's attempt to maintain homeostasis and to provide greater cohesion and unity to ensure the survival of the family. This unhealthy process allows family members to discharge the feelings created by the death of the child.

Issues with Surviving Siblings

When a child dies in a family it is not uncommon to hear parents assert that this was the "favorite" child, the "best" child, the "most sensitive" child, the "especially unique" child, and so forth. This assignment of sanctified qualities can intensify grief experiences for both parents and siblings. Parents are often worried that their other children will suffer in comparison to the idealized child. It also tends to make their own loss more painful. They have lost a child who had such wonderful qualities, at least in parental recollection after the death, that hopes and aspirations are retrospectively intensified. This means that parents are then called upon to relinquish and grieve for more.

Surviving siblings may find themselves in very vulnerable positions. All too frequently there is the expectation that these other children will fill the void of the deceased. This is an unhealthy expectation both for the children and their parents, often held in an attempt to keep the deceased child alive. Severe problems have been documented with regard to "replacement" children (Cain & Cain, 1964; Poznanski, 1972). Unfair burdens are placed on the new child, who is expected to live up to an image of the sibling she never knew. This is usually caused by one or both of the parents' inability to work through the intense anguish and grief over the loss of the deceased child. Often they have had extreme narcissistic investment in the child who died. Inappropriate identifications, dreams, and plans had been placed on that child. In these cases, the new child is essentially born into a world of mourning. Apathetic and withdrawn parents focus on the past and literally worship the image of the dead. The childrearing atmosphere is pervaded with sorrow, yearning, and depression. In the classic Cain and Cain (1964) study of replacement children, parents had not been interested in having another child until their child died. For many, the home was turned into a shrine, daily schedules were dictated by visits to the grave, and photographs of the deceased filled the house. Parents talked incessantly about their deceased child many years later. Frequently they imposed the identity of the dead child upon the substitute child and unconsciously identified the two. The deceased child was idealized and the new child could never hope to compete. Such replacement children have been found to have psychopathologies ranging from moderate neuroses to psychoses, to be filled with phobias and general fearfulness created by parental overprotection. They are characterized by somatization, hysterical identifications, morbid preoccupations, and identity problems. They evidence guilt for never being able to measure up and decreased self-esteem as a result. They engage in self-defeating activities and feeble attempts to reject comparisons and dismiss identifications.

Even for those parents who manage to avoid the difficulties that can result from overidealizing or replacing their deceased child, there are a number of other problems in caring for the remaining children. Parents who have other children must continue to function in the very parenting role they are trying to grieve for and relinquish. This places them in an enormously psychologically difficult situation, as they try to meet the competing demands of surrendering and maintaining the same function simultaneously. (See Chapter 2 for more on this topic.) It frequently also becomes difficult to deal with the other children because they serve as painful reminders of the child who died. If bereaved parents feel they are giving inadequate care to the surviving children due to their preoccupation with the deceased child or other problems secondary to the grief process, even more agony is added to their failure-frustration cycle. Often, the overwhelming stress of grieving for the deceased child leaves the parents with little to give to anyone else. In addition, the normal tendency in grief to displace hostility onto others in close proximity may result in anger being directed toward the surviving children. This can make parents feel even more guilty.

Still other problems can occur between bereaved parents and the remaining children. There may be excessive worry over how the surviving children are dealing with their grief, which prompts many attempts by parents to diminish this grief. There may be feelings of resentment that the other children continue to live or distress because it appears that they have adjusted too quickly or grieved insufficiently. Parents may become concerned that their relationships with the remaining children are less intense than the one they shared with the deceased child and may fear that they have lost the ability to love their children. Usually this is very temporary and can be worked through as the bereaved parent continues through the mourning process and starts to reinvest. At times it may reflect a desire not to invest in the other children because of fear of their potential loss.

Overprotection of remaining children is not uncommon, but it has negative effects. Often such behavior robs those children of the normal experiences of life, usually desperately needed following the abnormal event of losing a sibling. Further problems can ensue when overprotection denies them needed opportunities for psychological, social, and physical development or increases fears and anxieties that interfere with normal growth. Reactions such as hostility, resentment, anxiety, insecurity, counterphobic behavior, and estrangement from parents can result when remaining children are overprotected. The irony is that, in their attempts to hold on to their surviving children, many bereaved parents actually push them away.

It is crucial for parents to understand the different grief responses of their children so that they do not erroneously presume the children do not understand the loss or are unaffected by it. Parents must avoid assuming that they "know" what the children feel or think unless they have talked with the children. Knowledge about children's responses to loss and how they are similar to and different from those of adults also better prepares them to communicate with their children about death and loss and to help their children cope.

Parents must recognize the unique difficulties of surviving siblings. These children will live longer with the loss than anyone else. The closeness of the sibling relationship makes the death of a child particularly traumatic for the surviving sibling, since it profoundly illustrates that she can die too. Parents must realize that surviving children may be struggling with guilt over previous ambivalence, anger with the parents for failure to prevent the death, emotional turmoil resulting from family reorganization, and problems stemming from the parents' preoccupation with their own grief, as well as grief over the sibling's death. It is also important that parents become aware if the remaining children are setting up unrealistic expectations for themselves by trying to take away the pain from their parents, to be perfect, or to replace the deceased sibling.

The Mourning of the Family Unit

Parents must be cognizant of the fact that the family system as a unit will mourn the loss of the child and parts of itself, just as each individual mourns that child and the part of himself that had been invested in that person. Failure to appropriately grieve can lead to serious familial dysfunction. It can cause an "emotional shock wave" that can shake the extended family system's equilibrium for years afterwards (Bowen, 1976) and can leave the family members open to the serious sequelae of unresolved grief. Both individual family members and the family as a whole must develop a new relationship with the deceased child and new identities for themselves. (See Chapter 22 for further discussion about this.) They also need to know that, while their closeness may be supportive in their grief, it can also make them likely to displace blame, anger, and other hostile feelings onto one another. Family members may ask one another unanswerable questions about the death, avoid communicating, or place irrational demands on each other. They may also remind one another of the deceased child. The "multiplier effect" frequently comes into play. Sometimes the presence of so many grieving people under one roof may be stressful and painful as one family member's grief response can trigger another's. At other times it may be comforting and supportive, generating a sense of community, shared loss, and strength in numbers.

Because parents have felt such an assault on their parental identities since they were unable to protect their child, they may be even more susceptible to assuming guilt when they notice the pain of the family's grief. Nevertheless, they must avoid trying to "protect" the family from this. This reaction is especially prevalent in bereaved fathers, who may attempt to take away the pain from other family members since they could not take away the death of the child. It is unrealistic for parents to expect themselves to be able to shield the rest of the family from pain following the death of a child. To attempt to do so will only interfere with the healthy mourning process that must be allowed to occur. Many parents may be so concerned with their children's grief processes that they pay insufficient attention to their own. For some parents this is solely a natural outgrowth of their focus on their children, but for others it may be a way of avoiding their own grief.

In many families, grandparents are an important part of the family system. While all relatives or friends can help or hinder the grief experience of bereaved parents, it must be remembered that grandparents are in a particularly difficult role. They not only lose their grandchild, but they "lose" their child as well, as they cannot rescue their child from bereaved parent status. Many of the issues pertinent to bereaved parents are salient for bereaved grandparents.

A particularly difficult issue for families to contend with is the number of different and idiosyncratic reactions to grief family members will display. It is additionally complicated when asynchrony in grief inevitably arises. As with marital couples, family members must not expect each other to grieve in similar fashion along a similar course, and must not assume that each has lost the same relationship. Family members must allow for personal differences in the system, recognizing that the individual factors previously discussed will influence each person's reactions to the death more than will her presumed similarity to other family members. A delicate balance must be struck between meeting the individual's needs in the mourning process and meeting those of others or of the system as a whole. There is the highest probability for successful negotiation of this difficult process in families where open and fluid communication is allowed.

SOCIETY

Compared to other deaths, there is greater social concern over the death of a child. Kalish (1969) discusses several reasons why the death of the young child seems more stressful than the death of an older individual. He notes:

> The life of a child has great social value. He has not had a chance to live, and we feel he is entitled to this. Also, his general helplessness moves us. . . . Another factor is that we do not attribute the death of a child to "his own fault," to inevitability, or to a style of living of which we disapprove. . . . The child who dies in contemporary American society is not considered mature enough to be responsible for behavior leading to his death, and, unlike the elderly man, he cannot be considered to have died inevitably. (p. 102)

Glaser and Strauss (1964) also believe that the death of a child is considered a greater loss because the child has not had the opportunity to live a full life as compared with the adult or aged individual. They note that such an evaluation may be responsible for the better quality of care and personal treatment given to children by health caregivers.

Nevertheless, in much of the thanatological literature the pediatric ward is cited as the example of the ultimate situation of frustration, anguish, and personal/professional stress for the caregiver. A dying child appears to cause the greatest anguish for all individuals involved (Rando, 1984).

Societal Reactions

That society is significantly threatened and impacted by the loss of a child is evidenced by the manner in which it treats bereaved parents and the unhealthy and inappropriate expectations it maintains and enforces for them. The remainder of this chapter analyzes society's posture toward and reactions to the parental loss of a child.

The social evaluations just described, plus the role of the parent and the parent-child bond with its attendant responsibilities, determine society's uniquely strange and callous response to bereaved parents. Although all bereaved people are somewhat socially stigmatized and may experience altered social relationships, parents whose children have died appear to report more of this than other mourners. Other parents are clearly made anxious by bereaved parents as they recognize that this unnatural event could happen to them and their own children. Bereaved parents represent the worst fears of these other parents and they become the victims of social ostracism and unrealistic expectations as other parents attempt to ward off the terror generated within them by bereaved parents. It is common for bereaved parents to experience feelings of abandonment, helplessness, and frustration as reactions to their experiences with other parents. They often complain that they feel like "social lepers." Frequently they will be avoided by other parents or will be the subject of their anger when premorbid levels of activity and humor are not returned to quickly enough. Social invitations may dwindle or become nonexistent. Consequently, bereaved parents are often left without many of the social and emotional supports desirable for coping with the grief process. Fortunately there are many national, as well as local, organizations that are extremely helpful here. Such self-help groups as The Compassionate Friends or groups devoted to specific types of loss such as Mothers Against Drunk Driving (MADD) or those existing for support of parents who miscarry, have stillbirths, or lose their child to Sudden Infant Death Syndrome (SIDS), have arisen to meet some of the psychosocial needs of bereaved parents and to fill in the gaps left by other members of society. Unfortunately, this segregation lends further support to the common feeling that only other bereaved parents can offer solace and understanding.

Inappropriate Social Expectations about Grief

Society has made a number of erroneous assumptions about the grief process that have been transformed into expectations. They are clearly inappropriate in light of clinical evidence about grief; however, they are potent factors in any individual's grief work because they directly influence that individual's evaluation of self as compared to societal expectations and standards.

In a society that values attractiveness, youth, and productivity, the death of a child, who embodies these attributes, is particularly repugnant. In such a situation the normal difficulties encountered with social expectations about grief and mourning are exacerbated. Usually society's unrealistic expectations and inappropriate responses to a griever's normal grief reactions make the grief experience much worse than it has to be. Admonitions such as "be brave" and "keep a stiff upper lip" are well recognized for stimulating unnecessary conflicts about the expression of grief. When the death is that of a child, there are additional emotional factors that intensify the social myths about bereavement. Example of some of these myths are as follows:

- All bereaved parents grieve in the same way.
- Parental grief declines over time in a steadily decreasing fashion.
- When grief is resolved it never comes up again.
- Family members will always help grievers.
- Children grieve like adults.
- Feeling sorry for yourself is not allowable.
- It is better to put painful things out of your mind.
- Do not think about your deceased child at Christmas because it will make you too sad.
- Bereaved parents only need to ventilate their feelings and they will resolve their grief.
- Expressing feelings that are intense is the same as losing control.
- There is no reason to be angry at people who tried to do their best for the deceased child.
- There is no reason to be angry at the deceased child.
- Only sick individuals have physical problems in grief.
- Because you feel crazy, you are going crazy.
- You should only feel sadness that your loved one has died.
- Miscarriage, neonatal loss, or sudden infant death shouldn't be too difficult to resolve because the child was not known that well.
- Children need to be protected from grief and death.
- Rituals are unimportant to help us deal with life and death in contemporary America.

- You should feel better knowing that there are other loved ones still alive.
- Being upset and grieving means you do not believe in God or trust your religion.
- Your family will be the same after the death as before your child died.
- You will have no relationship with the deceased child after the death.
- Your experience of grief, its intensity, and its length are testimony to your love for the deceased.
- There is something wrong if you do not always feel close to your spouse or other children, since you should be happy that they are still alive.
- There is something sick about you if you think that part of you has died with your child.
- If someone has lost a spouse, she knows what it feels like to lose a child.
- When in doubt about what to say to a bereaved parent, offer a cliché.

Harmful Impact on Bereaved Parents

As a parent struggles to cope with the intense reactions of grief following the loss of his child, it is particularly difficult to have to contend as well with the insensitive and hurtful responses of others in his social world. The rejection of others is often internalized as further evidence of deficiency or lack of value. This usually occurs despite an intellectual recognition that people are probably responding to their own anxiety. It is especially harmful when the intensity of parental bereavement causes parents to feel that they are "going crazy" and that they lack the validation that they could get from others, if not about the painfulness of their grief, at least about ongoing reality. In sensory deprivation experiments it has been well documented that in the absence of others with whom to check out perceptions and communicate, individuals become disorganized and develop serious impairments in reality testing. Societal reaction to the death of a child places bereaved parents in this situation frequently. This not only robs them of needed support, but also exacerbates the already high levels of stress and anxiety under which they must operate. In other words, societal responses too often not only do not help, but actually hurt bereaved parents. It is interesting to note that while society appears to value the parent-child relationship above all others, it also abrogates its responsibility to support those for whom this relationship has been severed. However, this is true only in regard to a parent's surviving a child. There is much more support for a child who survives the death of a parent. This may provide further evidence that the anxiety generated by contemplation of loss of a child is so high that it makes it relatively easier to cope with children who lose parents than with parents who lose children.

Another indication of society's problems with bereaved parents is its expectation that their grief experience will adhere to the same criteria as that of other bereaved persons for successful resolution of mourning and identification of pathology. As noted in Chapter 2 of this book, parental bereavement needs to be conceptualized and analyzed in terms other than the general models of mourning or the accepted symptoms of pathological grief. Failure to recognize this precipitates further stress for bereaved parents, who must contend with unrealistic expectations and inappropriate diagnoses of pathology.

Interestingly, society has even failed to provide an appropriate term signifying the altered status of a bereaved parent. A child who loses his parents is an *orphan*. A spouse whose mate dies is a *widow* or *widower*. But there is no word to denote a parent whose child has died. There also are no social guidelines on how to answer the question that plagues bereaved parents, "How many children do you have?"

SUMMARY

The death of one's child presents a parent with a host of psychosocial issues unparalleled in any other loss. This type of death profoundly impacts not only the individual parents, but also the marital dyad, the family system, and society. Caregivers must recognize the uniqueness of the loss of a child if they are to ameliorate the potentially devastating sequelae of this unequalled tragedy.

References

Arndt, H. C. M., & Gruber, M. (1977). Helping families cope with acute and anticipatory grief. In E. R. Prichard, J. Collard, B. A. Orcutt, A. H. Kutscher, I. Seeland, & N. Lefkowitz (Eds.), *Social work with the dying patient and family*. New York: Columbia University Press.

Benedek, T. (1970). The family as a psychologic field. In J. B. Anthony & T. Benedek (Eds.), *Parenthood: Its psychology and psychopathology*. Boston: Little, Brown.

Bowen, M. (1976). Family reaction to death. In P. Guerin (Ed.), *Family therapy: Theory and practice*. New York: Gardner.

Bowlby, J. (1961). Processes of mourning. *International Journal of Psycho-Analysis, 42,* 317–340.

Cain, A. C., & Cain, B. S. (1964). On replacing a child. *Journal of the American Academy of Child Psychiatry, 3,* 443–456.

Cairns, N. U., & Lansky, S. B. (1980). MMPI indicators of stress and marital discord among parents of children with chronic illness. *Death Education, 4,* 29–42.

Clayton, P. J. (1980). Bereavement and its management. In E. S. Paykel (Ed.), *Handbook of affective disorders.* Edinburgh: Churchill Livingstone.

Clayton, P. J., Desmarais, L., & Winokur, G. (1968). A study of normal bereavement. *American Journal of Psychiatry, 125,* 64–74.

Fish, W. C., & Whitty, S. M. (1983). Challenging conventional wisdom about parental bereavement. *Forum Newsletter: Forum for Death Education & Counseling, 6*(8), 4.

Foster, D. J., O'Malley, J. E., & Koocher, G. P. (1981). The parent interviews. In G. P. Koocher & J. E. O'Malley (Eds.), *The Damocles syndrome: Psychosocial consequences of surviving childhood cancer.* New York: McGraw-Hill.

Freud, S. (1957). On narcissism: An introduction. In *Standard edition of the complete psychological works of Sigmund Freud* (Vol. 14). London: Hogarth Press. (Original work published 1914)

Furman, E. (1976). Comment on J. Kennell and M. Klaus, "Caring for the parents of an infant who dies." In M. Klaus & J. Kennell (Eds.), *Maternal-infant bonding.* St. Louis: C. V. Mosby.

Glaser, B. G., & Strauss, A. L. (1964). The social loss of dying patients. *American Journal of Nursing, 63,* 119–121.

Gorer, G. (1965). *Death, grief, and mourning.* New York: Doubleday.

Herz, F. (1980). The impact of death and serious illness on the family life cycle. In E. Carter & M. McGoldrick (Eds.), *The family life cycle.* New York: Gardner.

Jackson, E. N. (1977). Comments in section on "The Parents." In N. Linzer (Ed.), *Understanding bereavement and grief.* New York: Yeshiva University Press.

Kalish, R. A. (1969). The effects of death upon the family. In L. Pearson (Ed.), *Death and dying: Current issues in the treatment of the dying person.* Cleveland: The Press of Case Western Reserve University.

Kliman, A. S. (1977). Comments in section on "The Parents." In N. Linzer (Ed.), *Understanding bereavement and grief.* New York: Yeshiva University Press.

Lansky, S. B., Cairns, N. U., Hassanein, R., Wehr, J., & Lowman, J. T. (1978). Childhood cancer: Parental discord and divorce. *Pediatrics, 62,* 184–188.

Levav, I. (1982). Mortality and psychopathology following the death of an adult child: An epidemiological review. *Israeli Journal of Psychiatry and Related Sciences, 19,* 23–38.

Lindemann, E. (1944). Symptomatology and management of acute grief. *American Journal of Psychiatry, 101,* 141–148.

Macon, L. (1979, November). Help for bereaved parents. *Social Casework,* 558–565.

Miles, M. S., & Crandall, E. K. B. (1983). The search for meaning and its potential for affecting growth in bereaved parents. *Health Values: Achieving High Level Wellness, 7* (1), 19–23.

Montgomery, P. (1980). Grief in couples. *The Compassionate Friends Newsletter, 3,* 5. (Reprinted from *Omega Report,* April 1979)

Osterweis, M., Solomon, F., & Green, M. (Eds.). (1984). *Bereavement: Reactions, consequences and care* (Report by the Committee for the Study of Health Consequences of the Stress of Bereavement, Institute of Medicine, National Academy of Sciences). Washington, DC: National Academy Press.

Parkes, C. M. (1964). Effects of bereavement on physical and mental health—A study of the case records of widows. *British Medical Journal, 2,* 274–279.

Parkes, C. M. (1970). The first year of bereavement. *Psychiatry, 33,* 444–467.

Parkes, C. M. (1972). *Bereavement: Studies of grief in adult life.* New York: International Universities Press.

Parkes, C. M. (1974). "Seeking" and "finding" a lost object: Evidence from recent studies of the reaction to bereavement. In *Normal and pathological responses to bereavement* (Series on Attitudes Toward Death). New York: MSS Information Corporation. (Reprinted from *Social Science and Medicine,* 1970, *4,* 187–201)

Parkes, C. M. (1975). Determinants of outcome following bereavement. *Omega, 6,* 303–323.

Parkes, C. M., & Weiss, R. S. (1983). *Recovery from bereavement.* New York: Basic Books.

Poznanski, E. O. (1972). The "replacement child": A saga of unresolved parental grief. *Journal of Pediatrics, 81,* 1190–1193.

Rando, T. A. (1983). An investigation of grief and adaptation in parents whose children have died from cancer. *Journal of Pediatric Psychology, 8,* 3–20.

Rando, T. A. (1984). *Grief, dying, and death: Clinical interventions for caregivers.* Champaign, IL: Research Press.

Raphael, B. (1983). *The anatomy of bereavement.* New York: Basic Books.

Sanders, C. M. (1979–80). A comparison of adult bereavement in the death of a spouse, child, and parent. *Omega, 10*(4), 303–322.

Schiff, H. S. (1977). *The bereaved parent.* New York: Crown Publishers.

Schwab, J. J., Chalmers, J. M., Conroy, S. J., Farris, P. B., & Markush, R. E. (1975). Studies in grief: A preliminary report. In B. Schoenberg, I. Gerber, A. Wiener, A. H. Kutscher, D. Peretz, & A. C. Carr (Eds.), *Bereavement: Its psychosocial aspects.* New York: Columbia University Press.

Schwartz, A. M. (1977). Comments in section on "The Parents." In N. Linzer (Ed.), *Understanding bereavement and grief.* New York: Yeshiva University Press.

Shanfield, S. B., Benjamin, A. J., & Swain, B. J. (1984). Parents' reactions to the death of an adult child from cancer. *American Journal of Psychiatry, 141*(9), 1092–1094.

Shanfield, S. B., & Swain, B. J. (1984). Death of adult children in traffic accidents. *Journal of Nervous and Mental Disease, 172,* 533–538.

Singh, B., & Raphael, B. (1981). Postdisaster morbidity of the bereaved: A possible role for preventive psychiatry? *Journal of Nervous and Mental Disease, 169*(4), 203–212.

Stephens, S. (1974). Bereavement and the rebuilding of family life. In L. Burton (Ed.), *Care of the child facing death.* London: Routledge & Kegan Paul.

Vollman, R. R., Ganzert, A., Picher, L., & Williams, W. V. (1971). The reactions of family systems to sudden and unexpected death. *Omega, 2,* 101–106.

Wallace, J. (1967). Comment on "Family Functioning" in panel discussion on "Care of the Child with Cancer." *Pediatrics, 40,* 512–519.

Chapter 2

Parental Bereavement: An Exception to the General Conceptualizations of Mourning

Therese A. Rando

Therese A. Rando, Ph.D., is a clinical psychologist in private practice in North Scituate, Rhode Island. She received her doctorate in Clinical Psychology from the University of Rhode Island and has participated in advanced training in psychotherapy and medical consultation-liaison psychiatry at Case Western Reserve University Medical School and University Hospitals of Cleveland. Presently she is the Clinical Director of Therese A. Rando Associates, Ltd., a multidisciplinary team providing psychotherapy, training, and consultation in the area of mental health, specializing in loss and grief and the psychosocial care of the chronically and terminally ill.

As a consultant to the U.S. Department of Health and Human Services' Hospice Education Program for Nurses, Dr. Rando developed their program for training hospice nurses to cope with loss, grief, and terminal illness. Her research interests focus on mourning, the experience of bereaved parents, and the emotional reactions of rescue workers. She is the Co-investigator in The National Bereavement Study, a longitudinal multidisciplinary research project investigating the processes and effects of grief.

Dr. Rando has lectured nationally and written about grief and death since 1970. She has numerous articles and chapters in print on the clinical aspects of thanatology, and is the author of *Grief, Dying, and Death: Clinical Interventions for Caregivers* and the editor of *Loss and Anticipatory Grief.*

The author wishes to thank Vanderlyn R. Pine, Ph.D., for helpful comments on an earlier version of this chapter.

In respectful dedication to all the bereaved parents who have shared their pain with me.

It is becoming increasingly apparent from clinical observation and empirical investigation that parental bereavement cannot be adequately understood in terms of the general conceptualizations that are held for grief and mourning. Not only is it clear that the process described in general models of mourning is impeded by the dynamics of the parental loss of a child; but the criteria utilized for identification and classification of pathological grief commonly appear in parental bereavement. This makes it difficult to identify abnormality given the typical responses evidenced after this type of loss.

This chapter begins with an examination of parental bereavement in terms of a commonly accepted model of mourning (Worden, 1982) and then documents how loss of a child involves issues and dynamics that set up the parents for diagnoses of unresolved, pathological, or abnormal grief. The poorly fitting model and its resulting diagnoses create further distress for bereaved parents when erroneous assumptions are made and unwarranted demands are placed on them. The chapter concludes by advocating two changes designed to reduce the problems resulting from the inappropriate usage of general paradigms for grief and mourning with bereaved parents. First, a new model of parental mourning must be constructed that takes into consideration the particular difficulties inherent in mourning the loss of one's child. Second, acceptance of previously adopted criteria for pathological grief must be reevaluated in light of the intensification and prolongation of symptoms typically evidenced in grief over this type of loss.

Although the observations and arguments made in this chapter in some ways fit deaths other than those of children, the author believes that the constellation of factors inherent in child loss makes this experience totally unlike any other bereavement.

PARENTAL BEREAVEMENT AND
THE TASKS OF MOURNING

In Worden's (1982) model, there are four tasks of mourning that must be accomplished in order for successful recovery from grief to occur: (1) accepting the reality of the loss; (2) experiencing the pain of grief; (3) adjusting to the environment in which the deceased is missing; and (4) withdrawing emotional energy and reinvesting it in another relationship. Because of the distinctive circumstances of losing a child, these tasks are hard for the bereaved parent to achieve. The model of the four tasks appears to be more applicable to conjugal bereavement than to parental bereavement on a number of levels. Just as it recently has been recognized that children's grief is not sufficiently explained by the adult model of grief and that a new one is needed that is more suitable to the experience of the grieving child, so it must be seen that there is a mandate for a new model of parental bereavement.

Parents have trouble meeting the first task of grief, accepting the reality of the loss, because it is difficult to accept such a reality when it violates one of the basic functions of being an adult, defies the laws of nature and orderliness of the universe, multiply victimizes the parents, and savagely assaults their senses of self and their abilities. (See Chapter 1 for a full discussion of these and other considerations.) The fact that parents often have more than one child complicates the matter further. When a spouse is lost, there is no other spouse living in the same home and the loss is constantly present. The absence of the spouse and the lack of gratification of the needs to invest in and be invested in by that special person force the mourner to unremittingly confront the fact that the death has occurred. However, bereaved parents can often deny the loss of a child by displacing their affection, hopes, and dreams onto their surviving children. Parents are called upon to remain functioning in the same role that they occupied with the deceased child. When a spouse dies, there are no other existing spouses that still require the same role responsibilities and behaviors. In contrast, surviving children do continue to require and demand parental interaction and functioning from their parents. Parents must still perform parental role-fulfilling behaviors, while the widow would not be expected to assume conjugal role-fulfilling behaviors unless she had remarried.

One obstacle may occur when the child who dies is an infant. Too frequently there is a social negation of this type of loss, an absence of social support and/or funeral rituals to help promote realization, confirm the loss, and provide an opportunity for nurturance from others. At the other end of the age spectrum, bereaved parents of adult children who die often have difficulty accepting the reality of the loss because there is no dramatic absence to signal that the death has occurred. The child usually has been living away from home and the parents have already adjusted to an environment in which the child is missing (see the third task). The death is easier to deny because the parents do not expect to see their child in the home and thus do not have to confront the reality of the child's absence. In such cases it may take a long time and much psychological work for the parents to recognize and accept that, in addition to the child's no longer being present in their environment, she is no longer existing in another environment somewhere else either.

The second task of mourning is to experience the pain of grief. The agony of grief and suffering is intensified in bereaved parents because they not only grieve for the loss of the child, but also for the hopes and dreams invested in that child, as well as the parts of themselves and their immortality that are represented in that child. Because of the unparalleled closeness of the parent-child bond and the unique issues with which bereaved parents must contend (see Chapter 1), the premature separation from one's child would be expected to generate the most severe torment possible. This is what is believed to account for the findings of the studies mentioned in Chapter 1 that document the particular severity and length of parental grief as compared to grief over other types of losses. It explains the observation that the "death of a child is the most significant and traumatic death of a family member" (Clayton, 1980).

Experiencing the pain of grief is a task that frequently is subverted by the lack of social support encountered by bereaved parents. Consistent with research on grief in general, the lack of such support leaves mourners without the requisite reality testing, compassion, and nurturance they need to handle the painful emotions and confrontations demanded in grief work. The unrealistic expectations maintained for bereaved parents additionally alienate them from potential sources of support and victimize them further.

The third task, adjusting to the environment in which the deceased child is missing, is complicated when parents must continue to operate in the very same environment, performing the same roles for surviving children (as noted under the first task). Usually a redefinition of roles and responsibilities, combined with an assumption of new skills, is mandated after a death. These not only signal that a change has transpired, but assist the mourner in coping with the new world in which she finds herself. For bereaved parents, there is frequently an absence of major role redefinition and altered functioning, unless the loss is of an only child. Parents are in a new world, an environment without the deceased child, but they still must operate in the ways of the old world, functioning in the same roles, with the same types of parental demands.

The fourth task is a combination of decathexis and reinvestment, withdrawing emotional energy from the child and reinvesting it in another relationship. This task is terribly difficult because it requires parents to attempt mutually incompatible tasks, simultaneously holding on and letting go. They are called upon to relinquish the parenting role with the deceased child and at the same time continue it with the surviving children. They also are faced with the need to let go of the aspects of the self represented in the parenting role with the deceased child and embodied in the child herself while retaining them at the same time. The child has been an extension of the parent and has been invested with myriad symbolic meanings, along with parental hopes, dreams, needs, and wishes for immortality. As such, it is difficult to differentiate the child from the self, identifying those qualities that solely belong to the child or solely belong to the parent. Thus decathexis is exceptionally hard for parents because detaching hopes and feelings from the child seems tantamount to giving up on part of oneself. As the child represents an extension of the parent's self in more than just the interactional sense of self that is usually defined in a relationship between two individuals, the loss of a child is more of a personal loss of self than any other loss.

Because of this close relationship, it is difficult to form the new identity that is supposed to develop as an outgrowth of healthy grieving. A further problem appears because a new identity is partially reached through the process of identification, an operation that is easier to accomplish when the deceased is a peer or a parent. It is less problematic to identify with another adult than it is with a child. Identification, to be healthy, must be appropriate to the age and role of the parent and must occur in aspects of the personality and functioning that can be appropriately integrated into an adult.

In this regard, it is relatively easier to internally retain parts of the self that were in interaction with individuals who were in roles other than that of a child. For example, it is comparatively simpler to internally hold onto some part of the self that had been a daughter by remembering the experience of having been mothered than it is to preserve some aspect of having been a mother to a deceased child. To internally "mother" rather than "be mothered" appears to be a more difficult process, since it requires an interactive process precluded by the absence of the child. It is less a disregarding of reality to think "What would my mother say?" than to try to act as if one were still parenting a child, perhaps thinking, "What can I do to make my child comfortable?" when the child no longer exists. In the former case, the passivity of the position does not require any interaction beyond making a decision based on one's former knowledge of the deceased. It is more consistent with a recognition of the reality of the loss. In the latter, the active position inherent in the parental role mandates that the parent interact with an individual who is no longer there, a process that tends to foster denial. Consequently, it is easier to form the required new relationship with the deceased (recognizing her as someone who lived and died) and to find appropriate ways to relate to her if this individual is a peer, parent, or spouse than if she is one's child. The parental role usually involves "doing for" and "doing to" the child, behavior that requires an object. In other role relationships, one can be "done for," for example, by a parent, or "done with," for example, with a spouse or peer. In these cases, the mourner does not require the presence of an object in order to relate to the deceased in the same manner as she would if it were a parent-child interaction.

Furthermore, it may be a relatively less complex transition to develop a new identity when one loses a spouse and shifts from being a "we" to "I" than when one must make a similar shift in regard to a particular parent-child relationship yet still maintaining the previous identity with surviving children. This makes the taking on of new assumptions about the world more difficult. Changes are harder to discern since much of the world is still the same.

The second part of the fourth task deals with reinvestment of the emotional energy that has been decathected from the child. This is a task that again seems more readily accomplished by those who are conjugally bereaved. While it is certainly not easy to find and develop new adult relationships in which to reinvest, it is undoubtedly less problematic for an adult to look for a mate than it is for a parent to have another child. In other words, in conjugal bereavement there is more availability of people who are similar to, and able to return investment like, the deceased loved one. People can more easily marry than become a parent; a child cannot be replaced as easily as a spouse. Clearly, bereaved parents must free the emotional energy that is invested in the deceased child; however, the reinvestment of this energy will be relatively less in other people (as compared to a widow who develops new relationships with adult men) than in other beliefs, behaviors, goals, and activities. Of course, some of the emotion that was invested in the child can be reinvested in other people. However, the model of adult grief and decathexis must be recognized as being more possible for adults seeking to replace the loss of a significant adult relationship than it is for a parent who has lost a child. It should also be noted that the widow who grieves and then finds another husband is often supported, whereas the parents who have another child are often looked at with the suspicion that such a child will be a "replacement child."

PARENTAL BEREAVEMENT AND UNRESOLVED GRIEF

Astute clinicians have observed that normal parental grief appears to approximate commonly accepted descriptions of pathological mourning or unresolved grief. Research studies have documented that grief over the loss of a child is relatively more severe when compared to grief over other losses (Clayton, 1980; Clayton, Desmarais, & Winokur, 1968; Sanders, 1979–80; Schwab, Chalmers, Conroy, Farris, & Markush, 1975; Shanfield & Swain, 1984; Singh & Raphael, 1981). It has been found to be particularly complicated and long lasting (Osterweis, Solomon, & Green, 1984) and to evidence major shifts in intensity over time, with symptoms frequently increasing following a decrease or absence of them previously (Fish & Whitty, 1983; Levav, 1982; Rando, 1983). There are a number of factors inherent in parental bereavement that invariably set the stage for this type of grief experience.

Reasons for Failure to Grieve

In 1979, Lazare posited a constellation of psychological and social variables that contribute to a mourner's failure to grieve. A number of these are prevalent in parental bereavement. These are delineated here with a brief explanation of how they relate to the parental loss of a child. Whereas these issues can occasionally impede any mourner's grief work, they are usually a normal part of the typical parental grief process.

Lazare identifies six psychological reasons for failure to grieve. Not infrequently, bereaved parents typically must contend with five of them:

1. *Guilt.* Parents are incomparably susceptible to guilt for the reasons stated in Chapter 1.

2. *Loss of an extension of the self.* Parents qualify for this because the child, by definition, is an extension of the parent's self.

3. *Reawakening of an old loss.* The death of a child can precipitate the reawakening of an old loss, as any death can. However, in those not

infrequent cases where the relationship with the child was a way to rectify old losses or where the child was representative of someone else, it is highly probable that the parent will have additional difficulties mourning the child because the old loss is resurrected (Orbach, 1959).

4. *Multiple loss.* Although usually employed to describe a series of discrete losses over time or a number at once, it is legitimate to attribute this experience to bereaved parents because of the distinctive dynamics of the parent-child relationship. Because of the multiple investments placed in a child, the numerous meanings that child may signify to the parent, the changes often perceived and/or experienced in the marital relationship subsequent to the death, and the typical avoidance by other parents, the individual who loses a child actually experiences a number of losses. While this is not unlike other bereavements, in which individuals also sustain a host of psychosocial and secondary losses after the death of a loved one, the loss of a child is sufficiently multifaceted that the parent experiences relatively more losses and can qualify as experiencing this resistance to mourning.

5. *Idiosyncratic resistances to mourning.* A number of factors idiosyncratic to child loss contribute to a reluctance to grieve: the nature and role of the parent-child relationship and the sense of failure it gives rise to when severed; the fact that the loss is so unnatural and unfathomable; the loss of support encountered in the spouse and other individuals in society; the fact that the family is permanently changed and "lost" to some extent; and the parent's observation at close hand of bereavement overload of those he loves. Most importantly, the loss of a child is such an overwhelming assault on the self, resulting in a marked decrease in self-esteem, the shattering of parental identity, and the negation of hopes for immortality, that it significantly interferes with the bereaved parent's ability to address and complete grief. He simply cannot cope with it very well. These are factors that are generally encountered. Factors idiosyncratic to the individual parent can be expected to compound any resistance that already exists.

Four of Lazare's five social reasons for failure to grieve typically may be incorporated into the normal parental grief experience:

1. *Social negation of the loss.* This frequently happens when the death is of an infant or an older adult child. In these cases there is a lack of social validation of what the parent has lost. This leaves bereaved parents without confirmation of their loss and without the social support necessary to accomplish grief work.

2. *Socially unspeakable loss.* This also contributes to a lack of a support system for confronting and experiencing the grief process. It

is well documented that bereaved parents suffer relatively more than other mourners from an absence of support and actually are avoided by others precisely because of the anxiety-provoking nature of the loss that they represent. It horrifies and frightens other parents, who then leave them without the resources needed to address their grief and overcome the inappropriate social expectations maintained. In cases where the types of death themselves are socially unspeakable, for example, murder or suicide, the parent experiences additional alienation.

3. *Social isolation and/or geographical distance from social support.* This issue refers not only to the customary lack of social support that is secondary to the social isolation just discussed, but also to the lack of support that occurs when there is a physical distance between family members. This latter issue is increasingly problematic because of the mobility of Americans and the nuclearization of the American family. It also is frequently encountered when one is mourning the death of an adult child if this child had been living away from home with his family. There may be difficulty in connecting the grandparents with the spouse and children, which interferes with confronting the reminders of the deceased and reviewing the mutual relationship as is required for successful resolution of grief.

4. *Assumption of the role of the strong one.* This is a position that often impedes the griever's accomplishment of the tasks of grief. Often parents, most notably fathers, are victims of this role because of their desire to protect the family, not only from outside harm, but from their own grief as well. Since the expression of grief is often inappropriately construed as a sign of weakness, those in this role will strive to avoid it.

Negative Influences on Response to Loss

As noted in Chapter 1, there are a number of factors that have been documented to influence any griever's response to a loss (Rando, 1984). The parent is the victim of a host of these factors, which makes the loss of a child harder to cope with and the grief experience more difficult. Those factors that are an inherent part of the bereaved parent's experience include the following:

1. *The unique nature and meaning of the loss sustained or the relationship severed.* Typically a child is invested with multiple meanings, and the parent's relationship with the child is the most intense life can generate. It would be expected that the loss of a child would be the most problematic loss to resolve because of this.

2. *The individual qualities of the relationship lost.* Since the parent-child relationship is so strong and involves so much attachment, bereaved parents face additional complications in their mourning.

3. *The roles that the deceased occupied in the family or social system of the griever and the characteristics of the deceased.* The fact that the loss is of one's child makes this the most significant and arduous loss to contend with. As the child is younger than the parents, and especially when his age is associated with vulnerability and innocence, the grief is more difficult to cope with.

4. *The amount of unfinished business between the griever and the deceased.* There will almost always be unfinished business with this type of loss, since when a child predeceases a parent it will almost invariably be viewed as a premature death and the parent will have to confront the loss of unrealized hopes.

5. *The individual's perception of the deceased's fulfillment in life.* This perception is skewed toward the unacceptable, since parents rarely feel that the child has lived the allotted time.

6. *The death surround and the sudden versus expected death.* The deaths of children very often occur suddenly, as the result of accidents. Both factors make grief more intense, longer lasting, and more difficult to recover from.

7. *The timeliness of the death.* It is always untimely for a child to predecease his parents.

8. *The individual's perception of preventability.* This is a thorn in many parents' sides, as they feel that in their role as parents they should have protected their child from everything. As a result they are susceptible to unequalled feelings of guilt.

9. *The number, type, and quality of secondary losses.* Because of the number of parental hopes and dreams represented in the child, the meanings invested in her, and the marital and social reactions that often follow her death, the number and quality of secondary losses is expected to be quite high.

10. *The presence of concurrent stresses or crises.* The fact that this loss often creates stress in the marital relationship, robbing a spouse of her primary source of support, significantly compromises the parent's ability to manage her grief.

11. *The individual's social support system and the acceptance and assistance of its members.* The support system is often absent or negligent for bereaved parents and this can be expected to exacerbate their grief.

12. *The funerary rituals.* In cases where funeral rituals are omitted, most notably in the deaths of infants, or where they are decided by others who may not incorporate the parents' needs into the ritual, as in

the case of the death of the adult child whose spouse makes the decisions, bereaved parents do not receive the therapeutic benefits of such ceremonies.

Susceptibility to Unresolved Grief

The characteristics of relationships that lead to unresolved grief are typically found in parent-child relationships. Although they can certainly be found in other relationships, they are overrepresented in this unique one. Consequently, bereaved parents are, by definition, set up to experience this type of grief. Four categories of unresolved grief are noted here, with particular mention of the associated factors that are inherently found in the parent-child relationship.

Inhibited, suppressed, or absent grief often occurs when one simply cannot accept the loss. Because of the unnatural nature of the event of the death of a child, and because of the features of the parent-child relationship, along with other reasons cited in Chapter 1, parents are likely to encounter difficulty accepting the loss and to end up with symptoms of these types of unresolved grief.

Distorted/conflicted grief is grief in which there is an exaggeration or distortion of one or more of the manifestations of normal grief, while other aspects may be suppressed. Two common patterns are extreme anger and extreme guilt. Extreme anger is often seen after the loss of dependent relationships, when there has been a sudden or unexpected death for which someone is blamed, or where the loss is of something special and irreplaceable. All of these characteristics are pertinent to a parent's relationship with a child. The distorted/conflicted grief response can also be manifested in extreme guilt. This is a reaction to which parents are extremely vulnerable because of the unrealistic personal and social expectations placed upon them.

Chronic grief results after the loss of dependent and irreplaceable relationships, when there has been an unexpected death, and when there has been an extraordinary, and possibly pathological, investment in the person who died. All of these factors are consistent with normal attributes in a parent-child relationship and consequently these predispose the bereaved parent to chronic grief. Additionally, in a very unique way, bereaved parents "grow up with the loss" of their child (Rando, 1984). The times at which their child would have accomplished certain things, such as gone to college, gotten married, or had children, are marked by upsurges in grief, as the absence of these experiences causes the parents to reencounter their loss in poignant ways. Parents thus experience a grief process that is continually resurrected, more so than grief over other losses.

The unanticipated grief syndrome is marked by complicated recovery (Parkes & Weiss, 1983). Grief symptomatology persists much longer than usual, the griever's adaptive capacities are seriously assaulted, and there is significant difficulty grasping and accepting the full implications of the loss. Since frequently the death of a child before a parent is not expected since it violates the natural order, and especially when the death is due to a sudden accident (which is so common in children's deaths), bereaved parents are naturally susceptible to this type of unresolved grief.

NEED FOR A NEW MODEL OF PARENTAL MOURNING

There are myriad variables that predispose bereaved parents to be exceptionally vulnerable to unresolved grief: the intense types of psychological, social, physical, and financial investments in the child; the unique relationship of parental responsibility and child dependency; the parent's investment in the child in terms of hopes and dreams; the child's significance to the parents in terms of meanings; the irreplaceability of the parental role; the strong motivation to deny the loss; and the fact that parents are forced to "grow up with the loss." This proclivity toward unresolved grief coincides with the conclusion by the National Academy of Sciences' Institute of Medicine that "it is often observed that grieving for a lost child never entirely ends" (Osterweis, Solomon, & Green, 1984, p. 83).

Now that the realities of the grief experience subsequent to parental loss of a child are known, a new model of parental mourning must be developed. Unless major modifications are made, bereaved parents often will be construed as having failed to appropriately complete their grief work according to the general model of mourning currently utilized (Worden, 1982). New criteria are mandated for identification of pathological parental bereavement, since the normal experience of parental grief so closely resembles that commonly accepted as unresolved, pathological, or abnormal. Since the typical characteristics of the parent-child relationship are those that complicate any individual's grief response, it is inappropriate to evaluate parental bereavement with traditional criteria. Such criteria cannot discriminate among symptoms of a loss that is so qualitatively different from others.

While research on conjugal bereavement, the foundation for most of the conceptualizations about grief and mourning, has provided clinical information of inestimable value to all those in the field of grief, it is imperative that we now recognize its limitations. Perhaps, as Bowlby (1980) suggests, it is time to recognize that different types of affectional bonds will give rise to different experiences after their severing. Just as the diverse affectional bonds (e.g., child to parent, parent to child, spouse to spouse, sibling to sibling, friend to friend) cannot be regarded as identical, neither can the needs and experiences generated from their loss be considered the same. Bowlby suggests that it is time to study these differences, although he feels this will represent "a formidable undertaking." With regard to parental bereavement, the time is overdue and the consequences are too severe to overlook, both in terms of the inappropriate social expectations that are placed upon bereaved parents by society, as well as themselves, and in terms of the misdiagnosis of normal parental grief as pathological.

References

Bowlby, J. (1980). *Attachment and loss: Vol. 3. Loss, sadness and depression.* New York: Basic Books.

Clayton, P. J. (1980). Bereavement and its management. In E. S. Paykel (Ed.), *Handbook of affective disorders.* Edinburgh: Churchill Livingstone.

Clayton, P. J., Desmarais, L., & Winokur, G. (1968). A study of normal bereavement. *American Journal of Psychiatry, 125,* 64–74.

Fish, W. C., & Whitty, S. M. (1983). Challenging conventional wisdom about parental bereavement. *Forum Newsletter: Forum for Death Education & Counseling, 6*(8), 4.

Lazare, A. (1979). Unresolved grief. In A. Lazare (Ed.), *Outpatient psychiatry: Diagnosis and treatment.* Baltimore: Williams & Wilkins.

Levav, I. (1982). Mortality and psychopathology following the death of an adult child: An epidemiological review. *Israeli Journal of Psychiatry and Related Sciences, 19,* 23–38.

Orbach, C. (1969). The multiple meanings of the loss of a child. *American Journal of Psychotherapy, 13,* 906–915.

Osterweis, M., Solomon, F., & Green, M. (Eds.). (1984). *Bereavement: Reactions, consequences and care* (Report by the Committee for the Study of Health Consequences of the Stress of Bereavement, Institute of Medicine, National Academy of Sciences). Washington, DC: National Academy Press.

Parkes, C. M., & Weiss, R. S. (1983). *Recovery from bereavement.* New York: Basic Books.

Rando, T. A. (1983). An investigation of grief and adaptation in parents whose children have died from cancer. *Journal of Pediatric Psychology, 8,* 3–20.

Rando, T. A. (1984). *Grief, dying, and death: Clinical interventions for caregivers.* Champaign, IL: Research Press.

Sanders, C. M. (1979–80). A comparison of adult bereavement in the death of a spouse, child, and parent. *Omega, 10,* 303–322.

Schwab, J. J., Chalmers, J. M., Conroy, S. J., Farris, P. B., & Markush, R. E. (1975). Studies in grief: A preliminary report. In B. Schoenberg, I. Gerber, A. Wiener, A. H. Kutscher, D. Peretz, & A. C. Carr (Eds.), *Bereavement: Its psychosocial aspects.* New York: Columbia University Press.

Shanfield, S. B., & Swain, B. J. (1984). Death of adult children in traffic accidents. *Journal of Nervous and Mental Disease, 172,* 533–538.

Singh, B., & Raphael, B. (1981). Postdisaster morbidity of the bereaved: A possible role for preventive psychiatry? *Journal of Nervous and Mental Disease, 169*(4), 203–212.

Worden, J. W. (1982). *Grief counseling and grief therapy: A handbook for the mental health practitioner.* New York: Springer.

Chapter 3

Parental Grief: A Synthesis of Theory, Research, and Intervention

Vanderlyn R. Pine
Carolyn Brauer

Carolyn Brauer, B.P.S., graduated from Empire State College in 1984. She is interested in social service and health care and has worked with The Mental Health Association in Goshen, New York, and the Valley School in Newburgh, New York. Ms. Brauer is a bereaved parent.

Vanderlyn R. Pine, Ph.D., is Professor of Sociology at the State University of New York at New Paltz and the former chair of the department. He holds A.B. and A.M. degrees from Dartmouth College and a doctorate from New York University.

Dr. Pine is a noted lecturer on the subject of dying and death and has been involved with counseling and research in death education. He is a member of numerous professional associations and serves on the advisory boards of The Center for Death Education and Research, The Foundation of Thanatology, The Association for Death Education and Counseling, and The Hospice Association of Ulster County. He is the Co-investigator in The National Bereavement Study, a longitudinal multidisciplinary research project investigating the processes and effects of grief.

A prolific writer, Dr. Pine has authored, coauthored, or edited some 40 published pieces, including the books *Caretaker of the Dead: The American Funeral Director, Responding to Disaster,* and *Acute Grief and the Funeral.* His articles discuss such subjects as dying and death, funeral customs, social change, statistical analysis, and computerization. In addition, he serves on the editorial boards of *Omega: The Journal of Death and Dying, Death Studies,* and *Suicide and Life-threatening Behavior.*

This chapter is dedicated to the memory of
Joshua Matthew Brauer, whose brief life was
not in vain.

———

Even though the literature on parental grief and response to the death of a child is abundant and multidisciplinary, it is badly fragmented. A major goal of this chapter is to try to bridge the gap between theory and practice and to offer some practical suggestions about ways to understand and help those in grief. While our ideas may spur some research, that truly is a secondary intention. Instead, the main purpose of this chapter is to offer a middle-range theoretical/empirical synthesis of theories, symptoms, treatments, and ideas about parental grief.

To accomplish this, we first present a brief review of some of the pivotal theoretical literature on grief and bereavement. Second, we delineate a number of specific findings on parental responses to the death of a child. Third, we present a review of the literature on successful treatment methodologies for parents who have experienced the death of a child. Fourth, we isolate the salient common themes in the theoretical discussions, research findings, and clinical reports. Finally, we present a synthesis of points one through four, offering what we believe are reasonable and humane suggestions and a practical protocol for dealing with the death of a child.

It should be noted that there are reviews of the relevant literature, especially in theses and dissertations; however, they tend to be perfunctory. Sadly, there is a dearth of coherent, systematic syntheses of the abundant material. Our aim of developing a theoretical/empirical synthesis may be overly ambitious, and in scholarly writing that is risky business at best. Our very purpose may upset some empiricists in the thanatology movement, whereas the same purpose may upset some of the field's theorists for opposite reasons. We are sorry if we create such feelings, and our apologia reflects a certain discomfort on our parts; but we believe that by attempting to develop a middle-range synthesis, we have a better chance of clarifying some important human reactions to the death of a child.[1]

THEORETICAL LITERATURE ON GRIEF

We begin by briefly describing the seminal work done by Freud, Lindemann, Bowlby, and Parkes in the development of a theory of grief.

Freud

Sigmund Freud (1917/1959) distinguishes between mourning as a normal "reaction to the loss of a loved person" and melancholia as "a morbid pathological disposition." He notes that although grief "involves grave departures" from usual everyday life, after an appropriate but undefined period of time it is "overcome." Freud goes on to explain that any external interference with grief may be "inadvisable or even harmful." Unfortunately, this comment seems to have led some early psychologists to avoid clinical intervention in grief situations.

Freud calls grief a "painful" state of mind and sets out to analyze grief, loss, and pain in terms of the "economics of the mind." The concept of economics opens the possibility of treating grief as an exchange process, with psychological tasks and activities being carried out as "labour" in exchange for a kind of psychic "freedom" from the dead person. In this sense, "the work of mourning" takes place over time, and bereaved people are fully aware of the fact that their reactions are because of the death.

Simply put, the goal of what Freud refers to as "the work of grief" is to free the bereaved individual from attachments to the dead person, inhibitions to becoming a separate being, and conflicts of ambivalence over the lost love relationship. Freud expands upon the ambivalence issue because of its complicating features, and because even unconscious feelings of ambivalence may be unearthed following death. This provides the grieving person not only with the conscious problems of loss but also with unconscious feelings, the existence of which the bereaved person never may have been aware. He explains that:

> The loss of a love object constitutes an excellent opportunity for the ambivalence in love relationships to make itself felt and come to the fore. Consequently... the conflict of ambivalence may cast a pathological shade on the grief, forcing it to express itself in the form of self-reproaches, to the effect that the mourner himself is to blame for the loss of the loved one. (p. 161)

Freud goes on to explain that after "normal grief" accomplishes the "labour" of freeing the bereaved from the lost love object, it does not leave "traces of any gross change" in the bereaved person. Loosely interpreted, it may appear that completed grief work represents a cured condition. Once again, a faulty Freudian legacy is that some clinicians extend this perspective to see grief as being curable in the medical sense, which implies that grief is an illness. Unfortunately, this violates Freud's ultimate point, which was that the human psyche has the ability to cope naturally with loss.

It goes beyond mere coping, however, for Freud speculates that the grief process absorbs the psychic energy surrounding the loss by assisting the person to gradually come to grips with the reality "that the object no longer exists." Moreover, Freud posits that the "slow and gradual severence" of love attachments that grief provides dissipates the energy of loss by the time grief work is carried out. Notably, he does not make the common error of placing a chronological time dimension on the duration of grief. It is a recent tendency to ignore the use by Freud of psychosocial time in favor of the easily measurable chronological time. The important lesson in Freud's insight is that it is the *process* of grief work that one must accomplish, and when that has occurred, then enough time will have passed.

The essential tasks of grief work are rather straightforward. Freud explains that "by declaring the object to be dead and offering the [person] the benefit of continuing to live, it impels the [person] to give up the object" (p. 169). As mentioned earlier, these tasks involve freedom, separation, and ambivalence.

Freud sets the stage for a sensible approach to managing grief by observing that grief is "like a painful wound." With the wound analogy, Freud paves the way for therapeutic intervention and moves a solid step closer to a usable theory.

Lindemann

Erich Lindemann's (1944) classic descriptive work, "Symptomatology and Management of Acute Grief," remains one of the best accounts of grief. It is theoretically sound, empirically grounded, and clearly written. Lindemann covers most of the issues of grief in this brief article. He distinguishes between normal and pathological grief, suggests ways of dealing with repressed or delayed grief, and explains that grief may precede a loss, labeling such an occurrence *anticipatory grief*. In a brief footnote he even introduces the term *chronic grief*.

One of the important accomplishments of this study was to grapple with the idea of grief as a potentially *acute* psychosocial phenomenon. Previous work on the subject often treated grief in the religious-prohibitory sense. For example, the ancient statement in the Roman Catholic funeral mass urged mourners "not to languish in fruitless and unavailing grief." This view that grief should be "gotten over" quickly was shared by early psychologists and psychiatrists. Such early treatments motivated Lindemann to analyze the reality of war and mass societal trauma and the resulting acute grief with rapid onset, serious conditions, and (hopefully) treatable symptoms.

Lindemann delineates acute grief as a definite syndrome with psychological and somatic symptoms. The syndrome may appear immediately, or it may be delayed, exaggerated, or apparently absent. Furthermore, distorted reactions may appear, which represent specific aspects of the grief syndrome. Lindemann goes on to say that, through proper psychiatric intervention, distorted grief may be transformed into normal grief, which then can possibly be resolved. This is another of the unique and brilliant glimpses Lindemann provides regarding grief: with humane and humanitarian understanding *and* clinical intervention, something can be done about unresolved grief.

Lindemann identifies five outward signs or expressions of acute grief. He first cites easily recognizable symptoms of somatic distress, such as tightness in the throat, choking, shortness of breath, sighing, emptiness in the abdomen, lack of muscular power, and tension. The other outward signs include preoccupation with the image of the deceased, guilt, hostile reactions, and loss of usual patterns of conduct. Lindemann states that there may be a sixth characteristic, which is often shown by patients who border on pathological reactions. This is the assumption of traits of the deceased by the bereaved person. For example, bereaved people may experience symptoms of the illness suffered by the deceased or find themselves walking or talking in the same manner as the deceased.

Lindemann states that the duration of the grief reaction seems to depend on how well the person performs what he terms *grief work*. The grief process may be subverted when the bereaved try to avoid grief work because of the intense distress and emotion it generates. The goal of the process, according to Lindemann, is resolution. This includes "emancipation from the *bondage* to the deceased" (p. 143), readjustment to the environment, and the ability to form new relationships. The idea of the dead person holding the bereaved "in bondage" refers to the fullest interactive relationship between people. This bondage involves power so dominant that, once dead, the person remains not only in memory but also in control of the bereaved person's life. This control may go beyond mere bondage if the bereaved idealize the dead person. When there is also a preoccupation with the image of the dead, the bereaved are in the double bind of being in bondage and idealizing the dead person, further subverting the goal of resolution.

According to Lindemann, if a bereaved person is confronted with important tasks or feels responsible for maintaining the morale of others, that person's grief reaction may be delayed for weeks or even years. Later, grief reactions may be precipitated by the recall of circumstances surrounding the death or by a spontaneous occurrence in the person's life. With World War II as a backdrop, Lindemann correctly recognized the tendency to refrain from or to delay grieving. In one sense, this tendency to delay or postpone reflects the potentially overwhelming aspect of loss by death. So much is gone, in terms of everyday behavior, economic interdependency, togetherness, relationships, conversation, that the bereaved person experiences a kind of loss overload that blocks adequate grieving. It may be thought of as a variety of what later was termed *bereavement overload*, in which case the bereavement that causes the grief simultaneously and paradoxically prevents the resolution of the grief.[2]

Lindemann observes that the type and severity of a distorted grief reaction can be predicted to some extent by knowledge of the premorbid personality. For example, patients with an obsessive or depressive personality may exhibit an agitated depression after bereavement. He further notes that the relationship to the deceased, whether affectionate or hostile, can be a significant factor in determining the severity of the grief reaction.

Lindemann feels that with proper management of grief reactions, serious psychological or medical problems can be avoided or ameliorated. The psychiatrist, psychologist, or other caregiver first must share in the grief work by helping the bereaved person extricate himself from overattachment to the dead person. The caregiver then should help foster the formation of new patterns of conduct for the bereaved that are psychologically and socially acceptable.

It must be emphasized that Lindemann's intention in his pioneering article was not to explicate the overall course of grief longitudinally. Even so, the manifestations he describes can be extended readily, at least in part, to the death of a child. Furthermore, Lindemann observes that "severe reactions seem to occur in mothers who have lost young children" (p. 146); however, he does not elaborate on this point, nor does he describe any specific psychological or physical symptoms for such cases. Grief symptomatology for child death can be extrapolated from the general case. Therefore, recognizing the symptoms he gives can help in understanding grieving parents. Of even greater saliency in the context of this book is the fact that many child deaths are sudden and/or unexpected; thus clinicians must understand the dimensions of acute grief in order to be responsive to many bereaved parents.

Bowlby

John Bowlby (1969) presents a detailed analysis of the nature of human attachment, drawing on a wide range of studies of the effects of separation and loss in early childhood. He describes patterns of response that occur regularly in early childhood and then traces how similar patterns of response are discernable in the functioning of later personality.

Unlike Lindemann, Bowlby's starting point is not a symptom or a syndrome but an event or experience that is deemed to be potentially pathogenic to the developing personality. Bowlby's pathogenic agent is the loss of a mother figure during the period between about 6 months and 6 years of age. Children in anxiety-producing situations demonstrate behavior recognizable as love, hate, ambivalence, security, anxiety, mourning, displacement, and repression. According to Bowlby, attachment behavior does not disappear with childhood but persists throughout life, for "old or new figures are selected and proximity and communication maintained with them" (p. 350). The outcome of behavior remains the same, but the means for achieving that outcome become diversified as the child incorporates new elements of attachment behavior. For our purposes, Bowlby links ongoing and new attachments to experiencing loss, for without attachment, there cannot be loss. The absence of proximity and communication actually defines his meaning of loss. Bowlby's analysis of the origins of mourning behavior in humans provides another dimension of the nature of bereavement by illustrating the powerful strength of human attachments.[3]

Parkes

In his book *Bereavement: Studies of Grief in Adult Life* (1972), Colin Murray Parkes presents a readable, compassionate review of the psychology of grief. Bowlby's influence on Parkes is evident and directly acknowledged by Parkes. Parkes deals primarily with the loss of a spouse, but he also touches on other losses, including child and parent. He stresses that grief as a functional psychiatric disorder is of known etiology, has distinctive features, and has a relatively predictable course, yet it is neglected in the psychiatric literature.

As does Freud, Parkes recognizes a therapeutically critical dimension of the concept of grief when he likens it to a physical injury rather than to an illness. From this perspective, he posits that the "wound" gradually heals but that further injury can cause psychosocial complications, just as further injury would to a healing physical wound. In such cases, grief may be complicated by the onset of physical illness.

Parkes adds two factors that he feels play a part in the overall reaction to bereavement, namely stigma and deprivation. By *stigma* he means the attitude of society to the newly bereaved person. As people avoid the person or become uncomfortable in his presence, it is as if in some way the bereaved person has become tainted by death.

Deprivation refers to the absence of those psychological benefits that previously were provided by the lost person, such as love and security. Herein lies a key link between grief and bereavement. Bereavement is the state or condition of being bereaved. In this sense, it is the *fact* of loss, regardless of what has been lost. *Bereave* means to deprive, dispossess, or strip from. Its root word derives from the Old English word meaning "to rob more from." Grief is the psychosocial response to the loss. The benefit of this view is that it enables clinicians to identify the clear-cut elements of a particular bereavement (the losses) and then to assess the accompanying grief (the psychosocial reactions). This is especially important when trying to provide therapeutic intervention to parents grieving the death of a child because the reactions may be more complicated than in other grief situations.

Parkes goes on to discuss the physical and psychological stresses apparent among the newly bereaved. He mentions several clinically observable reactions. First, the newly bereaved have a heightened tendency to become ill or to die. Second, they may experience panic states, episodes of severe anxiety, psychological pain, or "pangs." Finally, they often are preoccupied with thoughts of the dead person.

Parkes considers the defense mechanisms used by the newly bereaved, such as disbelief and selective forgetting, to be coping strategies used to mitigate the pain of grief. In this light, they need not be seen as pathological. Recall that Freud refers to grief work as the activity by which the bereaved person tries to obtain psychic freedom from the dead person by adjusting awareness, recollection, and memories of the dead person. Parkes extends this by assuming that grief work has the function of preparing the bereaved individual for acceptance of the loss. In one sense, some losses are never recovered from completely, and this is neither abnormal nor pathological, especially with the death of a child. Furthermore, it is not really chronic grief in the sense of what Lindemann described. Rather, it takes the form of consciousness that the loss has occurred and is part of life's reality. Acceptance of the loss does not necessarily mean getting over it, but rather coping with it.

Parkes found anger to be a fluctuating emotional reaction to bereavement that alternates with periods of depression. The bereaved person often turns anger against self toward others. Guilt may accompany anger, especially following bereavement in an ambivalent relationship. An extension of Parkes's position on this subject lends credence to the notion that grief for a child by a parent will be complex and often guilt-ridden. The death of a child generally is intricately intertwined with perplexing feelings of ambivalence. These feelings may involve death wishes about the child in cases of lingering, disfiguring, and debilitating diseases. In other cases the feelings stem from a host of interpersonal consequences of the parent-child relationship. Whatever the case, as Freud observed, ambivalent feelings compound an already difficult situation.

Parkes points out that ambivalence in a relationship, inability to talk about feelings, and the absence of appropriate social expectations and acceptable rituals for mourning are likely to contribute to patho-logical reactions to bereavement. He feels that the role of the therapist in treating typical grief reactions is to be an accepting professional with whom the bereaved person may express feelings of anger, guilt, despair, and anxiety. Pathological grief then can be transformed into normal grief and proceed toward resolution. Parkes concludes by stating that the care of the bereaved is a communal responsibility, encouraging family, friends, and volunteer caregivers, along with the therapist, to continue to be empathetic and supportive of the bereaved person. Of course, in reality, there often is an absence of strong interpersonal support in cases of child death. This lack often leads grieving parents to feel isolated, lonely, and misunderstood.

The poignancy of Parkes's observation reflects the widespread tendency for parents to feel stigmatized and deprived because of their child's death. The sharpness of the double-edged sword of stigma and deprivation is stated poetically by Simon Stephens (1972) in his descrip-tion of the parents in the book *Death Comes Home*:

> The innocent victims of a conspiracy of silence, Margaret and Peter Robinson suddenly found themselves placed in a quarantine. Their son's death had made them contagious. They had become a threat to the Mickleforth Community and, as the Old Testament leper had been excluded from the life of his village until such time as he was pronounced clean by the priest, so the Robinsons found themselves deprived of community care. They were enshrouded in a community of silence, at the heart of which was the great unmentionable—Death! (p. 33)

SPECIAL ISSUES IN PARENTAL GRIEF

In much of the current literature on the subject of bereavement, researchers recognize that the grief process is "normal" in the sense that grief is an expected, reasonable reaction to loss. However, this does not mean that it proceeds through precise fixed stages or sequelae. We can view grief as a predictable outcome following the death of a child and use that as a guideline for understanding and helping bereaved parents. The theoretical views mentioned thus far provide valuable insight into the dynamics of the grief process and suggest possible intervention techniques for dealing with the bereaved. Let us now turn our attention directly to some significant points found in a selection of the works giving special consideration to parental grief.

Parental Reactions to Child's Death

Parental bereavement seems to be more intense than other forms of bereavement, although the parents' feelings about the child will affect their response. In Catherine Sanders's (1979–80) comparison of the intensities of bereavement reactions in three types of deaths, spouse, child, and parent, she notes significantly higher intensities of grief among parents surviving their child's death. Sanders's work lends credence to the contention that the death of a child is especially problematic for the surviving parents. Moreover, we believe that the death of a child magnifies feelings of grief. It is the intensity of these feelings that gives rise to the more powerful responses that parents have after a child's death. Sanders found that parental grief resulted in more somatic reactions and greater depression, anger, guilt, and despair than did the mourning of those subjects who had lost either a spouse or a parent.

Grief after the death of any child is further complicated by how the parents feel about the child. On the one hand, if parents (or one of the parents) feel ambivalence toward the child for any reason, there are likely to be extreme emotional reactions linked to feelings of guilt if the child dies. For example, if the child is an infant of the opposite sex from what the parents wanted, if an adolescent does not possess the athletic ability the parents hoped for, or if an adult child does not fulfill parental expectations in the selection of a career, then a sense of ambivalence may exist for the parents. On the other hand, if the parents have always had positive feelings toward the child, regardless of expectations, the reactions may be quite different.

Richard Kalish (1969) believes that the death of a child causes more stress than any other death. He feels that this is so because in today's society there is exceptional social value placed on the life of a child. Furthermore, our collective emotions are moved by the death of a young child, who is considered helpless and deserving of a chance to live, and whose death is neither his own fault nor inevitable. The child or adolescent who dies in our society is not viewed as mature enough to be responsible for behavior leading to his death. Nor, in contrast to, when the elderly person dies, is it believed that the child's death was inevitable.

Age of Child at Death

Even when the child is not young, death generally causes intense problems for the parents; but whether the age of a child is a determinant of the level of parental grief is a debatable issue. It is possible that the grief reaction is not determined by the age of the child but rather by the child's dying out of sequence with the parents. Bereaved parents and their dead children fall into all age categories, and regardless of the child's age when he dies, the parental emotional reaction is rooted in the pervasive societal belief that a parent should not outlive a child.

Schwartz (1977) calls the death of a child a blow to the family and a threat to its hope for symbolic immortality, saying that a child serves as a connection not only with the past, but also, and perhaps more importantly, with the future and with a sense of immortality. The matter of immortality is too complex to treat adequately given the scope of this chapter; however, it is not a minor issue. Regardless of the exact nature of parent-child relationships, there is the natural order, the conventional wisdom of life, aging, death, and something beyond. It is logical that one's offspring should be a significant part of the "something beyond."

Some scholars believe that an older child's death is the most difficult grief experience for surviving parents. For example, Geoffrey Gorer (1965) feels that the most distressing and long lasting of all griefs is the loss of a grown child. In such a case it seems to be literally true, and not a figure of speech, that the parents "never got over it." Gorer explains that, at least in peacetime, it is "against the order of nature" for a child to die before his parents.

There are those who believe that having a teenaged child die is the most problematic grief situation. Arthur M. Schwartz (1977) points out that it appears that the effects of the deaths of adolescents or young adults are exceptionally intense. Edwin S. Shneidman (1977) asserts, "To die of cancer in one's teens or twenties, in college, seems a particularly 'unfair' and tragic thing" (p. 75). Kalish (1977) concurs with this view, observing that in our society the death of a young adult is viewed as the most tragic of all. Young adults have not yet been able to utilize their lengthy schooling; their deaths are often sudden and unexpected; and they are viewed as having been deprived of their birthright.

Even though there is disagreement about the most critical age of a child who dies, we believe that the issue does not have much practical significance to parents who have had a child die. The death of a child of any age generally is a loss so profound and unsettling that parents react in similarly distraught fashion. They may feel cheated and betrayed, guilty and responsible, out of control and inadequate, inconsolable and desperate, or a combination of all. Such parents lose not only the child but also part of their selves and an important part of their future.

Effects of Bereavement on Marriage and Family

The impact of a child's death on parents as a couple or on the family as a whole is great. There are differing perspectives on how marital partners and families might best handle their grief.

In her book *The Bereaved Parent* (1977) Harriet Sarnoff Schiff, a bereaved parent, aims to help newly bereaved parents regain a level of normal functioning. Schiff believes that only a bereaved parent can know how another bereaved parent actually feels. She draws essentially from her own personal experiences and observations, making some mention of studies but not listing any specific references. Although this is not a truly empirical work, Schiff makes some excellent points.

She states that in addition to the emotional trauma of losing a child, family crises erupt in the majority of cases. The aftermath of a child's death may include separation, divorce, alienation, and/or alcoholism. She contends that it is almost impossible for parents to comfort each other when they are experiencing relatively equal grief. In her opinion, a major contributor to divorce after parental bereavement is that too much is expected of the mate and too little given. When this is combined with the harsh reality of the child's absence, emotional turmoil is created that may linger.

Schiff discusses the impact of bereavement on marriage. She strongly disagrees with the notion that the tragedy of the death of a child brings a couple closer together. Instead, the emotional bond holding the couple together often breaks. She believes that the best way for the marriage partners to handle their grief is to enlist the aid of a third party to counsel them. As an alternative to private counseling, she recommends social service agencies and self-help groups. She cautions parents to carry their grief alone rather than try to do it as partners, claiming that their grief cannot be shared. Each parent is asked to remember that the other partner would help if it were possible, but it is unrealistic to put demands on a mate who is feeling the same pain of bereavement.

We contend that labeling mutual sharing as an unlikely possibility presupposes failure. The success of efforts by organizations such as The Compassionate Friends suggests that parents experiencing grief can help each other.

Schiff also believes that the capacity to enjoy is one of the bereaved parent's most important survival tools. It is important for bereaved parents to realize that they can and will be able to experience enjoyment again. She feels that enjoyment does not mean that a bereaved parent is abandoning the dead child or the grief of the loss, and that the key to dealing with pleasure lies in knowing this.

Erna Furman (1978) brings together two areas of research, the area of parent-child relationships and the area of bereavement and mourning. Although she does not give specific references, her comments on detachment and identification are reminiscent of Bowlby's attachment theory (1969). Furman points out that our culture does not contain a support system for parents who have lost a child. She suggests that parents should share their grief with each other or with other people in similar circumstances through what could be called peer counseling. Here she is at odds with Schiff's (1977) opinion that the partners must work out their grief separately.

Furman believes that it is necessary to tolerate the pain and discomfort of grief consciously, and that parents should try to share these feelings with each other. However, she also adds that it is beneficial to have a professional person available to assist them and share the burden of grief with them using empathetic understanding.

Idealization of the Dead Child

Parents may try to cope with a child's death through idealization or "enshrinement" of the dead child. Beverley Raphael (1983) finds this to be a common theme in the mourning of children. She states that the child who has died is intensely idealized. Memories of a perfect child are maintained by the parents so that other children seem imperfect and fail in comparison. She feels that this is a way of trying to hold on to the dead child.

Walter Tietz, Laura McSherry, and Barbara Britt (1977) interviewed parents of leukemia victims and observed that in many of their homes a picture of the deceased child was prominently displayed. They note that the picture of the child was "large and lifelike as if the child were still present in the home, as if the child had not died at all" (p. 419). John Kerner, Birt Harvey, and Norman Lewiston (1979) did a study of parents who had lost a child to cystic fibrosis. They state that more than a year after the death many of the parents had preserved the dead child's room as a shrine or visited the gravesite at least weekly. They feel this contributes to or is a symptom of incomplete mourning. Such idealization seems to be potentially problematic and damaging to the family milieu, causing feelings of inadequacy, deprivation, and hostility.

Albert Cain and Barbara Cain (1964) discuss the replacement child syndrome, saying that it is most likely to take place when parents have suffered the death of an offspring during the childhood period. The authors state that although the dead child is enshrined by the parents, they do not seem able to give up their need for a child. Therefore, in addition to grieving for the dead child, some of them have a new baby on whom they impose the identity of the dead child. The grieving parents attempt to mold the new child into their generally unrealistic, idealized image of the dead child. This often leads to unfavorable comparisons between the replacement child and the dead child. Some children are overprotected, while others bear the brunt of much hostility. This syndrome also may involve a surviving sibling who is delegated the dead child's place in the family.

In contrast to the negative perspective just discussed, Lynn Videka-Sherman (1982) feels that the replacement of the dead child or the capacity to reinvest love may help the parent to adjust and cope with the loss of a child. She feels that early replacement illustrates an "active" adaptation to a loss. She considers either replacement with another meaningful role or another child to be coping strategies that allow parents to reinvest energy and love.

Contrasting views about the matter of a replacement child pose a serious dilemma. It is our opinion that encouraging replacement is potentially harmful. A key need for the bereaved person is to be reintegrated into society as a modified or altered being who will continue living without the dead person. This calls for *new* investments of energy and love into other relationships. However, replacement, like love on the rebound, starts a new relationship on a weak foundation.

Furthermore, a replacement child fosters ongoing death denial. In essence, a replacement child becomes a third person in a tragic triad consisting of the dead child, the live child, and the live child as a substitute for the dead child. Parental denial of the death is essential for this perverse relationship to exist, and the victim is the replacement child whose selfhood is oppressed by the image of the dead child. To put it bluntly, a replacement child never can substitute for the dead child and never can truly actualize himself.

The Search for Meaning

Another way parents can cope with a child's death is by trying to find meaning in the loss. It is a healthy way to recover from such a tragedy.

Yvonne Craig (1977), a bereavement counselor for The Compassionate Friends, writes that the primary task of the mourner and counselor is generally recognized as being the emotional relief of bereavement. She draws attention to the ways the bereaved understand their experience and reconstitute their family life. In her article she notes that recent studies of parents whose children have died in traumatic circumstances suggest that it is an essential part of grief work to resolve the meaninglessness of the crisis. Those whose children die following chronic diseases also need to find meaning in their tragedies. Bereavement is thus an experience of suffering, and the renewal of family life depends on the acceptance of separation and the regenerative use of its pain. These points are reminiscent of the works of Bowlby and Parkes.

Craig feels there are many ways in which society attempts to assuage the suffering of parents facing crises. Often it does this by imposing its current morality on them. For example, a bereaved woman may be told by a doctor that she should have another child, or tranquilizers will be given to a bereaved parent to enable the doctor to retreat from a threatening therapeutic relationship. All such tactics may have a negative effect on the bereaved parent and lead to dissatisfaction with professional intervention. Craig notes that when there is discontent with professionals, the need to reconstruct meaning following shattering experiences may lead individuals to strengthen themselves by activities such as forming self-help groups.

Margaret Shandor Miles and Eva K. Brown Crandall's (1983) findings from their studies of bereaved parents suggest that, following the death of a child, parents may embark upon an existential search for meaning.[4] This may ultimately lead to positive growth outcomes. The bereaved parents in the Miles and Crandall study noted positive effects such as "having a stronger faith, being more compassionate and caring toward others, and living life more fully because of an increased awareness of the preciousness and fragility of life" (p. 19). It is important to recognize the commonsense connection between their findings and the age-old awareness that discovering purpose and meaning is crucial in helping resolve grief.

Anticipatory Grief and Grief Over Time

Therese A. Rando (1983) investigated parental experience with and adaptation to a child's terminal illness. In the course of her study she explored the important topics of anticipatory grief and the course of grief over time. Several surprising results were found.

Researchers have previously asserted that a mother's more extensive participation during a child's hospitalization facilitates her anticipatory grief and subsequent adjustment following the death. However, Rando's data do not support this assertion. They show that although fathers were not as involved as mothers in behavioral participation during a child's hospitalization, they were almost equal in their amount of observable anticipatory grief behavior.

Her findings suggest that support to parents during the illness of a child facilitates the process of anticipatory grief, which seems to foster other positive experiences. Support to parents during the illness appears to be associated with less abnormal grief after the death. This indicates the potential for health care personnel to have a positive influence on parental grief by supporting parents during the illness.

Rando notes two variables that seem to identify parents who may be at high risk in terms of their grief and adaptation: long duration of the child's illness (longer than 18 months) and a high level of previous losses for the parents. Rando's assertions regarding long duration of illness are particularly noteworthy. According to her, long duration of the illness may lessen the coping abilities of the parents after death and increase their feelings of anger and hostility. She posits that when an illness lasts too long the stress of the experience works against adequate preparation for the death by the parents. Remissions, relapses, and possibly parental denial due to the long course of an illness may be important factors that inhibit adequate preparation. The ordeal of the child's illness may simply drain the parents' ability to cope as well as hinder their adjustment after the child's death.

One of Rando's most notable observations involves the effects of the passage of time. Contrary to the adage "Time heals all wounds," she has observed something strikingly different. In the third year of bereavement there may be an intensification of the grief experience, suggesting that parental bereavement may actually worsen with time. The originality of this concept is striking, but additional research needs to be done in this area. Such research would involve a well-developed, longitudinal study of bereavement patterns among a wide range of bereaved people, including parents. This research would provide better understanding of the temporal dimensions of grief.

As mentioned earlier, Freud sees time as an element in bereavement but chooses not to set the limits in chronological terms. In the same vein, but from a different perspective, Lindemann observes, "Patients in acute bereavement about a recent death may soon upon exploration be found preoccupied with grief about a person who died many years ago" (p. 144). The point is, as Rando so aptly points out, the verdict is not in yet regarding grief and time. Moreover, her findings fit into our synthesis, for we maintain that grief must be considered in relation to psychosocial time as well as chronological time. Thus, more specific knowledge of the vicissitudes of grief patterns over time is essential for a fuller understanding of the dynamics of the overall process.

Sudden Death

Unexpected deaths, which often happen to children, bring many emotional complications. They are particularly hard on parents, who believe it is their duty to protect their children from harm.

James Nixon and John Pearn (1977) report their findings from an investigation to evaluate the intra-family dynamics that occurred with 111 cases of childhood drowning and near-drowning in the city of Brisbane, Australia, between 1971 and 1975. Personal interviews were obtained with 77 of the families. The authors point out two specific themes that occurred throughout their investigation of these families, who had suffered the sudden loss of a child. First, the suddenness of the accident gives no time to anticipate the tragedy and anticipatory grieving cannot occur. Second, many such accidents are interpreted by one or both parents as having been potentially preventable. The authors conclude that acute grief may be compounded by parental self-accusation, guilt, helplessness, and aggression. It was their experience that the suddenness of the loss of a child from acute unexpected trauma commonly leads to forms of pathological bereavement, such as those initially described by Lindemann (1944) as morbid grief reactions.

The same themes consistently run through research concerning Sudden Infant Death Syndrome (SIDS) deaths and unexpected neonatal deaths. Eric Markusen, Greg Owen, Robert Fulton, and Robert Bendiksen (1977–78) discuss the survivor as a victim following a death from SIDS and relate the particularly problematic aftermath for surviving parents. The suddenness of the death, absence of a definite cause, abrupt severing of the mother-infant bond, sibling bereavement, and the legal system all contribute added complications to SIDS deaths. They point out the possible contributions of one caregiver who is often overlooked, the funeral director. The authors feel that the funeral director can be a very important figure in supporting the bereaved family by interfacing with clergy and health care personnel in the months following a SIDS funeral. The steps to accomplish this include making the funeral director aware of the role that he might play with respect to SIDS, determining how that role might be successfully carried out, and studying actual case histories to evaluate the effectiveness of varying modes of intervention.

Stillbirth and Neonatal and Infant Death

There are particular psychological and social problems related to stillbirth and infant deaths. The reality of the child's life and death is hard for parents to confirm, and society often sees the loss of such a young child as less important than other losses.

Glenn Davidson (1977) conducted a 5-year study of mothers who suffered a stillbirth or neonatal death. He discusses ways the women and the people around them coped with the loss of the child. Davidson describes the process by which the mothers in his study tried to move from disorientation to orientation. There were three points at which they were thwarted: first, when trying to confirm their loss perceptually; second, when reaching out for emotional support; and third, when trying to test their feelings against the perceptions of others. Davidson found that perceptual confirmation of having given birth is a crucial part of women's becoming reoriented after the baby's death. Those women who held and touched their babies, even at the moment of death, were found to adapt to their loss more successfully than those who had not.

This point will be further expanded in our protocol for helping bereaved parents; however, it is important to emphasize that in order to accomplish any sense of closure regarding the child's death, the matter of actually confirming the birth *and* the death cannot be overestimated. We believe that human perception of another human being at the personal level involves a complex set of interpersonal stimulants affecting all the senses. Therefore, seeing, holding, touching, smelling, and hearing the child all contribute to the confirmation of reality.

Davidson found that when mothers reached out for emotional support after the death, their feelings often were sacrificed to the anxieties of others. The failure of society to understand the mothers' feelings often led to anger and frustration on their part. Davidson further found that when people within the mothers' milieu acted as though nothing had happened and ignored the women's feelings, the women doubted their own perceptions and found themselves fearing that they would go crazy. Our contention that realistic knowledge of the dynamics of grief is a prerequisite in helping the bereaved is clearly supported by Davidson's work.

Thwarting of the reorientation process by society caused the women in Davidson's study to resort to seemingly bizarre behavior in attempting to avoid chronic disorientation. One woman in the study cradled vegetables or a rolling pin the size and weight of her baby in her arms to help her imagine what her child might have felt like. She was then able to confront her grief. We agree with Davidson that healthy mourning needs to be expressed in a pattern that permits the mourner to have a sense of "doing the right thing," to identify with an orderly process, and to feel release from the intensity of the loss.

In their study of mothers whose infants had died, Larry G. Peppers and Ronald J. Knapp (1980) found a significant number of mothers for whom grief resolution may never occur.[5] The majority of the women in their study felt that they would carry the burden of loss throughout their lives. It must be noted, however, that most of the women in this study did not receive professional intervention to help alleviate their grief. That a truly long-term examination of these women did not take place underscores the absence of solid evidence regarding the duration and severity of grief.

Thomas Helmrath and Elaine Steinitz (1978) present an excellent discussion of the failure of social support for parents who have lost an infant. They begin by stating that parents undergo intense grief reactions following the death of a newborn infant. However, these parents frequently fail to receive emotional support from family and friends. They state that this social response differs from that which occurs with the death of an older child or an adult.

The authors believe that because neonatal death is not anticipated, the parents are usually in a state of shock and disbelief. Yet health care professionals and society at large often seem to view parental grief following the death of an infant as not as severe or prolonged as that experienced with the death of an older child. This view discounts the effects of bonding by the mother, and possibly the father, to the fetus prior to birth. The death of an infant or a neonate produces intense parental grief, regardless of whether the parents actually saw or touched the child.

Helmrath and Steinitz studied seven white, middle-class married couples between the ages of 20 and 35 to explore the events and personal interactions that helped or hindered them following their infant's death. The authors found that with all couples the men and women differed in the characteristics of their grief, with the women feeling the loss more acutely and grieving for a longer period of time. Unexpected episodes of acute sadness with prolonged spells of intense crying were experienced by the mothers. Each felt the need to talk about her baby and review the details of the birth and death. Guilt was evident in all cases, and the mothers appeared to experience this feeling more intensely than the fathers. Moreover, the men in the study appeared to resolve their guilt feelings sooner than the women. In this regard, the men also felt that they had been socialized to be strong and unemotional and felt that they had to be strong for their wives and not break down.

Couples commonly were found to experience a sense of extreme isolation from friends and family and feel that society treated their baby's death differently from the death of an older child. Feelings of resentment were generated by insensitive comments, and couples found that their need to talk about their loss was not shared by friends and family. This situation caused severe distress for all of the couples.

Helmrath and Steinitz found that the parents felt society viewed the dead baby as replaceable and thus saw their grief as somehow inappropriate. The authors believe that this social response occurs because family and friends do not have the opportunity to become attached to the baby, and they usually have minimal feelings toward the infant.

In this study, sharing of feelings between the partners and the resulting mutual trust proved to be the most important factor in the resolution of parental grief. They found that once lines of communication were fully opened, grief resolution progressed. For all couples in this study, the quality of their relationship was seen to have improved, and some felt that the death actually provided them an opportunity for growth.

The study concludes with specific recommendations for health care providers on facilitating grief resolution in parents. The authors feel that those working in obstetrical services should understand the grief process and assist the parents to verbalize their feelings. They should encourage the parents to see, touch, and even photograph the dead baby if desired. The grief process should be explained to the parents, and an appointment for a counseling session should be set before the mother leaves the hospital. Autopsy data should be made available to the parents and continued support should be offered. Referral to a support group can be made if the parents so desire. Finally, the parents should be encouraged at all points in the grief process to select the alternatives they desire, regardless of the feelings of family and friends.

Gender Differences in Bereavement

The issue of gender differences in grieving patterns is debatable. Judith A. Cook (1983) found in her research that in most instances "behavioral expectations" of the overall society were reflected in the expectations bereaved parents had for themselves and their spouses, such as the "emotionally and verbally expressive mother" and "stoic, nonemotional father" roles. She states, and we agree, that assuming these roles often restricts the grief and resolution processes.

From this and other analyses of the gender issue, one could postulate that purely sex-linked differences should be studied. However, our view is somewhat different. Both personal experience and observation, as well as anecdotal evidence from others, has led us to the following hypothesis. We believe that gender differences may be a result of medical circumstances and social activities performed in addition to established socialization patterns. For example, in the case of a newborn death or stillbirth the mother generally is hospitalized and is often in a physically weakened state. This usually results in the father making most or all of the arrangements for the funeral and taking care of other details that may foster and/or constitute closure in relation to the death. In our view, there is a need to study the impact of such closure activities on bereavement and coping. The point is, if performance of closure activities leads to better coping, then the question of grieving styles may not be due to gender or socialization alone but rather due to activity orientation as well.

Practical Problems

Although seldom mentioned, there are additional problems beyond the psychosocial ones, and these real-life problems generally have a direct bearing on the way parents respond in dying and death situations. Anders Krueger, Karin Gyllensköld, Gunnel Pehrsson, and Stig Sjölin (1981) point out that practical problems such as increased expenses and the need for supervision of children at home should be discussed with parents at an early stage in a child's terminal illness. The authors feel these problems can be addressed if a hospital social worker steps in to work with the family at the time when parents are first given information about the child's diagnosis. This avoids bringing in an "outsider" during a crisis or when death is imminent. In this way, the social worker can serve as a valuable contact person for the family throughout the child's illness. The authors state that this type of continuity is important to the child as well as the other members of the family. They emphasize that social problems that affect the family in connection with the child's illness should be determined early, and steps to alleviate these problems should be instituted as soon as possible.

The literature reviewed thus far emphasizes the fact that no single work definitively treats all issues relevant to grief and bereavement. However, certain common threads are apparent throughout. All authors recognize certain psychological, emotional, physical, and social aspects of the grieving process. The consensus of opinion is that while bereavement reactions may become problematic, a program of supportive and specific intervention can facilitate the process of grief resolution.

TREATMENT PROGRAMS FOR PARENTAL GRIEF

We believe that while the literature indicates that much more research should be carried out in addressing the needs of all bereaved persons, the special problems of bereaved parents require separate consideration. While there are no universal professional programs specifically designed to help reorient parents after the death of a child, our research has uncovered some humane programs designed to assist bereaved parents in coping with their grief.

Out of the research, writing, and speculation, the concept has emerged that a child's death and the grief that accompanies it is a treatable tragedy. Treatment programs offer a chance for relieving the most destructive grief symptoms when they link the reality of the death to a sound theoretical and programmatic approach.

J. William Worden accomplishes this in the approach he describes in his book *Grief Counseling and Grief Therapy* (1982). His techniques for counseling grow out of the works of Freud, Bowlby, and others, and are designed to facilitate the carrying out of four basic tasks of mourning: accepting the reality of the loss, experiencing the pain of grief, adjusting to the environment without the deceased, and withdrawing emotional energy from the deceased and reinvesting it in a different relationship. He offers the following 10 "counseling principles and procedures" for helping people work through their grief:

1. Help the Survivor Actualize the Loss
2. Help the Survivor to Identify and Express Feelings
3. Assist Living Without the Deceased
4. Facilitate Emotional Withdrawal From the Deceased
5. Provide Time to Grieve
6. Interpret "Normal" Behavior
7. Allow for Individual Differences
8. Provide Continuing Support
9. Examine Defenses and Coping Styles
10. Identify Pathology and Refer (pp. 39–48)

Worden views the death of a child as a special type of loss and recommends "additional understanding and intervention modifications which go beyond" his 10 general principles. For example, he recommends careful handling of information about the death, sensitive intervention by professionals, allowing parents to actualize the loss of the child by viewing the dead body, clarification of the cause of death, information about subsequent emotional reactions, and other sensitized responses.

Let us examine some specific treatment programs that utilize these and similar suggestions. They have been organized to reflect a life cycle sequence. We hope it enables readers to make reasonable comparisons among such programs and to derive the benefits of creative combinations.

Pauline Seitz and Louise Warrick (1974) are obstetrical nurses, who focus on nursing help for the mother whose newborn or fetus dies. They provide an emotional and useful account of the psychological needs of mothers and fathers anticipating a stillbirth. The authors feel that before the delivery of a dead fetus, a nurse should talk to both parents together to encourage mutual empathy and understanding. The woman needs reassurance that her anger, depression, and helplessness are not abnormal or uncommon.

As the woman enters labor, a statement from the nurse acknowledging that her situation is understood will open communication in a tension-filled predicament. The nurse should be available to talk with the woman and allow her to express her feelings during her labor so that she may begin to accomplish her mourning tasks. Throughout the delivery, the nurse should create an atmosphere that is comfortable and promotes the expression of feelings.

As far as viewing the stillborn neonate is concerned, the authors agree that it is important to recognize and respect the feelings of the parents and to support them in their decision. They state that when parents are prepared for what will be seen during the viewing there are no hysterical reactions.

The authors also address the subject of critically ill babies in neonatal intensive care units. They feel that it is essential that women have physical contact with their dying baby in order to facilitate acceptance of the inevitable death. They conclude that acceptance of the infant's death is the most important factor in developing appropriate coping mechanisms needed by parents to adjust to the reality and finality of the death.

Kenneth Kellner, Elizabeth K. Best, Sandra Chesborough, William Donnelly, and Marjorie Green (1981) describe the Perinatal Mortality and Counseling Program (PMCP) at Shands Teaching Hospital in Gainesville, Florida. In this program an interdisciplinary team provides crisis intervention for families that have experienced a stillbirth. The team follows a very humane, compassionate protocol for dealing with the families.

The counseling team at Shands consists of an obstetrician, a social worker, a pathologist, and a psychologist. The medical team tries to communicate about the delivery of a stillborn as directly and honestly as possible, giving predelivery information to the parents and informing the medical personnel caring for the woman. The parents are given a copy of the baby's footprints and relevant birth data. The mother is seen by team members every day during her stay in the hospital. Parents may see and hold the dead baby. Events of the labor and delivery are reviewed and expectations for the grieving process are communicated by the staff.

The parents are seen 4 to 6 weeks later for medical examination and to meet with the counseling team. They are encouraged to express their feelings. When an autopsy is performed, the pathologist and team members meet with the parents to review the findings. Team members try to identify potential bereavement problems and make appropriate referrals when indicated.

Ann L. Wilson and Douglas J. Soule (1981) discuss how a self-help group can ease guilt and foster communication between the marital partners in couples who have experienced a stillbirth. The authors share our view that grief in problematic situations should be facilitated by professionals or trained lay persons, for not to do so could prolong disorientation of the newly bereaved. They feel that training those who have experienced a stillbirth to help other newly bereaved people validates their emotions and eases their anguish, as well as aiding others in grief resolution.

Lewis Cohen, Susan Zilkha, Joanne Middleton, and Nancy O'Donnohue (1978) state that the health professional's role does not cease with perinatal death but shifts toward primary prevention of psychiatric problems in the parents. Their study was done through a multidisciplinary service at the Downstate Bereavement Clinic at Downstate Medical Center in Brooklyn, New York. The authors found that an increased awareness of the process of viewing the dead body and experiencing final disposition diminishes fearful speculations both by parents and staff and allows them to cooperate more fully in dealing with the death. An unofficial policy evolved at Downstate by which mothers, and occasionally fathers and other family members of an infant who died, are given the option of viewing the body. Parents are generally in favor of this policy.

The authors state that as recently as 1974 there were over 70,000 perinatal deaths in the U.S. In the vast majority of cases, the parents were ignored and neglected after the death. The authors found that rather than denying the event, mothers who have perinatal mortalities seek to affirm that they have been pregnant, that they have given birth, and that the baby has died. Viewing of the body, review of obstetric and autopsy data, explanation of fantasies, and the substitution of factual for speculative information about burial all assist in the process of affirmation. They believe that pathological parental reactions such as chronic grief may be ameliorated when health care professionals become more aware of the mechanics and processes of death and honestly deal with their patients' and their own grief and frustration.

John Morgan and Rachael Goering (1978) talk about the special problems of parents who have experienced SIDS deaths and discuss how the family must cope with shock, grief, and guilt. The authors of this article discuss how a nurse can assist a grieving family. They concede that when a death is sudden, mysterious, and misunderstood by family, relatives, community, and health officials, the suffering can become endless for the surviving family members. Because it is so sudden, SIDS generally catches parents totally unprepared to deal with the death. Furthermore, the feelings such victims experience are intensified by the guilt and mystery that accompany SIDS. The authors feel that an effective support person can spare the victims months or years of needless guilt and anguish.

The authors also suggest that a public health nurse make follow-up visits to the home of the bereaved parents to provide support. A public health nurse is felt to be ideal because she represents some medical expertise to the family. It is important that the visiting nurse be familiar with the various reactions experienced by the grieving family. The authors stress that special attention be given to older siblings, who may have guilt feelings because they secretly may have wished that the new baby would "go away." They conclude by suggesting that the nurse direct the grieving family to a local chapter of the National SIDS Foundation, for this group can talk to the family in a way others cannot.

Joseph Lowman (1979) describes a statewide program in North Carolina that has nurses intervene with parents losing a baby to SIDS. The program, which provides support and helps parents relieve their guilt, appears to have significant preventive potential. Experienced public health nurses are given short-term but intensive training in psychological reactions to death. They visit the grieving families in their homes three times after bereavement, at 3 to 5 weeks, 7 to 9 weeks, and 4 to 6 months after the deaths. Data from a sizable sample of families support the belief that this type of program has a beneficial impact on the participants.

Dennis Drotar and Nancy Irvin (1979) found that an infant's death can have a profound influence on the mother's relationships with surviving children. The authors feel that parents internalize memories of deceased infants differently than memories of older deceased children. Parents of deceased infants do not base their mourning on actual experiences but rather on articulated fantasies and wishes.

In their work with bereaved mothers, Drotar and Irvin employed certain principles of re-grief therapy, which involves dealing with feelings concerning a prior loss and presenting memories in a brief but

highly intensive treatment. The authors found that the mothers' denial
and idealization of past losses did not change readily. Only the consistency and support of the therapeutic relationship allowed the gradual
recovery of painful memories. Most mothers then achieved increased
comfort with their surviving children.

The authors' observations suggest certain psychosocial interventions with families that have experienced an infant death or are
anticipating one. They suggest that intensive care nursery staffs support
parents who are visiting and encourage close physical contact with their
infants. This should help confirm the reality of the child's existence in
the event of the child's death. The parents should also be allowed to
express their ambivalence about their child's physical condition. Following the death, medical and nursing staff should help parents recognize
the reality of the loss. They should be helped to realize that their grief
is powerful but very normal and that they should not attempt to forget
or to deny their grief. Medical and nursing staff should be mutually
supportive, thereby fostering the discussion of painful questions with
the parents. The authors conclude that pediatric or nursing follow-up
visits are useful supports for the family. Close follow-up care also allows
early recognition of siblings' behavioral disturbances, which can signal
pathological family adaptation to the infant's death.

John J. Spinetta, Joyce A. Swarner, and John P. Sheposh (1981)
studied the characteristics of parents of dying children that facilitated
grief resolution on a personal or philosophical level. They found that
parents who were best adjusted after the death of their child were those
who had a consistent philosophy/theology/cosmology of life during the
child's life. Such consistency seems to help the family accept the
diagnosis and cope with its consequences. These well-adjusted parents
also had a viable and ongoing significant other as a support to whom
they could turn for help during the course of the illness. Finally, they
seemed to give their child the information and emotional support the
child needed during the course of the illness consistent with the child's
questions, age, and level of development.

The authors conclude by recommending that families that experience the death of a child receive professional assistance to help
strengthen their own adaptive capabilities and coping styles. This can
help the family maintain a relatively good quality of life during the
child's illness and give them access to sources of support.

Yvonne Craig (1977) observes that pediatric workers are becoming
more aware of the need to give consistent pre-bereavement support to
parents whose children are dying. She feels that the pediatric social

worker should be the key figure in integrating this care with that of the staff, and later in offering to refer bereaved families to community support groups. She goes on to suggest that the more intensively and sensitively a family is supported before the bereavement, the greater the possibility that pathological developments will be avoided and that further support will be accepted from the community support network.

She concludes that bereavement is not a problem for social workers to solve but an experience in which they are invited to be companions. They should listen with warmth and sympathy, accepting expressions of grief and giving significance to the death of the loved child.

It should be evident at this point that scattered research findings point out common themes relevant to parental grief following the death of a child. Although many questions remain unanswered, we believe that certain hypotheses can be formulated from the literature and that they can point toward tentative answers regarding grief resolution following the death of a child. Let us now draw together some of these common themes and present them as confirmed hypotheses.

SUMMARY OF RESEARCH FINDINGS

From our review of the literature we have come up with seven points summarizing common themes.

- *There are special grief problems following the death of a child.* All of the studies presented identify intense and unique problems following the death of a child. Some of these problems are magnified when the death is sudden or when there is an absence or weakness of social support, limited opportunity for anticipatory grieving, lack of communication with health care personnel, and incongruent grieving patterns between men and women. These problems have been shown to be serious and are worthy of professional consideration. Equally important is that by encouraging open communication between the parents and health care professionals, as well as between parents themselves, such problems can be broached and overcome.
- *The parents of a dead child should make every effort and be encouraged to share their grief work.* Most authors feel that the death of a child can become a growing experience for couples. Parents must make allowances for each other's individual coping styles, but should be encouraged to believe that they can help each other when the time is right.

The shared grief process can take many forms. Some parents will pass through various grief reactions at the same time and sequence, others will experience all the same reactions but in a different sequence, and so forth. Even if the reactions are not shared, it is better if they can be mutually understood and accepted.

We recommend that efforts be directed toward developing effective sharing mechanisms. In this regard, the matter of psychosocial timing is of profound importance. Too little attention has been paid to this dimension in favor of chronological time. The elusive but nonetheless real element of emotional time must be considered. For example, for some parents, the time will seem right to make certain life adjustments regarding the dead child; for others, now is just not right. Such interfamilial differences require patient, understanding treatment by professional caregivers, family members, and friends.

Another dimension important in shared grief is the communication process itself. There must be open communication about and mutual awareness of both the objective circumstances and the subjective thoughts and feelings. This allows for discussion of differences in style, intensity, scope, and depth of grief. When parents are able to recognize how these exist in each other, they can come closer to helping each other cope with the differences.

• *When it is possible, anticipatory grief responses to a potential death should be encouraged and facilitated.* Some research indicates that sudden deaths such as SIDS and drowning hinder parental grief resolution, and this is traced to the lack of opportunity for anticipatory grief. A sound case can be made for professional intervention in cases where either stillbirth or long-term illness is anticipated in order to facilitate grief both prior to and subsequent to the birth and/or death. The process of anticipatory grief should be considered not only beneficial but also necessary.

While health care professionals should do what is necessary to facilitate anticipatory grief, there are at least two possible complications involved in this, and they cannot be overemphasized. First, there is clear evidence dating at least to Lindemann that too much anticipatory grief can be detrimental. For example, if parents move through their grief for a dying child too completely, it is possible for that child to become isolated and feel abandoned. There may also be such intense anticipatory grief that the remaining family members feel ignored, offended, or just plain unimportant. Sadly, there is no way to know just how much anticipatory grief is too much. It does appear that there is an optimum amount. However, our point is that a humane under-standing of this complex process must include recognition of both the benefits and risks.

Second, grief in anticipation of a bereavement is *not* a substitute for the grief that occurs at the time of the loss or afterward. Those providing either professional or lay support should be careful not to act as if prior expectation will mean no at-death or post-death grief. Indeed, it is our belief that anticipatory grief can help in dealing with a loss but that it cannot be assumed to resolve it. Hence, treating a recently bereaved parent who antici-pated her child's death as if she should be over the grief can be a tragic error.

• *Special consideration should be given to the bereaved siblings in any child death.* All authors who mentioned bereaved siblings say that special attention to them is necessary. The guilt and confusion siblings experience at this difficult time can become problematic in later life. Sometimes the remaining children are ignored. Other times they or future siblings become replacements for the dead child. Bizarre anecdotes abound regarding name shifts or trans-ference of personality, athletic, or intellectual traits that attribute magical, almost reincarnation-like powers to a surviving sibling. Parents simply wishing for replacement can be difficult to help and should be assessed carefully.

We believe that the health care or social work professional who is aiding the family needs to pay special attention to the bereaved sibling(s) apart from the parents. Doing this is not easy; however, we offer the following six suggestions:

1. Make it a point to observe the home atmosphere and the reactions of the children for signs of maladaptive behavior on the part of the parents or children.
2. Encourage the parents to be alert to unusual behavior on the part of the children such as nightmares, compulsive behavior, allergies or illnesses, or any unexplained psychological symptoms.
3. Encourage the parents to maintain close contact with the school, looking for possible behavior problems or difficulty with schoolwork.
4. In many cases, use play therapy to identify problems with young children.
5. In many cases, employ family counseling.
6. Educate the parents about the effects of the loss of a sibling on the remaining children. It is our belief that some long-term

psychological damage may be done when well-meaning parents, ignorant of the dynamics of grief, become absorbed in their own pain and become oblivious to the fact that children also have feelings and fears of their own. For example, siblings who behave as if they are uncaring, playing with toy cars or shooting baskets after learning about a death, are simply trying to exercise some control over their environment and may need assistance in sorting out their feelings and pain.

• *The final disposition of the child's remains should be determined by what is personally best for the parents.* There is some evidence that an autopsy can be important because it may give parents a more definite answer about the cause of death. When this occurs, an autopsy may help alleviate some guilt feelings. There also is strong evidence that viewing the dead body can be helpful if the parents wish to do so. By all accounts, this helps the parents to affirm their feelings that the child was real and is now dead. However, we feel that hospital personnel should follow the parents' lead regarding autopsy and viewing. While this could cause discomfort and anxiety for hospital personnel in contact with newly bereaved parents, they should be encouraged to put aside their own feelings on the subject in the interest of assisting the parents toward grief resolution.

In some instances family members may not be able to be present during the customary funeral period. For example, in stillbirths or neonatal deaths the woman may be hospitalized, or in accidents either or both parents or other family members also may be hospitalized. In any such cases there may be important family members who are unable to participate in the funeral ceremonies for the child. When this situation occurs it is often advisable to postpone the funeral until those people can attend.

• *Whenever reasonably possible and warranted, professional intervention following the death of a child is advisable.* Almost all the evidence recommends professional intervention following the death of a child. Whether it is a nurse, social worker, psychologist, physician, funeral director, grief counselor, family therapist, minister, or others who render the service, the need for a trained professional in this area of bereavement seems evident. It may even be advisable for the professional to seek the bereaved family actively and provide the opportunity for counseling, even if it is not requested. In some cases, it is the only way that pathological responses can be controlled or avoided and the mental health of the family and the community maintained.

Of course, there is the opposite view that any therapeutic intervention should be given only when sought. This position reflects the notion that undue professional intervention may in fact enable unresolved grief. This occurs when the bereaved person avoids the process of grief by becoming overly involved in the process of therapy. Parkes has cautioned about this; however, our position is that even though therapy cannot and should not be forced on anyone, it must be offered and openly made available. This is especially important in our highly mobile society, in which customary support sources, such as the immediate family, often are not available.

It is quite clear that the health care professional should be available to facilitate communication within the family, to allow them to vent their anxieties, and to try to provide answers to questions concerning the child's death. Such attention by the professional is usually gratefully accepted by bereaved parents, and from our viewpoint the health care community must not shirk this obligation.

Additionally, there are several volunteer support groups, and referral to one such as The Compassionate Friends may be advisable. These groups provide the communication and social support so often withheld from bereaved parents. Many parents gain the strength and insight necessary to be supportive of other bereaved parents. This is a possible goal that should be seriously considered and perhaps even suggested by health care professionals and social workers assisting parents in achieving successful grief resolution.

• *Grief following the death of a child can be "resolved."* There is the inevitable issue of defining resolution and then measuring it. From our viewpoint it is more important to put resolution in everyday pragmatic terms than it is to be so precise that the definition has little practical application. Therefore, we define grief resolution as reaching a psychosocial point of adjustment to a death so that life can go on. This would include goals such as emancipation from the dead child's memory, environmental readjustment, and the ability to form new relationships without destroying old ones.

Some researchers have consistently found unresolved pathological grief reactions in the families they studied, while others have found grief resolution to be not just possible but quite probable as well. The apparent contradiction seems to occur primarily because the families manifesting unresolved grief had not received professional post-bereavement intervention and were already in crisis at the time of the study. Conversely, families who resolved grief successfully were those in the newly bereaved state who received professional intervention from the time of the death itself or shortly thereafter. We suggest that when professional counseling is readily available to the newly bereaved parent, pathological and chronic grief conditions can be avoided and/or ameliorated, and grief resolution can occur, except in exceptional cases.

Although we have not resolved all the issues, we feel many points indicate intervention techniques that can assist the grieving process for parents. Developing a professionally recognized and socially acceptable protocol for professionals dealing with bereaved parents strikes us as not only a worthwhile goal, but also a socially humane step for helping those in need.

PROTOCOL FOR PROFESSIONALS DEALING WITH BEREAVED PARENTS

Distilling ideas for approaches, treatments, and clinical interventions leads to several obvious and some not-so-obvious conclusions. Here are some of our conclusions interpreted as a suggested protocol to aid in dealing with grief reactions of bereaved parents. These suggestions are based on a wide range of theoretical and clinical studies, research experiences, and personal observations.

- *Death education and training are necessary.* All professionals who come in contact with bereaved parents should be trained in the dynamics of grief and bereavement. This holds true for those who have contact with the family before an anticipated death and at the time of death, including physicians, nurses, psychologists, hospice workers, social workers, and clergy. After death, during bereavement, the list of professionals would include those previously mentioned as well as funeral directors and pathologists. Ignorance of the grief process on the part of professionals can be counterproductive and even harmful to the newly bereaved. Therefore, a coherent program of professional education is a worthwhile goal.
- *Health care facilities should foster an interdisciplinary approach in dealing with bereaved parents.* All professionals involved should make a concerted effort to provide integrated sources of emotional support and valid information for the bereaved. Such professionals include physicians, nurses, social workers, psychologists, clergy,

hospice workers, and funeral directors. The extent of development of such an interdisciplinary approach depends partly on financial and material resources, but most importantly on a strong philosophical commitment to the concept. It is not always easy to elicit the cooperation of diverse professionals, so it may be necessary to seek cooperation from the highest administrative and professional levels. If there is direction from the top echelon down, interdisciplinary programs have a strong chance to achieve success.

- *In the case of a hospitalized child whose death seems imminent, certain steps should be taken.* Medical personnel and other professionals in contact with the family should make every effort to explain the child's condition and prognosis as honestly as possible so that anticipatory grief may begin. Visiting hours should be unrestricted for parents, and they should be encouraged to touch and hold their child.

- *In cases of sudden, unexpected, and/or unanticipated death, hospitals should abide by an emergency room protocol.* First, there should be professional contact with the parents before the death is declared to facilitate the process of anticipatory and/or acute grief. Second, the information about the child's condition and announcement of the death should be given by a medical professional, preferably the physician in charge of the case. Third, a social worker, hospice worker, psychologist, or other professional should remain with the bereaved family until their departure from the hospital. This person could help telephone other family members and/or the clergy, explain the process for release of the body, call the funeral director, assist in filling out the paperwork, remain with the family if viewing and/or holding the deceased child is desired, and give emotional support throughout the ordeal. Fourth, referral information should be given about a peer support group, a psychologist, a social worker, or other death counselor for the period following the death.

- *After the death of a newborn or in the case of a stillbirth, parents should be given the option of seeing and holding their baby.* Honest explanation of what the parents will see should precede this event.

- *The possibility of an autopsy to pinpoint the exact cause of death should be discussed with the parents.* The surgical procedure should be explained fully, and the value, benefits, and potential outcomes of a post-mortem examination should be honestly presented. Any misgivings should be discussed, and the parents' ultimate wishes and feelings in this matter should be honored.

- *A caregiver should be available in any trauma area of a hospital to give consistent emotional support to the parents before and after the death.* Such areas would include the emergency room, the intensive care ward, or the delivery area in the case of an anticipated stillbirth. The caregiver's task should include listening to the parents' anxiety, providing information about bereavement and the grief process, scheduling a follow-up appointment for approximately 2 to 4 weeks after the death to assess the family's situation, reviewing autopsy data, and making referrals to a peer support group or professional counselor.

  The value of a funeral consistent with the family's religious beliefs should be discussed as early as possible and appropriate in the anticipatory grief process, or certainly at least as soon as possible after the death. In instances of stillbirth or neonatal deaths, the inclusion of the mother in making the funeral arrangements is recommended. The joint efforts of the couple can not only help the mother but also provide the father with a sense of joint decision-making and togetherness. Making such emotionally charged decisions alone not only may seem frightening, but also may be disruptive to the marital relationship. The presence of the mother at any ceremony should be encouraged and facilitated. If it means delaying the service until her release from the hospital, then the counselor can help arrange this with the cooperation of the clergy and funeral director.

- *In cases where a professional counselor is recommended following the death, family assessment should be done.* Every effort should be made to assess the family's home life and the effect of the bereavement on the surviving siblings.

- *In no case should a family be left without follow-up support services following the death.* Follow-up support should include open discussion and exploration of the family's coping mechanisms and grieving patterns, discussion of the family's social milieu, and continued examination of their experience with the grieving process. The parents should be helped in developing effective mechanisms to share their grief. Even though this may be difficult, it is a crucial step in developing an open context of mutual awareness about the unique feelings each person may be experiencing.

- *Trite expressions of encouragement should be avoided.* Comments such as "You can have another baby," "It was God's will," and "At least you have other children" never should be made. Such phrases in no way aid in the resolution of grief and may often be a hindrance.

It has been a circuitous path from Freud to the present grief resolution practices. However, it is our hope that the suggested protocol will help parents along the road to healthy grief resolution. Although some of the points discussed are applicable to other groups of grieving people, the specific thrust of our synthesis is to assist parents in the resolution of their grief.

From the scientific perspective, we hope that this protocol will be tested professionally in a variety of clinical settings. From the humanitarian perspective, we hope that it is of assistance in dealing with an often neglected and ignored bereaved population. Based on the evidence presented and on our personal experiences, we are convinced that the suggested ideas can help avoid many psychiatric problems due to parental bereavement.

We anticipate that this protocol will be modified, reinterpreted, and expanded. Advances that may emerge from scientific and clinical investigations are eagerly awaited. However, the search for certainty and empirical verification can be arduous and time consuming. When a parent loses a child the pain is immediate, and sensitive assistance cannot wait for precisely confirmed scientific hypotheses. Therefore, we hope that our suggestions help immediately in addressing the deepest human needs of bereaved parents.

Notes

1. Our use of the term *middle-range theories* is derived from the work of Robert Merton, who refers to them as theories used to assist in empirical inquiry. Such middle-range theories lie between everyday, commonsense theory testing and systematic attempts to develop a unified theory that will explain all the observed regularities of social behavior and organization. For a full discussion see *On Theoretical Sociology: Five Essays, Old and New* (New York: Free Press, 1967), 39–72.

2. The term *bereavement overload* was introduced by Robert J. Kastenbaum to describe a specific condition affecting some elderly men and women. Kastenbaum explains that the elderly are more apt to have experienced the loss of many significant persons in their lives, as well as other important losses such as loss of physical abilities, employment, and social respect. He posits that the multiple losses accumulate and result in bereavement overload. For a full discussion see *Death, Society, and Human Experience*, 2nd ed. (St. Louis: C. V. Mosby, 1981), 231–232.

3. The parallels between Bowlby's stages of separation in early childhood to mourning behavior in later life are important. He describes the three phases of childhood separation as protest, despair, and detachment. Later, he identifies the four phases of grief as numbing, yearning, disorganization, and reorganization. Bowlby recognized the earliest phase, numbing, last and added it to his theory of grief in his more recent works. Bowlby

reminds us that Freud was caught in the bind of an inverse recognition of sequential phases of mourning and that he recognized early stages only after he had already described later ones. Bowlby (1969) explains that "always in the history of medicine it is the end-result of a pathological sequence that is noted first. Only gradually are earlier phases identified" (p. 28). We feel that Freud and Bowlby set admirable examples by admitting that existing theories may need to be discarded, revised, or augmented.

4. It is important to note that the sample for this study was a "small convenience sample of parents who, for the most part, belonged to self-help groups for bereaved parents." Miles and Crandall acknowledge the likelihood that these parents may constitute a special group, which may differ significantly from the general population of bereaved parents. Additionally, their attendance in a self-help group may enable them to find meaning and grow. We feel that this suggests the need for comparison studies that include a control group of bereaved parents who have chosen not to join self-help groups. Furthermore, Miles and Crandall point out that the period of time since the death of the child was not a factor considered in this study and that it may be an important variable.

5. Coauthor Carolyn Brauer was a participant in the Peppers and Knapp study. Approximately 1 week after the death of her first child in 1977, Ms. Brauer responded to a news release that described a preliminary study being done by Dr. Peppers and Dr. Knapp at Clemson University. The purpose of the study was to gain basic information about the effects of infant death on mothers. A lengthy questionnaire was completed and contact was maintained with the investigators until the study was published in 1980.

References

Bowlby, J. (1969). *Attachment and loss: Vol. 1 Attachment.* New York: Basic Books.

Cain, A. C., & Cain, B. S. (1964). On replacing a child. *Journal of the American Academy of Child Psychiatry, 3,* 443–456.

Cohen, L., Zilkha, S., Middleton, J., & O'Donnohue, N. (1978). Perinatal mortality: Assisting parental affirmation. *American Journal of Orthopsychiatry, 48,* 727–731.

Cook, J. A. (1983). A death in the family: Parental bereavement in the first year (Part 2). *National Reporter, 6*(12), 2–6.

Craig, Y. (1977). The bereavement of parents and their search for meaning. *British Journal of Social Work, 7*(1), 41–54.

Davidson, G. W. (1977). Death of the wished for child: A case study. *Death Education, 1,* 265–275.

Drotar, D., & Irvin, N. (1979). Disturbed maternal bereavement following infant death. *Child Care, Health and Development, 5,* 239–247.

Freud, S. (1959). Mourning and melancholia. *Collected Papers.* New York: Basic Books, 152–170. (Original work published 1917)

Furman, E. (1978). The death of a newborn: Care of the parents. *Birth and the Family Journal, 5,* 214–218.

Gorer, G. (1965). *Death, grief, and mourning.* New York: Doubleday.

Helmrath, T. A., & Steinitz, E. M. (1978). Death of an infant: Parental grieving and the failure of social support. *Journal of Family Practice, 6,* 785–790.

Kalish, R. A. (1969). The effects of death upon the family. In L. Pearson (Ed.), *Death and dying: Current issues in the treatment of the dying person*. Cleveland: The Press of Case Western Reserve University, 79–107.

Kalish, R. A. (1977). Dying and preparing for death: A view of families. In H. Feifel (Ed.), *New meanings of death*. New York: McGraw-Hill, 215–232.

Kellner, K. R., Best, E. K., Chesborough, S., Donnelly, W., & Green, M. (1981). Perinatal mortality counseling program for families who experience a stillborn baby. *Death Education, 5*, 29–35.

Kerner, J., Harvey, B., & Lewiston, N. (1979). The impact of grief: A retrospective study of family function following loss of a child with cystic fibrosis. *Journal of Chronic Diseases, 32*, 223.

Krueger, A., Gyllensköld, K., Pehrsson, G., & Sjölin, S. (1981). Parent reactions to childhood malignant diseases: Experience in Sweden. *The American Journal of Pediatric Hematology/Oncology, 3*(3), 233–237.

Lindemann, E. (1944). Symptomatology and management of acute grief. *American Journal of Psychiatry, 101*, 141–148.

Lowman, J. (1979). Grief intervention and Sudden Infant Death Syndrome. *American Journal of Community Psychology, 7*(6), 665–677.

Markusen, E., Owen, G., Fulton, R., & Bendiksen, R. (1977–78). SIDS: The survivor as victim. *Omega, 8*, 277–284.

Miles, M. S., & Crandall, E. K. B. (1983). The search for meaning and its potential for affecting growth in bereaved parents. *Health Values: Achieving High Level Wellness, 7*(1), 19–23.

Morgan, J. H., & Goering, R. (1978). Caring for parents who have lost an infant. *Journal of Religion and Health, 17*, 290–298.

Nixon, J., & Pearn, J. (1977). Emotional sequelae of parents and sibs following the drowning or near-drowning of a child. *Australian and New Zealand Journal of Psychiatry, 11*(4), 265–268.

Parkes, C. M. (1972). *Bereavement: Studies of grief in adult life*. New York: International Universities Press.

Peppers, L. G., & Knapp, R. J. (1980). *Motherhood and mourning: Perinatal death*. New York: Praeger.

Rando, T. A. (1983). An investigation of grief and adaptation in parents whose children have died from cancer. *Journal of Pediatric Psychology, 8*(1), 3–20.

Raphael, B. (1983). *The anatomy of bereavement*. New York: Basic Books.

Sanders, C. M. (1979–80). A comparison of adult bereavement in the death of a spouse, child, and parent. *Omega, 10*, 303–322.

Schiff, H. S. (1977). *The bereaved parent*. New York: Crown Publishers.

Schwartz, A. M. (1977). Comments in section on "The Parents." In N. Linzer (Ed.), *Understanding bereavement and grief*. New York: Yeshiva University Press.

Seitz, P. M., & Warrick, L. H. (1974). Perinatal death: The grieving mother. *American Journal of Nursing, 74*, 2028–2033.

Shneidman, E. S. (1977). The college student and death. In H. Feifel (Ed.), *New meanings of death*. New York: McGraw-Hill.

Spinetta, J. J., Swarner, J. A., & Sheposh, J. P. (1981). Effective parental coping following the death of a child from cancer. *Journal of Pediatric Psychology, 6*(3), 251–263.

Stephens, S. (1972). *Death comes home*. London: A. R. Mowbray.

Tietz, W., McSherry, L., & Britt, B. (1977). Family sequelae after a child's death due to cancer. *American Journal of Psychotherapy, 31*, 419.

Videka-Sherman, L. (1982). Coping with the death of a child: A study over time. *American Journal of Orthopsychiatry, 52* (4), 688–698.

Wilson, A. L., & Soule, D. J. (1981). The role of a self-help group in working with parents of a stillborn baby. *Death Education, 5,* 175–186.

Worden, J. W. (1982). *Grief counseling and grief therapy: A handbook for the mental health practitioner.* New York: Springer.

Chapter 4

Guilt in Bereaved Parents

Margaret Shandor Miles
Alice Sterner Demi

Margaret Shandor Miles, R.N., Ph.D., F.A.A.N., is Professor, School of Nursing, and Clinical Professor, School of Medicine, at the University of North Carolina, Chapel Hill. She has 25 years' experience in pediatric nursing both as a staff nurse and clinician and as an educator. The major focus of her clinical experience has been working with parents of critically ill children and bereaved parents. Dr. Miles's research interests also revolve around the responses and needs of parents when their child is seriously ill or has died. Among her publications are articles about parental stresses experienced when a child is in an intensive care unit and articles about parental grief responses.

Alice Sterner Demi, D.N.Sc., F.A.A.N., is Professor and Associate Dean of the Graduate Program, School of Nursing, Medical College of Georgia. She has been active in developing hospice and grief counseling programs in several states. Her research has focused on survivors of suicide, grief of parents, and grief of siblings. She serves as the ANA representative to the Professional and Technical Advisory Committee on Hospices for the Joint Commission on Accreditation of Hospitals.

Funding for part of this project was provided by the American Nurses' Foundation to Dr. Miles as Bristol-Myers Scholar, 1981. The authors also would like to thank the parents from The Compassionate Friends for their supportive cooperation.

Guilt, the feeling that one has done something wrong, failed to live up to one's expectations, or violated a standard, is a common human experience. At no time is guilt more prevalent than during the parenting years. The parent-child dyad is a unique relationship, with many societal expectations placed on the parenting role (Brown, 1978). Parents are expected to be superhuman lovers, protectors, educators, and nurturers. A sense of failure to live up to these expectations for a variety of reasons frequently leaves parents feeling guilty (McBride, 1973; Radl, 1979).

Because of this unique parent-child relationship, guilt is often one of the most insistent and profound reactions of parents when a child dies, regardless of whether the child died suddenly and unexpectedly or following a long illness. A large number of articles based on clinical studies, several books written by bereaved parents, and a handful of research papers about the grief experiences of bereaved parents all provide much evidence that guilt is a common and frequent reaction in bereaved parents (Friedman, 1974; McCollum, 1974; Miles, 1979, 1980, 1983; Schiff, 1977; Weinstein, 1978). Feelings of guilt in bereaved parents may be closely related to their sense of responsibility for the child's well-being, and their consequent sense of helplessness for not having been able somehow to prevent the child's death (Friedman, 1974; McCollum, 1974; Miles, 1983).

The commonality of guilt is especially evident in the literature regarding parents who experienced the death of an infant from Sudden Infant Death Syndrome (SIDS). This syndrome involves the sudden, unexpected death of an apparently healthy infant with no specific cause for the event being currently known. Weinstein (1978), in particular, notes that guilt feelings constitute a major source of the emotional distress in these parents. A number of clinical and research studies confirm the prominence of guilt feelings in these parents (Bergman, Pomeroy, & Beckwith, 1969; Cornwell, Nurcombe, & Stevens, 1977; DeFrain & Ernst, 1978; Miles, 1977; Smialek, 1978). Guilt feelings were predominantly related to parental perceptions of ways in which they might have prevented the infant's death or to ways in which they might have contributed to the death event.

The frequency of guilt feelings following other types of infant death has also been reported by many authors (Benfield, Leib, & Vollman, 1978; Hagan, 1974; Helmrath & Steinitz, 1978; Kennell & Klaus, 1976; Peppers & Knapp, 1980; Rowe, Clyman, & Green, 1978; Zahourek & Jensen, 1973). Guilt was reported to be especially common in mothers; guilt feelings were often related to maternal behaviors and feelings during pregnancy that might have contributed to the infant's death.

Literature on parental grief thus supports the view that guilt is a common and normal component of grief in parents when a child dies. Sources of guilt feelings are generally related to feelings of failure for not having prevented the death from occurring, to negative or ambivalent thoughts about the child or infant, to punishment for past or present perceived misdeeds, or for perceived failure to carry out other aspects of the parental role. In a recent study, Johnson-Soderberg (1983) examined 451 guilt statements made by 28 bereaved mothers and fathers. Her findings support the literature in that the sources of guilt often revolved around the parental role, around the child's illness and death, and around moral issues.

Although guilt feelings have been reported as a prominent feature of parental grief in clinical and research articles, little research has been done to clearly identify specific sources of guilt in bereaved parents, to evaluate how the guilt affects the overall grief process, and to identify parents who may be at risk for more intense guilt reactions. There is more research on guilt responses when a spouse dies; however, there are conflicting views on the frequency, intensity, and normalcy of this emotional response. Some authors view guilt as a universal and normal component of mourning (Averill, 1968; Bowlby, 1980; Cassem, 1978; Lindemann, 1944), while others report that the presence of guilt may be related to pathology and poor outcome (Glick, Weiss, & Parkes, 1974; Lieberman, 1978; Parkes, 1965; Parkes & Weiss, 1983; Raphael, 1975; Wahl, 1970). The latter group generally believes that guilt can lead to lowered self-esteem, self-punishment, isolation, emotional instability, and even suicide.

Since guilt can be a prominent and devastating component of the grief process when a child dies, studies about guilt are important in providing direction for assisting bereaved parents to cope with their guilt reactions, thereby minimizing potential sequelae. As a step in the development of a theoretical basis for more intensive studies of guilt in grieving parents, the authors present in this chapter a theoretical model that identifies a number of potential sources of guilt feelings experienced by bereaved parents, along with the thought process that results in these guilt feelings. This chapter also addresses important variables that may influence these guilt reactions and identifies strategies that parents may use to ameliorate their guilt.

The definition of guilt used in the development of this theoretical model is based on the various definitions previously reported in the literature (Izard, 1978; Lynd, 1961; Stein, 1968; Viscott, 1976). Guilt is defined as feeling accountable for violating a societal standard or for failing to live up to one's own expectations. Guilt may result from actual or perceived acts of omission or commission or from thoughts and feelings. Some of the following terms may be used to describe guilt: feeling unworthy, responsible, sinful, evil, wrong, ashamed, remorseful, blameworthy, and a failure.

A THEORETICAL MODEL OF PARENTAL BEREAVEMENT GUILT

In our model of parental bereavement guilt, guilt feelings in bereaved parents arise from a deep sense of helplessness in not having been able to prevent the child's suffering and death from occurring and from a sense of personal responsibility for the child's well-being (see Figure 4.1). As parents begin to deal with these two interrelated feelings, they may start to focus on how their own actions or feelings might have contributed to the child's illness or death, however indirect or irrational the connection. At the same time, parents often reflect back on their interactions with the child in the overall parental role.

In this process of self-evaluation, parents often review all the many events that occurred in the child's life and even events that occurred during pregnancy that may have had an impact on the child's life and death. As each parent has a perception of how he should behave or feel as an ideal parent, some retrospective perceptions of actions or feelings can fall short of ideal self-expectations, especially since the ideal often involves being all-knowing, always caring, and always available. The discrepancy between the ideal standard and the actual performance as a parent then results in guilt feelings.

Furthermore, parents may make a connection during these ruminations between the child's death and a past transgression that they believe violated their own moral code. This creates another type of discrepancy between expectation and performance that contributes to guilt feelings. Some of their behavioral and emotional reactions during the grief process also may create a discrepancy between their self-expectations and their performance as grieving parents, contributing further to feelings of guilt. Finally, because it is so unusual in our culture for a child to die before a parent, there is a perceived violation of a social standard that contributes to survival guilt and adds to the overall guilt reactions.

Figure 4.1. Development of Guilt in Bereaved Parents*

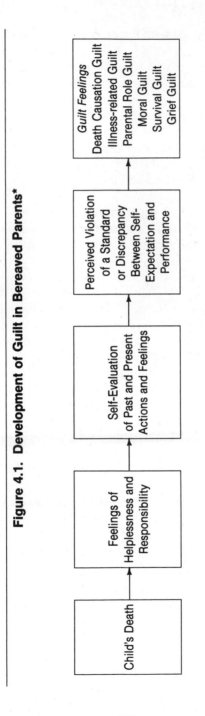

| Child's Death | → | Feelings of Helplessness and Responsibility | → | Self-Evaluation of Past and Present Actions and Feelings | → | Perceived Violation of a Standard or Discrepancy Between Self-Expectation and Performance | → | *Guilt Feelings*
Death Causation Guilt
Illness-related Guilt
Parental Role Guilt
Moral Guilt
Survival Guilt
Grief Guilt |

*Copyright, Margaret S. Miles and Alice S. Demi, 1983.

SOURCES OF GUILT IN BEREAVED PARENTS

In summary, then, the major sources of guilt feelings in bereaved parents seem to arise from experiences in the parent-child relationship. This includes experiences during pregnancy; during the course of normal parenting; during the child's illness experience, if the child was sick for a time before death; and at the time of death. Other sources of guilt may arise from the personal relationship with God or a higher being and with the relationships with significant others. Guilt also arises from the survival of self when a child has died. In the theoretical model developed by the authors, these various sources of guilt have been categorized into a typology of guilt sources.

The typology of guilt sources is based on the guilt and bereavement literature and on clinical and research data from bereaved parents. Various classifications that have been suggested previously for the feeling of guilt also were reviewed for their relevance to the grief typology model. These typologies for classifying guilt include real, neurotic, existential, legal, ethical, moral, and survival. Real guilt is based on actual acts of omission or commission that are recognized by others. Neurotic guilt is an irrational magnification of minor transgressions or of perceived transgressions that have no basis in reality (Stein, 1968). Existential guilt is based on failure to live up to one's full human potential (Buber, 1971; May, 1958). Legal guilt results from an act that is in violation of the law, while ethical guilt is based on violations of an ethical code and moral guilt is a violation of a moral or religious code (Tournier, 1962). Survival guilt is based on the experience of having lived when another person has died (Lifton, 1976).

Survival guilt, identified by Lifton (1976) in his study of the survivors of Hiroshima, is clearly a type of guilt that results exclusively from the death of another. Real, existential, legal, ethical, and moral guilt can be experienced by bereaved individuals; however, the type of guilt most commonly experienced by bereaved persons is similar to that usually labeled neurotic guilt, guilt based on irrational magnifications of minor transgressions or guilt that has no basis in reality. Usually the term neurotic implies psychopathology; however, in the bereaved it is common and normal to experience guilt that is based on irrational magnifications of minor transgressions or guilt that is not based on reality. The typology for parental bereavement guilt developed by the authors, while building on some of the previous categorizations, is directly related to sources of guilt arising from the grief reactions of parents. In particular, guilty feelings result from the parental feelings of helplessness and responsibility when a child dies and the resultant self-evaluation that follows.

In the development of this typology one of the authors had previously identified four sources of guilt in bereaved parents (Miles, 1979, 1980, 1983). These sources were related to the cause of death, the parental role, moral issues, and survivorship. The typology model was further developed, tested, and expanded upon in a small study by the authors. In this study, 28 bereaved parents who attended a workshop on guilt submitted their responses to four open-ended questions that elicited potential sources of guilt. Coding categories were preestablished based on the four typologies hypothesized earlier by Miles, but one additional category emerged from the data—grief-related guilt. This new category was related to the grief responses of the parents that contributed to guilt (Miles & Demi, 1983–84).

Recently an additional investigation with a larger sample has led to further revisions. In this second study, 33 parents of children who died in an accident and 30 parents of children who died following a chronic disease were asked to complete one open-ended question regarding potential sources of guilt. Again, content analysis was used to code and categorize the data. In this study, which included a larger sample of parents whose children had died of a chronic disease, a new category emerged—illness-related guilt (see Table 4.1).

The resultant typology of guilt sources found in bereaved parents, then, includes the following: death causation, illness-related, parental role, and moral, survival, and grief guilt. A more detailed definition of each guilt typology and examples of defining attributes are presented in Table 4.2 and discussed in the following paragraphs.

Death Causation Guilt

Death causation guilt is defined as guilt related to the parental belief that one either contributed to the child's death or failed to protect the child from death. Death causation guilt often occurs when bereaved parents begin to explore the cause of their child's death. During this process they may think about ways in which they may have caused or contributed to the death by sins of omission or commission. The parents' perception of the situation that caused the death may be based on the real situation but be colored by imaginings or irrational thoughts. Since protection of one's child is considered a responsibility of parents, such thoughts can lead to unconscious feelings that one has violated a standard for the parenting role.

Table 4.1. Sources of Guilt in Parents of Children Who Died of Accidents or Chronic Disease

	TYPE OF DEATH			
	ACCIDENTAL DEATH (N = 33)		CHRONIC DISEASE (N = 30)	
SOURCE OF GUILT	No. of parental responses	% of parents	No. of parental responses	% of parents
Death causation	15	45	7	23
Illness-related	2	6	8	27
Parental role	11	33	9	30
Moral	0	0	0	0
Survival	2	6	0	0
Grief	0	0	3	10

Note: Number of parental responses differs from the sample size because not all parents reported on guilt feelings, while others reported more than one source of guilt.

Some of the situations that contributed to death causation guilt in the parents in our studies include giving permission to the child to do some activity that resulted in the child's death (e.g., permission to attend a party, to cross the street, to go swimming); not being more vigilant about some aspect of the child's health (e.g., letting the child play outdoors with a cold, not getting another opinion about the child's illness, not taking the child to the hospital sooner); and being responsible for allowing the child to have the vehicle that caused the death (e.g., buying the car, bicycle, or motorcycle involved in the accident). Parents also reported feeling guilty for not being more vigilant about complying with treatment measures, for not being more inquisitive about the care provided by health care personnel, and for contributing to the disease genetically.

Illness-related Guilt

Illness-related guilt is defined as guilt related to the parental role during the child's illness or at the time of death. Although similar to

Table 4.2. Sources of Guilt

DEATH CAUSATION GUILT
> Guilt related to the belief that the parent either contributed to the child's death or failed to protect the child from death.

ILLNESS-RELATED GUILT
> Guilt related to perceived deficiencies in the parental role during the child's illness or at the time of her death.

PARENTAL ROLE GUILT
> Guilt related to the belief that the parent failed to live up to self-expectations or societal expectations in the *overall* parental role.

MORAL GUILT
> Guilt related to the belief that the child's death was punishment or retribution for violating a moral, ethical, or religious standard.

SURVIVAL GUILT
> Guilt related to violating the standard that a child should outlive her parents.

GRIEF GUILT
> Guilt related to the behavioral and emotional reactions of grief at the time of or following the child's death.

death causation guilt, illness-related guilt refers primarily to parental behaviors surrounding the dying child that are not related to feelings of causation but rather to feelings that they did not live up to their expectations in fulfilling the parental role with a sick or dead child. Again, the perceived situation may be related to acts of commission or omission or to thoughts and feelings.

Situations that parents reported as initiating this guilt included contributing to the negative quality of the child's life in the final days because of continued treatment measures that were painful or because of not electing to take the child home to die; feeling negligent for leaving the child's bedside to meet their own needs for rest and nourishment; and feeling unresponsive as a parent for not being with the child at the time of death. Another source of illness-related guilt was related to parental feelings of ambivalence in both wanting the child to live despite the pain and wanting the child to die.

Parental Role Guilt

Parental role guilt* is defined as guilt related to the belief that the parent failed to live up to self or societal expectations in the *overall* parental role. Guilt sources in this category are not related to the child's illness or death directly but are related more generally to the parent-child relationship before and at the time of the child's death. This source of guilt is more directly connected to societal concepts of the superhuman, all-knowing, always loving and available parent. Guilt may be related to things parents wish they had done better or things they wish they had not done at all.

Parents in our studies, for example, reported feeling guilty for not spending more time with the child who died; for not attending special events related to the child's activities, such as sport or theatre events; for not expressing their love to the child more often; for not providing more structure and/or discipline; for past impatient and angry episodes with the child; for punishing the child too much; and for being too lenient. A number of mothers reported guilt feelings related to their own overinvolvement emotionally in a divorce; to their fatigue from being both provider and homemaker, which minimized the amount of energy available for the child; and to their participation in their own work and/or school activities.

Moral Guilt

Moral guilt arises from the perception that the death was punishment from a higher being for the parent's past sins or transgressions. This type of guilt is more likely to be experienced by parents with an overly strict conscience or parents with religious backgrounds that emphasize guilt and punishment as part of the belief system.

In our studies of bereaved parents, few expressed guilt feelings related to moral aspects of their behavior; however, it is to be expected that such feelings are very intimate and would not be readily shared except in an intimate relationship. Clinical experiences of the authors with bereaved parents and data from the bereavement literature, however, suggest that such feelings are not uncommon and need to be considered. Having a pregnancy before marriage, extramarital affairs, poor church attendance, marriage outside of religion, or having had an abortion in the past are all events that may somehow irrationally be

---

*This source of guilt originally was labeled cultural-role guilt in a previous paper (Miles & Demi, 1983–84).

connected to the present loss when parents view the loss as a punishment for these past "misdeeds."

Survival Guilt

Survival guilt was identified by Lifton (1976) as guilt related to surviving an ordeal such as war when others, particularly esteemed individuals, did not live. In our model, it is guilt related to survival when one's child who is young and part of the future generation has died. Death of a child violates the standard that a child should outlive her parents, as it is considered unnatural in our society for the parent to bury the child. Children are expected to outlive parents; to carry on family names, traditions, and values; and to provide a sense of immortality to parents. Survival guilt, thus, is the resultant sense that somehow the parent should have died first. In our studies, parents implied survival guilt in the following responses given to complete the phrase "I feel guilty because . . .": "I'm here and she's gone; she had so much to live for"; "I'm still alive and enjoying life when she is dead"; "She died first." Parents who had some health problems themselves and older parents may especially feel survival guilt.

Grief Guilt

Grief guilt is guilt related to the behavioral and emotional reactions experienced at the time of or following the child's death. There seem to be three sequential phases related to grief guilt: guilt related to the parents' emotional reactions at the time of the child's death; guilt related to the parents' perception of their grief reactions during the active phase of grief; and guilt related to their recovery process as the grief feelings begin to abate.

In our studies, parents expressed guilt feelings because of how they behaved at the time of death. Some parents expressed guilt for overreacting and others expressed guilt for acting stoic and in control. During the phase of active grief, parents' guilt feelings mostly concerned their relationships with significant others. A number of parents felt guilty for the way they had treated their spouse or the remaining siblings in the family. Feelings of anger vented to family members or failure to meet the emotional and physical needs of other family members contributed to guilt. Recovery guilt occurred long after the child's death, when the parents began to feel better, to enjoy life, and to resume living without focusing on and putting so much energy into the grief process. Some parents feel that they are unfaithful to the deceased child if they ever again enjoy themselves. They seem to set a standard for themselves that "I will always grieve for him" or "I will always be unhappy without her." When parents inadvertantly laugh at something or relax and enjoy something, they may experience feelings of guilt because they have violated their own imposed standard to always grieve for their deceased child. Parents thus reported feeling guilt when they attended a party and had a really good time, when they planned and went on a special extravagant vacation, when they enjoyed a sexual relationship again, and even when the birth of a subsequent child brought immense joy to the family.

VARIABLES AFFECTING GUILT REACTIONS

As with all other grief-related emotions, individual bereaved parents experience a wider variance in the intensity, duration, and sources of guilt feelings. Clinical and research articles about the grief process of bereaved parents, as well as research with widows and widowers, suggest that many variables may influence guilt reactions. Based on this literature, our own clinical experiences with bereaved parents, and our model, we will put forth a number of parental, situational, personal, and societal variables that may affect the feelings of helplessness and responsibility, the process of self-evaluation, and the perceptions of violation of standards or discrepancies between self-expectations and performance (see Figure 4.2). By influencing these various emotional processes in bereaved parents, these variables can ultimately affect types of guilt reactions and the overall guilt responses of parents.

Parental Variables

Parental variables are aspects of the parent-child relationship that may affect the parent's feelings of helplessness and sense of responsibility toward a child. Although myriad variables could be detailed as important, only three will be discussed: ambivalence, dependency, and acts of omission or commission.

Ambivalence refers to the presence of conflicting parental emotions toward the child. Ambivalence has been reported as an important variable affecting the grief response of widowers and widows (Parkes & Weiss, 1983), but little research has been done with bereaved parents on this variable. Although ambivalence toward children is a normal and common phenomena, parents who have a large number of conflicting feelings about a child may have more guilt feelings when a child dies. For example, if a child has had serious behavior problems and has caused much pain and distress for the family, parents may have strong

Figure 4.2. Theoretical Model of Parental Bereavement Guilt*

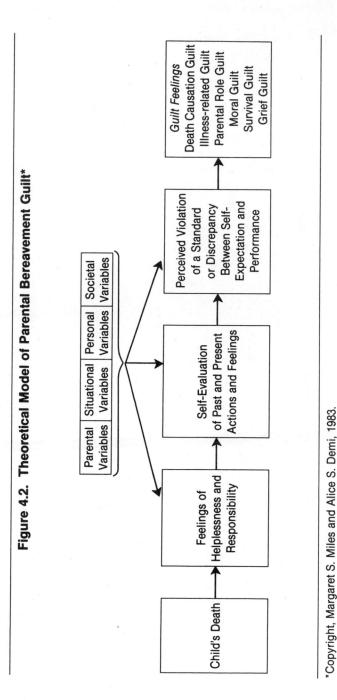

feelings of both love and hate toward the child. If a child has been terminally ill and has suffered for a long time, parents may both wish for him to continue living and also wish for him to die. Such ambivalent thoughts can be so unbearable that they are not allowed into conscious awareness. Thus, severe guilt feelings may be a clue that there is an underlying ambivalence that needs to be explored.

The level of dependence of the child upon the parents for physical and emotional needs also can affect the amount of guilt. The greater the dependence, the greater the potential for guilt because of the concurrent sense of responsibility. Infants and toddlers, for example, are very dependent on their caretakers for physical survival and safety. Hence, death of a child at this age may heighten guilt, especially if the death was accidental. With increasing age, children generally become less dependent for physical needs. In contrast, however, adolescence is a time when children are dependent on parents to set and enforce rules that protect them from harm. Parents and adolescents, then, are often in a struggle to gain an appropriate balance between dependence and independence. When an adolescent child dies, parents may then feel guilt for allowing too much or too little independence. In adulthood, children, if mature, are not dependent on their parents. Thus, if a child dies during adulthood, parents may grieve deeply, but generally do not have intense guilt arising from a sense of responsibility toward the child.

It is further suggested that perceived or actual acts of omission or commission in the parent-child relationship may influence guilt. Acts of omission involve things parents wish they had done or had done better as a parent, while acts of commission involve acts parents wish they hadn't done. Almost all parents experience guilt feelings resulting from such acts, but these feelings are usually fleeting and are far outweighed by remembrances of positive parenting behaviors. When a child dies, however, the acts of commission or omission can become exaggerated in parents' minds. Some parents also may recall actual deficiencies in their parenting activities, such as spending very little time with the child, not telling the child he was loved, severely punishing the child on a frequent basis, having many fights with the child, or unduly pushing the child to achieve more in school or other activities. These perceived or actual failures in the parenting role can be devastating to bereaved parents and the guilt related to them can be intense and long lasting. Thus, it is suggested that the more frequent and serious the perceived or actual acts of omission or commission, the greater the resultant guilt.

Situational Variables

Situational variables that may affect guilt reactions are the experiences of the child and parent during the terminal illness (if the child died of a chronic disease) or at the time of death, including the circumstances surrounding the death. Again, many aspects of the child's illness and death could contribute to guilt, but only three will be discussed: suddenness/anticipation, the care provided the child during the illness and at death, and the perceived preventability of the death.

Several authors have suggested that bereaved individuals who have had little or no warning of the loved one's impending death experience higher levels of guilt than those who have had a long expectation of death (Johnson-Soderberg, 1983; Parkes & Weiss, 1983). When a death is expected, parents may have time to ameliorate some of their guilt feelings by providing special love and attention to the child and to gain some sense of closure with the child. Sudden death, on the other hand, leaves the bereaved with no opportunity to say goodbye, resolve unfinished business, or mend wounds, and thus reach some level of closure.

At least one author has suggested that the quality of care provided to the loved one may influence the level of guilt (Cameron & Parkes, 1983). Parents of children who die after an illness may be left with guilt because of perceived inadequacies in the care given the sick child by themselves or by health care professionals whom they were responsible for engaging. In our recent study, we found that parents of chronically ill children had more illness-related guilt. Although many parents may feel some mild regrets related to care, actual or perceived large discrepancies may contribute to increased guilt responses. For example, if a child begged to go home to die but was kept in the hospital, guilt feelings following death may linger. Or parents might remember the severe pain and suffering caused by additional treatments that were attempted when the chances of remission were very slim. With sudden death, too, parents can experience long-lasting remorse. For example, following an accident that resulted in fatal brain injuries, parents can have intense remorse and guilt about having made the decision to turn off the respirator.

Any cause of death that is perceived by parents as somehow having been preventable can also affect guilt. Although there is no known cause and no known way to prevent Sudden Infant Death Syndrome (SIDS), parents often feel a sense of guilt for not waking the baby up sooner, not detecting some evidence in the baby's behavior prior to death, or not taking the baby to the doctor for a cold. Parents of children who commit suicide can view the child's death as preventable and expend much energy exploring the ways in which they might have prevented the death. Too, some parents may actually have committed an act that contributed to the child's death or neglected to do something that might have averted it. Resultant feelings of guilt may be so unbearable that these feelings can be blocked out of the conscious mind. However, the feelings may surface in other ways. A common manifestation of such guilt is seeking self-punishment. Unconsciously the parent feels "I'm guilty and deserve to be treated poorly or punished." Consequently, such a parent may set himself up to get in trouble with the law or act in such a way as to incite others to hurt him. Self-destructive behaviors such as gambling, drinking, or use of drugs could also be used to cope with guilt.

Personal Variables

Each individual's tendency to experience guilt is further determined by his personality structure. While there may be many personality variables that influence a parent's guilt response when a child dies, two are of particular importance here: the strictness and rigidity of the parent's conscience and the parent's sense of self-esteem or self-concept.

The conscience, a major part of the personality structure, develops early in childhood, primarily in the Oedipal period (ages 3 to 6). The strength of the conscience is directly related to the ability to experience guilt when a self-imposed or societal standard is violated. The stronger the conscience, the greater the guilt (Freud, 1938; Mowrer, 1960). Thus attentive, dedicated, and competent parents may feel a great deal of guilt, whereas other parents who were neglectful and incompetent may feel either little or no guilt. Although strictness of conscience is a difficult variable to assess in bereaved parents, some clues include being or having been a member of a religion that emphasizes guilt, having been reared in a family with much emphasis on blame, or reporting a history of guilt and self-blame prior to the child's death.

Self-esteem and self-concept are two closely interrelated concepts that refer to one's sense of competency and adequacy, which results from interactions with the environment, particularly with others (Wylie, 1974). As the death of a child can severely affect one's self-esteem, a preexisting weak or negative self-esteem can influence the grief process. In particular, poor self-esteem can affect the process of self-evaluation and lead to a great sense of guilt from all sources previously mentioned.

People with a rigid or strict conscience and poor or negative self-esteem are likely to be at risk during the grief process. Evaluation of these personality variables is complex and sensitive, requiring assessment of the bereaved parents' previous life experiences, perceptions of themselves, and ways of coping with other life stresses. Because these personality variables are preexisting, complex personality traits, such parents may require referral for grief therapy over and beyond the counseling provided in self-help and bereavement support groups.

Societal Variables

Many societal variables also can impact on parental guilt during bereavement. Society has values about the role of parents, the ideal parent-child relationship, the type of care that should be provided to a sick child, and the type of childhood death that can be tolerated. Generally, societal values affect parents through the attitudes and behaviors of family, friends, and others in the community. The amount of support provided, the level of social isolation experienced, the comments made, and the questions asked can greatly influence the guilt reactions of parents. Parents, for example, have reported that questions and comments of family members about the cause of the child's death often lead them into more self-blaming and hence more guilt. Sometimes the comments and even blame can come from a close family member such as a parent or spouse. In SIDS, for example, mothers have reported being blamed by a spouse for the infant's death; this triggered intensive guilt reactions and severe marital strife. Societal attitudes can particularly affect parents when a child has died of suicide or murder. Such families may be avoided by friends and neighbors or may even experience frank hostility.

COPING WITH GUILT

As guilt is a common and pervasive emotional response when a child has died, parents expend a great deal of energy attempting to come to terms with this feeling. Coping strategies used to deal with guilt feelings can be positive and helpful or negative and destructive. Continued negative self-evaluations leading to renewed guilt feelings, self-punishment, and use of alcohol or drugs to drown the feelings can be considered nonadaptive coping responses. Keeping busy and other attempts to avoid the feelings, while adaptive in the short haul, may only delay the guilt reactions. More adaptive responses include confronting and admitting to the feelings of guilt, exploring the various potential sources of guilt and sharing them with others in a supportive relationship, learning about the normality of these guilt reactions, relying on spiritual beliefs that might reduce guilt (forgiveness of oneself and/or focusing on positive destiny), and the use of rationalization.

Two studies that focused on how bereaved parents coped with guilt feelings revealed that indeed many of the adaptive coping mechanisms previously mentioned were used and found helpful. In our study, parents reported that rationalization, sharing, religious beliefs, and keeping busy were all helpful methods of coping with their guilt (Miles & Demi, 1983–84). Johnson-Soderberg (1983) mentioned in her study of guilt in bereaved parents that parents found talking, learning about grief, physical activity, drinking, "mind control," and time all helpful in reducing guilt reactions.

Confronting feelings of guilt means that parents openly admit that the feelings exist and then begin the process of examining the reality of the situation. In the process of examination, parents can be helped to accept the reality of the situation and restructure or reframe it into a positive solution (rationalization). For example, a parent might admit that indeed he had argued with his teenaged son prior to his death and then focus on the fact that the purpose of the arguments was to help his son deal with important issues in growing up into adulthood. In one situation, a mother reported feeling guilty for planning the party that resulted in her child's death. When she carefully examined her motives for planning the party, she began to realize that she was being a good mother in fulfilling her child's wishes. In another situation, a father who felt guilty about signing the operative permit for the surgery in which his son died realized he had made the only decision he could in an attempt to cure his son's heart ailment.

When rationalization doesn't work, parents may need assistance and permission to forgive themselves. As parents in our society seem to be very hard on themselves, forgiveness of self may be difficult to do. Writing a letter of self-forgiveness in a journal might be helpful. In addition, some parents have found it helpful to write a letter to the child who died that speaks to their regrets and to their need for forgiveness. Once the remorseful feelings are down on paper, they are often reduced or forgotten. Forgiveness can also be sought through spiritual beliefs.

Sometimes parents need assistance in identifying and changing irrational beliefs that might be producing guilt. Irrational beliefs are "shoulds," "musts," and "oughts" that recur over and over in one's regretful thoughts (Ellis & Harper, 1975). Some common irrational beliefs that can feed into bereavement guilt are "I must be perfect in everything I do," "Everybody must love me," "Everyone should always approve of what I say," and "My child's needs should always have come before my own." Once an irrational belief has been identified, the bereaved parent can be helped to change the belief into something more realistic.

Another related method for reducing guilt is having bereaved parents focus on the positives in their relationship and experiences with the child who died. Each time the parent begins to focus on guilt, he should be instructed to change that focus to a positive thought about something good that he did during the child's lifetime, during the illness, or at death.

Guilt may also be mitigated by helping others or contributing to society in some way. Turning the tragedy of the child's death into some method of helping others, such as developing a scholarship fund, providing leadership toward solving a societal problem such as reducing the number of drunken drivers, working in a group to help other bereaved parents, or providing assistance to other children can all be activities that reduce the feelings of guilt when a child has died.

SUMMARY

Because of the unique parent-child relationship, guilt is often one of the most insistent and profound reactions of parents when a child dies. In the theoretical model presented here, it is thought that guilt feelings in bereaved parents arise from the deep sense of helplessness and responsibility that parents often experience when a child dies. As parents begin to deal with these two interrelated feelings, they often focus on how their own actions or feelings might have contributed to the child's illness or death and reflect on their past performance with the child in the overall parental role. In this process of self-reflection, parents may perceive discrepancies between their ideal standards and actual performance as a parent, resulting in guilt reactions. Further, some parents may make a connection between the child's death and past transgressions for which they perceive they are being punished. The unnaturalness of a child's dying before a parent in this culture and aspects of parents' behavioral and emotional reactions during the grief process further contribute to guilt feelings. The theoretical model presented in this paper thus hypothesizes a typology of six potential sources of guilt that result from parental self-exploration: death causation, illness-related, parental role, moral, survival, and grief guilt. Furthermore, it is suggested that certain parental, situational, personal, and societal variables can influence parents' feelings of helplessness and responsibility, their process of self-evaluation, and their perception of having violated a standard or of a discrepancy between self-expectations and performance. These variables can ultimately affect the intensity, duration, and sources of guilty feelings.

As guilt is a common and sometimes devastating emotion of grief, bereaved parents often need help in accepting and coping with it. Just as parents have been taught that it is normal to feel sadness and anger, they must be provided information about the normality of guilt feelings during grief. When working with bereaved parents, caregivers may find it helpful to explore the various sources of guilt feelings and the parental, situational, personal, and societal variables that may be affecting parents' responses. Coping responses are very important in mitigating guilt reactions; it is thus important to assess the adequacy of the coping responses and to encourage adaptive responses. Rationalization, forgiveness, identification of irrational beliefs, positive reinforcement, and helping others are all important and useful ways of coping with guilt reactions. If guilt feelings persist and intensify over time, if parents seem to be coping with their guilt reactions in nonadaptive ways, or if parents appear to have an underlying personality trait such as poor self-esteem or a rigid conscience, referral for therapy may be important in overcoming and coping effectively with the guilt reactions.

References

Averill, J. (1968). Grief: Its nature and significance. *Psychological Bulletin, 70,* 721–748.

Benfield, D. G., Leib, S. A., & Vollman, J. H. (1978). Grief response of parents to neonatal death and parent participation in deciding care. *Pediatrics, 62,* 171–177.

Bergman, A. B., Pomeroy, M., & Beckwith, B. (1969). The psychiatric toll of the Sudden Infant Death Syndrome. *General Practice, 40*(6), 99–105.

Bowlby, J. (1980). *Attachment and loss: Vol. 3. Loss, sadness, and depression.* New York: Basic Books.

Brown, S. L. (1978). Functions, tasks, and stress of parenting: Implications for guidance. In L. E. Arnold (Ed.), *Helping parents help their children.* New York: Brunner-Mazel.

Buber, M. (1971). Existential guilt. In R. Smith (Ed.), *Guilt: Man and society.* New York: Doubleday.

Cameron, J., & Parkes, C. M. (1983). Terminal care: Evaluation of effects on surviving families of care before and after bereavement. *Postgraduate Medical Journal, 59,* 73–78.

Cassem, N. (1978). *Grieving for others: Practical management component of normal mourning.* Paper presented at the American Psychiatric Association Meeting, Atlanta, GA.

Cornwell, J., Nurcombe, B., & Stevens, L. (1977). Family response to loss of a child by Sudden Infant Death Syndrome. *Medical Journal of Australia, 11,* 656–658.

DeFrain, J. D., & Ernst, L. (1978). The psychological effects of Sudden Infant Death Syndrome on surviving family members. *Journal of Family Practice, 6,* 985–989.

Ellis, A., & Harper, R. A. (1975). *A new guide to rational living.* Englewood Cliffs, NJ: Prentice-Hall.

Freud, S. (1938). *The basic writings of Sigmund Freud* (A. A. Brice, Trans.). New York: Random House.

Friedman, S. B. (1974). Psychological aspects of sudden unexpected death in infants and children. *Pediatric Clinics of North America, 21,* 103–111.

Glick, L. O., Weiss, R. S., & Parkes, C. M. (1974). *The first year of bereavement.* New York: Wiley.

Hagan, J. (1974). Nursing interaction and intervention with grieving families. *Nursing Forum, 13,* 373–385.

Helmrath, T. A., & Steinitz, E. M. (1978). Death of an infant: Parental grieving and the failure of social support. *Journal of Family Practice, 6,* 785–790.

Izard, C. (Ed.). (1978). *Emotions in personality and psychopathology.* New York: Plenum Press.

Johnson-Soderberg, S. (1983). Parents who have lost a child by death. In V. J. Sasserath (Ed.), *Minimizing high risk parenting.* New Brunswick, NJ: Johnson & Johnson.

Kennell, J. H., & Klaus, M. H. (1976). Caring for parents of an infant who dies. In M. H. Klaus & J. H. Kennell (Eds.). *Maternal infant bonding.* St. Louis: C. V. Mosby.

Lieberman, S. (1978). Nineteen cases of morbid grief. *British Journal of Psychiatry, 132,* 159–163.

Lifton, R. J. (1976). *Death in life: Survivors of Hiroshima.* New York: Touchstone Books.

Lindemann, E. (1944). Symptomatology and management of acute grief. *American Journal of Psychiatry, 101,* 141–148.

Lynd, H. M. (1961). *On shame and the search for identity.* New York: Science Edition.

May, R. (1958). The origins and significance of the existential movement in psychology. In R. May, E. Angel, & H. F. Ellenberger (Eds.), *Existence: A new dimension in psychiatry and psychology.* New York: Basic Books.

McBride, A. (1973). The anger-depression-guilt go-around. *American Journal of Nursing, 73*(6), 1045–1049.

McCollum, A. T. (1974). Counseling the grieving parent. In L. Burton (Ed.), *Care of the child facing death.* Boston: Routledge & Kegan Paul.

Miles, M. S. (1977). S.I.D.S. : Parents are the patients. *Journal of Emergency Nursing, 3*(2), 29–32.

Miles, M. S. (1979). *The grief of parents: A model for assessment and intervention.* Unpublished manuscript.

Miles, M. S. (1980). *The grief of parents when a child dies.* Oak Brook, IL: The Compassionate Friends.

Miles, M. S. (1983). Helping adults mourn the death of a child. In H. Wass & C. Corr (Eds.), *Children and death.* Washington, DC: Hemisphere Press.

Miles, M. S., & Demi, A. S. (1983–84). Toward the development of a theory of bereavement guilt: Sources of guilt in bereaved parents. *Omega, 14*(4), 299–314.

Mowrer, O. H. (1960). *Learning theory and behavior.* New York: Wiley.

Parkes, C. M. (1965). Bereavement and mental illness. *British Journal of Medical Psychology, 110,* 198–204.

Parkes, C. M., & Weiss, R. S. (1983). *Recovery from bereavement.* New York: Basic Books.

Peppers, L. G., & Knapp, R. J. (1980). *Motherhood and mourning: Perinatal death.* New York: Praeger.

Radl, S. (1979). Breaking the guilt habit: A joyful mother's guide. *Ladies' Home Journal,* *96*(5), 103, 170–173.

Raphael, B. (1975). The management of pathological grief. *Australian and New Zealand Journal of Psychiatry, 9,* 173–179.

Rowe, J., Clyman, R., & Green, C. (1978). Follow-up of families who experience a perinatal death. *Pediatrics, 62,* 166–170.

Schiff, H. S. (1977). *The bereaved parent.* New York: Crown Publishers.

Smialek, Z. (1978). Observations on immediate reactions of families to sudden infant death. *Pediatrics, 62,* 160–164.

Stein, E. V. (1968). *Guilt theory and therapy.* Philadelphia: Westminster Press.

Tournier, P. (1962). *Guilt and grace.* New York: Harper & Row.

Viscott, D. (1976). *The language of feelings.* New York: Arbor House.

Wahl, C. (1970). The differential diagnosis of normal and neurotic grief following bereavement. *Psychosomatics, 11,* 104–106.

Weinstein, S. E. (1978). Sudden infant death syndrome: Impact on families and a direction for change. *American Journal of Psychiatry, 135,* 831–834.

Wylie, R. C. (1974). *The self concept.* Lincoln, NE: University of Nebraska Press.

Zahourek, R., & Jensen, J. S. (1973). Grieving and the loss of the newborn. *American Journal of Nursing, 73,* 836–839.

Section 2

Issues in Specific Types of Death

Chapter 5
Miscarriage

Ellen Fish Lietar

Ellen Fish Lietar, R.N., M.S., C.S., is a psychiatric clinical specialist who maintains a private practice in Providence, Rhode Island, and is on the faculty at Boston University School of Nursing.

"It happens to lots of women"; "Don't worry, you'll have another one"; "This baby would have been abnormal anyway"; "You were hardly pregnant"; "You'll get over this quickly." These are words often heard by a woman grieving after miscarriage. Miscarriage is described in one article as "gynaecological scrapings," in another as "tissue," and in still another as "products of conception."

Miscarriage, also called spontaneous abortion, is defined as the "unintended ending of a pregnancy before the time the fetus could survive outside the mother. This time is usually considered to be the twentieth week of pregnancy" (Borg & Lasker, 1981, p. 27). A review of the literature reveals that approximately 20% of all pregnancies end in miscarriage. Three-fourths of those end before 12 weeks and are termed early miscarriages. They often indicate a problem with implantation on the wall of the uterus or genetic mutation with ensuing abnormality of the embryo. Late miscarriages are those that occur from week 13 to week 20 of the pregnancy. Some common reasons for late miscarriage are structural problems of the uterus, problems with implantation, or an incompetent cervix.

The first trimester of a pregnancy is characterized by a process of binding into the pregnancy. The woman begins to incorporate the developing fetus as an integral part of herself. Even before quickening, the occasion where the mother feels fetal movement, she may alter her dietary habits, shop for a crib, and fantasize about her enlarging family. She may give up tobacco and alcohol, and plan to adjust her work hours. Her life begins to change.

Ambivalence is a part of the first trimester. Especially since the woman has not felt movement, the pregnancy is less of a reality. Attachment is often in a very early stage, and as a result it is common to see a high degree of ambivalence. The newly pregnant woman wonders if she will have enough love to share with a new baby. A career woman worries about compromising her position. A marriage may be threatened. As the woman accommodates to her pregnancy, the first trimester is a time of significant emotional upheaval and change. Although some degree of ambivalence is expected, it is well known that high degrees of ambivalence relate directly to more difficult bereavement after a miscarriage.

GRIEF FOLLOWING MISCARRIAGE

The first symptoms of miscarriage are cramping and bleeding. This is a frightening time for the couple. The woman is advised by her health care provider to rest in bed. She may become angry or disappointed that nothing more therapeutic is prescribed. Helplessness and anxiety are emotions most often felt by the woman who is beginning to miscarry.

The issue of control becomes important for the woman. Early signs of miscarriage are ambiguous, and neither the patient nor her physician can anticipate what will happen. This is often the time that a woman will come into the hospital. As a hospitalized person, she loses additional control. Her nightgown is replaced by a shirt that doesn't close, her case is discussed in a language that she can't understand, and she is poked and prodded. Because her medical treatment is uncomplicated, she is often put in a back room by herself until the need for a dilatation and curettage is indicated. Her grief and her need for control are largely ignored.

The issue of loss and grief in the medical setting is a difficult one. "Implicit in the medical education process is the concept that every death corresponds to a failure either of the individual physician or, more commonly, of medicine as a whole" (Bohrod, 1974, p. 811). Evidence of this is provided by the Knapp and Peppers's (1979) data, in which 100 parents who had experienced miscarriage were interviewed. The majority of respondents stated that frequently their obstetricians terminated their relationship abruptly, or were insensitive to their needs or aloof.

Compounding the problem of grief and loss in the health care system is the fact that the woman who miscarries has only an image to grieve. She does not have a viable fetus. She has nothing to see or hold. One woman described her miscarriage as a "passing of a dream." Thus, the bereavement response will relate strongly to the fantasies that a mother has had about the unborn child. The fantasized baby may represent a number of things to the parent-to-be: hope for resolution of an intrapsychic conflict; replacement of someone who has been lost; someone who will need and love the parent; someone with whom the parent can compensate for her own deprived childhood; evidence that the parent is mature, sexual, or attractive; or a weapon in a relationship with someone else (Raphael, 1983). A pregnancy can represent the replacement child to parents who have not resolved former losses and who may have planned to name the new baby after a lost child. All of these hopes, dreams, and meanings will have to be identified and grieved after the miscarriage. Because they are intangible and symbolic the grief process is more difficult, but no less important.

Notable in miscarriage is the lack of social support. Many women may not have told anyone about the pregnancy. Because there are no external signs of pregnancy, friends, relatives, and even the woman herself may deny that anything important has happened. Significant others do not have memories of a person who has died. This serves to isolate the woman, to whom the child has been very real. A couple is told "At least you have other children at home" or "You are young, you can always have another child." Many times, even if the pregnancy has been recognized by others, the loss of it will be minimized or negated. People frequently assume that since the baby was never born, the couple has nothing to grieve and can easily replace what has been lost. There is an absence of recognition that the parents, most especially the mother, already had a relationship with the unborn child in terms of all that it represented to her. The amount of grief over a miscarriage will not be determined by the time between conception and aborting, but by the meaning that the pregnancy held for the couple and a number of other factors such as the desire for parenthood, religious training, cultural mores, the positive value placed on the pregnancy by the couple's social and environmental milieu, and their understanding of pregnancy (Shaw, 1983).

It was once said that grief is like dirty dishes: "If you don't do them, they pile up!" If the loss is recognized, the normal process of mourning can take place. Caregivers, friends, and loved ones must give grieving couples permission to experience and express their sense of loss. They must be allowed to temporarily assume a dependent role: to cry, to be held, and to be cared for. After a period of relative decompensation and disorganization, resolution and restitution usually occur (Stack, 1980). If the loss is not recognized and validated by others, a social response that is critical in initiating and providing support for the grief process, the couple becomes susceptible to the malignant consequences of unresolved grief.

In 1980, Seibel and Graves studied 93 women who had experienced miscarriage. They found that the predominant concerns involved two questions: What caused the miscarriage? Why did it happen? Of the respondents 25% felt somehow responsible for the miscarriages, blaming themselves for such things as having had sexual intercourse, playing, or bowling. It was discovered that patients had often been misinformed and frequently required more accurate data about what had actually caused the miscarriage in order to dispel the illegitimate guilt that frequently occurred.

Since this is a major loss for many individuals, all the normal symptoms of grief can be expected. Additionally, women often struggle with the painful issue of worthlessness or of feeling like a failure or deficient in some way because they have been unable to produce a healthy child. If the miscarriage occurs when fertility has yet to be proven, the couple may experience anxiety about their ability to ever have children. There may be many thoughts about what the child would have been, could have been. Anniversaries of when the child would have been born may elicit brief upsurges in grief over the loss of this particular unborn child.

In many cases there is a discrepancy between the grief of the mother and the father. This reflects the difference in the investment in the unborn child. For the mother, investment occurs earlier and is reinforced by the bodily changes she experiences. However, some fathers bond with the child-to-be early in the pregnancy, and in these cases grief will be more similar to the mother's. Where there are large discrepancies between the grief experiences of mother and father, the woman can feel even more isolated in her grief.

INTERVENTIONS

In their work on crisis intervention, Aquilera and Messick (1974) define a person in crisis as someone facing a problem that he cannot readily solve by employing the coping mechanisms that have worked before. The principles of crisis intervention can be helpful when working with a couple after a miscarriage.

To help couples recover following a miscarriage, we first need to legitimize the loss. We then must assess the extent of the crisis. We must see if the woman is talking about the miscarriage, and whether or not she is using her support systems. The use of support systems is a healthy sign; we should encourage interaction with significant others, as their support is critical. We need to mobilize family and close friends to make themselves available to the woman. We also need to look at the family as a system. When one member of the family has experienced a crisis, such as a miscarriage, the others in that family will be affected also. Often fathers are especially neglected during the pregnancy/childbirth experience and when there is a miscarriage; whatever care and concern is offered centers around the mother. It is more difficult for men to find social support when they are bereaved, and this is especially the case in miscarriage. We must make special attempts to reach out to these men.

We must listen for guilt and feelings of responsibility. Most women feel somewhat responsible for the miscarriage and are reassured when the reason for the miscarriage is explained. If we can remember that guilt is almost always a part of the experience, communication can be directed toward relieving that guilt. We should ask whether the woman feels suicidal. Very few people will volunteer that information, but many will answer if questioned in a direct and concerned manner.

It is important in assessment of the couple after a miscarriage to know how much the miscarriage has disrupted their lives and how it has affected others around them. We must ascertain the couple's coping skills and strengths and then capitalize on them in our interventions. Miscarriage, as any other event, is different for everyone.

At the time of miscarriage, a woman may not look pregnant, she has not felt fetal movement yet, "she has not identified the fetus as a new person but rather has considered it part of herself. Grieving for the loss of one's self is often different and more difficult than grieving for the loss of an outside love object" (Stack, 1980, p. 100). Therefore, it is very important in our intervention to encourage a woman to verbalize all her feelings. We should not reassure her too soon, but allow her to express her guilt, ambivalence, sadness, and all other feelings of grief. Often, in a hospital setting, there is not sufficient privacy for a woman to express her sense of loss. It is recommended that isolation areas or grieving rooms be given greater priority.

Many couples find it very helpful to see the products of miscarriage. It helps to reinforce reality and to initiate the grieving process. Always give them a choice, however. Parents should not be made to feel guilty if they do not want to see the miscarriage products or the fetus. It is important to leave room for individual styles.

Many times a woman will ask her health care provider whether she should see the miscarried baby. Rather than answering directly, the provider should help her explore her own feelings. She will come to the decision that is right for her.

Case Example: Jane, age 30, began counseling 2 years after miscarrying at the 20th week of pregnancy. She had never seen the fetus. She wanted to call her obstetrician to see if he could tell her what the fetus looked like. "Part of me knows that is silly, but I have an overwhelming need to know."

Often Polaroid pictures are offered to parents, and they are treasured as concrete proof that the child existed.

Case Example: Elisa, age 32, had never seen her miscarried baby. On the mantlepiece was her photograph of her child—a framed copy of the ultrasound tracing!

The final principle of crisis intervention is to assume that there is resolution. Helping the couple to see that they are grieving and to identify their coping styles reinforces these adaptive coping mechanisms.

If we recognize the importance of this event in a person's life, we can facilitate the grieving process and pave the way for improved mental health in the future. We all must recognize that maternal grief has been documented to be the same for a miscarriage as it is for a stillborn or neonatal death (Peppers & Knapp, 1980). It is a serious, intense experience for those who undergo it. Because miscarriage is a medically common occurrence, many of us may forget that it is a highly significant event for the couple and that the loss should be treated as important, with the same care provided as if an older child were lost (Shaw, 1983). We can be especially helpful if we provide the couple with norms on grief reactions, the amount of time it takes to recover, and the impact on the marital relationship. Referral to a self-help group of other parents who have experienced a similar loss is often quite therapeutic. They can encourage the couple to have patience with themselves and to avoid the "shoulds" that they can impose on themselves, such as "I shouldn't be so upset over this," which frequently minimize the loss or interfere with healthy grief expression. If the couple decides to have another child, they should be encouraged to recognize the uniqueness of the new child and not use him to replace the lost child.

References

Aquilera, D., & Messick, J. (1974). *Crisis intervention: Theory and methodology*. St. Louis: C. V. Mosby.

Bohrod, M. D. (1974). Uses of autopsy. *Journal of the American Medical Association, 192*, 811.

Borg, S., & Lasker, J. (1981). *When pregnancy fails*. Boston: Beacon Press.

Knapp, R., & Peppers, L. (1979). Doctor-patient relationships in fetal/infant death encounters. *Journal of Medical Education, 54*, 775–780.

Peppers, L., & Knapp, R. (1980). Maternal reactions to involuntary fetal/infant death. *Psychiatry, 43*, 155–159.

Raphael, B. (1983). *The anatomy of bereavement*. New York: Basic Books.

Seibel, M., & Graves, W. (1980). The psychological implications of spontaneous abortions. *Reproductive Medicine, 24*, 161–165.

Shaw, C. T. (1983). Grief over fetal loss. *Family Practice Recertification, 5*, 129–145.

Stack, J. (1980). Spontaneous abortion and grieving. *American Family Physician, 21*, 99–102.

Chapter 6

Stillbirth

Sherrell Harter Hutchins

Sherrell Harter Hutchins graduated from Hanover College in 1957 with a degree in Human Relations. In 1958 she and her husband, John, a fifth-generation funeral director, returned to his hometown and joined the family business. Later that year a long-awaited son was born prematurely and died some 12 hours later. Ms. Hutchins has spent over 28 years in funeral service and 6 years in bereavement follow-up on the local level, plus 15 years in continuing education in funeral service on the state, regional, and national levels. Locally she is active in The Compassionate Friends, hospice volunteer training, and SHARE Outreach; she also has served on the National Funeral Directors Association Committees on Women in Funeral Service and Public Information, and as Chair of the Outreach Committee. She is a member of The Association for Death Education and Counseling and The National Perinatal Bereavement Coalition.

*Dedicated to our infant son, whose birth and
death opened first my heart and then my mind
to the needs of bereaved parents—those parents
who have since become my best teachers.*

Prior to the 1900s deaths of babies and children from natural causes were common. When babies were born at home, and sometimes died at home, there was no need for intervention to actualize the loss. Mothers, fathers, siblings, and grandparents were naturally involved in burial rites for their loved ones. But with the advent of hospitals in the 1900s our society entered a phase of protectiveness. We thought if we kept death behind high walls and closed doors, it might not hurt us.

In 1958, when my newborn baby died, it was common for the father and the funeral director to hurry to the grave site, leaving the mother in her hospital room never having seen the baby. The father, the grandparents, the doctor, and the funeral director all had good intentions; they wanted to protect the mother and surviving children. If mothers never saw the baby, the reasoning went, they (and society) could pretend that the loss never occurred. In some cases hospitals contributed to this conspiracy of protectiveness by disposing of the "tissue." To understand that era it must be remembered that grief was considered abnormal prior to the 1960s.

Today research (Benfield & Nichols, 1980) and personal testimonials from the survivors of perinatal death indicate that it is difficult and sometimes impossible to resolve the death of a dream. Parents want the opportunity to see, touch, and hold the baby that was so much a part of their lives and expectations prior to birth. They need the opportunity to say "hello" before they must say "good-bye" (Schwiebert & Kirk, 1981). Hospital personnel (and trained volunteers) are in a frontline position to offer them options for saying "hello." Funeral directors and clergy are critically important in encouraging a participatory "good-bye." Research clearly calls for such confrontation and closure as steps toward healthy grief resolution.

There also are other reasons for this emerging emphasis on the needs of survivors following perinatal death. Today family planning is possible, so pregnancy may be delayed for years. Infertility problems also are on the increase. When pregnancy finally occurs, it may have been long anticipated. If loss comes, the pain is multiplied by the years of expectation.

In the 1980s it is common for couples to delay pregnancy until they are in their mid-30s. By then both husband and wife may have their careers in order and feel they are financially and emotionally ready to rear a child. The birth is an event that may have been anticipated by the parents for a decade.

Consider the needs of the mother-to-be who has made a soul-searching decision and quit work in order to devote herself to the "wished-for child" (Davidson, 1979). In such cases, when birth results in death, it is a tragedy that bitterly mocks the dream of the perfect time for the perfect child. And the biological clock continues its relentless countdown. . . .

By contrast the unwed mother of 16 who is told her baby is dead may be haunted by guilt, riddled with anger at the teenage father, or seething with frustration at the cadre of protective grandmothers-to-be. Her needs may be different but just as intense.

Another increasing phenomenon today is the common occurrence of the second marriage and the accompanying desire to create a family that is not only blended, but bonded by the addition of a new baby. In this case, again, the parents are older and are under pressure of time.

TYPES OF PERINATAL DEATH OR TRAUMA

Pregnancies may fail in many different ways. Miscarriage or abortion may take place early in the term; premature labor, stillbirth, or death shortly after birth may arise later.

In the past the survivors of miscarriage were viewed by society as "illegitimate mourners" (Nichols, 1984). Today we are acknowledging their right to mourn. We now realize that parents begin to bond with their child long before the actual birth. With the first news of the pregnancy, the new mom and dad may have quietly celebrated and dreamed of the baby's first step, a family Christmas, the football hero, the wedding celebration, their own immortality. With the loss of the child, they also lose these dreams. They may need the doctor and nurse, the clergy, and the funeral director to grant them permission to grieve, to confirm their legitimate right to mourn. In addition the parents may need to see the dead child to verify their loss, and may find that a burial site serves as a focal point for resolving that loss.

The spontaneous abortion (also termed miscarriage) that occurs prior to 20 weeks is a life still in limbo. If it is not ruled a live birth, the bureau of vital statistics does not recognize it. The abortion may occur at home or in a hospital setting away from obstetrically trained nurses. Standard hospital procedure may be to dispose of "the tissue." The parents, on the other hand, may view "the tissue" as their very real baby. The trained crisis intervenor, whether it be a nurse, doctor, clergy member, a mental health worker, or funeral director, must listen for the signals from parents and explain the options before it's too late. In some cases it has been necessary to "rescue" the fetus from the lab and from the pathologist, who assumed that, following tests, hospital disposal was intended.

Clinicians are also researching the needs of the survivors of a planned abortion. In some cases, the tangled emotions surrounding the loss may require clinical intervention. (See Chapter 14 for more on this.)

Very often the mother in premature labor is in a state of emotional shock. She experiences paralyzing fear that the process cannot be halted, that the baby or babies cannot survive, that they are somehow abnormal. Depending on how long the labor continues prior to birth and on the mother's and family's coping styles, the birth and death may be anticipated and the grief process initiated. On the other hand, denial may be the defense and grief work may be delayed until later.

The parents experiencing a full-term stillbirth or death shortly after birth may be the least prepared. When the pregnancy has gone full term, there is usually a sense of relief. The danger zones have been passed. The nursery is ready, and the baby shower gifts await the new arrival. Siblings have been prepared, Father has completed the childbirth classes and is ready to coach, and Grandmother is set to appear at a moment's notice. And then the unthinkable occurs—the baby dies. At this point, it is especially important that the entire family participate in experiencing the baby, in saying "hello" at the hospital and in saying "good-bye" at the funeral or prayer service, and at the grave site.

The baby who, in addition to dying, is born with anomalies, may be more difficult for the caregivers to deal with than the parents. Medical caregivers will need to prepare the parents for the abnormalities, to wrap the baby in a (warm) blanket, to place a beehive dressing or a bonnet or cap on the baby, and to let the parents choose what they wish to see. They should focus on that which is normal—fingers like Mom's, hair like Dad's. Parents usually confirm that what they see is much better than what they had imagined. In the case of stillbirth, the parents and family need to be prepared for discoloration and any maceration (a deterioration of the child's body).

STILLBIRTH

The stillbirth experience is unique within the context of perinatal bereavement, as death is anticipated prior to birth. After months of feeling movement, the mother's first sign may be an unexpected stillness. When the stethoscope and the ultrasound machine verify the silence, it is a traumatic moment for parents and caregivers alike. Honesty and compassion are our only allies. There are decisions that must be considered at a time when judgment is dulled by emotional, sometimes physical, pain. Should the mother and father wait for natural labor to begin or choose to induce labor at some point in time?

Assuming that physical reasons to induce labor do not prevail, it seems only fair to explain to the parents that delay will inevitably lead to maceration. Parents have become conscious of their rights to see, touch, and hold their babies, and they expect to see a body that looks much like a normal baby. Those expectations extend to the funeral service as well, when viewing by family and friends is anticipated. The longer the delay, the more difficult it becomes for the funeral director to present a normal-looking body.

When the parents choose to wait for an extended period, does denial of the death persist? Is it better to initiate the grief work rather than prolong it? When the birth is delayed, will the mother be outside the circle of care that could be provided by trained crisis intervention teams of obstetric or neonatal intensive care staff? Will she feel isolated and be treated impersonally in the emergency room or surgery, where she may raise the anxiety levels of those not trained to care for her emotional needs? This does not mean there should be a hurried rush into induction of labor, but the realities must be acknowledged and considered.

The death of a baby *in utero* during labor or shortly before birth more nearly parallels a sudden death, with the surviving parents experiencing numbing shock and paralyzing fear, with little time for mythical bargaining. However, the stillbirth that is delayed may initiate anticipatory grief, bringing all the factors into play that accompany the diagnosis of terminal illness. A closer parallel might be found in the situation where life is sustained only by machines. It is a state of limbo where there is neither life nor the hard reality of death. In either case anticipatory grief may or may not be initiated.

Bereavement follow-up with the families of hospice patients clearly brings to light the differences in people's ability or willingness to anticipate grief. The patient and/or one or more of the family members may have progressed along the road to acceptance, while others may be out of sync, stranded in a state of denial. On the other hand, the patient herself may not acknowledge the impending death, in which case the entire family system may support the myth. In such cases only a skilled facilitator may open the door to honest communication between mates or among family members. Differences in coping styles; temperament (Keirsey & Bates, 1984); gender; life cycle stages; socioeconomic, ethnic, and religious background; and experiences with previous losses and compounded grief all play a part in the process.

Parents grieving for a stillbirth have a difficult course to travel. Charme Davidson, a psychologist specializing in perinatal bereavement, suggests that there is always a degree of ambivalence in perinatal bereavement. Past resentments over the loss of freedom the child would have brought might haunt the survivors of the death of even the most planned-for and wished-for child.

On the other hand, there is also the fact that, whether they have other natural children, adopt, or never have a child, they will always wonder what might have been. They will think of how the child would have looked on his first birthday, when he went to school, when he graduated and married. The future of that very special baby who never grew up is untarnished by truth. This may create problems, for dream children remain perfect, while real children test their parents, fail, and try their parents' patience. Yet it is hardly fair to judge reality by the standards of idealistic dreams.

In addition, the parents experiencing stillbirth or other perinatal death are most often young and inexperienced at dealing with death and loss. If the physician, nurse, clergy member, social worker, or funeral director does not create an awareness of the options, the parents won't know they exist. It is a time-limited opportunity. In bereavement follow-up I listen to frustrated parents who were either not assertive enough to make their feelings known or were not given information and the permission to choose.

Subsequent attempts to have a child, particularly for parents who have endured a previous full-term stillbirth of unknown cause, can be extremely stressful. If infertility has been a problem in the past, parents may wonder if they will ever have another child. If there is a pregnancy, there is a long 9-month ride on an emotional roller coaster; and at the end of the ride the parents may have a baby girl instead of the replacement baby boy of their dreams. Support from those who have experienced a successful, subsequent pregnancy and resolved any resulting parenting conflicts is of inestimable value.

Current research indicates that a waiting period prior to subsequent pregnancy is advisable, not only for physical reasons but for better psychological adjustment. A replacement baby is not considered a mentally healthy substitute for unresolved loss. However, this reasoning leaves the prospective mother in her 30s in a difficult bind. How do we counsel someone who is facing a biological barrier, who may have experienced previous bouts of infertility, who may have planned her children 2 years apart?

When grief was considered pathological and was often suppressed, when the survivors of miscarriage, stillbirth, and death shortly after birth were considered "illegitimate mourners" (Nichols, 1984), the unresolved grief could span a lifetime. Today, with the assistance of enlightened caregivers, perhaps it is possible that the tasks of mourning (Worden, 1982) for such a loss may be dealt with in a shorter time span, freeing the parents emotionally for a subsequent pregnancy.

The grief of parents who have been told they will never have another child is different. Their hope is gone, and their needs are long term. There is a stubborn buoyancy that carries parents following a first-time loss, but the bottom drops out if the unforgivable happens and another baby dies. These parents may be the ones who most need to make some sense of it all and eventually reinvest their energies in mutual support of others like themselves or in some worthy cause. In time they may come to see that creativity is not limited to childbearing.

Looking at the other side of perinatal loss, is it more difficult for the mother who has experienced successful pregnancies? She has previously cradled, cuddled, and nursed the fruition of months of pregnancy and hours of labor. When she (and the expectant father) return home with "empty arms" (Ilse, 1982), will the thwarted instincts be more intense than for the woman who has never experienced being a mother? Again shifting the focus, would parents feel less personally "defective" if they had previously experienced the birth of healthy baby? Would the feelings of failure be dispersed somewhat?

CHANGING ATTITUDES TOWARD PERINATAL DEATH

When I married a fifth-generation funeral director and returned to his hometown, funeral service was completely new to me. I had never experienced the death of a close family member. But early in our married years we had a much-anticipated first-born son who died. Miscarriage, both preceding and subsequent to our son's death in 1958, caused us to close that door and, we hoped, the risk of being hurt again. Some 3 years later our healing was facilitated when we adopted first a baby girl and then a boy, but an acute sensitivity to the needs of bereaved parents remained.

Today our "babies" are young adults and a dearly loved grand-daughter has extended our present family to four generations. In 1979, with a (sometimes) empty nest, I dusted off a degree in human relations and expanded my role in the family business to include community education and bereavement follow-up services. We began with program-ming for the widowed, but within a year I turned to focus on the bereavement that had touched us personally. In our small community the funerals we conduct are often for the families of friends and personal acquaintances. Whether that service is for a child, infant, teenager, or adult, the pain that we experience is not only for the significant survivors, but also for ourselves.

In the fall of 1980 our funeral home sponsored a conference for bereaved parents, providing a forum for them to explain to the caregiving professionals—medical practitioners, clergy, funeral directors, and mental health personnel—what hurt and what helped in the traumatic aftermath following the death of their child. That conference yielded an increase in public awareness of the long-term needs of bereaved parents and, perhaps more important, led to the formation of a chapter of The Compassionate Friends to serve our four-county area. Since that time many local families have received immediate and ongoing support from other bereaved parents, education from self-help literature, and the outlet of a small group in which to share their pain and their victories. How many others have been helped by the subsequent public education through the media, by the newsletters read privately in their homes, or by a doctor's new-found courage to speak with parents about their dead child, we will never know. But we do know that the results have been well worth the price of our efforts.

My full circle experience continued in the fall of 1981, when the Indiana Funeral Directors' Association sponsored an interdisciplinary seminar in South Bend, Indiana, that featured Dr. Gary Benfield, Director of Neonatology, Children's Hospital, Medical Center of Akron. Several nurses and a clergyman and his wife attended along with me. The minister and his wife, new to our community, had recently experienced loss through miscarriage. Two of the three home health care nurses who traveled with us that day had had newborns that died in years past. When the invitations were issued, I had had no knowledge of their previous histories.

Dr. Benfield's soft-spoken manner did not decrease the intensity of his message. He told us, funeral directors, clergy, and medical and mental health professionals, that grief is unrelated to birth weight; that the macerated stillborn may appear different to parents than to us; that the use of sedatives and clichés is paternalistic. He encouraged us to offer parents the option of seeing, touching, and holding their dead or dying baby.

For me, the circle was complete. With a growing sense of mission, I was pleased when the obstetric nurses at our local hospital asked me to help with an in-service seminar on perinatal death: "We don't know how to handle it. Maternity is supposed to be a happy place!" I shared

Dr. Benfield's research and made copies of The Compassionate Friends' publication *When a Baby Dies* (Church, Chazin, & Ewald, 1981) available to nurses and bereaved parents.

I would like to testify that our homefront consciousness-raising in 1982 had successfully changed the established patterns in our community, but continuing education is an ongoing need. In hospitals and in funeral service staff rotate around the clock, weekend and holiday staffs consist of extra help, and normal personnel changes create orientation gaps. Communication is difficult at best in 365-days-a-year, 24-hours-a-day operations.

On a more positive note, our son, a 1985 graduate of the Cincinnati College of Mortuary Science, has already proved his enlightened sensitivity to the needs of the survivors of stillbirth. The necessity for increased grief counseling skills was graphically illustrated in our blended family of five generations, with two sets of grandparents who had previously experienced the loss of a child. Such intergenerational grieving has the potential for creating both support and conflict.

CRISIS INTERVENTION EDUCATION

In the summer of 1984 I received a call from a childbirth educator who had been in attendance at a single-parent stillbirth at our local hospital. The educator felt inadequate, had not been satisfied with the nursing response, and asked for help. One of our mutual acquaintances had delivered premature twins at a nearby city hospital who subsequently died. That young mother and father's first experience with death was made easier by a trained crisis intervenor who visited them in their hospital room shortly after the death. The volunteer had explained to them their various options. I called that crisis intervenor, Betsy Dixon, who had herself experienced perinatal death some 15 years earlier. She consented to be our speaker for a crisis intervention education seminar. I later learned that she had done various in-service seminars and had written an article for the clergy entitled "When Birth Means Death."

The seminar was scheduled for late August. We met in the hospital board room and all crowded around a long table—nurses, bereaved parents, clergy, and funeral service representatives. For both the young and the older funeral directors in attendance, I could have asked for no better vehicle to convince them of the importance of viewing even an imperfect stillborn infant, of the value of encouraging participation of mother, brothers, and sisters in the funeral rites, of the continued frustration of families who were not given the options of "closure," and of the importance of crisis intervention as a form of prevention.

Afterward we formed a steering committee consisting of a child-birth educator, a chaplain trained in pastoral education, myself as a funeral service representative, and an obstetric hospital supervisor. Each of us had personally experienced a loss from miscarriage, still-birth, or newborn death. We met with the physicians on the obstetrics/gynecology committees of two area hospitals and kept them informed as we began to develop checklists. We listened to the experiences of bereaved parents. Then we planned and held a series of workshops entitled "Crisis Intervention For Caregivers and Families When a Baby Dies." The series created an opportunity for public education as well as for focused intervention techniques.

We also chose to affiliate with SHARE,* a support group that began with Sister Jane Marie Lamb at St. John's Hospital, Springfield, Illinois, and is now extending nationwide. The national SHARE news-letter is a helpful resource for newly bereaved parents.

The checklists we developed and the letter to the parents were written in the simplest of formats in the hopes of communicating with bereaved parents and hospital personnel even in the midst of crisis. Unlike obstetric high risk/neonatal intensive care units, smaller hospitals have personnel who are often newcomers to the trauma of "when birth means death." A brochure that could be given to the family by the funeral director or the hospital was another intervention tool we found useful during this period of time, when bereaved parents' concentration is limited.

Our first session, which dealt with hospital policies, included an introduction of hospital administrators and nursing supervisors and a discussion by two physicians on the normal and abnormal birth pro-cesses. Perhaps of most value was the fact that the physicians remained for the small group discussion among nurses, bereaved parents, and clergy that followed. I must give credit to physicians and other profes-sional authority figures who are willing to stay after imparting their expertise, for they risk having their frame of reference challenged. For instance, the term "monster" may be found in medical textbooks, but bereaved parents find it totally unacceptable and will make their feelings known, suggesting that the physician change not only the term but the textbook as well! There might be fewer lawsuits if time sharing and *two-way* communication became a standard part of prevention, intervention,

---

*For more information contact SHARE, St. John's Hospital, 800 East Carpenter, Spring-field, IL 62769

and postvention medical practice. Doesn't the isolation of the specialist make that specialist even more vulnerable to misunderstanding?

In the second session a representative from the mental health center discussed the grief process. The third meeting featured a physician specializing in genetic counseling. During the fourth, a clergyman with a doctorate in counseling discussed listening and communication skills, and the fifth and final public meeting dealt with caregivers working as a team and the SHARE outreach concept, as well as discussion of subsequent pregnancies and adoption considerations.

In a handout at the 1985 National Funeral Directors' convention I encouraged other funeral service personnel to locally develop such an educational project. Such continuing education can make us more responsive, even when it dictates that we must change. It can also validate the funeral process that includes confrontation to actualize the loss, participation to experience the pain, and ceremonies of closure to facilitate acceptance. The call for change reinforces a basic premise of funeral service: to deny the confrontation with grief is to delay it, to compound it, and to unnecessarily prolong it.

INTERVENTION SUGGESTIONS

Hospital staff need to know how to respond when a child is born dying or dead, possibly deformed. A checklist developed for our local hospital includes the following recommendations for medical caregivers taken from research and from personal testimony of surviving parents:

- If the mother is sedated, wait until she is alert before telling her what has happened.
- First speak to the parents alone. Explain honestly, but gently, what is happening or has happened. Reassure them that nothing they did is the cause of it (assuming this is true). Prepare them for what they may see if there are birth defects or if the baby was stillborn.
- Bathe the baby and wrap the child in a clean, warm blanket.
- Offer the parents and other family members the opportunity to see, touch, and hold the baby. Explain that it is better for them to experience the baby rather than delay grief and later feel that it is difficult to believe the child ever existed.
- Focus on that which is normal about the child.
- Allow for individual differences in the mother's and father's responses. Explain that it is normal for mothers and fathers to have different reactions and needs after the loss of a baby.
- Encourage the parents to name the baby.

- Give the parents time to make decisions. However, if the parents or grandparents think they may want the baby to be viewed at the funeral home, talk with the funeral director. If there is to be a delay, arterial work will be affected.
- Be alert to the overprotective interference of grandparents or the father.
- Save the child's footprints, bracelet, lock of hair, hospital certificate, or other mementos.
- Photograph the baby in as pleasant a setting as possible, such as being held. If parents do not want the photo at the time, keep it on file. Focus the camera on those portions of the child that are normal, perhaps the hands and feet (Kirkley-Best & Kellner, 1982).
- If an autopsy is recommended and the family anticipates viewing the baby prior to funeral services, the lab and pathologist should be informed.
- Ask the parents how you can help: Do you want us to call a member of the clergy to say a prayer or baptize the baby? May we call a volunteer to talk with you, someone who has also experienced newborn death? Do you want the funeral director to come to the hospital room so that both of you can participate in the arrangements?
- Encourage the involvement of mother and father, grandparents, siblings, and significant others in planning and participating in funeral rites. Siblings may want to share a toy, the grandmother a blanket, the mother a poem or lullaby. The father and grandfather may wish to be casket bearers. Make sure the family knows that in most cases the funeral can be delayed until the mother can attend.
- Provide literature on perinatal death and grief for parents to take home with them. Mental health caregivers should send a personal note to parents following hospital dismissal saying that they are available by phone or for visits.
- Follow up with a medical report to the parents reviewing the past events and considering the future.

It is important that children be included in, rather than left out of, the family's grief. They need to be reassured that no "magical" wish on their part caused the death of the baby.

Families often ask for resources for explaining death to children after a baby sibling dies. A mother who experienced an unanticipated stillbirth at 9 months said:

My 4-year-old and 5-year-old were so excited and primed for the new baby. It seems to be as difficult for them as for me. They keep asking when the baby is coming home from the hospital. If I had it to do over again, I'd have allowed them to see the baby at the funeral home. Now I wonder if they'll be frightened when, and if, they must be admitted to a hospital.

A mother whose newborn baby died shortly after birth had this to say:

They gave me a copy of *Newborn Death* (Johnson et al., 1982) at the hospital. My friend read it and said, "I think there are some suggestions in here you need to think about." That's when we decided to include the children and have a funeral.

The kids were next to me like glue the first 2 weeks after I was home from the hospital. I guess they were afraid they would lose me, too. I think right now they need a lot of consistent care—from me.

Another survivor of stillbirth said of her experience: "My 2-year-old has really regressed. I guess I was pretty upset all through the holidays, and now I have to leave him to go back to work. He won't sleep alone in his bed at night."

Some resource books available for reading to surviving children following the death of a baby sibling are *Where's Jess?* (Johnson & Johnson, 1982) and the books of the *Thumpy* series (Dodge, 1985; Lamb & Dodge, 1985).

Much has been written recently about the role of funeral service personnel when a baby dies. In our practice we have dealt with many such situations. Our experiences have led us to develop the following general policies:

- If at all possible visit the mother at the hospital or meet with her at home or at the funeral home to include her in decision-making. Call her by phone if an in-person visit is not possible.
- Before removing the baby from the hospital, check to be sure the parents and family have had the opportunity to see, touch, and hold the baby. Offer the same opportunity at the funeral home; however, prepare the family in advance for the differences in sight and touch.
- Tell parents what the possible options are: viewing that is private or for family and friends; a prayer service in the funeral home, hospital chapel, church, or at home; a graveside service; burial or cremation (if ashes are to be scattered, suggest that parents choose a specific place).
- Provide the family with opportunities to be involved: to choose how the baby will be dressed and to help with dressing; to select

a toy for, make a drawing for, or write a letter to the baby; to creatively participate in a personal good-bye, choosing music, poems, or scripture.

- Be alert to cultural differences. In our area families with Appalachian or Amish backgrounds might naturally assume that the baby will be viewed at home, perhaps with a funeral service at home, prior to burial. The Amish family would also furnish the casket. Within these cultures these are standard, accepted funeral practices.
- Be a resource for the family, offering self-help literature or audio/visual materials and links to personal or group support.

These crisis intervention options offer survivors the opportunity to complete the first task of mourning, accepting the reality of the loss, and to begin the second task, experiencing the pain of grief (Worden, 1982). Promoting the process may prevent long-term unresolved grief. To help parents with this second task, here are further points to remember in handling grief following the death:

- This will be a difficult time for both parents. The mother may feel almost a physical need to hold and care for a baby; the father may withdraw and seem distant, perhaps to protect others from his own pain.
- Parents may blame each other, the hospital, doctor, nurses, the funeral director, the chaplain, even God. It is human nature to shift the burden of grief when the pain is too much to bear.
- There will be a need for parents to talk about any guilt they feel. In the light of reality, the guilt may disappear.
- Surviving children need to be told that their parents' grief is normal and that nothing they did or said caused the baby to die. They should *not* be told that God took the baby away, for this may make them fear that the same thing will happen to them.
- Facing others for the first time will be hard. Well-meaning people may ask, "When did you have your baby? Was it a boy or a girl?" Later, when parents are able to talk about the loss, friends and family may feel uneasy discussing it. They will need to be reassured that talking about it is permissible and will help in recovery.
- Anger is normal. Most women have thoughts such as "Why me? Look at my neighbor! She did everything wrong, and yet she has a healthy baby!"
- Depression and low energy are to be expected. They are the result of the process of grief, plus hormonal changes.

- Some activities that might help in working through the grief are keeping a journal or creating a personalized craft item or symbolic painting.

THE CONTINUING STRUGGLE FOR CHANGE

By virtue of being part of a team, I have had the opportunity to extend my perspective from local to state, from regional to national. It is a focus that changes from wide-angle to close-up in a matter of hours. As a frontline caregiver and a national volunteer, I've had the opportunity to walk (sometimes run) on a two-way street, sharing insights gained from both directions.

In 1986 I am concerned about the voices that I continue to hear. A survivor of stillbirth, cared for in an "enlightened" city hospital asks, "Did I have to have the baby *alive* for someone to care?" Frustrated parents have to remind the funeral director, "Whose baby is it, anyway?" A group participant tells us, "The psychiatrist gave me drugs when all I needed was someone to understand my grief." I know we've only just begun.

Paternalism continues to abound, often within the power structures of the very institutions we are trying to change. When you mention, "infant death" and a glazed look replaces intelligent interest, you begin to wonder who is protecting whom? But in fairness let us consider the physician who views death as personal failure, the funeral director who was taught to protect, the pathologist who must focus on findings rather than feelings, the plight of the clergy member who's supposed to have all the answers, the nurse who carries an overload of secondary grief. For those who continue to hurt, we must sometimes walk in another's shoes and try to forgive.

Support groups, bereaved parents, and concerned professionals might wish to examine institutions and their members to see which have changed their 1950s patterns in response to the 1980s call for change. Even more essential to change is the review of each profession's schools of education. When the same old societal tapes are replayed over and over again, is it any wonder that gaps in awareness exist? If continuing education and consciousness-raising are our goals, how do we reach the doctor who has a crowded appointment schedule with patients who depend on her, as well as a family at home pleading neglect? How do we communicate with the Main Street funeral director who is tied to home base on 24-hour call? How do we get to the member of the clergy who already has a conflict between the personal crises of parishioners and institutional demands?

They may be unable to come to us. Perhaps we should reach out to them with audio tapes for the car, audiovisual aids for hospital in-service times coordinated with morning rounds, and cassettes for the home VCR. We can schedule community education meetings planned around the professionals, ask them to speak, and hope they stay for an informal exchange.

Perhaps the wonder is that some of the former protectionists have clarified their thinking, reviewed the mixed messages from the past, and actually listened to their very best teachers, the bereaved parents themselves.

References

Benfield, D. G., & Nichols, J. A. (1980, September). Living with newborn death: The need for focus. *The Dodge Magazine*, p. 6.

Church, M. J., Chazin, H., & Ewald, F. E. (1981). *When a baby dies*. Oak Brook, IL: The Compassionate Friends.

Davidson, G. W. (1979). *Understanding death of the wished-for child*. Springfield, IL: OGR Service Corporation.

Dodge, N. C. (1985). *Thumpy's story: A story of love and grief shared by Thumpy, the Bunny*. Springfield, IL: Prairie Lark Press.

Ilse, S. (1982). *Empty arms: A guide to help parents and loved ones cope with miscarriage, stillbirth and neonatal death*. (Available from Sherokee Ilse, P. O. Box 165, Long Lake, MN 44356)

Johnson, J., & Johnson, M. (1982). *Where's Jess?* Omaha: Centering Corporation.

Johnson, J., Johnson, M., Cunningham, J., Ewing, S., Hatcher, D., & Dannen, C. (1982). *Newborn death: A book for parents experiencing the death of a very small infant*. Omaha: Centering Corporation.

Keirsey, D., & Bates, M. (1984). *Please understand me: Character and temperament types*. Del Mar, CA: Prometheus Nemesis Book Company.

Kirkley-Best, E., & Kellner, K. R. (1982). The forgotten grief: A review of the psychology of stillbirth. *American Journal of Orthopsychiatry, 52*(3), 420–429.

Lamb, J. M., & Dodge, N. C. (1985). *Sharing with Thumpy my story of love and grief*. Springfield, IL: Prairie Lark Press.

Nichols, J. (1984, November). Illegitimate mourners. In *Children and death: Perspectives and challenges*. Symposium sponsored by Children's Hospital Medical Center of Akron, Akron, OH.

Schwiebert, P., & Kirk, P. (1981). *When hello means goodbye*. Portland, OR: University of Oregon Health Sciences Center, Department of Obstetrics and Gynecology.

Worden, J. W. (1982). *Grief counseling and grief therapy: A handbook for the mental health practitioner*. New York: Springer.

Chapter 7
Newborn Death

Jane A. Nichols

Jane A. Nichols, Bereavement Consultant to the Regional Newborn Intensive Care Unit of Children's Hospital Medical Center of Akron, Ohio, since 1978, is trained in Transactional Analysis and entered the field of thanatology as a licensed funeral director. As such, she was one of the pioneers of the adaptive funeral and ongoing supportive care for bereaved persons. Coauthor of "Funerals: A Time for Grief and Growth" in *Death: The Final Stage of Growth*, edited by Elisabeth Kübler-Ross, she has also chaired the Bereavement Committee of the International Work Group on Death, Dying, and Bereavement (IWG) which produced "Assumptions and Principles Regarding Bereavement." Ms. Nichols is a bereaved parent.

To my infant sons.

———

In many respects the grief of parents following the death of their newborn infant is similar to other kinds of grief. There are, however, some unique aspects that may require unique caregiver responses. If these are ignored, caregivers may unwittingly add to the bereaved family's pain, not because they mean to do harm, but because newborn death is not common in the average person's experience and people have not considered how to react therapeutically. This chapter will focus on the unique aspects of newborn death and offer some suggestions for caregiver response.

Before considering the special issues of newborn death, let's review some general knowledge. When a newborn dies, parents grieve (Benfield, Leib, & Reuter, 1976). Grief symptoms observed in parents following neonatal death are predictably individual responses not significantly related to birth weight, duration of life, the extent of parent-infant contact, previous perinatal loss, or parent age (Benfield, Leib, & Vollman, 1978).

When a baby dies, parents report a variety of grief symptoms. Some of the most commonly reported physical symptoms include emptiness, aching arms, a slight sense of unreality, body tension, exhaustion or fatigue, lack of appetite, and headaches. Emotional symptoms include sadness, anger, guilt, depression, death-related anxiety, and pining for what might have been. Mental symptoms, such as preoccupation with thoughts about the baby; hallucinations, fantasies, or dreams about the baby; fear of going crazy; and confusion have been noted. Social symptoms of grief that bereaved parents of newborns have reported include the desire to be left alone, difficulty planning for the future, and social distance from and problems communicating with one's mate.

There appear to be differences between male and female responses to the death of a baby. In general, mothers report more symptoms of grief than do fathers. Women also tend to experience their symptoms for longer periods of time than do men. For example, in our study at Children's Hospital Medical Center of Akron, Regional Neonatal Intensive Care Unit (NICU), mothers reported that they experienced "a sense of release" from the emotional pain caused by the death of their baby on the average of 18 months after the death. Fathers, on the other hand, indicated that this experience occurred between 6 and 12 months for them (Benfield, Nichols, & Newman, 1981). As with all parent bereavement, one of the most difficult tasks that the couple has is respecting the fact that each parent grieves differently, at a different pace, using different coping styles. These differences are frequently misinterpreted by partners as being insensitive or unloving and put a great strain on the relationship. Now let's look at some of the things that make newborn death unique.

DISCOUNTED GRIEF AND NEGATED DEATH

Following the death of their newly born infant many parents find that professional and lay caregivers engage in behavior that tends to discount or minimize their grief and/or negate the loss, depriving them of the opportunity to grieve legitimately with social support. The words and actions of many caregivers imply to the bereaved parents that their grief is not necessary or that the death (and the life) did not occur. Hence, caring others tend not to offer the compassion or the vehicles of mourning that are available to other grievers.

Discounted grief or negated death is one of the most unique aspects of newborn death. With few other exceptions, such as deaths of the disoriented old-old, our culture has come to expect that survivors will experience loss and therefore grieve. This is frequently not true for bereaved parents of newborns. People simply slough off the event and its potential impact and tend to respond "Too bad. What are you doing for lunch?"

One possible reason people discount the grief of parents is because newborn death is comparatively rare and there are few rituals of behavior prescribed for the occasion. Or perhaps it is because they are not acquainted with the baby and therefore do not join in the parents' grief. Perhaps it is because of the misperception that when a baby dies parents "don't go through so much," or if they do, it is very brief and most certainly not profound. This incorrect assumption seems to be especially prevalent if the baby is deformed or stillborn. Perhaps it is because the death of an innocent infant does not fit into philosophic-religious beliefs in eternal justice, universal goodness, or the fairness of life and so people pretend it did not happen.

Regardless of underlying reasons, examples of discounting and negating behaviors are widespread. Mothers' hospitalizations may be unnecessarily extended, which prevents them from having to deal with the "situation." At the same time, mothers are often moved from the obstetrical unit to another area of the hospital so as not to be reminded of their "experience," although nearly 50% of the mothers in our survey indicated they would have preferred not to have been moved. (However, it must be noted that some mothers are more pained by being placed in the obstetrical unit and witnessing babies being brought to other mothers to hold and feed.) In the case of miscarriage, mothers are frequently transferred to the surgical unit, and the subtle message is that they did not sustain a loss, but merely a surgical procedure. Some hospitals continue to offer to dispose of the baby's body on behalf of the parents, depriving them of this part of their parenting role.

Funeral directors tend to collaborate with grandparents or fathers to get "it" over with as soon as possible, with the least amount of parent involvement allowable. Mothers are often excluded from making arrangements for or attending the funeral, and many of them have expressed anger about the exclusion. Many newspapers have a policy of not printing death notices for newborns or stillborns, so others may not be aware of the death. The clergy speak of "rosebuds" in God's garden, rather than the loss of personhood. Friends or relatives frequently seek to remove from the home all preparations for the expected baby prior to the mother's hospital discharge. And until recently, few published resources were available for bereaved parents of newborns.

Mental health practitioners have been noted to treat symptoms of newly bereaved parents as if they were not related to grief. For example, one mother recently reported that the psychologist with whom she consulted about 6 weeks after the death of her baby diagnosed her as being depressed and suicidal, with no mention of these symptoms fitting into the framework of grief response. The infant's death was treated as superfluous to the symptoms even though there was no indication of previous psychological imbalance.

The list of discounting behaviors continues. Helping others have been quick to offer clichés such as "You're lucky you never got to take him home," as though loving and sorrow only began with that occasion. Parents have reported nonsupportive statements such as "You weren't *really* a mother; why are you acting this way?" Even within parent-to-parent support groups, bereaved parents of newborns have been discounted as not knowing what *real* grief is.

Parents themselves are frequently surprised by their grief response to the death of their baby. "When she first died, I cried a lot. . . . But I don't understand what's wrong now" (mother, 6 weeks after the death of her child). "I thought I would be over it by now" (father, 1 week after the death of his child). Fathers, whose grief tends to be shorter and less intense than that of mothers, are often among those caregivers who discount mothers' grief and therefore do not provide the necessary empathy and support.

As a result of behaviors and attitudes such as these, which negate the death and discount the grief response, parents of newborn infants who die are deprived of social support, understanding, and opportunities that, though often painful on a short-term basis, have been documented as facilitating grief work. This can be a hazardous combination of social factors that, as Lazare has pointed out, can complicate grief reactions (Lazare, 1979).

"When survivors are thwarted in their attempts to grieve honestly, they are forced to grieve less honestly, by unconscious means" (Davidson, 1979). Social negation encourages parents to ignore their grief; grief then can be delayed or otherwise complicated. If parents do acknowledge their grief, they are apt to find few people who will accept their expressions of grief and their grieving patterns as legitimate, necessary, or even appropriate. If opportunities for facing reality in supportive settings are omitted or limited, as when funerals are not held, reality can become distorted, its healing quality withheld. Further, these omissions may deprive parents of opportunities to gain closure. Friends, not having been informed of the death or having no special occasion provided during which they might respond, may come upon the information at inopportune times, when they have the least chance of responding in a helpful manner. Alienation and confusion may dominate the parents' experience.

Implications for caregiver response to this unique aspect of newborn death are clear: parents must stop getting the message that there is nothing *to* their baby's death and be offered opportunities for support, understanding, and grieving. To do that, caregivers must remember that when a newborn dies, parents sustain a *real* loss.

The approach to caring, then, is similar to bereavement care and grief counseling in other circumstances with these additional considerations:

1. The loss may need to be not only made real, but also validated, taken seriously, listened to, sympathized with, honored.
2. Parents are apt to need explicit and implicit permission to grieve.
3. Since mothers and fathers of newborns often have little knowledge about or experience with grief, it may be helpful to outline a model of grief, to provide a conceptual framework for their grieving and some idea of what to expect. I have found it wise to remind parents that the only thing a model is good for is to give them a perspective; it is not a series of hoops through which they will or must jump.
4. Caregivers may need to be particularly assertive in seeking occasions to talk to parents about grief and to confront grief

issues. These conversations could be initiated during childbirth education programs, at the time of death, or within an active post-death follow-up program.

5. Caregivers might create occasions to provide special death education for the broader circle of family and friends in order to enhance their awareness of the normality of parents' grief following the death of a newborn and the dangers of overprotection, as well as to enhance sensitivity and supportive care skills.

There are also implications for "upstream" caring, that is, caring with a broader scope.

1. Human resource educators could refer to dimensions of newborn death when discussing grief issues with the public in order to heighten general awareness.

2. Hospital personnel, funeral directors, and clergy might consciously review their policies and practices with an eye to the therapeutic value of parents being involved with their own destinies and their own realities.

3. Each professional caregiver could review his own attitudes and behavior toward survivors of newborn death to ensure that he does not discount or negate their experience.

OVERPROTECTION

Entwined with the attitudes that discount grief and negate newborn death is the common urge of caregivers to overprotect parents when their baby dies. The desire to overprotect seems contradictory to discounting and negation, yet in my experience this desire is almost always present and entangled with the other two. Many of the examples of discounting the death that were given are also examples of overprotection.

Behavior that seeks to protect frequently smacks of avoidance. Avoidance and overprotection can revictimize parents because they deprive parents of the chance to live through their experience. Parents sometimes do this to one another, as the following story illustrates.

Case Example: In a follow-up session with a young couple whose baby had died the year before, the father made this comment: "I felt it was my responsibility to arrange the funeral, to get it over with. Even though my wife had been discharged from the hospital before we had the funeral, I felt that she shouldn't go because she wouldn't be able to handle it. We really paid the price for that decision. If I had to do it over, I would do it differently" (Nichols & Benfield, 1980).

As the discussion continued, both parents described how difficult it had been for the mother to "get a handle" on the reality of her baby's life and death. Being excluded from the funeral was but one example of many incidents of overprotection that complicated the mother's grief.

Caregivers may find it helpful to think in terms of providing "gentled reality" rather than "protection" when dealing with bereaved parents. "Gentled" means kindly, serene, gradual, soft, soothing; it does not mean harsh, rough, avoiding, or evasive. Professional caregivers may also choose to clarify this difference with family members.

UNUSUAL REQUESTS

When a newborn dies, parents frequently make requests of caregivers that would be unusual or unlikely if the death were that of an adult, but which seem to fit an infant death and may reflect personal intuitive knowledge of what could be helpful and healing to a given parent. It is easy to respond to out-of-the-ordinary requests with a judgment that the request is inappropriate or too risky. When challenged with the question "Too risky for what and to whom?" the answer is often "Too risky for me, the caregiver, because I've never heard of it before and I don't know what to do." When caregivers deny an unusual request, they may block the healing process and lay an unnecessary burden on grievers, making it more likely that the grievers will become "stuck" in their grief. Here is an example of how one caregiver handled such a request from a parent.

> *Case Example:* At Children's Hospital NICU, it is our custom to invite parents to be present with their baby, especially when it appears that death will come soon. Many parents choose to grasp this intimate time to hold, rock, and talk to their baby. That is not unusual. On one such occasion, a mother asked the attending neonatologist if her dying 4-day-old son was able to suck . . . could she put him to her breast? This *was* unusual.
>
> Restraining his natural instinct to say no simply because the question was so uncommon, the physician questioned himself mentally: "Why not? . . . What is the worst that could happen? How would I handle that? . . . Is it in touch with reality?" He answered the woman in quiet honesty: "It's an unusual request. I

don't know if he has the energy to suck, but if you wish to try, I think the closeness would be good for both of you. Would you like me to stay with you?"

Later in follow-up the mother reported the event as having been positive for her. This is not to say that all mothers should be offered this option. Rather, it is to say that this unusual request, when thought out, seemed healthy for this particular mother. Other unusual requests may be productive for other parents.

Someone once said, "People can handle anything if they have information and human support." Many people can right themselves if their attempts to do so are not blocked by well-intentioned but mis-guided others. In order to avoid hindering grievers and yet protect themselves, caregivers might first react by asking parents, "Tell me more about your request," and then ask themselves the important safeguard questions: "What is the worst that can happen? Can I handle that? Is the request in touch with reality?" For example, if the baby is already dead, would it be in touch with reality to take him home to his own bed? No, dead babies don't go home to their own beds, they go to the funeral home. Caregivers should explain the rationale for their response to the person making the request.

LACK OF FOCUS

Another unique aspect of grief following newborn death is that it often lacks focus; it lacks a clear image. Frequently the baby dies before parents have experienced the reality of her being alive, much less the reality of her death.

Several factors account for the lack of focus. In a review done in our NICU, we found that half of the newborn deaths occurred within the first 68 hours of life, at a time when mothers were still confined to the obstetrical division and had had little opportunity to bring the infant's life into focused reality. Compounding the problem is the separation of mother and infant caused by regionalized health care. Currently most areas in the United States offer newborn intensive care in specialized regional units that often are separate from the obstetrical unit or many miles away from the hospital of birth. At-risk infants who are born sick are transferred to NICUs almost immediately after birth so that mothers, especially, have no time to get to know their new child. Further, the lack of focus could be heightened by the discounting behaviors outlined earlier.

For many parents, then, the baby's death occurs before they have had the opportunity to shift from knowing their baby on an extrarational level to knowing their baby in more concrete terms. Throughout the prenatal period, parent-child attachment has usually occurred on several levels. Imagery, fantasy, hopes, aspirations, psychological attunement, and physical awareness have all been a part of the pregnancy. The loss of these when the infant dies is no less real or painful than in other deaths, but it may be less focused, less easily defined, more vague. As one father said, "It feels like I have something to get off my chest, but I don't know what it is."

Parents have reported that they have difficulty identifying whom or what it is that they are grieving. There is an unsureness, a hazy reality. It is as though the pregnancy, labor, delivery, life, and death were a dream. Dreams are difficult to grieve. The phenomenon is similar to that experienced by survivors of men missing-in-action. Since it is highly likely that diffused grief is more problematic than focused grief, a lack of focus does not mean that parents will not grieve; it just makes dealing with grief more difficult. Caregivers are helpful and assist grief work when they seek to provide parents with opportunities to focus on reality. The reality is: they had a baby . . . the baby lived a while . . . the baby died.

Before listing some options that parents have reported as being helpful, it is important to note that there could be a tendency to use such a list as a recipe, a cookbook of things to be tried out on all parents. If used in that way, the suggestions could be harmful. Not all parents will want or choose all options. If decisions are to be made based on personal preference and knowledge of self, then options must be offered in a neutral way, without caregiver opinion. Coercion on either side of an option is inappropriate. A parent could thus be approached: "Many people have told us that 'this' was helpful for them" (legitimate information-giving). "Do you think 'it' would be helpful for you?" (the invitation). The invitation would *not* be weighted, as in "You *do* want to do 'this,' don't you?" In this way, each parent would be free to make a personal choice based on her own, not the caregiver's, sense of what is healthful to her. Although parents sometimes regret their decisions, in my experience most of them are pleased to have had the opportunity and do not become weighed down by errors in judgment.

Here are some suggestions that have helped parents focus on their reality.

1. Provide open means of communication and contact between parents and their baby and the baby's attendants throughout the baby's life and after death. For example, in our NICU we offer 24-hour parent and significant other visiting and WATS line by which parents can

speak directly to health care staff for daily information about their baby's status. We also have an instant-developing camera so that hospital-confined mothers may have pictures of their babies. With funds donated by parents, we are currently developing a hospital-to-hospital audio-video transmitting system.

2. Speak openly, candidly, and gently about the baby even after death. One mother reported, "People don't say anything about it. It's as though Tommy never lived."

3. Be supportive of the need to recall memories of this pregnancy, labor, delivery, and events in the nursery, as well as fantasies about and expectations of this baby.

4. Provide parents with opportunities to have some normal experiences centered around their baby. When a child is born well, people respond spontaneously with "What have you named him?" "Who does she look like?" "How much does he weigh?" The baby who is well is dressed. People gather around to see her. Parents of sick babies also seem to welcome the chance to share their focus in these ways.

5. Provide occasions for parents to see, touch, hold, talk to, give something to, or spend time with their sick, dying, newly dead, or embalmed baby (deformed or not). When offering these options, we have been cautious to encourage each parent to decide independently of the other; to prepare parents with a verbal description of what it will be like; to offer them the chance to change their minds; and to remain physically and/or spiritually available to give them emotional support no matter what they choose. If parents decide to see, touch, or hold their baby, caregivers can often lead the way by touching, holding, or "prizing" the baby themselves.

If the mother remains hospitalized, consideration can be given to arranging for an early discharge or a temporary pass, or to taking the newly dead baby back to the hospital of birth, so that the mother can be afforded this option.

6. Provide tangibles: a lock of hair . . . the hospital bracelet . . . footprints . . . pictures . . . birth and death certificates . . . a burial spot . . . a name . . . a death notice. After the funeral, parents may need some concrete items to help them stay in focus. These mementos and a few fragmented memories may be all they have to show for an experience that profoundly marked their lives.

7. Encourage funeral rituals and disposition of the baby's body in ways that are in keeping with family and local tradition and values and that provide the opportunity to gain closure. Adult funeral customs may not suit the unique circumstances of a newborn's death. However, ignoring the death is not a helpful alternative. Parents of newborns can

benefit from the values of a funeral: a framework of meaning, a context wherein social support is readily available, a further opportunity for reality testing and focus. Specially tailored funeral occasions could provide these benefits. If the mother remains hospitalized, funeral arrangements can be delayed until after discharge or made in the hospital room so that both parents will have the choice of participating in the planning and implementation of their baby's funeral.

GUILT, LACK OF INFORMATION, AND THE FUTURE

The two questions asked most often by parents after the death of their infant are "Why did it happen?" and "Will it happen again?" Reflected in these questions is a special concern that is unique to newborn death. Guilt and its counterpart, blame, which are almost always present among survivors when a death has occurred, take on a delicate shade of difference with neonatal death. Added to the sense that, as parents, they should have been able to protect their child, is the reality that this baby was so recently created out of the parents' genes and juices and that the mother so recently embodied the child. The cause of illness and death, then, may inappropriately be thought to be directly linked with genetic flaws, with physical defects, or with "poor" behavior on the parents' part.

Rationally or irrationally, self-blame and blame of others are very common. Imagination runs rampant when definitive information is not present. One mother wrote a list of 26 things she had done that she thought might have caused her daughter's premature birth and death. All were ill-founded, but she lacked the medical information necessary to check her perceptions against reality.

The second most-asked question, "Will it happen again?" is a very practical one. Of 700 consecutive deaths in our NICU, the mean maternal age was 23.8 years. For many couples, this was their first child. The likelihood of subsequent pregnancies is high.

Caregiver response to these questions is important. First, if parents are given accurate day-by-day information about their baby's condition and the attempts of medical and nursing staff to save the child's life, and if parents have the opportunity to be present in the NICU to see the use of sophisticated equipment and sense the high level of caring by the staff (assuming all of these are present), then they will be apt to recognize that everything that could be done was done. There is some consolation in that knowledge.

Second, for those parents who have a burning desire to know and understand why it happened, the need for doing an autopsy on the baby is particularly vital. It is the last chance for physicians and parents to learn all the facts. However, parents should not be coerced into a decision for autopsy. The most common reason parents in our study gave for declining autopsy permission was that "the baby had already been through too much for her short life." For these mothers and fathers, the desire to leave the baby in peace outweighed their need to know. Here again, varying perspectives of parents should be respected, if possible.

Third, whether or not an autopsy is performed, it is highly desirable for health care personnel to invite the family back for follow-up discussion. This interview is an excellent time to candidly review the baby's illness and care, provide medical information that might offset irrational guilt, discuss implications for future pregnancies, and suggest possible courses of action, such as a need for genetic counseling. If an autopsy was performed, a careful explanation of the findings should be presented. (The information does little good if it is kept a secret.) Parents can be asked about issues that trouble them or about any shadowy guilt they still harbor. Caregivers can tell parents about community resources, such as support groups, that are available. Follow-up is also an opportunity for parents to reflect upon their feelings and inner thoughts with a caring, knowledgeable other. Normal behavior can be described to allay their concerns. Worden offers a final word of caution to health care professionals in the follow-up setting.

> The husband feels powerless and his need to act strong and to be supportive may be misinterpreted by the woman as not caring. Out of this sense of helplessness, many husbands find an ally in the physician, who is often male and who focuses on the fact that the couple can conceive and have another child soon. Although this may make him feel less helpless and may be realistic in the situation, it may not be what the woman wants to hear at that particular time . . . . Do not try to minimize the loss by an upbeat focus on the future and the possibility of other pregnancies and other children. (Worden, 1982, p. 90)

CONCLUSION

In the end parents must heal themselves. It was their baby; it is their loss; it is their grief. They need to gain closure, to experience release, to look to their new future. Caregivers cannot do their mourning for them. Even if all of the suggestions in this chapter are gently and progressively implemented by knowledgeable caregivers, parents will still grieve. But they will grieve for the right reasons. They will grieve because their baby died, not because people in their support network added to or blocked their grief.

> We cannot keep them from suffering;
> But we can keep them from suffering
> for the wrong reasons.

—Anonymous

References

Benfield, D. G., Leib, S. A., & Reuter, J. (1976). Grief response of parents after referral of the critically ill newborn to a regional center. *New England Journal of Medicine, 294*, 975–978.

Benfield, D. G., Leib, S. A., & Vollman, J. H. (1978). Grief response of parents to neonatal death and parent participation in deciding care. *Pediatrics, 62*, 171–177.

Benfield, D. G., Nichols, J. A., & Newman, I. (1981). [The parent grief study]. Unpublished raw data.

Davidson, G. W. (1979). *Understanding death of a wished-for child.* Springfield, IL: OGR Service Corporation.

Lazare, A. (1979). Unresolved grief. In A. Lazare (Ed.), *Outpatient psychiatry: Diagnosis and treatment.* Baltimore: Williams & Wilkins.

Nichols, J. A., & Benfield, D. G. (1980, September). Living with newborn death: The need for focus. *The Dodge Magazine,* p. 6.

Worden, J. W. (1982). *Grief counseling and grief therapy: A handbook for the mental health practitioner.* New York: Springer.

Chapter 8

Sudden Infant Death Syndrome

Jacque Taylor
John DeFrain
Linda Ernst

Jacque Taylor has a B.A. and an M.A. from the University of Nebraska. She is currently Executive Director for the Freemont County Alliance Against Domestic Violence and Sexual Assault in Riverton, Wyoming. She is the Chair for the Wyoming Crime Victims Compensation Program and the Wyoming representative to the National Coalition Against Domestic Violence.

John DeFrain, Ph.D., is Associate Professor, Department of Human Development and the Family, University of Nebraska-Lincoln, and co-director of a joint graduate training program in marriage and family counseling. He has conducted more than a decade of research on how families cope with the loss of an infant and has coauthored four books, *Coping with Sudden Infant Death, Parents in Contemporary America, Secrets of Strong Families,* and *Stillborn: The Invisible Death.*

Linda Ernst, B.A., M.S., got her undergraduate degree in Social Welfare from the University of Minnesota and her masters in Human Development and the Family from the University of Nebraska. She did graduate work in Family Studies at Brigham Young University and is presently pursuing a doctorate in Education from the University of Minnesota. Her present area of interest is developing a values in family life education curriculum.

Special thanks to Charlotte Jackson, Clar Nelson, Nick Stinnett, Jan Stork, and Ginger Woodward, who all know why we're thanking them.

159

*This chapter is dedicated to parents who have
experienced a SIDS death. Their gift to us was
to teach us that pain is bottomless and we are
in awe of their strength. They made us take a
hard look at some of our basic values. We
found these wonderful people had changed our
lives forever.*

My babysitter found our eight-week-old boy dead during an afternoon nap, and I received a call at work. At first I was hysterical, then through the funeral I was numb and for about a week after I was very sad. I felt so lonely for my Josh. I longed to hold him, and felt guilty for having said, "Oh, I hope you sleep through the night because I'm really tired."

I felt bitter toward someone, but I never did figure out who (God was in the back of my mind). Then I thought that Josh might have thought he was a great burden to us and decided to leave us. After all, there is no reason for SIDS, so your mind thinks everything.

About a week after Josh died I visited our babysitter who had found Josh, and she told me she just found out she was pregnant. For an instant I hated her, because I felt that, "My baby died here with you and now you tell me that you will have a baby in eight months." I have trouble becoming pregnant and I am in a panic thinking I will never be able to have another baby. (pp. 17–18)

—a Missouri mother*

In the beginning I lost all sense of being. The second day after the funeral, I went out and tried to dig up her grave. I thought I could see her in her walker or hear her cry. I stayed up all of the day and night checking the other kids. I'd leave them several times a week and go to the cemetery and sit by her grave all afternoon. At the time I was four months pregnant. After my little boy was born, my husband and I took turns with four-hour shifts, watching the baby for several weeks. Then I would dress him in her clothes, until one day I put her shoes on him and I had to get my oldest child to take them off.

I wouldn't allow her to be put in a casket until the day of the funeral. We had taken pictures of her at the funeral home but my husband wouldn't allow me to look at them. But they seemed to be some sort of a help. I can't really explain in words how they helped me. I never had but one other picture of her and it was when she was a newborn. The best I can explain this was just being able to look at her, it seemed she wasn't so far away. The pictures from the funeral home were not taken of her in a casket and she looked as though she was asleep.

I still have periods of fear of losing the other children. Right after my baby died, my niece, four years old, drowned. Then my father was shot and killed. I lost all sense of reality. My husband started drinking

---

*All the quotes from parents are taken from J. DeFrain, J. Taylor, and L. Ernst, *Coping with Sudden Infant Death.* (Lexington, MA: Lexington Books, 1982).

and I hated him. I couldn't sleep. If I did I had dreams about bugs eating her, or I'd dream of the funeral. Somewhere in the back of my mind I decided if I could just stop loving the kids, my husband, and parents, I could never be hurt by anyone or anything.

I knew I needed counseling, but my mom and husband were totally against anything like that. It was only for crazy people. But I finally went to one doctor for almost a year, and I lived in my grief and could talk to him, and am thankful to God he told me what a selfish mother I was being. Oh, I hated him at the time, but he is the only one who really helped me out of the loneliness, because I'd shut myself off from any feeling relationships.

My stepfather made some harsh statements; some people thought we were really to blame. When it happened we were visiting my mother and the baby was in bed with us; my husband had been drinking and thought he had suffocated her. My husband wanted to send the pictures we had taken of her to his mother. I hated him and blamed him. She had awoken for a two o'clock feeding and we played and she laughed and cooed, and at six o'clock she was dead. My husband never said so in so many words, nor did I, but we just became distrustful of each other. (pp. 1–2)

—an Illinois mother

In this chapter we will describe the psychological issues involved in losing an infant and will define Sudden Infant Death Syndrome (SIDS), very briefly discussing the medical community's search for its causes. From there, we will go on to identify the unique factors exacerbating SIDS grief and will outline treatment issues for SIDS parents and siblings. Next, the grief of individual family members and bereavement issues will be discussed. The roles of others dealing with SIDS parents will be explored, and finally summary treatment recommendations will be offered.

For almost 11 years now we have been studying families in crisis. A good deal of that time has been invested in working with SIDS families. Though we all wear different hats in our professional lives—that of the teacher, the researcher, and the clinician—our primary contact over the years with SIDS families has been as researchers trying to better understand what happens after a death. Our assertions in this chapter are, therefore, based primarily on our research findings. A detailed discussion of our research procedures over the years is given in previous publications (DeFrain & Ernst, 1978; DeFrain, Taylor, & Ernst, 1982).

What, in short, happens when a baby dies for no apparent reason? "You wade into an ocean of sadness, and let its enormous energy strike you down in pain and awe."

And what, then, can others do to help those in misery? "Listen, and ache, and cry. Maybe even offer a few hesitant words of your own, even though they will seem banal and foolish. Just remember: the

sadness and confusion will last for a long time, and the person will
need a friend for a long time."

PSYCHOLOGICAL ISSUES IN INFANT DEATH

For the vast majority of us a baby is the very antithesis of death. A new
life, it represents hopes, dreams, and new beginnings. It embodies the
future, while providing an extension of the parent in the present and
symbolizing the parents' continuity and immortality. A baby represents
the potential for fulfilling dreams, starting over, rectifying past mistakes, putting into practice new insights.

Psychosocially the infant has a functional role in the family from
the time the parents are aware of its impending birth. It will be the
object of numerous aspirations and expectations. It also will dramatically change the composition of the family. This happens initially on
the level of fantasy and then becomes real when the birth occurs.

The birth of an infant requires adaptation on the part of the
preexisting family, as there must be a realignment of family power,
roles, and responsibilities to accommodate the changed equilibrium in
the family. Consequently, the birth of the infant demands response by
the family unit. This will engender stress during the period of adaptation. If an infant dies during the early months of life, the family is then
not only confronted with the loss of all the baby has symbolized, but
must also cope with the unresolved feelings stimulated by the stress
and demands of the new infant that had not yet been accommodated.
If the infant is a first-born, concerns about defective parenting and
inability to protect the child contribute to increased guilt. The parent-
child relationship is at its closest and the death of the infant viciously
rips away at the parent's own sense of self.

UNDERSTANDING SIDS

Sudden Infant Death Syndrome—the term alone can be confusing. It
sounds so precise, so definitive, so clinical. And yet it is a curiosity to
the nonmedical person, because it is almost, in essence, a nondefinition.

If a patient has cancer, the doctor can describe the condition to
him. If a patient needs a gallbladder removed, a simple chart will show
its location and the doctor can easily discuss the extent of the problem.
But SIDS is different. It's a term that doesn't say what doctors know,
but, rather, what they don't know.

The Second International Conference on Causes of Sudden Death
in Infants defined SIDS as the sudden death of any infant which is
unexpected by history, and in which a thorough post-mortem exami-

nation fails to demonstrate an adequate cause for the death (Bergman, Beckwith, & Ray, 1970). In short, performing an autopsy on the infant tells the doctors nothing definitive. They don't know what happened.

The parent plaintively questions: "Babies don't just die, do they?" The medical community's reply at this point is "We have not found the reason or reasons yet."

There may be any number of explanations as to why babies die that researchers have not yet uncovered. Beckwith has catalogued 73 different theories for the cause of SIDS, and noted that new ideas are being published almost on a weekly basis (Beckwith, 1978). Our experience with physicians tells us that SIDS is enormously frustrating to them, and they are driven by a need to find the causes of SIDS and prevent them, just as SIDS parents are driven to understand how and why.

The research literature on SIDS is enormous. When we sat down to write this short segment on SIDS causes, we found ourselves in dismay over the mountain of articles covering the desk. All had impenetrable (to us) titles like "Attenuated Responses of CO_2 and Hypoxia in Parents of Threatened Sudden Infant Death Syndrome Infants."

A telephone call to a friend whose baby died of SIDS was comforting. The woman is a statewide consultant for a SIDS agency, counseling parents and consulting to various organizations. She noted that the issue of causes for SIDS is "a morass," and from a practical standpoint we should "stay away from it."*

She added that the issue is "more of a nightmare now than ever." This, she went on to explain, is because so much attention recently has been focused on apnea (cessation of breathing) in infants. Many lay persons now associate apnea with SIDS, and this can cause a good deal of confusion and bad feelings. Bereaved parents whose baby dies of SIDS may be told, "If only you had had the baby on a breathing monitor, everything would have been OK." Consequently, two clinicians, Bakke and Dougherty of Children's Orthopedic Hospital and Medical Center in Seattle, go to great lengths to point out that recurrent infant apnea and SIDS are two different things. They outline a number of key distinctions in regard to the presentation and diagnosis of these two

---

*For those who wish to wade into the thicket of research on the questions of the causes of SIDS, we recommend J. Bruce Beckwith, *The Sudden Infant Death Syndrome*, rev. ed., DHEW Publication No. HSA 75–5137 (Washington, DC: U.S. Government Printing Office, 1978); Maria Valdes-Dapena, *Sudden Unexpected Infant Death, 1970 Through 1975: An Evolution in Understanding*, DHEW Publication No. HSA 78–5255 (Washington, DC: U.S. Government Printing Office, 1978); and Maria Valdes-Dapena, "Sudden Infant Death Syndrome: A Review of the Medical Literature 1974–1979," *Pediatrics*, *66*(4)(1980), 597–613.

phenomena and stress that SIDS cannot be predicted or prevented (Bakke & Dougherty, 1981).

What we do know is that SIDS is a leading cause of the deaths of infants between 1 week and 1 year of age in the United States, accounting for up to 10,000 deaths annually with a ratio of up to three SIDS death per 1,000 live births (Valdes-Dapena, 1970). During the third and fourth months of life this condition apparently accounts for more than half of all infant deaths, with a rapid decline thereafter that makes this a unique age distribution unparalleled by any other known medical condition (Beckwith, 1975). These sudden and unexpected deaths occur to otherwise healthy infants, almost always while the child is asleep. Subsequent post-mortem examinations reveal no usually accepted cause of death. The following are some basic facts about SIDS that have been taken from the writings of Lowman (1979) and the U.S. Department of Health, Education, and Welfare (1976):

- SIDS is a distinct medical disease entity and not simply a category of unexplained infant death due to a variety of causes. Nevertheless, there is no way SIDS can be predicted or prevented, even by a physician.
- Research to date indicates that the cause of SIDS is not suffocation, aspiration, or regurgitation. A minor illness such as a common cold may be present, but many victims are entirely healthy prior to death. There appears to be no suffering; death occurs very rapidly, usually during sleep. SIDS is not contagious in the usual sense. Although a viral infection may be involved, it is not a "killer virus" that threatens other family members or neighbors.
- SIDS is not hereditary; there is no greater chance for it to occur in one family than in another.
- SIDS is at least as old as the Old Testament and seems to have been at least as frequent in the 18th and 19th centuries as it is now. This demonstrates that new-environmental agents such as birth control pills, fluoride in the water supply, and smoking have not caused SIDS.
- The rate of deaths from SIDS appears to remain relatively constant in different countries (Valdes-Dapena, 1967) and during periods of physical deprivation, such as world wars, when rates of other illnesses have been shown to rise. SIDS is slightly more common during the winter months, but occurs at any time of the year.

- A significant association has been found between lower weights at birth and SIDS victims (Bergman, Ray, Pomeroy, Wahl, & Beckwith, 1972).

Having sound information about SIDS and understanding it as much as possible is a critically important treatment issue with this type of child death. "If onlys" will plague parents for a long time after a SIDS death. It is important that parents discuss these "if onlys" with medical professionals who can give them the answers to the questions they have and can tell them what is not known or uncertain. If parents don't understand what the doctors have told them about the death, we urge them to go back repeatedly until they are satisfied. Most doctors will be more than willing to be of service. If gnawing doubts still remain, we encourage parents to write or call the National SIDS Foundation.* The Foundation does an excellent job of monitoring the deluge of research and theory on SIDS that pours out each year and can assist parents in finding answers to the questions.

This issue of SIDS information is critically important for parents. Every time a new theory or study is reported in the media, parents relive the nightmare of SIDS. They have to mentally piece their way through what happened, and see if the new study or theory sheds any light on the death. This is a painful exercise for parents, of course, but we would hazard a guess that the "if onlys" will continue to haunt people occasionally for as long as they live. The pain of the baby's death will diminish as time passes, but there most likely will always be a soft spot in the person's soul, a place that cries out when touched for whatever the reason. Likewise, doubts will return again and again. As professionals continue to search for the causes of SIDS, parents will be forced to reenter that dark area of life from which they had hoped they had escaped.

UNIQUE FACTORS EXACERBATING SIDS GRIEF

There are a number of unique features of a SIDS death that complicate the grief and victimize the parents and family members left behind. Markusen, Owen, Fulton, and Bendiksen (1977-78) identified five critical ones. The first feature of SIDS that may produce a particularly traumatic grief reaction is the suddenness of the loss. There is absolutely no opportunity to prepare for the death. Previous research has confirmed that unanticipated death results in more complicated bereave-

*The National SIDS Foundation, 8240 Professional Place, Suite 205, Landover, MD 20785. Phone: (301) 459-3388 or 1-800-221-SIDS.

ment reactions (Parkes & Weiss, 1983). The dynamics of a SIDS loss are the same: there is no opportunity for preparation or for appropriate amounts of anticipatory grief; there is no chance to say goodbye to the infant or to absorb the reality of the loss gradually over time; the unexpected loss so overwhelms people that it reduces their functioning and compromises their recovery; and the physical and emotional shock of the infant's death undermines their capacity for regaining a feeling of security.

Second, the absence of a definite cause prevents a complete definition of the situation by family and caregivers. This increases the likelihood of intense guilt, since parents are given no rationale to feel blameless and others can create doubts through criticism of parental care or insinuations about their actions. In the absence of specific information, in a very ambiguous situation, it is not unusual for adults as well as children to assume responsibility and guilt, however inappropriately.

A third feature of a SIDS loss is that it evokes particularly problematic grief reactions. The intense and critical mother-infant bond is abruptly severed. This, plus the fact that it is the first loss experience many young married couples encounter, creates an extremely intense and harsh grief experience for the mother. Similar problems exist with the father-infant bond for many men, although culturally they may be less involved at this point than their spouses are.

Fourth, the issue of sibling bereavement complicates the situation. Siblings must suddenly struggle with guilt over the ambivalent feelings they had had about their new sibling. Additionally, they are compelled to cope with the disruption that their mourning parents' own grief creates for the family.

A fifth aspect of SIDS is the legal system's involvement. Because the death is sudden and of no known cause, families are forced to deal with the police, medical examiners, and hospital personnel who are designated to protect the interests of the child and the state by investigating unexplained deaths. There is all too often an insinuation that the death was caused by some act of commission or omission on the part of the family and this places an undue additional burden of guilt and pain on them.

Several other factors combine to exacerbate the grief response following a SIDS death. First, the infant dies at a time when the family is still oriented to taking care of her. The sudden absence of the baby and the futility of the parenting role after the loss make the situation seem more overwhelming. The lack of knowledge among the public and professionals about SIDS adds to the pain of the trauma, as parents often feel there must have been something they could have done to prevent the death. They may even suffer from a lack of support from professionals, whose ignorance of SIDS or increased death anxiety subsequent to a SIDS loss interferes with their supportive care of the bereaved family. Another factor sometimes involved is parents' lower socioeconomic status or youth, as lower socioeconomic status and younger parents (Bergman et al., 1972) are overrepresented in the SIDS parent population. Such parents may have limited emotional, experiential, and economic resources to cope with the trauma of SIDS loss. Finally, all too frequently a SIDS loss is not socially validated in the same way other deaths are. Others often fail to recognize that despite the brevity of the child's life the family's attachment to that child is strong and deep, and has been present in various ways, since the knowledge of conception. Parents are told they are lucky they didn't have the baby long enough to become too attached, or that they are young and can have other children. Such responses tend to invalidate the loss and may inhibit the necessary mourning that must occur. The family must adjust, and the dreams, hopes, and expectations that will never be fulfilled must be relinquished.

TREATMENT ISSUES

The SIDS Family Adjustment Scale has been developed to identify critical tasks and factors specific to SIDS. It helps health care professionals to predict individuals' adjustment based on how well they have resolved the delineated tasks; it also aids them in the development of appropriate intervention strategies (May & Breme, 1982-83). The family is rated on a 5-point continuum ranging from a maladaptive response indicative of poor adjustment to a highly adaptive response associated with good adjustment. The areas rated are noted here. Keep in mind that they also represent the critical tasks for resolution of a SIDS death.

- *Communication of feelings.* The more open communication is permissible, the better the possibility for successful readjustment.
- *Lifestyle resumption.* The degree of resumption of usual individual and family activities (e.g., work, school, social life) gives some indication of the individual and family adjustment to the disequilibrium caused by the infant's death.
- *Use and perception of community and family support.* Families who can utilize outside support seem to have better bereavement outcomes. This is critical in SIDS deaths when those outside the family may imply that parents were neglectful, thereby isolating the family in their grief.

- *SIDS information.* Providing factual information about SIDS to the family immediately after the death can help prevent subsequent emotional problems. It has been well documented that SIDS families have a strong desire for factual information and that providing rational explanations for such a confusing phenomenon is an intervention that has been vastly underestimated (Lowman, 1979). Early provision of this information is important to prevent the establishment of erroneous patterns of guilt, blame, and responsibility.
- *Preventability.* If the cause of a death is believed to have been preventable, the grief process will probably be prolonged. If the death is considered to have been unpreventable, grief may be shorter, but intense. In SIDS deaths the feeling of preventability is often mistakenly reinforced when a label other than SIDS is used. Such terms often seem to imply that there may have been symptoms that went undiagnosed and that, if the child had been treated in time, the death could have been prevented.
- *Subsequent children.* If the decision to have children is not made through thorough and rational discussion, the replacement child syndrome (Cain & Cain, 1964) may appear as parents attempt to assuage the grief. The decision to have subsequent children must only be made following some emotional resolution of the grief over the SIDS death.
- *Religion.* It appears that families having a deep religious orientation and spiritual values achieve a better emotional adjustment to the death than families without similar religious convictions and practices.
- *Family morbidity.* The prolonged existence of a number of physical symptoms in family members may reveal blocked or incomplete emotional expressions of grief.
- *Infant centrality.* Preoccupation with the deceased infant and prolonged ritualized behavior in which the infant remains in a central position within the family may indicate a failure to appropriately decathect, suggesting unresolved grief.
- *Family emotional health.* Extreme emotional dysfunction and lability in family members are concomitants of ongoing grieving and indicate a failure of resolution of grief at the time of assessment.
- *Functional role of the infant in the family.* The assigned role of the infant in the family (e.g., marriage stabilizer, family heir) may give an indication of the functioning needs of the family system. The death of the infant will create a change in the composition of the family and the absence of this functional role may result

in subsequent changes in family relations. To determine the functional role of the infant one must empathically ask parents how the infant changed the family lifestyle and pattern, what their motivation was for having this child, and whether the birth of the infant resolved a previous family conflict. The child's loss must then be evaluated within this context.

- *Family solidarity.* While deaths can bring family members closer, they may also precipitate isolation and confusion. The perceived changes in closeness of family members following a SIDS death will give an indication of the family's response to the loss. Family closeness may facilitate successful grief resolution and may fill the need for emotional support that exists after such a loss.

Basically, all SIDS families should be regarded as mourners of a sudden, unanticipated death, and treated with strategies appropriate to resolution of this type of grief. Consequently, they will need confirmation of the death through the funeral and mourning rituals, and repeated opportunities to talk about the loss. Social support is critical to validate the child's brief existence and to comfort the family.

The grief after a SIDS death is very intense for all family members. The mother often feels that her child has been torn from her. Searching for the baby, evidenced by a preoccupation with the infant's image, is a strong component of this grief. Anger, frustration, and irritability with others is common. This particular type of loss involves a major crisis for the bereaved family and consequently engenders any number of symptoms of grief, including family disruption; general symptomatology and distress; psychosomatic reactions; depression and other psychiatric illnesses; changes in interpersonal relationships, both within the family and outside of it; and parenting problems with subsequent children. Guilt, such a difficult issue for all parents who lose children, is often perpetuated by the unique factors of SIDS death cited previously. The entire family is disrupted, not only because of individual grief responses, but because the intense grief of the mother often renders her unable to provide any of the other nurturant functions in the family. Children are bewildered, communication is disrupted. Indeed, "the loss of the baby seems to cut at the heart of the family life" (Raphael, 1983, p. 260). As parents desperately search for a cause they may start to implicitly or explicitly blame one another. This is fueled by the unknown etiology of the death. Parents repeatedly review their behavior looking for some clue, as if could they only find that, they could undo the death. They not only search their own behavior, but their spouse's and surviving children's as well, in an effort to try to make sense out of what has happened. Communication may become disrupted as anger and guilt are projected onto one another.

There are a number of other clinical issues in SIDS grief. These are addressed next in terms of the grief of individual family members, bereavement issues, and the role of others.

THE FAMILY'S GRIEF

Some theoreticians have defined the process of grief as a series of five stages that begins with denial, then moves through anger, bargaining, depression, and acceptance (Kübler-Ross, 1969). Life, however, is not a stage theory. The order, length, and intensity of stages is very individual. In a family, all members are processing their own grief with an idiosyncratic agenda. The maintenance of relationships becomes extremely precarious, as family members will need to experience the same processes of denial, anger, bargaining, depression, and acceptance as part of the family system, as well as individuals. It is not surprising that a relationship might not survive. It takes a lot of strength for a man, woman, or child to simply survive, intact, as a functioning human being.

Denial, one of the most frequently misunderstood components of the grief process, can be temporarily the greatest of gifts: a numbing of the pain and the removal of reality to arm's length, where the feeling isn't as intense. It is a brief respite, and funerals have a way of ending many of the feelings of denial.

Each of the feelings and actions associated with the process of grief will be difficult to label. For example, a woman's anger may take the form of depression. She may find herself angry at the surviving children, which is one of the only places that a woman has societal permission to be angry. Her guilt at the anger can then lead to overprotectiveness which in turn may leave her feeling more depressed. Alternatively, a man may be able to deal with the anger in acceptable ways, but may find that he is angriest with a depressed wife who is trying to be "Super Mom." He often feels guilty at these feelings and the guilt will frequently be expressed as anger. The vicious cycle of the woman's depression (which often is anger turned inward) and the man's anger can continue and escalate, but will generally lead to bargaining. Anger is the hardest emotion for both individuals and supportive friends and professionals to deal with, since it is so socially unacceptable. Anger generally has been denied as an acceptable feeling from the first time we said, "I hate you, Mommy." In their letters parents expressed these kinds of feelings reflective of anger and guilt: "I hate it when they tell me to forget"; "I hate my husband for demanding sex"; "I hate my friend whose baby lived, maybe I even hate her baby." Then the other shoe drops: " . . . and I feel guilty."

> I felt an overwhelming feeling of guilt, coupled with remorse. Our baby had colic from about nine days old to four weeks old. That was very difficult for me to cope with. I resented her many times and sometimes wished I'd never had her. I even had fantasies I might harm her and they surprised and upset me. She was getting to be a real pleasure to have shortly before her death at four and a half months, but I have reflected on my resentment and horrible fantasies. (p. 2)
>
> —a Delaware mother

The guilt creates the need to bargain, which can cause more depression. This happens because the bargains struck are hollow and empty and will never take the place of the safe, orderly world the person used to live in—a world where babies don't just die, and a person's anger cannot become so intense it takes on a life of its own.

Finally, the process of acceptance begins. Acceptance of a new world where, yes, babies do just die; acceptance that things will never, ever be the same again and that it is going to be all right.

> Sometimes I've thought that I'd be able to change things somehow, like if I could find out what causes crib death, I could have Sara back again. But there is always this voice in my mind telling me that it really happened, I can't change it, and I have to accept what has happened. (p. 18)
>
> —an Indiana mother

> I have really found out that nothing is permanent and it really scares me. If my two-and-a-half-year old oversleeps, I'm afraid to go in her room for fear of finding her dead. (p. 7)
>
> —an Indiana mother

The Bereaved Father

Fathers traditionally are supposed to be the rock of strength in the family. When a crisis occurs, it usually falls to the men to make decisions and maintain the family. Culturally we do not allow fathers to mourn the way we do mothers; it is assumed that mothers are the primary caretakers and that they have lost more. Men, of course, having assumed the role of rock of strength, often find themselves not knowing how to grieve, or not allowing themselves to do so if indeed they do know how. Anger is one emotion they usually know well, but as suggested earlier, anger can be confusing and not always very functional in terms of processing all the stages of grief. While women grow up with a rainbow of emotions, learning early to differentiate and name them, men do not always know what they are feeling. Not knowing the words, they find it difficult to talk about the feelings. Consequently, they tend not to do so. This puts them into a response style that is usually quite different from the mother's, which allows for a more open expression of grief with longer time required for return to normal functioning. Often the father may be perplexed by what he considers his wife's preoccupation with the death.

The personal and societal prohibitions against feeling place men in a "What about me?" position, as one father shared with us:

> Those people who would comment about Jenny's death would say how sorry they were and then ask how my wife was. This concern for Chris was appreciated, for she was terribly shaken by Jennifer's death. Along with concern for Chris' well-being came words of wisdom or advice as to my conduct on how to handle my wife in this situation. People advised me to handle Chris with great care, for this was a loss like nothing she would ever have encountered before. "Show her great patience, more than ever before, be kind to her, and be extremely understanding." (p. 24)
>
> When is it my turn to cry? I'm not sure society or my upbringing will allow me a time to really cry, unafraid of the reaction and repercussion that might follow. I must be strong, I must support my wife because I am a man. I must be the cornerstone of our family because society says so, my family says so and until I can reverse my learned nature, I say so. (p. 25)
>
> —a Nebraska father

Feeling emotions of grief is tantamount to losing control for many men. And losing control is a significant issue with men, because they do not know what will happen if they do. Still, many men are struggling with learning about their feelings. Both their attempts and their feelings must be recognized and legitimized.

In their research, Mandell, McAnulty, and Reece (1980) observed paternal responses to the sudden unanticipated death of an infant. They found some interesting differences between maternal and paternal grief. They report that fathers experienced a necessity to "keep busy" with increased work; intellectualization of grief and blame; decreased self-esteem and sense of masculine power; self-blame because of a lack of involvement with the infant's care; a limited ability to ask for and accept help; and a sense of urgency about having another child.

The Bereaved Mother

Women are traditionally socialized to be more comfortable with emotional expression and with requesting and utilizing help from others. They feel the pain of SIDS grief intensely. Because they have been interacting so closely with the infant, the death robs them of their raison d'être. Each mother feels she has lost part of herself and becomes preoccupied with the image of her infant as she seeks to find and reunite with her lost child. She may ignore the needs of other surviving family members as she struggles with her own numbness, pain, longing, and grief.

Mothers express the most feelings of guilt. The "if onlys" and "I shoulds" pepper their responses to the grief they feel. Again, this appears to be a culturally prescribed role: women know how to feel guilty, but they don't know what to do about it. Women prepare themselves for the worst. Every time they hear the screech of car tires in the street they think, "Where are my children?" This almost automatic response is in no way a preparation for children being hurt, but rather a belief that eternal vigilance will keep children safe. SIDS destroys this sense of protection in parenting and the power to prevent is forever gone.

> I think the worst thing is guilt. I still think that I should have stayed up with her that night, and then she'd be alive today. She had a stuffy nose, and I felt that if I had only taken her to the doctor she would have been alive. I have even gotten up in the night to check the other kids. I know that crib death can't happen to them because they're too old, but I had to get up and check them anyway. (p. 18)
>
> —an Indiana mother

Getting back some sense of equilibrium is a slow process, and guilt can bog down a woman in depression. The light at the end of the tunnel may seem very dim. At these times all an individual may have is grit and a will to survive, but it will do, and most mothers are able to get past paralyzing guilt.

The Bereaved Siblings

A child's feelings during bereavement will be similar to an adult's; but due to different cognitive processes, children will think about the death of a sibling from SIDS in their own unique ways. To children, magical thinking works. After all, if Santa brings me just what I want, the same is true for jealous or angry thoughts about the baby who dies. Children will truly believe that they wished the baby away.

It will be difficult for a very young child to articulate these feelings, and parents need to begin these conversations themselves rather than wait for the child to talk. This will probably occur at a time when the child would just as soon not talk about the death or his feelings of responsibility for it, but delaying the discussion does not help. Parents must be careful not to brush aside the fears or misconceptions of the child as trivial. The child assumes he is powerful and that his wishes will come true. The child may also need continued reassurance that his own body is strong and will keep him alive.

The parental urge to be overprotective can be comforting to a child as long as it is temporary and done in moderation. At this time children themselves probably feel their lives are fragile, and extra attention is preferable to being shut out from their parents' grief. It is important for children to know that their parents are sad and that they can't always make everything turn out according to plan.

BEREAVEMENT ISSUES

How Long the Pain Lasts

Bereavement is not an illness that can be cured. It is a situational adjustment to a loss that may take a lifetime of work. Just when things are falling into place, the pain can come with such sudden agony that it completely shatters the fragile safety net of feelings that grievers have formed.

The process of grief doesn't have any clear rules. The person who bounces back quickly may be using denial or may be less grief-stricken because of a strong support system. The person who broods and mourns more publicly may get fewer positive responses, but be just as healthy. What is clear is that the grief process is much more individualized and takes much more time than previously expected. It proceeds on an up-and-down course over time.

> It has been almost a year now and we still have a hard time going into his room. It is hard to look at other babies, and I find myself looking for his face on other babies. He was my only child. I miss him terribly. Every holiday just reminds me of what I had thought about the year before. Thinking that would be the last holiday my husband and I would spend alone.
>
> At first I cried every day. Then, I just had an overall sadness intrude on all the times that would have been extremely pleasant before. We still want a baby. We wanted a boy and got one. Now we are afraid to try again.
>
> It has been one year, yet we have to face his birthday late in May and then his death date August first. Maybe then. (p. 7)
> —a Mississippi mother

> To put it bluntly, I feel I have been terribly beaten and weakened in some way that I know I will never be the same again. It's true that nothing or no one can ever take the place of the loved one you've lost, no matter how hard you may try. There will always be a terrible empty void that nothing will fill.

Every month that went by I would always think Matt would have been so many months old.

Every holiday, happy and yet unhappy because he will not be there to share it.

The day which would have been his first birthday was very hard.

Sometimes it is hard not to still feel bitterness, but that gets you nowhere, so you pick up and start again.

It hurts me very much because the son we wanted so badly is gone and we miss him terribly.

If I see other boys his age I ache, for I will never know what he would have looked like.

He was such a beautiful baby and touched so many people's lives in ways some people who live to be one hundred don't even accomplish. He filled us with love and warmth and we have many loving memories of him to cherish forever.

I feel very lost and empty a lot of the time. It can be very easy for me to feel sorry for myself. "WHY ME?" Everyone thinks it happens to everyone else until it hits home.

I feel I've gone through so much, sometimes I thought I'd never pull through, but I did and I seem to be stronger for it. (p. 55)

—an Iowa mother

Having Another Baby

Having another baby after experiencing SIDS can be anguishing for a family. They may feel anxious throughout the pregnancy and subsequent birth until the magic moment of reaching the deceased child's age is past. Parents contemplating another child must recognize the importance of this issue and work to avoid the pitfalls of the replacement child syndrome. This is best accomplished when the new pregnancy does not occur too soon following the SIDS death and the parents have appropriately mourned the lost infant and achieved some resolution of their grief. The child should be conceived because the couple wants another child, not out of a desire to avoid grief over the SIDS infant, resolve any lingering guilt, or prove their ability to raise another child. The new child must be seen as a unique human being, not just as a substitute for the lost infant. Parents also must recognize that in the months after a SIDS death they may experience some difficulty in the woman's becoming pregnant and carrying the baby full term (Mandell & Wolfe, 1975).

Attitude rather than time appears to be the major factor in the decision to have another child. The fear that SIDS will happen again is universal. Overprotection of the new child and the remaining siblings is a danger. The research on this point can give little comfort, but parents need to remind themselves that, if only one out of every 350 babies dies of SIDS, then 349 of them live.

THE ROLE OF OTHERS

Friends, Relatives, and Professionals

From the outside looking in, the process of grief cannot be easily understood in terms of theory. For example, although a woman's anger may be expressed in depression, it would be erroneous to conclude she is in the stage of depression per se, just one step away from acceptance. A man's depression may appear as tremendous anger, yet it must not be assumed that anger is the stage that he is in; it may be a symptom of another stage. Therefore, for those who offer support to the grieving family, it is essential not to label the griever without the full understanding of the dynamics of grief. Labeling is a safe business, and grief work is not safe at all. The caregiver must be willing to support in a nonjudgmental way, assuming that basically, unless she has had the experience, she simply will not understand. Platitudes and clichés should be left at home. They are also safe, but as the parents shared with us, they are rarely helpful:

> Some people tend to keep you feeling upset because they avoid you, because they don't know what to say or do. Some people act like they don't believe that SIDS exists. They want you to give another reason why she died so young. People also have said things like, "I guess it was better she died so young because you would have been more attached to her later in life." Others have said it was God's way of punishing us for our wrong way of life. (p. 32)
> —a Nebraska mother

The healing must come from within, and supporters can only offer Band-Aids from without. Singer Phoebe Snow says, "Anything that doesn't kill me makes me strong." Parents whose children have died know this. They also begin to understand that they are survivors, and as such find themselves separated from the rest of the "safe" world, with knowledge that no one else wants to hear.

All too frequently SIDS parents lack the critically important support of others. Those outside the family may never have seen the child, and thus may find it difficult to relate to the parents' loss. Or, worse still, they may tell the parents, "It's lucky you didn't really get to know the baby or else it would have been harder." People fail to recognize that the family's attachment to the infant begins long before the child's birth. This lack of validation and support only further alienates the family, which already feels strange after undergoing such a confusing experience as a SIDS death.

These families are isolated by their experience, and in the vacuum they often feel they must stifle feelings and behaviors that might make others uncomfortable. Their wish to make friends, relatives, and professionals feel at ease is in direct conflict with their feelings of loyalty to the dead baby and their need to talk about and remember each moment of the tiny child's life. Parents and children need permission to express their grief and confusion.

> Let the person suffering the death talk. I know myself, I need to talk. I don't want other people to forget Sara. I need to know that other people remember her, too. I have to tell people how I feel, I need to know that they really want to listen and not to feel that I'm going crazy because I need to tell people about it.
> Some people get upset when I mention the baby's name. They tell me to forget about it. I will never forget. (p. 32)
> —a Pennsylvania mother

It must be recognized that SIDS deaths affect professionals quite adversely. Such deaths stir up deep anxieties about the deaths of their own loved ones, especially children and grandchildren. Often this discomfort results in avoidance of SIDS parents or in disapproving or inappropriately hostile remarks. These only serve to exacerbate feelings of guilt, responsibility, and, in many cases, punishment. Caregivers must be especially attuned to their verbal and nonverbal responses to these particular mourners because of the unique factors in SIDS death. They must deal with their own fears and anxieties without displacing these feelings onto bereaved parents or being unsupportive.

Support Groups for SIDS Families

Participation in a support group of families who have experienced SIDS and other types of infant death is beneficial for most people. It is important that whoever facilitates the group have some skills in ethical communication. If the leaders have had a baby die from SIDS, they must have dealt with their own grief sufficiently that they can not only bring up their own tragedy, but also encourage others to share. One-upmanship has no place in any self-help group. Everyone needs to be heard. This is a difficult but not impossible challenge, and one that demands planning and persistence.

Sharing pain with others won't make it go away, but it can ease the feeling of being bad or crazy or both. Some individuals will benefit from seemingly little interaction with the group; simply the fact that they are there listening may be very therapeutic for them. Others may demand the spotlight, and will have to be redirected. At times they may even require referral to individual counseling, which may better suit their needs.

Couples or individuals coming into the group will be at different places in their grief. Nonjudgmental and accepting statements will need to be modeled by the facilitator. As time passes, the group may begin to set its own agenda and really take off. On the other hand, some groups just never get off the ground. This will be disappointing for the facilitator, but it occasionally happens.

SUMMARY TREATMENT RECOMMENDATIONS

Therapeutic intervention with SIDS parents and families is universally suggested in all clinical and empirical investigations in the literature. Intervention with SIDS parents has been documented to have a beneficial impact (Lowman, 1979). Lowman suggests three specific psychological goals for intervention with SIDS parents:

1. To reduce parental guilt by countering inaccurate explanations parents use to blame themselves or others for the baby's death
2. To encourage expression and acceptance of the emotions of grief and reassure parents that this normal process will eventually end
3. To support parents in coping with lingering guilt and sadness, others' false accusations, health and economic problems, and plans for the future

Beckwith (1975), too, asserts that it definitely is possible to deal effectively with the family that has lost an infant to SIDS. The cornerstones of success are (1) a positive attitude toward the diagnosis of SIDS; (2) a compassionate attitude toward all families of SIDS victims; and (3) the availability of a mechanism for rapid routine notification and follow-up of families. In terms of intervention the following points are critical:

• Autopsies are important and should be available for all infants, not only those whose families can afford them. However, they must be interpreted appropriately.
• Parents must be given an immediate diagnosis of SIDS. With rare exceptions when gross autopsy reveals no cause for death, a diagnosis of SIDS can be made for counseling purposes. It is an enormous relief to families to learn that it is not their fault, before erroneous patterns of guilt and blame become established. If subsequent laboratory findings reveal information of which the family should be made aware, such as unsuspected genetic disease, this can be communicated without changing their concept

of the immediate cause of death: "Your baby did die of SIDS, but during our routine study of the case we found something about which you should know" (Beckwith, 1975, p. 30).

- Printed material is of great help and should be provided to parents so they may look at it over time, as it may be difficult for them to absorb information in times of emotional distress.
- Follow-up contacts are very useful in order to reassure parents that the intense grief reactions and slow adjustment period they experience are expectable and that they are not losing their minds. During these contacts parents also can be advised on how to deal with other siblings and other family and social matters.

In summary, caregivers are urged to remember that while SIDS loss is a quite unique and traumatic event, compassionate and direct intervention along the lines just suggested can both facilitate and ameliorate the painful, but necessary, process of grief.

References

Bakke, K., & Dougherty, J. (1981). Sudden infant death syndrome and infant apnea: Current questions, clinical management, and research directions. *Issues in Comprehensive Pediatric Nursing, 5*, 77–88.

Beckwith, J. B. (1975). *The sudden infant death syndrome* (DHEW Publication No. HSA 75–5137). Washington, DC: U.S. Government Printing Office.

Beckwith, J. B. (1978). *The sudden infant death syndrome* (rev. ed.) (DHEW Publication No. HSA 75–5137). Washington, DC: U.S. Government Printing Office.

Bergman, A., Beckwith, J., & Ray, C. (Eds.). (1970). Sudden infant death syndrome. In *Sudden infant death syndrome: Proceedings of the Second International Conference on Causes of Sudden Death in Infants.* Seattle: University of Washington Press.

Bergman, A., Ray, C., Pomeroy, M., Wahl, P., & Beckwith, J. (1972). Studies of the sudden infant death syndrome in King County, Washington: 3. Epidemiology. *Pediatrics, 49,* 860–870.

Cain, A. C., & Cain, B. S. (1964). On replacing a child. *Journal of the American Academy of Child Psychiatry, 3,* 443–456.

DeFrain, J. D., & Ernst, L. (1978). The psychological effects of sudden infant death syndrome on surviving family members. *Journal of Family Practice, 6,* 985–989.

DeFrain, J. D., Taylor, J., & Ernst, L. (1982). *Coping with sudden infant death.* Lexington, MA: Lexington Books.

Kübler-Ross, E. (1969). *On death and dying.* New York: Macmillan.

Lowman, J. (1979). Grief intervention and sudden infant death syndrome. *American Journal of Community Psychology, 7*(6), 665–677.

Mandell, F., McAnulty, E., & Reece, R. (1980). Observations of paternal response to sudden unanticipated infant death. *Pediatrics, 65*(2), 221–225.

Mandell, F., & Wolfe, L. (1975). Sudden infant death syndrome and subsequent pregnancy. *Pediatrics, 56,* 774–776.

Markusen, E., Owen, G., Fulton, R., & Bendiksen, R. (1977–78). SIDS: The survivor as victim. *Omega, 8*(4), 277–284.

May, H. J., & Breme, F. J. (1982–83). SIDS Family Adjustment Scale: A method of assessing family adjustment to Sudden Infant Death Syndrome. *Omega, 13*, 59–74.

Parkes, C. M., & Weiss, R. S. (1983). *Recovery from bereavement.* New York: Basic Books.

Raphael, B. (1983). *The anatomy of bereavement.* New York: Basic Books.

U.S. Department of Health, Education and Welfare. (1976). *Facts about sudden infant death syndrome* (DHEW Publication No. NIH 76–225). Washington, DC: U.S. Government Printing Office.

Valdes-Dapena, M. (1967). Sudden and unexpected death in infancy: A review of the world literature 1954–1966. *Pediatrics, 39,* 123–138.

Valdes-Dapena, M. (1970). Progress in sudden infant death research 1963–1969. In A. Bergman, J. Beckwith, & C. Ray (Eds.), *Sudden infant death syndrome: Proceedings of the Second International Conference on Causes of Sudden Death in Infants.* Seattle: University of Washington Press.

Chapter 9

Accidental Death of a Child

Catherine M. Sanders

Catherine M. Sanders, Ph.D., is a psychologist in private practice in North Carolina. She is the Founder and Coordinator of the Loss and Bereavement Resource Center at the University of South Florida in Tampa. Her research into the symptoms and process of grief has led to a number of articles and chapters in professional journals and books. She also is the coauthor of the *Grief Experience Inventory,* an assessment tool for grief used internationally. Dr. Sanders is a bereaved parent.

There is no anticipation. No warning. There is only the raw, unequalled pain that even the initial shock cannot anesthetize. Part of oneself has been sliced away.

> It all began and ended for me on a Labor Day afternoon. One of those beautiful Florida days, a lazy day. We had opted to remain at home and not risk the dangers of the highway on a holiday weekend. Why leave? We had only recently moved to Florida and were enjoying living in a waterfront home with our own dock and swimming pool.
>
> Everyone had already had breakfast, even lunch, when my 17-year-old said he was going waterskiing with his friends. To Jim, happiness was a full can of gas for the boat.
>
> I watched as he walked down the dock, thinking to myself, "What a fine young man he is becoming." Tall, broad shoulders, a wonderful body, he was just beginning. That was the last time I saw him alive. An hour later, a boat came rushing toward our dock. Jim's best friend in the bow screaming, "Get an ambulance! Jim's been hurt!" The craziness surrounding the rescue attempts is foggy to this day. I'm not sure what really went on. But we didn't know the extent of Jim's injury until we arrived at the hospital after the ambulance. Until then, we didn't know that another boat had hit him when he was in the water. We didn't know he was dead.

Surviving this experience is what prompted me to begin a research project on grief (hereafter called the Tampa Study). My initial purpose was to find out what caused the awful pain, the physical, gut-wrenching pain. I eventually learned that the pain cannot be circumvented. It must be borne with full vengeance and awareness. What can help, however, is to understand as much as possible about grief even before it happens.

The death of a child has been described as the most distressing and long lasting of griefs (Gorer, 1965; Sanders, 1979–80). Add to that the shock of sudden death and you have a double-edged sword. Not only is there a narcissistic injury of gigantic proportions, but the suddenness of death can produce such systemic shock as to significantly diminish the capacity to cope. Bereavement becomes a total psychophysical experience of suffering (Craig, 1977). Full functioning may not be realized even years following the death (Fish & Whitty, 1983; Glick, Weiss, & Parkes, 1974; Rando, 1983).

The literature dealing with the sudden death of a child is meager. Most studies treat situations where the death has been anticipated, as in neoplastic disease. What has been reported on sudden death indicates that the shock component creates grief reactions that tend to be more intense and longer lasting than others (Parkes, 1975; Parkes & Weiss, 1983; Vachon et al., 1976). In a study comparing sudden death of a spouse to long-term illness death (Sanders, 1982–83) it was found that the suddenness of the bereavement left survivors with significant feelings of loss of control. They found it difficult to trust again. While there were no statistically significant differences noted between survivors of a sudden death and survivors of a chronic illness death, there were qualitative differences. Sudden death survivors reported more intense anger and frustration, as well as a larger number of physical complaints, particularly 18 months to 2 years following the tragedy. It was suggested that this could be attributed to the fact that the shock aspect lasted longer for sudden death survivors, creating prolonged stress that further debilitated and demoralized the mourners.

It would appear that parental grief follows the same trend as the previous study. While reported levels of grief are more intense and longer lasting for parents, the loss will be felt as deeply whether the child dies suddenly or dies from a chronic illness. However, because there is no psychological preparation for an accidental death, parents suffer a major insult requiring months, even years, to resolve (Woolsey, Thornton, & Friedman, 1978). Systemic shock appears to be the major divider between reactions to death from illness and sudden death.

Unquestionably, further research must be done before this can be fully determined. The focus of the remainder of this chapter is on the shock experienced, as well as other sequelae of parental grief, when a child has died from an accident.

SHOCK

What I experienced that Labor Day, the fogginess, the confusion, and the feelings of unreality, are typical of the initial reaction to grief. This is the shock response. The degree of shock will vary according to the variables surrounding the death. Who died, when they died, what the attachment is between the survivor and the deceased, what the coping ability is of the survivor—all will make a difference in the intensity of the shock.

When a child dies suddenly, these factors are compounded. Systemic shock affects the individual not only psychologically, but physically as well. Psychologically, shock acts as a buffer, briefly protecting the individual from a perception that would otherwise engulf him. Yet, when a child dies, this buffer acts as only a thin edge between the surviving parents and their pain. There is no context. No history. There is nothing leading up to it that could help prepare them.

Shock can be experienced in many ways: a need to yawn, dryness of the mouth and throat, uncontrolled trembling, weeping, loss of muscular power. Parents move into an unreal world where the impossible has happened. The foundation of their world has been destroyed, leaving them shaken and off balance. There is a preoccupation with thoughts of the child that seems to absorb all available energy.

Shock can also be intensified by the way the parents learned of the death. In cases of accidental death, emergency rooms become a major arena for death disclosure. One mother, telling of the death of her son following an automobile accident, described the hospital scene like this:

> They didn't tell us when we came in. We sat there for over an hour in a little examining room. Sat there and froze to death, shivering and shaking and all the time I knew he was dead.
>
> Nobody came in and finally my husband went out and said, "Can't you tell us something?" They said, "The doctor is busy right now and he will be with you in a few minutes." We just waited and waited and finally this doctor came in and he said, "I didn't see your son. The doctor who saw him has left. But, he is dead." Just like that.

The abruptness of this conversation jolted the dazed parents. Emergency room staff should be offered training in the treatment and care of newly bereaved people. On the other hand, continued support needs to be provided to the staff themselves. Theirs is a tough job.

Another serious problem can arise when caregivers are careless as they disclose the news of the death. One couple in the Tampa Study lost their 6-year-old daughter when she drowned in the neighbor's swimming pool. When the child fell in, the children with whom she was playing ran to tell the mother. She pulled the daughter from the pool and attempted resuscitation, but to no avail. When she arrived at the hospital, the attending physician told her that if she had gotten her daughter to the hospital sooner, the girl might have been saved. The young mother could not forgive herself and suffered endlessly over this remark. Hospital personnel, as well as friends and family, need to pay special heed to the vulnerable condition of bereaved parents. They will live with those remarks forever.

Physiological symptoms can become serious. One mother, whose son was killed in an automobile accident, reported what appeared to be a heart attack:

> They never did decide what it was . . . it started on the right side, my right arm, and worked over to my left side . . . and I had this terrific pain.
>
> I got [my husband] up and said, "I don't know what's wrong with me. I can't breathe. . . . I have such pain." And he got up and took me to the hospital. I was in intensive care for 2 days and they still don't know what was wrong. That was only a few weeks after our son was killed.

The large number of somatic experiences evidenced in the Tampa Study is a direct indication that survivors of the death of a child undergo a high level of stress and should be encouraged to consult their physicians as soon as possible for a checkup. These conclusions support those of other writers (Bozeman, Orbach, & Sutherland, 1955; Orbach, Sutherland, & Bozeman, 1955; Solnit & Green, 1959)who have indicated that in cases of fatal illness and accidents in children, the physician has a responsibility not only to the dying child, but to the entire family as well.

In their excellent book *Recovery from Bereavement* Parkes and Weiss (1983) discuss what they call the unexpected loss syndrome. They present sequelae of sudden death situations, such as difficulty believing that the loss really occurred and inability to face the loss, as well as social withdrawal from others who could offer support and comfort. In my opinion, these are all part of the shock reaction experienced in sudden death. In these cases shock goes on for months, partially cloaking the bereaved in an insulated sheath that protects them from experiencing the reality of the death too starkly. There is a tendency to remain closely attached to the deceased long past the time that others think they should be.

New shocks are sustained constantly as the bereaved person is reminded by one thing or another that the beloved child is no longer there. One mother reported that going to the grocery store and passing by the favorite food of the deceased child was a devastating reminder for months, even several years. Birthday cards did the same for another mother as she realized she would never again buy a special card marked, "To My Daughter On Her Birthday." Yet these reminders cannot be avoided, and they in turn keep the bereaved off guard and vulnerable.

In most cases, the shock phase in bereavement is over in the first few weeks after a loss. Not so in sudden death. Sudden death takes much longer to process. This phase could even last into the second year of grief. Inordinate patience is needed by both the bereaved and those supporting them. Bereaved parents of children who die suddenly need continued and extended encouragement not to push too hard nor too fast. Nurturance and support are the major tools of the caregiver at this juncture in the grief process. Just as shock is treated at the scene of an accident by applying warmth to maintain optimal body temperature, so nurturance acts as a blanket of concern to sustain the emotional balance of the bereaved in the shock phase of grief. Caregivers must act as a bridge to safety, insuring a resolution of grief sooner than would otherwise be possible.

EMOTIONAL SEQUELAE

The death of a child, whether sudden or anticipated, represents many social losses to the parents. Ideally, the child is the focus of love—a nurturing object. Family life revolves around the developmental process, and therefore a child's growth and well-being become central. Children, in turn, supply their parents with a feeling of purpose. Mothers, particularly, sense the importance of their roles as the "hub" of an active and growing clan. Fathers experience this in a more peripheral way as providers. As a result, parents feel loved by their children at the same time they feel responsible for them. Implicit in this exchange is the knowledge that if the job is done correctly they will receive the social status conferred on parents of successful children. A keen sense of continuing pride is the reward. Parents bask in the knowledge that their children will live on after them. Genes will be transmitted for generations to come. Their immortality is preserved. When a child dies, however, a part of the parent's hopes and dreams is slashed away. Continuity between the past and the future is broken. This represents a narcissistic injury of major proportion from which recovery may never be achieved.

In the Tampa Study, where several types of grief were compared, bereaved parents showed more intense grief reactions of somatic types and greater depression, as well as anger and guilt, than did those who had lost either a spouse or parent (Sanders, 1979–80). The single term "despair" described them best. Whether the death was caused by accident or illness made little difference in their response. In sudden death this high level of despair seems to result from the loss of control over a world that heretofore was organized appropriately. When a child dies suddenly, there is no time to rearrange the orderliness of events. There is no period in which to rehearse even the possibilities of such a tragedy. This kind of catastrophe leaves the survivors unable to know what to trust. An impressive body of literature has identified such lack of control and unpredictability as factors that adversely affect the person involved to a significant extent (Averill, 1973; Richter, 1957; Seligman, 1975; Weiss, 1970). This feeling of helplessness then leads to extreme frustration and anger. For example, one research study found that in comparison to an anticipated death, men show more anger at a sudden death for the first 2 years of bereavement (Fish & Whitty, 1983). In sudden death situations, in general, anger appears to be the outstanding reaction.

Since parents are given the responsibility of providing for and rearing their children, a child's death is seen by the parents as the ultimate failure. Recognizing an innate responsibility for their child's safety, they seem to feel that the death has occurred because they have somehow relaxed their guard. Blame is internalized as well as extended to the other spouse. This is often the root of marital conflicts that follow a child's death.

Estimates of marital discord, separation, and divorce following a child's death have run high (Schiff, 1977). In one study, where cases of childhood drowning and near-drowning were compared, it was found that 24% of parents whose children died separated following the death of the child. Where the child survived, none of the couples separated. These investigators found that the bereaved parents drank more, experienced sleep disorders and nightmares, and reported significant levels of anxiety (Nixon & Pearn, 1977). Although these symptoms would certainly produce irritation, it is often difficult to ascertain marital discord when the couple remains together. Nevertheless, even with these limitations and projecting more conservative estimates, there is still room for substantial unhappiness in bereaved parents.

The shock of a child's sudden death works negatively on the family as well. Just at the time when mutual support and understanding are needed, the greatest level of familial disharmony is felt. The buffer that serves to protect them from the raw pain of grief also serves to isolate them from each other's pain. They are like individuals standing in the rain, but each under her own umbrella. It is here that the caregiver, whether friend or professional, can help mobilize the family unit and reinstate closeness. Because caregivers are not caught up in family systems, their objectivity allows a broader view of the overall problem, enabling them to understand varying grieving patterns within the unit.

Family members do not grieve alike. Depending upon the relationship to the deceased child, each person sets up a unique agenda. Mothers will see the child differently from fathers. Siblings, grandparents, and extended family members will have different perspectives on what they have lost. Each of these losses must be acknowledged and dealt with as seriously and attentively as the next one. Caregivers will do well to appreciate each of the individual links that form the major grieving bond.

SEARCH FOR MEANING

In the Tampa Study, parents whose child had died had an intense preoccupation with thoughts of the child (regardless of age) that seemed to absorb all available energy. The impossibility of surviving their child remained foremost in their thoughts and the question of

"Why?" was an obsessive rumination. Several spoke of moving through an unreal world—of life not making sense. There seemed to be a general pattern among these bereaved parents of attempting to explain a mystery that surrounds the circumstances of the death and that troubles them greatly.

A father whose son had died in a car accident talks of his ruminations:

> When I talked with the police later I said, "Couldn't the roll bar have saved him?" They said there is no roll bar in that car. Well, he had two Sprites—one with a soft top and one with a roll bar. I was thinking of the roll bar, in fact, I had forgotten that he didn't have a roll bar in both cars.
>
> And they said the safety belt wasn't fastened and then we just went all to pieces trying to figure out why wasn't the safety belt fastened. It's a mystery to us and this mystery will always remain with us, I'm afraid.

The primary task of mourning is relinquishing the attachment to the deceased and resolving the meaninglessness of the event. In the sudden death of a child, the enormous shock makes this task difficult to accomplish. Confusion, rage, and guilt will prolong resolution. However, even when these emotions dissipate somewhat, the capacity to love others is jeopardized if the parents fail to relinquish the lost object. This has been referred to as interminable mourning (Aleksandrowicz, 1978). Under favorable conditions, bereaved families compensate for their loss by making shifts and adjustments in object love. Ties are strengthened by open sharing of grief and pain. In interminable mourning the family divides and deteriorates. The chief mourner harbors the grief and bars the remaining family members from expressing theirs. A crystallization of the split then occurs, blocking the family from resolution of grief. This often happens as one parent takes over the major role of grieving the lost child, leaving the other one in a tenuous position, unable to find appropriate expression. This one-sidedness creates tension that is often never resolved, leading to separation or divorce.

Resolving the meaninglessness of their child's death may become an impossible exercise for parents. In a culture that values youth above all, the death of a child is viewed as the greatest of all tragedies. It is more useful, perhaps, to focus on the meaning of the child's life instead. But rituals too often are of little help. The funeral comes too soon and there are no other opportunities for most to ritualize a celebration of life. The focus then must come from altruistic activities of the parents, such as establishing a memorial project that benefits others or participating in self-help groups. In a study examining coping abilities of bereaved parents, it was shown that parents with externally directed coping strategies, such as engaging in altruistic behaviors and investing in a new role or meaningful activity, became less depressed and moved further forward than those who did not (Videka-Sherman, 1982). The least adaptive coping mechanisms were found to be escape by not thinking about the death or by using drugs and alcohol, and persistent preoccupation with the deceased child.

Positive coping when a child dies suddenly will depend on many variables, as mentioned earlier. That it is extremely difficult, often approaching the impossible, has already been brought out. Yet, in their agony, parents will face the inevitable question, "If I have survived my child, what is the meaning of life?" Perhaps this is where altruistic activities have the greatest significance. This is a question for which each bereaved parent must find a personal answer.

CONCLUSION

In conclusion, the compelling task of bereavement is not to change the reality of the loss, but to adapt to it. This can be assisted in several ways. The parents should be informed of the death in a compassionate manner and should be nurtured through their shock. They should be provided emotional support and opportunities for ventilation of thoughts and feelings. This includes the time and opportunity to talk through the implications of their loss, place it in a context (in essence preparing themselves for a loss that has already occurred [Parkes & Weiss, 1983]), and react emotionally. Finally, they should be assisted in their attempts to search for the meaning of their child's death. The attachment may be successfully relinquished, but the memory of this special child will always be there, sometimes as a shadow, sometimes as a penetrating beam of light. We would not wish it any other way.

References

Aleksandrowicz, D. R. (1978). Interminable mourning as a family process. *Israeli Annals of Psychiatry and Related Disciplines, 16*(2), 161–169.

Averill, J. (1973). Personal control over aversive stimuli and its relationship to stress. *Psychological Bulletin, 80,* 286–303.

Bozeman, M. F., Orbach, C. E., & Sutherland, A. M. (1955). The psychological impact of cancer and its treatment. III. The adaptation of mothers to the threatened loss of their children through leukemia (Part I). *Cancer, 8,* 1–19.

Craig, Y. (1977). The bereavement of parents and their search for meaning. *British Journal of Social Work, 7*(1), 41–54.

Fish, W. C., & Whitty, S. M. (1983). Challenging conventional wisdom about parental bereavement. *Forum Newsletter: Forum for Death Education and Counseling, 6*(8), 4.

Glick, I. O., Weiss, R. S., & Parkes, C. M. (1974). *The first year of bereavement.* New York: Wiley.

Gorer, G. (1965). *Death, grief, and mourning.* London: Cresset Press.

Nixon, J., & Pearn, J. (1977). Emotional sequelae of parents and sibs following the drowning or near-drowning of a child. *Australian and New Zealand Journal of Psychiatry, 11*(4), 265–268.

Orbach, C. E., Sutherland, A. M., & Bozeman, M. F. (1955). Psychological impact of cancer and its treatment. III. The adaptation of mothers to the threatened loss of their children through leukemia (Part II). *Cancer, 8,* 20–33.

Parkes, C. M. (1975). Determinants of outcome following bereavement. *Omega, 6*(4), 303–323.

Parkes, C. M., & Weiss, R. S. (1983). *Recovery from bereavement.* New York: Basic Books.

Rando, T. A. (1983). An investigation of grief and adaptation in parents whose children have died from cancer. *Journal of Pediatric Psychology, 8*(1), 3–20.

Richter, C. P. (1957). On the phenomenon of sudden death in animals and man. *Psychosomatic Medicine, 19,* 91–198.

Sanders, C. M. (1979–80). A comparison of adult bereavement in the death of a spouse, child, and parent. *Omega, 10*(4), 303–322.

Sanders, C. M. (1982–83). Effects of sudden vs. chronic illness death on bereavement outcome. *Omega, 13*(3), 227–241.

Schiff, H. S. (1977). *The bereaved parent.* New York: Crown Publishers.

Seligman, M. E. (1975). *Helplessness.* San Francisco: Freeman.

Solnit, A., & Green, M. (1959). Psychologic considerations in the management of deaths on pediatric hospital services: I. The doctor and the child's family. *Pediatrics, 24,* 106–112.

Vachon, M. L. S., Formo, A. K., Freedman, K., Lyall, W. A. L., Rogers, J., & Freeman, S. J. J. (1976). Stress reactions to bereavement. *Essence, 1*(1), 23–33.

Videka-Sherman, L. (1982). Coping with the death of a child: A study over time. *American Journal of Orthopsychiatry, 52*(4), 688–698.

Weiss, J. M. (1970). Somatic effects of predictable and unpredictable shock. *Psychosomatic Medicine, 32,* 397–408.

Woolsey, S. F., Thornton, D. S., & Friedman, S. B. (1978). Sudden death. In O. J. Z. Sahler (Ed.), *The child and death.* St. Louis: C. V. Mosby.

Chapter 10

Death of a Child from a Serious Illness

Mary Jo Kupst

Mary Jo Kupst, Ph.D., is currently Research Psychologist in the Department of Child Psychiatry, Children's Memorial Hospital, Chicago, Illinois, and Associate Professor in Psychiatry and Pediatrics, Northwestern University Medical School. She is also in part-time private practice. Her major research interest is in coping with serious illness, and for the past 8 years, she has been doing research to study coping in families of children with leukemia.

The author wishes to thank Jerome L. Schulman, M.D., Principal Investigator of the Coping Project, for his leadership and knowledge of coping with serious illness. I am also grateful to those who worked on this project, including Lynne Tylke, M.A., Loy Thomas, M.A., Rhoda Kling, M.A., and Connie Stuetzer, M.A., who were the intervenors on the project; and Cathryn C. Richardson, Mary E. Mudd, Martha Schulman Stolberg, Ph.D., Betsy Gilpin, Ph.D., and Mary Fran Riley Maggio, who gave me invaluable aid as research assistants. I also wish to thank volunteers Alice Saar and Di Cross for their help in data collection and analysis, and Cheryl Klaub for her help in rating taped interviews.

This project was funded by the National Cancer Institute, Grant Number CA 19344, and by the Margaret Etter Creche Learning Center.

*To the families who participated in the Coping
Project, whose courage and openness have
taught us the meaning of coping.*

—————

Death of a child comes as an unexpected tragedy, since most parents do not expect their children to die before they do. It does not matter whether the "child" is an adult, an adolescent, a school-age youngster, or a fetus who never had the chance to be born. The death may be due to an accident or illness, sudden or prolonged, but it is always a situation of severe loss. Some parents learn to cope with their sorrow; others never recover from it.

This chapter covers the effects on the parent of a child's death from a serious and chronic illness. It is based on our work with families who participated in the Coping Project, a longitudinal study of family coping with pediatric leukemia. While some of the issues they faced are unique to that illness, the general overview holds true for many chronic and serious illnesses. Instead of being inevitably fatal as it was several years ago, leukemia has taken on the quality of a chronic illness. Because of the advances in treatment, more children are living through long-term remission, with many being called "cured." In our study, 44 out of 64 children are in remission and doing well 5 years after diagnosis.

Leukemia is, however, still a life-threatening illness. People still die, as did nearly a third of the patients seen in the Coping Project. This chapter will present some things we learned from working with these families, as well as families undergoing similar problems. The focus will be on some of the issues parents face when a child dies, and the intervention strategies used to help them cope. It is not intended to be a review of death and dying, nor of loss in general. Neither is it intended as a "how-to" explanation. Most professionals have, through their training and experience, evolved their own philosophies and styles. Each person who works with families of dying patients or of patients who have died discovers that some methods work better than others, given different patients and different situations. The material presented here is not the only way to understand these patients and families and to work with them, but it is based on commonalities found in the study. The intervention strategy is based on what was found to be helpful from our perspective and from the viewpoint of the parents.

COPING WITH A CHRONIC ILLNESS

Events prior to death often have a strong impact on how families cope. Death of a child from a serious and chronic illness differs from sudden death in that parents have more of an opportunity to anticipate the loss. Several authors (Chodoff, Friedman, & Hamburg, 1964; Futterman & Hoffman, 1973; Knapp & Hansen, 1973; Knudson & Natterson, 1960; Townes, Wold, & Holmes, 1974) have espoused the idea that adequate time for anticipatory mourning helps the grieving person to cope better with the death. Pediatric leukemia is a particularly good example of an illness that allows numerous instances for anticipation of the death.

Illness

The diagnosis itself involves issues of loss and possible death since, for many people, cancer carries with it the implicit sentence of death. Some parents reported that among their initial reactions to the diagnosis were thoughts of buying a cemetery plot and planning a funeral. Uninformed relatives and friends frequently reinforce issues of death by acting as if the child were dying.

With pediatric leukemia, especially in cases of acute lymphocytic leukemia, the illness is presented differently by medical staff. Newly diagnosed patients and their families are given a generally optimistic view of treatment efficacy, and the fear of death is often replaced with hopes for achieving remission. Attention centers around the treatments and procedures themselves. Patients and parents become more concerned with the discomforts of the bone marrow aspirations and lumbar punctures, and the side effects of the medications. In most cases of acute lymphocytic leukemia, remission is induced, and the family tends to feel more optimistic about the patient's chances. The longer remission lasts, the more the family may deny the likelihood of death ("We feel she's one of the lucky ones who've made it"; "He's cured"; "I used to have leukemia").

As remission goes on, life returns to a more normal pace. Patients are involved in school and social life, in their jobs, in leisure activities. Parents can refocus on their own lives, work, and activities, and on the needs of their other children. It almost seems as if it never happened. Then, when relapse occurs, it comes as a shock. Patients may feel cheated and angry that they endured the discomforts of the treatment only to have their early fears realized. Parents may feel similarly. Relapse reawakens the feelings of impending loss. It is sometimes the first time that parents really begin anticipatory mourning. Parents have reported that they were so occupied at the time of diagnosis with details of admission and treatment that they did not have time to feel much. At relapse, they may acknowledge and talk more about the possibility of death, as may the older child or adult patient.

Usually induction procedures are begun again, and the family again hopes for remission, but with less optimism and more fear. Results of blood counts and bone marrows become more crucial. There may be cycles of relapse/remission/relapse, each one getting shorter until it becomes clearer and clearer that the treatment is not working. When the family comes to accept the inevitability of death, the mutual goal of staff and family becomes one of making the patient as comfortable as possible, with attention to the issues of dying. Decisions must be made about whether to take the patient home, what to tell other family members, how to relate to the dying patient, how to plan the funeral, and so forth. Parents must make the shift from coping with the illness to coping with death.

Impending Death

Parents and patients deal with death in many different ways. One finding of our study was the lack of a common pattern or set of phases that holds true for most families. Some parents keep fighting, searching for alternative treatment, struggling to find a cure, denying that the patient is dying. They frequently become angry at staff who fail to save their child. Other parents deal with impending death by beginning to pull back from their children. (Spinetta, Rigler, and Karon [1974] have also shown that children do this as well as they near death.) While some distancing is normal and necessary for parents, it can be negative. In one case, a 14-year-old boy had been the main source of psychological support for his mother during a very difficult time in her life. She had become increasingly dependent on him for the support she did not get from her husband or friends. When it became clear that her son was dying, her distress at losing him resulted in her becoming distant and unavailable to him. While he became more open in trying to talk about his own impending death, she withdrew even further, sometimes leaving his room for long periods even when it was clear that he wanted his mother near.

Other people come to accept the reality of death and to plan for it. A 13-year-old girl was a striking example of openness and willingness to confront the reality of her illness throughout treatment, as were her parents. She wrote a series of articles about having leukemia and preparing for death, some of which were published in local newspapers. Along with her mother and a hospital chaplain with whom she became close, she planned the details of her funeral, taking care that it would be as positive as possible for those who would be there. She gave her parents instructions about the disposition of her belongings and other details. She even asked that after her death her mother contact another girl she had known in the hospital to tell her to "keep up the good fight." Her courage and openness were inspiring to all.

Most people seem to fall in between the extremes, vacillating between trying to conquer death and accepting its inevitability. They generally maintain hope, even at the end: "The only thing that kept me going, and I can't say it's advice for anybody else, was hope. And it kept me going up until the very last minute." And sometimes parents see death as a relief from the pain and discomfort suffered by the patient throughout treatment. The mother of a 30-year-old woman who had gone through a great deal of physical discomfort was heard to say as her daughter lay in a coma, "Please go to God. You've suffered enough already." When her daughter died, this bereaved mother was still profoundly affected by the loss, but found comfort in the fact that there would be no more pain.

After death occurs, the family usually participates in a funeral or other type of service during which they share the loss with other family members and friends, as well as hospital staff who were involved with them. The service often functions as a structured and sanctioned way to say good-bye to the person who died and to show support to the family. Support from friends and relatives is usually available at this time, but after a while it lessens and the family must face the void left by the death of the child alone.

In time, the wounds usually hurt less, but they don't heal completely: "You don't ever really get over this one." Yet we have found that most parents learn to cope with the death of their child, especially with the passage of time. Intervention can be helpful to these parents; they and staff reported a number of things to be helpful to them in fostering good coping.

INTERVENTION WITH PARENTS

Intervention with parents whose child is dying or has died from a serious illness does not differ greatly from other interventions with the parents of a deceased child, most of which are presented elsewhere in this book. Several points will be made that we felt were particularly important for this population, but the list will not be an exhaustive accounting of how to intervene in the case of a child's death in general. Because our involvement preceded the death of the child, many of the strategies take place before death. Some strategies for after the death are presented, but in general these do not differ from other types of interventions for survivors.

The caregiver who has not been fortunate enough to have had pre-death involvement with the parents is at a relative disadvantage, but this does not preclude effective treatment. It does mean, however, that the caregiver will have to work harder with the parents to establish trust, convey an appreciation of the unparalleled demands of chronic life-threatening illness, and gain an understanding of what these particular parents' experiences were during the child's illness and death and how the parents cope with stress and grief.

One point that holds true for all who work with parents of children who have died is a personal one. It is presumed that the intervenor has had experience and training in counseling and psychotherapeutic techniques, many of which are useful in this situation. But even trained professionals who have worked with complex psychological problems can find working with these families very difficult, frequently because they themselves have not adequately worked through their own issues of loss and death. Before beginning this type of intervention, it is important to be aware of and to deal with one's own reactions and previous experiences with death, some of which can be powerfully reawakened. Another issue is the feeling of impotence in one's inability to remove the pain or to save the patient from death. We found that by sharing these feelings with other professional staff in peer supervision and other similar group situations we gained support in dealing with these issues.

Intervention before the Death

Prior involvement with the families has certain advantages: (1) the family already knows and presumably trusts the intervenor; (2) the family background and typical coping responses are known to the intervenor; and (3) there is an opportunity to prepare the family for death and to be with them when it occurs.

Many parents reported that the most important thing at this time was the availability of the intervenor, who frequently just sat with them in the hospital room. While intervenors felt that they were not doing much in terms of intervention, parents later remembered their presence and said it meant a great deal to them. One parent said that to be helpful, one should "just be there" for them. Availability meant being on 24-hour call, coming to the hospital at all hours, and allowing parents to call at odd times. Parents were encouraged to let the intervenors know when they wanted to be alone as well. It was just as important for the intervenors to be aware of when to step back from the families.

Throughout treatment the role of the intervenor included being a liaison between physician and family, which became crucial at the time of death. It meant facilitating communication between them, and supporting the physician in being straight with the family regarding the patient's chances. We were fortunate to work with medical and nursing staff who were open and straightforward with families, but this is not always the case.

When the child was dying, involvement of other family members, especially siblings, was encouraged, and in most cases families complied. It was generally supportive and helpful, although some family members had difficulty dealing with the child's death and were not supportive of the parents. Intervenors then backed the parents' decisions to limit those family members' involvement.

Perhaps the primary focus was on the patient, who was encouraged to talk about her own feelings about what was happening. Even very young children quickly became aware of the anxiety and tension surrounding them. Basically they were often very afraid and fearful of being alone, as well as worried about pain and discomfort. Intervenors worked with parents to provide support to the child and to be open in their feelings and answers to the child's questions. Along with parents, they reassured the child that she would not be left alone and would be kept comfortable. In many of the families, parents and children were open enough to be able to say good-bye, to hold each other, and to support each other.

After the child died, intervenors attended the services and maintained contact with the family through telephone calls and occasional home visits. They reminded parents that they and other professionals would remain available and advised parents of several self-help groups in the area. A follow-up study of these families is ongoing.

Intervention after the Death

When one sees a parent of a child who has died from a serious and chronic illness, it is important to become familiar with what that parent experienced during treatment. Much of the early discussion will involve events during treatment, experiences with hospital staff, and other illness-related situations.

Parents may begin by presenting problems connected with the child's death, such as the existence of still unmanageable emotional reactions, or the child's death may surface as an issue during a discussion of other problems. Generally, the intervention would involve the same elements as other interventions following a death. (See Chapter

22 for an in-depth discussion of treatment interventions with bereaved parents.) We felt, however, that it was important to make certain assessments at the beginning, because they related to parental coping in our study.

Length of time since the death was an important factor. Parents look very different when seen immediately after the death as opposed to 3 years later. Some families that we thought would cope poorly over time due to intensely angry and divisive behavior shortly after the child's death turned out to do quite well 3 to 5 years later. As one mother said, "The first year or two I don't think you're living. You just go through the motions. As time goes on, you really get the feeling of wanting to be a part of life again." How one judges coping often depends on the point in time at which the parents are seen. Strong emotional reactions that were very appropriate at the time of death may be inappropriate 5 years later.

Openness of communication within the family was also a factor in coping. Families who could share their feelings openly with each other seemed to cope better than those who did not want to discuss the death of the child. In cases where the communication was not good, the intervention involved facilitating communication among all family members.

Parental attitude was also found to be related to coping. Those who coped very well were found to be people who could acknowledge the negative aspects of a situation, but who could focus on the positive ones. Instead of focusing on their loss of the child, they could eventually come to appreciate the time they had had when the child was living and the quality of their own lives. Intervention involved strengthening this aspect of coping and presenting positive aspects at appropriate times.

Another common function of the intervention was to help parents work toward a philosophical resolution of the meaning of the child's death. Parents varied widely in the way they resolved issues of meaning, but in general seemed to have a need to achieve some type of perspective, especially after the intense grieving reactions had lessened.

Parents who coped well tended to have good support systems. The intervenor's role was to strengthen existing supports and to help parents locate new ones. Most parents reported that they received support from each other, friends, relatives, the intervenor, and hospital staff. They differed in their readiness to participate in self-help groups such as The Compassionate Friends. Very few required additional psychosocial intervention, and only one family saw an outside psychiatrist several years after the death.

Based on our follow-up assessments, most of the parents coped remarkably well over time, but not without feelings of intense sorrow, loss, and sometimes anger at the death of the child. Although it is a void that will remain with them throughout their lives, most are able to manage their emotional reactions, to gain a perspective on the death, and to proceed with life without the child. While no one would wish such an unfortunate experience upon anyone, it is true that several families showed positive adjustment and even growth in terms of closer family relationships, improved individual functioning, and appreciation of life. However, one must remember that coping is a long-term process of adjustment and adaptation to a very painful experience.

References

Chodoff, P., Friedman, S. B., & Hamburg, D. A. (1964). Stress, defenses and coping behavior: Observations in parents of children with malignant disease. *American Journal of Psychiatry, 120,* 743–749.

Futterman, E. H., & Hoffman, I. (1973). Crisis and adaptation in families of fatally ill children. In E. J. Anthony & C. Koupernik (Eds.), *The child in his family: Vol. 2. The impact of disease and death.* New York: Wiley.

Knapp, V., & Hansen, H. (1973). Helping the parents of children with leukemia. *Social Work, 18*(4), 70–75.

Knudson, A. G., & Natterson, J. M. (1960). Participation of parents in the hospital care of fatally ill children. *Pediatrics, 26*(3), 482–490.

Spinetta, J. J., Rigler, D., & Karon, M. (1974). Personal space as a measure of a dying child's sense of isolation. *Journal of Consulting and Clinical Psychology, 42*(6), 751–756.

Townes, B. D., Wold, D. A., & Holmes, T. H. (1974). Parental adjustment to childhood leukemia. *Journal of Psychosomatic Research, 18*(1), 9–14.

Chapter 11

Death of a
Child by Suicide

Iris Bolton

Iris Bolton, M.A., is Director of the The Link Counseling Center, a private, nonprofit counseling center in Atlanta, Georgia. She is a graduate of Columbia University and holds a master's degree from Emory University in Suicidology. She is a grief counselor and Co-founder of the North Atlanta Chapter of The Compassionate Friends, a national, self-help organization for bereaved parents. She is the founder of a support group in Atlanta called Survivors of Suicide, for anyone surviving the suicide of a friend or loved one. She conducts workshops and seminars in suicide prevention, intervention, and postvention, working with parents, lay people, professionals, and the media to bring insight into coping with the complex problem of suicide and the resolution of loss. Ms. Bolton is a bereaved parent.

With empathy, love, and gratitude I dedicate
this chapter to the many courageous parents
with whom I have shared pain, love, and
healing.

———

Since the beginning of time, people have struggled with the complexities of life, with its mysteries, with its frustrations and injustices, with the ambiguity of "to be or not to be." Many cultures have chosen not to speak of self-destruction, to shroud it in silence and to deny it. And because we as a people so often deny death as part of life, it has enormous power in our lives. I believe that those things we can bring to light and deal with will lose their destructiveness. Those things we deny and speak not of claim power in our lives, often destructive power. We must learn that death gives meaning to life so that we can value today, and each other, and now.

There are no perfect formulas for living through the loss of a loved one who has completed suicide. There are no absolutes, no real guidelines—only the sharing of common experiences and reactions.

No words can adequately explain the phenomenon of self-destruction. Nor can spoken language instruct a family in how to survive. As yet, we know no final answers. Hence, we must be satisfied with partial explanations, with guesses, and with the knowledge that each incident is different. True, there are common denominators, but ultimately we must search for our own piece of the truth by living through the questions.

What is certain is that death is a life event, a life change, a rite of passage. It elicits powerful feelings from deep levels within ourselves, feelings not usually evident in day-to-day living. A suicide in the family may magnify these feelings and impose a heavy burden on those left behind. The deed may involve more than the destruction of the person who pulls a trigger or swallows an overdose. Too often it destroys others in the family, devastating them with the stigma of suicide, with personal guilt, often shattering lifetime relationships. A father whose 16-year-old daughter took her own life says, "Suicide is not a solitary act. A beloved person thinks she is killing only herself, but she also kills a part of us."

GRIEF RESPONSES AFTER A SUICIDE

Much has been written about the stages of grief. I prefer to summarize the impact of grief as I have experienced it and to share what many people typically go through. I remember the words of one bereaved parent: "You build your own grief process, and you build your own recovery. It's not right or wrong, good or bad. It just *is*."

The impact of suicide is felt emotionally, physically, intellectually, and spiritually. Emotional trauma includes painful feelings, fears, and longing for the absent one. Exaggerated guilt and anger are common. A sense of shock and disbelief may accompany outcries of protest. Physical reactions include aching, crying, upset stomach, inability to sleep, and loss of appetite. They also include searching for the physical presence of the deceased, and painfully regretting not being able to touch or feel that person again. One may also experience a sense of an actual wrenching away of part of one's own body, leaving what feels like a gigantic hole within oneself. The intellectual response is asking how, when, where, and especially why. One struggles in vain to understand what has happened and to make rational sense out of the confusion and the calamity. The spiritual response is difficult to capture in words. A suicide seems to batter one's soul so violently that it is altered forever. At first, one feels utter emptiness, a void as if the spirit had died. In time, this sensation somehow seems to connect one to universal truth, to the mystery of life and death, and to the collectiveness of mankind.

What happened to me was typically blinding, maddening, and paralyzing, but it subsequently provided me with insights as a grief counselor following the traumatic suicide of my own 20-year-old son in 1977. On a Saturday morning in February my second-born son, Mitch, shot himself in his bed with two guns while talking to his exgirlfriend on the telephone. He was a bright, popular, attractive young man whose sadness prior to his death had seemed to be related to being rejected by his girlfriend. We now believe his depression was masked and that it covered a deep despair and overwhelming pain so paralyzing and debilitating that he chose to die rather than live with it.

I shall try to describe my personal tidal wave in the hope that I might add a dimension to the healing of others through affirmation of themselves and their own process, and through renewed hope of survival.

I felt confused, shocked, bewildered, and dazed. I felt guilty and somehow responsible. "It must be my fault," I said. "I've failed my son. I should have been able to see the signs. I should have been able to stop him. Looking back, I now remember hearing him speak of giving up on life; now I see his despair. How could I have been so stupid as to miss his cries for help!"

I felt personally rejected, which leads to self-pity. "He preferred death to living with me," I imagined.

Somehow in my agony and in my grandiosity I believed that I had failed him, that I was not good enough or wise enough to keep him alive. I was abandoned and cast aside for Death. My unworthiness was so immense that I believed myself to be foul and I, too, wanted to die. My single-minded thought was of being willfully deserted by my son. It didn't occur to me that he was also leaving others. My only conscious awareness was of my own overwhelming loss. Had I been a better mother, he would be alive today, I thought.

The ripple effect of my squashed self-esteem evidenced itself in my relationships with others, in returning to work, and in my future survival. In relating to others I felt contaminated and believed that my foulness would somehow be as destructive to them as it had been to my son. I feared for my peers and for the rest of my family. My self-loathing was to isolate me, while at the same time I yearned to be close to others, to be told I was still OK.

Any thought of returning to work was quickly dismissed because I felt incompetent and inadequate. How could a failed mother ever be in charge of anything again? I was to struggle endlessly with my value as an employee. I had no energy to give to a job; but even more debilitating was my sense of worthlessness. I had nothing to offer anyone.

Rejection, desertion, and my feeling of responsibility and guilt left me hopeless and desperate. I saw no future. I wanted none. If I lived, I would only hurt someone else and perhaps cause that person to give up on life, too. My mind was filled with meanderings of self-doubt, self-loathing, and self-hate.

I asked, "Why me, God? What have I done to deserve this?" My self-destructive thoughts questioned, "Am I being punished? If so, for what . . . and what must be my penance?"

I felt rage, violent and consuming. I was angry at God, then at myself, and eventually at my son. Sometimes I even felt guilty because I was so angry at my beloved child. A sense of inescapable injustice haunted me.

I felt embarrassment. I asked myself, "What must my friends think of me and of our family? How can I ever face them again? I am so humiliated."

I felt isolated, even though people were all about. It was so easy to say "Nobody loved him the way I did. No one even understands my pain or can empathize with it. Worst of all, nobody wants to talk to me about what happened. Everyone avoids the subject."

I felt helpless, weak, and lifeless. "I can't change my child's death," I thought. "I can't start my life over, and I can't cope."

I felt depressed, hopeless, and suicidal. The pain cut deeply into my soul. "I can't go on. I want to die, too."

At the same time I experienced a conflicting sense of relief. I thought, "At least he is no longer suffering. He can't hurt anymore, and perhaps he is even at peace now." There was an onslaught of guilt and shame about this feeling. I needed assurance that this was common and normal. I had no concept of what was normal or to be expected, as these feelings were all foreign and new to me.

I experienced all of the emotions I've described. Some parents have told me they felt exactly the same way. Others have experienced only some of these feelings. Grief is unique to each individual, and one's process need not be judged.

Almost everyone experiences fear. Fear is the Mount Vesuvius of emotions. It can rise up from nowhere and turn into a raging volcano. It happens by day and by night and always when you least expect it. In its wake are perhaps the cruelest and most poisonous thoughts known to man, such as the following comments from grieving parents:

"I'm going crazy. I set the table for him again today, which makes at least a half-dozen times. And I can't stop crying. All day long, I keep asking myself if I'm crazy."

"I'm hopeless. I can't make it, can't cope, can't live through this pain. Will it ever go away?"

"I'm losing control of myself. If I ever let myself express my guilt and anger, I'll explode all over the place. All I can do is stuff it down inside and pretend."

"I can't stop reliving that moment. It's up there in my mind, burning like a red hot coal. My nightmares run on through the whole night."

"They say suicide is inherited. Who is going to kill himself next? It could be me. Is suicide contagious? Will it spread through our family?"

"I'm just plain bad . . . contaminated . . . foul; I must be or he'd still be alive. If I've caused one death, maybe I'll cause another. I hate myself. I hate living with this agony."

"I'm told I need help but nobody can help me, not even professionals. They can't understand it if they haven't been there."

"I'm confused and keep forgetting things. I can't even perform simple tasks sometimes. Will I ever be normal again?"

These fragments are only a fraction of the parade of thoughts that follow in the wake of fear.

HEALING ELEMENTS

As the first days passed, not a single ray of hope penetrated the blackness that gripped my mind. Literally, I can still remember the exact words that introduced me to postvention therapy and made my recovery possible. "You will survive," the man said. His gaze locked my eyes to his. I sensed his sincerity and his determination that I should share his vision. The man was Dr. Leonard T. Maholick, an Atlanta psychiatrist and an old friend. "You will survive," he repeated firmly, "if you choose to." I wanted desperately to believe him. It was a beginning. Disintegration is not inevitable. The destructive burden can be lifted and one's desperation can be turned from the agony of mourning to the wonder of survival.

During the weeks and months that followed, my husband and I and our three remaining sons were to experience the healing balm of a mosaic of services and experiences. The funeral was the first "rite of passage" that aided our grief process. It served as a ritual through which our feelings could be vented and acted out when it was too difficult to talk about them. The funeral served to affirm basic assumptions about life that were shattered by our son's death. We had to look at the meaning and purpose of life and death. The ceremony also helped us to face the truth about his death. It gave us an opportunity to say good-bye.

Our decision, as a family, was to survive this crisis together, facing the truth and reality of the horror of suicide. We would deal with the stigma in the community, and we would not cover up the ugliness of this kind of death. We talked about how we could blame and destroy one another or we could survive together. We made funeral decisions in family conferences as we huddled together, seeking comfort and understanding from one another. We talked and shared and clung to each other and, somehow, our collective pain was eased.

The presence of relatives arriving from all over the country to attend the funeral was crucial. They held us, fed us, encouraged us, and loved us in spite of the stigmatizing tragedy that had befallen us. This was the burgeoning womb from which our healing was to grow. The throngs of friends and acquaintances with outstretched arms who listened and kept a steady vigil throughout the endless blurring of days and nights added curative power. Weekly therapy sessions that provided regular venting and purging of emotions served as a guide for survival and provided a sense of hope that we would survive.

TREATMENT RECOMMENDATIONS

Postvention, as described by Dr. Edwin Shneidman (1981), is "activities that serve to reduce the aftereffects of a traumatic event in the lives of survivors" (p. 358). He explains, "Its purpose is to help survivors live longer, more productively, and less stressfully than they are likely to do otherwise" (p. 358).

To that end, he has developed a set of commonsense principles that I have found useful in my own work. They are paraphrased here:

1. A caregiver should begin working with "survivor victims" as soon as possible.
2. Caregivers should be aware that most survivors eagerly welcome opportunities to talk to a professional.
3. Caregivers should expect to encounter powerful negative emotions. Shneidman names irritation, anger, envy, shame, and guilt. All these emotions must be explored and ventilated eventually.
4. A medical examination by a physician is useful; Shneidman even calls it crucial. Examination findings can provide a baseline for estimating improvement or deterioration in a client's physical or mental status.
5. All conversational banalities and Pollyanna platitudes must be avoided.
6. The process of recovery from the traumatic loss of a loved one is often long, slow, and punctuated by setbacks. Shneidman says that postvention takes at least 3 months, and may take up to a year. Occasionally it is needed to the end of life. It is my experience that 1 or 2 years are required for this process, at a minimum.
7. A comprehensive program of mental health care should include preventive, interventive, and postventive elements.

Postvention is truly a many-faceted miracle. Unfortunately, it remains a grossly neglected aspect of family therapy; but some of us who practice it diligently are turning it into an effective instrument for healing. To summarize my own experience and that of my family, and to add to Dr. Shneidman's principles, I suggest these few imperatives:

1. Assure family members they can survive. It is their choice.

2. Encourage the family to talk openly wherever possible about the experience, the pain, and the bafflement.
3. Teach the process of recovery from grief. I say it is like climbing a series of stairsteps, one at a time, and occasionally stumbling and falling back, only to start climbing again.
4. When survivors insist that they want to die, let them know this is a normal and common reaction and that it should pass.
5. Teach survivors to reach out to other family members and to friends. Friends and family are like a parachute. The fewer they are, the smaller the chute, the faster one falls. Reaching out insures survival.
6. Suggest the idea that guilt can turn to regret if one forgives oneself based on no malicious intent.
7. Clarify that the suicidal act, which felt like a rejection, was probably more of a statement about the individual than about anybody else.
8. Discuss how one's grandiosity can lead one to believe she could permanently stop anyone from killing himself if he were really determined. Hindsight is 20/20.
9. Teach survivors that suicide is not inherited and that it need never happen again in the family if there is courage to deal with it openly and honestly. It can, in fact, help everyone to appreciate and value life more than ever before.
10. Help the family understand that grief is unique for each person and must be done at one's own pace. There is no right or wrong way to grieve. It's an up and down process and takes a long time. The hope is that the spirit is resilient and, though your life will never be the same, you can find meaning and purpose and joy again. Remember that a wound always leaves a scar. Clients say, "I can never forget what happened." Of course not. But time helps healing. You will one day remember the life of your loved one, not the death. Your life will never be the same again, nor will you ever be exactly the same person; but it is up to you individually whether or not you live the remainder of your life as an angry, hostile person or as one who is caring and compassionate.

J. Eugene Bridges, a psychotherapist at The Link Counseling Center in Atlanta, Georgia, recently summarized his work with families in the aftermath of suicide as follows (Bolton & Mitchell, 1983):

First encourage them to know it's all right to sit down and remember their life with the person. In this way the family member or members who have come for counseling are helping to bring order into their lives, and—in a mystical way—helping to bring order out of the chaos which erupted with the suicide. The sitting down is the beginning. Second, is the remembering. And with remembering, acceptance begins to set in, and after a while, the people are ready to adjust and to get up and to move on. My belief is that in therapy they sit down and remember and that will enact the healing process and the grief process which have been tragically disengaged by the person's choosing to take his life into his own hands. (p. 94)

In assisting family survival in the aftermath of suicide, Nancy Hogan (1983) speaks to the importance of "commitment to the survival of the family," as well as "commitment to the memory of the deceased." These two aspects are essential for positive resolution.

Whether the suicide is completed by a child, a parent, a spouse, or a sibling, the family system will be "in a crisis state as all of the pieces that fit together to make it a special family become disorganized and are then reorganized into a new, smaller family" (p. 5). She adds that family members "need to be assured that the disorganization that occurs with tragedy is normal and that in time your family will have understandable rhythms again" (p. 6).

SURVIVAL

As one bereaved father put it, "You never get over it, but it does get better." Families need to know it will get better and that they will survive. *How* they survive is their choice. Some families blame and separate, while others pull together and become a stronger, more bonded group. The choice may depend on the overt hope for survival and the commitment to remembering the deceased.

In my own family, following my son's suicide, decisions were made as a group. We had consensus on the beliefs that we would survive together, that we would always remember his life, that we would never fully understand why suicide had occurred in our family, and that we didn't have to know in order to go on with our lives. We didn't understand it; we didn't have to. We didn't like it; we didn't have to. What we did want to do was to choose to survive as a family and as individuals in that family. We would value life and value each other in a way not possible before, making meaning out of the meaninglessness of suicide.

Several months after my son's death I was asked to co-lead a self-help group for parents whose children had died. I wasn't sure I could handle it, but agreed to try. The purpose of the group was to provide an accepting atmosphere in which parents could ventilate their feelings, share with one another, and give and receive support, encouragement, and hope that they would survive. The group was well attended and eventually became a chapter of a national organization called The Compassionate Friends (see Chapter 30 for how to contact them). More than 400 chapters around the country assist parents and siblings in gaining insight and understanding about the healing process. The members offer love and support to one another as they are able to reach out to the newly bereaved.

The group setting is not for everyone, due to personal differences, needs, and support systems. It has, however, helped thousands of parents to help themselves and has filled a need for many families.

Professional counseling is also helpful to many parents, while others prefer to handle their grief by themselves. It was crucial in my healing and gave me a safe place to struggle with powerful emotions. I learned about the phases of grief and what to expect with its ups and downs. I gained insights about myself and about life and death. I learned that the pain eventually subsides and that there is hope for survival, and even joy once again.

The impact of Mitch's death on my three sons is their own story. I can say here that their survival and their healing has been a part of mine and that of my husband. We have hurt and cried together. We have felt guilty and angry together. We have laughed, shared, and healed together. We have faced the truth. Today, no secrets haunt us. I know that makes a difference.

After 32 years of marriage, my husband and I are facing our future with a firm sense of who we are. Our marriage has survived the statistics that say that parents of a child who kills himself often divorce each other. We have survived, I believe, because we were determined that our bonds of loving and struggling should not be broken. We had suffered one loss; we didn't want another.

We did our grieving within our own beings, in the stillness of our private souls, separate and alone. And we healed in our own ways and according to our own timetables. But at the same time, we shared our sorrows and so received the wonderful kind of healing that comes from dividing a burden. Sometimes we did very well, and sometimes we did not do well at all. But we did it. Often it was difficult because we had no energy to give to each other. Having different needs, it became tempting to blame.

Gradually, our guilt turned to regret, as we continued to share and talk. Our strength returned, bearing the gifts of laughter without guilt, of joy, of faith in God, and of confidence in the future.

We now know that we cannot control what happens to us, but we can take charge of how we respond. We can choose to survive or we can choose to be devastated. I can no longer change the destiny of my loved one, but I can be sure that my life will be more meaningful as a result of this experience. I can survive. As Albert Camus said so beautifully, "In the midst of winter, I finally learned that there was in me an invincible summer" (1954, p. 158).

My 92-year-old aunt, Sarah Reeves, wrote these words of hope:

> These days are the winter of the soul, but spring comes and brings new life and beauty, because of the growth of roots in the dark . . . spring comes and brings new life and beauty, because of the growth of roots in the dark.

Two years ago, as a part of my healing, I wrote a book titled *My Son . . . My Son . . . A Guide to Healing After a Suicide in the Family* (Bolton & Mitchell, 1983). I strongly recommend writing out one's feelings as a therapeutic intervention in the grieving process. It is often helpful to write a letter to the deceased child in order to say good-bye and to get a sense of closure. I heard recently of the suggestion for the parent to write back to herself in the words of the child, saying what the child might have said to the parent. This was a powerful healing experience for a mother who struggled through this.

The following words summarize my feelings 7 years after the suicide of my son, Curtis Mitchell Bolton. He was known to his family and friends as Mitch. I quote here the last two paragraphs of my book:

> My son . . . my son . . . your life indeed was a precious gift. Unbelievably so were the lessons I learned from living each day for itself, knowing that there may be no tomorrow, but whatever happens I have this day to love, to value, to be. I must have thought that you were immortal, if I thought of it at all, for I never even considered that you might die. Now, you have taught me to revere life. I see that it is precious and fragile and can vanish in an instant. I now look with "seeing" eyes and "hearing" ears. I'm intent on cherishing the moment. What a treasury of lessons your sacrifice has uncovered. Would that I never forget. And if I do . . . because I am human . . . let my scarred heart remind me gently with pangs of missing you.
>
> And help me to be aware always that it is through suffering that we humans meet one another, knowing no strangers, and that life can regain its meaning through that precious kinship. (Bolton & Mitchell, 1983, p. 98)

References

Bolton, I., & Mitchell, C. (1983). *My son . . . My son . . . A guide to healing after a suicide in the family.* (Available from Bolton Press, 1325 Belmore Way N.E., Atlanta, GA 30338)

Camus, A. (1954). Retour a tipisa, *L'ete.* Paris: Gallimard.

Hogan, N. (1983). Commitment to survival (Part One). *The Compassionate Friends Newsletter,* 6(3), 1, 5.

Shneidman, E. S. (1981). Postvention: The care of the bereaved. *Suicide and Life-Threatening Behavior,* 2(4), 349–359.

Chapter 12
Murder of a Child

Joan D. Schmidt

Joan D. Schmidt, B.S., got her degree in Home Economics from Cornell University. She taught in New Jersey public schools for 18 years and for the New York State Extension Service for 4 years. With her husband, Bill, she is Co-leader of the Central New Jersey Chapter of The Compassionate Friends; she is also editor of the chapter's newsletter. Ms. Schmidt is a bereaved parent.

*In loving memory of our son, Fred, who
worked so hard to "grow us up," a fine young
man we remember with love and pride; and in
grateful appreciation to all those who reached
out to help us in our desperate need.*

Murder is not a four-letter word. But it certainly is dirty! Murder is the ultimate egocentricity, the ultimate selfishness. "You're in my way. I'll fix it so you *never* talk to anyone again!"

THE MURDER

Frederick Alexander Schmidt was murdered very early in the morning on July 15, 1978. It was a brutal slaughter. He did not want to die. Shortly before his 25th birthday, he was full of dreams and hopes and carefully considered plans to implement his goals. He wanted to marry in October or November and start rather soon on the proposed family of four children that he and his wife-to-be considered ideal. The first would be a boy, Frederick William, after Fred and the two grandpas.

We'll never know what he'd have done if the first were a girl. Nor what they'd have named the other three children.

THE IMMEDIATE CRISIS

Notification of the Death

When a child has been murdered, the immediate problem is to tell the parents. It's a job police hate, but inherit. If the town is small enough so police know families, I'd suggest they turn the task over to a *compassionate* clergy member or family friend. The person who does have to tell the family should be briefed on as many details as possible. They won't be needed at once. Later on, parents will have questions which should be answered simply and kindly. That's when they'll need a friend who may be able to tell them. Still later, as the tangled mess unfolds during investigation and trials, they can acquire the painful minutiae.

Having been given the job, how do you do it? The coldest, most cowardly way is over the phone. *Don't!* Do make this an in-person call. Get someone who's intensely practical to go with you if you're afraid to go alone. When you get there, the simple fact of two at the door will convey part of your message. So will your general demeanor.

Once inside, don't be long-winded. Don't blurt out your news either. Simply, one sentence at a time, say:

"I have bad news."

"Your child has been hurt."

"Your child is dead."

Pause between your sentences. You can catch your own breath, and the parents can grasp a truth at a time. Make sure you use the child's name, both to humanize the child and to avoid an awful guessing game. Do not deliver your news to another child or family member. Parents deserve to know first.

The primary reaction will most likely be shock, disbelief. Then is when you must add the simplest details: the child was murdered, where, perhaps briefly how, and where the child is now.

At this point, the reaction may still be shock, a complete draining, or rage. If it's rage, it's an involuntary storm. Stand back until it passes. You may have to repeat details, especially when and where they can receive their child. Although you may have brilliant homilies at the tip of your tongue, this is not the time for them. The "Why?" you hear is not a question. It's the parent's statement that "we hate this."

The Funeral

This child will need the most highly skilled technician available. The coroner, medical examiner, or homicide police may well know who is the best craftsman. Parents probably don't. Anyone acting in a helping role should try to help them find the best, perhaps the most experienced at working with homicide victims.

Viewing is most likely *not* for the general public. But it is important for parents, brothers and sisters, and some friends and family members. Those who loved this child most dearly, who will be most affected by the death, should be allowed to see him. When the crime has been discovered, the body found early, this is easily within possibility. There may need to be warnings about what not to touch, but that's manageable. If the body has gone undiscovered for a time, the presentation problems are magnified. It is still best to let at least parents and siblings see something of the child—even if only the sole of his foot, a big toe. Better to see only a small part than to spend the rest of your life convinced that he's out there somewhere, unable to call home.

Parents should be given time alone with their child, individually as well as together. Brothers and sisters should be offered the opportunity of time alone, as a group, and as a family group. A child under 10, however, ought to be accompanied.

Finnish customs decree that a photograph be taken of the deceased in the coffin. Although not everyone agrees, I strongly do. Take a photograph of the open coffin and the body in it. It is not for public display. It is not for the album. It is to be there should it be needed by the family.

A lock of hair, clipped, tied, and put in a small envelope, may sound Victorian. But it would be another comfort to a sentimental mother. Both the picture and the hair can be simply included in the folder of papers every funeral director gives families.

This farewell, from a family to a part of itself, is for a long time. Don't rush them. Give them time.

Do beware of voyeurs, sometimes a part of the extended family. Spare the parents the screaming soprano, crowding for a better look at the now-notorious child. This viewing might well be scheduled at an inconvenient hour, and when the parents are not there. For the public funeral, a closed coffin and picture of the child are just fine.

Police may be at the funeral as friends of the family, to direct traffic, or to look for a suspect. If they are there in an official hunting capacity, they should be available to protect the family if needed, but should keep a very low profile and remain unobtrusive.

The press should be barred from a murdered child's funeral services. Unless they happen to be close friends of the family, they are there only to sensationalize the event. Their fleeting pleasure may well be a lingering sorrow to the parents and family, caught off guard in mid-grief.

THE AFTERMATH

As murder victims, we face a long haul. We have all of the problems any other parents have after the death of their child, plus the knowledge that someone *wanted* our child to be dead and killed him. As details unfold in the media and trials, we uncover our child's last hours or minutes. We can reconstruct the struggle, the fight, the anguished pleading, the attempt to escape. I learned from newspaper headlines that the "Slay Scene" was a "Detectives' Dream, Detectives' Nightmare." There were clues all over, my son's blue eyes were opened wide in horror and disbelief, and his blood was everywhere.

Your child is no longer your child. Your child and many of his possessions are the state's property, held as evidence. Some people have not had a body released for burial for a number of years. The evidence must be kept open until all appeals are exhausted. This doesn't end until the murderer's dead or has served some time and gotten out. Frequently murderers are very cunning and can con mental health professionals into believing that they are rehabilitated or need psychiatric care rather than imprisonment.

As murder victims, we have major enemies. Aside from the murderer(s), there are lawyers and courts, the media, and well-meaning imbeciles.

Swift and speedy justice does not exist. It would be the victim's ally. But it's the criminal's enemy. And so there is always a lawyer to find a loophole (it's his bread and butter); a judge to grant a stay, overturn a conviction, give a delay, release the latest opinion to the press. Friends are surprised: "Is that *still* going on? I thought that trial was over!" Until the criminal is freed, he'll appeal.

The worst part is hassling with the criminal justice system. It's incredibly bad and no one knows until they've had to cope with it. People who are not involved are unaware of the never-ending repeat action in the criminal justice system. It's not prosecutors nor trial judges. They seem to aim for upholding the law and protecting society. It's lawyers and appeal courts who go for the picayune and frivolous to simply create delay and set precedents, which can then be used for further delay and so on for millions and millions of taxpayers' dollars. It becomes a tearing-down process to which the family's rebuilding efforts are prey.

The media, as well as the justice system, is in business. With the latest court pronouncement in hand, they catch me off guard in search of my reaction. They do what they think will sell papers or air time, according to their own individual bent. So some are compassionate, in search of the other side of the story. And some are merciless, cruel, and tacky. If I refuse to talk to the media, I may well be unaware of what's going on in the legal process. And I deny myself my right to free speech. I have a point of view. I deserve to be heard as much as any criminal.

Police are also people who do it their way. Catching criminals has to be the most discouraging, most futile of occupations. Yet there are police who are gentle and kind in their work. And there are those who cast themselves as adversaries to victims.

Those blue, blue eyes are shut, closed by a skillful hand. Our dreams of grandchildren from our first-born son will not be realized. Our ordinary problems are those of many parents. Our extraordinary problems are what continue to plague us in our life's rebuilding.

REBUILDING

The usual things apply to a murder parent, too. I need food, rest, exercise, some small dash of cheer each day. I'm better off (as any other bereaved parent) without mood-changing drugs. Self-help groups, where there are others who understand, are a great aid. Chapters of The Compassionate Friends are easier to find than a Parents of Murdered Children group. Some parents may shy away, but there may be others whose child was murdered. Encourage me to write: a journal of my feelings for my eyes only; prose or poetry to share with other parents. Drawing or painting, no matter how poorly done, can give me something to concentrate on and may be a key to unlocking my feelings. Please refrain from pronouncements that I "must," "must not," "should," "should not." If it's really and truly important, take time, go the long way 'round, and con me into wanting to myself. Or, just put a brush in my hand and say "Paint!" Feelings are my problem, and words don't work well.

God was busy, so you came instead? Go away then. For me, God is on tenuous ground. Where was He when my child fought evil? Omnipotent, powerful, wise? Listen to me. Hear me out. And be most careful in your choice of Scripture with which to end our interview. "The sins of the fathers . . ." is not a good one.

The special things you can do to help me are these:

- Be honest with me. Be honest about facts, if you have them. Be honest about your inability to help, to hear, to relate to my woe. Or, if you are truly willing to try to help, be honest about that, too.
- Rejoice with me when I have a small victory. When the murderer is caught, rejoice. If it should happen that the murderer is given a suitable punishment, rejoice again with me.
- Support me in my determination to attend trials. I should be there. My son should be represented. Please do not go on about "opening up all that all over again." I have a right and a need to be there, to stand by my child. If it's a reasonable distance and you can go with me, go. If it's too far away for you to go, wish me well in what I must do.
- Spare me your views on capital punishment. Instead, you listen to mine. My views are relevant. My reasons are sound. Since I'm talking from a victim's experience, probably you *do* need to know my feelings. Capital punishment is written into law. It is not intended as a resurrection measure. It is to *punish* for a crime committed. Used, it would punish. It would also prevent further murders committed by freed murderers. There is no parole, no pardon, no reprieve for my son or our family.
- Spare me also from your agitation over criminals' sorry lot. Convicts in prisons chose to do wrong. I'm not convinced they

deserve large, cheery, amenity filled cells. My child is serving a sentence he did not want, nor earn, nor deserve. I doubt you'd play devil's advocate for a cancer virus. You'd hardly recommend a drunk be behind a steering wheel. Be just as intelligent when it comes to murder.

- Allow me my fantasies. I have those common to every bereaved parent, plus some special to my lot. Don't get upset if I dream aloud of well-placed lightning, if I describe what I'd like to do. Allow me to express my feelings. The odds are strong that murder goes unpunished. So let me dream—guilt-free.
- Write letters with me when you agree with my position and want to help support it. Laws are made by legislators who pay attention to mail volume. So do governors. And the newspapers present a forum for letter writers.
- Intercede if you can make yourself available. Step between me and one of the well-meaning imbeciles. Answer the phone when things are especially tough. Winnow out the calls designed to hurt.

CONCLUSION

I did not bring my misfortune upon myself. I am in no way dirty or unclean. My son was not doing anything he should not have been doing. And he was not someplace he should not have been. He wasn't looking for, nor inviting, trouble. He was going about his business, finishing a day's work, making sure all the details were attended to.

Being in the wrong place, doing the wrong thing—it's the murderers who own those labels. Look askance at them, never at the victim nor his family. If snide remarks are your natural way of expression, save them for the true criminals—the murderers. Make your nasty insinuations to the murderer's family, not to the victim's.

> I run in little circles.
> I do my idiot jobs.
> For if I don't keep moving,
> I'll surely drown in sobs.*

Please don't let, or make, me run in circles. There's a long haul ahead of me, whether or not I choose to fight transgression. It'll take a lot to keep my head together. So let me "drown in sobs." I'll have to

---

*The author's poem was originally printed in the July, 1981, *Newsletter of the Central New Jersey Chapter of The Compassionate Friends*, p. 4.

sink or swim. You might be able to help me swim; but please don't make me run in circles. Isn't that the path to insanity?

You cannot insulate me from the world. If you want to help me, walk beside me while I learn to tread on thorns.

Chapter 13

Death of
the Adult Child

Therese A. Rando

Therese A. Rando, Ph.D., is a clinical psychologist in private practice in North Scituate, Rhode Island. She received her doctorate in Clinical Psychology from the University of Rhode Island and has participated in advanced training in psychotherapy and medical consultation-liaison psychiatry at Case Western Reserve University Medical School and University Hospitals of Cleveland. Presently she is the Clinical Director of Therese A. Rando Associates, Ltd., a multidisciplinary team providing psychotherapy, training, and consultation in the area of mental health, specializing in loss and grief and the psychosocial care of the chronically and terminally ill.

As a consultant to the U.S. Department of Health and Human Services' Hospice Education Program for Nurses, Dr. Rando developed their program for training hospice nurses to cope with loss, grief, and terminal illness. Her research interests focus on mourning, the experience of bereaved parents, and the emotional reactions of rescue workers. She is the Co-investigator in The National Bereavement Study, a longitudinal multidisciplinary research project investigating the processes and effects of grief.

Dr. Rando has lectured nationally and written about grief and death since 1970. She has numerous articles and chapters in print on the clinical aspects of thanatology, and is the author of *Grief, Dying, and Death: Clinical Interventions for Caregivers* and the editor of *Loss and Anticipatory Grief.*

The author gratefully acknowledges the thoughts of Art and Ronnie Peterson, which have been incorporated into this chapter, and the helpful comments of N. Claire Kowalski, M.S.W., on an earlier version of this chapter.

This chapter is dedicated in loving memory of
my grandparents, Samuel Felix Rando and
Rose Bruno Rando, who learned all too well
about the death of an adult child.

As a child grows older the parents' relationship with him necessarily changes. There is less physical, "hands on" caretaking, and more offering of advice and sharing of mutual interests. The relationship becomes more egalitarian and peer-like, an adult-to-adult connection marked by more reciprocity and equal access to power and resources than before. As time passes, there is a gradual shift in responsibility. Role reversals or dependency shifts may occur, with the child caring for the parents. While earlier parental nurturance is not forgotten, the maturing of the child adds new facets to the relationship. This contributes new depths to the parent-child relationship, but it may also add new dimensions to the loss when this relationship is severed by the death of the child.

This chapter covers some of the salient issues and experiences of parental loss of an adult child. An adult child is herein defined as a child who has attained the age of majority. For purposes of discussion, it will be assumed that the adult child is living outside of the parental domain and is actively engaged in substantial responsibilities, with many other individuals depending upon him. He clearly is not at the age where he would have been perceived as having lived his allotted time. The age of the parents discussed in this chapter is typically 40 or older. Obviously, the age of both parent and child will have a significant impact on the relationship that exists and the subsequent mourning of it after the child's death. The parents of an 18-year-old would be expected to be in a significantly different situation than those of a 60-year-old. Nevertheless, in both cases the couple are now the bereaved parents of an adult child. For purposes of illustration of the dynamics of such losses, this chapter highlights the situation of the "older" parents of the "older" adult child, that is, those parents in their mid-50s and older who lose a child who is approaching or has reached middle age. This is *not* to devalue the experience of younger parents of adult children who die. It is merely to typify the critical issues that arise in this bereavement. These can then be adjusted to fit the situation of the younger bereaved parent who loses a young adult child of college age or older.

The primary thesis of this chapter is that the unique relationship that exists between the adult child and his parents presents those parents with special losses and demands that can complicate normal parental grief and mourning following the child's death. This is an area that has been virtually neglected in the study of parental bereavement. However, it is one that begs for examination, since with increasing life expectancy there will be greater numbers of older adults who will experience the death of an adult child.

It is assumed in this chapter that the reader has a command of the general issues regarding parental bereavement and normal grief symptomatology after child loss, as articulated in Chapter 1. This chapter will focus only on the unique issues of the loss of an adult child that differentiate it from the loss of young children. Hopefully it will become clear that many of these issues are like double-edged swords: they have the potential to both help or hinder the parents' coping with grief.

UNIQUE FEATURES OF
BEREAVEMENT FOR AN ADULT CHILD

A classic description of the bereavement of parents who lose an adult child has been provided by Gorer (1965), who posits why it is such a particularly traumatic event as compared to other deaths.

> The most distressing and long-lasting of all griefs, it would seem, is that for the loss of a grown child. In such a case it seems to be literally true, and not a figure of speech, that the parents never get over it . . . it would appear that, at least in time of peace, it is "against the order of nature" that a child should die before his or her parents; and it seems as though the parents, in some obscure way, interpret this as a punishment for their own shortcomings . . . it seems as though their self-image may be destroyed. . . . Perhaps a reliance on the orderliness of the universe has been undermined. (pp. 121–122)

This may account for the results reported by Fish in Chapter 23. In his investigation of bereaved parents he found that there was less incongruence between the grief experienced by mothers and by fathers after the death of an adult child than after the death of a younger child. However, this type of loss precipitated the most severe grief of all for fathers. (Mothers remained at similar levels of grief intensity relative to their own or their child's ages, while fathers exhibited steadily increasing intensity relative to their own or the child's ages.) The specific symptoms of parental grief associated with the death of an adult child appeared to "portend a crumbling sense of the meaning and stability of life." In the clinical picture provided by the research, there was an extreme intensity of rumination and preoccupation with thoughts of the adult child, for whom there is more to remember. Along with this, anger, despair, and depersonalization were prominent in mothers, while a great sense of isolation and desolation, accompanied by feelings of loss of control and a considerable fear of death, was present in fathers.

Additional information about how the grief of bereaved parents of adult children differs from that of parents of younger children can be extrapolated from Rosenblatt's superb work, *Bitter, Bitter Tears* (1983). In this book he amends the contemporary theory of grief following careful analysis of 19th-century descriptions of how people dealt with the loss of a loved one through death or separation. Rosenblatt notes that there is a different time course for grief work on memories than on hopes. From data on grief over the deaths of children of different ages, it seems that people confront hopes much more at the beginning of grief. The first grief work struggles are concentrated fairly heavily on hopes. Later, memories are dealt with more. Thus, the time course of grief over a relationship built largely on hopes, as with the younger child, may be somewhat shorter, but relatively intense at first. The time course of grief over a relationship rich with memories, as with the adult child, may or may not be relatively intense at first, but it will last much longer, possibly as long as one lives.

These parents may also feel an acute and painful sense of unfairness by seeing their child robbed of life and the enjoyment of reaping the fruits of his labors. Such a death violates the almost sacred goal in our society of a long and healthy enjoyment of affluence and material goods and services (Kalish, 1969). Although many parents can take comfort in what the adult child managed to accomplish in his allotted time and may have gratitude that he lived long enough to have certain life experiences that are reserved for adults (e.g., sexual maturity, college graduation, owning a home), some will feel bitter disappointment, believing that their long-term, multifaceted investment in the child has come to naught. In such a situation they cannot help but wonder if that means that their investments were insufficient, or worse, insignificant.

Incredulity over the death frequently arises because the child has been reared successfully and safely through more dangerous times. He has avoided harm as a youngster and the perils of adolescence did not result in serious injury. Because of this, parents often feel they can let their guard down and relax now. Their job has been successfully accomplished. They have protected their child and he can now protect himself. The death of the adult child viciously points out the fallacy of any parent's ever being able to feel truly secure. The parents' world becomes chaotic and unreal following their child's death as they struggle to understand what happened. Infants die of Sudden Infant Death

Syndrome. Young children succumb to cancer. Adolescents drink, drive recklessly, and die in automobile crashes. Sometimes disturbed people kill themselves. Yet it seems incomprehensible that someone who has survived all of this should die before his natural life expectancy is reached.

The death becomes even harder to fathom when the parents see the child's responsibilities left unattended with his death: the children left fatherless, the company without its director, the projects that will remain incomplete. The child is perceived as having been cheated out of a portion of his birthright. Depending on the age of the child and the developmental tasks in which he was engaged personally, professionally, and socially, there will be a number of contexts in which his absence will be acutely felt. The tragedy of this does not go unrecognized by his parents. Although they themselves have doubtlessly known other losses, none are as outrageous or as intolerable as this one. They are likely to be deeply disturbed and feel their own deaths to be far more preferable. The incompleteness of the child's life leaves the parents with a gaping void.

THE PSYCHOSOCIAL SITUATION
OF THE BEREAVED PARENT

There are a number of psychosocial factors present in parents' lives preceding and following an adult child's death that can contribute to the anguish of this particular loss.

As parents of adult children themselves are older, lifespan and developmental issues specific to the older person influence grief over the loss of an adult child. Frequently these parents are experiencing other losses and relinquishing those things that had previously helped to define them. The end of the corporate climb up the ladder, retirement, widowhood, relocation, or loss of contemporaries—all these create a psychosocial situation in which the death of a child can be more difficult to contend with. Issues of midlife crisis and the aging process must always be taken into serious consideration when looking at the experience of these bereaved parents.

These parents are already feeling a loss of control as a consequence of the natural aging process; it is dramatically increased when their child dies. For many of these parents "Why not me?" is an even more salient question than it is to younger bereaved parents. Many are at an age where their own deaths would be seen as more timely than before. Therefore, it seems even more "unnatural" for the child to predecease the parent at this time. It is this untimeliness that makes the loss harder to adjust to, despite the fact that some degree of separation from the child has already occurred in the normal context of adult development and independence.

To many parents, in the midst of their own developmental transitions and losses, the death of the adult child robs them of a significant source of vicarious ego-gratification. With the death they lose a way of retaining meaning and achieving the sense of continuity and generativity (Erikson, 1950) so important to successful aging. It should be noted that the parent need not have been pathologically invested in the child for this to occur. Within limits, such vicarious gratification is a normal experience reflecting the child's being an extension of the parent. For those whose investments were unhealthy, with the child serving solely as a narcissistic extension of the parent without appropriate differentiation or recognition of individuality, the deprivation is even worse.

As with all other losses, the meaning of the relationship to the mourner, the characteristics of that relationship, and the roles the deceased played in it will determine what must be grieved by the bereaved parent. For example, some parents will lose social status with the death of their child. The parent who had been accorded particular respect because of being the mother of a star athlete not only loses her child, but also suffers a major secondary loss when her special status disappears with his death. If this type of status is one of the main supports of the parent's self-esteem, such a symbolic loss will prove even more devastating. The roles the child played in the life of each parent must be evaluated in order to understand the parent's unique loss and subsequent experience of grief. The more roles the child occupied, the more the parent will have to grieve.

With parents whose own worlds may be diminishing socially, the loss of the child who occupied numerous roles will be felt in many more ways. Where a role reversal may have commenced, the parents may have become dependent on the child in a variety of ways: financially, psychologically, socially, and physically. This may predispose some parents to feel more guilt after the loss of their child, because they feel anger over the dependency needs that are left unmet with his death. They are then subject to the difficulties in mourning that can develop when there is grief over the loss of a dependent and/or irreplaceable relationship. Previous research has found that often this results in chronic grief, in which high intensity grief reactions continue and mourning fails to draw to its natural conclusion (Parkes & Weiss, 1983; Raphael, 1983). Intense yearning and an inability to go on with life are quite common. Of course, it must also be kept in mind that because these deaths are considered to be untimely, many of them may also be unanticipated. This subjects bereaved parents to the significant difficulties in grief resolution and adaptation that are encountered by victims of unanticipated losses (Parkes & Weiss, 1983). (See Chapter 22 for more on chronic and unanticipated grief.)

Some parents may experience conflicted grief. This exists when there is an exaggeration or distortion of one or more of the manifestations of normal grief, commonly extreme guilt or anger, while other aspects of the grief are suppressed (Raphael, 1983). In cases where the parental relationship with the child was marked by a high level of ambivalence, a syndrome of conflicted grief is often found in which there is an exaggeration or distortion of guilt while other signs of normal grief are minimal or absent. Conflicted grief is also often witnessed following sudden or unexpected deaths for which someone is blamed (e.g., failed or negligent medical care or when the deceased died violently, as in an accident or disaster) or after the loss of a dependent relationship. In these cases the grief is marked by extreme anger, with little else evident. This type of grief reaction can be abnormally prolonged. (See Chapter 22 for more on conflicted grief.)

In addition to problems with the successful resolution of grief, practical problems can arise when a child dies on whom the parents have become dependent. Isolation, economic instability or devastation, and unmet responsibilities around the home or business may ensue. These parents lose someone to care for them at some point in the future, if the child was not already doing so at the time of death. The parents may then be confronted with serious questions pertaining to their physical, emotional, and financial livelihood. Along with this, they are deprived of a source of solace at a time in their development when it may be needed to help them appropriately manage and integrate their lives.

BEREAVEMENT PROBLEMS CAUSED
BY THE LOSS OF THE ADULT CHILD

The loss of the adult child presents parents with five issues that adversely affect the normal grief experience: (1) the compromising of the successful completion of the four tasks of grief work; (2) the exclusion of the parents from the concern of others; (3) the preponderance of factors contributing to unresolved grief; (4) the parents' significant lack of control before, during, and after death; and (5) the number and kind of secondary losses faced by the parents.

The Compromising of the Successful
Completion of the Four Tasks of Grief Work

There are four tasks that must be accomplished in order to successfully cope with a death: (1) acceptance of the reality of the loss; (2) experience of the pain of the grief; (3) adjustment to the environment in which the deceased is missing; and (4) withdrawal of emotional energy and reinvestment of it in another relationship (Worden, 1982). A number of unique factors may impede these tasks and contribute to unresolved grief for parents who lose an adult child.

  · One of the most striking problems that confronts the bereaved parents of an adult child involves the difficulty these parents often have in meeting the first task, accepting the reality of the loss. This is a critical task that must be successfully addressed if mourning is ever to occur. Ironically, this difficulty is prompted by the parents' having already partially achieved the third task of mourning, adjusting to the environment in which the child is missing. It is precisely because they have already adjusted to such an environment, with their child's having moved outside of the family home, that they may have difficulty confirming the reality of the death. For them there is no dramatic absence to signal that the death has occurred. It may seem more unreal to these parents, who are accustomed to not seeing their child on a daily basis and who must struggle to adapt to a loss that is more difficult to recognize and accept. The death of the adult child is easier to deny because they are not faced with the frustration of expecting to see their child and then not having him appear. Contrary to parents whose children are at home, these parents do not expect to see their child frequently, and most of his belongings have long since been moved out of the home. Consequently, it may take a very long time and much psychological work for the parents to realize that, in addition to the child's not being "here," in the home, he is no longer "there" either, where he had been living with his own family.

  If the adult child had not been in close communication with his parents, or if his spouse had taken over the communication for him, it may take a long time before the absences in contact are internalized by the parents as being permanent absences indicating the child's death. These parents have "lost" their child before, but he has always popped up again when he came to visit or when he telephoned. For this reason, holidays and family gatherings may become painful occasions. Since these may have been the only times of the year when the parents did see the child, they may be the only events that will signal his death, the only times his absence is actually perceived. Added to the difficulties every bereaved family experiences on holidays is the crushing realization that the death has really and undeniably occurred, a fact previously not real (Ronnie Peterson, personal communication, 1984). In those cases where there was a lack of opportunity to say good-bye, additional complications such as the presence of unfinished business and problems with lack of closure are imposed upon the parents. All of these issues combine with the natural urge to deny that the death has occurred, leaving these bereaved parents with the potential for having more difficult issues to address in their grief work.

The point should be made that, although intellectual acceptance of the death is harder because normal maturation has led to less frequent contact with the child, emotional readjustment may be *relatively* easier than it would be if the child had been present in the home and the parent had to contend more with the reminders and the more acutely perceived absence. This is consistent with Rosenblatt's (1983) observation that both coresidence with and involvement in the care of dying individuals (with such active caring involvement usually a function of normal parenting of younger children) may lead to heightened grief. As opposed to parents whose children still live at home or nearby, parents who have not been sharing a residence or having frequent contact with their child have fewer current linkages of behavior patterns and fewer reminders of memories that have to be grieved. They also do not lose the important day-to-day interactions with the child that help define their sense of self and reality.

Depending on the age of the parents and the opportunities available to them, there may be diminished strength, abilities, and options for reinvestment and nurturance following the death of the adult child. Decreased opportunities to reinvest emotionally leave these parents in situations where their ability to fulfill the fourth task of grief, withdrawing emotional energy and reinvesting it in another relationship, is severely compromised. For example, because of their age there is usually an inability to have subsequent children. They may have no other ways in which they can assure their own immortality or create other extensions of themselves. Or there may be an absence of healthy ways to cope with their grief. They may lack the diversions of employment or have physical difficulties that restrict their opportunities to alleviate the loss, such as limited mobility that interferes with attendance at self-help groups or failing eyesight that makes it impossible to read. Moreover, they may not have the energy required to try to change the conditions that contributed to their child's death (e.g., raise money for cancer research or work to stiffen drunk driving legislation) or to become involved in altruistic behaviors for the good of others or in memory of their child—both consistently demonstrated to be therapeutic outlets and appropriate reinvestments for bereaved parents. Parents of this age may suffer from the absence of a support system. Many have lost friends or have friends who do not know how to react to the loss because they see no observable changes in the lives of the bereaved parents and did not know the child well, if at all. Many of these parents feel hopeless because there is no way to compensate for or adapt to the loss as a younger parent might. This does not mean that they want to "replace" their child in an unhealthy fashion, but that there are often few opportunities to engage in activities that could help them assuage the loss or cope with it better.

On the other hand, many of these parents have had to cope with trauma previously in their lives. A large majority will have dealt with other bereavements. Although the research data are mixed as to whether previous losses are associated with better bereavement outcomes for parents who lose children (Shanfield & Swain [1984] found it was; Rando [1983] found it was not), it appears reasonable to assume that successfully resolved losses that indicate that grief can be managed and survived can be helpful to bereaved parents. In this regard age and experience can be positive factors for parents who lose older children.

**The Exclusion of the Parents
from the Concern of Others**

Parents who lose adult children suffer discrimination that is different even from that suffered by other bereaved parents. With the loss of an adult child the focus of attention usually centers around that child's spouse and children. Because the deceased is an adult, concern is directed toward her own immediate family and the responsibilities she left unattended. Frequently there is little appreciation that this individual, despite being a parent or grandparent herself, is still a child to her own parents. With the focus on the spouse and children, the parents are usually excluded. Consequently, bereaved parents of adult children are left with a lack of validation of their unique loss. In this regard, bereaved parents of adult children are not so dissimilar from parents who have suffered miscarriage, stillbirth, or infant death in that their loss is less readily recognized and legitimized by society. Interestingly, even in the literature on bereaved parents, there is little about the loss of an adult child. Most of the writing focuses on the loss of a younger, usually school-aged, child. It appears as if children who are too young (those who are miscarried, stillborn, or suffer infant death) or who are too old (the adult child) are accorded relatively less professional, as well as social, attention. Even in the media, the drama of a youngster combatting a terminal illness attracts more attention than the similar plights of very young or adult children.

This exclusion of the parents not only leaves them invalidated and missing crucial social support but it also means they may be omitted from important activities following the death that could help them cope with the loss. For example, while the adult child's spouse and children would certainly be invited to a ceremony in which a scholarship is given in her name, it would not be uncommon for the elderly parents to be overlooked and not be included. The focus is simply not on them, as it would be if the child were a youngster.

There is also a curious social phenomenon in which older individuals are expected to be less grieved by death. Some assume that previous loss has made them immune to grief, or that advancing age means that they are comfortable with death since they are closer to it. Research suggests that these assumptions are not necessarily valid. Clinical observation indicates that frequently the opposite is true, and that the older bereaved parent of the adult child who dies is in an extremely vulnerable position.

The Preponderance of Factors
Contributing to Unresolved Grief

As a consequence of the phenomena just described, as well as of the normal aging process, the bereaved parents of an adult child may find themselves with a diminished support system. The lack of support and acceptance interferes with parental mourning. Both social negation of the loss and social isolation from support are among the primary social reasons for failure to resolve grief (Lazare, 1979). Additional problems along these lines may develop when one of the parents is widowed, or when parents have relocated far away from family or friends.

Bereaved parents of adult children also face other impediments to the successful completion of mourning. In addition to the guilt normally found in parental bereavement, these parents frequently experience intensified guilt because of the unnaturalness of their child's predeceasing them at their age. This guilt may be intensified if they fail to appreciate that increased independence, with its consequent increase in psychological and geographical distance, is a normal part of a relationship with an adult child. Sometimes parents regret the independence they granted their child, magically thinking that if they had kept him at home they could have protected him from harm. This further exacerbates not only their guilt, but their anger, depression, and marital stress. Combined with all this, as with other bereaved parents, they too have lost extensions of themselves with the death of their child. And, when the child's death occurs when the parents are suffering from the deaths of their peers, or from other developmentally related losses, these parents become susceptible to bereavement overload (Kastenbaum, 1969). Taken independently, the guilt, the loss of an extension of self, and the multiple losses are all psychological reasons for a failure to grieve (Lazare, 1979). Taken together, as in the situation of parents who lose an adult child, they further complicate the bereaved parent's mourning process because of their cumulative effect.

Another factor that contributes to unresolved grief is the parents' physiological state during bereavement. Because of their being older, with increasing infirmities and decreasing physical abilities, there may be additional somatic difficulties. There are often more problems with nutrition, rest, physical health, and exercise—all of which are well documented as physiological factors that influence the mourner's grief response (Rando, 1984). Inappropriate amounts of these will compromise the bereaved parents' grief response. Furthermore, parents of this age are more frequently prescribed medication for emotional distress. Overreliance on medication during the grief process can retard, if not prevent, healthy grief work. For these reasons these bereaved parents are more vulnerable to malresolution of grief on purely physiological grounds.

The Parents' Significant Lack of Control

Parents of adult children generally have much less contact with and control of or decision-making power over their children than parents of younger children. This is usually (but not always) accepted by both the parents and child as they mature. However, the child's dying or death may stir up various feelings about control in parents. Some may feel a desire for more control; others may feel relief that they no longer must be responsible for the child, which does not signify a lack of love but is a normal surrendering of parental duties. In any case, the lack of control and involvement that typifies a parent's relationship with an adult child can cause bereavement problems not experienced by parents of younger children.

It is highly probable that parents of adult children will not be involved in the child's last days or in his life in general. This may be the result of emotional or geographical distance, or may reflect a desire to keep the parents only peripherally involved for their own protection or the child's. This may mean that in situations of illness parents are precluded from participation in care, with preference given to the child's spouse and children. Appropriate amounts of participation in the care of younger terminally ill children has been found to be associated with numerous indices of better coping during the illness and more positive adjustments subsequent to the death (Rando, 1983). Too much or too little of it has been associated with problems for bereaved parents. *If* the same concerns apply to older parents, despite the diminution of their direct caretaking duties because of the age of their child, denial of adequate opportunity to participate in the care of their child would be expected to be harmful. The desire not to interfere in the decisions made by the child and his family often prompts these parents to not assert their own needs, and their mourning may be complicated by these needs being unfulfilled.

There are often situations in which the child has been maintaining a lifestyle or making medical treatment decisions of which the parents would not approve. Such unacceptable behavior on the part of their child may contribute to ambivalence and other uncomfortable feelings such as anger, disappointment, and guilt, as well as some relief—all of which can compromise the grief process.

The decreased control and lack of everyday contact may mean that bereaved parents must struggle with incomplete information as they attempt to understand the life and circumstances that preceded their child's death. Frequently they may not have all their questions answered. This negatively influences grief resolution. Concerns about the child's emotional and physical state, worries as to whether everything possible had been done to prevent the death, and anxieties about whether their child's needs were met are all reactions with which parents may be forced to contend. Additional complications arise in the grief process if parents feel that problems existed prior to the death with which they could have been helpful. Anger at in-laws may erupt if there is a sense that the spouse and children failed to provide the type of environment or care for the child that the parents would have wanted. Guilt about having given independence to the child, regret over lack of physical or emotional closeness, a sense of unfinished business, feelings of disconnection, and lack of involvement may contribute additional stress to the mourning process.

Another related issue that impacts on parental bereavement is the parent's limited control, if any, over the decisions regarding funerals and funerary rituals. Most often the child's spouse is in the decision-making position, often influenced by her own parents. This leaves the parents of the deceased child in a position where they may be forced to endure rituals that are distasteful to them, or, more often, must suffer the absence of those that would be helpful and meaningful to them. Decisions that are deemed inappropriate or repugnant to parents often complicate their grief. For example, the increasing trend toward cremation is more readily accepted by the younger population, but may be intolerable to older parents. Because of the deritualization of contemporary society, there may be a lack of religious ceremony, which may leave the parents of the deceased child not only without psychosocial and religious support, but with angry and hostile feelings as well.

The parents' image of their child and what they believe he would have wanted is often in contradiction to what the surviving spouse knows to be true. This can become quite problematic, since many decisions are made based on the person's knowledge of the deceased. The discrepancy in viewpoint between parents and daughter-in-law often causes significant conflict. The parents may remember the little child who was the altar boy and be unfamiliar with the adult who eschewed his former religion. The missing religious ceremony is then even more painful. The parents' memories are all they have, and when they are incompatible with a spouse's current assessment, the situation often results in one party's losing what it wants or needs. Most often this is the parents. They cry, "I can make no decisions, yet he was my flesh and blood!"

The Parents' Secondary Losses

In addition to the previously mentioned losses that the parents of the adult child must endure, there are a number of other secondary losses. Secondary losses are those losses that develop as a consequence of the death (Rando, 1984). They may be physical or psychosocial in nature. Bereaved parents are forced to confront many fears around these secondary losses. There is usually a major fear that the parents will lose contact with the grandchildren, and often with a beloved in-law. When the family has lived nearby, there is the real possibility of their moving away. Seeing the surviving in-law start dating or watching someone take over the deceased child's role in the family is particularly painful for parents. Remarriage, the surviving in-law's renewed dependence on her own parents, and increased reliance on others to support the deceased child's family emotionally and physically are actions that poignantly illustrate to the parents the absence of their own child and stimulate further concerns about the emotional and physical loss of the child's family. It is not uncommon to fear that the grandchildren will forget their real parent and/or not be reared in ways the parents feel their child would have wanted. This, when combined with the real lack of control and input on the parts of these parents, contributes to increased frustration and loss.

Witnessing the pain of the child's family and being unable to do anything about it exacerbates the parents' own. They are unable to answer the grandchild's question, "Why didn't you die instead of my daddy? You are so much older"—the precise question with which the parents themselves struggle. Looking at their grandchildren and seeing living reincarnations of their own child can be an additional stress or a blessing. Some parents are concerned about having to assume caretaking duties for their grandchildren at a time when they are emotionally and/or physically depleted themselves. While some manage this successfully, others are less fortunate. Those unwilling or unable to do so may have to contend with guilt and other repercussions as a result.

Other secondary losses that may accrue to parents after the death of their adult child are the loss of the family business or the loss of the family name if there is no one else to carry it on. Depending on the relationship with the child's family and/or the existence of other children, many bereaved parents feel particularly deprived at not having someone to whom to bequeath important and symbolic heirlooms, critical for a sense of personal and family continuity and immortality. Or, if they have already been given to the child and are retained by the family, the parents may have to face the awkward situation of wanting them back.

TREATMENT RECOMMENDATIONS

In addition to the treatment recommendations outlined in Chapter 22 "Individual and Couples Treatment Following the Death of a Child," the following treatment recommendations are made.

Psychosocial Issues

- Recognize and validate the loss of the adult child in order to legitimize the experience of grief and socially validate the experience.
- Assist parents in understanding and appreciating the very unique difficulties in their mourning for the loss of an adult child. Work to facilitate the appropriate resolution of these.
- Identify the issues that complicate the tasks of mourning for an adult child and those factors that promote unresolved grief. Help the parents successfully work through these.

- Work with parents to help them adjust to the reality of the permanent loss of the child, which is unlike previous losses when the child would leave the environment but return on occasion.
- Help parents to integrate the loss of their child at a time when they may be experiencing other developmentally related losses.
- Maximize the control that these parents do have when in the process of losing so much in addition to their child. Help them deal with that lack of control with which they must cope.
- Encourage parents to discuss their deceased child and their grief with their peers, even if these peers never knew the deceased child.
- Help parents to find the information that is important for them in order to successfully cope with the death of their child; for example, questions about what occurred at the time of death or what precipitated the heart attack.
- Help parents to understand that decreased contact and increased independence, with its consequent increase in psychological and geographical distance, is both natural and normal. Attempt to ease inappropriate guilt and to help these parents appreciate the reality of a relationship with an adult child in order to cope with the loss of it.
- Work to help these parents cope with the discrepancies between what they would have wanted for their child and the choices they would have made, and what others actually did before and after the death.
- Help parents deal with their anger, resentment, and feelings of exclusion because they are not given primary, or many times sufficient, attention after the death of the adult child and because they are not in decision-making roles.
- Work with these parents to help them finish any unfinished business with the child and say the good-byes that may have been precluded by the circumstances of the death.
- Help these parents identify and, as far as is possible and appropriate, find substitutes for the roles the child fulfilled. Make sure they will be able to survive not only psychologically, but also economically, physically, and socially. If not, intervene in these areas.
- Predict particular difficulties on holidays and during family gatherings, which will now poignantly illustrate to parents that the child is no longer alive. This is the time when most adult children who had moved away would have returned to see their parents.

Relationships with the Family of the Deceased Child

- Help bereaved parents work out an agreement with the surviving spouse regarding physical and emotional contact with the family and what can be done to keep the child "alive" to the grandchildren. Encourage appropriate contact.
- Include these parents with the family in funeral decisions and psychological treatment, if possible and appropriate. In cases where the parents cannot be combined with the child's family, work to give the parents their own time and space in order to deal with their loss and meet their own needs.

SUMMARY

The relationship between the adult child and his parents has a number of characteristics that can make the child's death particularly difficult to address. In addition, the psychosocial situation of older parents frequently complicates their bereavement experience. There are a number of psychological and social impediments to the successful resolution of grief when parents of this age lose an adult child. Caregivers must recognize the unique issues, problems, and demands of this type of loss in order to effectively serve this traditionally overlooked population of bereaved parents.

References

Erikson, E. H. (1950). *Childhood and society.* New York: Norton.

Gorer, G. (1965). *Death, grief, and mourning.* Garden City, NY: Doubleday.

Kalish, R. A. (1969). The effects of death upon the family. In L. Pearson (Ed.), *Death and dying: Current issues in the treatment of the dying person.* Cleveland: The Press of Case Western Reserve University.

Kastenbaum, R. J. (1969). Death and bereavement in later life. In A.H. Kutscher (Ed.), *Death and bereavement.* Springfield, IL: Charles C. Thomas.

Lazare, A. (1979). Unresolved grief. In A. Lazare (Ed.), *Outpatient psychiatry: Diagnosis and treatment.* Baltimore: Williams & Wilkins.

Parkes, C. M., & Weiss, R. S. (1983). *Recovery from bereavement.* New York: Basic Books.

Rando, T. A. (1983). An investigation of grief and adaptation in parents whose children have died from cancer. *Journal of Pediatric Psychology, 8*(1), 3–20.

Rando, T. A. (1984). *Grief, dying, and death: Clinical interventions for caregivers.* Champaign, IL: Research Press.

Raphael, B. (1983). *The anatomy of bereavement.* New York: Basic Books.

Rosenblatt, P. C. (1983). *Bitter, bitter tears: Nineteenth-century diarists and twentieth-century grief theories.* Minneapolis: University of Minnesota Press.

Shanfield, S. B., & Swain, B. J. (1984). Death of adult children in traffic accidents. *Journal of Nervous and Mental Disease, 172*(9), 533–538.

Worden, J. W. (1982). *Grief counseling and grief therapy: A handbook for the mental health practitioner.* New York: Springer.

Section 3

Socially Unacknowledged Parental Bereavements

Chapter 14

Induced Abortion

Betty Glenn Harris

Betty Glenn Harris, R.N., Ph.D., is an assistant professor at the University of North Carolina at Chapel Hill School of Nursing where she teaches maternal/ infant nursing advanced diagnostic process. Currently, she is doing research on the psychological impact of spontaneous abortion. She is also a childbirth educator. For many years, she has taught a course on parenthood for university students.

In general, induced abortion* is not considered to be a cause for grief. Although individual circumstances may be viewed as unfortunate, and the occurrence of guilt, depression, or anger with abortion has been studied, the occurrence of grief has received little attention. This chapter will survey the information available on grief as a reaction to abortion and consider ways in which caregivers may help to diminish the likelihood that unresolved grief will interfere with effective functioning in their clients.

Almost all literature on the topic focuses on the reactions of women to the experience of having undergone abortion. Although there is reason to conclude that men are also affected, this chapter will concentrate more heavily on the women's experiences. Further research into men's reactions is needed.

PSYCHOLOGICAL EFFECTS OF ABORTION

Some of the psychological reactions of women to their abortions have been extensively studied. Osofsky, Osofsky, and Rajan (1973) reviewed the literature available on the topic in 1973 and analyzed separately the literature written before abortion's legalization and studies published during the early years after legalization. They concluded that there was little evidence from either period to conclude that abortion was associated with intense negative reactions. A minority of women experienced depression, sadness, or guilt, but these feelings usually subsided within several weeks to a few months. They noted that, during the prelegalization period, most women who had abortions were given permission to abort because they were judged at high psychiatric risk. When those women who were granted abortions (presumably the ones with more intense pathology) were compared several months later with those who were denied abortions, it was found that the women who had undergone abortions were significantly less troubled than were those who had given birth.

More recent studies have found a similar pattern. After reviewing the literature, David (1978) concluded that "legal induced abortion does not carry a significant risk of psychiatric trauma, and . . . whatever psychological risk exists is less than that associated with carrying a pregnancy to term" (p. 97). In general, David concludes that post-abortion psychiatric disturbances are more likely to be related to

---

*Hereafter, when the term abortion is used, it will refer to induced abortion, unless otherwise indicated.

prepregnancy adjustment than to the abortion procedure. That is, those women who have difficulties with adjustment prior to pregnancy are more likely to have increased difficulty following the stress of an abortion than are women who are well adjusted in general.

Doane and Quigley (1981) reviewed more than 250 articles on psychiatric and related aspects of therapeutic abortion. Although many of the studies they reviewed suffered from methodological inadequacies, Doane and Quigley concluded that approximately 5% of patients reported feeling worse several months after their abortions. The most commonly reported symptoms, accounting for 57% of adverse effects, were "depression, with or without grief, guilt, and crying spells" (p. 429). When information was gathered from patients a year or more following their abortions, almost no such symptoms were reported.

It is tempting to conclude that abortion is an innocuous procedure insofar as the risk of negative emotional sequelae is concerned. The tendency to discount potential problems may also be affected by sociopolitical factors. The original impetus for stressing the ease and safety of abortion grew out of the need to convince the public that legal abortions were safe, certainly when compared with illegal terminations. Preserving access to abortion requires that it be viewed as a procedure with minimal inherent risks, and, in general, the physical and emotional risks of abortion have been found to be quite small. For some individuals, however, probably no more than 10% (Fogel, 1981), an abortion has had more intense consequences.

Since the proportion of clients who experience negative reactions is relatively small, such a client may be missed unless the caregiver is sensitive to the possibility of emotional trauma. The problem of identifying the client in need may be compounded by her unwillingness to admit to grief, sorrow, or sadness. Such reluctance may arise from the client's feeling that she chose the abortion and therefore should not experience, or admit to, any detrimental effects. As Raphael (1983) notes:

> For many women there will be grief to follow and often an undue burden of guilt as well. It is particularly difficult for the woman that she seeks on one hand to be rid of the pregnancy, yet at the same time mourns its loss. Often she is expected to feel grateful that she had been able to obtain the termination, as well she may. Those to whom she might turn for support give her a covert message that her affects should be of pleasure and relief rather than sadness, failing to recognize that the two may coexist. The woman may have required a high level of defensive denial of her tender feelings for the baby to allow her to make the decision for termination. This denial often carries her through the procedure and the hours immediately

afterward, so that she seems cheerful, accepting, but unwilling to talk at that time when supportive counseling may be offered by the clinic. (p. 238)

Masking of emotional responses may thus occur both at the time of abortion and in later contacts with professionals. If grief persists, moreover, it may surface in disguised form and be expressed behaviorally or through psychosomatic symptoms.

HIGH-RISK FACTORS FOR ADVERSE EMOTIONAL EFFECTS

While any woman (or man) involved in an abortion may grieve the loss of the pregnancy, certain groups have been shown to have greater potential for adverse emotional reactions. At greater risk are those who have had previous emotional illness, experienced pressure to have an abortion, undergone a second-trimester abortion, or had abortions for medical reasons, such as to terminate a defective fetus. Very young women are at special risk for some of these reasons.

Predisposing Emotional Problems

Undergoing an abortion, even when it is ardently desired, causes some stress in most women. For those with a prior emotional disturbance, the experience of finding themselves pregnant, deciding to have an abortion, and then actually having one can prove especially stressful. Belsey and her co-workers concluded that the dominant factor affecting emotional response to abortion was the degree of emotional adjustment existing before the pregnancy (Belsey, Greer, Lai, Lewis, & Beard, 1977). The most common forms of emotional maladjustment, they found, were a history of psychosocial instability, poor or no family ties, few friends, a poor work history, and lack of contraceptive practice. The psychological vulnerability of such a client may be increased when the necessity for dealing with an unwanted pregnancy confronts the woman with unpalatable facts, such as her lack of financial and emotional resources or her personal unreadiness to assume the responsibility for a child. That stress may serve to worsen her emotional state. On the other hand, some women find that the experience of confronting and coping with an unwanted pregnancy contributes to increased maturity and competence (Belsey et al., 1977; David, 1978; Donovan, Greenspan, & Mittleman, 1975).

Pressure to Have an Abortion

Women who undergo abortions when they would prefer to continue their pregnancies are at special risk for emotional reactions. Donovan et al. (1975) concluded that "[A] vulnerable woman who is coerced into abortion or accepts it reluctantly. . . appears to be more likely to decompensate than does a vulnerable woman whose decision is made with little ambivalence on the basis of pressing reality factors" (p. 16). If she experiences, or perceives, pressure from her parents, mate, or health professionals, she may consent to have an abortion. She may also choose abortion because of her social circumstances or her own current needs. If full emotional consent to the procedure is lacking, however, the potential for feelings of exploitation, anger, and grief are increased.

Second-trimester Abortions

Review of the literature on second-trimester abortions suggests that women having these procedures are likely to be young (under 21), black, Protestant, high-school dropouts with no other children. They are likely to have been referred from a prior health care provider and not to have been using contraception (Kaltreider, 1973). Kaltreider did in-depth interviews with 18 women before an abortion and again a few days after the procedure. She compared those seeking abortions during the first trimester with those already in their second trimester. Emotional factors that were identified as contributing to delay in seeking abortion included fear of sterility, fantasies of replacing an earlier loss, and disturbed relationships with mates or parents. The women in their second trimester tended to deny the possibility of pregnancy for a prolonged period.

However, Kaltreider found that women in their second trimester also spoke of "this baby" or "a child." Women having abortions during the first trimester more often used terms such as "the pregnancy" or "a fetus." The experience of pregnancy and abortion is very different for second-trimester aborters. Those having early abortions may not perceive the fetus as a real being since quickening has not yet occurred and abortion is accomplished through some form of evacuation procedure. The abortion is over quickly and usually involves minimal pain. The woman has no direct contact with the products of conception that are removed. In contrast, women aborting at 16 weeks or later have often become aware of fetal movements, which tend to make the fetus seem much more real. Such abortions are usually done with instillation of prostaglandins or hypertonic saline. After a wait of 24–36 hours, there is a period of labor and the delivery of a recognizably human fetus. The entire process is much more like giving birth, and there is far more pain. Kaltreider found that 72% of first-trimester patients felt positive about their experience; this was true of only 37% of the second-trimester patients.

Medical Indications

The experience of women having abortions for medical reasons is even more at variance with the norm. Although accounting for only about 5% of all abortions, these women and their families are at highest risk for emotional trauma. Not only are these women usually in their second trimester, but to a much greater extent their pregnancies occur in a family context and are desired. The largest number of medical indications involve women pregnant with a defective fetus. Accurate assessment of fetal development and detection of anomalies or chromosomal aberrations often requires waiting until approximately 16 weeks gestation in order to do an amniocentesis. Laboratory evaluation may require another 2–4 weeks. As a result, most women are well into their second trimester before their test results are known. During the early weeks of pregnancy, the possibility that the fetus is normal and will be carried to term permits an emotional involvement with the fetus as a potential child. Much anticipatory bonding may occur during these weeks. When it becomes known that the fetus is not viable or not normal, the decision to have an abortion disrupts the bonding process. In general, there is a wait of at least 24–48 hours between the time the decision is made for abortion and the time the procedure is carried out. For the woman, this period—waiting to terminate the life of a moving fetus—can be agonizing (Adler & Kushnick, 1982). The situation's difficulty is further complicated by the nature of a second-trimester abortion. When genetic factors are involved, the reaction of both the woman and her mate may be further influenced by their feelings of responsibility for the defect, and they may experience a decrease in self-esteem as a result.

The parents' sense of responsibility attaches not only to the fetus's imperfection but also to the abortion. It would be easy to assume that both parents, even if suffering the effects of an altered self-concept and diminished self-esteem, would experience relief at escaping from the necessity for bearing and caring for a chronically or terminally ill child. This is often, but not universally, true. Some women feel afterward that they should have gone on and borne the child. The potential for the occurrence of grief reactions is therefore enhanced. Two recent studies illustrate this finding. In their study of 48 women undergoing second-trimester abortions for fetal malformation, Lloyd and Laurence (1985) found that 77% of the women interviewed experienced an acute grief reaction following termination of their pregnancies. Forty-six percent (22 women) remained symptomatic 6 months after their abortions. Similarly, Furlong and Black (1984) found that 9 of 15 families (60%) found the decision to abort very difficult. The researchers also assessed the effect on other children in the families and found negative behavioral changes in 19 of 22 children after the abortions. To some extent, these children may have been responding to anxiety and grief in their parents. Many, however, had received full explanations of the situation and the reasons for terminating the pregnancy. No doubt some identified with the fetus and were anxious about their own safety. Others, especially the older children, undoubtedly had personal grief about the loss of an anticipated sibling.

In summary, medically indicated abortions carry a profound threat to the self-esteem of both parents, who may see the defect of the child as indicative of a defect in themselves. This is particularly true of the woman, who may have had a deeply symbiotic emotional, as well as physical, relationship with the developing fetus. Although the abortion may appear to be the only practical response to the situation, the parents may grieve for the child who is lost, and for all the unmet expectations, hopes, and dreams that the child embodied.

Very Young Age

The pregnant adolescent is more vulnerable to a number of issues that may lead to a forced decision for abortion. Not only does she lack economic independence, but she may need the emotional support of her parents more deeply than does an older woman. At the same time, her own strength and ability to make autonomous decisions and take responsibility for the outcomes is still in the process of development. When the physical and emotional changes of pregnancy are superimposed on a young woman still unaccustomed to the changes in her body posed by puberty and adolescence, her vulnerability to real or imagined pressure for abortion is increased. At the same time, as Raphael (1983) notes, she may hesitate to verbalize her ambivalence for fear the abortion will be denied to her, or she may fear she will not have the strength to carry through with the procedure if she allows herself to recognize any wish to bear the child. Under such circumstances, she is more likely to suffer psychological distress after the abortion.

SOURCES OF ABORTION-RELATED STRESS

A major source of abortion-related stress is the disparity between the fact of having an abortion and the requirements of the individual's value system. Individuals have widely varying values relative to many of the issues concerned with abortion. However, in Western society at this time, pronatalist values are common. Most people grow up expecting to have children. This expectation is especially true for women, who often feel that having a baby validates, in important ways, their femininity. Those who choose not to carry a particular pregnancy to term may find that this decision conflicts with their emotional expectations. The conflict may be related to moral or ethical issues, or to the perception of the fetus as a person and to guilt or grief over feeling one has either killed one's child or refused it the possibility of life. As Simone de Beauvoir (1961) wrote in *The Second Sex*, "Many women are intimidated by a morality that for them retains its prestige even though they are unable to conform to it in their behavior; they inwardly respect the law they transgress, and they suffer from this transgression" (pp. 461–462). She goes on to describe the feelings of conflict that may affect a woman having an abortion.

> [In] her heart she often repudiates the interruption of pregnancy which she is seeking to obtain. She is divided against herself. Her natural tendency can well be to have the baby whose birth she is undertaking to prevent; even if she has no positive desire for maternity, she still feels uneasy about the dubious act she is engaged in. (p. 462)

Even though external or internal reality may dictate termination of a pregnancy, a client's self-concept may still suffer as a result. Grief may then attach either to the loss of the fetus (and the potential for nurturance or motherhood inherent in the fact of pregnancy) or to the loss of self-esteem or altered self-concept accompanying the abortion, or both.

A poignant example is the account written by Linda Bird Francke (1978). She and her second husband had three adolescent children when she found herself pregnant again. Her husband was contemplating a career change at the time, and Mrs. Francke had finally returned to the job market after being away from it for several years. A baby simply didn't fit into their lives at that time—financially, emotionally, or practically. So she had an abortion. But 2 years later she wrote:

> It certainly does make more sense not to be having a baby right now—we say that to each other all the time. But I have this ghost now. A very little ghost that only appears when I'm seeing something beautiful, like the full moon on the ocean last weekend. And the baby waves at me. And I wave at the baby. "Of course, we have room," I cry to the ghost. "Of course, we do." (p. 7)

Other couples Francke interviewed discussed their feelings after having experienced an abortion. Although their reactions ranged over the emotional spectrum, some did articulate a pervasive and enduring sense of loss or grief at having terminated their pregnancy. This was true for men as well as for women.

Religious background may contribute in important ways to a sense of guilt and sin, and these emotions may complicate feelings of grief. The viewpoint of the Catholic church is clearly and repeatedly communicated—that abortion is murder and a sin. Other religious denominations convey similar prohibitions. If religion is an important part of the inner life of the expectant parent, these messages may be very difficult to reconcile with another form of reality, which makes continuation of the pregnancy seem impossible. The individual may feel separation from an important source of support at the same time that the need for such support is particularly intense.

A THEORETICAL PERSPECTIVE

According to Rambo (1984), loss is defined as "being deprived of a valued object or person. What is valued varies widely and is highly individualistic" (p. 281). She further suggests that loss can be classified into one of the following categories: loss of (a) a significant or valued person, (b) some aspect of the self, (c) developmental skills, and (d) external objects. Although the emotional impact or meaning of pregnancy is highly variable, the loss of pregnancy may fit into any of these four categories. It may be perceived as loss of a valued person, particularly if the fetus is highly desired or if the woman or her mate personalize the fetus through fantasy. Especially for the woman, the symbiotic tie with the fetus may lead to perception of the abortion as a loss of part of herself. Developmental skills, while not specifically lost, may go unnurtured because they are not being practiced or implemented through parenting a child. Finally, external objects help people carry out their roles in life, and abortion of a fetus, which is in one sense an external object, may lead to feelings of loss of the potential parental role.

One of the factors that contributes to pathological grieving is the experience of multiple losses during a short period of time (Rambo, 1984). For some women, an abortion is only one of a constellation of losses. For example, the termination of the relationship through which the pregnancy occurred frequently compounds the problem. If the loss of a significant other occurs in combination with the loss of anticipated parenting—and possible diminution in self-concept—then the possibility for excessive or slowly resolving grief is increased.

THE CAREGIVER'S ROLE

The attitudes of caregivers play a major role in their ability to perceive post-abortion grief as a problem and to be willing to deal with it in an effective manner. Their attitudes, like those of other citizens, vary widely. While some individuals reject abortion completely, others accept abortion under some, but not all, circumstances. Abortion is widely accepted when the fetus suffers from an anomaly that would make the child's life difficult or short. Abortion for a pregnancy following rape or incest is also widely accepted. For some individuals, it is more difficult to accept an abortion that is performed for social rather than medical reasons. It is essential in all circumstances that caregivers clarify their own feelings and be able to hold them in abeyance when necessary. If this is not possible, then the client should be referred to someone who can listen nonjudgmentally and be realistically empathic and supportive.

The first of the useful abilities that a person should possess to be effective in dealing with post-abortion grief is a well-developed awareness that grief may follow abortions. Pathological or unresolved post-abortion grief is not a common occurrence. For those individuals affected, however, accurate identification and exploration is important. Women and their partners are not always aware that grief, anxiety, or sadness reactions are related to the fact of the abortion. Or, if aware, they may be reluctant to raise the issue—and this is especially likely to be the case in circumstances in which there is a sense of grief and loss involved. Having made the decision to terminate the pregnancy, it may seem inappropriate to the woman now to express, or even feel, grief as a result of that decision. She has "nobody to blame but herself" and so may choose not to share her feelings either out of a sense of personal responsibility or for fear of blame. In such a situation, the potential for losing sight of reality is increased. In addition, the individual may not make the connection between her current state and the abortion if the emotional impact is delayed. For these reasons, it is perhaps more important in dealing with post-abortion grief than with grief from other sources that the caregiver be aware of the potential for grief and take the initiative in exploring the client's perceptions and reactions.

Benoliel (1971) notes that some research suggests that a person is unlikely to grieve during the stages of impact and initial adaptation to loss. Grief appears as the person becomes more fully aware of the loss that has occurred. This is another reason, along with the initial relief patients feel at termination of the stress-producing situation, that professionals in the hospital or clinic where abortions occur may not see these negative effects. As relief at having completed the process without complications subsides, the reality of what has occurred comes to the fore. Health care providers involved in follow-up services or working in unrelated areas are more likely to be confronted by resultant emotional problems. At the same time, it is particularly important to be aware that grief reactions may not be identified in the health care setting. Women suffering from profoundly negative feelings about an abortion frequently miss follow-up appointments because they do not wish to be reminded of the place or the people connected with that experience (Raphael, 1983). Professionals in other areas may have a greater opportunity to identify problems and to intervene effectively.

In addition to remaining aware of the possibility for post-abortion grief, caregivers should be aware that, for some women, certain times may cause increased vulnerability. These include the time when the pregnancy would normally have reached term and the baby would have been born and anniversaries of the abortion or expected date of birth (Cavanar, 1978). The woman may then find herself with fantasies of how the baby would have looked, what it would have been named, and how she would have nurtured the child. Helping clients to identify any association between these vulnerable times and the onset of symptoms may help them to perceive the relationship between their symptoms and the abortion more clearly.

Caregivers should be aware that grief related to an abortion may also be found in other situations. For example, when a woman who has had a previous abortion later becomes pregnant, she may find that the abortion experience is reawakened and processed in a different way. Occasionally, professionals in a prenatal clinic or childbirth education class find that counseling to help the client separate the current pregnancy from the previous one is necessary, or the expectant mother may need help in dealing with emotional reactions precipitated by the fact of again being pregnant. In addition, women who later experience a spontaneous abortion or have fertility problems often feel that the abortion that they had may be in some way responsible. One young woman, who had two abortions followed by an ectopic pregnancy, was in the hospital for evaluation of a threatened spontaneous abortion. She told the nurse giving care, "Sometimes I wonder if I used up my chances with the abortions."

In order to give effective support, a caregiver needs to identify how the client sees herself, the values and beliefs that direct her behavior, and the stimuli causing her to act as she does. In the case of abortion, such identification involves assessing the reaction to the fact of abortion that grows out of the client's values and beliefs, and the impact of each of these factors, taken together, on the self-concept of the client. Questions that may be useful include "How do you see (or feel about) abortion in general?" "How do you respond to other people who have abortions?" and "Was deciding to have an abortion a difficult decision for you?" Open-ended questions that permit a client to explore and articulate her ideas and feelings will be most helpful. Such assessment may be difficult when the caregiver also has unresolved or negative feelings about abortion. If a caregiver is ambivalent, it may be difficult to listen with patience and empathy. As noted earlier, in such a situation it is essential that the patient be transferred to someone who is capable of dealing with the issues involved in a more straightforward manner. Caregivers working in an area where abortions are performed can refuse to work in a specific abortion situation if they have ambivalent feelings, and they often have resources available to assist in dealing with ambivalence. These options may not be available to the professional working in other areas where post-abortion grief may first appear. The ability to identify post-abortion grief as a possibility and make alternative arrangements when ambivalent feelings get in the way of helping the client is important.

There are specific activities that may be useful to an individual in exploring and dealing with clients who are experiencing post-abortion grief. The measures suggested in the treatment chapters of this book will be applicable here as well as in other grief situations. Rambo (1984) suggests that the following activities are appropriate interventions in dealing with grief in general. As paraphrased here, her categories are used as a framework for a discussion of dealing with post-abortion grief.

Be accepting of the griever's feelings and experiences. While acceptance is important in dealing with any topic that is highly charged emotionally, it is particularly important in working with post-abortion issues. The client in this situation is often highly ambivalent about the abortion and its effects. In essence, she is faced with negative, often unanticipated effects of an action that was deliberately chosen—or at least to which she agreed. Guilt and regret, therefore, are most often present in the individual suffering post-abortion stress, although the client may still judge abortion to have been the most appropriate choice. In addition, anger is common and may be projected onto other family members, the mate, society, or health care providers. It is important to listen—both to provide an opportunity for the client to verbalize feelings that are being experienced and to help clarify and label those feelings. It is essential for the caregiver to communicate an active intent to listen and to understand. Nonjudgmental responses that communicate an effort to understand will be most useful.

Encourage the griever to avoid making unnecessary or unreasonable demands on herself and to seek ways to reduce additional stresses. Abortion procedures, especially those taking place during the first trimester, are usually done on an outpatient basis, with the woman returning to her usual activities after a day or so. Even second-trimester abortions require only 1 or 2 days of hospitalization, and the expectation is for rapid physical recovery. Abortion is, however, in addition to being a termination of a pregnancy, "a surgical procedure that causes a complex of feelings related to invasion of the body" (Fogel, 1981, p. 532). Even when physical convalescence is rapid, a client may require a longer period for full emotional recovery. When sadness, anger, guilt, or other negative feelings are involved, it is important for the client to permit herself time to process the information, integrate what has happened into her self-concept, and deal with the emotions that have been aroused. Pressing herself to continue with daily activities as if nothing had happened may pose an additional stress. Recovering from abortion requires time—often several weeks to a few months, or even years. The client needs to feel justified in taking time to recuperate, even if this only involves giving herself permission to feel sad and distressed.

Similarly, the woman may not give herself permission to feel, or to express, sadness or other negative feelings about the abortion. Having chosen to terminate the pregnancy, the client may feel that it is inappropriate in some manner to then experience distress. It is important that the person working in a caregiving capacity help the woman to recognize that these two feelings are not incompatible. Relief may coexist with grief, and both feelings need to be accepted and worked through during the grieving period (Rando, 1984).

Explore, with the griever, what it is that makes her feel that the situation is hopeless or irreparable or that she is worthless and life is not worth living, and search for ways to overcome these conclusions. Frequently, dealing with these issues will elicit discussion of the patient's values and moral beliefs and a description of her stress over not having lived up to her values. Certainly, it is not possible to undo the abortion. The client may be asked about plans for another pregnancy since repetition and searching for a different outcome are not infrequent in these patients. This situation is particularly true in circumstances in which the original pregnancy, later aborted, was an attempt to solve some emotional issue. In general, grief over the current loss should be realistically dealt with and largely resolved before another pregnancy is attempted. If the external realities have not changed, then such a repetition may be catastrophic. Supporting the client emotionally may be necessary as she deals with her feelings about selecting an abortion.

A related function that the caregiver can fulfill is that of reality testing. Helping a client to review the situation as it was at the time the decision to abort was made can be helpful. This function may include reviewing the dynamics behind the occurrence of the pregnancy as well as the options that were available and the decisions that were made. Subsequent information or changes in circumstances might have made a different decision possible or desirable; however, the client made the decision for abortion based on information that was available to her at the time. Helping her to retrieve an awareness of the circumstances as they were thus may be helpful in reducing stress and regret. The hope is that the client will conclude "I made the best decision that I could make, given the circumstances as they seemed at that time."

Protect and bolster the griever's self-esteem and self-confidence. The opportunity to achieve these goals grows out of the process of interaction more than out of specific words of reassurance. As the client reviews her situation, the experience of being listened to and accepted by the caregiver, just as things are, may serve to remind her that she is worthy of regard and acceptance. Recognizing and commenting on instances in which the client dealt with difficult issues in a straightforward manner or with good intent (and one hopes with good results) can increase her awareness of her coping skills and her ability to handle difficult issues. If nothing else, the fact that she is talking about her distress communicates a desire for greater health and a willingness to work for that health. Recognition of that desire may help to bolster health-seeking activities during the times when painful feelings are dominant.

Buckles (1982) describes a technique that she finds useful in helping "stuck" clients work through post-abortion grief. This technique involves first helping the woman deal with the reality of the fetus and say goodbye to it. The procedure does not require forgetting the fetus but rather achieving a degree of detachment from the feelings associated with it. The second part of the process involves establishing positive remembrance of the significant meaning of the fetus's existence to the woman. From examples that Buckles gives, it appears that this step often takes the form of a specific activity (taking a trip, planting a tree, creating a picture) that expresses, for that woman, her attachment to the fetus and recognition of the part it played in her life. These symbolic activities may allow the woman to move beyond her grief and resume her life without undue sorrow.

CONCLUSION

The proportion of women who experience significant post-abortion stress is relatively small. Probably no more than 10% of all women having abortions respond negatively to the experience. Of these, almost all will have resolved the issues satisfactorily, without outside assistance, in 4-6 months. A few, however, perhaps 1% of those selecting abortion, will have grief, depression, or guilt reactions that more drastically interfere with their ability to function effectively. Caregivers who work with clients in all areas should be aware of the potential for post-abortion grief and of the need to assess the clients' recovery and coping strategies. Clients may not be aware of the relationship of their anxiety or depression to the abortion or may be unwilling to express their feelings for fear of blame or because of self-blame. Professionals, therefore, should maintain an awareness of the potential for this situation and be prepared to help clients explore and deal with residual feelings from an abortion experience.

References

Adler, B., & Kushnick, T. (1982). Genetic counseling in prenatally diagnosed trisomy 18 and 21: Psychosocial aspects. *Pediatrics, 69*, 94–99.

Belsey, E. M., Greer, H. S., Lai, S., Lewis, S., & Beard, R. W. (1977). Predictive factors in emotional response to abortion: King's termination study IV. *Social Science Medicine, 11*, 71–82.

Benoliel, J. Q. (1971). Assessments of loss and grief. *Journal of Thanatology, 1*(3), 182–194.

Buckles, N. B. (1982). Abortion: A technique for working through grief. *Journal of the American College Health Association, 30*, 181–182.

Cavanar, J. O., Jr., Maltbie, A. A., & Sullivan, J. L. (1978). Aftermath of abortion: Anniversary depression and abdominal pain. *Bulletin of the Menninger Clinic, 42*, 433–444.

David, H. P. (1978). Psychosocial studies of abortion in the United States. In H. P. David, H. L. Friedman, J. van der Tak, & M. J. Sevilla (Eds.), *Abortion in psychosocial perspective: Trends in transnational research* (pp. 77–115). New York: Springer.

De Beauvoir, S. (1961). *The second sex.* New York: Bantam.

Doane, B. K., & Quigley, B. Q. (1981). Psychiatric aspects of therapeutic abortion. *Canadian Medical Association Journal, 125*, 427–432.

Donovan, C. M., Greenspan, R., & Mittleman, F. (1975). Post-abortion psychiatric illness. *Nursing Digest, 3*, 12–16.

Fogel, C. I. (1981). Abortion. In C. I. Fogel & N. F. Woods (Eds.), *Health care of women: A nursing perspective* (pp. 524–538). St. Louis: Mosby.

Francke, L. B. (1978). *The ambivalence of abortion.* New York: Random House.

Furlong, R. M., & Black, R. B. (1984). Pregnancy termination for genetic indications: The impact on families. *Social Work in Health Care, 10*(1), 17–34.

Kaltreider, N. B. (1973). Emotional patterns related to delay in decision to seek legal abortion. *California Medicine, 118*(5), 23–27.

Lloyd, J., & Laurence, K. M. (1985). Sequelae and support after termination of pregnancy for fetal malformation. *British Medical Journal, 290*, 907–909.

Osofsky, J. D., Osofsky, H. J., & Rajan, R. (1973). Psychological effects of abortion: With emphasis upon immediate reactions and follow-up. In H. J. Osofsky & J D. Osofsky (Eds.), *The abortion experience: Psychological and medical impact* (pp. 188–205). New York: Harper and Row.

Rambo, B. J. (1984). Coping problems of the self-concept. In *Adaptation nursing: Assessment and intervention*. Philadelphia: Saunders.

Rando, T. A. (1984). *Grief, dying, and death: Clinical interventions for caregivers*. Champaign, IL: Research Press.

Raphael, B. (1983). *The anatomy of bereavement*. New York: Basic Books.

Chapter 15

Solomon's Mothers: Mourning in Mothers Who Relinquish Their Children for Adoption

Samuel Roll
Leverett Millen
Barbara Backlund

Samuel Roll was born in Colombia, South America. He received his doctorate from Pennsylvania State University and did postgraduate training at Yale. Currently, he is Professor of Psychology and Psychiatry at the University of New Mexico and is a consultant to the Instituto de Salud Mental in Monterrey, Mexico. He holds a diploma in both Clinical and Forensic Psychology. Dr. Roll has helped people work through bereavement under both normal and more unusual circumstances, such as sudden infant death, loss by adoption, and death from AIDS.

Leverett Millen received his doctorate in Clinical Psychology from Pennsylvania State University in 1973 and is a Diplomate in Clinical Psychology. He is currently Director of Training for the Doctoral Program in Counseling Psychology at New Mexico State University. In addition to his clinical and research interests, Dr. Millen has maintained a long-term active involvement in human rights and peace issues.

Barbara Backlund is a graduate student in the Department of Counseling and Educational Psychology at New Mexico State University. Her research interests include the bereavement process in women who have experienced the loss of a child and children's fear of nuclear war.

In some ways, every important human loss is like every other important human loss. The inevitable experience of loss that is a part of being human allows tragic art and literature to be understood by people of all cultures. Michelangelo's *Pieta*, in which the Blessed Virgin Mary holds her dead son on her lap, has a precise meaning for Christians. However, it also has an appeal that transcends Christianity and Western culture and addresses an issue that exists in the history and fearful anticipation of every human being—that is, the loss of a loved one and especially one's child.

Each individual loss also is unlike every other individual loss. The Blessed Virgin Mary contemplating the dead Christ, the Latin American mother contemplating her child killed in an act of terrorism, the anguished mother sitting at the bedside of her child dying of cancer— all of these women experience loss in a highly individualized and unique way that cannot be understood separately from the individual context and the highly subjective interpretation of a lifetime of experiences.

Loss of a child as a result of relinquishing the child for adoption is in some ways like every other loss. There is the inevitable and ubiquitous growing sense of attachment between two individuals. There is the problem of knowing that someone who was once part of you is no longer available. As with every loss, the mother who has relinquished a child can neither give nor receive protection, comfort, or support . . . and, if she gives love, it is love that cannot find its mark and must remain forever unrequited. It is frequently assumed that a woman who has relinquished her child for adoption has severed any emotional ties that have developed and has resumed her life with few adjustment problems. Our work with such women has contradicted this assumption. The experience of motherhood does not cease with the signing of surrender papers. Although the woman returns to her life, the child's existence— and her feelings of separation from that existence—becomes a painful part of her reality.

The mother who has relinquished her child for adoption is like the mother who holds the crucified Christ, the mother whose baby has been destroyed by an act of war, or the mother whose child has been taken by disease. Like all of these mothers, the mother who has given her child for adoption must go through the steps of mourning or be faced with haunting shadows of recurrent depression, waves of loneliness, and feelings of detachment and separation. But there is something special in the experience of the mother who has relinquished a child for adoption. Having been taught from birth that women are defined as mothers, mothers-to-be, or nonmothers, the mother who has relin-

quished her child is at best an anomaly and at worst a mystery to herself
and an object of scorn to self-righteous others.

THE "SOLOMON'S MOTHER"

The mourning of the mother who has given up her child for adoption
is special, and obstacles to her completing her mourning are legion.
Even our clumsy phrase "mother who has relinquished a child" reflects
our collective inability to find a conceptual framework to understand
and assist these women. Various other names have been offered—
equally clumsy and equally incomplete (Sorosky, Baran, & Pannor,
1978). The term "birthmother" expresses a biological reality, but it is
cold and uncaring and suggests the uncomfortable analogy of woman
as incubator, as if giving birth and motherhood were analogous. The
term "real mother" is doubly pejorative. It insults the mother who
adopts since she is the "nonreal" mother and insults the mother who
has relinquished the child since "real" is a belittling adjective and
underscores the notion that if one were the *real* mother one would *really*
have the child. The term "biological mother" has some of the same
drawbacks and reflects some of these same difficulties.

In seeking a term that would convey the psychological reality of a
woman who relinquishes her child for adoption, we turned to the Old
Testament. Most appropriate to our purpose was the incident in which
two women asked King Solomon to decide who was the actual mother
of the child they both claimed. Solomon decreed that the child would
be cut in half, with one part of the child to be given to each woman.
According to Scripture, the mother of the child, though she yearned to
be with her son, was willing to forego a relationship with the child so
that he would not be harmed. Solomon concluded that this sacrifice
revealed the depth of this woman's feelings for the child and acknowledged her as the mother. The term "Solomon's Mother," though not
perfect, does reflect the psychological reality of offering up one's child
in the hope of making the child's life better despite the prospect of
great pain. It also addresses an historical injustice. In the biblical story,
the lesson is that the people of Israel saw that the wisdom of God was in
Solomon. The other unspoken and unheralded lesson is that women are
often forced into the position of letting their children be separated
from them under the real or imagined belief that the children will be
better off. The story of Solomon does not so much concern the wisdom
of a judge as it illustrates the nobility of a woman. That the two women
in this tale were presented as harlots only adds to the appropriateness

of our choice. A harlot is defined as an immoral woman and is subject to the same biased and unsympathetic judgments that the relinquishing mother faces. The stigma of bearing an illegitimate child has a great impact on the decision to relinquish a child. This judgment of immorality also contributes to the lack of social support, which will make the relinquishing mother's situation more difficult.

Although the term "Solomon's Mother" reflects a psychological rather than biological reality and addresses the inherent nobility of women who have children they cannot keep, it is still an imperfect description. There cannot be a perfect term for these women and their experience, to which our society responds unjustly, unfairly, and inhumanely.

THE PROCESS OF MOURNING IN THE SOLOMON'S MOTHER

If actually relinquishing the child for adoption is the most difficult task to be faced by the Solomon's Mother, then her second most difficult trial is to experience the process of mourning for the loss. Through our work with women who have relinquished babies for adoption— some as recently as 3 months ago and some as long as 22 years—we have gradually learned how Solomon's Mothers have dealt with this second most difficult task. We must caution the reader that, in order to abstract what is common about these women, we have necessarily focused on group characteristics. We must continually remind ourselves and each other that we can abstract patterns but that these abstractions do not reflect the intensely individual suffering and uniquely courageous victories of the women with whom we have worked. There is one more warning: it is too easy to forget that, although the Solomon's Mother will undergo some experiences as a result of her status as part of this special group, her mourning is an example of the process of the universal and human attempt to deal with a very specific and particularly painful loss. Like everyone else, the Solomon's Mother must go through mourning and grief. It is useful to take a look at the process in this specific group in light of what we know about grief and mourning in other situations. A most thorough analysis of the grief experience is found in the work of Parkes (1972) and his colleagues, who have studied adult bereavement, primarily in widows. They delineated the following features of the typical post-death grief reaction:

1. A process of realization
2. An alarm reaction
3. An urge to search for and to find the lost person

4. Anger and guilt
5. Feelings of loss of self or mutilation
6. Identification phenomena

In the following discussion, we will attempt to describe each of these features in the grief reaction of the Solomon's Mother.

In the typical post-death grief reaction, it is through the process of realization that the bereaved moves from denial to acceptance of the loss. To come to terms with a loss, the individual must accept the loss as permanent. The yearning and searching impulses present in the grief reaction must be recognized as expressions of longing but cannot be used to deny the finality of the loss.

Like the person dealing with a death, the Solomon's Mother denies the permanence of her loss through a persisting experience of the child's presence in thought and fantasy. Many of our patients report repeated dreams of reunion with their children, a fact not surprising when considered in light of research done by Sorosky et al. (1978), which revealed that 82% of the birthmothers they interviewed were interested in a reunion with their relinquished child. The dreams of the Solomon's Mother, like those of other grieving persons, may be an attempt to deny finality of loss, but for the Solomon's Mother the continued existence of her child in reality is an added complexity.

Alarm, the second feature of the grief reaction, is a stress reaction often expressed through somatic symptoms and restless anxiety. Most of the widows in Parkes's study found the world had become a threatening and potentially dangerous place. Their somatic complaints included increased muscle tension, change in appetite, difficulty in sleeping, digestive disturbances, and headaches. Feelings of being panicky, irritable, tense, jumpy, and in a turmoil are symptoms of the phenomenon Parkes calls restless anxiety.

In his discussion of the situations that produce alarm, Parkes defines the lack of a haven or home in which the individual can feel secure as being especially alarming. For the Solomon's Mother, this same situation can exist, for the security of her life can be shattered as those around her begin to withdraw emotionally. At the same time that she is trying to deal with this emotional withdrawal, she often must leave her home until the birth of her child.

Loss of child in any circumstance is a situation clearly capable of producing a high state of alarm, and the relinquishment of a child is potentially devastating for the Solomon's Mother. This sense of alarm is seen in the words of one patient:

I was constantly on edge and felt as if I had to be on the watch out for something, but I was never sure what. Although I had never had physical problems before, every system in my body seemed to be calling out. Sometimes alternately and sometimes in combination, I would have headaches, backaches, joint aches, and even trouble seeing. I made frequent trips to doctors, only to be told there was nothing wrong with me. The worst is over. I still have periods in my life which I can only describe as being on edge.

The next component, searching, is an expected element in the typical post-death grief reaction. Although the bereaved can acknowledge that search for the dead person is irrational and futile, the impulse to search, in both thoughts and actions, is strong. The grieving person will scan a crowd looking for the dead person—someone with a certain walking gait, color of hair, or familiar article of clothing will momentarily become the deceased. The mannerisms or traits will have momentarily tied into the grieving person's visual memory of the dead person.

The Solomon's Mother also develops a visual picture of her relinquished child based on her own physical appearance, that of the child's father, or both. This picture helps to sustain fantasies of an accidental meeting with the child. Typical is the report of one of our patients, who tells of being startled by any child with large dark eyes and black hair. These were the features she visualized for the child she had given up 6 years earlier.

The urge to search is complicated for the Solomon's Mother since her searching impulses are not irrational, and further, may not be futile. Unlike the grieving person who eventually comes to terms with the fact that the lost person is truly dead, the Solomon's Mother knows her child is alive. Future contact has a possibility of being more than a fantasy. Beyond the hopes of an accidental meeting is the reality of successful reunions between Solomon's Mothers and their relinquished children. Such meetings may result from individual searches by the child or the mother, or from searches facilitated through such organizations as Orphan Voyage or Adoptees' Liberty Movement Association. These possibilities foster conscious and unconscious hopes in the Solomon's Mother that she may eventually be reunited with her child and thus discourage the resolution of search fantasies. This unresolved search component also interferes with the realization process in grief.

The fourth feature of the grief reaction concerns the feelings of anger and guilt. Bowlby (1963) has shown that the angry protest seen in grieving is a normal reaction to separation. The anger felt by the bereaved can be experienced toward oneself for not preventing the loss, toward the lost person for leaving, or toward third parties who are perceived as having helped bring about the loss.

Self-reproach and guilt in the typical post-death grief reaction most often are part of a constellation of feelings focusing on not having done enough to prevent the loss. With time, there is a diminution of self-reproach as the bereaved person realizes that the loss was inevitable and beyond her control. Unlike the typical grieving person, the Solomon's Mother feels guilt and anger at herself that intensify with the passage of time as she comprehends her role in setting up her loss and experiences consequent feelings of remorse and grief. One of our patients expressed this frequent realization in a dream 4 years after relinquishing her son:

> I am walking with a child in a city. I allow the child to wander off. I begin to be apprehensive that the child is too far from me and go to retrieve him, but increasingly large numbers of people file in between me and my son. I search frantically, but am unable to find him and I realize that it is my fault he is lost.

The guilt experienced by the Solomon's Mother is intensified because, unlike the person who suffers a loss through death, she is blamed by herself and others for the loss since it is she who actually relinquished the child.

According to Parkes, during a grief reaction, anger at the lost person takes the form of personalizing the loss with such questions as Why did you leave me? and Why have you caused me this pain? Generally, the passage of time and the expression of such reproaches mitigate this anger. The Solomon's Mother, however, sees the child's absence as a result of her own actions and thus cannot justify any anger. Intensifying this lack of justification for her anger at the lost person is the reality of a child as helpless and innocent. Given these factors, the Solomon's Mother is unable to allow herself to feel anger, let alone express anger toward the child.

It is only in a dream 9 years after relinquishment that this Solomon's Mother was able to explore rage at her lost child:

> In this dream, I am reading or sewing, I can't tell which. My child comes to me and interrupts. Initially, I push her away. Eventually, I push her away with such vehemence that she is smashed right against the furniture. I realize that I had hurt her more than I intended.

This kind of feeling needs to be expressed and understood to mitigate anger and guilt. However, the Solomon's Mother's situation does not readily allow for expression, exploration, or mitigation of these frightening feelings. Anger and guilt may not be eased with time as is the case in the normal grief process.

In addition to anger at themselves and at the lost persons, many of the widows in Parkes's study expressed anger and reproach at the medical personnel who had been unable to prevent the loss of the women's husbands. Although acknowledging that some of this anger, which took the form of complaint about failure and delay in diagnosis, may have been justified, Parkes interprets such bitterness as part of the bereavement process. Attempting to assign blame and responsibility for the death to third parties is seen as an effort to somehow prevent or undo the loss. With acceptance of the finality of the loss, the urge to blame and attribute responsibility to third parties diminished.

In contrast, the Solomon's Mother's anger at third parties appears to intensify rather than diminish with time. Her experience with third parties includes contact with professionals whose words are those of encouragement and comfort, yet whose actions involve manipulations at a level many Solomon's Mothers perceive as coercive. Anger may also be directed toward family members who are unable to offer the necessary support. Most of our patients told of deep bitterness toward many of the third parties involved when they relinquished their children. Most reported that social workers and counselors offered no options, emphasized that others could provide better lives for their children, and insisted that they should leave past mistakes behind them. Even parents who had been supportive during the pregnancy required that the mothers omit any mention of this part of their lives following the relinquishment of the child. Clearly, the bitterness of many Solomon's Mothers toward third parties was legitimate, and it was a bitterness that deepened and distorted the bereavement process.

The fifth feature of the grief reaction is characterized by feelings of loss of self and mutilation. With time, the intensity of these feelings of emptiness and destruction diminishes as the bereaved individual resumes and reconstructs her life without the lost person. One Solomon's Mother describes her experience of loss of self like this: "I felt like pieces of a person, instead of a whole person." Another of our patients conveys the continual feeling of emptiness in this way, despite a full life that includes a child and a career, a life that she defines as fulfilling: "No matter what happens, no matter how much happiness surrounds me, there is a haunting shadow of sadness." Yet another patient reports the feeling as follows: "Even in my happiest moments, there is an almost physical sense of loss; sometimes it is accompanied by a gnawing feeling in my abdomen halfway between discomfort and pain."

A further elaboration of the sense of loss and mutilation is vividly depicted in this Solomon's Mother's description of a dream:

> I had a dream during which I felt an intense pulling and stretching. I put my hand under my blouse to try to touch where I had the feeling. No matter which part of my body I touched, the tugging and pulling moved to some other part. I finally woke up and found I was sweating and for the rest of the day, I was haunted by the feeling of being broken or damaged in some undefinable way. I sometimes feel I will never be complete.

The grieving person's experience of emptiness and loss of self are exacerbated in the Solomon's Mother by the reality of the child's having indeed been a part of her physically as well as emotionally.

The sixth component of the bereavement reaction, the feeling of identification, was noted by Freud when he wrote, "If one has lost a love object or has been obliged to give it up, one often compensates oneself by identifying oneself with it" (1933/1964, p. 63). Like most other mechanisms designed to avoid the painful reality of loss, identification is only partially successful. The bereaved person gradually accepts a sense of separateness from the lost person and rebuilds a new identity that includes the lost person and her changed life situation.

Identification phenomena in the Solomon's Mother are intensified as a result of the 9 months of carrying the child within her. The reality of the pregnancy facilitates the woman's sense of a presence of the lost child and slows down the letting go necessary for the working through of grief and the building of a new identity separate from the lost person. One of our patients reports that 3 years after her pregnancy she still experiences some of the sensation of the baby's moving inside of her, as occurred during the pregnancy. For this Solomon's Mother, the sense of the child's continuing presence reduces her ability to deal with her feelings of loss.

It is apparent from this comparison of grief following death with grief following the relinquishment of a child that the Solomon's Mother confronts some special problems in coming to terms with her feelings. First, in the Solomon's Mother, the process of realizing loss may be incomplete because the actual existence of the child intrudes on her acceptance of finality. Second, her alarm reaction may be shattering because it involves not only the loss of a child, but also involves the loss of her home and the support of those around her. Third, in addition to compounding the problem of realizing loss, the existence of the living child may complicate the urge to search because the possibility for reunion is real, unlike the possibility of reunion with a person lost through death. Fourth, working through guilt and even anger in this group is more complicated than for those mourning a loss through death: the Solomon's Mother may feel particularly responsible for giving up her child and may thus experience a heightened sense of self-reproach. She may be unable to express, or even acknowledge, anger toward the lost child since that child can be perceived only as being helpless and innocent. Further, the working through of anger and guilt are impeded because of the secretive, often shameful nature of her experience. Fifth, the bitterness the Solomon's Mother feels toward others may in many cases be justified; frequently, she experiences little sympathy or understanding from parents, social workers, and society at large. Finally, the feelings of loss of self and the identification phenomena typically experienced after death are distorted and con-founded in this situation by the connection that had developed during the pregnancy between the Solomon's Mother and her child.

The foregoing discussion enumerates the ways in which the major aspects of the bereavement reaction are confounded and impeded in the Solomon's Mother. We must conclude from this information that her experience of mourning is inhibited and prolonged.

RECOMMENDATIONS FOR FACILITATING GRIEF WORK

What we have learned from our work with Solomon's Mothers is that the emotional bond they develop with their children must not be denied, overlooked, or denigrated. Rather, the connection must be viewed as valid, and the break occurring at the time of relinquishment must be recognized and grieved. Among those factors delaying or suppressing grief that we found to be most relevant to the experience of the Solomon's Mother are the following:

1. The loss may be socially stigmatizing (Bowlby, 1963).
2. External events prevent the expression of the feelings of loss (Volkan, 1970).
3. Uncertainty may exist as to whether or not there is an actual loss (Greenblatt, 1978).
4. There may be an absence of mourning at the normal and expected time (Volkan, 1970).
5. Mourning rituals are often lacking (Lindemann, 1944).

The following recommendations are made in the effort to address these factors and to facilitate grief work with Solomon's Mothers.

Destigmatizing the Relinquishment

A loss viewed as real and valid can be more easily grieved than a loss shrouded in secrecy and shame. We are aware that destigmatizing the relinquishment decision will be a slow, difficult process since that decision directly confronts certain social values about women, the nuclear family, and adoption. We are therefore recommending that graduate schools and professional associations sponsor workshops exploring the issues of women as mothers, legitimacy, and open adoption.

Counseling during the Relinquishment Process

1. *Exploration of alternatives.* It is imperative that a woman who is considering relinquishment be satisfied that this decision is the result of a process of exploration of all possible alternatives, including single parenthood, foster care, and abortion.

2. *Examination of previous experiences with loss.* Researchers have suggested that failure to work through prior experiences with separation and death predisposes the bereaved to pathological grief reactions (Lindemann, 1944; Volkan, 1970). We are therefore proposing that an indispensable aspect of counseling with a Solomon's Mother is an in-depth probing of her history of loss.

3. *Realistic appraisal of expectations regarding a possible grief reaction.* A number of our patients reported that social workers, family, and friends assured them that any sadness or anguish about the relinquishment would quickly subside. Our work with Solomon's Mothers, as well as prior research, clearly testifies to the intensity of the continuing emotional trauma set off by the relinquishment (Lifton, 1979; Sorosky et al., 1978).

Support for the Mourning Process

In light of the observation that absence of mourning distorts the grief response, we are recommending the following types of support for the mourning process:

1. *Availability of mourning ritual.* Symbolic leave-taking ceremonies, such as funerals, have a long history as an acknowledgment of loss. We are convinced that, for the Solomon's Mother, it would be useful to have a rite or an alternate method to publicly acknowledge loss.

2. *Grief counseling.* The Solomon's Mother's expression of grief is distorted and delayed by denial of her loss, both by herself and others. The counseling process must validate the reality of this loss and aid the Solomon's Mother in exploration and expression of her guilt and anger, both toward herself and toward those around her.

An adjunct to grief counseling can be dream analysis. If a dream is taken as a statement of internal experience and represents notions about the dreamer's world, then the dream will be valuable for reflecting the Solomon's Mother's unique construction of her world and will help facilitate her grief work (Roll & Millen, 1979).

It is not clear from presently available data to what degree the Solomon's Mothers who make up our clinical sample are similar to or different from Solomon's Mothers who have not sought psychotherapy or mothers who have lost a child through stillbirth or during infancy. In our clinical sample, at least, it is evident that the experience of relinquishing a child provokes feelings of intense loss, enduring panic, and unresolved anger; episodes of searching for the lost child in waking life or dreams; a sense of incompleteness. We recommend that steps be taken to reduce the intensity of this inhibited mourning.

Throughout this discussion, we have written in terms of "we" and "they." However, the characteristics that differentiate those of us who are and are not Solomon's Mothers are accidents of gender, circumstance, and history, not the result of differences in personality, values, and morality. If we learn about Solomon's Mothers and do not learn about ourselves, we learn about neither.

References

Bowlby, J. (1963). Pathological mourning and childhood mourning. *Journal of the American Psychoanalytic Association, 11*, 500–541.

Freud, S. (1964). *New introductory lectures on psychoanalysis* (Vol. 31). (J. Strachey, Ed. and Trans.). London: Hogarth. (Original work published 1933)

Greenblatt, M. (1978). The grieving spouse. *American Journal of Psychiatry, 135*(1), 43–47.

Lifton, B. J. (1979). *Lost and found: The adoption experience*. New York: Dial.

Lindemann, E. (1944). Symptomatology and management of acute grief. *American Journal of Psychiatry, 101*, 141–148.

Parkes, C. M. (1972). *Bereavement: Studies of grief in adult life*. New York: International Universities Press.

Roll, S., & Millen, L. (1979). The friend as represented in the dreams of late adolescents: Friendship without rose-colored glasses. *Adolescence, 14*(54), 255–275.

Sorosky, A. D., Baran, A., & Pannor, R. (1978). *The adoption triangle: The effects of the sealed record on adoptees, birth parents, and adoptive parents*. Garden City, NY: Anchor/ Doubleday.

Volkan, V. (1970). Typical findings in pathological grief. *Psychiatric Quarterly, 44*, 231–250.

Chapter 16
Missing Children

Gweneth M. Lloyd
Carolyn Zogg

Gweneth M. Lloyd received her Master of Social Work in 1983 from Columbia University School of Social Work in New York, and her B.A. degree in Elementary Education and Social Work in 1979 from Skidmore College in Saratoga Springs, New York. She is currently a clinical social worker at the Psychological Counseling Center at the State University of New York, College at New Paltz. In addition she works as a part-time consultant at the IBM Employee Assistance Program. She is also a member of the Child Find Board of Directors.

Carolyn Zogg is Associate Director of Child Find of America, Inc., one of the oldest private, nonprofit agencies that registers, searches for, and assists in the location of missing children. A graduate of Syracuse University with a B.A. degree, Ms. Zogg is also a licensed lay reader in the Episcopal Diocese of New York.

Although the family in our culture does not function as an isolated entity, immunized from life's daily problems and crises, its health is largely contingent upon its ability to ward off external threats to its emotional, physical, and financial well-being. Thus, an overall goal of the family as it goes through the family life cycle is to achieve homeostasis, or equilibrium, between internal and external forces. The family's ability to successfully reach and maintain that state of equilibrium is determined by many factors, including the family structure, and particularly the clarity of boundaries between parental and sibling subsystems, the family's ego strength, its coping capacity, its problem-solving skills, and its ability to effectively utilize external support systems.

Even the most intact family frequently exhausts its crisis-meeting resources when dealing with the internal crisis resulting from the abduction of a child. The following statement from one mother of a missing child indicates some of the stress and emotional problems with which the family must cope:

> I cannot very well explain my feelings toward what happened. The only thing I can say is that I am very sad and depressed. Since that day I feel something is wrong with my mind. I sometimes forget things. I forget what I'm doing. There is not a day that passes by which I don't pray for him [her missing son] and beg God to bring him back to me. No one here knows how I feel, but people ask me if I have found him. I feel desperate. I just say no. I wish this not to happen to any mother—not even to my worst enemy.

According to the National Center for Missing and Exploited Children, approximately 15 million children are missing from their homes every year, from every social, economic, geographic, racial, and ethnic group (Gelman et al., 1984 March 19). The reliability of any statistics on the number of missing children is controversial, but the figures do suggest the degree of vulnerability of children and the number of parents and other family members who are traumatized by the crisis.

The crisis a family experiences when a child is missing may totally disorganize the family system, destroying the level of homeostasis. Family members are suddenly confronted with behavior changes in other family members—sometimes manifested through hostility, abusive language, drinking, breaking the law, and severe depression—as means of adapting to stress. Extended family members, friends, neighbors, classmates, clergy, and other people external to the immediate family structure become involved with the victim's family, contributing to its disorganization and dismemberment. The loss of a child also brings about a sense of demoralization, isolation, guilt, shame, and diffidence within family members, particularly parents. Lives may be drastically and permanently altered. A statement of one parent illustrates the depth of demoralization and structural change that can be experienced: "When my child was stolen many years ago, people knew nothing of the problem, and I received so much criticism from ignorant people that I began denying I had a child to avoid the pain."

FAMILY REACTIONS

The family's response to the crisis of a missing child can be compared with the bereavement process experienced by families confronted with the death of a family member, although the family suffering loss through death must accept, at least eventually, the finality of death. For the family of a missing child, there is no final acceptance. To accept that the child will never be found—whether dead or alive—is to deny the very existence of the child; it also signifies the loss of hope. As a result of the lack of acceptance, however, family members spend the remainder of their lives living in hope and disarray within the family structure. The child is often living in hope and disarray as well: hope of one day being found or hope for a stable lifestyle. Neither the family nor the child is able to achieve a state of equilibrium until the crisis is finally resolved.

Kübler-Ross, in her book on terminally ill patients and their families (1969), cites different stages of adjustment experienced by both patient and family in dealing with death and the process of dying. As identified by Kübler-Ross, the five stages the terminally ill patient experiences when confronted with the inevitability of death are denial and isolation, anger, bargaining, depression, and, finally, acceptance. Meanwhile, the family goes through similar stages of denial and anger, followed by stages of guilt, resentment, and preparatory grief as a form of acceptance. During these stages the family system becomes highly disorganized, and it remains in turmoil until the family is able to accept its loss and resolve its grief, as evidenced by the ability to remember completely and realistically the pleasure and disappointments of the lost relationship (Engel, 1964).

Families of missing children go through similar stages as they struggle to cope with the loss of their child and the uncertainty of the child's fate. Stages of denial, anger, guilt, and depression are clearly identifiable, and there is no resolution until the child is located and reunited with the family or his fate is known.

Denial is a major defense against the acceptance of reality, and it is the primary defense used by the parents and family of a missing child. Initially, the parents and family members react with shock and disbelief;

the possibility of their child being abducted is the last thought on their minds. This shock and disbelief is succeeded by a period of action-oriented momentum in which the parents frantically contact friends, other family members, school, neighbors, and organizations to which the child belonged in an effort to locate the child. When this approach fails, search crews consisting of family, friends, neighbors, local organizations, and law enforcement officers are organized. The search may last for days or weeks, with little or no evidence of the missing child. To the parents and family, the search is endless.

Law enforcement authorities and other concerned agencies are often, ironically, a common source of the anger experienced by the family of a missing child. A parent or family member, already panic-stricken and looking toward the authorities as a "salvation," may be told that nothing can be done unless the child has been gone for 24 hours. Or the search may be terminated after a few days by authorities who have a long list of unsolved cases, including missing child cases in which parents are demanding special attention.

The stages of guilt and depression experienced by families are triggered by feelings of helplessness and impotence often precipitated by ongoing but unproductive efforts of helping agencies. Self-blaming is a primary manifestation of the guilt. Parents begin to question their accountability for the tragedy and will sometimes insist on accepting full responsibility for abductions. This reaction seems to be most prevalent when the abduction is by the other parent. Parents whose child is taken tend to feel they could have predicted and perhaps prevented the abduction. This guilt complex is further exemplified by obsessive thoughts of things never done for the child prior to the abduction.

While much of the depression parents and other family members suffer stems from guilt, anger, and helplessness, a larger part is caused by external factors. Frequently, the parents' financial resources are severely depleted, if not exhausted, through hiring private detectives or traveling from one end of the country to the other to investigate clues. Siblings in the family subsystem become highly susceptible to emotional deprivation and may begin to gradually have emotional and behavioral problems if the parents' attention remains focused on the missing child. That emotional deprivation and resulting problems may cause the sibling to seek attention by acting-out behavior, ranging from school truancy and drug and alcohol abuse in the older siblings to enuresis or violent temper tantrums in the younger family members. Additionally, two-parent families must deal with stress in the marital relationship. During the crisis over a missing child, a parent's physical and emotional energies become overextended and focused on internal and external family matters. Whether the marriage or relationship will survive depends largely on the state of the relationship prior to the crisis.

IMPLICATIONS FOR PRACTITIONERS

Appropriate intervention can be best realized if health care practitioners first make a thorough assessment of family system dynamics. The assessment should focus on: (1) the family's psychosocial history, (2) the family's previous and present coping style—particularly for crisis situations, (3) the family's use or abuse of alcohol and drugs, and (4) the family's ego strengths and weaknesses. Additionally, clinical consideration must be given to the family in the following areas:

Coping with work

Coping with routine matters

Dealing with reality and family finances

Dealing with the community

Dealing with the authorities

Dealing with siblings

Dealing with the spouse

Dealing with the media and rewards

Dealing with "crazies"

Dealing with celebrity status (exposure to the media)

Dealing with an emotional roller coaster (self)

Dealing with suspicious and self-enforced isolation

Dealing with loss of self-confidence and self-esteem

Dealing with guilt

Dealing with feelings about giving up the search

Laughing and finding humor in life

Dealing with the family's communication style

Changing family roles

Dealing with the family's value system

Each of these factors must be carefully assessed to determine the degree of stress that each imposes on the family and the specific way in which the family is affected by it. In the field of victimology, the biochemical nature of stress is unknown. Therefore, practitioners must also be aware of the somatic complaints of families of missing children in order to assess the psychosomatic manifestation of the stress related to such a crisis.

Practitioners need to pay particular attention to the communication style of the family, which may be best dramatized in the practitioner's office. In some families the missing child may be a taboo subject, resulting in strained or closed communication in the family, with everyone making an effort to avoid mention of the child's name or related issues. In other families, the opposite effect occurs. Discussion of the missing child may supersede any other topic of discussion and remain the central family conversation piece. This type of communication may be equally as closed since it prohibits discussion of other relevant family matters. In still other families, the missing child is a scapegoat for other family problems, including those precipitated by the crisis itself. The practitioner will need to be aware of these problems, and when other family issues are being avoided, carefully plan intervention strategies.

A safe environment conducive to ventilation of feelings and facilitation of discussion around such feelings is also a must for the effective practitioner. The family may develop a sense of paranoia, which must be carefully assessed so as to avoid misdiagnosis as thought disorder. Parents may become overly protective of their other children, which may be dysfunctional, particularly if the children are middle to late adolescents. Siblings may also develop phobic reactions, such as fear of being outside or away from the family. How parents and siblings deal with the anniversary date of the abduction, Mother's Day, and the child's birthday is critical for intervention purposes. Some families choose to keep everything of the missing child exactly as the child left it. Some parents may even continue to buy birthday and other special holiday gifts for the missing child.

Parents of abducted children are a relatively ignored group. They suffer and have significant pain, guilt, and confusion, but little psychological and emotional help is available to them. The role of the practitioner must be to assist the family in (1) mourning the loss of a loved family member, (2) reestablishing a functional level of family homeostasis by clarifying roles and boundaries, and (3) establishing effective patterns of communication. The practitioner must avoid being pulled into the family dilemma of whether or not the missing child will ever be found. Therapeutic work cannot be accomplished if the practitioner gets involved in that dilemma; instead the focus of work should be on the here and now.

Untold numbers of people experience severe and continuing trauma due to personal tragedy. In order to survive as individuals and families, they must learn to cope and endure that trauma, especially in the case of missing children. Recognizing the factors at work in their response to the trauma and taking the first steps to this awareness helps people come to grips with their life and take positive actions to improve it. The walls individuals build to survive need the doors and windows of family and community opened for nurturing and support. While no one can understand how a victim feels—a victim child, brother, sister, grandparent, cousin, aunt, uncle, friend, or classmate—identifying and acknowledging the problem is the first path to recovery and survival. The evidence overwhelmingly points to the need for support, the need to meet other victims traumatized by shock, and the need for clinical practitioners to recognize the severe clinical depression and stress that can be found within the family and community of a missing child.

References

Engel, G. (1964). Grief and grieving. *American Journal of Nursing, 64*(9), 93–98.

Gelman, D., Agrest, S., McCormick, J., Abramson, P., Finke Greenburg, N., Zabarsky, M., Morris, H., & Namueth, T. (1984, March 19). Stolen children. *Newsweek,* pp. 78–86.

Kübler-Ross, E. (1969). *On death and dying.* New York: Macmillan.

Chapter 17

Missing in Action

Edna Jo Hunter

Dr. Edna Jo Hunter received her B.A. from the University of California at Berkeley, her M.A. from San Diego State University, and her Ph.D. from the United States International University. She is currently on the faculty of the United States International University where she serves as Research Professor and Director of the Family Research Center. During the 1985–86 school year, she was a Distinguished Visiting Professor in the Department of Behavioral Sciences and Leadership at the United States Military Academy. From 1967 to 1978, Dr. Hunter served as a research psychologist at the Naval Health Research Center (NHRC), San Diego. At NHRC she devoted 5 years to sleep research and 7 years to a longitudinal study of Vietnam POW/MIAs and their families while she served as Acting Director, Administrative Director, and Head of Family Studies at the Center for Prisoner of War Studies. Dr. Hunter is a licensed psychologist in the state of California. In 1983 she was named "Distinguished Military Psychologist" by the American Psychological Association. She has written/edited over 100 journal articles and book chapters and 8 books.

The author acknowledges the assistance of Dr. Therese A. Rando in the writing of this chapter.

*This chapter is dedicated to all mothers and
fathers whose sons were listed as missing in
action during wartime. These parents wait
and hope for resolution of their grief in a
vacuum their tears have been unable to fill.*

There is a special group of parents who suffer from a particular type
of bereavement that casts them into chronic unresolved grief. These
are the parents of men who still remain missing in action after the
release of 566 American servicemen in 1973 from prisoner of war
(POW) captivity in Vietnam. According to figures issued through the
National League of Families of American Prisoners of War and Missing
in Southeast Asia (1985), 2,441 Americans remain missing and unac-
counted for—1,797 in Vietnam, 556 in Laos, 82 in Cambodia, and 6
elsewhere. As of November 1, 1985, there had been 805 reported
firsthand live sightings of American POWs in Indochina. Most of these
reports (85%) are thought to relate to individuals who have since left
Indochina, men who have died, and possibly fabricated reports. However, 119 men reportedly seen in the 805 live sightings remain unac-
counted for, a fact that causes continuing ambiguity for the parents
and nurtures the persisting hope that their sons may still be alive
somewhere in Southeast Asia. It must be remembered that after the
French defeat at Dien Bien Phu, Vietnam continued to release live
POWs for 16 years, which also gives faint hope to these parents who
wait.

The stress of these parents' unresolved grief continues today—over
20 years after the conflict began in 1964. The words of one MIA
mother, Sally Kennedy (personal communication, 1986), aptly describe
the emotional experience of attempting to cope with this unique type
of grief:

> My son, Jack, was a U.S. Air Force pilot and 24 years old when he
> became missing in action in South Vietnam. . . . I think the worst
> emotion I have experienced is the frustration of not knowing if Jack is
> alive or dead. Such frustration, as no one can imagine, takes over
> when there is no one to turn to who can find out what happened. . . .
> The real tragedy comes with the devastating realization of how slow
> the government process is, particularly with this issue. After the peace
> treaty and our men came home, no one wanted to talk or hear about
> the Vietnam war. So we spent years of heartbreaking work with the
> National League of Families of American Prisoners and Missing in
> Southeast Asia trying to get our government and the peoples of the
> world interested enough to do something about resolving this issue. . . .
> Besides the tragedy of losing a son, the indifference of the government,
> other people, and even friends, is difficult to deal with. There have

been many, many times when I think I'll just have to give up on this; we are not getting anywhere. Then almost immediately I realize I can't give up. My son might be alive and if I don't do all that is humanly possible, how could I deal with that? How can anyone turn away from this nation's obligation of determining what happened to all those missing men who went to Vietnam when called? (S. Kennedy, personal communication, May, 1986)

This chapter examines the unusual experience of being the parent of a serviceman missing in action. Most of the research with MIA families has focused on POW/MIA wives and children, not on the parents. Nonetheless, as part of the planning stage for the 7-year family study carried out at the Center for Prisoner of War Studies (CPWS) from 1971 to 1978 (Hunter, 1984), all "dependent" Army, Navy, and Marine Corps POW/MIA parents (those receiving monthly allotments from their sons) were interviewed by the research staff. However, that particular group of family members was not included in the longitudinal study of the Army, Navy, and Marine Corps families, and little is known of how they have coped over time.

As with bereaved parents in general, MIA parents have received insufficient attention, despite the preliminary CPWS finding that their grief and suffering in fact may be deeper and more long lasting than that of the wives and children of the missing men. This chapter attempts to reconcile this oversight by examining the unique stresses of MIA families and integrating what is known about the grief of *any* parent who loses an adult child, and then extrapolating that knowledge to MIA parents. The chapter concludes with treatment suggestions for caregivers working with this special population.

THE UNIQUE STRESSES OF MIA FAMILIES

Perhaps by relating an incident that occurred shortly after the return of the POWs in 1973, a point can be made about how all-encompassing the MIA situation had become. One MIA family member related a dream she had had the previous night. This particular woman was a real estate salesperson and usually spent considerable time each day driving about town in her automobile. In this dream she was going about her job as usual. However, in the backseat of the station wagon was the body of her missing husband. Nonchalantly, she continued showing property to her clients, going about her job as if there were absolutely nothing unusual about having her husband's body in the backseat.

"Dr. Hunter," she exclaimed, "that's precisely the way it is. I'm *sure* he's dead, and yet I can't bury him. He's always with me wherever I go" (Hunter, 1982). Such is an example of one of the MIA family members whom I have frequently referred to as "combat casualties who remain at home" (Hunter, 1980).

These MIA families continue to grieve because there is no way their losses can become reality. They continue to wait and hope and pray for resolution. Stuck in an emotional limbo, not knowing for certain if their loved ones are alive or dead, they experience unresolved grief as a way of life. The stress for family members is both prolonged and indefinite. Moreover, the situation is ambiguous and without guidelines. It includes the threat of death or permanent loss of the family member, but without confirmation. This threat is ongoing; it does not end in 1 hour, 1 week, 1 month, or even 1 year. Despite the continuing passage of years, the families often cannot "accept" the loss of their missing members. Consequently, both chronic and intermittent feelings of helplessness, hopelessness, powerlessness, anger, guilt, and rage combine to prevent rapid and effective coping strategies from developing within the family system.

According to Robert White (1976), there are three major tasks that must be met if successful adaptation to a crisis is to be achieved: (1) adequate information about the environment must be obtained, (2) satisfactory internal conditions both for action and for processing information must be maintained, and (3) freedom of movement or autonomy must be secured. If we examine those three requirements one by one, it becomes apparent MIA parents possess none of the requirements necessary for adaptation.

First, *adequate information about the environment* must be obtained. MIA parents do not have adequate information. Parents and families had little, if any, information about the details of their loved ones' casualties during the war years. They were not even allowed access to the men's casualty files to assist them in reaching their own decisions as to whether or not the men might return at the end of hostilities.

The second requirement for successful adaptation is that *satisfactory internal conditions for action and for processing information* must be available. In the early years of the Vietnam conflict, families were told not to tell others their sons (or husbands) were missing. They were expected to be "good" and "brave," not to give up hope, and not to grieve over their loss. They were cautioned not to discuss their missing loved one with *anyone*. They were warned that talking about the situation might bring harm either to themselves or their loved ones in captivity. In actuality, this restriction was more likely made to protect the government's contention of noninvolvement in Southeast Asia. Only "next of kin" were informed of the casualty initially and then updated on new developments should there be any. There were instances in which daughters-in-law did not share the information of their husbands' missing status with their in-laws and in which wives did not confide in their children concerning the loss of their fathers. Thus, there was no support from other family members or friends who could have assisted these MIA families with their grieving process. How different for families whose loved ones were killed in action (KIA) in Vietnam. Their loved ones were dead; thus, the families could begin the grieving process and get it over with.

The third and final requirement for adaptation to crises is that *there must be freedom of movement or autonomy.* For the most part, MIA parents did not have this freedom. Most missing men were married. The wives, not the parents, were considered "primary next of kin." If speeches were to be made or trips to be taken to foreign embassies to advocate for better treatment for POWs or an accounting of MIAs, it was the wives, not the parents, who were usually the active participants. Research at CPWS showed that *direct action,* even in helpless, hopeless situations, is a very effective coping mechanism (Hunter, 1984). Often parents had to remain in the wings and wait, even though they had the time to participate.

Parents also were often no longer in the working force. Wives, on the other hand, were filling a dual parental role and were busy with households and taking care of minor children. Few worked outside the home in those early years. As time passed and children matured, however, many MIA wives pursued further education or careers, in addition to their household and childcare functions. In painful contrast, most MIA parents lacked similar foci for their time and energies, and the separation, pain, and helplessness were accentuated and thus exacerbated.

Psychological crises can translate into physical problems. For example, in a study of healthy, functioning families, Lewis and associates (1976) found evidence that individuals are predisposed to illness under certain specific circumstances such as when:

- A great many life changes are experienced in a short time
- One's social and interpersonal environment is perceived as highly unsatisfactory
- A prolonged affective state of hopelessness or helplessness is developed

These very circumstances characterize the MIA experience. Consequently, in the CPWS study (Hunter, 1984), it was predicted with some degree of confidence that MIA family members would be likely to show physical and psychological pathology in greater degrees than the families of servicemen whose status was less ambiguous. Because of this factor of ambiguity, it was expected that adjustment would *decrease* going from the group of military wives whose husbands were not POWs and had not been killed, to POW wives whose husbands had returned, to wives of men killed in action, and, lastly, to MIA wives. The MIA families were expected to manifest the greatest number of psychological and health problems. Results bore out this prediction. Four samples of these types of families were compared on an index derived from a health inventory completed 4 years after the POWs' release, and the hypothesis was supported. In other words, the MIA group reported significantly poorer physical and emotional health than the KIA group, the returned POW group, and the comparison group; that is, wives of military men who were not in any of those categories (Hunter, 1980). Extrapolating from those findings, it could probably also be predicted that parents of men killed in action would have fewer adaptation problems than parents of men missing in action.

COPING WITH LOSS

Men missing in the Vietnam war remained listed as missing for an unprecedented length of time, even when there was good evidence they probably had not survived. In the first months of the Vietnam conflict the decision had been made at top levels *not* to change any statuses from MIA to presumptive findings of death until the war ended. The assumption was that the war would undoubtedly end within 6 months to a year. The families of MIAs continued to receive full pay and allowances of the missing men because changes in status were withheld. However, the war did not end quickly; it dragged on and on for 9 long years, and the families waited. Although the policy of keeping men listed as MIA provided substantial increases in monetary benefits to MIA families as compared to KIA families, these MIA families paid a high price in terms of the inability to complete the grieving process. Also, there were no group supports in the beginning—not until the families themselves banded together and formed the National League of Families of American Prisoners and Missing in Southeast Asia and went public in late 1969.

When any family member is lost, either temporarily or permanently, the family is profoundly affected. A primary emotion experienced by MIA parents and family members, especially during the initial weeks, was fear. As time passed, feelings of isolation, alienation, anger, guilt, hostility, and depression developed. These feelings are experienced in a type of emotional roller coaster pattern which finds family-member reactions ranging from hope to despair to rage and remorse (Figley, 1980). At the time of the plight of the waiting Iranian hostage families in 1980, one Vietnam era MIA family member made the following observations based on her own personal experiences:

> The families of the hostages are probably experiencing all of Kübler-Ross's steps of the grief cycle, on a "temporary" basis. They are bouncing back and forth within that cycle. . . . They are experiencing a sense of helplessness; they cannot control their own lives. . . . Their once-secure family now rests on the whims or fickleness of captors who are highly suspect. . . . They cannot take charge of the issue that has disrupted their lives; it is far too big. . . . Wives will experience intense fear for their husband's safety. They will also be angry, because they have been left alone, and then they will feel guilty because they are angry. . . . The final outcome is uncertain; the "limbo" could end tomorrow or next year. . . . Some wives may be able to reach decisions, based only on their husband's pre-stated wishes. . . . Others may be able to demonstrate more independence or autonomy. Some may be paralyzed. (Foley, 1980, p. 2)

Despite the presence of the feelings that are part of the grief process, the normal process of grief is unresolvably stuck. In grief over any loss that is confirmed, the final phase in resolution of that grief ideally involves the mourner coming to grips with the permanent loss. Many MIA parents and families, however, have not been allowed to reach this final phase. When it is not known whether one is a parent or a bereaved parent, a wife or a widow, there can be no final stage of acceptance or adequate coping with the loss. Indeed, as Worden (1982) points out, unless the primary task of mourning can be met, that is, accepting the reality of the loss, the mourning cannot continue. As resolution of the grieving process becomes exceedingly difficult, if not impossible, the unresolved grief can prevent a person from "getting on with living." The CPWS family study found that usually after 2 to 3 years, most wives made a conscious decision to close out the husbands' roles—at least partially (Hunter, 1984). They reported they had to do so in order to cope with the pragmatics of everyday living. On the other hand, parents of the MIAs, without the concern for the emotional health of small children still at home, had no pressing need to close out the memories of the sons.

With MIA families, the first stage of grief lasts for such a long time that there is a tendency to blame. There is much guilt for parents, as well as for wives and children. There are ruminations about what could have been: "We could have done so many things together"; "Perhaps I didn't raise him to be strong enough to survive"; "Why didn't he get out of the military?" Later the blame, anger, and hostility may shift from self to the military: "The war was wrong"; "He shouldn't even be over there"; "They're not trying hard enough to find him."

Most wives discovered eventually that they had to force themselves to shed the guilt and anger in order to function effectively for their children (Hunter, 1982). Parents had more difficulty doing so because of the typical exacerbation of guilt experienced by parents due to their own and society's unrealistic expectations of the parental role (see Chapter 1). The parental role and the meaning and implications of the loss of a child compromise the MIA parents' ability to resolve the grief:

> Today the plight of the parents of MIAs is particularly poignant. Still suffering are those elderly parents who will probably *never* be convinced that their sons are dead and will always hope that they will one day return home. As one mother said, "You wives can still have another life; he was my only son. I shall never have another. I shall always hope that some day he will come walking through that door." (Hunter, 1983, p. 177)

From the CPWS studies (Hunter, 1984) it was learned that parents went through the same stages of grief as wives and suffered physical symptoms such as anorexia, insomnia, and fatigue, as well as psychological reactions such as preoccupation with the image and memories of the missing son. Some parents felt the Vietnam war was totally unjustified, and therefore their sons' casualties could not be reconciled by reference to the "traditions of our country" and "the price of freedom." For others, however, the tragedy could be explained by reaffirmation of their own beliefs in these patriotic values.

Other parents emphasized the importance of looking at the entire situation through their sons' eyes: "He loved the military and wouldn't have been happy doing anything else"; "He knew the risks and was willing to take them because he believed in what he was doing, even if it meant the possibility that he would die in combat."

Despite such reasoning, parents nonetheless found it difficult to accept their loss. Some parents set aside an entire section of their homes to display their sons' photographs, awards, and memorabilia—a shrine to their sons' memories. More parents than wives reported religion had helped them cope with their situations. For some parents, their beliefs in religious teachings were the only possible way to explain the casualty and the hardship and pain they had endured over the months and years. Through prayer they sustained hope; through their beliefs they gained understanding (Hunter, 1983).

Differences in grieving were found between fathers and mothers of MIA servicemen (McCubbin & Metres, 1974). Attention was focused on the parents' grief during a series of religious retreats held for MIA families in the summer of 1973 shortly after the return of the POWs from Southeast Asia. At that point in time, MIA families had been forced to contend with the fact their loved ones were not among the repatriated. Mothers, especially, showed a need to talk about their experience, their grief, frustrations, and aspirations, whereas fathers appeared to seek help in expressing their feelings and getting in touch with their anger and frustrations that still lay hidden beneath a facade of understanding silence. Unlike the mothers, most fathers did not appear willing to express their feelings openly or to discuss the personal meaning of their sons' casualties.

Compared with wives of MIAs, these parents differed in their reasons for attending the retreat. The wives' attendance appeared to be for the opportunity for respite or vacation. Perhaps wives, coping with the practicalities of raising children, pursuing careers, or establishing new lifestyles, had already come to terms with themselves and their future plans. In contrast, mothers were still struggling to come to terms with their feelings about their loss. In other words, wives were asking, "How do I cope?" while mothers still asked, "Why did it happen and what are the chances he will return?" (Hunter, McCubbin, & Benson, 1974). At the time of these retreats, MIA parents still faced dilemmas and had to work out equitable and personally satisfying balances between conflicting sets of tasks, such as:

- Acknowledging and accepting the ultimate loss of a son and yet maintaining hope for his eventual return,
- Concentrating on commitments to other family members and devoting greater energy toward reconciliation of the MIA situation,
- Pursuing a personal, active, and unrelenting cause for obtaining a full accounting and still demanding support from governmental agencies,
- Moving forward with their lives but remaining committed to a life centered around their absent sons. (Hunter, 1983, p. 178)

MIA wives and parents did have in common feelings of helplessness and powerlessness. In an attempt to gain control over the situation, some had virtually let it become a way of life. They were totally involved in local and national POW/MIA activities such as letter writing, campaigning, and talking to local civic groups. As some parents slowly began to realize their sons probably were not coming home, they repressed the thoughts because of the guilt that they aroused.

By 1973, however, some parents were beginning to ask, "When do I stop?" Nevertheless, a few parents implicitly believed their constant and never-ending preoccupation with their sons' survival was in fact the very force that kept the men alive. One mother said, "I have often felt guilty for not having thought about my son every moment." Understandably, other children in the family were affected by their parents' preoccupation with the missing child. Not unlike the siblings of dying or deceased children, these brothers and sisters of MIAs often were forced to cope with their parents' relative neglect. As one adolescent boy blurted out, "My parents always talk about my dead older brother, but I'm alive! I guess I'll have to commit suicide to get them to care about what I do" (Hunter, 1983, p. 175).

Once the POWs returned in 1973, the military began to review all information on those men who had not returned and began to change statuses from MIA to presumptive findings of death, only to be faced with a class action suit to prevent them from doing so. The parents and wives who filed the suit feared that once the government declared the men dead, no further effort would be made to learn what had happened to these men, nor would there ever be any effort to have their remains returned from Vietnam for burial.

When the government learned the suit was to be filed, word was quickly spread that if wives wanted their husbands' files reviewed they should request it be done immediately. Such a request was usually followed by an immediate change of status to a presumptive finding of death, which many wives wanted in order to get on with their lives. There were instances of splintered families where daughters-in-law requested the review against the violent protests of the missing men's parents. The end result for a few families was that parents not only lost a son in Vietnam, they also lost access to their grandchildren because of the ill feelings engendered by the government's placing the onus of requesting a review of the MIA's status on the shoulders of the primary next of kin.

TREATMENT IMPLICATIONS

In responding to the needs of MIA parents, caregivers who are most effective are those who are informed, empathic listeners. The first task in dealing with MIA families may simply be one of educating the family members about typical stress reactions to assure them their responses are "normal" reactions under the circumstances. The caregiver must be nonjudgmental so that family members can feel secure enough to share their feelings and to ventilate anger and hostility without fear of being labeled "good" or "bad." It is imperative that the caregiver not "feel sorry" for MIA parents who must be allowed to face the reality of their loss. Nor should the remark be made to them, "I know exactly how you feel." They will quickly remind you there is no way you could possibly know how they feel. The caregiver must realize that each person must find individual coping mechanisms. There are differences between family members as well as differences between each family system. For example, contact with the news media may be welcomed by one person, but abhorred by another as an added stressor (Hunter, 1983).

The special problems of MIA parents include the chronic nature of the stress, the up-and-down cycle of stress, and the fact that MIA parents have an experience that inherently contains all five of Lazare's (1979) social reasons for failure to grieve (uncertainty of the loss, lack of social support, socially unacceptable loss, social negation of the loss, and the assumption of the role of the strong one). All MIA parents suffer from the dilemmas of bereaved parents in general and from the issues involved in the loss of an adult child in particular (see Chapter 13 on the death of an adult child for an in-depth examination of these issues).

Feelings of helplessness and increased anger often occur because of the nature and purposelessness of the death (for some parents, at least). Other problems unique to MIA parents are the difficulties of reaching closure without feeling they are betraying their sons, guilt that not only comes from any parental loss of a child, but also at times from the wishful confirmation of death so they can continue their lives, and the ongoing concerns about what may be happening to their sons if they are still alive.

Specific recommendations for caregivers who counsel MIA parents include the following:

1. If possible, parents should be kept informed by the appropriate governmental agency on a regular basis, even when there are no new facts to report.

2. One of the most effective support systems for MIA parents is other parents who are, or have been, in a similar situation. The government should support and fund opportunities for these families to meet together and discuss their plight, especially during the first weeks subsequent to loss.

3. Parents should be encouraged to take charge of their own lives in whatever way they can. This action will help fight their helplessness and feelings of inability to control their own lives. Normalcy of family routines should be encouraged (e.g., birthdays celebrated and vacations taken). Anything that can promote positive and direct action stimulates a feeling of power or control, even when little exists.

4. Parents should be urged to express their feelings and be allowed to develop their own conclusions about the missing members' status and their own methods for coping with this stressful situation. Long-term adjustment can be achieved only when parents accumulate a personal history of being able to cope with their stress over a period of time.

5. Experiencing an ambiguous situation, such as the MIA experience, causes emotions to swing from highest hope to deepest despair with, for example, a single news broadcast. Parents should be urged to neutralize this roller-coaster effect. A crisis hotline should be available for the parents' use at any time, day or night, to verify information obtained from various sources and to dispel rumors with no basis in fact.

6. As parents begin to understand and accept the possibility that their sons will not return, feelings of guilt and frustration may simul-taneously increase. After years of maintaining hope in the face of overwhelming odds and keeping alive the active search for satisfactory answers, any inclination toward "giving up" will bring on feelings of guilt and self-condemnation. Nonetheless, during the period when the parents await word from governmental agencies about the fate of their sons, the caregiver can play a valuable role by assisting in the alleviation of these anxieties and feelings of guilt—feelings normally associated with the process of "acceptance" of the possibility of the sons' never returning (Hunter, 1983).

7. Feelings about the political climate and the responses of Amer-icans who appear to wish to forget about Vietnam only serve to increase the anger, frustration, and sense of helplessness for MIA parents. These feelings, especially when coupled with convictions about the preventability of the death (a factor that can make the death harder to resolve), may provoke in some parents strong reactions about the senselessness of the Vietnam war and the fact that their sons are still missing. "Missing for what?" they may think as they try to find some meaning in a meaningless situation.

8. The normal concerns about starting to get on with life after a loss are heightened in this situation. Without the knowledge of whether or not one's child is alive, concerns about betraying the child by going forward are very prominent. Also, there is a demand for continued work on the part of many of these parents as they try to take action that could either improve their son's welfare or confirm his death (e.g., letter writing, applying political pressure).

The grief of MIA parents cannot be successfully resolved in the same way as resolution of grief subsequent to confirmed losses. Only when the family has some confirmation of the death will they be able to come to the type of resolution that would be *ideal* after a loss. In the absence of this, caregivers must be advised that even in the presence of positive steps to continue with life, the MIA parent may always experience some form of grief and "waiting" for news, along with the press of unresolved and unfinished business with regard to their missing son.

When three sets of remains of MIA servicemen were returned from Vietnam in the summer of 1981, one distraught mother of one of the servicemen who had been missing for 13 years referred to other family members who still did not know the fate of their loved ones and remarked, "We are the lucky ones. . . . *Our* wounds will now heal."

References

Figley, C. R. (Ed.) (1980). *Mobilization I: The Iranian crisis: Final report of the Task Force on Families of Catastrophe.* West Lafayette, IN: Purdue University.

Foley, B. (1980, February). *Reflections of an MIA wife.* Paper presented at a meeting of the Task Force on Families of Catastrophe, West Lafayette, IN.

Hunter, E. J. (1980). Combat casualties who remain at home. *Military Review, 60*(1), 28–36.

Hunter, E. J. (1982). Marriage in limbo. *Naval Institute Proceedings, 108,* 27–32. .

Hunter, E. J. (1983). Captivity: The family in waiting. In C. Figley & H. McCubbin (Eds.), *Stress and the family: Coping with catastrophe* (Vol. 2, pp. 166–184). New York: Brunner/Mazel.

Hunter, E. J. (1984). Treating the military captive's family. In F. Kaslow & R. Ridenour (Eds.), *Treating the military family: Dynamics and treatment.* New York: Guilford.

Hunter, E. J., McCubbin, H. I., & Benson, D. (1974). Differential viewpoints: The MIA wife vs. the MIA mother. In H. I. McCubbin, B. Dahl, P. Metres, E. Hunter, & J. Plag (Eds.), *Family separation and reunion* (Cat. No. D–206.21:74–70, pp. 189–197). Washington, DC: U.S. Government Printing Office.

Lazare, A. (1979). Unresolved grief. In A. Lazare (Ed.), *Outpatient psychiatry: Diagnosis and treatment.* Baltimore: Williams & Wilkins.

Lewis, J., Beavers, W., Gossett, J., & Phillips, V. (1976). *No single thread.* New York: Brunner/Mazel.

McCubbin, H. I., & Metres, P. J. (1974). Maintaining hope: The dilemma of parents of sons missing in action. In H. I. McCubbin, B. Dahl, P. Metres, E. Hunter, & J. Plag (Eds.), *Family separation and reunion* (Cat. No. D-206-21:74–70, pp. 169–178). Washington, DC: U.S. Government Printing Office.

National League of Families of American Prisoners of War and Missing in Southeast Asia (1985, November 8). *Newsletter.*

White, R. W. (1976). Strategies of adaptation: An attempt at systematic description. In R. H. Moos (Ed.), *Human adaptation: Coping with life crises.* (pp. 17–32). Lexington, MA: D. C. Heath & Co.

Worden, J. W. (1982). *Grief counseling and grief therapy: A handbook for the mental health practitioner.* New York: Springer.

Section 4

Subjective Experiences of Death

Chapter 18
Grief of Fathers

William H. Schatz

William H. Schatz, with his wife, Barbara, cofounded the Seattle-King County Chapter of The Compassionate Friends after the death of their 9-year-old son. He has been a member of the national Compassionate Friends' board of directors, and served as President of The Compassionate Friends for a year. Mr. Schatz has presented many workshops and lectures on the topic of men's grief. He is the author of the booklet *Healing a Father's Grief*.

To all who search for meaning in their lives,
but especially those bereaved mothers and
fathers who, after the death of their child,
search, scratch, claw, and wrestle with what
life has given them, and then discover new
values that will create a full and meaningful
existence for themselves and all whom they
touch in their lifetimes.

———

A father's reaction to grief is as multifaceted as anyone else's. The significant difference is that much of what goes on inside a man concerning the loss of a child stays inside and only becomes apparent in some indirect way. I have come to this knowledge through personal experience, through confirmation from other bereaved fathers during 5 years of work with The Compassionate Friends, and through workshops and seminars I have conducted for groups of fathers and groups of mothers. What will be presented here will not apply to all fathers, as there are differences depending on the pre-death relationship between father and child. However, such an overwhelming majority of fathers have corroborated my material that I feel comfortable in presenting it. One further note: much of what I say will also apply to single female parents who are bereaved, those single mothers who have had to be both mother and father to their children.

The pre-death relationship affects the paternal response to a child's death. Where the pre-death relationship of a father and child was very close, for example, when the son worked at his father's business after school and all during the summer months, responses more like the typical bereaved mother's will be produced. One will see very open emotions, with frequent crying; inability to go to the place of work, where the memories are; and possibly even sale of the family business. More typical reactions for a father are emotional outbursts and irritability; low energy and depression; frantic activity, as manifested by the workaholic; and any behaviors that keep him from thinking about what has happened until he reaches exhaustion. Yes, he will experience shock and numbness immediately after the child's death. However, when he finally realizes what has really happened to him and his family, he will have a difficult time handling the emotional, painful part of grief.

IMPEDIMENTS TO A FATHER'S GRIEF

I believe that men are taught to grieve the way they do.

As I grew up I learned how the American male is supposed to behave. Through an *unconscious* process, we all learn the role that is *modeled* for us by parents, teachers, relatives, heroes, television and movie characters, and others. This *social conditioning* applies to both men and women and is one way a culture passes its values and patterns to the next generation. Fortunate is the child who is surrounded by strong, positive, loving models, both male and female. But there may be negative elements. The fact is: Typical male roles tend to interfere with grieving. Men are *conditioned* to grieve, or not grieve, in certain ways that are not healthy. We need to look at this conditioning. (Schatz, 1984, p. 4)

There are a number of male roles that negatively affect fathers in dealing with their grief. These include:

- The role of being strong, a macho man who always controls his emotions
- The role of competing, of winning in a crisis and being the best
- The role of being the protector of family and possessions
- The role of being the family provider
- The role of being the problem solver, fixing things or finding someone who can
- The role of being the controller, controlling actions and the environment
- The role of being self-sufficient, standing on your own two feet

Socialization in these roles impedes the father's successful resolution of grief. Each role has prescribed behaviors that work against the open expression of feelings and confrontation with powerlessness and vulnerability that is an inherent part of the grief experience. Macho men are not supposed to express feelings. As a competitor, the father is defeated when his child dies. As a protector, he has failed in his role. As a provider, he has difficulty because grief impairs his functioning at work. Whereas he could always be a successful problem solver in the past, he cannot solve the problem of his child's death. He has lost the control of life that he could previously maintain; everything is out of order and control after the child's death. And, as a man who is supposed to be self-sufficient, he will eschew the assistance and support of others. With the roles that have previously defined him now seriously compromised with the death of his child, the father's ego and sense of self are severely assaulted. He could not assume these roles successfully enough to keep his child from death and cannot control the pain and trouble experienced by his family, as well as himself. Guilt and a sense of failure result, which further compound his grief and make him more resistant to attempting to address it.

In a situation where the wife is at home as the primary caregiver and the father has gone back to work, it is more probable that the mother will be engulfed in the pain and suffering aspect of grief before

the father. When this takes place, the father reacts to his role expectations and attempts to fix the situation. This usually fails, as each person
must work through her grief in her own way and her own time frame.
The father feels rebuffed. As pain grows worse for his wife, he feels
like things are getting out of control. He feels totally helpless to do
anything for her, something he has been capable of doing before. He
thinks that the least he can do is remain strong, control what is going
on inside himself, and set the example for his wife and family. Besides,
logic tells him that if he started to fall apart or lose control, then
everything would deteriorate. Who would hold this bereaved family
together? This phenomenon is common and results in many fathers
postponing their grief work until they think it is safe, until other family
members are better, or until they just cannot control the upheaval going
on inside anymore.

While he is trying to remain strong and emotionally controlled, the
father may begin to display inappropriate anger, a pound of anger for
an ounce of stimuli. This occurs when the normal emotional reserve we
all have to sustain us over the small emotional irritants in life has been
depleted by a child's death. The father no longer has this reserve to dip
into when a minor annoyance comes along. He reaches for his emotional
reserve and it is gone. Consequently, an inappropriate emotional out-
burst occurs. I call it "Saving Up Your Green Stamps." Little events that
normally do not even get the father's attention now put green stamps
in his book. And it doesn't take very long before the book is full. This
is because most of his energy is used in controlling the emotions
(sadness, hurt, and pain) evoked by grief and in getting through an
abnormal workday. The result is a very volatile, explosive father trying
to remain in control while other members of the family are working
through the toughest parts of their grief work.

I can remember my own emotional outbursts. They occurred over
the slightest things. And then afterwards, recovering from my emotions,
I'd ask myself, "What was that all about?" or "I can't believe I just did
that, what's wrong with me?" Little did I know at the time, but this was
the only way my conditioning would allow me to express my emotions.
In discussions with other fathers, they not only related to my outbursts,
they also shared similar experiences. Some fathers admitted later on in
their grief work that they had started to drink because they could not
stand themselves after these emotional explosions, especially when they
were directed at members of their family. As you can imagine, if there
were any preexisting unsettled issues in the marriage or family, this
climate could give rise to all types of arguments. I believe that if this

response pattern goes unchecked, it becomes one of the factors in the high divorce rates among bereaved parents.

If fathers feel that it is necessary to be strong and delay or postpone their grief, they may feel resentful. They may ask themselves such questions as "How could I work on my grief even if I wanted to, since everyone else is unfinished? When is it my turn? What about me? I've got feelings, too! I loved my child, too! Nobody asks me how I feel or how I'm doing—they always ask me about my wife!!"

Despite its perceived necessity, delay or postponement of grief can only last so long. The powerful emotional forces at work inside will eventually emerge in some fashion. They may come at a time when they are least expected, after it seems the worst is over. For me, it was 18 months after David died, and my wife was over her heavy grief work. Postponed grief seems to need some sort of catalyst to get things started. For me, it was a picture of David on our last vacation together, combined with the unconscious decision that the environment was safe enough to let the real feelings under the anger come to the surface. As I went by that picture, I began to cry. Then I cried for 30 minutes. It seemed like I cried for all the times I had not cried since David had been diagnosed with leukemia—7 1/2 years before. Each weekend for 4 weeks the same thing happened. It was a tremendous relief! I never thought that crying could feel so good. No one could have convinced me that it could relieve some of the hurt inside. One significant note: when I cried the first time, I was terrified that I would not be able to stop. Yet it felt so good that I soon forgot the scared feeling. It is also important to note that no one ever knew this was taking place. Only after I was sure that it was over did I even share it with my wife. Other fathers have related parallel experiences using a catalyst of some kind, for example, a picture, a toy, sports equipment, some special place or music (Schatz, 1984). There are other fathers who have told me a different story—that once they cried, they were then able to cry easily with their wives. However, these men seem to be in the minority. Unfortunately, there are very few alternatives to dealing with the grief. They range from several forms of escape to many physical and emotional illnesses caused by the stress of unresolved grief.

SEARCHING

As soon as there is some constructive emotional release like crying, many fathers enter a period of deep searching. This is unlike the initial questioning of early grieving, when the "Why?" questions are asked, such as "Why did this happen?" "Why did this happen to my child? To our family? To me?" "Why do children die anyhow?" or the statements associated with guilt are made, such as "If I only would have taken her to the doctor sooner!" "If I only would have told him not to drive in snowy weather!" "If I only would have prevented him from going swimming at night!" "If I only wouldn't have let her go to the party!" "If I only. . ." These questions and statements are necessary and normal, but there is a deeper search that follows all of them. It is the search for the meaning in all this, the meaning of life and death. Some answers to make it all worthwhile.

The first penetrating search for us as bereaved fathers is to come to full confrontation with our own mortality—our own death. If our child can die, then so can we! Those of us who have had many experiences with death, especially with the death of someone under 30 or a close family member, may have done some serious thinking about our own death. But those of us who are like the average person, where death has been limited to grandparents or older parents, aunts, and uncles, probably have done little thinking about it. This personal confrontation with death brings up other latent feelings: fear and anxiety about what is after life. What's it like to stop breathing? Is this all there is? How long will I live? What if I won't be here in 10 years? 5 years? 2 years? Next year? The impact on the present and the implications for the future are mind-boggling and usually cannot be thought of all at once, or for an extended period of time, without some feelings of despair or depression.

However, as soon as we begin to feel comfortable with the fact that we are not going to live forever, a new, deeper probe creeps into our mind. What's it all about anyway? What is this life all about? What are we here for? Where is the meaning or purpose in what we're all doing? As I look back on it now, this deep searching can be likened to a "mid-life crisis" situation. I personally reflected on what I had done in my life up to that point. I had a family, two children, a job with certain achievements, a house, a certain standard of living, an amount of money, some other possessions—none of which seemed to make any difference to me at the time. When our child dies, a part of us dies with him. Nothing else can replace him. Therefore, during this grief period we search and question everything we have. We reexamine what is meaningful to us, what in life is really important. This takes a long time, as we try to put into perspective our relationships with others, our job, our family, our marriage, our religious beliefs, our own vulnerability, our ego, our possessions, and our purpose for being alive. This process can take from several concentrated months with the help of a professional to 3 or more years. I personally feel that the entire process is never finished; life will be evaluated continually in the future in terms of the new values we have established during the grief period.

Some of the values clarification issues that we face are connected to the values that were instilled in us by our parents as we grew up. Many of the admonitions given to us by our parents, and in which we truly have invested, turn out to be little help or consolation to us after the death of our child. Such important reminders as "Don't spend all your money, but save some for a rainy day" or "Wait until you can afford it before you take your kids to Disneyland" really have little application after a child has died. Save for what? For whom? Our parents told us, "Work hard and you'll get ahead. It's worth it!" We may need to reexamine the whole aspect of work. Should I be working at a job that pays a lot of money, but gives me very little personal satisfaction? Is it worth all the company politics and pressure to get ahead just to be involved with more politics and more pressure? What for? Achievement? For whom? Does it really make a difference after your child is dead?

Don't forget the religious beliefs! Past values from our parents tell us to lead a good life and everything will turn out OK. Go to church, give a percentage of your income to the poor, and God will take care of you and your family. It is difficult to reconcile the facts when you believe God controls everything and then your child dies. More questions! Why would God do this? Is this a loving God to let children suffer and die before they live a full life? Have I done something terrible that God should punish my family by taking my child? Is there a merciful and loving God? Is there a God at all? In my personal searching, the most important work I have found to date was written by another bereaved parent, Rabbi Harold S. Kushner. It is a book entitled *When Bad Things Happen to Good People* (1981). A suggestion is made, which has some credibility for me and others, that God may not choose to control everything. And since we live in an imperfect world, sometimes things just happen, like disease and accidents. This concept may have saved my faith until I could review my religious values on a less emotional basis and on a more theological level.

In an attempt to make sense out of all this, a father may do some very foolish things. If the marriage was unstable before the child died, some fathers try to find meaning in another relationship, either temporary or permanent. They say that the reminders are not there, that another woman who is not in grief can support them, and that they feel they can start a new relationship without going through any more pain. Unfortunately, this usually complicates everyone's life; and the father, no matter how hard he tries, cannot escape his own grief. The inevitable grief work must be done in order to heal the tragic hurt. There are just too many documented cases of divorced bereaved fathers who have returned to their grief work many years after they have separated from their families.

Another foolish means of escape that fathers employ is staying away from home. They may try doing this by working extra hours. While overtime may sometimes be necessary due to the low energy level brought on by grief, excessive overtime is generally a socially acceptable excuse for not going home. If that doesn't work, they may become overly involved in service organizations, community clubs, and sporting events. Another means of escape is stopping off at the local bar or using drugs. This adds obvious complications to an already difficult situation. One of the more serious problems is that alcohol or drugs remove any remaining control of emotions, and the angry emotional outbursts previously mentioned become more frequent. Consequently, the bereaved father is either feared or fought with by the rest of the family. If reliance on alcohol or drugs persists, it can become another factor contributing to divorce among bereaved parents.

A value that is reexamined is that of planning for the future—fulfilling one's dreams. When a child dies, not only do dreams die, but planning for any future event seems meaningless. It is a kind of summary of all the other areas of search. Fathers have told me, "What's the use of planning for the future? There are no guarantees anyway!" As fathers we feel helpless to do anything to control our own lives or our families'. We feel cheated, ripped off! Are we all just puppets dancing at the end of someone's string? Are we completely insignificant; does anybody really care about us? It is easy to understand why many fathers enter a period of depression until they can adequately complete their search. Only after we find our own personal answers, new values to direct our lives, and ways to cope with the loss of our child will the curtain of depression begin to lift.

COPING WITH PATERNAL GRIEF

The timing and sequence of the events in the search are not important. What is important is that they occur at all! Here are some suggestions that other bereaved fathers have found helpful, suggestions that gave them time to conduct the search and tools to facilitate it.

- Lighten the load, back off on any extra activities.
- Talk to your family, and explain that men grieve differently than women.
- Set aside time to think, to sort things out.

- Learn to cry, for crying is the most natural response to being hurt.
- Express anger constructively by being mad at things, not people.
- Find a support system by reaching out to other bereaved fathers, a group, or a professional. (Schatz, 1984)

The time taken to record in a journal can be especially valuable, as it provides personal feedback when it is reread. Sharing with the same person, one-on-one, can also provide a form of feedback. In some way your personal story of grief needs to come out. If groups or interpersonal sharing are not acceptable to you, the personal journal is the best substitute. If you can share, or are willing to participate in a group, even just by listening, you should find your local chapter of The Compassionate Friends. To my knowledge, this is the best self-help group for bereaved parents. It is a group where you learn that you are accepted no matter what your situation is, that your reactions to grief are most probably normal and healthy, and that you are not alone in your struggle with grief.

Personal answers and values will be different for each one of you, but I guarantee that you will continually test them in the years after your child dies. Some fathers have told me that they have had false starts in discovering new values, some involving foolish escape attempts. However, when they have continued to pursue the search they have discovered what the most important things are in their life, and in the lives of their wife and family.

SIGNS OF HEALING

Is it over? How do you know? It probably is never really over, but signs of progress can be visible. Looking back at your personal journal is one way you can see for yourself. There are several other ways to see "signs of healing" (Schatz, 1984). You can have confidence you have begun to heal when:

- You begin to look outside yourself at how others in your family are handling the loss.
- You no longer feel the need to escape from your emotions.
- You feel more comfortable about your grief and are willing to talk about it.
- You have a day without emotional stress.
- You can discuss, observe, or experience memories (good and bad) without having feelings that overwhelm you.
- You see your socially conditioned behavior return and it feels comfortable.

- You realize that no matter what happened, both you and your wife did the best you or anyone else could have done under the circumstances.
- You begin to find glimpses of new or renewed meaning in your life again.
- You begin planning for the future again.

Finally, there is the area of your wife's progress. One question that seems to plague bereaved fathers more than anything else is "Why does it take so long for my wife to get over her grief?" A chapter relating to the grief of mothers is in this book and is well worth reading by all fathers, especially those with the above question. If that chapter does not provide the necessary understanding, then the best recommendation that I can give is to have patience, as your wife may need time to complete her own unique grieving process as a mother.

It is my sincere hope that this chapter is a small beginning in the examination and understanding of a father's grief. The unfolding of a man's emotions may result from a child's death. May bereaved fathers be the pioneers for all men, so that we may all experience life to its fullest as long as we are here.

References

Kushner, H. (1981). *When bad things happen to good people*. New York: Schocken Books.

Schatz, W. (1984). *Healing a father's grief*. Redmond, WA: Medic Publishing Company (Box 89, Redmond, WA 98052).

Chapter 19

Grief of Mothers

Barbara D. Schatz

Barbara D. Schatz, B.S.W., M.C., with her husband, Bill, cofounded the Seattle-King County Chapter of The Compassionate Friends after the death of their 9-year-old son. She holds a bachelor's degree in Social Work from the University of Washington and a master's degree in Counseling from Seattle University. Ms. Schatz has done numerous workshops at Compassionate Friends' conferences, and she currently maintains a private practice as a therapist specializing in grief and loss issues. In addition she provides community education and acts as a consultant to therapists and to churches establishing grief ministries.

To my children . . .
My son, David . . .
whose birth I will never regret,
whose life I will ever celebrate,
and whose death I will always grieve.
My daughter, Bethany . . .
whose life and love continue to bring me
pride and joy as a mother.

———

Successful intervention by a professional caregiver is dependent upon a solid understanding of what it means, in very practical terms, to be a bereaved mother. The impact of a mother's loss must be viewed in the context of how her loss affects her daily life and the meaning that child gave to her life.

The literature reports high levels of stress and somatic complaints for families after a child dies, indicating the need for a strong support system that may include professional help. Why, then, do bereaved parents consistently report dissatisfaction with professionals' interventions? My feeling is that in general professionals earnestly seek information about the grief process and have a genuine desire to help the bereaved parent. What seems to be lacking is recognition of the multiple facets of parental grief that make it different from other kinds of grief.

The grief process for a bereaved mother is both intense and lengthy. In this chapter factors will be examined that contribute to the intensity and duration of maternal grief: age of the child at the time of death, circumstances surrounding the death of the child, and role of the child in the family system. Consideration will be given to the unique sensory involvement of a mother with her child and the impact of the loss of that involvement after a child's death. Suggestions for professional intervention will be offered, with emphasis placed on the needs of the bereaved mother.

PERSPECTIVES ON MATERNAL GRIEF

After the death of her child, a mother begins to grieve for what might have been—for the loss of the future and for what will be no more. Her process entails learning to live without her child. She struggles to hold on to memories from the past while letting go of dreams for the future with her child. The life and death of her child compose a bereaved mother's story, which continues to unfold as she works through her grief. It is vital to the health and healing of a bereaved mother that she be allowed to repeatedly tell her story. Parts of the author's own story are contained in this chapter.

Recently my husband and I were asked to join a small group to begin a year-long planning program for our community. As the meeting began, each member introduced himself; many shared the names and ages of their children. As my turn approached, I became aware of an uneasiness in the pit of my stomach. My son is a part of my "story," and I wanted to acknowledge him. I said, "I have two children, a daughter who is 18 and a son who died 5 years ago at age 9." My experience was not unique. In my work with The Compassionate Friends I have spoken with hundreds of bereaved mothers and have heard similar stories often repeated. Years after the grief has softened and a significant amount of grief work has been done, mothers feel a need to acknowledge their child or children who have died. This phenomenon is not easily understood by those who have not personally experienced the death of one of their children.

The grieving process for a bereaved mother seems far more complex than working through a series of stages. Mothers routinely experience intense emotional pain that is frightening and overwhelming. As one mother reported, "I wanted to scream, but was unable to utter a sound for fear of shattering some delicate thread within, which was holding me together." There seems to be little relief from the suffering, even after the first year of bereavement. My own expectations for relief from pain at the end of the first year were not met. I felt duped by the literature which assured me that "normal grief lasts 6 months to 1 year." Other mothers concur; there is no magic timetable to guarantee how long the intense pain of loss will last. At the end of a year, I had returned to college as an undergraduate and was involved in The Compassionate Friends. Friends and acquaintances commented on how well I had "gotten over" my son's death. But my level of functioning and productivity was in no way a measure of the pain I still felt. A common complaint of bereaved mothers is "Everyone thinks I am 'over' my child's death. I will never 'get over' it, I'm just learning to live with it." The role of the professional caregiver is that of a facilitator who helps the bereaved mother as she works on the task of learning to live without her child.

FACTORS AFFECTING THE GRIEVING PROCESS

Let's examine some factors that may contribute to the intensity and duration of a mother's grief.

Age of Child at Time of Death

A bereaved mother will frequently say that her child died at a special age. It doesn't matter what the age of the child was, because mothers tend to attribute specialness to their children at every age. A mother whose infant died will discuss the tiny toes and fingers, the features that resembled a parent or relative, and the budding personality of her infant. She also will talk of the dreams for the future of her son or daughter that will never be realized. The sparsity of memories will plague her, as she may be heard to envy a parent whose child was older at the time death occurred. One mother whose infant died at 6 weeks of age said, "I have reviewed each day of those 6 weeks, searching my mind for some small detail I might have forgotten. Six weeks of memories seem too few to last me an entire lifetime."

For me, a special age is 9. Each time I hear of a child who dies at 9 I experience an extra twinge, since that was the age of my son, David, when he died. I think of 9 as a time when little girl or little boy features begin to fade. In spite of his long eyelashes and soft blond hair, David was beginning to look more grown up. His permanent teeth seemed too large and his smile anticipated orthodontia. His shoulders began to broaden and his legs were long sticks, his growing feet covered with huge, tattered sneakers. Reading became easier and sports were more of a challenge. He began to identify with his father and I found myself forced into stealing an occasional hug or kiss. After he died, I often wished for just a few more years, to be able to see him as a teenager. How wonderful, I thought, to see in a son some of the qualities I admire and love in his father. I am convinced 9 is special, and not a good age for a child to die.

The teenage years are often fraught with child-parent disputes as independence becomes a goal for the teenager. When a child dies at this age, a mother has a glimpse of the future young man or woman. She regrets being unable to know the finished product, the young adult who emerges out of youthful struggles. Her memories of her child may be colored with painful disagreements or arguments which are often a routine part of the growing-up years.

When an adult child dies, a mother has worked through the difficult developmental years with her child and often has a relationship involving mature friendship. Sometimes mother and child share common interests, hobbies, or a job. One mother was in partnership with her daughter in a small antique store. She said, "We did what we liked together, building a business, sharing the delights of new discoveries or profitable sales. I never thought I could enjoy one of my children so much. She was a part of my life for over 35 years . . . it seems impossible to live without her." Other mothers whose adult child dies may have grandchildren who are a constant reminder of the deceased son or daughter. "It is a blessing, I know," said one mother, "to have my grandson, but it is like watching my son grow up all over again, knowing it isn't really him."

There seems to be no "good" age at which a child dies, at least not in the eyes of a bereaved mother. Her investment in her child, at any age, her hopes and plans for the future, and her memories of the past all contribute to a deep sense of loss and longing for "just a few more years." The specialness attributed to the age at which a child dies may contribute to the intensity of a mother's grief.

Circumstances Surrounding Death of Child

Conversations with a newly bereaved mother will ultimately evolve into a description of the circumstances that resulted in her child's death. How it happened—illness, accident, suicide, or homicide—is an integral part of the story of a mother's deceased child.

Frequent attendance at and participation in a support group such as The Compassionate Friends fosters in a mother the realization that all who have experienced the death of a child are faced with the task of working through grief. One mother said, "We are all in the same boat. One of our children died, and our grief is over that loss, no matter how it occurred." It is important to note, however, that the circumstances causing the death do result in variations in the way a bereaved mother seeks resolution of her grief. Initially, circumstances become a focal point for expression of some of the normal emotions of grief. For example, anger, prevalent in many bereaved mothers, is often directed at the person who "caused" the death. This may be a drunk driver whose car was out of control, the murderer in a homicide, or the doctor who was unable to cure an illness. If a bereaved mother remains locked into focusing on the cause of death, she can avoid or postpone the other components of grief work that need to be broached no matter how the death occurred, such as anger about the death itself.

Circumstances resulting in a child's death will be different in each individual case, even if the documented cause of death is identical. Each mother, therefore, will need to carefully examine her own story and work through an acceptance of "how it happened." It is not wise to neglect this aspect of the grief process. Consider the mother who was primary caregiver for a terminally ill child for many years. Her grief process involves a period of mourning for the years of suffering she observed in her child and the pain she experienced actually or vicariously. She may question not only the reason for the death, but also the suffering to which she was privy.

In conclusion, the circumstances resulting in a child's death will affect the bereaved mother's initial focus of her grief work. It is essential for a mother to work through feelings related to "how it happened." As healing continues, a mother will be able to see the big picture that reveals a bitter truth: one of her children has died. She can then address the more general issues of grieving, such as the unfairness of death at an early age.

Role of Child in Family System

In her lectures, the well-known family therapist Virginia Satir often uses the metaphor of a mobile to illustrate the dynamics of the family system. She describes the disturbance of balance in a mobile when one part of the mobile is absent. After the death of a child there is an imbalance or upset in the equilibrium of the family. Bereaved mothers often talk about "not seeming to be a family anymore" after a child's death.

A mother's explanation will relate to the role of the child in the family: "John was our athlete," or "We could always rely on Sally to cheer us up," or "Milt was our serious-minded student." Since mothers are aware of the diverse talents and personality traits of each of their children, the absence of a child highlights the absence of that child's contribution to the family.

When the child who dies is the only boy or girl, or is an only child, a mother is faced with the loss of her only son or daughter. Her grief is complicated by the loss of the relationship with this son or daughter. One mother whose only son died said of her experience, "I am unable to have more children. When my son died I knew it was the end of my dreams to see my son as a father, to have a daughter-in-law, to have a young man I could remember as my little boy. My dreams for seeing my husband with our son, playing ball, going fishing, or just being together also ended."

Mothers are often "comforted" with the suggestion that they have other children, in some way implying that living children will take the place of the child who died. Yet mothers will universally state that each of their children is different, each is unique.

The bereaved mother loses a part of herself with the child's death, while also witnessing and experiencing a loss of a part of her family. She grieves not only for the loss of the relationship with her child, but also for the loss of the once delicately balanced family system. As other family members struggle with their own grief, both individually and collectively, a mother realizes that "things will never be the same." She can never replace the missing child, because there will never be another person identical to the child who died.

With certain cultural or ethnic backgrounds, the birth order of a child can have special significance. The first-born son may be expected to take over the family business. The youngest daughter may be considered the caretaker for aging parents. Families have their own expectations or rituals, sometimes unspoken, that only become verbalized after the death of the child expected to perform in a traditional manner. When the loss is of an only child, a bereaved mother is jolted into the realization that she has lost her own role as mother; what once was a family becomes a couple.

SENSORY STIMULI AND THE BEREAVED MOTHER

After the death of her child, a mother is faced on a daily basis with stimuli that remind her of the deceased child. Her memories of the child are triggered by environmental cues that directly relate to her personal sensory experience with that child. The stories of many bereaved mothers confirm this universal experience, which points to an important hypothesis: the grief of a bereaved mother is intensified as she yearns for the sensory experiences that were a part of her nurturing, caregiving role. This might explain why mothers who are told by well-meaning others that their memories will bring them comfort often say, "The memories are painful, because with them comes the realization that I'll never be able to see or touch or hear my child again." Mothers who describe this feeling seem to be referring to a kind of sensory deprivation, in which they are no longer able to demonstrate their love for the child or receive from the child the sensory feedback that says "I love you, Mom."

A thousand such reminders, different for each mother, arouse an awareness of previous experiences with the deceased child. The sound of a noisy muffler, the smell of crayons in a school classroom, the sound of a school bus moving up a hill, the laughter of a young man or woman, the sight of a sailboat on a clear summer day, the taste of freshly baked chocolate chip cookies—these are but a few examples. Each of the mother's senses becomes tuned to the touches, tastes, sights, smells, and sounds of the past as they relate to her child. She is keenly aware of her deprivation and with each stimulus the pain of her loss is accentuated.

Case Example: "I was unable to finish my grocery shopping," reported one mother. "Then, as I approached the produce section and saw the fresh carrots, I was overcome with a flood of memories about Terri, who loved carrots. Her favorite after-school snack was carrot sticks dipped in peanut butter. I remembered her so vividly, sitting at the kitchen table telling me about her day in school while munching on a carrot. The sight of those carrots was so painful I ran from the store in tears and sat in my car and sobbed."

Another mother said, "I felt OK when we entered church several months after the death of our infant. But the sound of a small baby crying several pews behind us was more than I could take. I left church in tears and want to hide in my house from now on so I won't be exposed to the sight and sound of a baby. I long to cuddle and feed my baby, but I know I'll never be able to do that again."

My own experience caught me unawares, almost 3 years after the death of my son. On a cold autumn day, my husband, daughter, and I clustered around the fireplace for the first fire of the season. It seemed a perfect time for hot chocolate with big marshmallows floating in a mug. With my first taste of that sweet, steamy liquid came a flashback and instant tears as I remembered David's face and heard him saying, "I eat my marshmallows before they melt."

Any bereaved mother can list her own examples of the times her memories have been called forth by simple, daily occurrences, times in which she relives a previous sensory experience with her child. One might argue that as humans we all perceive the world through our senses, no matter what or whom we are experiencing. But the world of a mother and her child is one in which the senses of a mother play a vital role from a period before the birth of the infant.* Reflect momentarily on what happens when a mother cares for her infant. She bathes and grooms the baby, patting and powdering; she feeds the infant, testing food temperature by bringing it to her lips, and stroking as she

---

*In discussions with bereaved mothers, it is rare to find someone other than a mother as the primary caregiver for children. Mothers who work full time are usually responsible for taking their child to daycare, school, or other activities. It is the mother who most often takes a sick child to the doctor or stays home from work when a child is ill. With the preponderance of single parent households in the United States headed by women, this is particularly true. This is not to say that in some two-parent households parenting responsibilities are not shared or that such a shared arrangement would not be more ideal. It is merely to note that the present norm is one in which mothers are more involved in child care.

burps the infant; she touches a feverish forehead or rubs a fresh bruise, often completing these activities with generous hugs and kisses. She awakens to the sound of a small voice in the middle of the night calling "Mommy." She watches a tooth erupt through a tender gum, or sees a tiny round head sprout tufts of curly hair. A mother is involved in a sensory way in caring for her infant. The activities change as the infant grows and becomes more independent, but always, even as the child becomes an adult, the mother has a relationship with her child that involves sensory experience. During teenage or adult years, the pat or hugs exchanged between mother and child are meaningful. Mothers still delight in preparing a child's favorite foods or hearing the child share new adventures. The meaning a mother attributes to these sensory experiences is most often associated with loving and caring about her child.

INTERVENTION BY THE PROFESSIONAL CAREGIVER

The general stages of grief quoted in the literature often are applied to intervention with bereaved parents. One mother said, "My therapist kept telling me I was in the angry stage, but that didn't help me at all. I knew I was angry; I wanted her to understand what I was angry about." Labeling a bereaved mother's emotion simply identifies that which she is expressing, whether it be sadness, anger, or guilt. A bereaved mother does need reassurance that her feelings are a normal response to loss. However, beyond that there is a deep need to be understood. Many bereaved parents argue that only another bereaved parent can truly understand their pain. At some level this is true, but I have been helped, along with many other bereaved mothers, by the nonbereaved caregiver.

How can the professional caregiver who has not experienced the death of a child be helpful to the bereaved mother? No amount of technique or practice can make the nonbereaved professional qualified to successfully help the bereaved mother; it requires a willingness to enter into the pain of the bereaved mother. The rare caregiver who attempts this will become acquainted with a pain that will annihilate attempts at professional distance or demeanor. He must recognize the mother as expert, while acknowledging his own limited role as a facilitator and source of support.

One of the keys to understanding the multiple facets of an individual mother's grief is to understand the process of parental grief. Since that process varies from parent to parent, the caregiver must hear the "story" of each bereaved mother with whom he works. Only after becoming familiar with that story can the caregiver address the question that is central to understanding the process of parental grief: "What is it like for you now, learning to live without your child?" The answers to this question will be similar, but never identical, among bereaved mothers. The answers will also vary for each individual with the passage of time and the ebb and flow of daily emotions.

My suggestions for intervention are limited, but allow for a thorough journey through the painful grief process with a bereaved parent. First, listen to the "story" of each bereaved parent. Remember, it does not end with the death of the child. The parent is examining and reexamining the pieces of the "story," sorting information that may once have seemed insignificant. As her "story" unfolds, a mother begins to recognize the time spent each day caring for her child, either directly or indirectly, or planning for activities with her child. After her daughter's death, one mother said, "My entire day seems consumed with reminding myself I no longer need to do the routine things I once did for Bobbie. I don't need to pick her up at school, I no longer make cookies for her class or take her to ballet lessons, or help her with homework or fix her hair. I still do these things for my other girls, but I'm aware every day of what I can no longer do for Bobbie." The "story," then, involves not only facts about the birth of the child and anecdotes about the life of the child, but also circumstances surrounding the death of the child and all of the emotions, past and present, relating to the life *and* death of that child. This brings us to the second suggestion for intervention.

Part of a mother's ongoing story is her experience of day-to-day life without one of her children. Ask the question "What is it like for you now, learning to live without _____ ?" (It is important to always refer to the child by name, rather than as "your son or daughter," which tends to depersonalize the child.) Implicit in this question is the knowledge that grieving is a learning process that takes a bereaved parent time to master. It is no easy task to finish one's relationship with one's child. Parents are no longer prepared to live without one of their children, because in today's society it is expected that children will not precede their parents in death. The process, then, involves learning what seems unnatural. A parent learns slowly what it means to have a child missing on holidays, or special occasions, or at the evening dinner table. More importantly, a parent learns slowly that a part of life will always include some sadness over the loss of a part of self, a loss of love. In the book *The Bereaved Parent* Harriet Schiff states, "To bury a child is to see a part of yourself, your eye color, your dimple, your sense of humor, being placed in the ground. It is life's harshest empathetic experience and must therefore be the hardest one with which to deal" (p. 23).

The mother who is learning to live without her child is faced with a lifelong task. At each milestone in her own life and that of her family she is cognizant of the fact that one of her children is missing. The marriage of a surviving sibling, the birth of grandchildren, each of her birthdays and anniversaries—these are all events during which she will try to imagine how life would have been different if her deceased child had lived. A small part of each bereaved mother grieves forever. This presents a conflict with a stage of grief the literature refers to as *acceptance*. It seems this stage has erroneously been interpreted to mean freedom from pain or sorrow as a result of having finished grieving. My personal experience, and that of numerous other bereaved mothers, points to another definition of *acceptance* for the bereaved mother. *Acceptance* means recognition that I will live the rest of my life without one of my children. I will think of that child during the sad times in my life and wish that child could be with me to share the happy times. My joy will always be somewhat diminished and my sorrow more poignant because a part of me is gone forever.

Consideration of this new definition by the professional caregiver will ensure realistic expectations for treatment of the bereaved mother. Her sadness on the anniversary of her child's death or her occasional "blue day" will be seen as a normal part of her ongoing process. The misused label *unresolved grief* will be replaced with a practical understanding of what it means to be a bereaved mother. Such understanding on the part of the professional caregiver includes recognition of the following realities.

A bereaved mother needs to tell her story. A bereaved mother's story will include her unique relationship with her child, the meaning she attributed to that child's life, the circumstances surrounding the death of the child, a description of the child, anecdotes about the child, and the details of her emotional struggles as she learns to live without her child. The healing of a bereaved mother's grief is dependent upon the willingness of both the caregiver and others to listen as the "story" of a bereaved mother unfolds.

A bereaved mother will never forget her child who died. No matter how briefly or how long a child was a part of a mother's life, that child will never be forgotten. The healing of grief and the ability of a bereaved mother to continue life in a meaningful way does not mean she no longer thinks about or remembers her deceased child. A bereaved mother wants to remember her child as a special part of her life, and her love for her child continues as long as she lives.

A bereaved mother will never be the same. The death of her child, at whatever age, brings irrevocable changes in a bereaved mother. These changes can be positive if she is allowed to grieve. After the death of a child, a mother has new attitudes about the meaning of life and love. She may appear "different": she may be more direct, she may acquire new interests, and she may express her emotions more openly. Unfortunately, all too often the changes in her are viewed as negative by others when this is not necessarily the case.

A bereaved mother will recover. The intense pain and debilitation of a bereaved mother's initial grief will not last forever. With love, support, and encouragement to express her feelings she will be able to find new meaning in her life. She will laugh again, experience joy again, and love again. Her pain may temporarily weaken her, but the healing of the grief of a bereaved mother promotes inner strength and brings with it a new confidence and purposefulness.

References

Schiff, H. S. (1977). *The bereaved parent.* New York: Crown Publishers.

Chapter 20

A Single Parent Confronting the Loss of an Only Child

Evelyn Gillis

Evelyn Gillis is a past member of the Greater Providence Area Chapter of The Compassionate Friends. She was the developer and facilitator of the surviving sibling group. Currently she is the Co-director of the Rhode Island Attorney General's Victim Assistance Program, for which she has developed a statewide computerized letter notification system to inform victims of each step of the criminal justice system, and provides personal in-court assistance to trauma victims of felony crimes during Superior Court proceedings. Ms. Gillis is a bereaved parent.

My daughter, Lorena Mary Main, age 22,
died with my sister, Mary, in an auto accident,
April 26, 1981.
Good night, sweet Lorena.
I'll see you in the morning.
Mom.

———

The word "alone" screams at a single parent. Those of us who become single parents—either through death or divorce—find most physical, emotional, and financial support severed. We must learn to accept independence from our spouse and assume full responsibility for our child. Daily life for our broken family must be maintained and sustained. It becomes necessary to live as normal a family lifestyle as possible.

After we recover from the emotional trauma of death or divorce, we create a new family unit of parent and child. As the child ages, and if we do not remarry, our relationship evolves beyond that of parent and child. Our lives become closely entwined. The child becomes a companion and helpmate. All of our parental love and caring is given to this one child.

Upon the death of the child, we face the absence of support from another adult who would share the same feelings of loss and grief. After being told of the child's death, we alone carry the responsibility of the funeral arrangements. Even when help is offered by friends and family, we must face those difficult final decisions alone.

After the funeral, when other people return to their own homes and families, we are left to face the reality of the child's death, alone in a house that offers nothing but silence. In the first few months we may charge into a whirlwind of activity. Dinner invitations, nights of visiting, weekends away, and even a movie alone—we'll try anything to get away from the emptiness and silence at home. Eventually, physical exhaustion limits such activity. And what is left? Nights alone in a silent house.

We cry out to have another person alongside who knows, really knows, what the death of the child means, someone who shares those special memories of how our family once was. And that person could be anyone. We reach out to family, friends, and sometimes even strangers, only to find it isn't enough. They did not know the child as we did. They cannot understand and return the depth of feeling. They cannot because they do not feel it. We are alone, trying to cope with the insane madness of grief and unable to share our emotions or remembrances with another. During those terrible times when we lose control of our mind and body there is no one to touch us, hold us, and reassure us that we are not crazy. In the midst of this madness there is just silence. From somewhere we have to find the strength to regain self-control. We are totally responsible for ourselves.

Within a week or two after the death we must return to our job and profession. For 8 hours a day or more we are confined with co-workers who expect us to produce and be as normal as possible. During these hours we must suppress our intense feelings of sadness, anger, hate, despair, and fear, for society will not accept our expressing such negative emotions. And we ourselves consider this unacceptable public behavior. These emotions are intense. When they grab hold of the body, most of us cannot control our reactions. The flowing tears, the shaking, nausea, vomiting, and the inexplicable pain through the body erupt as though they had a will of their own.

Conditions in the home change as well. There is no desire to clean house, shop for and cook food, entertain. Doing these things for one person is not enough. What does it matter if the refrigerator's bare insides all but echo? Food sustains life, and life is now a burden. Within us, a storm of fear and self-doubt rages. Why am I unable to function? Why can't I maintain my job and home? Why did my child die? Was it my fault? Am I a bad person? Am I being punished? Who will help me in all of this? No one. We must totally shoulder the feelings of doubt, guilt, and blame. If we had custody of the child, we may be blamed by the other parent, thereby increasing the feeling "I am to blame." An ugliness and hatred for the other parent may grow, especially if that parent has remarried and has other children. At night, at home, the hours crawl until it is time to sleep.

Perhaps we have one glass of wine to help us sleep. Sleep does not come. One more glass. Still sleep eludes us, as exhausted as we are, and we are alone. Be it one glass of wine or enough wine to bring us to the point of insensibility, hoping to deaden the pain, there is no one to help. There is no one to say "You don't need that," "Come to bed," or "We can talk." And most times there is not even the strength to make a phone call to ask for help. And who to call at this time of night? Friends and family would understand a call for help once or twice, but certainly not for the many months that these conditions exist. We are part of an exclusive club that all members wish they had never joined.

After hours of raging pain perhaps there is some sleep, but sleep, in its lack of mercy, does not last long. There are nights when we awake screaming from nightmares and we are in the dark alone, too frightened to try to return to sleep for fear the nightmare will return. In the morning, in this condition, we must present ourselves at our place of business, knowing that we must maintain the standards of our profession. Anything less may put us in jeopardy of losing our income, and this cannot happen because we are responsible for ourselves.

Having been responsible single parents and realizing that we are no longer can be devastating. Our need to be comforted by another adult is great. This realization takes time. It could be months before we are aware we are not coping as well as we could. For this reason we must not always be alone. We must reach out to family and friends. Best of all we should join a self-help group of bereaved parents. They alone will be there for us in the many months and perhaps years that are needed to learn to cope with the death of a child. We need understanding adult companionship to help us become strong, secure, childless, single adults.

Our children are our roots of family. With the death of an only child we know that this is the end of any family life. One day we were parenting, the next—nothing. We will never again hear those words "Hi, Mom"; we no longer have a person who is truly ours. Where once was a happy family now exists a solitary person. What was once "we" is now "I." In a family-oriented society we find ourselves personless, with no one to share the joys and sorrows of life as do a child and parent. We feel the absence in our homes of any activity concerning children. There is nothing to do for our child; we are no longer needed. We begin to feel a sense of aloneness. How different this feeling is from feeling lonesome or lonely. Those feelings can be corrected just by being social with family or friends. I became so affected by this feeling of aloneness that when ordering carry-out food from a restaurant I was unable to order just one dinner; I had to order at least two. A feeling would come over me that if I ordered one dinner everyone in the restaurant would know that I was truly alone. It is difficult to be a family of one.

Gone are the graduations, birthday parties, proms, and the dream of my child's wedding. Those once wonderful holidays, Thanksgiving and Christmas, will never be celebrated again as a family, if indeed celebrated at all. The thought of Christmas in my home with a tree, decorations, gifts, and a turkey, without this precious person, is unbearable. My grief on normal days was so intense that with the approach of these holidays I feared for my sanity. How would I ever pass these days without becoming insane? Not having other children for whom a pretense of holidays would have to be made, my home was barren at Christmas. I also was unable to accept invitations from family and friends to share these holidays in their homes. I could not face being in the presence of their children knowing that my child was dead.

I will never become a grandparent, never see my family grow through my daughter and her family, never have anyone to whom I can pass on my family china. What will happen to me as I grow old? Who will come to me on holidays? If I become ill or infirm, who will care about and for me? Yes, I know there are people who care for me, but I also know they have families of their own, and that makes the difference. All these things and more contribute to that feeling of aloneness. Never again in social situations will I be able to say "This is my daughter, Lorena" and know the love and pride I felt in having her. Instead, when asked that cruelest of questions, "How many children do you have?" I know the answer: "I had a daughter; she's deceased." Before the death of my daughter I did not realize how much that question was a part of life. Being childless, learning to answer that question became one of the most difficult adjustments. And saying it reinforced that feeling of aloneness.

My visits to the cemetery were overly long. Sometimes I sat by her grave for 5 to 6 hours. Although I knew I should leave, being alone, I could not find the strength to go to my car and drive away. Nor did I want to. This became the place where I felt I belonged. I would trace my fingers along the indentations of the newly laid grass, digging little holes to see how far down into the earth I could dig, all the while telling Lorena, "Don't be afraid, I'll get you out of here. I'll take you home with me." During this period my thoughts of suicide surfaced. At first it was just a strong urge to follow her. I could not accept on blind faith that she was safe and free from harm. I had loved and protected her in life and I wanted to love and protect her in death. Some spark of self-preservation brought me to a suicide counselor. She called me daily. Hour after hour she would listen to me talk about Lorena, how agonizing the pain was and how I could not bear it one more minute. She helped me to understand I really did not want to die. I just wanted the pain to stop, and suicide seemed the way to become free from this pain. It is because of her day-after-day patience and understanding that I am alive today.

For my life to change, I had to give to someone the love and caring I had for my child. But I felt it was better not to love, not to give, to protect myself from pain. It was many months before I could reach out to others. Later I became the chapter leader of a sibling group in The Compassionate Friends' organization. If I had not learned to love and give again, I would always have had that feeling of aloneness.

Chapter 21
Grief of Siblings

John Stephenson

John S. Stephenson, Ph.D., is an Assistant Professor of Sociology at San Diego State University. He is the author of the book *Death, Grief, and Mourning,* and he has written many professional articles dealing with the grief process. In addition to his teaching and research, Dr. Stephenson is a family therapist in private practice. Dr. Stephenson is a bereaved parent.

> In losing a sibling the child loses a playmate, a companion, someone
> who is a buffer against the parents, someone who may love and comfort
> him, someone with whom he identifies and whom he admires. In short
> he loses someone dearly loved as well as perhaps envied and rivalrously
> hated. (Raphael, 1983, p. 114)

The purpose of this chapter is to review the literature on grieving
children with special emphasis on those who have lost a sibling. Much
of the information in this chapter is applicable to peers as well and can
be extrapolated to them depending on the strength of their relationship
with the deceased child.

FACTORS INFLUENCING CHILDREN'S
REACTIONS TO LOSS OF A SIBLING

To begin to understand siblings' grief, we have to remember that much
of how siblings grieve will be determined by the fact that they are
children, not adults. Their thoughts and feelings, and the way they are
expressed, will be shaped by their age, developmental level, and previous
experience with death. This is particularly true when considering a
child's ability to understand death. Other factors that will influence the
way a child reacts to loss of a sibling are the child's personality, her
relationship to the deceased sibling, and the manner in which the
sibling died.

The Child's Understanding of Death

In order to understand how children react to a death, it is important
to know what death means to them. If a child has no conception of the
finality of death, then the person's absence will seem as temporary as a
parent's trip to the supermarket. The death will be met with the same
emotional response a trip to the store might evoke. Thus, a child who
does not appear to be grieving should not be viewed as uncaring; she
may simply be unable to fully comprehend the death of a sibling.

The early work of Nagy (1948) showed that children's understanding of death can be correlated with chronological age. Nagy suggested
that there are three levels of cognition in children under 10. Under 5
years of age the child sees death as a reversible state, like sleeping.
Between 5 and 9 years of age, death becomes personified and something
one can avoid. After 9, the child begins to recognize the finality of
death. It should be noted that Nagy's finding of the personification of
death has been called into question, and is considered culture-specific
by many (Kane, 1979; Koocher, 1974).

More recently, studies have related children's conceptualizations of death to Piaget's theories of intellectual development (Koocher, 1973; Salladay & Royal, 1981). The child involved in preoperational thought (ages 2 to 7) often engages in magical thinking, which would account for Nagy's finding that death is initially seen as reversible. Concrete operational thinking (ages 7 to 11) relates to death in physical terms, with an emphasis upon causation. For example, a child at this stage is aware that death can be caused by illness or trauma to the body, such as stabbing. She realizes that death causes the failure of the body, and that it is irreversible. The formal operations stage (11 and over) allows the child to understand more abstract aspects of death, such as parts of the body wearing out or the possibility of death occurring to self and others in the future.

A child's conception of death is also affected by life experiences. Studies of children who are terminally ill reveal that these children often display an understanding of death and their own impending deaths that belies their years, but certainly not their experiences (Spinetta & Deasy-Spinetta, 1981). This "advanced" understanding of death may also hold true for children who have experienced the death of a member of their nuclear family (Kane, 1979). Reilly, Hasazi, and Bond (1983) studied children's death experiences and their understanding of death itself. They concluded that children's concept of death is a function of both their cognitive developmental level and their life experiences.

The Child's Personality

Obviously the personality—the emotional makeup of the child—will be a factor in how the child reacts to death. Like any other trauma, the death of a loved person places emotional demands upon the survivor. Those children with stronger, more developed personalities will stand a better chance of withstanding the vicissitudes of bereavement.

The Child's Relationship to the Deceased Child

Describing Rogers's (1967) study, Rosen and Cohen (1981) point out that no specific syndrome of responses to sibling loss was discovered, but birth order was found to play an important role. Older children felt more guilt over their wishes that the younger child would disappear, while younger children felt more of a burden to replace the lost child. Rosen (1986) states that the nature of the sibling relationship will affect the survivor's grieving. Citing Bank and Kahn's (1982) paradigm, Rosen describes sibling relationships as lying somewhere along a bipolar continuum, with a symbiotic, fused relationship being one extreme, and strongly "negative and distant relationships, where anger, hostility, and rigid differentiation predominate" at the other extreme (p. 6). The closer the children's relationship was to one of the poles, the greater the chance there will be an extreme grief reaction on the part of the surviving sibling.

The Cause of the Sibling's Death

Another factor that will affect the child's reaction to the death of a sibling is the cause of death. Children who lose siblings through illness need to have a clear understanding of the causes of the disease that has taken the life of their brother or sister (Weston & Irwin, 1963). When children are not given a complete explanation that they can understand, they tend to fill in the gaps themselves. The author knows of one child who believed that her brother contracted cancer because he broke a mirror, and that his illness (which later claimed his life) would go away at the end of 7 years. This is a good example of a child seeking to make sense out of life-threatening illness by using the information available to her. Fortunately this remark was noticed by an adult, who was able to help correct her misconception of the illness.

In addition to understanding the illness that is threatening or has taken the life of a sibling, children need to be assured that they are in good health themselves. Some physicians are sensitive to this, and will take the time to give a brief "physical" to a dying child's sibling to assure the child that she is not ill. It would seem prudent for the parents of the sibling of a terminally ill child to request a routine check-up, if for no other reason than to demonstrate the parents' concern for the health of the well child as well as the ill one.

Accidental or violent death may produce its own particular issues for the surviving sibling, as accidents often imply fault or preventability. Cain, Fast, and Erickson (1964) described instances of families refusing to discuss the accident, to avoid provoking their suppressed anger over the perhaps preventable loss. In addition, an open discussion of the accident might implicate the surviving children, thus dealing another blow to the already grieving parents.

Death by suicide leaves the sibling with a difficult burden to carry. Not only must the child cope with her grief, but also with the social stigma of being a suicide survivor (Stephenson, 1985). Rudestam (1977) states that the family of a child who commits suicide often works to deny the reality of what has taken place, even inventing a new version of the death and suppressing any further discussion of the event. This may lead to the sibling's manifesting disturbed grief reactions later.

Each of these types of deaths discussed—illness, accidental and violent death, suicide—may have its own kind of contingencies that can affect the grieving sibling. The emotional and physical demands of a terminal illness may leave the surviving children feeling abandoned by parents who have devoted their time and energy to the dying child. The sudden trauma of an accidental or violent death may leave unanswered questions of cause or blame that remain unresolved within the family. The suicide of a sibling may leave the surviving children to cope with their feelings of rejection by the deceased child, the family's emotional upheaval over the death, their own grief over the loss, and society's negative and stigmatizing view of suicide. To the author's knowledge, no study has been made of children's reactions to a sibling death that takes into consideration the nature of the death that occurred. It does not seem rash, however, to speculate that sibling death by suicide would place greater demands upon the survivors than other forms of death.

CHILDREN'S REACTIONS TO LOSS OF A SIBLING

The death of a member of the family is certainly a major event in a child's life. Like any other major event, it will have a lasting impact upon the child. Because of our cultural image of children, whom we see as both innocent and vulnerable, we tend to view the intrusion of death into a child's world as something that can do great damage (Stephenson, 1985). While this certainly is possible, we should be aware that most children will be able to successfully grieve the loss of a brother or sister. Stehbens and Lascari (1974), in examining 64 siblings of leukemia victims, found that 70% of the siblings were reported to be back to normal relatively soon after the child's death. Twelve children were reported to have suffered depressions, enuresis, abdominal pain, or restless sleep, but they returned to normal in a short period of time. Seven were reported to have done poorly in school for a few months, but only two displayed lasting emotional problems after the death of a brother or sister. The citing of these studies is not meant to dismiss the grief of children as a transitory phenomenon; rather, it is meant to emphasize that with proper emotional support and normal cognitive functioning usually the child can overcome the trauma of sibling death. The finding that grief reactions after the death of a sibling need not invariably lead to dysfunction is supported by other researchers as well (Osterweis, Solomon, & Green, 1984; Raphael, 1983). While we will be focusing upon the problems that may arise after the death of a sibling, these data indicate that incapacitating grief reactions are not typical after the death of a brother or sister. Perhaps Rosen and Cohen (1981) summed up children's grief over the death of a brother or sister best when they wrote:

> In general, the reactions of children to sibling loss are varied in intensity and duration, and are dependent upon many factors operating in the child's life. Severe pathology is not a necessary outcome. Among the common reactions cited are guilt and depression; distorted concepts of illness, death, doctors, hospitals, and religion; death phobias; comparisons, identifications, and misidentifications with the dead child; disturbances in cognitive functioning; loss of appetite and psychosomatic disorders; separation anxiety; behavior problems and change of role within the family. (p. 217)

Two emotional responses typical of children when a sibling has died are ambivalence and guilt. The ambivalent, love-hate emotions that a child feels may be based in part on thoughts that are the natural outgrowth of sibling rivalry. For the younger child, feelings of omnipotence have not yet been tempered by reality, and the child's thoughts can take on a kind of magical power. The death of a sibling, loved and yet often hated, may lead to confusing emotions concerning the loss. A straightforward acknowledgment of the commonality of such feelings can do much to ease the child's fears about his grief reactions.

The guilt that a child feels after the death of a sibling may spring from various sources. First, there is guilt that arises because the child was in some way responsible for the death that has occurred. Second, there is guilt as the result of magical thinking, whereby the child believes his thoughts brought about the sibling's death. Third, there is guilt that is manifested in order for the child to get a sense of control over his life (Osterweis, Solomon, & Green, 1984). By accepting the blame for the death, the child avoids the existential dilemma of living in a world of randomness and chance. Cain, Fast, and Erickson (1964) suggest that guilt may also be imposed upon the child by the parents when the child does not outwardly mourn the death to the degree that the parents might have expected. Finally, Rosen and Cohen (1981) describe Jaglon's (1973) study, which argues that children may manifest a kind of survivor guilt, feelings that they, the less worthy, should have died rather than the sibling.

There is a debate in the literature concerning the importance of guilt in children's grieving. On the one hand, Brice (1982) claims, "I have never encountered a case of childhood mourning where the child has not believed that he/she caused the death" (p. 318). On the other hand, Cain, Fast, and Erickson (1964) state:

> Our growing case material soon served to demonstrate the limitations of perhaps the one notion of any currency about the import of sibling death, namely, the concept that the primary if not exclusive patholog- ical impact of a sibling's death upon the surviving child is one of guilt over rivalry-bred hostile wishes which, through the early omnipotence of thought, are seen as having been fulfilled by and responsible for the sibling's death. (p. 742)

While there is a lack of unanimity about the amount of guilt present in children's grieving, there appears at least to be agreement that guilt is a common and primary emotion felt by surviving children after the death of a sibling.

Like guilt, denial is a defense mechanism that is common in the literature on grief and that takes on special significance when seen in children. In this poignant example, Furman (1970) describes a child's efforts to deny the loss that has occurred.

> A six-year-old who always had a lively interest in school lost his mother. He suddenly stopped bringing home any of his school papers. He forgot them, leaving them in his desk at school. The boy was not able to explain this to his father. Overhearing one of these conversations, his older brother said, "I know why. There is no mother home to bring the papers to. It would make him too sad so he forgets them at school." (p. 79)

Kliman (1968) suggests that one of the tasks of childhood grieving is to test the reality of the loss. With fantasy and magical thinking so powerful in children's thinking, especially younger children's, it is easy to see how denial could become a powerful defense against the reality of death. As we shall see when we investigate the role of the family in childhood mourning, much can be done to help the child to accept the reality of the loss. We must be aware, however, that a child's seeming lack of grief over a death is not necessarily repression or denial at work. As noted before, the child may not grieve in the open manner typical of adults. The import of the loss is not as easy for the child to comprehend, and the child's grieving may be more subtle as the impact of the death is slowly realized (Stephenson, 1985).

At the other end of the emotional spectrum, Weston and Irwin (1963) report that occasionally a child will openly grieve with as much intensity as the parents. The child may never have seen his parents express such strong emotions. Unable to openly grieve with the same intensity, the child imitates the parents' feelings. For example, the author experienced the open crying of a 9-year-old at the news of the death of his stepbrother. Some time later, he commented that he never cried when his stepbrother died. In fact, the strong emotions displayed by the parents evoked in him a sympathetic reaction. This reaction was the source of his tears, and not the death that had occurred.

Adolescents may have other motivations to suppress their grief. Their need to conform to their peer group may mean avoiding the stigma of being one who has experienced a loss, of being one whom death has touched. In fact, the adolescent may endeavor to appear unscathed by the loss of a sibling in order to maintain his social and emotional equilibrium (Garber, 1985).

EXPLAINING DEATH TO CHILDREN

Children need to know what has happened to their brother or sister. They will often ask why the child died, inquire about what "dead" and "death" really mean. In responding to the questions a child might ask, we often fall back on four strategies: overly simplistic explanations ("She's living up in the clouds"), incomplete religious interpretations ("God took him"), obfuscation ("Your sister has succumbed as the result of a massive allergic reaction"), or the ever-popular parental response to stressful questions, "We'll talk about it some other time." We should be aware that these strategies may negatively affect the child's understanding of the death and his subsequent grieving.

Simplistic explanations usually convey two messages. The first is that death, at least in part, is mysterious. As a result of learning this, the child may make up his own explanation. Oversimplification leaves too many questions unanswered, and thus the child must rely on his own resources to fill in the blanks. For example, if the child is told that his dead sister is "living in the clouds," the child may then come to believe that airplanes can take him to see her. One child reasoned in this manner: His sister was in heaven. Heaven was in the sky. Birds fly in the sky. Did this mean that birds were going to eat his sister? (Cain, Fast, & Erickson, 1964). The second message that may be conveyed by an overly simplistic explanation of death is that the adult does not want to discuss the matter any more. Children are quick to pick up on this, and will not feel comfortable in bringing up further questions.

Religious explanations of human events have an important role in many families. However, it can be difficult for children to deal with a concept as abstract as God, let alone theology. Rosenblatt (1969) gives us a good example of how a misinterpreted prayer could cause difficulties for a child. Martin was brought in for therapy after the death of his sister, Suzy. Martin said that he worried a lot, especially after reciting the prayer, "Now I lay me down to sleep, / I pray the Lord my soul to keep. / If I should die before I wake, / I pray the Lord my soul to take." Rosenblatt states that Martin

> thought that Jesus had taken Suzy "because he wanted an extra angel." At a later point I said that it was a help to think of the power of Jesus when a person was frightened, but this very power must be frightening to him. "You must think that whenever Jesus needs another angel he might suddenly decide to pick you," I said. Martin gave an emphatic "yes" to this. (p. 327)

Rosenblatt gives us a good example not only of a child's misinterpretation, but of an empathic intervention made by a therapist.

Obfuscation in responding to a child's questions results in the child's having a confused understanding of death or illness. While there is no substitute for direct and simple language, adults need to realize that it is all right to say "I don't know." There are things we don't know about death, and we should not try to shield that fact from children. At that point, we can continue the conversation by telling the child what we believe to be true about what happens to people when they die.

Avoidance of the subject of death or dying leaves the child with no explanation at all. In its extreme form, this leads to a "haunted child" affect, according to Krell and Rabkin (1979). "In such situations, the living child is haunted by something mysterious and uncertain, knowing and yet not knowing, and afraid to ask for clarification" (p. 474).

Cain, Fast, and Erickson (1964) report that the children they studied who had exceptionally strong or morbid reactions often had "confused, distorted concepts of illness, death, and the relationship between illness and death" (p. 745). For example, some believed that only old people die, and had to struggle to reconcile this belief with the death of their sibling. Some children, seeing an older sibling die, decided that to get older meant to die. They thus regressed to a more infantile passive and dependent state. This fearfulness of reaching the age at which the sibling died may also be manifested as an unexplained sense of doom or depression experienced by the child as he reaches that same age.

Grief is a process that begins when a loss is recognized. This means that the child's grieving will be powerfully influenced by how he understands that loss. We can help children who have lost a brother or sister by providing them with a clear understanding of illness and death.

THE FAMILY'S INFLUENCE ON CHILDREN'S GRIEF

The family is the environment in which the child most usually comes to grips with the death of a brother or sister.

> Generally, the child will try to fit into the climate created by the parents. If the circumstances of the tragedy are clear, adaptation is possible. If the circumstances are ambiguous, the atmosphere tense, the climate hostile, then it will be difficult for the surviving child to sort out his or her involvement in the matter. (Krell & Rabkin, 1979, p. 472)

This quote emphasizes the theme of this section: children's grieving will be powerfully influenced by the family. Children look to their parents to give meaning to a particular situation, especially a situation that is unfamiliar and emotionally tinged. A death in the family is a relatively rare phenomenon, and it is not unusual for children to grow to adulthood without any personal experience with death. When a loss occurs, the children look to the parents or other significant adults for cues as to how to behave, both socially and emotionally. When adults are unable or unwilling to communicate with children, the children are left to their own devices as to how to cope with their own feelings of despair, anger, and sadness. Rosenthal (1980) agrees with this, noting that lack of communication with their parents following a death in the family is a common experience among children referred for psychiatric counseling.

Stephenson (1985) views the family as a system that relies upon mutually held images to give meaning to events and actions. A closed family is one that tends to be rigid and insensitive. People are locked into strictly defined roles, with little room for innovation and change. The open family system, on the other hand, is much more dynamic and sensitive to events and feelings both within and outside of the family structure. Each individual in the open family is seen as unique and worthy, and role behavior is influenced by the immediate family needs as well as those of the person in that particular role.

In confronting the loss of a child, the closed family is more likely to deny the impact of the death. Locked into strict ways of thinking, feeling, and behaving, the family is unable to react appropriately to the loss. What appears to be almost bizarre family behavior in the face of the death of a child may, in fact, be the result of an inability to respond to the situation. Family members may revert to modes of behavior that have always been appropriate in the past, even if they do not fit the situation now. Children, especially younger children, are caught up in this inappropriate "reality." For them there is no alternative—they are forced to respond to the death as their parents deem appropriate.

Cain, Fast, and Erickson (1964) give us several examples of pathological behavior on the part of families unable to accept the loss of a child. They report that some fathers who had lost their only sons began to masculinize their daughters. A mother who acted out her anger through one daughter's rebellious behavior sought to turn her sister, the "good" daughter, into a rebellious child after the "bad" daughter's death. In another example of projecting feelings on a surviving child, Tooley (1975) describes parents who transfer their own guilt for the death onto a surviving sibling, making this "bad" child one in need of much punishment and abuse. Cain, Fast, and Erickson (1964) describe a closed system family of four that stayed together on the unspoken agreement that each parent possessed one child. Upon the death of one of the children, the family immediately disintegrated. All of these examples describe a family system that is locked into a rigid view of itself, with no room for the reorganization and working through of feelings mandated by the loss of a child.

The more dynamic, open family can, on the other hand, support the surviving siblings in their grief. By validating the children's feelings, the family gives them permission to deal with the loss and its emotional and social ramifications. By sharing their feelings and thoughts openly, the adults pattern the children's responses as well. Raphael (1983) states that children need to see their parents grieve. This shows them how much their parents cared for their dead sibling, and the siblings learn that they, too, would be mourned should they die. The surviving children can also facilitate the parents' grieving. Weston and Irwin (1963) point out that children's continued questioning concerning death (as a way to work through the loss) may function to lessen the parents' impulse to deny the loss.

Children in single-parent families may feel an additional burden of attempting to meet the adult needs of the parent. Fulmer (1983) describes children who try to distract their mothers from grief by presenting some behavior disorder. The child's misbehavior serves to distract the mother from her sadness. Of course this does not resolve the mother's grief, but rather leads to habitual unhealthy behavior on the part of the child and continued unresolved grief for the mother.

Another important aspect of childhood grief is that surviving siblings often are given a lower priority by society than the parents. This can result in the child's feeling doubly abandoned; first by the sibling, and then by society, which chooses to focus on the parents' grief. The author has seen this process at work in a large family that experienced the accidental death of an adult son. As family members gathered, the focus was upon the grief of the mother and father. Since all but one of the family members were married, they arrived with their respective spouses. In the middle of the evening, the youngest child, an adolescent girl still living at home, cried out, "Where is someone for me?" The family quickly understood that everyone else had the support of a spouse, while she was left alone with her grief. She was encouraged to call a friend to come and be with her, which provided some support for her during her initial grieving.

HELPING CHILDREN COPE WITH THE DYING AND DEATH OF A SIBLING

What should we keep in mind when talking with a child about death, dying, or illness? As we have seen, the child's reasoning ability and past experience with death will affect how much the child can understand. The child also may have a tendency to deny both the reality of death and the feelings the subject evokes, especially if the child is young (Rosen & Cohen, 1981). Thus, after giving a direct and clear explanation for what has occurred, we should ask the child to relate back what she has heard. This will give us an opportunity to look for any misinterpretations or confusions in the child's mind. We also should provide an open environment for the child, so that she feels comfortable in bringing up her own troubled or confused thinking.

Schultz (1982) offers the following suggestions for talking with a child about a death:

1. Get on eye level. Do not talk down to the child, either physically or mentally.
2. Always touch. "During times of stress, fear, pain or grief the victim can deal with the problem much better when there is skin touch. If the message is too difficult to deal with, touch alone can convey caring and support" (p. 30).
3. Let the child know what to expect. Tell the child what the dead or dying child will look like. Explain what is being done for the sick child. Tell the child that sometimes, despite everything that we do, some people don't get better; they die.
4. Give the child meaningful tasks to perform. Suggest meaningful things that the child might do for the dying or dead brother or sister. For example, if there will be active participation in the funeral service by those attending, see that the surviving siblings have an opportunity to take part.

Coping with a Dying Sibling

All too often the siblings and friends of a dying child are not given a high priority. Of course the dying child is the focus of most of the attention, usually followed by the parents. Schultz (1982) puts it this way:

> A doctor may pat a child on the head but he relates to the parents. Social workers give permissions and encouragement to the parents. A minister may greet the child with a sentence or two but he comforts the parents. . . . Nurses care deeply about a grieving child but communicate with the parents. Who is the child's advocate in a crisis situation? Who is primarily interested in the child first and then the family as it relates to the child? (p. 27)

Feinberg (1970) describes five aspects of his therapy with two siblings of a dying child. These guidelines are valuable for the lay person as well as the helping professional:

- *Forthrightness.* This involves being ready to tell the truth when asked, and establishing a relationship based on openness and trust. Feinberg suggests beginning by asking children for their understanding of the sibling's illness.
- *Immunizing discussions.* In order to put death and dying in a context that is easier for children to manage, Feinberg uses discussions of losses of pets or people outside of the immediate family. This allows the children to relate to the dynamics of loss without immediately and directly confronting the impending sibling loss.
- *Allowance for catharsis.* All too often, the typical reaction to children's strong feelings is an attempt to suppress them. This may be accomplished by distracting them or reacting negatively to their feelings. Conversely, by validating those feelings, we may help children to understand their emotional responses to the impending loss. By allowing them to openly express their feelings, we give them permission to vent feelings of anger and sadness surrounding the death of a brother or sister.
- *Emphasis upon reality.* We should work to ensure that children have a clear and correct understanding of what is happening. The events surrounding the illness, the treatments that are being given, death, and what is happening emotionally to others are all important topics for discussion. "Confusion and ambiguity have a way of being contagious; mourning cannot effectively occur when a child is burdened by misconceptions, misperceptions, and fantasies" (Feinberg, 1970, p. 658).

- *Initiation of mourning.* Children need to receive permission to share memories and feelings concerning the dead sibling, and to receive validation of their thoughts and feelings. The helping professional can also allow children to share feelings that might be seen initially as unacceptable in the family context (Schumacher, 1984). For example, anger may be felt for the pain the dead child has caused the parents, or for the overprotectiveness that the surviving children have been burdened with as a result of the sibling's death.

The importance of Feinberg's guidelines can be seen when we look at Koocher and O'Malley's (1981) findings in interviews with over a hundred siblings of children with a life-threatening illness. Many of their more negative findings could have been alleviated by implementation of Feinberg's approach. Some of the pertinent themes Koocher and O'Malley reported were:

> Having a brother or sister with cancer had a sustained and profound impact on their [sibling's] lives.
>
> Emotional concerns such as feeling left out, jealousy, resentment, and fears for their own health were relatively common in the siblings.
>
> It may be that siblings aged 6–10 at the time of cancer treatment are particularly vulnerable to feelings of rivalry and the attendant difficulties.
>
> Closed communication systems in families may contribute to the development of behavioral and emotional problems among the cancer patient's siblings.
>
> Many of the siblings' problems could apparently have been prevented or ameliorated by providing direct factual information at the time of diagnosis and during treatment. (pp. 110–111)

Coping with the Death of a Sibling

Children are sometimes at a disadvantage in grief because people try to protect them from the reality of death. Occasionally parents will not allow their children to attend a sibling's funeral. The child should be given the opportunity to attend, and what will take place should be openly discussed. If the child chooses not to attend, that decision should be honored, once it has been established that the child has a full understanding of what the funeral entails.

Schumacher (1984) interviewed surviving siblings between the ages of 9 and 13 in 15 families. In addition to the issues raised in other studies and already cited, several other concerns were often mentioned by the survivors. Guilt appears to be the most difficult emotion for the surviving child to recognize and understand. Often these children reported wishing that they had died instead of their siblings. The surviving children also evidenced concerns about what to tell their friends, often feeling that they had become social outcasts as a result of the death of a sibling. The children also expressed some fearfulness at getting on with life, lest their happiness or moving forward with their lives be seen as evidence that they didn't care about their dead sibling or their parents' grief.

Because the child is so dependent upon the family for understanding reality and interpreting feelings, much of the clinical literature on facilitating childhood grieving has focused upon working within the family context. Krell and Rabkin (1979) cite three tasks of family therapy. First, the therapist must encourage the family to work through suppressed and unresolved grief. Second, the family structure should be loosened so that new or changing roles and identities can be developed. This process allows the family to adjust to the loss of a member. Third, the communications between and experiences of family members need to demystified and openly shared and understood.

Fulmer (1983) suggests the therapist use the technique of "joining" to frame the feelings of family members as grief, which is normal and will diminish over time. Unexplained feelings, such as dysthymic and hopeless feelings, should be reframed as grief. Similarly, children's acting-out can be redefined as attempts to help the parents, thus avoiding blame and strengthening the bonds between the children and parents. Fulmer also suggests that the helping professional work to break "the rules of the system," thus allowing for expressions of grief that may have been taboo in the closed family system.

There is a great deal of similarity between techniques used to help the child cope with a dying sibling and those used to help the child come to grips with the sibling's death. Open and nonjudgmental communication is necessary in both cases.

THE REPLACEMENT CHILD

We now turn to a particularly unhealthy coping mechanism of parents that directly affects children. No discussion of sibling death would be complete without mentioning the phenomenon of the child who is deliberately conceived in order to relieve the parents of their grief by being a substitute for the dead child. This does not mean that parents should avoid having any more children because they would only be creating a replacement child. The concept of the replacement child is not always clearly understood by the public, who, distrusting their own intuitions, may fear having another child because it will somehow become a replacement child.

There are several distinctions cited in the literature between the dynamics that produce a replacement child and those that produce the normal child. Cain and Cain (1964) report that the replacement children they studied were conceived by parents who suffered exceptional grief reactions, who had another child in order to relieve themselves of their grief, and who expected the replacement to emulate an idealized image of the dead child. Interestingly, the parents in the Cains' study all reported having decided not to have any more children prior to the death of their child. Replacement children are not allowed to develop their own identities, but are constantly viewed as inferior reflections of the dead sibling. All of Cain and Cain's sample had been referred to a clinic for psychiatric evaluation. Haunted by a dead sibling from whom they could never be emancipated, the children appeared to be fearful, without a sense of their own identity, and all reported that they did not expect to live to adulthood.

Idealization of a dead child by parents is a common enough event. The author has often seen scrapbooks and heard stories of the wonderful actions of dead children. While this is not unusual, when this idealization is exaggerated to the point of perfection and then changed into expectations placed upon the replacement child, it becomes a psychologically intolerable burden.

As we saw earlier, parents may transfer some of their expectations and needs from the deceased child to a living sibling. This is probably quite common, as parents seek to find substitutes for the rewards found in the dead child. Poznanski (1972) points out that this may be done unconsciously by the parents. The question then becomes the degree to which this seeking is imposed upon the surviving child and controls that child's life.

Helping professionals need to be aware of the replacement child syndrome, and to work with grieving parents to understand their motives in wanting another child. (Many parents in the Cains' study reported being advised by professionals to have another child.) Allowing sufficient time for grieving over the lost child is obviously important, and parents may need to be advised that having another child will not diminish their present grief (Poznanski, 1972). In fact, by subverting the grieving process, having a replacement child may render them unable to reach closure with the dead child.

CONCLUSION

The child's reaction to the loss of a sibling will be influenced by many factors: the child's cognitive development, past experiences with death, personality, and relationship with the sibling; the nature of the death; and existing family dynamics. While this chapter has been focused on the negative aspects of children's grief, it should be noted that there may be positive results as well. The author has witnessed families using the death of one of their members as an opportunity to become more united and to share feelings more openly. Roles and values may be reassessed. The survivors may develop a greater sense of family and individual strength. The result of sibling death does not necessarily have to be a life of unresolved grief. Given the opportunity to understand and express his own feelings, and to adapt in healthy ways to the loss that has occurred, the surviving child can overcome the trauma of the death of a brother or sister.

References

Bank, S., & Kahn, M. (1982). *The sibling bond.* New York: Basic Books.

Brice, C. W. (1982). Mourning throughout the life cycle. *American Journal of Psychoanalysis, 42*(4), 315–325.

Cain, A. C., & Cain, B. S. (1964). On replacing a child. *Journal of the American Academy of Child Psychiatry, 3*, 443–456.

Cain, A. C., Fast, I., & Erickson, M. (1964). Children's disturbed reactions to the death of a sibling. *American Journal of Orthopsychiatry, 34*, 741–752.

Feinberg, D. (1970). Preventive therapy with siblings of a dying child. *Journal of the American Academy of Child Psychiatry, 9*(4), 644–668.

Fulmer, R. H. (1983). A structural approach to unresolved mourning in single parent family systems. *Journal of Marital and Family Therapy, 9*(3), 259-269.

Furman, R. A. (1970). The child's reaction to death in the family. In B. Schoenberg, A. C. Carr, D. Peretz, & A. H. Kutscher (Eds.), *Loss and grief: Psychological management in medical practice.* New York: Columbia University Press.

Garber, B. (1985). Mourning in adolescence: Normal and pathological. *Adolescent Psychiatry, 12*, 371–387.

Jaglon, M. (1973). Reactions of three schizophrenic patients to their brother's death. *Annals of Psychiatry and Related Disciplines, 11*, 54–65.

Kane, B. (1979). Children's concepts of death. *Journal of Genetic Psychology, 134*, 141–153.

Kliman, G. (1968). *Psychological emergencies of childhood.* New York: Grune and Stratton.

Koocher, G. P. (1973). Childhood, death, and cognitive development. *Developmental Psychology, 9*, 363–375.

Koocher, G. P. (1974). Talking with children about death. *American Journal of Orthopsychiatry, 44*(3), 404–411.

Koocher, G. P., & O'Malley, J. E. (1981). *The Damocles syndrome.* New York: McGraw-Hill.

Krell, R., & Rabkin, L. (1979). The effects of sibling death on the surviving child: A family perspective. *Family Process, 18*, 471–477.

Nagy, M. (1948). The child's theories concerning death. *Journal of Genetic Psychology, 73*, 3–27.

Osterweis, M., Solomon, F., & Green, M. (1984). *Bereavement: Reactions, consequences, and care.* (Report by the Committee for the Study of Health Consequences of the Stress of Bereavement, Institute of Medicine, National Academy of Sciences). Washington, DC: National Academy Press.

Poznanski, E. (1972). The "replacement child": A saga of unresolved parental grief. *Behavioral Pediatrics, 81*(6), 1190–1193.

Raphael, B. (1983). *The anatomy of bereavement.* New York: Basic Books.

Reilly, T. P., Hasazi, J. E., & Bond, L. A. (1983). Children's conceptions of death and personal mortality. *Journal of Pediatric Psychology, 8*(1), 21–31.

Rogers, R. (1967). Children's reaction to sibling death. In E. Dunlop, in collaboration with M. N. Weisman (Eds.), *Psychosomatic medicine: Proceedings of the First International Congress of the Academy of Psychosomatic Medicine.* Amsterdam, NY: Excerpta Medica Foundation.

Rosen, H. (1986) *Unspoken grief.* Lexington, MA: DC Heath.

Rosen, H., & Cohen, H. L. (1981). Children's reaction to sibling loss. *Clinical Social Work Journal, 9*(3), 211–219.

Rosenblatt, B. (1969). A young boy's reaction to the death of his sister. *Journal of the American Academy of Child Psychiatry, 8*(2), 321–335.

Rosenthal, P. (1980). Short-term family therapy and pathological grief resolution with children and adolescents. *Family Process, 19*, 151–158.

Rudestam, K. E. (1977). Physical and psychological response to suicide in the family. *Journal of Consulting and Clinical Psychology, 45*(2), 167–170.

Salladay, S., & Royal, M. (1981). Children and death: Guidelines for grief work. *Child Psychiatry and Human Development, 11*(4), 203–211.

Schultz, C. (1982). Grieving children. *Critical Care Update, 9*(2), 26–32.

Schumacher, J. D. (1984). Helping children cope with a sibling's death. In J. C. Hansen (Ed.), *Death and grief in the family.* Rockville, MD: Aspen Systems.

Spinetta, J. J., & Deasy-Spinetta, P. (1981). Talking with children who have a life-threatening illness. In J. J. Spinetta & P. Deasy-Spinetta (Eds.), *Living with childhood cancer.* St. Louis: C. V. Mosby.

Stehbens, J. A., & Lascari, A. D. (1974). Psychological follow-up of families with childhood leukemia. *Journal of Clinical Psychology, 30*(3), 394–397.

Stephenson, J. S. (1985). *Death, grief, and mourning.* New York: Free Press.

Tooley, K. (1975). The choice of a surviving sibling as "scapegoat" in some cases of maternal bereavement—A case report. *Journal of Child Psychology and Psychiatry, 16*, 331-339.

Weston, D. L., & Irwin, R. C. (1963). Preschool child's response to death of infant sibling. *American Journal of Diseases of Children, 106*, 564–567.

Section 5

Professional Help for Bereaved Parents

Chapter 22

Individual and Couples Treatment Following the Death of a Child

Therese A. Rando

Therese A. Rando, Ph.D., is a clinical psychologist in private practice in North Scituate, Rhode Island. She received her doctorate in Clinical Psychology from the University of Rhode Island and has participated in advanced training in psychotherapy and medical consultation-liaison psychiatry at Case Western Reserve University Medical School and University Hospitals of Cleveland. Presently she is the Clinical Director of Therese A. Rando Associates, Ltd., a multidisciplinary team providing psychotherapy, training, and consultation in the area of mental health, specializing in loss and grief and the psychosocial care of the chronically and terminally ill.

As a consultant to the U.S. Department of Health and Human Services' Hospice Education Program for Nurses, Dr. Rando developed their program for training hospice nurses to cope with loss, grief, and terminal illness. Her research interests focus on mourning, the experience of bereaved parents, and the emotional reactions of rescue workers. She is the Co-investigator in The National Bereavement Study, a longitudinal multidisciplinary research project investigating the processes and effects of grief.

Dr. Rando has lectured nationally and written about grief and death since 1970. She has numerous articles and chapters in print on the clinical aspects of thanatology, and is the author of *Grief, Dying, and Death: Clinical Interventions for Caregivers* and the editor of *Loss and Anticipatory Grief.*

Some of the material in this chapter is taken or adapted from *Grief, Dying, and Death: Clinical Interventions for Caregivers* by T. A. Rando. Published by Research Press, Champaign, Illinois, 1984. Reprinted by permission.

In memory of Patrick John Sherlock,
who knew how to live.

In order to provide effective therapeutic intervention for bereaved
parents, it is necessary for the caregiver to (1) have a command of the
tasks and processes of grief and mourning in general and how these
specifically apply to bereaved parents; (2) be familiar with the psychological, social, and physiological factors influencing the grief response;
the forms, symptoms, and causes of unresolved grief; and the techniques of grief assessment; and (3) be able to competently utilize the
techniques of grief facilitation and intervention. The commonly experienced symptoms of parental grief have been delineated in Chapter 1.
This chapter looks at the specific tasks and processes of grief and
mourning that give rise to these symptoms. It examines the methods
and information involved in assessment of individuals or couples, and
then concludes with intervention strategies for bereaved parents.

The material offered in this chapter is applicable both to individual
and couples treatment following the death of a child. Interventions have
been delineated that facilitate the normal process of grief, with a small
section at the end devoted to the treatment of unresolved grief.
Depending on the individual case, interventions used to facilitate
normal grief may also be employed, with some modifications and
additions, in the treatment of unresolved grief. Issues specific both to
individuals and to couples are treated. That these are intermingled,
rather than separated out, reflects the fact that there is constant
interplay between individual and couple concerns, whether one is
dealing with a parent alone or the marital dyad as a unit. The caregiver
must be aware of both individual and couple concerns in this type of
loss because it strikes at both dimensions.* Hopefully there would be
the opportunity for some couple contact whenever there is treatment of
an individual bereaved parent. While this is an ideal in many types of
situations that require intervention, it is especially pertinent to the
parental loss of a child for the reasons noted in Chapter 1.

THE TASKS AND PROCESSES OF GRIEF AND MOURNING

The terms *grief, mourning,* and *bereavement* are employed continuously
when discussing loss. At some times they have been assigned specific

------

*Please note that a third critical dimension, that of the family's need for intervention, is
addressed in Chapter 24, "Family Therapy after a Child's Death."

meanings in the literature, while at other times they have been used interchangeably. As used in this chapter, they mean the following:

GRIEF: The process of psychological, social, and somatic reactions to the perception of loss. This implies that grief is (a) manifested in each of the psychological, social, and somatic realms; (b) a continuing development involving many changes; (c) a natural, expectable reaction (in fact, the absence of it is abnormal in most cases); (d) the reaction to the experience of many kinds of loss, not death alone; and (e) based upon the unique, individualistic perception of loss by the griever, that is, it is not necessary to have the loss recognized or validated by others for the person to experience grief.

MOURNING: This term has historically had two meanings. The first, derived from psychoanalytic theory, is a wide array of intrapsychic processes, conscious and unconscious, that are prompted by loss (Bowlby, 1980). It is a process whereby the bereaved individual gradually undoes the psychological bonds that bound him to the deceased, a reversing and undoing of processes that have gone into building the relationship (Raphael, 1983). The second meaning is the cultural response to grief. This implies that there is no one style of grief, but that it is a reaction that, like other reactions, is socially and culturally influenced. As used in this chapter, the term *mourning* recognizes both meanings, but will be used interchangeably with *grief* because of its connotation of the same role and experience in that role for the griever. Likewise the terms *griever* and *mourner* will be interchanged.

BEREAVEMENT: The state of having suffered a loss.

Types of Losses

Losses may be of two kinds: physical (tangible) or symbolic (psychosocial). Examples of a physical (tangible) loss include losing a child or having a house burn down. Examples of a symbolic (psychosocial) loss include getting a divorce or losing status because of a job demotion. Usually a symbolic loss is not identified as a loss per se, so it is not recognized that one must take the time to grieve and deal with feelings about it. Although often symbolic loss is not validated, it will initiate a process of grief just as physical loss will.

Most people find that their most difficult experiences in life have involved a loss of some kind, either physical or symbolic. For many individuals, if the difficult situations they were undergoing (e.g., a divorce, the break-up of a love relationship, a move to another city, development of a chronic illness, retirement) had been interpreted as a "symbolic death," they would have seen that their intense reactions were part of a grief process that they had been unaware they were experiencing. This understanding probably would have enabled them to cope better at the time. In all of the different forms of therapy, one of the main ways in which the caregiver helps is by assisting the client to recognize that a loss has occurred and must now be grieved, or by pointing out that the client's symptoms themselves are a form of grief reaction over the loss. As caregivers, it is critical to identify symbolic losses for clients. When these losses are not identified, individuals will fail to grieve appropriately, or will not recognize or understand the reactions they are undergoing and often suffer additionally as a consequence.

A concept that pertains to all bereaved individuals is the notion of secondary loss (Rando, 1984). This is a loss, either physical or symbolic, that develops as a consequence of the death of the loved one. For example, depending on the roles the deceased fulfilled, the mourner may have to suffer a change of environment, a loss of status, an alteration of relationships with other family members, and other losses because the deceased is gone. At times these secondary losses cause more problems for the griever than the initial loss of the death of the loved one. For bereaved parents, some of the secondary losses might include loss of the hopes and dreams invested in the child, loss of a person to parent, loss of an extension of self, loss of someone to carry on the family name, loss of a confidant, loss of someone to take care of them in old age, loss of a baby-sitter, or loss of status because they are no longer the parents of a notable person. Existing and potential secondary losses must be identified and appropriately predicted with parents, in a manner that does not overwhelm them or establish a self-fulfilling prophecy, so that these losses can be prepared for and grieved. The more secondary losses there are, the greater the amount of grief work that is mandated for the parent.

Specific Tasks and Processes

There are a number of tasks and processes in grief that must be successfully addressed for each physical or symbolic loss to be resolved. Worden (1982) has synthesized the classic conceptualizations of Lindemann (1944) and rearticulated his tasks of grief work. He posits that four tasks must be accomplished for recovery from grief to take place: (1) acceptance of the reality of the loss; (2) experiencing of the pain of grief; (3) adjustment to an environment in which the deceased is missing; and (4) withdrawal of emotional energy and reinvestment of it in another relationship. The goals of grief work, and of all therapeutic grief intervention, are to satisfy these four tasks.

Rando (1984) has added additional clinical observations and suggests that there are several cognitive and intrapsychic processes that must accompany the affective procedures of expression of feeling, catharsis, and reinvestment in grief. Too often caregivers have an incomplete understanding of the importance of the cognitive and intrapsychic aspects of grief work. They tend to focus solely on the reactions to the external world, the emotional responses to the separation from the loved one, and not enough on the changes in the inner world. This is why grievers are often left wondering why they have failed to resolve their loss despite having expressed their emotions: "But I cried for my son"; "I saw a therapist and we talked about my child's death." The three cognitive and intrapsychic processes of grief that mandate changes in the inner world are: (1) decathexis; (2) development of a new relationship with the deceased; and (3) formation of a new identity. Although they will be discussed here individually, they are not mutually exclusive; in fact, they are quite interdependent.

Decathexis

Decathexis is the first cognitive and intrapsychic process that must occur. The early psychoanalytic theorists gave the clearest explanation of it. Freud (1913/1955) said, "Mourning has a quite precise psychical task to perform: its function is to detach the survivors' memories and hopes from the dead" (p. 65). To reach this end, the process of decathexis must occur.

When a parent experiences the loss of a child, she wants to deny that it has happened. However, repeated frustration of the desire to unite with and obtain gratification from the lost child finally convinces the parent that the loss has indeed occurred. In order to avoid the overwhelming feelings that accompany recognition of the separation, the parent creates within her mind a representation or mental image of the deceased. In this way she attempts to hold on to the deceased child. This process is called introjection. It is from this introjected image of the deceased child that the parent must withdraw her emotional energy. All the feelings, thoughts, memories, expectations, hopes, and fantasies that bound the parent to the child are gradually worked through by being revived, reviewed, felt, and loosened. This is a crucial intrapsychic procedure that must be accomplished in order for the bereaved parent to successfully resolve the loss and have unattached emotional energy to invest in subsequent relationships. The operations of decathexis can be summarized as follows:

> The process of mourning, then, involves the following steps: under the influence of the reality that the object no longer exists, the ego

gives up the libidinal ties to the object. This is a slow piecemeal process in order that the ego will not be overwhelmed by a flood of feeling. The mourner pursues this task by introjecting the relationship with the lost object, and then loosening each tie to the now internalized object. For a normal person it is apparently easier to loosen ties with an introjected than with an external object (Fenichel, 1945, p. 394), presumably because in this case our inner world is more tractable than the world around us. Thus, introjection acts as a buffer by helping to preserve the relationship with the object while the gradual process of relinquishing is going on. The ties of relationship are represented by hundreds of separate memories, and the dissolution of the tie to each one of these takes time (ibid., p. 393). In this process, of course, the relationship to the lost person is not abandoned, but the libidinal ties are so modified that a new relationship can be established. (Siggins, 1966, p. 17)

All too frequently caregivers fail to assist the parent to sufficiently review and appropriately process the feelings, thoughts, memories, expectations, hopes, and fantasies that she had about the child. As a result the parent is still emotionally bound to the deceased child in an unhealthy way.

Worden (1982) discusses this particular procedure in task four, withdrawal of emotional energy and reinvestment of it in another relationship. He notes that many people misunderstand this task and feel that if they withdraw their emotional attachment they are somehow betraying or dishonoring the memory of the deceased. Or they are frightened by the prospect of reinvesting their emotions in another relationship, since this, too, might end with a loss. If they do not complete this task they become hindered by holding on to past attachments rather than going on and forming new ones. The therapeutic completion of this task is noted by Worden in relating the words of the teenaged girl who was successfully moving through this process after the death of her father: "There are other people to be loved," she wrote, "and it doesn't mean that I love Dad any less" (Worden, 1982, p. 16).

Development of a New Relationship

The death of the loved one does separate the parent mourner from the deceased child. However, it does not constitute the end of their relationship. As the parent's life is reorganized in the absence of the deceased child, a new relationship must be structured. This relationship is one based largely on recollection, memory, and past experience (Irion, 1966). It is possible for this relationship with the deceased to be a healthy, life-affirming, and life-promoting one in which the physical presence of the loved one is absent, but there is appropriate, sustained, loving, and symbolic connection with the dead (Attig, 1986). Relinquishing the concrete loving of a present person and replacing it with the abstract loving of the absent deceased is the second cognitive and intrapsychic process that must be undertaken.

The grieving parent must decide what the new relationship with the child will be like. First, the deceased must be remembered in context as someone who lived *and* died. A clear, realistic image of the deceased child needs to be developed, reconciling all the differing aspects of the child's personality and all the experiences the parent had with that child. It is also necessary for the parent to consciously decide which parts of the old life and relationship should be retained, and which must be relinquished. This includes finding ways to healthily remember and "interact" with the deceased child as life continues, without impeding decathexis and reinvestment in others. Some possibilities are rituals, anniversary celebrations, prayers, commemorations, memorializations, caring about the concerns and values of the deceased, and healthy identification.

Formation of a New Identity

The third cognitive and intrapsychic process that must be accomplished for successful resolution of grief is the formation of a new identity. This begins when the griever develops different expectations, beliefs, assumptions, and knowledge about the world, a new world in which the child no longer exists. For instance, with every day that passes she gradually learns to stop including the child in her daily plans, to stop thinking about what can be done for the child. Time and again she catches herself looking for the child, or beginning to talk to the child, as she comes to grips with the reality that the child is gone. These changes in looking at the world eventually bring about changes in the griever's identity.

The loss of the loved one also changes the griever personally. Part of an individual dies when one with whom she has been emotionally involved dies. This is because there is a loss of those interactions that help define one's sense of self and of reality. The interactional part of the self created by the unique and special relationship between them becomes one that exists only in memory. For example, the death of a son destroys that part of the interactional self that was the son's mother (Weigert & Hastings, 1977). However, the mother can augment herself as she adjusts to the loss. She can adopt new roles, skills, behaviors, and relationships. She will relinquish certain hopes, expectations, experiences, values, and fantasies after the death and incorporate new ones.

One of the parts of this process is identification. Identification with the deceased first occurs as a way of perpetuating the mental image of the lost loved one to prevent the pain of the loss from being felt. By temporarily preserving the loved object, it allows the griever to work at the process of decathexis without becoming overwhelmed. Later it helps to partially conserve the lost loved one while it adds to the ego, thereby contributing to the enrichment of the personality (Furman, 1974). Just as the ego is constructed in childhood by the process of incorporation of and identification with others, the griever's identity may be changed through her identification with the deceased child. For example, the bereaved parent may alter her personality and sense of self by taking on the child's values, acting on his concerns, adopting his mannerisms, or feeling as he would have felt. Of course, depending on the age of the child, it may be somewhat difficult to have much to remember or with which to healthily identify. This does not automatically mean, however, that parents cannot find some healthy ways to identify with the child, no matter what the age. For instance, it is not uncommon for parents to point out the strength, perseverance, or endurance of their small child during a battle for life. These positive qualities have often been taken up by parents as a way they can incorporate part of their child into themselves permanently. It must be recognized, however, that when incorporation and identification become ways to avoid experiencing the loss and relinquishing the loved one, rather than aids to decathexis, the process has become pathological and must be vigorously confronted.

The griever needs to develop a perspective on what has been both lost and gained as a consequence of the death. That which has been changed, either positively or negatively, must be recognized and grieved for; that which continues must be affirmed; that which is new must be accommodated. It is important to define and integrate the new and old selves and to explore the new life options available. There should be an awareness that a transition is taking place as the new identity shifts from "we" to "I."

Reviewing the information just presented on the tasks of mourning and the cognitive and intrapsychic processes of grief, it should be evident that it is easier for these to occur when the person that has been lost is a peer or a parent, rather than a child. In fact, parental bereavement involves such unique issues that it is poorly explicated by the general model of mourning, with its associated cognitive and intrapsychic tasks. There is an urgent need to develop new models for parental mourning and new criteria for identification of pathology. (Please see Chapter 2, "Parental Bereavement: An Exception to the General Conceptualizations of Mourning" for further discussion of and support for this critical claim.) Evaluating parental bereavement by and with the commonly accepted conceptualizations of grief and mourning appears unwarranted and inappropriate in light of current evidence.

Expectations for Grief

In addition to having a command of the tasks and processes of grief and mourning, the caregiver must be knowledgeable about appropriate expectations for them. One of the most helpful interventions is providing bereaved parents with realistic perspectives of how grief will change over time and how long it will take for them to adapt to the loss.

Frequently *time* is viewed as a healing factor in the process of grief. It is not uncommon to hear "Time heals all," "It just takes time," or "Time will ease the pain." However, time can be helpful in the grief process *only* if the bereaved parent is dealing with the loss, not if he is denying, inhibiting, delaying, or otherwise not working through the loss. It is similar to the healing of a wound. If the wound is cleaned and properly dressed, with time and treatment it will heal. However, if the wound is not appropriately cleaned and tended to, time will not be helpful. In fact, it will only mark the progress of festering infection. In grief, time is therapeutic in that it can allow the griever to put things in perspective, adapt to change, and process the feelings and attend to the tasks of grief work. The passage of time plus these experiences reduces the pain. But, for the person who seeks to avoid his grief, time is distinctly malignant. It only increases the pressure and strengthens the resistance to healthy mourning, providing fertile ground for the development of other pathology. For the griever who has not attended to his grief, the pain is often as acute and fresh years later as it was the day after the death. During these years, other symptomatology has probably developed as well. In contrast, the griever who has successfully completed his grief work will still feel a sense of loss, but time will have helped the healing and the pain will be more in memory than experienced at that moment. In sum, the passage of time can help the individual successfully adjust and adapt to loss, but only if this is accompanied by the active undertaking of grief work.

In general, grievers assume that they should be over grief in only a fraction of the time that it actually takes to recover. The intensity of grief will fluctuate over time and this must be identified, predicted, and legitimized for the griever.

"The *course of the bereavement process* for parents may be considerably longer and more complicated than was previously believed" (Osterweis, Solomon, & Green, 1984, p. 80). Grievers will need to be informed that bereavement does not follow a decreasing linear pattern. It has many ups and downs, twists and turns. It may be difficult to determine where a person is in his grief at any given time. Hardt (1978-79) found that there was a series of stages that the bereaved individual passes through prior to being able to accept the death of a loved one, and that in several of those stages the mourner appears to have a greater acceptance of the death than in fact has been internalized. The research of Rando (1983) on parental grief and adaptation suggests that parental bereavement symptoms may initially subside over a period of time, then increase again long after the death. Fish and Whitty (1983) found corroborating evidence indicating major shifts in parental bereavement symptomatology over time, with intense periods striking bereaved parents years after the loss. Further suggestion of an intensification of symptoms over time is found in Levav's (1982) reanalysis of the classic Rees and Lutkins' (1967) data, in which he found no differences in the mortality rates between bereaved parents and controls in the first year following bereavement, but discovered very great differences over a 5-year period. Fluctuation can also be expected over a shorter range of time. Even the person who is acutely grieving may not evidence it 24 hours a day, since grief must sometimes be put aside for the demands of living.

It should be noted that the grief of bereaved parents has been found to be particularly intense and long lasting. A recent report from the National Academy of Sciences' Institute of Medicine noted that "it is often observed that grieving for a lost child never entirely ends" (Osterweis, Solomon, & Green, 1984, p. 83). As a result, the expectations that are normally appropriate for grieving individuals suffering the loss of someone other than a child may be quite inappropriate for bereaved parents. In all cases the duration of grief is variable and will depend upon the factors influencing the grief response. The research that has been conducted on the duration of grief is scant and inconclusive; it is also artificially biased, since the follow-up period is usually only 18 months, precluding knowledge of what happens after this time period. This prohibits making valid, generalized statements about the length of grief. A rule of thumb is that as long as a grieving behavior is not severely dysfunctional (physically or psychosocially) for too long, harmful to long-term adjustment, or representative of more severe pathology, it can be viewed as not abnormal and seen as part of the process of grief. This allows for a wide variety of reactions and fluctuating symptom intensities.

In general bereavement theory (which usually refers to conjugal bereavement specifically, since it is easier to investigate) it was once held that the *duration of the symptoms* of grief was only 6 months. Now it is known that some of the symptoms may take up to 3 or more years to be resolved, with most of the more intense reactions of grief subsiding within 6 to 12 months. However, the saying "Once bereaved, always bereaved" still remains true. There are some parts of the loss that will continue to be with the griever until he dies. It should be remembered that *no* evaluation can be made about grief and its duration without taking into account all of the psychological, social, and physiological factors that influence a specific grief response. In this regard it must *always* be kept in mind that the loss of a child has been found to be sufficiently different that it warrants consideration of new norms for duration of parental grief response.

Anniversary reactions are to be expected. These are brief upsurges in grief that occur during certain times of the year (for example, during anniversaries of important events or dates related to the child's death, holidays, birthdays) or in the presence of certain stimuli (for example, a special song, photograph, location), and they are normal within limits. All of us have an unconscious time clock within us that keeps track of anniversary dates whether or not we consciously recognize it. It is very common for someone who is experiencing an inexplicable increase in symptoms to later realize that it is the anniversary of a significant event. It should be predicted for bereaved parents that they may feel more vulnerable at anniversary times and that this is quite normal. Continued vulnerability to these intermittent pangs of grief is not incompatible with recovery, as long as the defense against the vulnerability does not take too much effort, reduce grievers' capacity for gratification, or interfere with their functioning (Parkes & Weiss, 1983).

It can also be predicted that certain experiences later in life may temporarily resurrect intense grief resulting from earlier losses. These new experiences may make aspects of the lost relationship important that were insignificant at the time of the bereavement (Siggins, 1966). For example, the bereaved father whose brother becomes a grandfather; the bereaved mother who has no one to whom to pass on her heirlooms; the family who attend the high school graduation to receive the child's diploma posthumously; the bereaved parents who lament the fact that their son is not present to witness the First Communion of his daughter—all these individuals may experience a recurrence of normal grief reactions occasioned by events that poignantly illustrate to them the loss they have sustained. Within appropriate limits these, like anniversary reactions, are normal and expectable.

It is often unrecognized that parents must "grow up with the loss" in a grieving process spanning the years. For example, times at which their child would have graduated, gotten married, or had children are often marked by upsurges in grief. Since parents are rarely prepared for these occurrences, and frequently are unaware of their source, they may feel that they are acting abnormally or have insufficiently addressed their grief. For this reason, parents need to have this phenomenon explained to them in advance.

Criteria for the Successful Resolution of Grief

What indicates the ending of grief? Freud (1917/1957) summed up his criteria for the successful resolution of the grief process rather succinctly. He felt that the work of mourning was complete when decathexis was accomplished and the ego became free and uninhibited again. Others feel that grief is ended when the individual completes the final mourning phase of reorganization (Bowlby, 1980; Parkes, 1972). Lindemann (1944), Worden (1982), and Parkes and Weiss (1983) assert that their respective tasks of grief work must be effectively carried out prior to being able to call the grief process complete. These are quite abstract concepts and difficult to operationalize. For this reason, the following four lists are presented to offer specific criteria pointing to resolution of grief.

Some behavioral criteria suggested by Lazare (1979) indicate the resumption of life with successful resolution of grief. As with other aspects of grief, these will be evidenced in a waxing and waning fashion.

- The depressive symptomatology of bereavement disappears.
- The individual's time sense goes back to normal—she can let time go on now.
- There is a different kind of sadness, a change from a bitter sadness to a sweet sadness.
- The individual displays more equanimity when discussing the loss.
- The individual starts to enjoy holidays again.
- The "searching" for the lost loved one ceases.
- The individual relates better to others.
- There is a healthier relationship with the deceased.

Ten general areas of assessment reported by Parkes and Weiss (1983) appear to capture all the various facets of recovery for the bereaved individuals they studied:

- Level of functioning comparable or better than before the death
- Movement toward solution of outstanding problems
- Acceptance of the loss, including an absence of distortion (belief in the permanency of the death and a realistic image of the

deceased), comfort in talking or thinking about the deceased, and a socially acceptable, rational explanation for the death
- Ability to socialize as effectively as before the death
- Positive and realistic attitude toward the future
- Health back to pre-bereavement levels
- Appropriate general level of anxiety or depression
- Appropriate general level of guilt or anger
- Appropriate general level of self-esteem
- Ability to cope with future loss

Schatz (1984) delineates the signs of healing of a father's grief. These are equally useful for a bereaved mother.

- You begin to look outside yourself.
- You can live with your emotions.
- You begin to have times without emotional stress.
- You are comfortable with your grief.
- Depression does not follow exposure to grief.
- Socially conditioned behavior returns.
- You realize that you and your spouse did your best.
- You find glimpses of meaning in life.
- You start to plan for the future.

The Compassionate Friends, the international self-help group of bereaved parents, distributes the following guidelines entitled *You Know You're Making Progress When:**

- You can remember your child with a smile.
- You realize the painful comments others made are made in ignorance.
- You can reach out to help someone else.
- You stop dreading holidays.
- You can sit through a church service without crying.
- You can concentrate on something besides your child.
- You can find something to thank God for.
- You can be alone in your house without it bothering you.
- You can talk about what happened to your child without falling apart.
- You no longer feel you have to go to the cemetery every day or every week.
- You can tolerate the sound of a baby crying.

---

*Prepared by The Compassionate Friends, Carmel/Indianapolis Chapter, IN. Reprinted with permission.

- You don't have to turn off the radio when his or her favorite music comes on.
- You can find something to laugh about.
- You can drive by the hospital or that intersection without screaming.
- You no longer feel exhausted all the time.
- You can appreciate a sunset, the smell of newly mowed grass, the pattern on a butterfly's wings.

Most of the bereaved eventually come to terms with their grief and carry on with their lives, but total resolution of grief, in the sense of completely finishing the mourning, never truly occurs. The following description was originally written about widows, but the sentiments and observations are equally as true for bereaved parents, although the time frame may be somewhat longer:

> In our earlier formulations we had thought that a widow [bereaved parent] "recovers" at the end of the four to six weeks of her bereavement crisis on condition that she manages to accomplish her "grief work" adequately. We believed that thereafter she would be psychologically competent to carry on with the tasks of ordinary living, subject only to the practical readjustments demanded by her new social roles. We now realize that most widows [bereaved parents] continue the psychological work of mourning for their dead husbands [children] for the rest of their lives. During the turmoil and struggles of the first one to three years, most widows [bereaved parents] generally learn how to circumscribe and segregate this mourning within their mental economy and how to continue living despite its burden. After this time, they are no longer actively mourning, but their loss remains a part of them and now and again they are caught up in a resurgence of feelings of grief. This happens with decreasing frequency as time goes on, but never ceases entirely. (Caplan, 1974, p. viii)

ASSESSMENT

Before any intervention for bereaved parents is planned there must be an accurate assessment of where they are in their grief and of the significant factors that influence it. Intervention without appropriate understanding of the dynamics of a given bereavement situation may not only be inappropriate, but may possibly do more harm than good. The areas that must be assessed include: (1) the psychological, social, and physiological factors influencing the grief reaction; (2) the degree of resolution of the grief or the symptoms and form of the unresolved grief if there has been a disturbance of the normal progress toward grief resolution; and (3) the reason for failure to complete the grief work, if parental grief is unresolved. A knowledge of how to conduct a therapeutic assessment to determine these factors is essential and is provided in the final section of this topic.

Factors Influencing the Bereaved Parent's Grief Reaction

For interventions to be effective they need to be individually tailored to specific grief reactions. Each parent's grief will be idiosyncratic, determined by a unique combination of psychological, social, and physiological factors. These factors will provide the context within which the individual must be evaluated. The loss of the same child does not guarantee that one spouse's reactions will be similar to the other's; nor do all bereaved parents experience the same grief responses because they have all had the same experience of losing a child. The following factors will be more influential in forming a particular bereaved parent's grief response. While explained here in terms of individuals, the factors identified can be extrapolated to bereaved couples as well.

Psychological Factors

The unique nature and meaning of the loss to this bereaved parent. Not everyone responds the same way to the same loss. It is not enough to use solely one's own standards to determine the impact of a loss on another human being. Instead, one must view the loss from that particular person's frame of reference and understand the idiosyncratic meaning it has for that individual. Caregivers must be wary of making assumptions based on their own feelings about the loss.

This is a very critical concept with regard to bereaved parents. It stems from the fact that, more than individuals in any other relationship, parents tend to project myriad thoughts, feelings, hopes, and identities onto their offspring. These must be understood because they help define the parent's loss. For example, in those cases where the child has served as a symbolic extension of another person, or where the death of the child reactivates earlier disappointments and losses because the parent had attempted to compensate for them with the interaction with the child, mourning will not be limited to resolving emotional ties with the deceased child. It will also involve coming to terms with the reactivated past injuries and the abandonment of hope for repair of the earlier losses (Orbach, 1959). In cases where the child was expected to fulfill the parent's unrealized aspirations and heighten the parent's self-esteem, new adaptive techniques will have to be evolved to replace the dependency on the child to achieve these. In essence, the numerous particular meanings this child had for the parent must be both thoroughly identified and explored in order to understand precisely what it is that the parent has lost, and must grieve for, with the death of this child.

The individual qualities of the lost relationship. The psychological nature of the relationship severed and the strength of the attachment will influence the mourner's capacity to complete grief work. For example, a relationship characterized by extreme ambivalence is more difficult to resolve than one that is not as conflicted. If there is a small degree of attachment in a relationship, it will be relatively easier to cope with the grief for that relationship than for a closer relationship where more is felt to be lost.

The roles that the child occupied in the family or social system of the parent. Each family member plays a variety of roles and performs a number of functions within the family unit. The losses resulting from these unoccupied roles must be identified and grieved. For example, the child who dies may have been a tension reliever, a scapegoat, a marriage stabilizer. The death of a child who served to bond the parents together into a tenuous relationship may bring about serious marital conflict. Whatever the roles the child occupied or the functions he performed, their unfulfillment following the death will significantly affect the adaptation of the bereaved parents. First, it will demand a reorientation for them personally. It also will force them to cope with an altered, out-of-balance family system until homeostasis can be reached again. This results in further secondary losses. Additional stressful demands are placed on family members, by the reassignment of roles and responsibilities necessary for reorganization after a death in the family.

The bereaved parent's coping behaviors, personality, and mental health. These psychological attributes will influence the response to grief just as they influence all other responses in life. The bereaved parent will tend to grieve in much the same manner in which the rest of his life has been conducted. Obviously people can sometimes change; however, most will cope with grief using the responses with which they have become familiar. That is why it is critical to have an assessment of the parent's past coping behaviors in order to support those that are the most healthy and offer alternatives for those that are nontherapeutic. This information also helps to establish realistic expectations for a particular bereaved parent. For example, if a person has consistently coped with crises by running away, it is probable that this same behavior will occur in the grief situation. Many other aspects of the personality will also affect the parent's response to grief: self-esteem, conscious and unconscious conflicts, emotions, beliefs, attitudes, values, desires, needs, and strengths. The parent's relationships, current and past state of mental health, and ego strength are also factors influencing the grief response.

When evaluating a couple, interpersonal factors will be critical in addition to the individual ones. These include such variables as communication style; couple rules, norms, and expectations; quality and characteristics of emotional relationship; role assignments; established patterns of transaction; decision-making processes; and habitual methods used to resolve problems or overcome crises.

The bereaved parent's level of maturity and intelligence. These personality attributes have a direct influence on the type of relationship the parent had with the child, the degree of the parent's cognitive understanding of the meaning and implications of death, and the types of coping resources available to the parent. Maturity and intelligence have been found to be consistently and positively correlated with effective coping skills and with favorable resolution of loss.

The bereaved parent's past experience with loss and death. Past experiences will not only set up expectations, but will also influence the coping strategies and/or defense mechanisms used by grievers. This influence can be either positive or negative. Previous unresolved losses generally hinder effective grief resolution. Too many past experiences with death (either occurring simultaneously or over a span of time) can leave the griever depleted emotionally and unable to adequately address the current loss. However, past experience can be helpful. For example, successfully resolved losses can provide the parent with the reassurance that intense grief will diminish if properly addressed.

The bereaved parent's sociocultural, ethnic, and religious/ philosophical backgrounds. These factors will influence how the parent's grief is understood, expressed, and dealt with. They will shape the beliefs, meanings, and values held by the parent for life, death, and life after death.

The bereaved parent's sex-role conditioning. The parent's sex-role conditioning will determine which aspects of grief expression are acceptable and which are conflicted. In Western cultures, males are traditionally conditioned to be controlled and to avoid the expression of feelings. This leaves them with difficulty coping with such emotions as sadness, loss, depression, and loneliness. It interferes with their requesting assistance from others. Consequently, when a male is grieving he may experience conflict, as the expression of feelings necessary for resolution of the grief is often contrary to previous sex-role conditioning. Traditionally women have experienced less conflict between their sex-role conditioning and requirements for successful resolution of the grief. The feelings and behaviors most often prompted in response to a loss are well tolerated in females. However, women tend to have relatively more difficulty in dealing with anger and assuming control and decision-making.

In therapy the parent's sex-role conditioning must be recognized as a strong determinant of the grief response. It should be noted that it is not the function of the caregiver to "de-condition" the parent, but to make the parent just comfortable enough with the necessary responses to grief that the grief work can be resolved.

Obviously, sex-role conditioning is based on stereotypes. For this reason the individual's unique background must be taken into account. Assumptions not based on specific information about that particular individual's upbringing should be made most carefully.

The age of the bereaved parent. The age of the parent is associated with other factors relating to loss, such as the past experience with loss and death and the level of maturity and intelligence. One of the trends that has been found in bereaved mortality studies of conjugal loss is that the loss effect is strongest in the younger widowed and weakens with increasing age (Stroebe, Stroebe, Gergen, & Gergen, 1981-82). Some preliminary evidence suggests that among bereaved fathers the reverse is true, with fathers exhibiting steadily increasing grief intensities relative to their own and their child's ages. (See Chapter 23, "Differences of Grief Intensity in Bereaved Parents," for more on this.) Mothers appear to exhibit relatively constant levels of intensity across their own and their child's ages. This suggests that the age of the father makes a greater difference in grief intensity than the age of the mother, although further investigation of this variable must be conducted.

The characteristics of the deceased. The particular interactional role that the deceased occupied in relationship to the mourner influences the grief response. In the case where the deceased is the child of the mourner, the grief can be expected to be more intense than that following the death of a spouse or parent. Moreover, the age of the child and the type of person he was also will play a large part in the type of reaction the mourner will have. There is a social tendency in our society to approve of grief for those considered "good" and "worthwhile," but not for those who are "bad." However, although the death of a delinquent teenager in the midst of a robbery may not arouse much social concern, it will nevertheless be highly significant to his parents, who will need to grieve accordingly.

The amount of unfinished business between the parent and the deceased child. Unfinished business refers to those issues that were never addressed or which lacked successful closure in the relationship. While it also refers to practical matters such as setting up estates or tying up loose ends in business, the term as used here primarily focuses on the psychosocial issues between the parent and the deceased child. Were they able to express the things they needed or wanted to express to one another? Did they come to some closure about their mutual relationship? Were there any loose ends in the relationship that were not addressed? For example, could one finally explain to the other why he had been so hurt and angry at a specific point in time? Were past conflicts resolved? Were regrets and thank you's stated? Did they get to say good-bye to each other? Unfinished business remains just that— unfinished. This lack of completion is anxiety-provoking and frequently causes a griever to restlessly search for an opportunity to come to closure with the deceased.

Many grievers feel they cannot relinquish their grief, and so fail to grieve, until they have brought some ending to that which was unfinished. The parent may seek to find some way to say the never-said "I love you," "I needed you," or "I'm sorry." The smaller the amount of unfinished business between the parent and the child, the better, for it means that there is less emotional baggage for the parent to cope with subsequent to the death. However, for parents, this factor is a particularly thorny one, since by virtue of the child's death one of their main tasks, that is, protecting the child and successfully rearing him until their own deaths, remains permanently unfinished.

The bereaved parent's perception of the child's fulfillment in life. The more the mourner perceives the deceased as having had a fulfilling life, the more readily can the death be accepted and the grief work completed. This is an additional reason why the death of a child is so difficult to comprehend and accept, since frequently from the bereaved parents' perspective the child did not have the opportunity to have a fulfilling life.

The death surround. This refers to the immediate circumstances of the death, including the location, type of death, reason for the death, and degree of preparation for it. To the extent that the death surround can be accepted by the parent the grief will be more amenable to management and resolution. When the circumstances of the loss are unacceptable, they may be harder to resolve. For example, it may be relatively more difficult to cope with a child's death by decapitation in a car accident than from an illness that ended at home, with family and friends present at the time of death.

The timeliness of the death. This refers to the psychological acceptability of death for this person at this specific time. The death of the young in our society is always viewed as untimely. However, even among older individuals whose deaths would be socially viewed as more timely, the mourner's perception of the acceptability of the death will depend less on social stereotype and more on what is happening in the relationship at the time of the death. For example, when a middle-aged adult dies, it will be untimely for his parents that he predeceases them and it will seem especially unfair since he is unable to enjoy the fruits of his labors. Of course, for parents it is rarely acceptable or appropriate for their child to die, but what is referred to here is their feelings about the specific timing of the loss. Circumstances prior to the death, such as recent conflict or reconciliation with the child, or the child's having just turned over a new leaf or finally achieved a long-desired goal, may make it more difficult for the parent to accept the fact that the death occurred when it did.

The bereaved parent's perception of preventability. The perception of death as preventable appears to affect the duration and severity of grief (Bugen, 1979). Sometimes this is based on a realistic appraisal of what in fact could have been done; at other times it is derived from unrealistic expectations that the griever holds for himself. In the normal process of grief, in which the individual recalls all his guilty feelings over negative acts and things he neglected to do, or unfavorable thoughts and feelings that inevitably arose from the normal ambivalence in the relationship, the preventability issue will always be raised. If it is unclear whether or not the death could have been prevented, or if the griever assumes responsibility for having had the power to prevent it, but failing to do so, grief will be greater and more guilt will arise to further complicate the mourning process. Because of the expectations that stem from the parental role, problems in this area are often seen in parents whose children die.

The sudden vs. expected death. When a death has been anticipated, even though it may put tremendous emotional demands on the individuals involved, coping capacities are directed toward an expectable end. When loss occurs, it has been prepared for. The forewarning has allowed time for experiences of anticipatory grief—finishing unfinished business, preparing for the consequences of the loss, mourning what has been and will be lost, and absorbing the reality of the loss gradually over time. (See Rando, 1986, for a further discussion of the components of the three interrelated processes of anticipatory grief.) When this preparation is lacking, and the loss comes unexpectedly, grievers are shocked and their ability to cope is seriously impaired. They painfully learn that major catastrophic events can occur without warning. As a result, the grievers develop a chronic apprehension that something unpleasant may happen to them or their loved ones at any time. They tend to become insecure. This lack of security, combined with the experiences of being overwhelmed, being unable to grasp the situation and having one's adaptive capacities assaulted, accounts for the relatively severe bereavement complications that occur after cases of sudden death.

Length of illness prior to death. Research has indicated that both too short a period of forewarning, as well as too long a period, can predispose bereaved parents to poorer outcomes (Rando, 1983). In too short an illness there is a critical lack of preparation and parents appear to suffer sequelae similar to those seen after sudden death. They lose the benefits of an appropriate amount of anticipatory grief. In an illness that is too prolonged, caring for the dying child requires large psychosocial, physical, and temporal investments which lead to progressively more social isolation, physical debilitation, emotional exhaustion, psychological conflicts, and family problems.

Anticipatory grief and involvement with the dying child. Research suggests that anticipatory grief will affect the type and amount of involvement parents have with the dying child during the living-dying interval (Fulton & Fulton, 1971; Rando, 1983, 1986). It can bring parents closer to the child or cause them to decathect from him before death. Whatever the experience is, it will definitely color the parent's bereavement period following the death.

The number, type, and quality of secondary losses. The physical and symbolic losses that develop as a consequence of the death of the child will necessarily contribute to and help define the grief of the bereaved parent. Such losses must be identified so that they can be prepared for and grieved. Some of these losses may cause more problems for the parent than the initial loss of death; for example, loss of someone to parent, loss of hopes for the future, loss of an extension of self, loss of a confidant, or loss of someone to assist with chores.

The presence of concurrent stresses or crises. The bereaved parent may be confronted with ongoing stresses unrelated to the death that may make the bereavement experience more difficult. For example, unemployment, physical illness, divorce, or developmental crises will add to the burden of grief and compromise the parent's ability to cope with it. Research has indicated that the presence of concurrent life crises is associated with poorer bereavement outcomes (Parkes, 1975; Raphael & Maddison, 1976).

Social Factors

The bereaved parent's social support system and the acceptance and assistance of its members. The type of support the griever will receive will be based on how the griever and deceased are valued by members of the social system, and the manner and circumstances of the death. As compared to other bereaved individuals, bereaved parents notoriously have had to endure major losses of support and unrealistic expectations from others. The tasks of grief work require appropriate expectations from others and their encouragement, empathy, and sustenance. Problems usually develop in their absence (Maddison, 1968; Parkes, 1972; Raphael, 1977; Sheldon, Cochrane, Vachon, Lyall, Rogers, & Freeman, 1981; Vachon, Sheldon, Lancee, Lyall, Rogers, & Freeman, 1982). The presence of supportive and positive relationships is so important that some clinical observation suggests that emotional discharge, when it occurs in the absence of others, is relatively less effective.

The timing of the social support is also crucial. While the presence of supportive relationships is valuable at the time of death, it has no significant association with later recovery (Parkes & Weiss, 1983; Vachon, Lyall, Rogers, Freedman-Letofsky, & Freeman, 1980). More important to fostering recovery is whether the support is available and utilized as time proceeds.

The bereaved parent's sociocultural, ethnic, and religious/ philosophical backgrounds. These will help or hinder grief work as they influence the parent's attitudes toward the expression of grief and determine the type of support available.

The educational, economic, and occupational status of the bereaved parent. A lack of education, financial resources, or occupational skills will only magnify the stresses on the grieving parent. They may compromise her ability to sustain and replenish herself (literally and figuratively) after the death and may contribute to additional secondary losses. This is a particularly significant issue when there are large medical care or funeral expenses after the child's death that take financial resources away from the current needs of the family. It is not unusual for parents to struggle with intense anger and a sense of injustice when they find themselves receiving bills following the child's death for the unsuccessful operation they had hoped would save her life. It adds insult to injury when these debts interfere with taking care of present family needs.

The funeral rituals. Rituals that promote realization and confirmation of the loss, assist in the expression of affect and memories, and offer social support to the bereaved parent will be truly therapeutic. The absence of these rituals, or their inappropriate use, can be detrimental to the grief process.

Physiological Factors

Drugs and sedatives. Drugs that are calming or anesthetizing are nontherapeutic in that they keep the griever from experiencing the pain and realizing the loss that ultimately has to be faced. Frequently bereaved parents are drugged during the wake and funeral, the precise times at which they should be encouraged to give vent to their emotions. This leaves them to confront their loss later on, at times when there may not be the social support that is usually available during the initial period following the death. This is not to imply that there is no point at which drugs are a useful tool for the bereaved. Although heavy sedation to block the mourning process is not wise, mild sedation to prevent exhaustion and severe insomnia, and illness resulting from them, may be quite therapeutic. Since the bereaved need energy for their grief work, such medication may be helpful. Complications of the mourning process, for example, clinical depression that is agitated or retarded, psychosis, elation, or phobic anxiety states, will require the skilled evaluation of a psychiatrist and may be reduced by psychopharmacological intervention, as may other indices of unresolved grief.

Nutrition. It is not uncommon for bereaved parents to be anorexic or, if they do eat, to complain of the altered taste of food and impaired gastrointestinal functioning. Despite this, they must be encouraged to maintain adequate nutritional balance and eating habits. Inadequate nutrition will only compromise their ability to cope with the loss, meet the continuing demands of daily life, and overcome the numerous physiological symptoms generated by the stress of grief.

Rest and sleep. Some degree of sleep disturbance is normally expected in the grief process. However, a lack of sufficient sleep may predispose the bereaved parent to mental and physical exhaustion, disease, and unresolved grief. If the requisite energy to undertake grief work is impaired, medication may be warranted.

Physical health. Grief assaults the body, just as it assaults the psyche. The bereaved parent's physical condition and the responsivity of her nervous system will influence how the stress of grief is handled by her body. A certain amount of physical disturbance is a normal component of grief. However, physical symptoms should be cared for to preserve the parent's energy for grief work and to reduce the potential for morbidity and mortality.

Exercise. Adequate exercise not only keeps the body in good physical condition, but also provides an outlet for the stressful emotions of grief. It allows for a reduction of aggressive feelings, a release of tension and anxiety, and a relief of depression. These emotions are then less likely to be somatized as psychosomatic illnesses.

Unresolved Grief

Given the multitude of factors that combine to determine an individual's unique grief response, it is not surprising that there are a number of variants on the typical process of grief described in Chapter 1. These variants are termed *unresolved* because there has been some disturbance of the normal progress toward resolution. In each there are components of denial or repression of aspects of the loss or of the feelings generated, as well as an attempt to hold on to the lost relationship. The following sections will describe the different forms of unresolved grief and the symptoms of this state.

Forms of Unresolved Grief

Caregivers must be familiar with the diverse forms of grief in order to implement appropriate intervention strategies, since the same techniques have differing impacts depending on the form of unresolved grief to which they are applied. The following descriptions of forms of unresolved grief have been taken from the analyses of Averill (1968), Parkes and Weiss (1983), and Raphael (1983).

Absent grief. In this situation feelings of grief and mourning processes are totally absent. It is as if the death never occurred. It requires either that the mourner completely deny the death or that he remain in the stage of shock.

Inhibited grief. In this form of grief there is a lasting inhibition of many of the manifestations of normal grief, with the appearance of other symptoms, such as somatic complaints, in their place. The parent may be able to relinquish and mourn only certain aspects of the deceased child and not others, for example, the positive aspects but not the negative ones.

Case Example: Alice came to therapy because her deteriorating physical condition suggested a significant depression. She was compliant and eager to please in treatment. Investigation revealed that her estranged son had committed suicide several years earlier. She had attended to the tasks of the funeral and then resumed her life as if nothing had occurred. There were no behavioral expressions of grief and there was no internal processing of it. Shortly afterwards Alice developed severe gastrointestinal difficulties and the next several years were devoted to focusing on her physical complaints.

Delayed grief. Normal or conflicted grief may be delayed for an extended period of time, up to years, especially if there are pressing responsibilities or the parent feels he cannot deal with the process at that time. A full grief reaction may eventually be initiated by another loss or by some event related to the original loss. For instance, a pet's death can trigger a response for a loved one who died years earlier, but who had never been mourned because the griever felt he had to be strong to take care of other family members. Meanwhile, only an inhibited form of grief may be observed.

Case Example: Tom was in medical school when his daughter died from Sudden Infant Death Syndrome. Tom knew he had to be the strong one and he kept in his feelings to protect his wife as well as himself. He threw himself deeper into school and never took time to grieve. Several years after the death of his daughter, Tom was at a post-mortem examination. However, instead of seeing a cadaver on the table he "saw" his own little daughter. This initiated an acute grief reaction.

Conflicted grief. In this grief there is frequently an exaggeration or distortion of one or more of the manifestations of normal grief, while other aspects of the grief may be suppressed at the same time. Two common patterns are extreme anger and extreme guilt. Extreme anger is often associated with a previously dependent relationship or with deaths that are sudden and unexpected and for which someone is blamed (for example, a medical caregiver's failure or negligence, or where the deceased died violently, such as in an accident or disaster). Extreme guilt is often associated with having had a markedly ambivalent relationship with the deceased.

Case Example: Felicia's 10-year-old son died from acute appendicitis 8 months prior to her referral for therapy. Felicia was an overemotional woman who for years had become hysterical whenever she had to contact the pediatrician about her son. She had strong ambivalent feelings toward her son because of his father's having deserted her when she discovered she was pregnant. At the time of the appendicitis attack, the pediatrician had heard Felicia exaggerate her son's symptoms once too often and consequently responded too slowly to save the child's life. Felicia's grief continued unabated as she constantly blamed herself for not convincing the pediatrician of the gravity of the illness, and she was filled with self-reproach for the resentment she frequently had felt for her son.

Chronic grief. In chronic grief the mourner continuously exhibits intense grief reactions that would be appropriate in the early stages of grief. Mourning fails to draw to its natural conclusion. There is an inability to relinquish the deceased and it almost seems that the mourner keeps the deceased alive with his grief. Intense yearning is symptomatic of this grief. Such grief typically is evidenced after the loss of dependent and irreplaceable relationships, deaths that are unexpected, and deaths of children. It usually indicates that the bereaved had extraordinary (and sometimes possibly pathological) emotional investment in the deceased. For this reason also, it frequently follows the deaths of children.

Case Example: John was a shy, insecure man who was devoted to his adult son who lived with him. John's wife had died when the son was 14 and the two of them constituted each other's emotional worlds. The son handled all the family finances, organized whatever social schedule they had, and looked after all his father's needs. Most of John's social contacts with others were through his son. After his son died from cancer at age 38, John was both deeply depressed and isolated. He undertook only minimum attempts at communicating with others, often being fearful of them. He spent most of his time alone and made no changes in the house that would reflect that his son was no longer there. He even set his son's place at the dinner table. Four years later he had made no changes since his son died.

Unanticipated grief. This is a form of grief reaction that only recently has been discussed in the literature (Glick, Weiss, & Parkes, 1974; Parkes & Weiss, 1983; Rando, 1986). It occurs after a sudden, unanticipated loss and is so disruptive that recovery is usually complicated. In unanticipated grief, parents are unable to grasp the full implications of the loss. Their adaptive capabilities are seriously assaulted and they suffer extreme feelings of bewilderment, anxiety, self-reproach, and depression that render them unable to function normally. There is difficulty in accepting the loss, despite intellectual recognition of the death, and the death may continue to seem inexplicable. Grief symptomatology persists much longer than usual.

> *Case Example:* Elliott's daughter was hit by a drunken driver one afternoon following a Girl Scout meeting. Elliott was completely overwhelmed when informed of the accident and this feeling stayed with him for almost a year. He could not believe that the death had actually occurred and frequently had to remind himself that his daughter was not going to return. Most of his grief symptoms persisted for an abnormally long period of time. Although he was able to go through the motions of putting his life back together again, Elliott became chronically anxious and apprehensive, always expecting another trauma to befall himself or one of his family. Although Elliott continued to be superficially involved with his family, he was never able to again deeply invest in any family members for fear that they, too, would be taken from him.

Abbreviated grief. This reaction is often mistaken for unresolved grief. In fact, it is a short-lived but genuine form of grief. It may occur because of the immediate replacement of the deceased or an insufficient attachment to the deceased. Sometimes it occurs when a significant amount of anticipatory grief has been completed prior to the death. After the death occurs the individual grieves, but much of the grief work has been accomplished, so that the post-death bereavement period, while painful, may be relatively shorter.

> *Case Example:* Becky's son succumbed to cancer after an extended illness of several years. Becky had gone through a long process of anticipatory grief during the illness and consequently, after a short but intense grief reaction at the time of her son's death, was left with few acute grief symptoms. Becky was able to pick up her life because she had received therapeutic intervention during the illness that had allowed her to continue to maintain some outside interests that could sustain her after the death. She had been prepared for the emptiness that would ensue when she would no longer have someone to care for and had made

appropriate plans to occupy herself with other caregiving functions. Although she missed her son deeply, acute grief was not long lasting.

Symptoms of Unresolved Grief

Sometimes bereaved parents will evidence symptoms that indicate the lack of resolution of grief, although either there are not enough of them to have coalesced into a formal condition of unresolved grief or they are not solidified enough yet to officially qualify for that diagnosis. Caregivers must be aware of the symptoms of unresolved grief and use them not only as diagnostic indicators, but also as "red flags" for areas requiring intervention.

Three primary variables indicate unresolved grief: absence of a normal grief reaction, prolongation of a normal grief reaction, and distortion of a normal grief reaction (Siggins, 1966). To make a determination of unresolved grief it is necessary to know the full range of normal grief against which the behavior in question is being compared, as well as the psychological, social, and physiological variables influencing the individual's grief response. Without an understanding of and appreciation for these variables and how they affect a particular individual's grief experience, *no* valid judgments legitimately can be made about the bereaved parent's grief response.

The following lists adapted from Lindemann (1944), Lazare (1979), and Worden (1982) delineate some symptoms indicative of unresolved grief. These individual symptoms are unremarkable during the acute stage of grief. However, they are the major signs of incomplete grief work when they are manifested *beyond* the expected time for resolution of grief. The more of these symptoms and behaviors the mourner evidences, the stronger the likelihood of unresolved grief.

The following manifestations of unresolved grief reactions were put forth by Lindemann (1944):

- Overactivity without a sense of loss
- Acquisition of symptoms belonging to the last illness of the deceased
- Development of a psychosomatic medical illness
- Alteration in relationships with friends and relatives
- Furious hostility against specific persons somehow connected with the death (e.g., doctors, nurses)
- Wooden and formal conduct that masks hostile feelings and resembles a schizophrenic reaction in which there is a lack of emotion
- Lasting loss of patterns of social interaction

- Acts detrimental to one's own social and economic existence (e.g., giving away belongings, making foolish economic deals)
- Agitated depression with tension, agitation, insomnia, feelings of worthlessness, bitter self-accusation, an obvious need for punishment, and even suicidal tendencies

The following diagnostic criteria for unresolved grief were proposed by Lazare (1979). When one or more of these symptoms or behaviors transpires after a death and continues beyond 6 months to 1 year, he considers the diagnosis of unresolved grief. Recent research and clinical observation suggest that with parental bereavement these time frames may very well need to be extended.

- A depressive syndrome of varying degrees of severity since the time of death, frequently a very mild, subclinical one often accompanied by persistent guilt and lowered self-esteem
- A history of delayed or prolonged grief, indicating that the person characteristically avoids or has difficulty with grief work
- Symptoms of guilt and self-reproach, panic attacks and somatic expressions of fear such as choking sensations and shortness of breath
- Somatic symptoms representing identification with the deceased, often the symptoms of the terminal illness
- Physical distress under the upper half of the sternum, accompanied by expressions such as "There is something stuck inside" or "I feel there is a demon inside of me"
- Searching that continues over time with a great deal of random behavior, restlessness, and moving around
- Recurrence of symptoms of depression and searching behavior on specific dates, such as anniversaries of the death, birthdays of the deceased, or holidays (especially Christmas), that are more extreme than those anniversary reactions normally expected
- A feeling that the death occurred yesterday, even though the loss took place months or years ago
- Unwillingness to move the material possessions of the deceased after a reasonable amount of time has passed
- Changes in relationships following the death
- Diminished participation in religious and ritual activities that are part of the mourner's culture, including avoidance of taking part in funerary rituals or visiting the grave
- An inability to discuss the deceased without crying or having the voice crack, particularly when the death occurred over a year ago
- Themes of loss in an interview with the mourner

In addition to a number of symptoms already mentioned, these symptoms of unresolved grief were suggested by Worden (1982):

- A relatively minor event triggering major grief reactions
- False euphoria subsequent to the death
- Overidentification with the deceased leading to a compulsion to imitate the dead person, particularly if it is unconscious and the mourner lacks the competence for the same behavior
- Self-destructive impulses
- Radical changes in lifestyle
- Exclusion of friends, family members, or activities associated with the deceased
- Phobias about illness or death

These lists are not all-inclusive. Mourners can be expected to manifest widely varying symptoms of unresolved grief. Caregivers will place differing amounts of importance on the presence or absence of specific symptoms depending upon the norms they develop over time as they work with the bereaved. A critical point to keep in mind is that when working with bereaved parents one must appreciate the intensity of this particular grief response and allow extraordinarily wide latitude in the margins used to demarcate resolved from unresolved or normal from abnormal grief. (See Chapter 2 for further discussion of this point.)

Reasons for Failure to Grieve

In addition to assessing whether or not the bereaved parent has unresolved grief over the loss of the child, the caregiver needs to understand the reasons for the failure to successfully resolve the grief. Jackson (1957) feels that two conditions may provoke difficulty in accomplishing grief work and thereby predispose the parent to unresolved grief. In the first condition, the parent is unable to tolerate the emotional distress of grief and resists dealing with its necessary tasks and feelings. In the second condition, the parent has an excessive need to maintain interaction with the deceased child. In this case the parent denies the loss and fails to appropriately decathect from the child, consequently failing in the requisite tasks of grief work. Of course, all of the previously discussed factors influencing the grief response have the potential to interfere with the completion of grief.

Lazare (1979) has delineated a number of psychological and social reasons for failure to grieve. For any parent, the failure to adequately mourn results from the complex interaction of the social milieu, the nature and meaning of the loss, and the characteristics of the bereaved individual.

Psychological Factors Promoting Unresolved Grief

Guilt. Unresolved grief may occur when parents are afraid to grieve because reviewing their relationship with the deceased child would resurrect remembrances of actions, omissions, or feelings directed toward the child that could make the parents feel too guilty. Guilt arising from other sources (see Chapters 1 and 4), a normal aspect of grief, can also block the grief process if parents feel that they are unable to confront it.

Loss of an extension of the self. Some mourners may be so dependent upon, or place such a high value on, the deceased that they will not grieve in order to avoid the reality of the loss. In this case, the deceased had been recognized as an extension of the self and to recognize the loss and grief would constitute a severe narcissistic loss to the self. While in other losses such an attitude is markedly unhealthy, the loss of a child, by definition, normally promotes such feelings.

Reawakening of an old loss. In some cases parents are reluctant to grieve because the current loss reawakens a more profound and painful loss that has not yet been resolved. An example of this would be the woman who cannot allow herself to grieve over her miscarriage because it resurrects the memory of the death of her mother, for whom she never appropriately grieved.

Multiple loss. Those who experience multiple losses, such as the death of an entire family or a number of sequential losses within a relatively short period of time, sometimes have difficulty grieving because the losses are too overwhelming to contemplate and deal with. Essentially they are suffering from bereavement overload (Kastenbaum, 1969). In the case of losing multiple family members it is additionally complicated because those who might usually support the griever no longer exist.

Inadequate ego development. Persons with severe ego impairments are often unable to adequately complete the grief process because they cannot meet the necessary intrapsychic tasks. Instead they frequently experience feelings of intense hopelessness, rage, frustration, depression, anxiety, and despair that they cannot defend against. Often psychotic behavior results when their primitive defense mechanisms fail. For instance, one borderline mother could never adequately grieve over her daughter because she was incapable of maintaining a consistent mental image of her daughter from which to decathect.

Idiosyncratic resistances to mourning. There are parents who do not permit themselves to grieve because of specific psychological issues that interfere with the process. For example, some are afraid of losing control or appearing weak. Others are afraid that if they start crying they will never stop. Still others are afraid to relinquish the pain because it binds them to their child. Any individual fear, conflict, issue, or conditioned response that interferes with the parent's yielding to the normal process of grief will constitute a resistance to mourning that will have to be identified, interpreted, and worked through.

Social Factors Promoting Unresolved Grief

Social negation of the loss. In this situation the loss is not socially defined as a loss, for example, a miscarriage or a neonatal death. Although grief work is necessary, the social support for it is inadequate or nonexistent. This occurs in many cases involving symbolic psychosocial losses.

Socially unspeakable loss. In this case the loss is so "unspeakable" that members of the social system cannot be of any assistance to the bereaved. They tend to shy away out of ignorance of what to say or moral repugnance. Examples include death by murder, suicide, or an overdose of narcotics. Frequently, the death of a child is a socially unspeakable loss because of its anxiety-provoking nature.

Social isolation and/or geographic distance from social support. In this instance the parent is either away from social supports at the time of mourning or there are none available for assistance. Geographical distance from support is becoming increasingly common in our mobile society. In addition, death may occur in places or at times when people may be unable to travel conveniently or quickly. When parents have no social support in the first place, they often fail to grieve. Social reasons for this lack of support include the breakdown of the nuclear family, the decline in primary group interactions with subsequent depersonalization and alienation, and the diminished importance of religion. Bereaved parents especially tend to suffer from a lack of social support because the nature of the loss makes them so anxiety-provoking to others that they are ostracized. Parents whose adult children die after having moved away may also suffer from a lack of social support from the child's family when that family is at a distance, or from peers who had never known their child.

Assumption of the role of the strong one. There are certain people who become designated to be the "strong one" by those around them. They must make all the funeral arrangements, bolster the morale of others, and not reveal any emotion. Frequently this is the role assumed by bereaved fathers, although mothers may also assume this role in an effort to protect their family from their own grief. These individuals then miss the opportunity to deal with their own grief due to the behaviors required or prohibited in the roles they attempt to maintain.

Uncertainty over the loss. In cases where a death is uncertain, such as when a child is lost at sea, is kidnapped, or is missing in action, the parents and their social systems are often unable to commence grieving until they know the precise status of the child. (See Section 3 for chapters discussing grief over a child whose fate is uncertain.) They cannot begin to address the first task of mourning, that is, accept the reality of the loss (Worden, 1982), because it has not been verified or made real for them. This is why so much time, money, and effort is spent searching to recover missing bodies and confirm the deaths.

Whenever working with bereaved parents who are not grieving appropriately or who have not resolved their grief within expectable time frames for this type of loss, the caregiver must ascertain the specific reasons for a parent's failure to successfully resolve grief so that these can be addressed.

GUIDELINES FOR CONDUCTING A THERAPEUTIC ASSESSMENT

Prior to planning any intervention with a bereaved parent the caregiver must have an accurate assessment of where the parent is in his grief and of the significant factors that influence it. Raphael (1983) suggests the following therapeutic assessment, which not only yields information, but also facilitates the expression of emotions and promotes the mourning process.

Can you tell me a little about the death? What happened? What happened that day? This gives the parent permission to talk about the death. It provides information on the nature and circumstances of the death; how the parent heard of it; whether it was expected or unexpected, timely or untimely; what effect it had on the parent; whether the parent's presence or absence at the time of the death may have been a source of guilt; whether it occurred at a time when there were special conflicts or stresses in the relationship. The parent's capacity to talk about the death and his pattern of emotional responses to it will become obvious. Defenses of denial and avoidance may become clear. It will also become apparent from the discussion whether the parent had the opportunity to see the body and say private good-byes.

Can you tell me about him, about your relationship from the beginning? This allows the caregiver to get the history of the relationship from the start, determining the expectations and disillusionments that went into it, as well as determining the images and interactions it involved. It clarifies the quality of the relationship with the deceased child, the level of ambivalence and dependence it involved. There is also an opportunity to assess the degree to which the bereaved parent still is denying the loss. The degree to which the parent can talk of the child in real terms, recalling him truthfully rather than in an idealized fashion, will become apparent. This information may help to determine risk factors from the relationship and can provide indications of the appropriateness of the parent's progress as well as of the quality of mourning at this point after the loss.

What has been happening since the death? How have things been with you and your family and friends? This permits exploration of the patterns of family and social response and the support that is perceived to be available. It yields information about the experience of the parent, his feelings about the absence of the lost child and the finality of death. It also provides for assessment of other crises or stresses that have occurred or of blocks to the resolution of the grief.

Have you been through any other bad times like this recently or when you were young? This area of inquiry allows for more specific assessment of concurrent crises and stresses and also of other earlier losses.

Several other issues must be addressed in this assessment. They will provide further information about the parent's status in the grief process and the impediments to or complications of that process. In addition, they will furnish the data essential for perceiving the loss from the parent's idiosyncratic perspective and for legitimately evaluating the grief within the context of a particular loss occurring to a particular individual.

Determination of the completeness of each of the four tasks of mourning. The focus of treatment should be on helping bereaved parents with any task they seem unable to meet. Using Worden's (1982) schema, they first must accept the reality of the loss. If they do not, treatment must focus on the fact that the child is dead and the parent will have to let him go. Then they also must experience the pain of grief, not merely intellectually accept the loss. Treatment is aimed at making it safe to feel positive and negative emotions so that parents can work through them. Part of this task is the redefinition of the parents' relationship with the deceased child. Parents must then adjust to the environment in which the child is missing. Here problem solving is a large part of the treatment. Parents are taught to overcome their helplessness by trying out new skills, developing new roles, and returning to living. The final task is the withdrawal of emotional energy and the reinvestment of it in other relationships, objects, activities, or beliefs. Parents must learn to stop acute grieving, say a final good-bye, decathect from the child and establish a new relationship with him, and cultivate new emotional investments.

Evaluation of the presence of illogical or magical thinking. This mode of thinking is not unusual in adults under stress. It is especially important to evaluate in bereaved parents since they have internalized many unrealistic expectations about the parental role that can foster such thinking.

Detection of increased feelings of guilt and responsibility. These feelings are almost always present in bereaved parents. Their existence, intensity, and focus must invariably be explored.

Description of what the loss means to the parent by the parent. This gives the parent the opportunity to point out his most salient concerns and to reveal his unique perspective on the loss.

Analysis of all the psychological, social, and physiological factors influencing the parent's grief response. All these factors must be analyzed for each parent. Special attention should be given specifically to the sociocultural norms that influence the overt expression of grief.

Collection of a complete history of prior losses. These include not only normal losses, but those events not normally perceived as losses, such as psychosocial losses or socially denied losses such as abortion.

Medical evaluation and treatment when symptoms warrant. It is critical to recognize when medical treatment is necessary to prevent mortality or morbidity or to manage physical symptoms of psychological distress that interfere with the grief process. For example, vegetative signs of depression, such as prolonged inability to sleep or eat, must be properly attended to.

Any assessment of the grief process will need to be continuously updated. Recent research suggests that there are previously unexpected fluctuations in the experience and needs of bereaved parents (Alexy, 1982; Fish in Chapter 23; Levav, 1982; Rando, 1983). An initial assessment without subsequent revisions will be inadequate. Grief is a process; it is not static. It will be constantly changing, responding to internal and external cues. The timing of any intervention is a critical variable influencing its effectiveness. It must be based on where the parent is in his grief at a given point in time.

Treatment may be carried out either during the crisis following the loss or at a later point in time. Raphael (1983) believes that the optimal time for preventive intervention is probably between the first 2 to 8 weeks, perhaps even up to 3 months, after the death. In the first several weeks many people are so preoccupied by the necessary practical tasks and family matters that they are not usually ready to talk and work through the various aspects of their loss. Since after about 6 to 8 weeks some of the urgency of the crisis settles and old defenses return, it is important for the caregiver to intervene before the griever is less open to influence and has developed maladaptive grief responses. This is consistent with crisis theory, which states that a little help rationally directed and purposefully focused at a strategic time will be more effective than more extensive help given when the person is less emotionally accessible.

Another reason for conducting a thorough and ongoing assessment stems from the recent evidence suggesting that, in regard to unresolved grief, some types of intervention that are appropriate for one type of bereavement are useless or even harmful in others (Parkes & Weiss, 1983). For instance, the most effective treatment following the loss of ambivalent relationships that have led to conflicted grief is intervention that stimulates and facilitates normal grief. The aim is to promote the overt expression of all of the feelings of grief. However, in contrast, when working with the chronic grief often found after the loss of dependent relationships, such attempts at promoting expression of grief would only make the situation worse. It has been going on in this fashion for too long. It requires some work leading to delimitation of this type of grief expression. In such cases it is better to insist on forward movement and increased autonomy for the parent, and to encourage him to play a more active role in developing goals and making decisions. As a further contrast, those bereaved from unanticipated losses require repeated opportunities to talk through the implications of their loss and to react emotionally. They must make sense out of the loss and bring order to their lives to diminish the feeling of being overwhelmed with stress and insecurity.

INTERVENTIONS

The interventions discussed next are suggested to assist the bereaved parent through the normal process of grief. Intervention for unresolved grief will be addressed later in this chapter, although much of it relies on the special use of the interventions described here.

The goal of the caregiver is to assist the bereaved parent in releasing emotional ties to the deceased child despite the discomfort and sorrow it causes, and in subsequently finding new objects of reinvestment. The parent must be persuaded to therapeutically yield to the process of grief, and this involves accepting the pain of looking realistically at the loss. The parent is encouraged to participate actively in the work of mourning instead of trying to escape or deny it, and to realize that the grieving period can be delayed but not postponed indefinitely, for it will be carried on directly or indirectly. What the bereaved parent needs most is acceptance and nonjudgmental listening, which will facilitate the expression of emotions and the necessary review of the relationship with the lost child. She will then require assistance in integrating the past with the new present that exists.

There are a number of specific strategies that can assist bereaved parents in meeting the goals of grief work. These strategies have been grouped into seven broad phases, roughly corresponding to the process of grief from initial shock to reintegration into normal life.

Make Contact and Assess

Initially the caregiver must attempt to make a connection with the grieving parent. In the early aftermath of bereavement parents are dazed, often in shock, with little energy or motivation to help themselves. The main tasks for caregivers at this time are to establish a relationship and simply be present. As noted before, it is imperative to conduct an assessment of the bereaved parent in order to plan the most appropriate interventions for this particular individual.

Since the bereaved frequently do not have the energy to initiate contact and often feel overwhelmed, caregivers must reach out in practical and concrete ways. While the professional therapist may be slightly more limited here, and may need to remain somewhat more nondirective for ethical and professional reasons, others can be very specific in the types of help offered to the newly bereaved parent. For example, instead of merely expressing concern, caregivers can make specific offers of assistance: "How about if I call your sister to accompany you to choose the casket?" "Why don't you let me help you arrange for a baby-sitter so you can attend The Compassionate Friends meeting?" Caregivers must determine what it is the bereaved parent needs, what they can offer, and then offer it as specifically as possible. They must recognize that this offer may be refused, but this should not stop them from offering assistance again at another point. A refusal should not be unduly discouraging or be taken personally as a rejection. It is simply a statement of the griever's emotional, social, and physical state in which she is temporarily unable to respond to or appreciate attempts at care and consolation. The bereaved parent may require a number of offers of help and will benefit in the long run from the continued efforts of concerned individuals who do not give up on her because of a few rejections. This is a true test of the empathic caregiver.

It is critically important to be present physically, as well as emotionally, to render the bereaved parent security and support. This is especially important during the initial period of shock and disorganization, in which consistent physical presence and physical contact (hugging, hand-holding, touching) not only convey to the parent that she is not alone, but help reorient her to the world that has gone out of focus and control with the loss of her child. This physical support will become critical again at the time when the true implications and reality of the loss sink in, weeks and months after the death.

Caregivers must realize that feelings about the child's death are only a part of the experience for the newly bereaved parent. Demands such as making funeral arrangements, notifying relatives, and dealing with the responses of others all engender further emotional reactions. While it is helpful to encourage the expression of feelings by the bereaved parent, immediate treatment should also be aimed at minimizing the tendency of the bereaved to become overwhelmed and unable to function. Consequently, intervention should be geared toward helping the family focus on problems one at a time, addressing solvable problems to which practical solutions can be found before progressing to the more complicated issues at the feeling level (Berlinsky & Biller, 1982). This is not to deemphasize or negate the critical importance of facilitating expression of feelings as soon as possible. However, if bereaved parents become so engulfed in the immediate demands for decisions and actions that they become convinced of their inability to cope with the situation or they abrogate all responsibility, an unhealthy passive tone is set for the rest of their grief experience.

Especially during the early period of shock and disorganization, it may be helpful for caregivers to point out that friends or relatives can legitimately take charge of some of the routine functions and responsibilities of the bereaved parents, such as providing meals or doing errands. During this time it may also be therapeutic to render the security of some direction, as bereaved parents may be unable to provide their own. Such things as reminding parents to eat, making sure they get adequate rest, suggesting priorities, helping them with funeral decisions, or gently confronting unrealistic or precipitous plans are examples of this type of support.

Because grief is such a foreign experience, and since it inherently contains many traditionally unacceptable thoughts and feelings, the bereaved parent will often consciously or unconsciously seek permission from others to grieve. If this permission is denied, implicitly or explicitly, the bereaved parent will censor her expressions in an effort to be socially acceptable. Consequently, caregivers must demonstrate verbally, and through nonjudgmental attitudes and behaviors, that the expression of grief is not only appropriate but essential for therapeutic resolution of the loss.

At this point in time the bereaved parent must not be allowed to remain isolated. Social support is critical throughout the entire grief process. It enables the parent to tolerate the pain of loss and provides the acceptance and assistance necessary for completion of grief work and reintegration back into the social community. Research repeatedly confirms that one of the most significant factors contributing to the failure to appropriately resolve grief is the absence and/or inappropriateness of social support and interaction. Especially early after the death, bereaved parents may require the presence of concerned others in order to feel grounded in the midst of the chaos. At a time of such intense emotional reactions, it is particularly helpful to have the accompaniment of other individuals to lend security, order, and a sense of reality—all of which are missing for the bereaved parent. This is why it is so tragic that bereaved parents are so socially isolated because of the anxiety-provoking nature of their loss. Caregivers must work to connect these grievers with appropriate social supports if these are lacking in the parents' own social system.

Because of the nature of the loss and the resulting difficulties with social support, it will usually be very therapeutic to refer bereaved parents to a support group. These groups have proven to be critically important resources to parents and are frequently cited as the major therapeutic agent in assisting bereaved parents to cope with their tragic loss. Options include groups such as The Compassionate Friends, an international self-help group for all types of bereaved parents (see Chapter 30 for how to contact them), or other local or national self-help groups devoted to particular causes of parental bereavement, such as Mothers Against Drunk Driving (MADD), or the National Sudden Infant Death Syndrome Foundation (NSIDSF). (The chapters in Section 6 describe various self-help groups for bereaved parents.) Through mutual sharing, support, modeling, learning that they are not "going crazy," and helping others, bereaved parents are supported in their grief. This is especially critical for these mourners, as they often have significant problems gaining needed emotional and social support for the expression and resolution of their special grief.

In working with the bereaved parent it will be important to maintain a family systems perspective and to recognize how family members and their grief impact on one another. The caregiver must recognize that the bereaved parent is not only dealing with the loss of the child, of that special relationship between herself and the child, and of a part of herself; she is also struggling with the irretrievable loss of the family as she has known it. With the permanent absence of the child, the family will never be the same again. This is a loss that must be grieved as well.

Maintain a Therapeutic and Realistic Perspective

Prior to discussing the appropriate caregiver perspective, it is critical to underscore the importance of viewing the loss from the griever's unique perspective. Caregivers cannot make presumptions based on their own values or points of view. Assumptions must be thoroughly checked before proceeding with interventions, for what is believed to be distressing by caregivers may not be for particular grievers. This means that caregivers must help bereaved parents to define and decide for themselves what is most problematic for them, to prioritize their concerns, and to deal with those concerns as therapeutically as they are able. Most importantly, caregivers must suspend personal value judgments about the meaning of a particular issue or loss to the parent. For example, a parent may be conflicted about what to do with the child's blood-soaked clothes from the accident, while it may seem "clear" to a particular caregiver that they should be cleaned or thrown away. The seriousness of any loss or dilemma must be evaluated in the context of the individual bereaved parent's perspective and cannot be compared to other concerns for other people.

In order to be most helpful to bereaved parents, caregivers must be realistic about the extent to which they can relieve the parents' suffering. Despite their best efforts caregivers cannot rectify the situation that is agonizing the parent—they cannot bring back the deceased child. This does not mean the caregiver has nothing to offer. It merely means that she must be realistic about what can be accomplished. A caregiver can only make the experience relatively better than it would be if she were not there, by being present to listen to the parent and facilitate appropriate grief. This critical value of the "gift of presence" cannot be overstated. Despite the fact that caregivers are more comfortable when able to "do" something, since this combats their feelings of helplessness, they will often be called upon to just "be" with bereaved parents and to share their pain of loss, since they cannot "do" anything to take it away.

Caregivers must be aware that they will often feel helpless when bereaved parents are in pain. Nevertheless, they must not allow this feeling to interfere with their being with the parent or their intervening.

Neither should they allow the bereaved parent's appearance of being unapproachable, inconsolable, or out of control dissuade them from making therapeutic contact.

Caregivers will have to learn to tolerate the intense angry protest and other hostile emotions that are often directed toward them by bereaved parents in the early stages of bereavement. They must be prepared to deal with the fact that this comes not only from the normal displacement of hostility that occurs during grief, but also from the parents' finding caregivers ineffective in gratifying their strong wish to be reunited with the deceased child. The pushing away that may result must be understood in these contexts. When appropriate, these feelings and what gives rise to them can be gently interpreted to the parent. Caregivers must understand and appreciate the excruciating pain of the bereaved parent and how much she desperately misses the child, although at times limits may have to be placed on the parent's inappropriate acting-out of anger.

Trying to rescue parents from grief is not therapeutic. Caregivers must resist the temptation to say or do things that, while intended to be comforting, will not ultimately help the bereaved to complete the painful but necessary work of grief. All interventions must promote the healthy resolution of grief; those that don't should be avoided, for example, admonishing the grieving parent about crying or censoring her guilt. Caregivers must never let their own needs determine the experience for the griever. It would be distinctly unhelpful, for example, to stop a conversation about the child because it hurts to see the parent so tormented. Caregivers must constantly ask themselves if the interventions they are considering are for their own benefit or for the bereaved's.

Related to this, caregivers ought to avoid attempting to explain the loss in religious or philosophical terms too early or asserting to the grieving parent that she should feel better because there are other loved ones who are still alive. These rob the parent of her legitimate sadness. People cannot be replaced and clichés such as "It's God's will" or "Everything happens for a reason" will not be therapeutic when parents need to rail, to ventilate their anguish, and to verbalize their irrational thoughts. Later on such explanations may assist them in finding some meaning and/or perspective in their loss. What eventually is most helpful is the compassionate acceptance of the parent's feelings and experiences signaled by the caregiver's willingness to remain present. This encourages the necessary review and processing of the loss experience.

Caregivers have no reason to be afraid to be emotionally moved by the sadness of the griever, if in fact this is prompted in them. If the reaction is a direct response to the present situation, and does not solely reflect the caregiver's own personal issues, the bereaved parent often perceives it as a confirmation of her loss, a normalization of her feelings, and a sign of acceptance and empathy on the part of the caregiver. It often is very therapeutic for bereaved parents to know that caregivers care enough about them to be emotionally touched by their situations. If the caregiver personally knew the deceased child, appropriate comments sharing her reaction to the loss are often especially meaningful and helpful to the parent. However, it is critically important to maintain an appropriate distance from the grieving parent. While a caregiver must be close enough to share in the bereaved parent's suffering, she must not be so close that she succumbs to despair or encourages inappropriate dependence. It is a fine line to walk.

Caregivers must avoid trying to unrealistically "pretty up" or minimize the situation. It must be legitimized as the difficult one that it is. Psychological healing is facilitated when bereaved parents are acknowledged as victims and then encouraged to talk about, share, and master the feelings of grief, loss, helplessness, guilt, and rage that accompany victimization (Kliman, 1977). It is more therapeutic to say "It is very painful now" or "You are right, it does not make any sense!" than to act as if something could happen to lessen the pain, and to behave as if the griever could run away and escape from it. This does not preclude the hope that the situation will improve, for hope is critical in sustaining the bereaved parent through the pain. It is the unrealistic, falsely cheerful responses that must be avoided.

Indeed, caregivers must not forget to actively plant the seeds of hope for the bereaved parent: hope that someday the pain will decrease, hope that someday there may be a reunion with the deceased child, hope that life will have some meaning again at some point. These are not unrealistic hopes offered in a way that denies or invalidates the current intense experience of grief or the permanent changes that will result from it. Rather, they are realistic aspirations that can offer the bereaved parent needed support and comfort. The reassurance that some day they will be in less pain is critical in allowing bereaved parents to carry on.

Along with hope, the caregiver must not fail to hold out the expectation that the parent will successfully complete the tasks of mourning. The parent needs to believe that she *can* successfully address the tasks of mourning. She needs to know that as long as she continues to deal with her grief, she can look forward to overcoming the pain and carrying on with her life, albeit a changed one. This self-assurance and confidence will support her through the many doubts that arise in the course of grief. Caregivers must not only be compassionate, sensitive, and empathic, but must insist that the bereaved parent continue to make forward progress through the grief process. Excessive commiseration or tolerance of inappropriate dependency or chronic grief will not help the bereaved parent. Certainly previous expectations of rapid recovery from grief were inappropriate for bereaved parents, but it is equally inappropriate to fail to encourage the griever to once again participate in life when she is ready and it is time.

Encourage Verbalization of Feelings and Recollection of the Deceased Child

In order to successfully complete grief work, the bereaved parent needs repeated opportunities to be heard nonjudgmentally, to express the pain of the separation, to accept the finality of the loss, to articulate and process the many different feelings about the loss and its consequences, and to engage in the recollection and review procedures that will facilitate healthy decathexis.

First, the caregiver must help the bereaved parent to recognize, actualize, and accept the loss. Failing to do this, the loss will not be real to the parent and he will not have to grapple with its implications or his feelings about it. For the bereaved parent there is naturally a need to deny the reality of the loss, especially early in the bereavement. Acceptance of the reality of the loss will take continued review of the relationship and discussion of the loss, the events that surrounded it, and its meaning and implications. It also will take the continued frustration of the ability to gratify needs with the child, the many times that the parent aches to see, hold, and interact with the child but cannot. The caregiver can facilitate gradual acceptance by listening nonjudgmentally with permissiveness and acceptance that will allow the ventilation of all thoughts and emotions of grief, including those that are unacceptable and guilt-provoking to the parent.

The caregiver must assist the parent in identifying, accepting, and expressing all the various feelings of grief. This is one of the most critical processes in grief. Failure of it prevents grief resolution. For some bereaved parents, there initially may be a need to work through certain societal, cultural, ethnic, religious, or idiosyncratic resistances to accepting particular symptoms of grief as tolerable or normal. For example, some bereaved fathers may need to have the behavior of crying reinterpreted for them as a natural expression of pain after a major loss, and not a symptom of weakness. Other grievers may require assistance in combining their emotions and their religious beliefs. For example, they may need help with understanding that their experience of grief over their child's death does not mean that they disbelieve their child is happy in heaven. Unless parents can be made more comfortable with these feelings, they will be incapable of working them through.

In grieving the loss of the child, each feeling must be identified and expressed in order to achieve appropriate decathexis. In the early phases of grief bereaved parents will feel painful yearning and angry protest. They require aid in recognizing some of the causes of their distress, such as their unfulfilled needs. Often simply naming the feeling or experience the parent is undergoing helps. For example, identifying emotions by saying "It sounds like you're feeling frustrated by your inability to change this situation" or "It makes you ache so painfully because you cannot hug your child" allows the griever to understand and perceive himself as more in control of the experience. It can clarify and help normalize unacceptable, unrecognized, or unexpected thoughts and feelings and make them more manageable.

If the bereaved parent appears to be resisting the grief process, the caregiver must carefully explore the griever's defenses to discover the reasons behind it. Often the resistances will be idiosyncratic to the individual parent. Many bereaved parents are afraid to express the emotions of grief, fearing they will lose control or break down. There may be excessive dependency, anger, or guilt that is interfering with the normal grief process. These feelings can be explored directly. The absence of expectable feelings can be queried with statements such as "People often seem worried about things that didn't go right at a time like this—an argument or misunderstanding or something they meant to do and didn't before the person died. Have there been any concerns like this for you?" (Raphael, 1980, p. 163). Of course, feelings cannot be demanded from bereaved parents. However, their resistances have to be worked through before they can progress any further in resolving the loss of the child.

Men, especially, will need assistance in dealing with the socially conditioned responses that block grief resolution. They will require permission to grieve and assistance in learning how to cry, discussion with other fathers, and support for the idea that fathers cannot "fix" everything despite their roles as protectors and problem solvers. Fathers must understand that it is unrealistic and unhealthy to attempt to protect the family from the effects of grief, both his and their own. Women must be helped to express their feelings of anger, which traditionally have been suppressed. They may require assistance in avoiding internalizing too much guilt, which they are often socially conditioned to accept.

Frequently there is a resistance to dealing with such feelings as anger and guilt because the parent will not want to look at the less-than-positive aspects of the relationship with the child. It sometimes helps to tell the parent that, while it is not unusual for people to be afraid of dealing with anger for fear of finding there was nothing positive about the relationship with the child, it is only if the anger is worked through that the parent will be able to see the positive aspects of the relationship. Other parents may not want to relinquish the anger or other intense emotions because they feel it is the only thing that binds them to the deceased child. In this case, they need to be told that by relinquishing the inappropriate emotion they will be able to remember the deceased more clearly and feel closer to him. In grieving they will be able to formulate a relationship with the child that will bring him closer than perpetuating their unresolved grief ever could.

Anger often requires legitimization by the caregiver. Because grievers have so much trouble facing this emotion, it may need to be relabeled before they can deal with it. Lazare (1979) suggests the use of words such as *irritate* or *annoy*. Worden (1982) uses the word *miss* by asking "What do you miss about him?" and allowing the person to respond in positive ways, then asking "What don't you miss about him?" and eliciting the more negative feelings. This balances the positive and negative feelings and teaches the bereaved parent that both kinds of emotions can coexist.

Another emotion that often poses significantly difficult problems for the parent is guilt. This arises when the griever feels he has fallen short of his self-image or has violated conscious or unconscious standards. Guilt is present to some degree after all deaths, but is particularly problematic for bereaved parents because of the unrealistic standards and expectations maintained for and by parents. Guilt that is out of proportion to the event is termed *illegitimate guilt*. Treatment requires that bereaved parents discuss their guilty feelings, and the acts, omissions, thoughts, or feelings that generated the guilt, with nonjudgmental others. They must rationally examine the events to determine if, given the amount of information available at the time, they did in fact act in the best way possible. They must examine the standards against which they are negatively judging themselves to determine if those standards are appropriate and realistic. Parents may have to be reminded that they are human, and consequently make mistakes and have ambivalent relationships. They must be helped to see the positives that existed in the relationship and be cautioned against overemphasizing the negative. Bereaved parents will need to forgive themselves, find constructive ways to expiate their guilt, and change the unrealistic standards or irrational beliefs that foster the guilt. However, these interventions must not be made too soon. Premature reassurance will deny these grievers the necessary opportunity to ventilate their guilt feelings.

Legitimate guilt occurs when there is a direct cause-and-effect relationship between what the parent did or failed to do and serious harm resulting to the child. In this situation, where guilt is appropriate, it must be acknowledged and plans must be made for restitution and expiation. This guilt can become destructive if it is used as self-punishment. When legitimate guilt warrants punishment, the parent should do something constructive about it, such as doing something altruistic for others as a way of atoning. Guilt that cannot be expiated must be accommodated. The parent must learn to live with it and not continue to punish himself. If this cannot be accomplished, the stage is set for unresolved grief. (See Chapter 4 for more on the topic of guilt.)

Bereaved parents must be allowed to repeatedly cry, talk, and review without the interruption of the caregiver's sanity. Each story told, each memory relived, each feeling expressed represents a tie to the child that the parent must process by remembering, feeling the emotions generated by it, and then letting it go. Caregivers must encourage such expression without analyzing or interpreting it. Limits can be imposed later, if therapeutically necessary. The parents repeatedly will need to review their attachments and relationship to the child and the circumstances of the death. Not only the dramatic memories, the ones that bring tears, need to be reexamined—they all do. This means going over the entire relationship, back to its earliest origins and the hopes and fantasies that formed it. The parent must discuss all of its ups and downs, its course and development, its crises and joys—all aspects of it through the years. As these events are gently unfolded, associated feelings can be examined, such as anxiety, ambivalence, and guilt. Only by repeatedly reviewing this unique relationship, which for the parent began at the moment of notification of conception, will the parent be able to identify the feelings that must be processed and slowly begin to complete grief work. This repetition is part of the critical process of decathexis. It is only by repeatedly seeing that their needs, feelings, hopes, desires, and expectations in regard to the child are being frustrated that parents start to accept the finality of the death and to appropriately decathect from the child. They may need to go over situations obsessively in an attempt to understand how things occurred, put them into perspective, and find some meaning and sense in them.

Initially most bereaved parents will idealize the deceased child. However, over time they usually become more realistic and see him as having had both positive and negative traits. To reach this point, repeated discussion of the negative as well as the positive aspects of the child and the parent's relationship to him is necessary. Raphael (1980) suggests how to gently open areas of discussion that may be somewhat negative: "You've told me a lot about the happy times you've shared; could you tell me a little bit about the times that were not so happy?" (p. 157). It will be critical for parents to develop a realistic composite image of the deceased child, one that adequately represents the *real* person and the *real* good-bad relationship (Raphael, 1983). This is especially required for legitimizing ambivalent or negative feelings about the child that necessarily must be worked through.

In the process of all of this caregivers must not be afraid to mention the deceased child to the parent. It is important to incorporate the name of the child in conversations in order to personalize the situation, make it more real for the parent, and confront the natural urge to deny and distance. Fear of prompting an emotional response should not inhibit mentioning the name of the child, for it is these feelings that must be addressed if grief is to be resolved adequately. In many cases parents are actually gratified to hear the name of the child spoken aloud. It is a way of having the child remembered and kept "alive" in a healthy way. It illustrates to them that they are not alone in remembering and caring that their child existed.

A therapeutic modality that is insufficiently used is writing. It is useful for bereaved parents on two dimensions. First, it can serve as a form of communication between a couple when they are unable to talk with one another. Letters and notes suit this purpose well, although the caregiver must caution couples about overusing them and compromising ongoing verbal communication. Still, the merits of letter writing should not be overlooked as a method of contact when painful and confusing issues need to be addressed in a manner that can provide some distance and clarity.

Second, personal journal keeping can be quite therapeutic for the individual bereaved parent on a number of levels. It allows for ventilation without fear of judgment or censor. The process of writing allows the writer to get more control of thoughts and feelings and renders them relatively less confusing as they are bound and grounded in the written word. Journal keeping also serves as a source of feedback to the parent when entries are reread over time. This is an important function, as parents frequently question their progress. Writing and journal keeping is especially helpful for bereaved parents in facilitating the necessary process of review. The possibility of forgetting even the smallest detail of the child's life is a great fear for them. A journal will allow them to record all the details of the child's life from the pregnancy through the day of death. Pictures, remembrances of friends and relatives, thoughts and feelings that occur to them can all be included. The negative as well as the positive acts of the child should be included in order to remember the child as he really was and to stimulate the parent's processing of the feelings, thoughts, and memories connected to the child. The parent can be encouraged to pour out his feelings to the child, such as telling the child of his love, anger, guilt, and longing for him. Finishing unfinished business can be prompted by writing down such things as what he wishes he had said or not said, done or not done; what he wished the child would have said or not said, done or not done; what he is regretful, angry, or resentful about; what he remembers fondly; what expectations and hopes he had for the child that will never be realized; and what he still owes the child, and what the child owes him, to finish the relationship.

Help the Bereaved Parent Identify and Resolve Secondary Losses and Unfinished Business

It is not enough for the bereaved parent to mourn the death of the deceased child. The parent must also mourn the secondary losses that occur as a result of the death. Too often these secondary losses are not identified and grieved for, especially when they are symbolic, such as the loss of parenting the child or the loss of a part of the self. Additionally, the parent must grieve for the dreams, hopes, fantasies, and expectations that he had for and with the child. The lack of ability to fulfill each one of these is a significant and highly painful symbolic loss. Such secondary losses, and any unfinished business that remains between the parent and the child, interfere with the successful completion of grief work and impede healthy readjustment to life without the child. Consequently, the parent must be helped to delineate and mourn current and potential secondary losses (both physical and symbolic) resulting from the death, and to identify any unfinished business with the child and find appropriate ways to come to closure.

At times this process may require sophisticated psychiatric techniques, but often it may be resolved by having the parent say aloud in the presence of a caring witness those things that were unsaid to the deceased child. Frequently in-depth discussion of what the parent would have wanted to say or do can be most helpful. The journal keeping suggested before also offers a vehicle for finishing unfinished business. The parent himself should be asked what he feels he must do in order to achieve a sense of completion. Then the caregiver can help him discern its appropriateness and, when therapeutically advisable, support his attempts at closure.

A prime secondary loss that develops after the death of a child is an altered marital relationship. Adjustments will be mandated as a result of the parents' not being the same people after the loss as before. A major loss always changes an individual to some extent. This does not necessarily have to be a negative change; it can be positive. However, even positive changes are stressful and constitute a loss of the status quo. Something is left behind. As a result, changes in parents will lead to changes in the marital relationship, and these constitute a major set of secondary losses. This places an additional burden of grief, loss, and adaptation on couples already overwrought with responsibilities and demands.

It is crucially important for bereaved parents to understand that they cannot overestimate the effects of grief on their relationship. (See Chapter 1 for a fuller discussion of this topic.) To minimize potential negative effects caregivers must encourage and facilitate communication between spouses. This is one of their most critical tasks. They need to assist parents in learning to keep the communication channels open despite their individual pain or their desire to protect the other or themselves. Bereaved parents often require encouragement and assistance in letting each other know what they need and expect from their partner. Frequently caregivers can help parents by educating them about the possible effects of grief on marriages (although this must not be done in such a way that it establishes a self-fulfilling prophecy or causes them to give up) and then having them discuss with one another how it has affected their marriage and how they can cope with it therapeutically. For some couples it will be easier to talk in the presence of a caregiver; for others it will be inhibiting. Some may benefit from the suggestion of talking in environments outside of the home, since at home they may feel there will be too many memories; others will profit from being in an environment that elicits memories of their child. If parents have difficulty communicating spontaneously, caregivers can suggest they schedule their discussions.

Parents need to reach an understanding of the problems that develop due to the grief process. (See Chapter 1 for a delineation of these problems and other related issues.) They must be helped to avoid the normal tendency to place blame on each other, and to deal with their unmet expectations when they find they grieve in different ways and have differing coping behaviors and interests. Since recovery will proceed for each of them in different areas at different rates and times, they must recognize this and give one another the time, space, and respect each requires. They will need support to remember that despite such differences, and the painful and volatile feelings resulting from the loss, they still love one another. Both of them need to treat each other as very fragile people who require patience and understanding in order to survive and recover from the loss, individually and together. They should be taught to be alert to the signals indicating what their partner needs at the time, for example, when one of them requires solitude or desires company. Time-outs both from one another and from the rest of the world can be suggested as legitimate coping strategies. Parents must recognize that grief most probably will have an impact on their sexual relationship for a while, and that this may be totally unrelated to their feelings of love for one another. The impact is usually a result of grief, depression, and fear of intimacy or future loss, although certainly at times it can reflect one spouse's response to another's behavior. They must also come to accept the fact that the loss of their child will change each of them individually, as well as their marriage and the family as a whole.

Parents will benefit from education about the unique issues inherent in child loss. These must be discussed with them, not to give them more to grieve for, but to legitimize their pain, help them see where it comes from, and assist them in understanding the need for reevaluating their standards when they are unrealistic. Caregivers should encourage parents to seek and reach out to individuals who can best meet their needs and support them.

Parents often will need help to see that the age of the child is inconsequential to their being bereaved, but that it will determine some of the issues that arise during the bereavement. Caregivers must especially try to legitimize grief for parents who grieve for a miscarriage, stillbirth, or neonatal or SIDS death, for too often there will be a social negation of this type of loss. They need to point out that the older parents of the adult child who dies may be in a uniquely vulnerable situation, as most of the support will be given to the child's spouse or children, and not to the parents. In some cases these parents fear losing their grandchildren after their own child has died. When it is a grandchild who dies, grandparents also may be in a difficult position. Caregivers can help legitimize this grief and work with them to cope with seeing their own child suffering with the loss of his child when there is nothing that they can do.

Support the Bereaved Parent in Coping with the Grief Process

This phase of intervention is the broadest. Actually, it is part of all the other phases as well, since the grief process spans the entire time during which intervention would be offered. It is discussed here in depth, and is placed at this point, to incorporate the interventions discussed previously and to supply the foundation for the bereaved parents' experiences, and for the interventions that will be helpful to them, later on in the grief process.

Before beginning, caregivers should attempt an understanding of each parent's personality so that they can maximize the chances of reaching that particular person. It may take time to learn about the individual parent, but it can make the interventions much more effective. For example, a husband might find it less threatening to discuss his reactions to the death of his son in the context of a discussion of family responses, rather than in an individual session focused on his own personal feelings.

For any caregiver to deal effectively with bereaved parents, and to be successful in encouraging them to ventilate their feelings, that caregiver must communicate her realistic understanding of the pain and the parent's natural wish to avoid it. The bereaved parent must be helped to recognize that despite the pain she must yield constructively to the grief process. There is no way to go around, over, or under grief—she must go through it. Parents must be helped to understand that grief cannot be delayed indefinitely, for it will erupt in some way, directly or indirectly. Especially for bereaved parents, when there is so much outrage at the unnatural event of a child's predeceasing a parent, questions of fairness and responsibility are often raised. However, whether or not their loss was fair is of no consequence. Whether or not they deserve what is happening does not matter. The inescapable fact is that they have sustained a major loss, requiring a painful period of readjustment that demands excruciatingly hard work and causes more pain and trouble if not attended to. Caregivers must put it in the context that, although the pain is distressing to the bereaved parents, the experience and release of it is a healing part of the process.

The grieving parent frequently has unrealistic expectations about both herself and the grief process. To help her cope with and productively yield to the grief experience, caregivers must correct these misconceptions and give her support in coping with the pain, along with permission to care for herself. This is partially accomplished by providing the bereaved parent with normative data about the grief process in order to alleviate fears of going crazy and to enable her to understand those issues she needs to address. The parent must be educated about grief, since unrealistic expectations about and negative feelings toward essentially normal grief reactions cause the majority of problems with the working through of grief. Part of the difficulty for bereaved parents is that currently it is unclear whether the normative data for grievers in general are appropriate for bereaved parents specifically. If any restructuring of normative data is required, it will be to indicate that the grief experience of bereaved parents routinely appears to be more intense and long lasting than that of other grievers. (See Chapter 2 for more on this.)

Parents often compare themselves to other grievers in general, and other bereaved parents in particular, without recognizing the significant similarities and differences. Often they berate themselves inappropriately for the discrepancies these comparisons generate. In order for bereaved parents to be fair to themselves, which is so important if they are to tolerate the pain and vicissitudes of grief, it is imperative that they understand that each parent's response to grief is distinct and unique. Even marital partners must recognize that although they have lost the same child, their grief responses will be colored by the personal attributes of themselves and the child, the distinctive relationship between themselves and the child, and their own idiosyncracies. Their tolerance of themselves in the grief process should reflect this.

The grieving parent must be helped to understand that her grief will affect all areas of her life. She may find herself experiencing feelings that are out of the ordinary for her. She also may encounter changes in concentration, work performance, social interest, and physical energy. Predicting the widespread nature of the effects of grief should not frighten parents or establish a self-fulfilling prophecy, but rather prepare them for the unexpected intensity and extensiveness of the experience. In this way, too, the grief will not precipitate other problems. For example, with this knowledge a couple may be able to see that the increased tension experienced in their marriage is a symptom of their mutual grief, and not necessarily of another loss about to befall them.

Bereaved parents require assistance in developing and maintaining appropriate time and course expectations for their grief. They need to know that research data suggest that parental bereavement may not automatically decrease with time (Rando, 1983). Symptoms may diminish for a while and then increase again. There also will be upsurges of grief at specific points in time that would have been salient for their child, for example, when the child would have graduated or gotten married. This is not abnormal and does not necessarily constitute unresolved grief. It is a normal part of "growing up with the loss," as grieving parents react to those times that dramatically signal to them that their child is dead and gone. Anniversary and holiday upsurges in grief should also be explained and predicted, and it should be suggested that significant events in the life of the parent (for example, getting remarried or having other children) or other symbolic stimuli may trigger new transient feelings of grief.

The loss of a child may be so devastating that parents may feel they will be unable to continue to survive. They must be urged to adopt a "one day at a time" perspective to help them avoid being overwhelmed. Grief is a choppy, "two steps forward, one step back" experience that will continue for much longer than they had anticipated, will expose them to feelings they never knew they could have, and will wax and wane over an extended period of time. Bereaved parents must be helped to regard difficulties as a normal part of the grief process and to take time to work on them.

Bereaved parents should be encouraged to be patient and not to expect too much of themselves. Hopefully, providing normative data will help them refrain from imposing undue "shoulds" on themselves about the grief process. Parents will need to learn to put appropriate limitations on their own expectations of themselves, as well as others'. They must recognize that they cannot do everything: they cannot be "supergrievers" and "superparents." If bereaved parents do not recognize the normal limits imposed by their being human, and insufficiently appreciate the toll grief takes on normal functioning, they will set themselves up for failure and for stress overload and burn-out.

All interventions should be designed to capitalize on the bereaved parent's positive coping skills and compensate for deficient ones. When the bereaved parent is doing healthy things, such as talking about the deceased child, it should be encouraged. When she is choosing unhealthy ones, such as drinking too much, alternative behaviors or other sources of help should be suggested. Caregivers should encourage parents to adopt coping strategies within their own personal styles that are active and externally directed, as these have been found to be most useful to parental adjustment. Videka-Sherman (1982) found that both altruism and investment in a new role or meaningful activity preceded reduction in depression of bereaved parents. The least adaptive coping mechanisms were found to be escape by not thinking about the death or by using drugs or alcohol, and persistent preoccupation with the deceased child.

Caregivers must be aware of the understandable, albeit self-defeating, tendency for some bereaved parents to try to cope through drug, tobacco, caffeine, or alcohol abuse. Others will turn to distractions such as excessive work or extramarital affairs to help them avoid confronting the loss. Many times the distraction is camouflaged through social behaviors that give the appearance of new and healthy reinvestments, such as overinvolvement with civic groups. Anything or anyone that inappropriately directs too much of the focus and energy away from the grief process and from the marital relationship constitutes an escape that, while perfectly understandable as a wish for release from pain, must be confronted and redirected. It will eventually cause more pain than it relieves.

Caregivers must be attuned to attempts by bereaved parents to cope by moving, taking a vacation, or making significant changes too early. Often such actions may appear viable and productive to the bereaved. However, they frequently only contribute to further disorganization or stress. If they occur prematurely, parents will find themselves stripped of their roots and the security of familiar surroundings. In the future, such changes may be very helpful to parents who are attempting to relinquish some of the past and integrate new roles into their lives and personalities. Yet those that happen too soon will result in more loss for individuals who are already overwhelmed by many losses. As a result, caregivers must work to prevent unnecessary changes in order to minimize the secondary losses to be encountered by the bereaved. Grievers should be discouraged from making important decisions if at all possible during the first year of bereavement.

Caregivers must also be aware of the practical problems that develop as a consequence of the death. Not only emotional matters require attention in grief; practical ones do as well. This is usually less of an issue when a child dies than when a spouse or parent dies. However, it still may be a salient concern for some bereaved parents. This is especially true if they are burdened by strained finances resulting from the child's illness or death, or if they had been financially dependent upon the adult child to support them. This does not mean that caregivers must become involved in all practical matters, but does suggest that it is important to recognize their significance to grievers and to at least refer them to appropriate sources of assistance.

Coping with the grief process requires major energy. It will drain the bereaved parent on many levels. Consequently, it is important to assist the parent in maintaining appropriate expectations and limits for herself, as well as in finding a variety of ways to replenish herself, following the severe depletion resulting from the loss of the child. The frequently unabating strain of grief on the griever, in which she is continually giving out and giving up for an extended period of time, makes it essential for her to nurture herself. Intellectual stimulation, religion or philosophy, literature, art, and the media can aid the grieving parent in finding meaning in the loss or in simply escaping reality for a while. Adequate rest and nutrition are essential. Optimum physical health must be actively promoted if the bereaved parent is to endure the arduous grief process and avoid psychosomatic complications. Freedom from drugs, a balanced diet, and special attention given to calcium, vitamin D, and phosphorus, which are depleted by the stress of grief, are all important in the bereaved parent's ability to sustain herself through the stress of grief. Physical activity or sports should be suggested to release the pent-up feelings, frustration, and anger that accompany this loss. Research has indicated that physical activity works to reduce tension and anxiety, externalize aggression, and relieve depression. Such activity also helps prevent further somatic and psychiatric problems resulting from the grief process.

Sometimes the caregiver may suggest these types of interventions and find that they are resisted by the bereaved parents. This is because the parents may have difficulty understanding that they should grant themselves a respite from the grief. They must be made to understand that it is not a betrayal of the deceased child to take a break from their grief, or to enjoy their other children and other aspects of their lives. This point may have to be repeated frequently, since it is not uncommon for parents to want to punish themselves for failure to protect the child and for other perceived violations of the parental role.

Notwithstanding all the suggestions just given, bereaved parents must be urged to find their own ways of doing things that are comfortable for them. Caregivers can provide an atmosphere in which bereaved parents are able to choose their own style of grief and then keep them on track within this style, as long as they are continuing to therapeutically address their grief work. It must be kept in mind that there is no one correct way to grieve. As long as the tasks of grief are being attended to and the parent is not causing additional stress for herself by her coping behaviors, the bereaved parent should be allowed the freedom and flexibility to navigate the grief process in her own way. Caregivers can warn her about the inadvisability of heeding all the advice offered by well-meaning others, encouraging her to critically evaluate its usefulness for herself.

Related to this, caregivers must assist bereaved parents in expressing their needs to others. Many people desire to be supportive, but are at a loss for what to do. Even though they are grieving and are the ones who should be extended to, bereaved parents may often have to take the initiative in reaching out to others and assertively stating what they need and want from them, or suggesting how they can be most helpful.

Help the Bereaved Parent to Accommodate to the Loss

As a bereaved parent progresses through the process of grief, caregivers can be especially helpful by assisting her in developing new ways to maintain a healthy relationship with the deceased child. The interventions mentioned here are suggested when the bereaved parent is well into her grief work and will be inappropriate if used too early in the grief process.

Bereaved parents will need assistance in getting and maintaining the proper perspective on what resolution of their grief will mean. In this context, resolution means successfully adapting to or adjusting to the loss, learning to live without the child. It is not meant to suggest that the loss can be dealt with once and for all, with feelings about it never to arise again. Bereaved parents will never be "over it" or "done with it"; their only legitimate hope is to be able to cope with the death of the child sufficiently over time so that they can continue to live and function somewhat meaningfully. However, the loss will always be there, albeit in the background many times.

Parents will need to understand that they will survive, although they will not be the same. They must recognize that a major loss always changes an individual to some extent, both positively and negatively. The bereaved parent must anticipate this and be aware of the transformation in herself. Parents also need to know that they will never forget. The emptiness will remain, but the pain will diminish and they can learn to live with the tragedy. Although there will always be reminders of such a significant loss, the goal is to help the bereaved parent recognize this fact and continue living, to reinvest in other relationships, goals, or activities without inappropriately clinging to memories of the deceased child. (This must be phrased so as not to cause parents to fear that their child will be forgotten, a prospect that terrifies some.) One thing that bereaved parents may need to be cautioned about is the tendency to equate the length and amount of their suffering with some kind of testimony to their love for the deceased child. Suffering must not be seen as a bond to the deceased or as proof of the value of the relationship. These types of beliefs will only promote unresolved grief. Parents must understand that healthy grief does not mean abandoning the deceased child.

Caregivers also must help bereaved parents to realize that a healthy new relationship with the child must be formed. Although death has separated them physically from their child, it has not ended the relationship. The relationship simply has changed from one based on the child's presence to one relating to memories of the past and/or one representing healthy, appropriate, sustained, but abstract, love and symbolic connection with the deceased child (Attig, 1986). This transition occurs during the grief process as the parent reorganizes and restructures life without the presence of the child. It is important for the parent to achieve the proper balance and perspective on this new relationship. While it is distinctly unhealthy for the parent to attempt to bring back the child by clinging to memories, neurotically perpetuating the relationship through illusion, neither is it healthy to extinguish all memories of the child, wiping out part of the parent's own past life. The child needs to be remembered as one who was once alive, but is now dead (Irion, 1966).

Caregivers must ask the parent in what appropriate ways she will keep the child's memory alive and continue to relate to her. It is critical for the parent to find healthy new ways to relate to the deceased child. Anniversary celebrations, family rituals, prayers, commemorative donations, mention in grace over dinner, and appropriate acting on the child's concerns or espousing her values are all examples of ways to relate to the deceased child while maintaining the proper perspective on the new relationship. Parents must decide what portions of the previous life with the child will be retained, such as special holiday activities, family routines, and symbolic mementos, and how reminiscences can be kept life-promoting, rather than death-denying. The message must be communicated to bereaved parents that "Learning how to treasure the irreplaceable memory of the missing member in your family is a healing part of grief" (Hogan, 1983, p. 6). The caregiver can help these parents develop appropriate meaningful rituals for the therapeutic expression of their grief and for the continuation of a healthy relationship to the deceased child. (The therapeutic use of rituals will be discussed in greater depth later in this chapter.)

After major losses, bereaved individuals have altered identities. Bereaved parents can be helped to discover their new identities by looking at the psychological and social roles that must be assumed or relinquished as a consequence of the death. Where once there was a "we" in the parent-child relationship, now there is an "I." This is a highly significant and painful transition to make. The parent should be asked what experiences, roles, expectations, values, opportunities, and fantasies she has had to give up, and what new ones have had to be adopted. Some amount of identification is normal in the grief process, and the parent needs to determine how healthy and appropriate identification with the deceased child has added to or changed her previous identity. Ask her to consider how she has identified with the child, confronting self-destructive ways and supporting therapeutic ones. Of course, much of this will depend upon the age of the deceased child; yet even adults can identify with the courage of a young child or the fun-loving nature of a toddler. The key issue for bereaved parents is that in order to be healthy this identification must be appropriate to their age and role. For example, to identify with a child by becoming increasingly immature would be pathological. Bereaved parents must choose to identify with aspects of their child that can be appropriately integrated into their adult personalities. This is less of an issue when an adult loses a spouse, for example, when the attributes to be identified with are already consistent with adulthood.

Another shift in identity that must be accommodated is the delicate task of disengaging from the parental role with the deceased child while maintaining this role with surviving children. This is a dual, mutually incompatible task. It will require much discussion to clarify the issues and separate the deceased child from the surviving siblings, and it demands of the parents the processing of feelings attendant to the task, such as anger at surviving children or regret over the loss of this particular child.

Parents must identify and grieve for each of the specific changes in themselves, both losses and gains, that have stemmed from the death and its sequelae. They also must identify what has remained constant despite the trauma of the loss of their child. Many times this will mean, among other things, acknowledgment of the continued existence of a loving family. This process of identifying what remains unchanged must be done in a way so as not to insinuate that it should replace or minimize the loss, but to illustrate that security and continuity still exist in the parents' lives.

Caregivers must provide bereaved parents with information about family reorganization after the death of a family member to prepare them for the stress and dynamics that occur as the family struggles to regain homeostasis. They need to work with the parents specifically to insure that they do not erroneously interpret the remaining children's reactions, assume they know what the children feel or think, psychologically abandon them, or place them in unhealthy or replacement roles.

Parents must be given information about how to communicate with the surviving children about death and loss, and how to help these children with their grief. Also, parents need to make sure these children do not adopt unrealistic expectations for themselves, such as trying to take the pain away from the parents or attempting to replace the lost sibling. Bereaved parents will benefit from normalization of their feelings and concerns for surviving children, such as resentment that the children are alive or appear to be insufficiently grieved, concerns that relationships with them are too intense or less intense than the one with the deceased child, and fears of losing them as well. Active guidance and intervention is important in all these areas so that parents do not further victimize themselves or their children. (See Chapter 1 for more on problems with family systems following a child's death.)

One of the most critical things a caregiver can do is to assist bereaved parents in reestablishing a system of belief or meaning in their lives. A major loss often precipitates a quest for meaning, not only for the loss itself, but also for the griever's life. When parents have lost a child, it is particularly important to understand why the event has occurred, since it is such an unexpected and incomprehensible tragedy. Bereaved parents will need guidance in answering those questions that can be answered (for example, the cause of death) and accepting the fact that some cannot be answered or understood (for example, why it had to happen). They will have to arrive at a point where they can live with the unknown and accept, or at least resign themselves to the fact, that they may never understand why the death occurred, although there well may be a reason that just cannot be ascertained. As parents struggle to put their lives back together, caregivers can help them by reframing their questions. Instead of looking for an answer to why the loss happened to them, they can be encouraged to decide what they are going to do about it and with it now that it has occurred. Although the tragedy lacks meaning, parents can give it meaning by what they choose to do to respond to it.

If an individual can find a "why" to live (for example, human relationships, altruistic or spiritual goals, dedication to the child's memory), she will be able to find a "how" to survive (Slaby, Lieb, & Tancredi, 1981). Accordingly, caregivers must strive to help bereaved parents identify those beliefs and actions that will provide a renewed sense of purpose in their lives. Some bereaved parents achieve this by honoring the memory of their deceased child through determining that some good shall arise from the loss. Many times this involves their changing themselves as a result of their encounter with death. For example, parents can become more sensitive to others, can reprioritize their lives, or become closer to remaining family. They may start to work to help others. Activities not formerly significant can become meaningful, such as campaigning for stiffer drunk-driving legislation after the death of a child in an auto accident (one purpose for the establishment of Mothers Against Drunk Driving) or establishing a chapter of a bereaved parents' self-help group. In this way the child can appropriately "live on" as the parents do things in her memory. To those for whom death has provoked a crisis of faith and previously held beliefs, new or renewed religious and philosophical ideals may supply reason and order. At first parents may feel there is no reason to go on, and they will have to be reassured that in time meaning can be restored.

Caregivers must continue to challenge the unrealistic expectations that may be harbored by bereaved parents about themselves in their roles. Where there have been unrealistic expectations that may have been taken seriously and now engender guilt (for example, the idea that they could have protected their child from everything), it is critical to assist the parents in working through their ensuing guilt, finding ways to forgive themselves for failing to live up to societal expectations for perfect parenting, and reestablishing appropriate expectation. At this point, caregivers can then help bereaved parents identify ways to make the tragedy meaningful and discover goals and activities into which they can appropriately channel their intense feelings.

Caregivers can provide assistance to bereaved parents in going forward with their lives by working with them to set appropriate goals for their continued existence. Parents must not relinquish goals for themselves, although after the child's death they may be changed somewhat. The reestablishment of goals is a major step in healing, as goals give the parents meaning and an organizational focus that can pull them forward. These goals, of course, must be realistic and frequently can be combined with those activities conducted to give the child's death meaning.

Work with the Bereaved Parent to Reinvest in a New Life

As bereaved parents continue to move well along into the grief process, interventions must be directed toward appropriately supporting reinvestment in a new life. This does not mean that bereaved parents are pushed into new relationships before they are ready. For many, this is an insult to the memory of their child and is an unbearable burden if it occurs precipitously. The decision to encourage a parent to enter into new relationships or find new activities will depend on the individual bereaved parent, the specific loss, and the progress that has been made through the grief process. However, at the appropriate time, encouragement to find rewarding new things to do and people to invest in will offer bereaved parents new persons, objects, activities, causes, or goals toward which their emotional energies can be directed in the absence of their loved child. Anyone or anything that would gratify the appropriate needs of the griever could serve as an outlet. Again, this does not mean that the deceased child is forgotten or betrayed. The relationship is altered to be sure, but it still exists in a very special way in the heart and mind of each bereaved parent. What is changed is that parent's ongoing investment in and attachment to the child as a living person who could return the investment. The energy that previously went into keeping the relationship with the child alive now must be channeled elsewhere, where it can be returned. This is difficult, but necessary, after any major loss. Sometimes this will involve the activities mentioned before that are undertaken to provide meaning in the parent's life. Frequently they are activities done for enjoyment, or out of duty or obligation. Some may be chosen simply for reinvestment purposes, in order to give the parent something in which to put energy and interest or to offer diversion.

Reinvestment may be particularly problematic for those who have been involved with caring for a child with a long-term chronic illness prior to the death. In this case, much of their time has been focused on the care of the dying child, and now time may weigh all too heavily on their hands. In these and other cases, grievers may require specific direction in getting back into circulation. Caregivers must help these grievers find the support they need to adapt to the loss and to form new relationships with others. It may come through family, friends, or self-help or other helping groups. If they are encouraged to choose new tasks to accomplish and new causes to invest in, these bereaved parents may also find supportive people in social, educational, religious, or political groups.

Bereaved parents can also be helped by being assisted in identifying the gain that has been derived from the death of the child. In every loss there is a gain that accrues, although this is not to dismiss the intensity of the bereavement experience or minimize its tragedy. For example, although a man loses his son, the situation may force him to recognize that he should spend more time with his other children. In this case, the gain is that the man now becomes more closely involved with his surviving children than he previously was. This does not mean that he is glad that the loss occurred, or that he would have wished for his son's death. The point is that at times it is helpful for parents to recognize these gains and to capitalize on them for their recovery process. It can help them to cope with the painfulness of the loss by putting it in the perspective of the gains and losses that continually ebb and flow through life, and by giving it some positive meaning through its consequences, despite its tragedy.

As a final note, it should be remembered that all of these treatment suggestions only hold true within certain limits. Grief that is absent, distorted, or too prolonged or intense will require more in-depth treatment. For those who are not trained in mental health intervention, referrals to mental health professionals may be necessary for some bereaved parents. There will also be times when caregivers will need to be more directive and assertive with particular bereaved parents. For, although the bereaved require nonjudgmental acceptance and support, there will be occasions, after a period of time, when they can benefit from a gentle, caring, and well-timed nudge in the direction of meeting the goals of appropriate grief work.

RITUALS*

Rituals can provide powerful therapeutic experiences that symbolize transition, healing, and continuity (van der Hart, 1983). Consequently, they can address and catalyze many aspects of the parental grief process. Like funerals, they can initiate the process of grief. However, they are not magic. Their power comes from the faith that the individual has in their ability to provide meaning.

> *Case Example:* Al's teenaged son committed suicide by shooting himself in the head with a shotgun in a field near their house. Now that Al can finally admit to the feelings of anger and betrayal that have complicated his grief, and has worked them through to a large extent, he is able to return to the spot of his son's demise and plant a tree to mark his son's life and to offer something living in place of death.

As discussed here, a ritual is a specific behavior or activity that gives symbolic expression to certain feelings and thoughts of the actor or actors individually or as a group. It may be a one-time occurrence or may be habitually repeated, such as an anniversary Mass or a yearly trip to the cemetery on Memorial Day. Rituals can be particularly helpful in assisting an individual or family to successfully resolve grief,

---

*Adapted from "Creating Therapeutic Rituals in the Psychotherapy of the Bereaved" by T. A. Rando. Published in *Psychotherapy*, 1985, 22(2), 236–240. Adapted with permission.

both prior to and after the death, ideally building successfully on the therapeutic foundation supplied by the funeral. These rituals need to be tailored to help the bereaved individual or family accept the reality of the loss, express and work through the feelings attendant to that loss, and accomplish all the tasks of grief work.

For the bereaved parent, rituals provide a structured way to recall the lost child and to make some statement about the parent's feelings. They encourage the necessary formulation of a new relationship with the child by acknowledging the physical loss, while allowing the memory and symbolic interaction to continue. In terms of the social group, rituals can work to solidify family relationships and realign family roles. Like funeral rituals, therapeutic rituals can increase group cohesion following the death of a child in several ways: they give the group a commonly experienced symbolic behavior; they provide a way to cope with the separation; they make a statement of communal support; and they provide meaning to counteract the loss of meaning experienced after the death. Rituals have many specific properties that are especially useful in assisting bereaved parents in coping with the death of their child.

The power of acting-out. Acting-out enables the parent to constructively do something to overcome the feelings of emptiness and powerlessness that often accompany parental bereavement. It gives the parent a sense of control, cutting through intellectualization and other resistances to mourning to directly reach the emotions. The physical reality of ritual behavior touches upon the parent's unconscious feelings far more effectively than any words can. It allows the grieving parent to externally express his inner feelings, and it may help him in expiating his feelings of guilt.

The legitimization of emotional and physical ventilation. Rituals give the parent permission to outwardly express his feelings, providing acceptable limits and symbols to focus upon.

The delimitation of grief. Grief can seem overwhelming when it is experienced as a diffuse, global reaction. Rituals can channel feelings of grief into a circumscribed activity having a distinct beginning and ending with a clear purpose, making the feelings more manageable.

Case Example: The Barclay family has a special dinner at a McDonald's restaurant in memory of their deceased toddler, Jonathan, on his birthday. It had been his favorite restaurant and was where he had celebrated his last birthday. This provides them with an activity through which they can demonstrate their love for the child and illustrate to themselves and others that they have not forgotten him. Consequently, the Barclays find it less stressful and not a betrayal of Jonathan if they do not feel constant pain throughout the anniversary date. They find it easier to give themselves permission to experience whatever joy is available to them on this day without as much guilt.

A ritual designed to express but also to limit grief, such as this one, can be especially therapeutic during holidays and other anniversary times.

The opportunity for the parent to "hang on" to the deceased child without doing so inappropriately or interfering with grief work. Participation in ritual behaviors may give the parent a chance to interact intensely with the memory of the child for a limited period of time without crossing over into pathological dimensions. Ritual legitimizes such emotional exchanges.

The provision of assistance in mourning and in confronting unresolved grief. Rituals allow the parent to state consciously and unconsciously, implicitly and explicitly, that a loss has occurred. Through them the parent can channel his feelings of grief or finish unfinished business. Rituals aid in the process of decathexis.

The learning gained through doing and experiencing. Participation in ritual behavior "teaches" the parent that the deceased child is gone. It provides the experience necessary to validate the loss and prepares him to adjust to the environment in which the child is missing.

The provision of structure for ambivalent or nebulous affect and cognition. Rituals provide a focus that is especially helpful in managing the confusing disorganization and loss of control commonly experienced in the parental loss of a child.

The provision of experiences that allow for the participation of other group members. Collective rituals promote the social integration that is a requisite for successful grief resolution and reintegration back into the social group.

The structuring of "celebrations" of anniversaries and holidays. Participation in ritual activities commemorating a special date may provide an unusually effective way of tapping into or confronting parents' anniversary reactions, which are not always easily recognized or owned by parents.

Certain variables must be assessed and taken into account in designing a therapeutic ritual: the psychological, social, physical, cultural, and religious/philosophical characteristics of the parent; the nature and extent of his psychosocial support; the specific characteristics of the loss; and the parent's present phase in the grief process and the issues and conflicts attendant to it. A ritual may be created to assist grievers in the normal process of their grief work.

> *Case Example:* Michaela, a 17-year-old girl, was killed in an automobile accident. Her family was told they needed to commemorate her at Christmas, a day they were dreading. They decided to burn a candle throughout the holiday to symbolize that she was still an important part of their lives, although in a radically different fashion. At dinner her empty chair was occupied by a senior citizen who otherwise would not have had a holiday feast.

It may also be a tool to help those whose grief has been unresolved.

> *Case Example:* Barbara was accompanied by her therapist as she visited the grave of her daughter, who died 19 years ago. Since that time she had been unable to appropriately adapt to her loss and emotionally go on with her life. At the cemetery she laid a bouquet of flowers on the grave, spoke of what she had lost in the intervening years, and talked of when she would reunite with her child. She then divided the bouquet in half, taking one half home with her and leaving the remaining flowers on the grave. She had told herself symbolically that while she had lost the physical presence of her daughter forever, her relationship continued based on loving memory. She had been fearful that if she acknowledged the death and grieved her loss, she would lose her daughter permanently. However, the ritual enabled her to acknowledge the death, grieve her loss, and still keep her daughter's memory.

Once the impediments to successful grief resolution are known, an appropriate ritual can be designed to overcome them. For instance, in the case described at the beginning of this section, Al needed something to symbolize that he could forgive his son for committing suicide. Consequently, he chose planting the tree in his son's place of death to illustrate that even though his son had died Al had a living attachment to him, as represented by the tree. Ritual does not have to be dramatic, but it should be tailored to the needs of the griever if it is to be meaningful and helpful. There must be an appropriate amount of emotional distancing for the ritual to be effective. Rituals that are too overwhelming (under-distanced) or do not have enough emotional meaning or content to the griever (over-distanced) will be nontherapeutic (Scheff, 1977).

It is important to recognize that therapeutic rituals can be as effective in dealing with the terminally ill as they are with the bereaved following the death. The same therapeutic properties exist since grief work is being addressed by both populations.

THERAPIES FOR UNRESOLVED GRIEF

Formal psychotherapy must often be utilized when normal grief turns to unresolved grief. The following section provides brief descriptions of some of the forms of grief therapy that are presently available. It should be evident that they contain many of the previously mentioned interventions utilized to facilitate normal grief.

Focal Psychotherapy

Raphael (1983) provides a model of focal psychotherapy that involves assessment of the particular form of pathological bereavement response and specific treatment to manage it and address the etiological processes involved. The goal is to convert the pathological bereavement response into one in which the individual is able to grieve more appropriately.

Focal therapy may be conducted either during the crisis following the loss or at a later point in time. Focal psychotherapy as applied to three categories of pathological (unresolved) bereavement will be discussed here. Although many of the strategies described in the preceding "Interventions" section are used in this therapy, only those specific to particular categories will be mentioned.

Inhibited, Suppressed, or Absent Grief

The caregiver must explore the reasons why the bereaved parent cannot accept the death. Among the possibilities are dependence on the deceased child, fear of the emotions of grief, and guilt about the death. The caregiver's principal task will be to repeatedly review the parent's relationship with the child, a process that will reveal the parent's defenses. Mourning itself will be facilitated by this process. An absence of appropriate affect may be due to the parent's fear of releasing emotions. It may be interpreted as such by the caregiver, who must also communicate recognition of the bereaved parent's inner pain, the purpose of her defenses, and her reluctance to experience grief.

Distorted (Conflicted) Grief

In this grief there is some suppression or inhibition of grief along with powerful distortions, usually extreme anger or extreme guilt.

Angry distortion is often found following the loss of a dependent relationship when there is a sudden or unexpected death for which someone is blamed, or when the deceased died violently. Aims and techniques for treatment of distorted anger are similar to those described for inhibited, suppressed, or absent grief. However, there will be particular emphasis in the treatment on assisting the bereaved parent in working through the displacement aspects of the anger and the problems created by the loss of a very dependent relationship and one that symbolized something special and irreplaceable for the parent.

The pattern of distorted guilt is usually found when the relationship between the bereaved parent and the child has been one of intense ambivalence, sometimes involving hostile actions, possibly even filled with conscious or unconscious wishes for the death or departure of the child. The guilt may be borne personally or projected onto others. Promotion of mourning will be the goal of treatment. As with unexpressed grief and angry distortion, the caregiver must explore the circumstances of the death, the lost relationship, and the support available to help with resolution of ambivalence. The latter is especially problematic for bereaved parents. There is a special need here to explore the origins of ambivalence in the relationship, its links to earlier repetition compulsions, and the parent's own parent-child relationships. Early in treatment, the caregiver must refrain from reassuring the parent that she did her best or all that she could for the deceased child. In most cases the parent is well aware on some level of the extent of her anger. She will only receive assurance when this anger (and possibly a resulting "death wish") is brought into the open and faced with a caregiver who can assist her in coming to terms with it—a major step toward resolution. If guilt is legitimately linked to real behaviors, the caregiver will need to help the parent accept it and learn to live with it. For the most part, however, the guilt of these parents has its origins in fantasy and has to be worked through in therapy. This group of bereaved individuals may relish the pain of their guilt and use it to pacify the deceased child. If the guilt becomes unmanageable, they may sink into a psychiatric depression. If there are fantasies of reunion with the deceased child, suicidal preoccupations may have to be assessed.

Chronic Grief

This form of bereavement is similar to acute grief but it has been prolonged. It is often seen following the deaths of children or individuals with whom the bereaved were in dependent and irreplaceable relationships, and after deaths that were unexpected. It usually indicates that an extraordinary, and possibly pathological, emotional investment had been maintained in the deceased. Many individuals experiencing this type of grief are not motivated to relinquish it, for it assists them in keeping the deceased "alive." Specific treatment goals are to explore why the relationship has such a special meaning and cannot be surrendered. It will be critical to explore the roles and identities that the parent had in terms of the deceased, since decathexis may only result following the adoption of new roles and identity. It must be noted that chronic grief can develop as a method of controlling and punishing others, eliciting their care, and receiving secondary gain. The caregiver may want to establish a set of concrete tasks for the chronic griever to complete, for example, sorting through the child's effects or decreasing visits to the cemetery. The grieving parent needs to develop other sources of gratification and to create an alternate role for herself. However, such grievers are notoriously difficult to treat and frequently retain their symptoms unremittingly. Parkes and Weiss (1983) caution against using traditional treatment modes that stimulate or extend grief expression with chronic grievers.

Unanticipated Grief

Although technically not attributable to Raphael's focal psychotherapy, the syndrome of the unanticipated grief reaction as discussed by Parkes and Weiss (1983) is amenable to treatment utilizing the focal psychotherapy approach. This is a form of grief reaction that occurs after a sudden, unanticipated loss. In this case, the loss is so disruptive that the adaptive capacities of the bereaved are seriously assaulted as they struggle not only to deal with the impact of the loss, but to cope with the effects of its suddenness and lack of warning: bewilderment, anxiety, inability to put it into a context or make sense out of it. The disruption caused by the impact of its coming from out of the blue is shocking both psychologically and physically to the griever, and as a result recovery is usually complicated. The caregiver must give the griever the time and opportunity to repeatedly talk through the death and its implications and to react emotionally to them. In essence, although the death has already occurred, the bereaved have to "prepare themselves for an event that has already occurred" (Parkes & Weiss, 1983, p. 239). They will require continued opportunities to share feelings, make real the events of the death, cope with the feelings of chaos and insecurity stimulated by this kind of unanticipated loss, and to work through the unfinished business that could never be addressed because of the lack of warning.

A major problem specific to bereaved parents is that the typical bereavement responses stimulated in them may approach these pathological grief reactions more often than not. Caregivers must be exceptionally careful in evaluating the pathology of parental bereavement, since it may not lend itself to evaluation with the criteria usually employed for diagnosis of unresolved, abnormal, or pathological grief. (See Chapter 2 for further discussion of this critical issue.)

Other Therapies

There are several other types of therapy that are also well suited to addressing unresolved grief. Volkan has written extensively on re-grief therapy (Volkan, 1971, 1975; Volkan & Showalter, 1968), which is designed to assist the parent in bringing into consciousness memories of the deceased child and the experiences she had with the child in order to test them against reality; have her accept with feelings, especially appropriate anger, what has occurred; and free herself from excessive bondage to the child.

The criterion for utilization of this treatment is intellectual acknowledgment of the loss accompanied by emotional denial 6 months or more after the death. The parent has a chronic hope that the child will return and consequently is fixated in the initial reaction to the death. Many of these grievers did not fully participate in funeral rituals and never saw nor believed the final interment to have taken place. There is usually great ambivalence toward the deceased child.

In the beginning of therapy rational distinctions are made between what actually belongs to the parent and what belongs to the deceased child. The individual is helped to form boundaries demarcating herself from the deceased through the taking of a detailed history of the deceased and the lost relationship. Sometimes a photo of the deceased is brought in to clarify the differentiation. The grieving parent is helped to understand why she could not permit the child to "die." The circumstances of the death are carefully examined. Next the caregiver focuses on the parent's *linking objects*, which are highly symbolized objects representing the deceased child and providing contact with her. The caregiver asks the griever to bring these to the session and they are used to stimulate memories and make the parent aware of the magical ties with the child. The concepts that are symbolized by the linking objects are identified and interpreted to loosen the parent's contact with the deceased. Further review of the circumstances of the death is conducted and emotional release is encouraged. Dreams and fantasies are analyzed, and the parent is encouraged to take responsibility for her feelings of anger, ambivalence, and guilt. This is a short-term therapy and the parent is usually seen four times a week to promote intensity.

Behavioral approaches are best suited for chronic pathological bereavement that contains strong phobic avoidance components. A number of researchers have suggested that a modified flooding technique of confrontation with pain-evoking stimuli breaks down denial and evokes the affects of grief, which can then be desensitized and extinguished.

Guided mourning is a treatment in which individuals with unresolved grief are exposed both in imagination and in real life to avoided or painful memories, ideas, or situations related to the loss of the child (Lieberman, 1978; Mawson, Marks, Ramm, & Stern, 1981). Individuals are asked to repeatedly describe such thoughts, feelings, or ideas until the distress that initially prompts the phobic avoidance response is diminished. They are encouraged to say good-bye to the lost loved one by writing notes or visiting the cemetery. There is an intense reliving of painful memories and feelings associated with the bereavement. Individuals are given instructions to write about the deceased, think about that person, force themselves to face the grief, and look at a photo of the deceased each day. Several studies have suggested that when compared to a control group that had been encouraged to avoid thinking about the death or the deceased, those who had received guided mourning intervention evidenced modest improvement, especially for the phobic avoidance aspects of their experience. However, improvement in levels of depression was less than expected, suggesting less of an association between mood disturbance and avoidance of bereavement cues than previously assumed.

A treatment method for those suffering from unresolved grief has been developed that uses present-time guided imagery (Melges & DeMaso, 1980). The process begins with preparation for making the decision to re-grieve and clarification of the procedures. This is followed by guided imagery for reliving, revising, and revisiting scenes of the loss. The griever is asked to relive a sequence of the loss by viewing it in her mind's eye as if it were happening now. She is then told to revise that scene in order to remove the barriers or binds that inhibit grieving. Finally, she is instructed to revisit the revised scene in the present tense as if it were taking place here and now in order to acknowledge the finality of the loss and experience the full range of grief that was previously prohibited. In many cases the individual is encouraged to engage in dialogues with the deceased in order to acknowledge the finality of the loss; differentiate herself from the deceased; express tears and rage; deal with ambivalence and misdirected anger; tease apart interlocking grief reactions; emancipate herself from unspoken binds; reveal secrets and deal with unfinished business; express love and forgiveness; and get permission for new relationships and options. Following this the caregiver works with the griever to build new hopes and plans of action following completion of the intense work of grieving. Often the griever's decision to re-grieve is therapeutic in and of itself. Results have been found to be good, sometimes dramatic, after 6 to 10 sessions. In most instances this type of therapy has been integrated with other forms of therapy. One of its greatest advantages is that present-time guided imagery or components of it quickly get at the core issues needing resolution. It serves to highlight the obstacles and binds that are often only dimly perceived when a bereaved person talks about the loss in the past tense.

SUMMARY

The death of a child presents a parent with an unequalled loss that must be addressed. To be of assistance caregivers must have a command of the tasks and processes of grief and mourning; be familiar with and able to assess the factors that influence grief and the forms that grief may take; and be able to employ interventions that will facilitate resolution of grief work and adaptation to this uniquely disorganizing loss. Parental loss *can* be coped with successfully, but it requires enormous amounts of psychological work on the part of these parents and clinical knowledge and social support on the part of caregivers.

References

Alexy, W. D. (1982). Dimensions of psychological counseling that facilitate the grieving process of bereaved parents. *Journal of Counseling Psychology, 29*, 498–507.

Attig, T. (1986, April). *Grief, love and separation.* Paper presented at the Eighth Annual Conference of the Forum for Death Education and Counseling, Atlanta, GA.

Averill, J. R. (1968). Grief: Its nature and significance. *Psychological Bulletin, 70*, 721–748.

Berlinsky, E. B., & Biller, H. B. (1982). *Parental death and psychological development.* Lexington, MA: D. C. Heath, Lexington Books.

Bowlby, J. (1980). *Attachment and loss: Vol. 3. Loss, sadness and depression.* New York: Basic Books.

Bugen, L. (1979). Human grief: A model for prediction and intervention. In L. Bugen (Ed.), *Death and dying: Theory, research, practice.* Dubuque, IA: William C. Brown.

Caplan, G. (1974). Forward. In I. O. Glick, R. S. Weiss, & C. M. Parkes (Eds.), *The first year of bereavement.* New York: Wiley.

Fenichel, O. (1945). *The psychoanalytic theory of neurosis.* New York: Norton.

Fish, W. C., & Whitty, S. M. (1983). Challenging conventional wisdom about parental bereavement. *Forum Newsletter: Forum for Death Education & Counseling, 6*(8), 4.

Freud, S. (1955). Totem and taboo. In *Standard edition of the complete psychological works of Sigmund Freud* (Vol. 13). London: Hogarth Press. (Original work published 1913)

Freud, S. (1957). Mourning and melancholia. In *Standard edition of the complete psychological works of Sigmund Freud* (Vol. 14). London: Hogarth Press. (Original work published 1917)

Fulton, R., & Fulton, J. (1971). A psychosocial aspect of terminal care: Anticipatory grief. *Omega, 2,* 91–100.

Furman, E. (1974). *A child's parent dies: Studies in childhood bereavement.* New Haven: Yale University Press.

Glick, I. O., Weiss, R. S., & Parkes, C. M. (1974). *The first year of bereavement.* New York: Wiley.

Hardt, D. V. (1978–79). An investigation of the stages of bereavement. *Omega, 9,* 279–285.

Hogan, N. (1983). Commitment to survival (Part Two). *The Compassionate Friends Newsletter, 6,* 5–6.

Irion, P. (1966). *The funeral—Vestige or value?* Nashville: Parthenon Press.

Jackson, E. N. (1957). *Understanding grief: Its roots, dynamics, and treatment.* Nashville: Abingdon Press.

Kastenbaum, R. J. (1969). Death and bereavement in later life. In A. H. Kutscher (Ed.), *Death and bereavement.* Springfield, IL: Charles C. Thomas.

Kliman, A. S. (1977). Comments in section on "The Parents." In N. Linzer (Ed.), *Understanding bereavement and grief.* New York: Yeshiva University Press.

Lazare, A. (1979). Unresolved grief. In A. Lazare (Ed.), *Outpatient psychiatry: Diagnosis and treatment.* Baltimore: Williams & Wilkins.

Levav, I. (1982). Mortality and psychopathology following the death of an adult child: An epidemiological review. *Israeli Journal of Psychiatry and Related Sciences, 19,* 23–38.

Lieberman, S. (1978). Nineteen cases of morbid grief. *British Journal of Psychiatry, 132,* 159–163.

Lindemann, E. (1944). Symptomatology and management of acute grief. *American Journal of Psychiatry, 101,* 141–148.

Maddison, D. (1968). The relevance of conjugal bereavement for preventive psychiatry. *British Journal of Medical Psychology, 41,* 223–233.

Mawson, D., Marks, I. M., Ramm, L., & Stern, R. S. (1981). Guided mourning for morbid grief: A controlled study. *British Journal of Psychiatry, 138,* 185–193.

Melges, F. T., & DeMaso, D. R. (1980). Grief-resolution therapy: Reliving, revising, and revisiting. *American Journal of Psychotherapy, 34,* 51–61.

Orbach, C. E. (1959). The multiple meanings of the loss of a child. *American Journal of Psychotherapy, 13,* 906–915.

Osterweis, M., Solomon, F., & Green, M. (Eds.). (1984). *Bereavement: Reactions, consequences and care.* (Report by the Committee for the Study of Health Consequences of the Stress of Bereavement, Institute of Medicine, National Academy of Sciences). Washington, DC: National Academy Press.

Parkes, C. M. (1972). *Bereavement: Studies of grief in adult life.* New York: International Universities Press.

Parkes, C. M. (1975). Determinants of outcome following bereavement. *Omega, 6,* 303–323.

Parkes, C. M., & Weiss, R. S. (1983). *Recovery from bereavement.* New York: Basic Books.

Rando, T. A. (1983). An investigation of grief and adaptation in parents whose children have died from cancer. *Journal of Pediatric Psychology, 8*(1), 3–20.

Rando, T. A. (1984). *Grief, dying, and death: Clinical interventions for caregivers.* Champaign, IL: Research Press.

Rando, T. A. (Ed.). (1986). *Loss and anticipatory grief.* Lexington, MA: Lexington Books.

Raphael, B. (1977). Preventive intervention with the recently bereaved. *Archives of General Psychiatry, 34,* 1450–1454.

Raphael, B. (1980). A psychiatric model for bereavement counseling. In B. Mark Schoenberg (Ed.), *Bereavement counseling: A multidisciplinary handbook.* Westport, CT: Greenwood Press.

Raphael, B. (1983). *The anatomy of bereavement.* New York: Basic Books.

Raphael, B., & Maddison, D. (1976). The care of bereaved adults. In O. W. Hill (Ed.), *Modern trends in psychosomatic medicine.* London: Butterworth.

Rees, W. D., & Lutkins, S. G. (1967). Mortality of bereavement. *British Medical Journal, 4,* 13–16.

Schatz, W. H. (1984). *Healing a father's grief.* Redmond, WA: Medic Publishing Company.

Scheff, T. (1977). The distancing of emotion in ritual. *Current Anthropology, 18,* 483–490.

Sheldon, A. R., Cochrane, J., Vachon, M. L., Lyall, W. A., Rogers, J., & Freeman, S. J. (1981). A psychosocial analysis of risk of psychological impairment following bereavement. *Journal of Nervous and Mental Disease, 169,* 253–255.

Siggins, L. (1966). Mourning: A critical survey of the literature. *International Journal of Psycho-Analysis, 47,* 14–25.

Slaby, A., Lieb, J., & Tancredi, L. (1981). *Handbook of psychiatric emergencies.* New York: Medical Examination Publishing Company.

Stroebe, M. S., Stroebe, W., Gergen, K., & Gergen, M. (1981–82). The broken heart: Reality or myth? *Omega, 12,* 87–105.

Vachon, M. L. S., Lyall, W. A. L., Rogers, J., Freedman-Letofsky, K., & Freeman, S. J. J. (1980). A controlled study of self-help intervention for widows. *American Journal of Psychiatry, 137,* 1380–1384.

Vachon, M. L. S., Sheldon, A. R., Lancee, W. J., Lyall, W. A., Rogers, J., & Freeman, S. (1982). Correlates of enduring stress patterns following bereavement: Social network, life situation, and personality. *Psychological Medicine, 12,* 783–788.

van der Hart, O. (1983). *Rituals in psychotherapy: Transition and continuity.* New York: Irvington.

Videka-Sherman, L. (1982). Coping with the death of a child: A study over time. *American Journal of Orthopsychiatry, 52*(4), 688–698.

Volkan, V. (1971). A study of a patient's "re-grief work" through dreams, psychological tests and psychoanalysis. *Psychiatric Quarterly, 45,* 225–273.

Volkan, V. (1975). "Re-grief" therapy. In B. Schoenberg, I. Gerber, A. Wiener, A. H. Kutscher, D. Peretz, & A. C. Carr (Eds.), *Bereavement: Its psychosocial aspects.* New York: Columbia University Press.

Volkan, V., & Showalter, C. (1968). Known object loss, disturbance in reality testing, and "re-grief" work as a method of brief psychotherapy. *Psychiatric Quarterly, 42,* 358–374.

Weigert, A. J., & Hastings, R. (1977). Identity loss, family, and social change. *American Journal of Sociology, 82,* 1171–1185.

Worden, J. W. (1982). *Grief counseling and grief therapy: A handbook for the mental health practitioner.* New York: Springer.

Chapter 23

Differences of Grief Intensity in Bereaved Parents

William C. Fish

William C. Fish, Ed.D., is currently Associate Professor of Education at Oakland University, Rochester, Michigan. A graduate of Amherst College, Yale University, and Columbia Teachers' College, Dr. Fish teaches a course on death and dying every year at Oakland and conducts research on parental bereavement. He also teaches courses on ethical issues in health care and has published an article on suicide and children in *Death Education*.

To Sarah, and all our children,
Who make us who we are,
While we have them.

———

The study described in this chapter was conducted to investigate incongruencies in parental bereavement and to describe the clinical implications these have for caregivers providing treatment to bereaved parents. The findings reveal that there are interesting and important discrepancies between the grief experiences of mothers and fathers. Some of these findings question long-held clinical assumptions about bereaved parents; others confirm previous clinical speculation. In all cases, important treatment strategies are suggested.

The specific results of the study indicate that there are significant differences in intensity of parental grief relative to the length of bereavement, the age of the parent and the age of the child at the time of death, the sex of the child, and the manner of death. In addition, the evidence indicates that the incongruence between mothers and fathers often increases after the first 2 years of bereavement, is greater in the loss of daughters than sons, is greater in the loss of infants than of older children, and is greater in anticipated deaths than in sudden deaths. Even though most parents in grief do not seek clinical help for their grief, they may seek help for marital difficulties. Knowledge of these variables may help clinicians diagnose grief-related roots of marital difficulties in clients who also are bereaved parents. As with all statistical studies, it is important for the clinician to remember that any particular client may be atypical of the general trends reported here. With this caveat, the conclusions of this study will be stated.

Schiff (1977) and Simpson (1979) have estimated that as many as 75–90% of bereaved couples are in serious marital difficulty within months of the death of a child and may divorce if professional help is not sought. Sanders (1979–80) found that the death of a child produced significantly higher intensities of grief than the death of a spouse or parent. Wiener (1970) asserted that the death of a child is the most devastating experience a family can suffer, affecting siblings and grandparents as well as parents. Binger et al. (1969) observed that bereaved parents have an extremely difficult time helping each other, especially if their marriage was weak before the death of the child. In order to help clinicians more accurately assess the very painful and explosive dynamics of parental bereavement, we* have analyzed the experience

———

*Research for this study was begun in 1981 in collaboration with Sally M. Whitty, undergraduate and then graduate research assistant, Oakland University.

of 112 bereaved parents to determine the nature and scope of incongruence in mothers and fathers whose children have died. Even though this study does not verify the high divorce rate suggested by Schiff and Simpson, we do find evidence of significant incongruence in the grieving styles of fathers and mothers that without informed clinical intervention could provoke separation or divorce.

For this study, two questionnaires were administered to 77 women and 35 men who had been bereaved from 1 month to 16 years. One questionnaire, the *Grief Experience Inventory* (GEI) developed by Sanders, Mauger, and Strong (1979), consists of 135 true/false questions that measure intensity of grief in nine categories: despair, anger, guilt, social isolation, loss of control, rumination, depersonalization, somatization, and death anxiety. The other questionnaire, written by the investigators, asks for demographic information and perception of differences in the grieving styles of the spouses, differences in the treatment of the spouses by others, and effects of the death and grief experience on the marriage, work performance, and religious beliefs. The data have been organized to compare differences of grief intensity within and across bereavement periods (less than 2 years, 2 to 4 years, 5 or more years), by age of the parents at the time of the child's death, by sex and age of the child at death, and by the manner of death (sudden or anticipated). Supplementing the data from the questionnaires, lengthy (2 hours or more) interviews were conducted with 18 parents.

EFFECT OF LENGTH OF BEREAVEMENT

Common sense says that intensity of grief will decline steadily over time. Grief is often compared to a wound and we normally expect wounds to heal with time as the restorative capacities of the body do their silent, steady work. As useful as the metaphor is, grief is not, in fact, a physical wound and the healing process seems to be quite different from the steady cellular restoration associated with physical healing. The loss of a child is more like dismemberment than a bruise, requiring adaptation to an irretrievable loss. What is experienced is not so much healing as the gradual acceptance of a pain that fluctuates episodically in intensity and changes in complexion over time, but does not necessarily diminish and never disappears. As one adapts to the loss of a limb, so one adapts to the loss of a child, but there is no restoration to a point of prior normalcy. One can no more alter the status of being a bereaved parent than one can reverse the aging process; the rest of one's life is indelibly defined by a condition for which there is neither a reversal nor an adequate prosthesis.

Contrary to common sense, this study indicates that grief in mothers is more intense after 2 years than it was before. Analysis of the GEI scores for mothers of children of all ages (stillborn to 31) and both sexes shows an overall mean increase after 2 years of bereavement, with significantly higher levels of anger, guilt, and social isolation. After 5 years, the measures of intensity diminish to levels only slightly below those of the first 2 years, except in loss of control, which is higher, and in rumination, which is significantly lower. Fathers, on the other hand, do show a steady decrease in seven of the nine categories after 2 years and in all categories after 5 years.

Anger

What this means for the clinician is that grief may be much more difficult for mothers after 2 years have passed, when most social support has been withdrawn and their own husbands are suffering much less intensely. The high level of anger in mothers is especially worth clinical attention because not only are their husbands much less angry after 2 years, but also, according to the self-perception questionnaire, they are not very aware of their own anger; only 7% saw themselves as more angry than their husbands. Since the object of the anger, the dead child, is missing, there is a tendency to direct the hostility outward toward the husband and friends, creating more marital tension and social isolation, or to direct it inward, increasing guilt and despair. Clinicians may need to intervene aggressively to help mothers focus on their intense anger at the child for causing the pain of their dismemberment. There is often resistance to such direct focusing, since the child is usually seen as the blameless victim of his own death. But the parent is also the victim of the child's death and it is not irrational to be angry at the death event as the cause of suffering, even though the child cannot be held responsible for it as an intentional act. The expression of anger as protest of the event rather than blame of the child is a significant and appropriate therapeutic goal, especially for mothers in their third and fourth years of bereavement.

Incongruence between Husbands and Wives

Another popular belief is that intense common experiences bind people together. Applied to bereaved parents, the expectation might be that the shared loss would knit the parents' lives more closely together than they would be otherwise and that, as the years pass, the togetherness would increase. Unfortunately, this increased togetherness occurred only in 24% of the sample; 70% reported significant marital stress related to the loss, and the GEI scores indicate dramatic differences in the intensity levels of the father and mother. As noted previously, there is an overall incongruence between the men and women in this sample that increases in the second through fourth years and declines only slightly after the fifth year.

In Table 23.1, the *t* scores for all the bereavement scales of the GEI have been averaged to show the increase in incongruence to nearly a full standard deviation after 2 years of bereavement. This incongruence is more dramatic when certain categories are compared between the first 2-year period and the 2- to 4-year period (Table 23.2).

As will be discussed later, the sex and age of the child, the age of the parent, and the manner of death also make a difference in the degrees of incongruence, but these comparisons indicate significant general changes in the degree of disparity over the bereavement years.

In addition to the major difference in anger already discussed, clinicians may look for symptoms of these other differences in maritally stressed bereaved couples. The greater despair of mothers may show itself in lower self-esteem and a more pessimistic outlook on life. The intensity of depersonalization means that mothers may be more over-

Table 23.1. GEI Mean *t* Scores of Parents by Sex and Years of Bereavement

YEARS OF BEREAVEMENT	MOTHERS	FATHERS	DIFF.
Less than 2	52.6	49.6	−3.0
2–4 Years	55.0	46.0	−9.0
5 or More	51.4	43.0	−8.4

Table 23.2. Parental Differences in GEI Mean *t* Scores by Category and Years of Bereavement

	YEARS OF BEREAVEMENT	
CATEGORY	0–2 YEARS	2–4 YEARS
Anger	−4.7	−16.4
Despair	+0.4	−10.8
Depersonalization	+1.3	− 9.3
Guilt	+3.2	− 7.9
Social Isolation	+2.2	− 7.9

whelmed by and less able to cope with daily stress than are their husbands. Therefore, mothers may more strongly resist returning to "normal" levels of pre-death activity, especially normal sexual relations.

Sexual Difficulties

One of the most serious problems between bereaved parents, according to the self-perception questionnaire, is in the difference between sexual expectations. Nearly 60% of wives are aware of serious sexual distress, mainly in their loss of interest and inability to find pleasure in such activity. Nearly 40% of the husbands complained about the change in the sexual part of their marriages, some claiming it had become non-existent since the death of their child.

Sexual difficulties may also be related to the high intensities of social isolation and guilt. The sense of isolation, especially from one's spouse, may make sex seem inappropriate, as purely physical rather than an expression of closeness. Guilt may lead wives to deny any right to physical pleasure as a form of self-inflicted punishment; at the same time, awareness of failing to meet their husbands' sexual needs can contribute to their sense of guilt and isolation. Therapists can help couples become aware of the vicious circle of emotions behind their sexual distress and reduce those behaviors that contribute to it, especially blaming and inducing guilt in each other.

Guilt

Guilt makes spouses especially vulnerable to accusations in blaming. In this study, 30% of the husbands and 10% of the wives showed a tendency to blame the other for the death of the child. The greater intensity of guilt in the mothers' GEI scales indicates that women internalize this affect much more than do men and therefore may need more active clinical intervention. In those cases where the parent did materially contribute to the death of the child, it can be helpful to distinguish between acts that were intentional, for which the parent may hold herself responsible, and acts that were unintentional or accidental, for which the parent is not responsible. It is also useful to use the "What realistically could have been known?" rule in assessing responsibility even for intentional acts. That is, parents should not blame themselves for not knowing everything that could have been known before acting; rather, they should honestly assess what was realistic for them to know at the time they acted and judge responsibility accordingly. In most cases, guilt is not so much related to a concrete act of parental failure, but rather to a general sense of failure as a parent ("I didn't do all that I could have done for my child"). In such cases therapists can help parents more rationally assess responsibility for what, in fact, was intended and what, in fact, was realistically knowable. Parents, especially mothers, may also feel guilty for still being alive when their child is dead. Therapists might try to explore the beliefs behind this feeling to see if they can be unloaded through frank appraisal. The belief that life is a gift, for example, has a connotation of reward that makes death a punishment. The pain of grief often makes it easy to believe that death is a punishment so that, to reverse the logic, if one is being punished, then one doesn't deserve to live. The most effective way to unload such a guilt producing belief is to assess the rationality of viewing death as a punishment. Other possible beliefs, such as that it is "wrong" for parents to outlive their children, need similar identification and assessment as possibly confused moral judgments creating unnecessary guilt. Most of all, therapists can help couples struggling with guilt by not reinforcing blaming accusations, especially by husbands of wives, and by stressing a more rational process of assessing responsibility for the death.

Social Isolation

The greater social isolation of mothers is an expected outcome of intense despair, depersonalization, sexual denial, and guilt. Actual withdrawal from social contacts and imagined withdrawal of others are natural consequences of living with a bundle of socially unacceptable feelings. Not only do bereaved parents have less real energy to give to relations with others, but they also may suspect that they are *persona non grata* to friends and relatives who are uncomfortable dealing with grief. There may be oversensitivity and apprehension of anticipated rejection that compounds the isolation, which a therapist may be able to help reduce. Therapists also may be able to help husbands understand that wives' greater sense of isolation may partially account for the complaints that wives make about a lack of communication. In the self-perception questionnaire, 67% of the wives expressed distress over what they felt to be inadequate communication with (mainly from) their husbands. It is probably true that husbands do withdraw as a means of dealing with their grief, thus contributing to the marital isolation; but it could also be that wives are perceiving greater distance out of their own greater sense of isolation. It would be clinically beneficial if wives could understand that their husbands may have a greater need to grieve alone than they do, and if husbands could understand that their wives may be suffering with feelings of more intense isolation and have a need to communicate more than they do. Such mutual insight could lead to a higher tolerance of differences and a willingness to relate to each other's needs.

A further comment about the tendency of men to withdraw is in order here. Criticism is often leveled at men in the grief literature for being noncommunicative about their grief. The assumption is that this is a debilitating inhibition foisted on men by macho conditioning and that they would resolve their grief sooner if they were more expressive. This assumption, shared by the investigators at the beginning of this research, may be questioned in light of this study. If fathers were indeed suffering from pathological inhibitions to grief expression, one would expect their sense of social isolation to increase over the bereavement years and to be greater than their more expressive wives'. As it turns out, fathers do show slightly greater social isolation than their wives in the first 2 years of bereavement following the death of male stillborn or teenaged children. But, as indicated in Tables 23.1 and 23.2, that isolation steadily diminishes in intensity after 2 years, while the sense of isolation in mothers increases or remains at a higher level. Since some might suspect that men are simply denying feelings of isolation, it is important to note that the GEI contains a denial scale and that men are not significantly higher than women on that scale. Much more needs to be known about the distinctive dynamics of male grief expression, but we can at least be wary of assuming pathology or assuming that men would be better off if they imitated the more verbal behavior of their wives. It may be that men have distinctly different needs in the resolution of their grief and that, however difficult it is for their wives to tolerate male solitude, it is unwarranted to assume that men have greater difficulty in resolving their grief because they talk less than their wives. This does not mean that therapists should not encourage men to express their feelings, but it does suggest a need to respect what may be an alternate style of grieving.

EFFECT OF SEX OF CHILD

Another popular assumption is that parents do or should love their children equally so that grief over the death of a child would be unaffected by whether it was a son or daughter. Even though we know that parents often feel closer to one particular child than to another, the preference is seldom generalized to a recognition of a more intense grief associated with the loss of sons than daughters. Since bereaved parents individualize the loss of their own son or daughter, it seems to them that the loss of either would be the same. It is also contrary to the parenting myth to imagine greater grief over the loss of one child than another, whatever its sex.

A comparison of GEI scores indicates that there is a sex-related factor in grief and that it is related to parental incongruity. In Table 23.3, mean *t* scores of the GEI are summarized to indicate the degree of sex-related difference and incongruence.

The dramatic difference indicated in these scores is in the greater intensity of grief felt by fathers over the loss of sons and the greater incongruence between parents over the loss of daughters, at least in the first 4 years. An analysis of the specific categories in the second through fourth years of bereavement in Table 23.4 indicates that there are significantly different grief responses between parents depending on whether the child who dies is a son or daughter. In all these categories, mothers have significantly more intense grief than fathers.

Table 23.3. GEI Mean *t* Scores of Parents by Sex of Child and Years of Bereavement

YEARS OF BEREAVEMENT	LOSS OF SONS			LOSS OF DAUGHTERS		
	MOTHERS	FATHERS	DIFF.	MOTHERS	FATHERS	DIFF.
Less than 2	54.6	51.3	− 3.3	50.8	40.3	−10.5
2–4 Years	54.4	48.3	− 6.1	54.5	42.4	−12.1
5 or More	53.0	42.5	−10.5	52.5	(Insuff. data)	

Table 23.4. Incongruencies of More than 1 Standard Deviation at 2–4 Years with Respect to Loss of Sons and Daughters

LOSS OF SONS
Anger
Rumination

LOSS OF DAUGHTERS
Anger
Rumination
Despair
Guilt
Depersonalization
Somatization
Death Anxiety

The clinical significance of these differences has more to do with the incongruence than with the higher intensity of grief in fathers who lose sons. To fathers who lose daughters, it is irrelevant that fathers who lose sons grieve more intensely. But the clinician may expect more serious problems of communication and lack of mutual understanding in parents who lose daughters. One may rue the implicit sexism of this evidence and speculate about its causes, but such inquiry has dubious clinical relevance. One possible cause—the identification of fathers with their sons—does suggest the clinical importance of therapists encouraging both parents, but especially fathers, to talk about the lost futures represented in the loss of a child, especially a son.

EFFECT OF AGE OF CHILD AND AGE OF PARENT

Although it is not often talked about, when comments are made about the effect of a child's age on parental grief, the assumption seems to be that the older the child who dies, the greater the grief. This turns out to be mildly true for fathers but not descriptive of mothers, and the reason for the phenomenon in fathers may have as much to do with the age of the father as it does with the age of the child. Another surprise in this analysis is that the incongruence between mothers and fathers decreases with the increased age of the child. Focusing on parents in the second through fourth years of bereavement, the mean t scores of the GEI bereavement scales in Table 23.5 indicate interesting factors in parental disparity of grief when losing a child at different ages.

The disparity in grief over the death of an infant seems to reflect the strength of maternal bonding in pregnancy, a thesis confirmed by the grief of similar intensity in mothers of stillborns (GEI mean: 54) in the same bereavement period. Another factor in the disparity of grief over infant death is that parents of infants tend to be younger than parents of teenaged or adult children, and younger fathers seem to grieve less intensely than older fathers. Age does seem to make a difference in the grief intensity of men, as Table 23.6 indicates.

Table 23.5. GEI Mean *t* Scores of Parents Bereaved 2–4 Years by Age of Child

AGE OF CHILD	MOTHERS	FATHERS	DIFF.
Infants (0–1)	55.0	38.9	−16.1
Children (1–10)	54.4	44.5	− 9.9
Teens (11–19)	50.7	45.8	− 4.9
Adults (20+)	56.1	52.4	− 3.7

Table 23.6. GEI Mean *t* Scores of Parents Bereaved 2–4 Years by Age

MEAN AGE	MOTHERS	FATHERS
31	54.2	42
47	54.4	50

Younger fathers may grieve less because they expect to have more children or because the child who died was younger than the child of an older father. Only an analysis of a data pool larger than that currently available could discern whether it is the age of the child or the age of the father that accounts for this difference. At this point, all that can be said is that the age of the father seems to make a greater difference in grief intensity than the age of the mother. Mothers are at similar levels of intensity relative to their own age or the age of the child, while fathers exhibit steadily increasing intensity relative to their own and their child's age.

The consistency of maternal grief intensity relative to age of child does not mean that there are no significant differences. As Table 23.7 indicates, there are significant changes in the dominant emotions for both mothers and fathers relative to the age of the child who died.

Table 23.7. GEI Mean *t* Scores for Parents Bereaved 2–4 Years by Categories of High Intensity

AGE OF CHILD	MOTHERS	FATHERS
Infants (0–1)	(62) Despair	(51) Guilt
	(62) Loss of Control	(46) Loss of Control
	(60) Social Isolation	(44) Social Isolation
Children (1–10)	(59) Guilt	(58) Guilt
	(58) Depersonalization	(48) Loss of Control
	(56) Despair	(47) Despair
	(56) Anger	(45) Rumination
Teens (11–19)	(59) Anger	(55) Rumination
	(56) Death Anxiety	(50) Death Anxiety
	(55) Despair	(50) Loss of Control
	(52) Rumination	(50) Depersonalization
Adults (20+)	(60) Rumination	(59) Rumination
	(59) Anger	(58) Social Isolation
	(58) Despair	(55) Loss of Control
	(58) Depersonalization	(52) Death Anxiety

Interesting similarities and differences emerge from this comparison. Despair is consistently high in mothers; loss of control is consistently high in fathers. This might be seen as typical of the different constellation of feelings in mothers compared to fathers. As they see themselves, mothers are immersed in feelings of hopelessness, plagued by low self-esteem, confusion, and depersonalization. Toward others, mothers are angry, irritated by perceived insensitivity, acting-out. Fathers, on the other hand, seem more directed at self-control and more disturbed by the loss of control provoked by their grief. They are more inclined to feel guilt than anger, aiming at self-control rather than control of others. They are more inclined to ruminate, to be preoccupied with thoughts of the deceased, rather than to ventilate.

It is also instructive to note the distinctive characteristics of grief related to the age of the child. Along with the difference noted between maternal despair and paternal guilt, parents who have lost infants are similar in the sense of lost control of emotions, inexplicably frequent mood changes, a sense of isolation from others, and a perceived lack of understanding by others of the severity of losing a child who was "only" an infant. Parents who lose children between the ages of 1 and 10 share high levels of guilt, self-blame, and despair; they differ in the mother's tendency to act-out in anger compared to the father's tendency to seek control of emotions and thoughts. Parents who lose teenaged children are similar in preoccupation with thoughts of the deceased, reflecting the greater abundance of memories of an older child and the more intensely specified future expected of an older child. It is significant that rumination is most intense for both mothers and fathers in the loss of an adult child, for whom there is more to remember. Despair and depersonalization in mothers, and loss of control coupled with death anxiety in fathers, all portend a crumbling sense of the meaning and stability of life. Fathers feel a particularly keen sense of isolation in the loss of an adult child, reflective of the dissonance between the depth of their felt grief and the understanding by others, including their own wives, of their condition. Fathers who have lost adult children are at the highest level of grief (for men) in every GEI bereavement category except guilt.

The clinical significance of these findings is as follows:

1. For parents who have lost infants, expect high levels of disagreement and misunderstanding between the parents, much higher levels of grief in mothers than in fathers, greater eagerness in the father to return to normal (especially in sexual relations), and consequent high stress on the marriage and consideration of divorce, especially by mothers.

2. For parents who have lost young children (ages 1-10), expect high levels of guilt and significant despair in both parents, with somewhat greater anger in mothers and concern about loss of control in fathers.
3. For parents who have lost teenaged children, expect high anxiety about their own death in both parents, more intense anger in mothers, and more concern about loss of control in fathers.
4. For parents who have lost adult children, expect extreme preoccupation with thoughts (memories, broken dreams) of the deceased and a great sense of isolation and desolation in fathers and despair in mothers, with considerable death anxiety in fathers. Though the intensity of grief is high in both partners, communication is not fluid since different dimensions of grief dominate each parent.

EFFECT OF MANNER OF DEATH

It seems to be the conventional belief that sudden death is much more traumatic than anticipated death, and that therefore the sudden death of a child would produce more intense grief than an anticipated death. This turns out to be true for fathers but not for mothers, yielding yet another factor that may contribute to incongruence in parental grieving. A summary of mean GEI t scores (Table 23.8) shows that scores for mothers are consistently higher in anticipated deaths than in sudden deaths, and scores for fathers are the reverse.

Table 23.8. Comparison of Parents Bereaved by Sudden vs. Anticipated Death by Years of Bereavement

YEARS OF BEREAVEMENT	GEI MEAN t SCORES			
	MOTHERS	FATHERS	DIFF.	SUDDEN/ANTICIPATED
0–2	52.0	49.0	− 3.0	Sudden
0–2	54.0	46.1	− 7.9	Anticipated
2–4	53.5	46.8	− 6.7	Sudden
2–4	56.4	44.0	−12.4	Anticipated
5+	50.4	46.7	− 3.7	Sudden
5+	53.8	42.3	−11.5	Anticipated

In each bereavement category there is significantly greater incongruence in grief over an anticipated death than a sudden death, and in the periods after 2 years the difference is more than a standard deviation. The clinical significance of this finding is that the manner of death does give another diagnostic clue to the possible severity of incongruence in a bereaved couple. Couples who suffer sudden death losses may be less incongruent in general intensity of grief than couples who suffer anticipated losses, though there may still be severe disparities of particular affects.

CONCLUSION

Parental bereavement places stress on the marital relationship. Contrary to some popular opinions, suffering the common loss of a child does not draw marriage partners together as often as it drives them apart. One major reason for this divisive effect is that each parent has sustained a severe dismemberment of self and is simply incapacitated, unable to help the other. Another reason, documented by this research, is that mothers and fathers grieve differently and therefore are often out of synch with one another in their grief; when mothers are dealing with intense anger, fathers may be in the grip of intense guilt, and neither will be able to minister to the other. Differences in parental grief intensity are traceable to sex and age of child, age of parent, manner of death, and length of bereavement. Clinicians may be of greater help to bereaved parents if they are aware of these specific disparities.

References

Binger, C. M., Ablin, A. R., Feuerstein, R. C., Kushner, J. H., Zoger, S., & Mikkelsen, C. (1969). Childhood leukemia: Emotional impact on patient and family. *New England Journal of Medicine, 280,* 414–418.

Sanders, C. M. (1979–80). A comparison of adult bereavement in the death of a spouse, child, and parent. *Omega, 10,* 303–322.

Sanders, C. M., Mauger, P. A., & Strong, P. N. (1979). *The Grief Experience Inventory,* U.S. A. Copyright, 1979.

Schiff, H. S. (1977). *The bereaved parent.* New York: Penguin Books.

Simpson, M. A. (1979). *The facts of death.* Englewood Cliffs, NJ: Prentice-Hall.

Wiener, J. M. (1970). Reaction of the family to the fatal illness of a child. In B. Schoenberg, A. C. Carr, D. Peretz, & A. H. Kutscher (Eds.), *Loss and grief: Psychological management in medical practice.* New York: Columbia University Press.

Chapter 24

Family Therapy after a Child's Death

Lawrence C. Grebstein

Lawrence C. Grebstein, Ph.D., is Professor of Psychology and Director of the Clinical Psychology Training Program at the University of Rhode Island. He was formerly Director of the Psychological Consultation Center, the university's training clinic, has served as a consultant to a variety of agencies, and maintains a part-time independent practice in family therapy. He is a Diplomate in Clinical Psychology of the American Board of Professional Psychology, has been a Fellow in Family Therapy and Family Research at the Center for Family Research, George Washington University Medical Center, and has served as Visiting Professor of Psychology at the University of Bergen, Norway. Dr. Grebstein is the author of several articles and chapters on eclectic family therapy and has edited a book, *Toward Self-Understanding: Studies in Personality and Adjustment.*

*To my loving father, Sigmund Grebstein, and
in memory of my loving mother, Sylvia
Grebstein*

The original underlying assumption of family therapy, which clearly differentiated it from individual psychotherapy, was that symptoms that occur in an individual person actually reflect problems in the family system. The initial rationale for doing family therapy was based on this belief of *systems causality*. More recently, the concept of *systems effect* has been added as a second rationale for family therapy. Systems effect is the belief that symptomatic behavior on the part of any individual in the family affects the other members of the family, regardless of the cause. Contemporary family therapy is based on the dual theoretical assumptions that disruptions in the family system can be a cause and/or effect of individual symptomatology.

Although present approaches to family therapy differ in theoretical emphasis and techniques, all the major theories share the belief that the family unit is the focus for therapeutic intervention. The present chapter will focus on an eclectic approach to dealing with the death of a child from a family systems perspective. It will include an examination of the impact of a child's death on the family, describe several different approaches to assessment, and discuss specific goals and interventions in treatment.

IMPACT OF A CHILD'S DEATH ON THE FAMILY

A basic concept of family functioning is the notion of balance, homeostasis, or equilibrium. This fundamental assumption portrays families as systems of interacting persons who maintain predictable relationships with each other. When some family member's behavior changes radically, this will lead to some sort of compensatory behavior on the part of one or more members of the family so that family functioning can be maintained. Jackson (1957) coined the term *family homeostasis* to describe this important pattern of family interaction. Family homeostasis conceptualizes the family as a closed information system in which variations in the behavior of any of the family members are fed back in order to correct the system's response. The death of a family member is an event that will disrupt the family system, alter the family homeostasis, and thus require a readjustment among the surviving family members.

Bowen (1976) uses the concept of the family's emotional equilibrium to explain the impact of a death. According to Bowen, a family is in emotional equilibrium when each family member is functioning at reasonable efficiency and the family is calm. The addition or loss of a new family member will disrupt the family equilibrium. In the case of a death, the degree of disruption is determined by the degree of the emotional reaction. This, in turn, is influenced by the functioning level of emotional integration in the family and/or by the importance of the person who dies. The death of a family member creates an "emotional shock wave" that is "a network of underground 'after shocks' of serious life events that can occur anywhere in the extended family system in the months or years following serious emotional events in a family" (p. 339). This shock wave most often occurs following the death of a family member and is related to the emotional dependence of the family members on each other, not to the usual grief or mourning reactions. The death of a child is especially traumatic for a family. As Bowen notes, "The death of an important child can shake the family equilibrium for years" (p. 341).

Two additional factors are cited by Bowen (1976) as being important in determining the impact of the death on the family. The first is the degree to which the surviving family members deny the death in their own minds. The second is the extent to which the family is a closed relationship system. Families can be described as having open or closed relationship systems. A family with an open system is one in which a person feels "free to communicate a high percentage of inner thoughts, feelings, and fantasies to another who can reciprocate" (Bowen, 1976, p. 335). A closed system is "an automatic emotional reflex to protect self from the anxiety in the other person, though most people say they avoid the taboo subjects to keep from upsetting the other person" (p. 336). The death of someone will affect the lives of all the family members. However, death is likely to have greater impact on those families with closed communication systems and higher denial. While Bowen's beliefs are theoretical and based on his clinical observations, there are research data to support his assertions. It has been reported that families with effective communication systems adjust better following a death (Vollman, Ganzert, Picher, & Williams, 1971; Williams, Polak, & Vollman, 1972).

In addition to the degree of openness of the family system, there are three additional factors that have a significant impact on the degree of disruption to the family following the death of a family member (Herz, 1980): (1) the timing of the death in the life cycle; (2) the nature of the death; and (3) the family position of the dead member. It is most disruptive to family functioning when the death is to a person in his prime years because the family is most dependent on him then.

Although the death of a child is not especially damaging to the instrumental or task-oriented functioning of the family, it can be very damaging to the emotional functioning of the family. For the parents, this is related to the degree to which the parents experienced the child as a extension of themselves. Using Bowen's concept of the "family projection process," Herz (1980) describes how the more incomplete the parents' emotional selves are, the more likely they are to see their children as "extensions of their own hopes and dreams in life" (p. 227). The more this occurs, the more disruptive the child's death will be on the family. It is important to point out that the effects of the loss are not limited to "emotionally incomplete" parents, and that to some extent children are always extensions of their parents in various ways. The pain associated with the death of a child spares no parent, regardless of the preexisting level of adjustment. The extent of the impact of a child's death on the family is indicated by the fact that separation or divorce occurs in an exceedingly high percentage of families following the death of the child (Herz, 1980).

Whether a child's death is prolonged or sudden can have different effects on the family, according to Herz (1980). With a prolonged death, the family has the opportunity to prepare for the death and separate from the victim, but the family undergoes a long period of stress. Watching a loved one die and not being able to do anything to prevent it is an emotionally draining experience. Sudden death, by contrast, involves a different source of stress because the survivors have little time for preparing, saying good-byes, or using other processes to help separation. After an initially intense grief reaction, the family may cover over the loss, and it may become a "taboo topic" that the family avoids mentioning. The underlying anxiety and other emotions can affect a sensitive or vulnerable family member, producing psychological or physical symptoms. A major difficulty for the family in the case of a sudden death is to resolve the loss.

An example of the magnitude of the effects of a child's sudden death on the family is provided by Sudden Infant Death Syndrome (SIDS) or "crib death," which creates an "emotional crisis of enormous proportions" for the surviving family (May & Breme, 1982, p. 61). Reported problems among surviving family members include disturbances in eating, sleeping, thinking, and working characteristic of depression; feelings of responsibility for the death, which may be experienced as personal guilt or sometimes be projected onto others (e.g., a physician or surviving sibling); difficulties in conception for the grieving mothers, including higher than average rates of infertility and spontaneous abortion following the loss of the child (Mandell & Wolfe,

1975; Markusen, Owen, Fulton, & Bendiksen, 1977–78); and severe stress on the surviving siblings, who have to deal both with their own irrational feelings of guilt and responsibility and with their parents' grief (May & Breme, 1982).

The death of a child can be particularly traumatic because it violates the usual pattern that grandparents, parents, and older persons die first. As Rando (1983) points out, the death of a child before the parent is unnatural and can have the effect of raising the anxiety of the survivors because it defies the usual expectancies. Change is often anxiety-producing. When the change is an unexpected death, the amount of ensuing anxiety can be substantial.

The effects of loss are produced even when the death is of an unborn child. Herz (1980) points out that families form emotional attachments to unborn children, and pre-birth deaths, such as still-births, miscarriages, and abortions, can affect the family. In pre-birth death, as in the case of the loss of an existing child, the reaction of the survivors is related to the emotional significance of the child who dies. Generally the more important the child is to the family, the more disruptive the child's death will be to family functioning. An unborn child always represents a source of hope and expectancy for existing family members. In its unborn state, the anticipated child is often idealized or is in other ways shaped to fit the fantasies of the family members. For example, to an existing child, the unborn baby may represent a desired baby brother or baby sister. The parents may have a variety of expectancies associated with the yet unborn child. The amount of loss and its effects are directly related to the kinds of expectancies associated with the child. The death of the child takes away hopes and dreams for the future.

Guilt and shame almost always play a part in a family's reactions to the death of a child. It is natural in the process of growing up for children to fight and disagree, and it is also natural for parents to get angry and punitive. These behaviors take on special meaning when a child suddenly dies, possibly producing guilt and shame in the survivors for the way they treated the dead person. The amount of guilt will be influenced by the extent to which the surviving family members feel responsible for the death. In some cases, the feelings of guilt are irrational or exaggerated to the extent that the death was not the result of any particular negligence on the part of any family member. However, there are instances in which a family member's negligence, usually a parent's, did contribute to the death of the child. In these instances, the feelings of guilt are legitimate, and they are based in the reality of the situation.

Case Example: A married couple separated following a long history of friction related to increasing differences of opinion about child-rearing practices, lifestyle, and values. One spouse had a traditional value orientation that emphasized hard work, responsibility, and self-discipline. The other spouse attached more importance to pleasure-seeking and personal freedom, including the use of marijuana and other drugs. This long-simmering feud between the parents was expressed in the family primarily through the behavior of their oldest daughter, who had a long history of adjustment difficulties and rebellious behavior, including sexual acting-out and minor drug use. The daughter's behavior reflected the pain and stress of her divided loyalty and helped hold the marriage together by focusing both parents' concern on her. Throughout this girl's adolescence the parents had disagreed on issues such as how much personal freedom to give her, particularly with regard to sexual behavior and drug use. The daughter had left home in her late teens but remained in the same community. The parents divorced after the daughter left home. Following the divorce, the young woman moved to a large city. She killed herself by jumping out of a window while under the influence of drugs. It was not clear whether the death was an intentional suicide or an accident resulting from distorted perceptions and beliefs produced by the effects of the drugs she was taking. Following her death, it was learned that one of the parents had been sending drugs to the young woman.

The ramifications resulting from a death such as the one just described, in which it appears that one of the parents actively contributed to the cause of death, are very different from the effects of a death for which no one can be considered at fault or to blame.

Rando (1983) describes two important effects a child's death can have on the parents. First, the bereaved parents can experience altered social relationships and be socially stigmatized. The death of a child raises the anxiety level of other parents to such an extent that they often find it difficult to associate with the surviving parents. Association with the bereaved persons serves as a reminder that "it could happen to me." The obvious consequence of this is the loss of an important source of social support at a time when it is needed most. Second, the parents may be unable to support each other because the death affects both of them. One of the nurturant functions of a marriage is for the spouses to support each other when one of them is stressed. While it can happen that both partners are simultaneously stressed, it is more typically the case that one can support the other. With both grieving the loss of a child, they may be unable to support each other and may displace their negative feelings of anger, blame, and guilt onto each other or the surviving children, thereby increasing the stress level in the family. Since each parent had a different relationship with the lost child, each may experience the loss in very different ways, which can further interfere with their capacity to support each other. Sexual contact and intimacy may be disrupted, and the couple may not be able to manage the ordinary problems of daily living because of their preoccupation with their loss. As Rando (1983) notes, even the sight of each other serves as a painful reminder of their loss. "Part of the couple together is lost irretrievably, both in terms of the past they have shared and the future of which they dreamt" (Rando, 1983, p. 2).

EFFECTS OF A CHILD'S DEATH ON SURVIVING SIBLINGS

Until recently, much of the attention has been on the impact on the parents when a child dies. However, a child's death can have a significant and sometimes devastating effect on the surviving siblings. This is especially true in contemporary society because of the smaller size of families. As Bank and Kahn (1982) point out, the loss of a child in a two-child family leaves the remaining child an only child, and this can have an extraordinary effect on the identity formation of the remaining sibling. Also, surviving children typically have to live with loss for a longer period of time by virtue of their greater longevity in comparison with parents. The effects of a child's death on the surviving children in the family can come from two general sources. The first is from the preexisting relationship between the siblings themselves. The second results from the parental reactions to the death and how their behavior influences the remaining siblings.

When siblings are close and generally get along, the surviving children have the usual feelings of loss, sadness, regret, and anger. These feelings may or may not be expressed and worked through depending on the family's tolerance for and usual "rules" about expressing emotions. It is important to realize that even in healthy, well-functioning families siblings rarely have only positive feelings toward each other. Especially for siblings close in age, there are likely to be rivalry, competition for parental attention and affection, and bickering over a variety of specific, daily occurrences, such as household responsibilities, TV programs, or the use of each other's things. As a result of these inevitable conflicts, children often feel a variety of negative emotions, such as frustration, anger, jealousy, and envy, as well as positive feelings toward their siblings. These mixed feelings are especially likely to occur in the case of serious chronic illness when, as a result of the illness, the sick child gets special treatment, such as extra time, attention, and affection from the parents and exemptions from household tasks and responsibilities. The healthy siblings may develop feelings of resentment because of their being neglected. This may occur even when they understand the situation and recognize the necessity for extra care.

When a sick brother or sister dies, the surviving siblings often feel guilt, remorse, and shame for the negative feelings they previously experienced. It is not uncommon for healthy siblings to have death wishes for their sick siblings, motivated by resentment, frustration, or a more positive desire for the sick child to stop suffering. If a child dies after a sibling has had death wishes or fantasies, this can create tremendous guilt and feelings of responsibility for the death in the surviving child, who may feel as if she caused the death by "willing it." This is especially true when the relationship between the siblings was not a good one prior to the death. The surviving child may initially feel joy or relief. How and whether these feelings are resolved will be determined in part by the family's willingness to face their emotional reactions to the death openly and directly. It is important that the parents recognize the complex emotional reactions that the surviving children may have and be available and willing to help their children deal with these feelings.

Bank and Kahn (1982) indicate that while many circumstances of a child's death can determine the effects on surviving children, clinicians should consider four factors: (1) the horror of the death and how directly the surviving sibling(s) witnessed it; (2) how long it took for the child to die; (3) whether the death could have been prevented and whether the surviving sibling feels she could have done something to prevent the death; and (4) the age of the survivor. Bank and Kahn point out that younger children, especially those below the age of 10, are more likely to have magical fantasies, misunderstandings, or distortions about the death than older children and adolescents.

The effects of a child's death on the remaining siblings is highly influenced by the parents' reaction to the death and how they treat the surviving children. Children often look to their parents as models for how to handle their own grief. Krell and Rabkin (1979) describe three pathological mourning processes that can have negative effects on the children. First, parents may establish a spoken or unspoken rule of silence and secrecy in which the family members are not allowed to talk about the death. The motive for this behavior is to avoid blame. Ironically, the result may be an increased feeling of guilt on the part of the remaining children, because they feel that the parents' unwillingness to discuss the death is an accusation of blame or fault. This silence can also be motivated by unstated family collusion to protect each other from the pain of the loss. A second parental reaction is overprotection. This results from the parents' perceiving the surviving children as more highly valued and precious. Consequently, parents may subsequently overreact to any minor symptom or behavior in a surviving child that reminds them of the dead child. The ensuing overprotectiveness can produce a timid, frightened child. The third reaction is substitution and replacement, in which the remaining siblings become living representatives of the lost child and have the increased burden of living two lives, their own and that of the dead sibling. When a child dies, the family is forced to redefine itself, shifting roles, responsibilities, emotional attachments, and expectancies among the remaining siblings. The change in family structure can result in confused identity and other problems. The loss of a child permanently alters the family constellation. This requires considerable adjustment on the part of the surviving children as well as the parents.

The death of a child does not always have only a negative effect on the family. As Bank and Kahn (1982) point out, the honesty of the children's reactions to the death can have a positive effect on the family by motivating the parents to complete their mourning, thus serving as a force for change and healing in the family. They further suggest that a death in the family can lead to mastery and creativity on the part of the survivors. This is consistent with the psychoanalytic concept of sublimation as an adaptive defense or coping mechanism for dealing with anxiety. Goldberg (1973) also notes that a death can have a positive impact on a family by increasing the solidarity or cohesiveness of the survivors. He cites Cobb's (1956) work which indicated that spouses who have a good marriage report increased closeness in facing the death of a child. Increased solidarity can also result if the family member who died was a major cause of conflict in the family.

There is little doubt that the death of a child has a major impact on a family. However, the nature of that impact and the extent to which it is disruptive to the functioning of the family or some of its members will vary and will be influenced by some or all of the factors already discussed. The alteration of family composition produced by the death of a child is a strong impetus for change. The change can lead to positive as well as negative consequences for the surviving family members. A thorough understanding by therapists of the range of possible impacts of the death of a child on a family is a prerequisite for helping grieving families.

FAMILY ASSESSMENT TECHNIQUES

Before discussing specific techniques for assessing the impact of a child's death on the family, it is important to distinguish between two different referral problems. One is the situation in which the death is a recent one that is consciously acknowledged by the family, and the death is the designated problem for which the family is coming for help. The other situation is when the death is more remote in time and/ or is not recognized by the family as a troublesome event, and the family is referred for another problem. One of the first assessment tasks of the clinician is to find out which of these situations exists.

The emphasis here will be on describing a variety of assessment techniques that are useful in determining the extent and nature of the problems in the family, whether family or other forms of treatment are needed, and, if necessary, what therapeutic procedures to use. Goals for a family assessment include obtaining information on the nature of any specific problems occurring within the family; the family's history and significant prior events; current family functioning on a number of relevant behavioral dimensions; existing interaction patterns among family members; and changes the family would like to make.

The assessment of a family begins during the initial contact usually made over the telephone. The first decision to be made is whom to include in the first interview. Family therapists go from the extreme of those who insist that all the members of the immediate family be included in the interview to those who will work with any portion of the family that is motivated. Although there are clinical and theoretical justifications offered for a variety of different approaches, there is no research evidence to suggest that any one approach works better. My own preference is to request that the entire family be present at the first interview. This request often serves to elicit potential problems when the caller, usually a parent, presents reasons why a particular family member or members cannot or should not be there. It has been my experience that parents most often object to the inclusion of young children, yet the presence of the children turns out to be one of the most helpful and revealing sources of information about what is going on in the family. In the case where there has been a death in the family, there is a particular tendency to want to exclude the children in order to protect them. However, as Hare-Mustin (1979) points out, parents often think they know what their children think and feel but are wrong. For example, in one family I worked with the mother and father were surprised to find out that their youngest daughter had visited the grave of her oldest brother daily, sometimes for as long as 4 hours at a time, for over a year after his death. The mother had also visited the grave daily and did not know of her daughter's visits. Even though the death had occurred 5 years prior to treatment, the family had never discussed their reactions to the death in sufficient detail to learn even the simplest facts about their respective mourning rituals.

The initial phase of the first family assessment interview is what Haley (1976) has described as the social stage and involves introductions and the usual greeting rituals. As soon as this is completed, the therapist moves on to more specific assessment techniques. It is at this point that family therapists differ in their approaches and are likely to use procedures reflecting different theoretical systems or preferences based on their clinical experience. My own preference is to use an assessment procedure that includes four main components: (1) obtaining a detailed description of the family's presenting problem(s); (2) taking a family history by using a genogram (Guerin & Pendagast, 1976); (3) assessing the family's current functioning using the McMaster model (Epstein & Bishop, 1981; Epstein, Bishop, & Levin, 1978); and (4) observing family interaction patterns from the point of view of structural family theory (Minuchin, 1974). It is important to point out that it is not always possible or necessary to do such an extensive or detailed assessment. Depending on the circumstances of the presenting problem and the specific characteristics of the individual family, the assessment process can be modified in keeping with the observations and clinical judgment of the therapist. For example, when the referral problem relates to the sudden death of a child, the SIDS Family Adjustment Scale (May & Breme, 1982) is a useful assessment procedure. The process described next is a model for a comprehensive assessment, designed to obtain a thorough evaluation of the family.

Beginning the formal assessment process with a description of the presenting problems in the family serves several purposes. As Haley (1976) notes, it informs the family of a shift from the social stage to the business at hand and sets an appropriate tone for the rest of the interview. Although asking for a description of the problems in the family can raise anxiety, it is also reassuring by communicating the therapist's willingness to understand and deal with the family's troubles in a direct, immediate, and forthright manner. It is important to note who takes the initiative in presenting the problems and the extent to which there is agreement or disagreement among the family members.

Regardless of who makes the initial presentation, the therapist should ask every person attending the session for an opinion before ending any discussion of the presenting problems.

After a complete description of the family's current problems has been obtained, I move on to either taking a family history using a genogram or doing an assessment of current family functioning based on the McMaster model. The order in which this is done varies with the particular family. One of my main objectives during the assessment phase of family therapy is to keep the family level of anxiety, threat, and emotionality as low as possible. A second objective is to have the interview make sense and appear relevant from the family's standpoint. Taking both of these factors into consideration, I will make a judgment at the time about which procedure to use next. It has been my experience that both the genogram and McMaster model assessment tend to be nonthreatening procedures.

Herz (1980) notes that families do not usually seek therapy for problems related to a recent or past death. Rather, they seek treatment for some other problem in the family. Even though the presenting symptoms may be related to the death, the family may not see the connection and will not mention the death. In order to find out that a death has occurred in the family, the therapist will have to do a genogram. The genogram (Guerin & Pendagast, 1976) is a structured family history in which the therapist diagrams the family tree and chronology of important life events. Typically, it covers the past three generations and is especially useful in discovering potentially "toxic" events for the family, such as divorces, "nervous breakdowns," and deaths. The genogram is based on Bowen's (1976) theory that the effects of major losses, such as deaths, can be transmitted to subsequent generations if they are not worked through by the family when they occur. In doing the genogram, it is important to obtain detailed information on all prior deaths in the family, including names, dates, and causes of death. Further exploration of the impact of thè deaths on the surviving family members is either done at the time of initial assessment or postponed to later interviews, depending on the clinician's assessment of how well the family is able to tolerate discussion of the deaths. The following case illustration provides an example of how a genogram can be clinically useful by eliciting information that might not otherwise be revealed.

Case Example: A mother called requesting an appointment because she was concerned about recent "unusual" behavior on the part of her youngest son, a man in his early 20s. She also stated that she did not think he would come in voluntarily for help. An initial family session was scheduled that was attended by the entire family except for the identified patient, who refused to come to the session. After obtaining a complete description of the parents' concerns, a genogram was done. In the process of completing the genogram, the parents mentioned that their oldest son had died a few years earlier in a tragic accident while still in his 20s. The family's ethnic background was one in which great importance is attached to the role of the eldest son. This was certainly the case with this family. The father, who was a self-made, successful businessman, had looked forward to his eldest son's joining him in the family business and eventually taking it over.

After learning of the son's death, the therapist directed a series of specific questions to the father aimed at obtaining information about how the father functioned after his son's death. The questions were essentially a standard assessment for clinical signs of depression. The father's answers clearly suggested that he had many of the symptoms of a serious and long-standing depression. This man, who had been a vigorous, energetic, and hard-working man for all of his adult life, described a pattern of withdrawal, loss of interest in work and community affairs, low energy, and sadness. After completing this series of questions, the therapist commented that it sounded as if the man had been depressed since his son's death and that he had put his own life on hold. The therapist then turned his attention to finding out how other members of the family reacted to the death of the son. At the next interview, the father spontaneously reported that he had thought a lot about what the therapist said about his depression and not living his own life. He stated that he now realized this was true and had decided that it was time to "bury his son" and get on with the business of living.

This case illustrates two important points: that a genogram can be used to discover important clinical information from the past that might not be revealed, at least initially; and that an assessment technique can have therapeutic effects and benefits. Although assessment and therapy can be conceptually separated, in actual practice they are often intertwined. Therapy begins in the assessment phase, and assessment continues throughout the therapy as the clinician gathers new information and learns more about the family.

It is important to obtain a detailed family history, but it is equally important to assess current family functioning. A major assessment task for the clinician is to determine the effects of the death on the family. The McMaster Model of Family Functioning (Epstein & Bishop, 1981; Epstein, Bishop, & Levin, 1978) is a comprehensive system for obtaining a detailed description of the current family functioning. Based on the study of nonclinical families (Epstein, Sigal, & Rakoff, 1962), the McMaster model provides a structured and thorough way of exploring the family's present behavior and is very useful in revealing areas of dysfunction that might be related to the prior death.

The assessment technique based on this model uses a straightforward procedure that consists of four stages: orientation, data gathering, problem description, and clarification of and agreement on a problem list. The data gathering stage is the focus of attention here. It consists of gathering information about the presenting and other problems in the family and current family functioning in six major areas: problem solving, communication, affective responsiveness, affective involvement, behavior control, and roles. *Problem solving* refers to the family's habitual ways of resolving both instrumental (task-oriented) and affective (feeling-related) problems. *Communication* involves assessing the family's style of exchanging information, with particular emphasis on exploring communication patterns along the parameters of clear vs. masked communication and direct vs. indirect communication. *Affective responsiveness* is the family members' capacity for responding emotionally. Assessment on this dimension involves clinical judgments of the range, appropriateness, and degree of emotional experience and expression that each family member is capable of. A closely related but separate dimension is *affective involvement.* This dimension refers to the degree to which family members value, care for, and show interest in each other. A family can range from overly close, enmeshed relationships (symbiotic involvement) to detached, distant, uninvolved relationships. *Behavior control* describes the methods a family has for monitoring the behavior of its members in different situations. The means of discipline adopted by the parents is an example of behavior control. *Roles* are the "recurrent patterns of behavior by which individuals fulfill family functions" (Epstein & Bishop, 1981, p. 466). It is this dimension that is especially sensitive to the effects of the death of a child.

While all of the dimensions of family behavior can be affected by the loss of a child, family role allocation is particularly likely to change as a result of the death. The roles carried out by the deceased child must be reassigned to surviving children or other family members. How much reorganization this requires is a function of both the number and types of roles involved. Some roles are easier to replace than others. For example, routine tasks, such as household chores, are easily reassigned to other siblings. However, the effects of this role reassignment may be to increase the amount of responsibility and diminish the amount of leisure time or availability for social activities for the surviving siblings. This results in what Rando (1984) refers to as *secondary loss,* the additional losses that accrue as a result of the death. Other roles of the deceased child may not be easily replaced. For instance, if the child had been successful in activities outside the home, such as school or organized sports, the parents may expect the surviving siblings to be more successful in order to replace the lost source of family pride. It is important for the therapist to ask detailed questions about what role changes have occurred in the family and the consequences of these changes.

Unlike the two previous approaches, the structural approach to family therapy does not have a formal assessment procedure that is separate from the ongoing process of family therapy. Rather, assessment is a continuing process in which the therapist observes various aspects of family interaction and categorizes them according to the concepts of the theory of structural family therapy. The family structure refers to the repetitive or characteristic organization of the family's interaction patterns. Family structure is defined in terms of various subsystems through which the family functions. Subsystems can be based on generation, interest, or function. For example, typical subsystems in a family include the spousal subsystem, sibling subsystem, and parental subsystem. These subsystems operate according to unwritten "rules" that affect who participates in the subsystem and how the subsystem operates within the family. These "rules" serve as boundaries that describe how the subsystems interact. For example, boundaries can be rigid, in which case the subsystems are distant and perhaps impervious, or, at the other extreme, they can be enmeshed so there is no separation of subsystems. Well-functioning families tend to be characterized by clear boundaries. The structural approach provides a useful conceptual scheme for classifying and understanding complex family interactions. Since the death of a child often has a major impact on the family structure, it is an important and useful tool for assessment.

As noted earlier, the effects on the family of a prolonged death, as in the case of chronic illness, are quite different than when the death is unexpected or sudden. Sudden Infant Death Syndrome (SIDS) or "crib death" is perhaps the prototype of the trauma of an unexpected and unexplainable death of a child. May and Breme (1982) have devised a method for assessing family adjustment to SIDS. This method, the

SIDS Family Adjustment Scale, involves the identification and rating of 12 factors that may be useful in predicting family adjustment following a SIDS death. The scale can also be useful for assessing family adjustment after any sudden death of a child, regardless of the specific cause. Some of the factors involved are communication of feelings; the resumption of normal lifestyle; the use of community and family support systems; cognitive beliefs about the preventability of the death; the religious faith and spiritual values of the family; physical symptoms in surviving family members; preoccupation with the dead child; the functional role of the deceased child in the family; and the closeness or solidarity of the family following the death. In addition to describing the salient factors involved in assessing family adjustment following sudden death, May and Breme (1982) suggest a number of specific interventions with regard to these factors that may be helpful to the bereaved family.

A careful assessment is an important first step in dealing with a referred family. If the death is acknowledged at the time of the referral, the assessment enables the clinician to determine the specific effects of the death on the family and what, if anything, needs to be done in subsequent therapy. If the death is not the referral problem, a detailed assessment is essential to discovering the death, the facts accompanying it, and the specific nature of its effects on the family. Most important, the assessment should provide information about the family's strengths and weaknesses, its need for treatment, and its motivation for family therapy. A detailed assessment is an essential first step in developing a useful treatment plan. If the clinician fails to do an adequate assessment, therapy may begin prematurely or be conducted in a manner that is unacceptable to a family. It is important to determine in advance, insofar as possible, what a family needs and wants, rather than to forge ahead and discover in the middle of therapy that the goals of the family and therapist are at odds.

FAMILY THERAPY INTERVENTIONS

In dealing with a family in therapy following the death of a child, the therapist will follow his usual theoretical and technical preferences. It is not possible to review here the variety of family therapy techniques and intervention strategies available to the clinician. But regardless of the individual differences that exist in the various approaches to family therapy, there appears to be a common assumption underlying all family therapy: the family therapist is a guide and, given the proper guidance, the family system will mend itself. This attitude distinguishes family therapy from other forms of therapy by placing the primary "healing" or "curative" forces within the family system, rather than within the therapist. This does not mean that the family therapist is unimportant. On the contrary, the completion of a successful journey is often highly dependent on the availability of a good map or knowledgeable guide. This section will describe some specific goals, interventions, and techniques that can be helpful in guiding the family through the difficult journey of recovering from the loss of a child.

Although it has been emphasized that a thorough assessment should be completed before beginning therapy, it is important to realize that therapy begins with the initial contact. It has been my experience that for many people psychotherapy is associated with feelings of failure, weakness, embarrassment, or other self-denigrating judgments. These feelings of discomfort may be especially prevalent in family therapy for two reasons. First, family therapy is a relatively new and unfamiliar therapy. Second, the reassurance of being able to talk privately is missing. In individual therapy, a person can express negative feelings about family members with the knowledge that these feelings will remain confidential. In family therapy, the very people with whom you are having difficulty are going to be in the same room with you. It may be necessary to share negative feelings or other uncomfortable information, and this can be especially anxiety-provoking. Because of this anxiety, family members are likely to avoid communicating directly and openly with each other. This is especially true in the case of an emotionally charged event like the death of a child. Thus, when the suggestion is made that the entire family come in, they may be reluctant.

Hare-Mustin (1979) points out that family therapy following the death of a child can be particularly difficult because doctors may be perceived by some or all of the family members as impotent in view of their inability to prevent the death. Therapists, particularly if they are working in a hospital or clinic setting, may be associated with doctors and can be targets for the family's displaced anxiety. The therapist should be sensitive to the possiblity of the family's discomfort and inquire about or acknowledge the family's feelings about seeking help early in the therapeutic process. This often reassures the family and helps engage them in therapy.

Probably the single most important task for the therapist is to help the family to talk openly about the death, its impact on them, and their emotional reactions to it (Bowen, 1976; Goldberg, 1973; Hare-Mustin, 1979; Herz, 1980). This is a complex task and can be difficult for the therapist to accomplish. One of the major obstacles is that different family members may be having quite varied emotional reactions to the death. Family members have different relationships with each other. When a child dies, the surviving family members have lost the same person but not the same relationship. As a result, the family members may not be able to understand or accept each other's responses. In some cases it may be necessary, at least initially, to see different family members in separate sessions. The following case illustrates this point.

Case Example: A family consisting of two middle-aged parents and two college-aged siblings contacted me out of concern for the son, the younger of the two children. The initial session was attended by the parents and their daughter, since the identified patient, the son, refused to attend the session. During the assessment, the parents reported a number of marked behavior changes in their son, which included a sudden decline in grades and subsequent dropping out of college after a very successful freshman year; noticeable increase in tension, irritability, and emotional lability; a dramatic increase in overt conflict with the father; grandiose ideation; and threats of suicide. It was further learned that the eldest son had died suddenly in an accident 5 years earlier. It was clear that the parents had never completed their mourning for this son and continued to idealize him in a variety of ways. His death had been a blow from which they had never recovered, and they kept his memory alive by constantly singing the praises of his many accomplishments and preserving his room as a shrine. In a subsequent individual interview with the youngest son, he painted a very different picture of his deceased older brother. He described his dead brother as having had many negative qualities, complained of having been picked on by him, and expressed both resentment and envy that his brother had been the favorite of his parents. While he was upset that his brother had died, he was also glad to be rid of a rival for his parents' affection and respect. Although the surviving son did not know it, the parents were aware of their youngest son's resentment of his older brother and probably could have tolerated his expressing it directly in a family session. The son, however, was unable to communicate his negative feelings to his parents. In this case the clinical judgment was made to help the son deal with his feelings in individual psychotherapy, rather than force him to attend family sessions. It is interesting to note that the son ultimately did attend family therapy.

This case illustrates that dealing with siblings' emotional reactions to the death of a brother or sister is a complex and delicate task that requires tact and sensitivity on the part of the therapist. It is particularly important for the therapist to realize that the surviving siblings may have feelings that they may be reluctant to express in a family session. As Bank and Kahn (1982) note:

> The therapist must be careful not to assume that all siblings can easily be united and that brothers and sisters can always be supportive of and cooperate with one another. . . . When using a family therapy approach, a number of sibling-specific techniques can be employed, but to rally siblings in the cause of someone they envy or hate, to ask them to cooperate when rifts exist, will only compound hurt in an already injured group of siblings. (p. 334)

When the therapist suspects there are issues for one or more of the siblings or the parents that the family as a whole is not yet ready to accept, these should be explored in separate sessions with the concerned individual or family subsystem.

Research comparing the reactions of grieving parents with other bereaved persons indicates that the grief of parents is particularly severe (Rando, 1984). Rando (1983) suggests a number of specific treatment techniques, including the following: challenging unrealistic expectations the parents may have about their ability to protect the deceased child or prevent the death; identifying and predicting particularly difficult times that might produce a sudden increase in grief, such as birthdays, graduations, and other reminders of the dead child; encouraging the couple to give themselves permission to take a "vacation" from their mourning and to enjoy their other children; assisting the parents in separating from their parental role toward the lost child and, at the same time, helping them maintain or strengthen their role as parents to the surviving children; and referring the parents to an appropriate support group, such as a self-help group of bereaved parents or a chapter of The Compassionate Friends.

Herz (1980) states that the major purpose of family therapy following the death of a child is to prevent family symptoms and dysfunction from developing and suggests several important interventions:

1. Use open, direct, clear, and factual language, avoiding the use of euphemistic and technical language.
2. Combat the family's tendency to avoid issues related to the death by establishing at least one open relationship in the family. It is essential that the death be discussed within the family. The use of provocative tapes, films, or reading materials is a specific technique that can be used to open up a family system that is treating the death as a taboo topic to be avoided.

3. The therapist should remain calm. Families often seek help when their stress or tension level is high and they have been unable to reduce it. While the therapist may experience strong emotions, if his therapeutic interventions are determined by emotional reactivity, it can increase rather than decrease the stress level in the family. Therapists who have not adequately resolved their own emotional reactions to this death or to other significant losses in their own personal lives may inadvertently collude with the family to avoid facing their reactions to the loss.

4. The therapist should encourage the family to mourn the death in ways consistent with their personal and religious customs, rituals, styles, and beliefs.

Family therapy often involves a strong educational component. After a child has died, the therapist may have to help the family be aware of the shifts in family dynamics that are likely to occur. For example, parents may withdraw from the remaining children in order to protect themselves from further hurt, or develop unrealistic expectations for the children. It may be necessary to legitimize the expression of grief for fathers who might feel it is unmanly to cry or otherwise show their feelings. Each family is different, and the therapeutic interventions required may vary considerably. If there is a single therapeutic prerequisite for doing family therapy after the death of a child, it is that the therapist be sensitive to the uniqueness of each family's reaction.

Successful therapeutic intervention following the death of a child requires a combination of well-developed family assessment and therapy skills, a knowledge of issues related to death and dying, and the capacity to cope personally with the powerful emotions associated with the loss. Often it is necessary for the therapist to maintain a balance between having the family revisit the past to express unresolved feelings of grief and encouraging them to face the future so that family life can continue to develop. Unexpressed feelings do not evaporate: they go underground. The single most important function of the therapist is to help the family to openly discuss and resolve their feelings about the loss. This is no easy task. Helping a family cope with the death of a child is a complex and delicate task requiring skill, tact, sensitivity, courage, and wisdom on the part of the therapist.

References

Bank, S. P., & Kahn, M. D. (1982). *The sibling bond.* New York: Basic Books.

Bowen, M. (1976). Family reaction to death. In P. J. Guerin, Jr. (Ed.), *Family therapy: Theory and practice.* New York: Gardner.

Cobb, B. (1956). Psychological impact of long illness and death of a child on the family circle. *Journal of Pediatrics, 49,* 746–751.

Epstein, N. B., & Bishop, D. S. (1981). Problem-centered systems therapy of the family. In A. S. Gurman & D. P. Kniskern (Eds.), *Handbook of family therapy.* New York: Brunner/Mazel.

Epstein, N. B., Bishop, D. S., & Levin, S. (1978). The McMaster model of family functioning. *Journal of Marriage and Family Counseling, 4,* 19–31.

Epstein, N. B., Sigal, J. J., & Rakoff, V. (1962). *Family categories schema.* Unpublished manuscript, Family Research Group of the Department of Psychiatry, Jewish General Hospital, in collaboration with the McGill Human Development Study, Montreal, Canada.

Goldberg, S. B. (1973). Family tasks and reactions in the crisis of death. *Social Casework, 54,* 398–405.

Guerin, P. J., Jr., & Pendagast, E. G. (1976). Evaluation of family system and genogram. In P. J. Guerin, Jr. (Ed.), *Family therapy: Theory and practice.* New York: Gardner.

Haley, J. (1976). *Problem-solving therapy.* San Francisco: Jossey-Bass.

Hare-Mustin, R. (1979). Family therapy following the death of a child. *Journal of Marital and Family Therapy, 5,* 51–59.

Herz, F. (1980). The impact of death and serious illness on the family life cycle. In E. Carter & M. McGoldrick (Eds.), *The family life cycle.* New York: Gardner.

Jackson, D. D. (1957). The question of family homeostasis. *Psychiatric Quarterly Supplement, 31,* 79–90.

Krell, R., & Rabkin, L. (1979). The effects of sibling death on the surviving child: A family perspective. *Family Process, 18,* 471–477.

Mandell, F., & Wolfe, L. C. (1975). Sudden infant death syndrome and subsequent pregnancy. *Pediatrics, 56,* 774–776.

Markusen, E., Owen, G., Fulton, R., & Bendiksen, R. (1977–78). SIDS: The survivor as victim. *Omega, 8,* 277–284.

May, H. J., & Breme, F. J. (1982). SIDS family adjustment scale: A method of assessing family adjustment to sudden infant death syndrome. *Omega, 13,* 59–74.

Minuchin, S. (1974). *Families and family therapy.* Cambridge, MA: Harvard University Press.

Rando, T. A. (1983). The particular difficulties of bereaved parents: Unique factors and treatment issues. *Forum Newsletter: Forum for Death Education & Counseling, 6,* 1–3.

Rando, T. A. (1984). *Grief, dying, and death: Clinical interventions for caregivers.* Champaign, IL: Research Press.

Vollman, R. R., Ganzert, A., Picher, L., & Williams, W. V. (1971). The reactions of family systems to sudden and unexpected death. *Omega, 2,* 101–106.

Williams, W. V., Polak, P., & Vollman, R. R. (1972). Crisis intervention in acute grief. *Omega, 3,* 67–70.

Chapter 25

Communicating with Surviving Children

Joan N. McNeil

Joan N. McNeil, Ph.D., is on the faculty of the Department of Human Development and Family Studies at Kansas State University and is the past President of the Association for Death Education and Counseling. Her research interests are family communication about death and the effects of death and grief on siblings and stepsiblings. She recently completed a study of how families are affected by disasters. Dr. McNeil is coeditor with Charles Corr of the book *Adolescence and Death*.

451

To Carolyn and to John, who shared.

———

I wanted to talk to my brother about it—I knew he was dying, but we never talked about it at home. We still don't talk much about him. I remember I spilled things to a friend at school when D. was taken to the hospital for the last time. But not to anyone in the family—no way! The worst thing is, I never told him I loved him—just couldn't get up the nerve! He meant the world to me. I wish we could've talked. . . .

This poignant statement by an adolescent girl recalling her brother's illness and death gives us several clues to the ordeal often suffered by siblings of children who die. There is a strong sense of regret and frustration in that statement, the realization that old mistakes cannot be mended, the guilt that there were no words of love. There is also a clear picture of "knowing but not telling," the awkward closed communication patterns in a family unable to express and share painful or tender feelings.

Although little empirical research has been done on siblings of children who die, some important clinical reports have revealed the profound effects of a child's losing a brother or sister. In their work with sibling survivors, Krell and Rabkin (1979) have pointed out that "the immediate effect of sibling death is to precipitate grief, expressed or not, and *to increase the psychological vulnerability of the remaining child*" (pp. 471–472, italics mine).

Sibling survivors are often overlooked in the general shock and grief endured upon the dying and death of a child. But there can be little doubt that the death of a brother or sister is a devastating blow to surviving children in a family, and that their "psychological vulnerability" increases greatly from the time a sick sibling is diagnosed as terminally ill, or from the moment of knowledge that the child will die or has, in fact, died.

REACTIONS OF SIBLINGS

Powerful and confusing feelings of sorrow, anger, fear, and guilt are incorporated in the loss experience of all immediate family members when a child dies. Whatever the age of the surviving child, bereavement takes its toll in many ways, and has been shown to affect adversely children's schoolwork, personal relationships, and later development. Balk (1983) reported effects on adolescents of sibling death, including a variety of emotional responses, difficulties in sleeping and eating, thoughts of suicide, frequent thoughts about the dead sibling, hallucinations, detrimental effects on academic work, and changes in peer and family relationships. Some acting-out behaviors can also be noted. In younger children, clinging to parents and whining behaviors are common. In older children and adolescents, intense feelings of frustration may result in extra boisterousness, hostility and fighting, destruction of property, or even self-destructive behaviors such as recklessness or self-mutilation. All these feelings and behaviors can be directly related to the experience of loss. (See Chapter 21, "Grief of Siblings," for more on this topic.)

What exactly has been lost? Certainly, through the death of a sister or brother, a significant person has been removed from the pattern of a young person's life, someone who has filled many roles: a peer, a companion and friend, a rival for the affections and approval of parents and friends, a younger admirer, or perhaps an older role model. This loss provokes a serious threat to identity formation. Another major loss is the blow to the security of the family system, which must undergo an unwanted change to a new reality of the family without the dead child.

Because "the parents' methods of coping play a large part in determining how the surviving child copes" (DeSpelder & Strickland, 1983, p. 238), a heavy burden descends upon them. Suffering deeply themselves, parents often do not have the energy or freedom to deal with their other children. They, and other adult observers, may assure themselves that surviving siblings are "doing fine" in the first months after the death. Children may indeed behave with model propriety during a crisis, in a desperate attempt to keep things "the way they were." Many children also seek refuge from unbearable reality in denial, coping by pretending that the death has not occurred and keeping painful thoughts at a distance. Thus, their real needs may not be apparent, and can be overlooked. Or if their grief is eventually revealed in such behaviors as aggressiveness, whininess, or inattention to schoolwork, adults may lack patience with them out of misunderstanding.

Bereavement after the death of a child often becomes a private matter in families, in which each person attempts to conceal sadness, anger, or confusion and suffers in a helpless "conspiracy of silence." This difficult situation can be attributed to the major painful emotion compounding grief in such families: *guilt*. Krell and Rabkin (1979) point out that the question of blame faces every family member.

> Parents and child come to share a powerful bond through the spoken or unspoken feeling that, if any one of them had somehow acted differently, the child might still be alive. The guilt maintained by these unrealistic beliefs remains intact and intense, with each individual

locked in a struggle with his own conscience and unable to share painful feelings. (p. 473)

When parents and surviving children feel that the death was somehow preventable and that they are responsible, communication about the lost child becomes difficult, vague, unclear. Somehow each feels that open discussion might reveal terrible truths about "whose fault" the death was, and that certainly this would trigger other painful feelings and thoughts, unbearable memories of past transgressions.

The young child's egocentric thinking can cause him to believe that in some way he must have played an awful part in the death of his sibling. When parents offer no explanation for the mysterious death, and in fact seldom mention the dead child out of a mistaken idea that this would "upset" the remaining child, the silence becomes an ominous clue that convinces him he really *is* guilty. The parent keeps silent because he believes talking would disturb the surviving child, and the child keeps silent because he is convinced the parents would be upset to talk about the dead child. "Constricted in circles of mutual protection and self-protection, the sibling never fully faces the loss" (Bank & Kahn, 1982, p. 275). In a study by Pomerance (1973) of a group of young women who had experienced the death of a brother or sister, the critical issue affecting the survivor's mental health was open communication about the dead person within the immediate family. If the family suppressed communication and pretended life had not changed with the death, there was a greater risk that the remaining sibling's mental health would suffer.

OTHER FACTORS IN BEREAVEMENT

Other factors must be considered in understanding the feelings and responses of the bereaved siblings. The age of the child may determine her understanding of the events involved in her brother's or sister's death, as well as her behaviors and needs. The child's relationship with her sibling is important, since the strength of those bonds will affect the depth of pain suffered. The circumstances of the death are significant, especially when the survivor has been involved in any way, perhaps having witnessed the sibling's dying or death. It also matters whether the dying took place during a long illness or after a sudden, unexpected incident such as an accident.

As previously mentioned, when silence is imposed by parents after a child's death, a remaining sibling may be "haunted" by guilt. Two other parental responses can strongly affect a surviving child's feelings and behaviors (Krell & Rabkin, 1979). When parents become especially fearful about their remaining children's safety and survival, they can become overprotective and overcautious. Their surviving children, being "bound" by smothering restrictions on their healthy strivings for separateness, can try desperately to break away, often to the point of taking unnecessary risks. Adolescents are especially likely to live more recklessly under such pressures, driving cars or motorcycles too fast, or experimenting with drugs and alcohol. Or, when parents unconsciously attempt to "replace" their dead child by comparing the survivor to her in various open or subtle ways, the living child must struggle with two identities—her own and that of her dead sibling. Thus she becomes a "resurrected child" who cannot escape the burden of living out a treasured lost child's identity.

These common parental attitudes and behaviors are communicated in a variety of ways as the family tries to work through the heavy tasks of mourning. And because of the complementary nature of the parent-child relationship, in which the parent takes the superior or primary position and the child plays the inferior or secondary role (Watzlawick, Beavin, & Jackson, 1967), the needs of the person related down to (the child) are often overlooked. What are those special needs?

NEEDS OF SURVIVING SIBLINGS

Certainly the bereaved child's needs are similar to those of adults in many ways. No matter the age of the grieving person, each feels especially vulnerable. However, there are at least four major needs of surviving siblings to which parents and other helpers must address their attention:

1. A need for release from the painful tension of feelings of sorrow, anger, and guilt, and a need to share those feelings with others who understand in order to face the loss coura-geously and begin to work through the grief
2. A need to feel loved and valued for themselves and their uniqueness—not as carbon copies of the dead sibling—and to have their bruised and shaken self-esteem bolstered
3. A need to find security in trustworthy bonds of loving family support that are not constrictive, but reassuring
4. A need to discover a personal and shared meaning in the life and death of the lost sibling, so that their own lives can be lived more fully and creatively in the present and future

Most of these needs of surviving siblings can be met through concerned attention within the family. However, because the death of a child deals such a serious blow to the family system, each member's ability to cope will be severely tested. "Survivor families are clearly families at risk, and immediate, sensitive support should be offered to help them bear their sorrow" (Krell & Rabkin, 1979, p. 476).

Therapeutic approaches to assisting children in such families may include various ways of "making contact" through use of the senses in communication, as Virginia Satir has recommended (1976). For example:

1. *Seeing*, or perceiving the child as he really is, not just as he is imagined to be. Seeing *beneath* a behavioral facade is often difficult, but "if we don't look, we make it up," Satir insists. If we judge that a child is "too young" to understand the death of his sibling, or that he is feeling no pain because he acts blandly unaffected, we may miss important opportunities to help the child deal with his fears and confusion.

2. *Hearing*, which involves, of course, listening. But listening with acceptance, affection, and more than a little patience to what a child is trying to tell us, making sure there are no interruptions that judge or interpret, such as "Oh, you don't really mean that!" or "Don't feel that way." Sometimes a child may have difficulty in expressing what his thoughts and feelings are, and may need some gentle questions, such as "How did that make you feel?" or "Tell me what you thought about when . . ." He may need reassurance that what he is revealing is appropriate, and that we sometimes have felt the same way.

3. *Touching* or showing concern through physical closeness is an important part of communicating comfort. In some families touching is not often permissible behavior; unspoken taboos about touching exist in many human relationships. Biologists (such as Morris, 1971) remind us that intimacy expressed through body contact is often necessary to calm anxious feelings. Inviting a child to sit on one's lap, or offering a shoulder to cry on, or just holding him in a warm embrace can provide some immediate comfort. A college student wrote about his family after his sister's death, as follows:

> I remember when Chris and I had to take some things to the funeral home . . . We sat most of the way without a word to each other. I could feel tears beginning to well up inside me and I extended my hand to her. I *needed someone to touch.* Chris grasped my hand just as a tear started down my cheek. We just sat there, physically and emotionally bonded for that moment. Not a word was spoken, but I soon became calmer and calmer. It was her love that helped me. . . . Suddenly I was very thankful to have my family.

4. Finally, *talking*, although difficult in times of emotional stress, is undoubtedly a helpful way of dealing with problem situations. Families differ in their styles of relating to each other, and open discussions of emotion-laden topics like death are more often resisted and avoided than not (McNeil, 1983). Family habits of expressing or not expressing thoughts and feelings are usually of long-standing origin and not easy to change, although a disruptive event such as a death may alter these patterns. However, everyday communication styles in a family tend to set the tone for what will happen after a crisis has somewhat abated. Early reactions to a loss are obviously more emotion-laden than communications occurring months afterward. But there comes a time when words will be needed to put reality to the test, when the open expression of the thought "He is dead" comes as a welcome relief from the unbearable tension of knowing but not telling. Speaking thoughts aloud, about how it feels and what has happened and what it means, over and over, to someone who understands and cares, can start a healing process.

To share in the warmth of family memories may also be a source of special comfort, as this girl's journal relates:

> My dad wasn't able to talk to us about my brother for a long time. One night at dinner, he began to reminisce about some crazy things D. used to do, and we all laughed and talked about him in such a happy way, it was almost like he was there with us again. It felt good.

Sometimes spoken words may not be forthcoming, but written words can fill the same need. Many nights when she could not sleep, one student confided, she arose to write her thoughts in a journal and even produced some poetry expressing intense emotional evaluations of her experience with death. A journal can be an uncensored aid to the writer's catharsis, and provide eventual glimpses of recovery.

Most importantly, however, sharing thoughts and feelings with trusted friends and empathic family members can bring the courage to continue, plus a desire to forge new and worthwhile meanings from the experience of tragic loss. As Bank and Kahn state (1982), "The death of a brother or sister, of no matter what age, forces the group of siblings to reorganize their roles and relationships to one another and their parents. Under certain circumstances, the death jolts the surviving brothers and sisters into being alert, sensitive, and actively concerned as never before" (p. 293).

The young girl who spoke of her difficulty in communicating with her family and her dying brother has expressed her recent recovery and ability to integrate her feelings in a positive way:

When I talk about him now, I can really remember him. And I feel like I know him better now than I did when he was alive. People come up to me and tell me they knew him—he has touched people's lives, he affected other people, they felt the loss, too! That comforts me. . . . His death has made me aware of others' pain. Now I want to become a counselor, so I can help other people to understand their feelings, to *talk* about their losses, to accept and to cope.

And a teenaged boy wrote in his journal:

This experience has shown me that love is very powerful and can be used to survive in this world. I thank God for my family and the love we share.

References

Balk, D. (1983, January). Effects of sibling death on teenagers. *Journal of School Health,* pp. 14–18.

Bank, S. P., & Kahn, M. D. (1982). *The sibling bond.* New York: Basic Books.

DeSpelder, L. A., & Strickland, A. L. (1983). *The last dance: Encountering death and dying.* Palo Alto, CA: Mayfield Publishing Company.

Krell, R., & Rabkin, L. (1979). The effects of sibling death on the surviving child: A family perspective. *Family Process, 18,* 471–477.

McNeil, J. N. (1983). Young mothers' communication about death with their children. *Death Education, 6,* 323–339.

Morris, D. (1971). *Intimate behavior.* New York: Random House.

Pomerance, R. N. (1973). Sibling loss in young women: A retrospective study (Doctoral dissertation, Boston University, 1973). *Dissertation Abstracts International, 34,* 1757B.

Satir, V. (1976). *Making contact.* Millbrae, CA: Celestial Arts.

Watzlawick, P., Beavin, J. H., & Jackson, D. D. (1967). *Pragmatics of human communication.* New York: Norton.

Chapter 26

Advice from a Bereaved Parent to Physicians

Eugenia L. Wild

Eugenia L. Wild, M.A., N.C.C., is a counselor in private practice in Hope Valley, Rhode Island. She is a bereaved parent whose daughter died of leukemia 13 years after diagnosis. During that time Ms. Wild coauthored the *Parent's Handbook on Leukemia*, published by the American Cancer Society, and developed the position of Parent Consultant in Pediatric Oncology, providing liaison and advocacy for parents of children with cancer at Rhode Island Hospital.

No matter how well the course of the child's illness is handled, there will be profound grief for the parents when the death of a child occurs. This sentence could be the end rather than the beginning of a paper by a bereaved parent offering advice to the physician. The reason for beginning with this obvious point is to underscore that what follows is an attempt to suggest ways to ameliorate that pain, not prevent it. The intensity of pain is directly proportional to the intensity of the involvement. This primary pain is immutable. It is the secondary pain that can be dealt with by appropriate management. The secondary pain is the "what if's," the "if only's," and the "I wish I had's." These second guesses can be minimized by maximizing parental involvement and control through participation as a treatment team member. Initially this may seem impossible, but given a chance each parent can be a full participant in caring for her child.

When I first see you, you focus your attention on my child: diagnosing, treating, stabilizing. You, the physician, are at your most competent. At the onset of an illness the course of treatment is usually clear and you can proceed with the full confidence of the medical establishment behind you. Even with the worst diagnosis, there is always something you can do—start an IV, give pain medication.

In contrast, I, who have no degree in parenting, am feeling most vulnerable. I have been given this child to take care of, and I have not done a good enough job, or else she wouldn't be sick. Since no one is certified as a good parent in our society, we parents each carry the fear that we will fail and be found out. This illness can be seen as the public admission of our incompetence. We are frightened and guilty.

Thus, in the initial stages of the illness, I am not at my best. The news that you have just given me is the worst a parent can hear. My mind is reeling with the shock because it is impossible to believe that my child could have a fatal illness, may die before me. While my body keeps functioning, part of me has gone off like a hurt animal to tend its wounds and is simply not available. Is it any wonder that at this point I give you complete power over my child? I'm sure you feel this giving over, and because of your certainty of how to proceed, it must be very comfortable for you to help out and take over.

It will take me some time to come to a place where I can bear this diagnosis, and I will never fully believe it until the death occurs. Don't take this creature you see for the real me, for much of me is absent. On the other hand, I need you to keep treating me as though I really were all right, because if you begin to "protect" me we may set up an interactive process in which I may never regain my full functioning.

One doctor told me, "Parents pay me to do the worrying." There is no way to keep me from worrying, so treating me with kid gloves merely serves to perpetuate unreality. Please don't mistake my backing off initially for a desire for you to take over forever. And, in fact, don't do that to yourself. Parenting my child is a 24-hour-a-day, 365-day-a-year job. You simply are not in a position to take over my job, any more than I am to take over yours. No matter how involved you are with her care, the time will come when I have to take her home, away from all the conveniences and aids of the hospital. At that point it will be well if I have regained some of my confidence to care for her, and you have let go of some of your being in charge. I'm sure you can see how handicapping it would be for me to feel that I couldn't make appropriate decisions and needed to call you every time a question arose.

When we leave the hospital, my child's bed will be filled and you will have yet another family in distress. I can imagine how exhausted you would get if you had to carry each child like a parent does. You see, as much as I'd like to, I can't pay you to do the worrying. So, from the beginning, could we resolve to do our own jobs? I will be the parent and provide that 24-hour-a-day caring, and you will be the doctor and provide the medical knowledge and resources to help her and me as long as is appropriate.

The issues of competency and control will be ever present for me in the course of my child's illness, however long its duration. Once the initial emergency has stabilized there are a number of things you can do that will help me regain confidence in my ability to parent, even under all these new circumstances, and to make appropriate decisions regarding my child's life, as I would have had this illness not occurred.

You will be helping me if you teach me about my child's illness again and again. In the beginning, I will seem to have difficulty learning, but as I get more used to this experience I will be able to take in more and more information. I will need this learning to help my child and me lead a "normal life." Ongoing exposure to the facts of her illness will help combat the false hope that is growing in me that, as the treatment is working and she looks better, the diagnosis was wrong and we are home free.

However, as much as I'd like to forget what happened, I will never be naive in the world again. Before this I could believe in the order of things; now, my faith in logic has been exploded. I need to fill its place, and so will concoct any number of superstitions to put the world right. (I remember promising that I would never again hunt for four-leaf clovers, something I seemed to have a knack for, if my daughter would be all right. And I consider myself a reasonable person.) As I try to reconstruct my cosmology, you will speak to me with the logic of medicine, giving me statistics and probabilities. Please remember that those numbers belong to a world that I have ceased to be a part of, and I no longer place much faith in them. After all, the statistics were one chance in X that my child would be fatally ill and she is.

Connecting me with other health care workers will have benefits for both of us. I will be able to get support and learn from them, making me less dependent on and demanding of you. There are so many facets of life that are changed by this diagnosis; I can be overwhelmed thinking about them. Knowing that there are team members who have special knowledge to offer is helpful: nurses, social workers, child psychologists. I may be able to let go of my belief in your omniscience when I meet those from whom you learn and get support. If you have help, perhaps it is all right for me to have help, also, and I will need to question my competency as a parent less.

Introducing me to other parents who are facing similar problems is a special help. Much of how I have functioned in the world has been normed by watching those about me. But I don't know anybody in my community who has this to deal with in her life and so I have no peer group. Meeting other parents who are surviving this experience will let me know that I can, too. It will be good to talk to people who have walked through everyday life with a child who may die. Their ways of coping with relatives, friends, and the community, and dealing with school situations, discipline, and marital stresses will be hints to me about how to proceed. Their helping me will rebuild their self-confidence, and when I pass the help along, mine. When their children die and I see them continue to live, I will believe I can, too. Since we each "walk in the same moccasins" we will be able to console each other.

The benefits of all this will become clearest when relapse happens. I will be shaken, but I won't be the novice I was initially. Since the treatment with proven efficacy is first to be tried, your best medical approach has failed. In some perverse way I will enjoy the fact that the statistics are once again irrelevant to my situation. My altered view of the universe, which occurred as the result of my child's diagnosis, has been proven right. Your belief in the efficacy of medicine will seem as naive as mine in a benign universe. We are both now at the mercy of the same capricious fate, which puts us on a more equal footing.

If I have been encouraged to be an active participant in my child's care, you will be amazed at what a competent ally I have become. I will still be stricken with pain, but having lived with the illness, I will be more prepared. Now that your position as all-knowing has been challenged, I will feel more like I can contribute as an equal.

For you, it was easier to tell me the truth in the beginning, although the diagnosis was awful to have to share, because the way to proceed was clear. Now being truthful is harder, since it involves sharing that you don't have "the" answer. There is usually no correct way to proceed. Initially, I would have moved heaven and earth to comply with the treatment plan. Now, if you can share with me the uncertainties, I can have input into which less-likely-to-succeed plan will be tried, based on the family's needs for less disruption of our daily lives, our finances, our cosmology. You with your skills and I with mine can truly work together to care for my child.

Perhaps there will be more remissions, good times, and relapses, scary events that try our ability to cope. These give us more information to use in the final stretch, when we all know that death is inevitable.

When you are able to admit to yourself that this life won't be saved, please tell us. I know this isn't easy (it's hard enough to admit it to yourself). It goes against all your training to accept that there is nothing more curative that can be done. But your acceptance of this will enable you to be truly with us in the final phase. Your honesty about the inevitability of the death will help us to take charge, to have these last stages in a style that fits our cosmology. Your medical support of pain medication, transfusions, and just sitting by the bed with us will carry us through. In the end, as in the beginning, it is necessary for someone to take the lead. It will be best for all if I and my child are allowed to make choices in ways that fit best with our needs and lifestyle. But we will definitely need help from you, for without your active support and information we will not have the knowledge and equipment necessary to deal with this time in the best way.

As we head down the last part of my child's journey, if we have done our work well, you and I will be able to separate the failure of medical technology from you the physician. We may want hospital care right to the end, or we may choose to be at home. Either way, we have a need for you, the person, who has shared the process with us for so long. Don't shortchange us or yourself by thinking that lack of medical need means your time is best spent elsewhere. We all need closure. You and I each need to say good-bye to this child. And we need to finish the situation by acknowledging the ending with each other and our work together in the process. This will enable us each to move on.

Throughout this process, please avoid developing a standard of appropriate behavior for families. Every child, parent, and family will have his own unique response to this situation and should be allowed to express it. If you have an idea about the best way to be, I may feel I need to do that to please you, or to get the care my child needs. I am also vulnerable to the community's view of appropriate behavior, and I will need to guard against that, also. Encourage me to be all that I can be, be truly myself. Then I can make choices based on what my and my child's needs are, not based on some outside standard. Then, after the death, I won't need to second-guess myself; to grieve all I didn't do that I wanted to, or the things I allowed that were against my belief of what was best, but seemed to be what you or "they" wanted. I will be able to finish the situation for myself in a way that feels consistent with my standards and desires. I then will be able to let go of the details of the experience and do the real work of mourning, mourning the unique human being who was my child and my special role in her life which has now ended. All my life I will miss that person to whom I gave birth and who was a separate and unique individual in the world, whom I loved and in whom I invested so much. Help me let go of the mundane and move into the profound contact with life that death provides.

Chapter 27

Advice to Clergy on Counseling Bereaved Parents

Rev. Kenneth J. Czillinger

Reverend Kenneth J. Czillinger is Pastor of Immaculate Heart of Mary Church, Cincinnati, Ohio. He has helped form over 20 support groups for bereaved parents, including chapters of Parents of Murdered Children and Survivors after Suicide.

*To the many bereaved parents who've taught
me so much about death and new life.*

———

Since July 1975 I have helped to organize more than 20 support groups for bereaved persons in the Greater Cincinnati area. These support groups include Parents of Murdered Children, Survivors after Suicide, Mothers Supporting Mothers (for women who've experienced miscarriage, stillbirth, or newborn death), and a local chapter of The Compassionate Friends, an international network of support for bereaved parents. In this chapter I will share four major insights I've received from this challenging ministry.

RISK ENTERING HELPLESS-HELPLESS BONDS

I have never experienced the death of a child. Therefore, I must watch my language when I am trying to help bereaved parents. I avoid language like "I understand what you're going through," "I know what you're dealing with," or "I can imagine what it's like." I do not know what it is like to be without a child 24 hours a day, 7 days a week. I cannot imagine what it is like to face holidays, birthdays, graduations, weddings, vacations. I cannot fully understand what it is like to go grocery shopping and pass a child's favorite food or to see a new baby right after one's baby has died.

Years ago I realized that in many ways I was really helpless in dealing with bereaved parents. However, my helplessness has become a gift, a source of strength and not weakness. What do I mean by the experience of helplessness?

To be helpless may mean I am powerless to change an event that has happened—to cure a life-threatening illness, to bring a dead person back to life. To be helpless may mean I am speechless, that I feel inadequate, out of control, frustrated, because I have no answers and feel absolutely useless to a bereaved family. It may mean I am afraid of failure, of making mistakes, of saying the wrong things.

I became a priest in order to serve others, to be a giver. Being helpless has taught me that often I first must risk being a receiver. Ultimately, to be helpless means getting deeply in touch with myself as poor, disarmed, and vulnerable.

However, the more I was able to walk this road of helplessness, the more I realized that bereaved parents were helpless, too. I had the opportunity to form a helpless-helpless bond with them. The more of these helpless-helpless bonds I formed, the more new languages I learned. I learned about the unique language of miscarriage, of stillbirth, of newborn death, of suicide, of murder, of violent death, of sudden death, of death through illness.

Through these helpless-helpless bonds, I began to break through many barriers both to my personal and my professional growth. I learned to love more universally and more unconditionally. I permitted myself to feel and share things that, as a man, I had not shared before. I did a lot of rethinking about my sexual background, my ethnic background, my religious upbringing, and my seminary training. Through my sharing with these bereaved parents, I was becoming more fully human.

Through these helpless-helpless bonds, I began to see a whole new ministry emerging for me. I was able to spend many hours *listening* to bereaved parents, but never could I *identify* with them. Gradually I discovered the importance of forming support groups, so that bereaved parents could come together and identify with each other. My role would be to organize, to facilitate, to enable and, at times, to intervene with wisdom I had learned from so much communion with the bereaved.

In my opinion The Compassionate Friends is a very important gathering place for parents who have experienced the death of a child, no matter what the cause. But I believe that some types of death have their own language. Parents of murdered children need to be together. Survivors after a suicide need to be together. Mothers who have experienced miscarriage, stillbirth, or newborn death need to be together. At times mothers need to be together, fathers need to be together, and siblings need to be together.

In light of my experience I think that it is crucial for the clergy to be *students*. I believe I can write with some authority about bereaved parents because I have spent many, many hours in the role of student. Once, while sharing with a young woman seriously ill with cancer, I got up from my chair and sat on the floor at her feet. "Diane," I said, "I cannot identify with you. To my knowledge cancer is not inside my body. You are my teacher. I am your student. Tell me your story." This is one way to form a helpless-helpless bond, the full power of which cannot be contained in words.

BE SENSITIVE TO THE TENSION MANY (NOT ALL) BEREAVED PARENTS EXPERIENCE BETWEEN GOD'S PRESENCE AND GOD'S APPARENT ABSENCE

In April 1980 I presented a workshop entitled "Anger, God and You" at the annual conference for The Compassionate Friends. More than

200 bereaved parents attended the workshop. I gave all participants a questionnaire that attempted to help them reach their angry feelings. Approximately 85 of these questionnaires were returned.

When I tabulated the responses, I realized that many bereaved parents experience a tremendous loss in their relationship with God. Before the death of the child, God had been experienced as present, just, caring, gentle, nonviolent, wise, in control, forgiving, and faithful. After the death of the child, God was described as absent, unfair, unjust, unloving, cruel, vindictive, stupid, crazy, not as powerful as previously thought, unmerciful, unreliable, a failure.

One mother, who had survived the deaths of two sons by suicide, responded that God was "not my father as I was taught, but a lousy shepherd." This uprooting of a previously close bond with God, this deep experience of the opposite of the biblical images of God, must be respected by the clergy and responded to with great sensitivity.

Clergy members need to watch their language about God. Beware of interpretations, statements, opinions about "God's will" and "God's plan." In some cases the more specific the clergy get about what God intends in a particular situation, the more they may be on shaky ground, unless they've received some direct intervention from God. I've never received such an intervention.

The healing journey for many bereaved parents involves being permitted to lash out at God for his nonintervention, for his seeming absence in a time of overwhelming need. The clergy must help the bereaved to lament, to give voice to their suffering. Sometimes this may mean helping people direct their protest toward God, because they cannot understand what has happened to them nor why it has happened.

In my relationships with bereaved parents, I've noticed a paradox. Sometimes the journey to a deeper praising of the Lord only comes after a period of intense cursing of the Lord. Hopefully the bereaved do not get stuck in cursing the Lord, but, like the psalmists, move through curse to praise.

Clergy members must be alert to those who may be trapped in guilt, believing that their child died because of some punishment from God. I believe God gives food to the hungry and drink to the thirsty, not punishment. Those bereaved who travel the road of guilt need skilled companions.

Many bereaved parents need help from the clergy in order to pray more spontaneously. The bereaved need to be more capable and more comfortable praying from where they are and offering to God the prayers of the lost, the confused, the bitter, the lonely, the jealous, the doubting, and the protesting.

BE AN EFFECTIVE PLAYER/MANAGER FOR A SUPPORT TEAM OF CARING PERSONS

Most people can work through most crises in their lives if they receive the gift of knowledge and the gift of human support. Rarely is one helping person capable of bringing the fullness of both these gifts to the bereaved.

Where possible I try to play the role of a "switchboard operator" and connect bereaved parents to the knowledge and support they need. First, I listen carefully to their story. Then I try to link them to other bereaved parents who can identify with them and be effective support persons. Not every bereaved parent is effective in helping others. Sometimes a screening process is necessary.

I stress the importance of sharing with those who can identify with them. A support group is one of the best ways to accomplish this need to share, to learn that they are very normal and not alone in their grief. Those who have not been there are limited in their ability to help.

I am also prepared to connect bereaved parents to sensitive professional persons—funeral directors, psychologists, psychiatrists, spiritual directors, oncology social workers, or attorneys.

I encourage people to seek professional therapy when they are stuck in denial, anger, guilt, depression, or any combination of these emotions. Usually people recognize when they are stuck and we reach a consensus that they need help. I also encourage people to seek therapy when they are overwhelmed. They may be overwhelmed by a number of significant losses in a relatively short period of time. Sometimes one significant loss triggers unresolved grief regarding past significant losses and this whole process overwhelms them. Sometimes people are overwhelmed by the circumstance of the death—for example, suicide, murder, fire, death of an only child, or death of all one's children. I do my best to have people contact me when they have followed though and set up an appointment for their therapy. I appreciate professional persons sending me a note indicating that people have contacted them.

When appropriate I'm not afraid to assume the role of teacher in dealing with bereaved parents. Since I've spent so many hours as a student in their midst, I've accumulated wisdom that can be handed on to other bereaved persons. I recognize my limitations. I do not pretend I have been there. I give credit to those who have enabled me to teach. But I do have something to offer to bereaved parents and I assert myself in sharing it.

Clergy members must be prepared to make home visits immediately after the death and then during the weeks and months ahead. They must acknowledge their helplessness, then go and listen to the bereaved. It is necessary to head into and not away from the pain and sorrow the bereaved are experiencing.

The clergy must take the lead in planning a meaningful funeral liturgy/service. In Cincinnati an increasing number of congregations are forming bereavement committees. These committees are composed of lay persons qualified to help the family plan a funeral liturgy. They go to the family as representatives of the pastor and the local church community. They work in partnership with the celebrant of the service. The family participates in choosing the readings, prayers, music, and other parts of the service. Other members of the bereavement committee specialize in follow-up ministry, visiting the home after relatives and close friends are no longer present or when the family is in need of additional assistance.

The clergy must preach more effectively. I serve on a committee reviewing the celebration of funeral liturgies in our archdiocese. At one meeting we discussed homilies and sermons and developed some recommendations for preaching. A homily should be personal. It should not be superficial, repetitious, or a canned product hauled out for every funeral. It should reaffirm faith in life without denying or ignoring the painful reality of death. It should refer to the dead child by name. The homilist should have some contact with the family beforehand. One benefit of this contact is to help the homilist get the facts straight. Unfortunately, funeral directors, music directors, bereavement committee members, and others can tell tragic stories about factual errors made by the clergy in their homilies.

Clergy members must be committed to giving bereaved parents options. Once a funeral director told a group of us about a parish in which "whatever Father wants, he gets." The clergy must abandon this type of thinking. They need to know liturgical options, support group options, and resource material options.

I get angry when I hear stories about those in the clergy who try to function as "lone rangers," doing everything for the bereaved by themselves. Often they are not qualified to do everything they are doing. Their unwillingness to let go and work as a member of a team shuts out other people from using their talents and gifts.

I also get angry when I hear stories about clergy members who are ignorant of available resources, like support groups, for bereaved parents. The clergy must become better resource persons, better "switchboard operators." They are open to legitimate and harsh criticism if they fail in this role.

"THOU SHALT TAKE CARE OF THYSELF"

This is one of my great commandments in caring for the bereaved. Helping bereaved parents is a draining experience. Nobody can give and serve 100% of the time. I must structure time for myself, time to get away for a while from suffering, death, grief, and hurt.

I need to be refreshed, to recharge my batteries. I take great pride in the work I do as an instrument for the Lord. I try to be as prepared as possible, as alert and as creative as I can be in each situation. I expect a lot of myself, but generally I am realistic in my personal expectations.

Chapter 28

Advice to Funeral Directors on Assisting Bereaved Parents

Royal Keith

Royal Keith received his B.A. from the University of Washington and graduated from the San Francisco College of Mortuary Science in 1959. He is President of the Keith and Keith Funeral Home in Yakima, Washington, where he has practiced funeral service for over 20 years. Mr. Keith has held all offices of the Washington State Funeral Directors Association, chaired several of its committees, and served as its president in 1969. He was elected to the board of the National Funeral Directors Association and served as its president for 1977–78. In addition he was Chairman of the Association's Task Force on Professional Certification in 1975 and a member of its Task Force on Membership Structure, and is presently Chairman of its 21st Century Committee. He has done extensive lecturing and writing on dying, death, and bereavement.

> Words cannot express how much you helped to ease the hurt we felt
> so deeply. Your assistance and support helped us work through an
> experience I didn't believe we could possibly endure.

For the funeral director who has served parents after their loss of a
child through death, words such as those quoted above are the most
rewarding in his professional life. Yet they are the most difficult to earn
or deserve. There is no death situation entered into by funeral directors
that fills them with such ambiguity, inner doubt, and personalized grief
as when they are called to help parents whose child has died. "What
can I do? What should I say? Should I suggest what they should do?
What have the parents gone through before I was called? Will each
parent have the same needs and will they be able to agree on what is to
be done? Will I be able to listen carefully to them so I can hear their
special needs? Do I as a person have the emotional reserve to go
through this crisis with them?" These and other questions flood the
funeral director's mind when a child dies.

For other caring professionals, and for the bereaved parents, these
same questions can focus attention on the issue of what should be done
when a child dies. Should there be a funeral? Should it be public or
private? Should the parents view the child? Should the casket be open
for other members of the family and friends? Where should the body
be buried? Should cremation be considered? Where and when should
the funeral be held? Decisions such as these must be made by the
parents in a matter of hours. What they decide will impact on their
adjustment to the loss for years to come. Yet for many parents these
issues are not highly important during the first moments and hours
following their child's death. Those times are reserved for the normal
responses of shock, disbelief, numbness, and despair. It is obvious that
a critical issue has arisen before we can even attempt to explore *what*
decisions should be made by the parents. That issue is *when* the parents
should make these decisions.

In addressing this issue, let us erase the common assumption that
parents must make these decisions immediately following the death of
their child. Repeated over and over again to funeral directors, and in
the literature where bereaved parents offer recollections of their experiences, are statements such as: "I felt I should go to the funeral home
the next morning [after my child's death]," "My friends told me I should
get it [the funeral] over with as soon as possible," "We felt we *had* to
make the decisions right away, but we really didn't feel like it." All
persons involved—bereaved parents, their families, helping professionals, and funeral directors—can take more time for these decisions.

There is no reason the family cannot wait 2 or 3 days before most of them are made.

By taking more time for these decisions the parents can explore more deliberately all the options available to them. For some parents, a list of options for them to discuss would be helpful. This could be provided by the funeral director. In one instance, a minister took the parents out to dinner 2 days after the death and at that time the options were given and the arrangements were discussed. To delay the decisions does not prolong the grief. Rather it can extend the time in which there can still be decisions and activities that involve the child. And, although there is no way to guarantee the correctness of those decisions, taking more time will give parents the best opportunity to make choices with which they will feel comfortable in the months and years ahead.

THE GRIEF SUPPORT SYSTEM

The feelings of hopelessness and helplessness of the bereaved parent cannot be adequately described in words. But the fact that others have made it through the experience must provide a ray of hope. In order for us to assist bereaved parents today, it is important to identify and understand what has enabled others in the past to survive their grief.

Within all cultures throughout history there has been a support system for persons in grief. This support system contains four basic elements: a close-knit family unit; a caring community of friends and neighbors providing a social fabric of reinforcement and support; a deep-rooted philosophical or religious attitude toward death; and the continuity and stability provided by known and repeated ceremonial forms and rituals. The full resources of these basic elements are needed for bereaved parents. But these elements of the grief support system cannot be stereotyped or rigid in their application.

Most times a family unit is brought closer together at a time of crisis. This cohesion is the key element in the early stages of parental bereavement. However, there are situations in which the crisis can become divisive and the family is not as supportive as it should be. For example, the two sets of grandparents may give different signals to the bereaved parents as to what should be done. In this instance, rather than expending time and energy resolving the conflict between grandparents or other family members, the parents may be better off to look to the other support elements for help.

Within recent years, the caring support of friends has reemerged as a significant element in the grief support system. For a time during the 1950s and 60s, friends and neighbors stayed away from the parents when they lost a child. This was done with the mistaken notion that "They would rather be alone" and "There is nothing I can say or do to help." Today it appears that the caring community is aware that just to be present is a statement of support. There still are some well-meaning people who suggest to the bereaved parents that a private funeral will be "easier" for them. Nevertheless, the evidence strongly supports having a funeral to which all may come. It then becomes the occasion where the silent statement of presence can be made. And it becomes a shared experience that can be the basis for future interactions with the bereaved parents.

Many studies have shown that the death of one's child causes more stress than any other event that can occur in a person's lifetime. For this reason, with their hurt, pain, and anger, the bereaved parents will search for answers to the age-old questions of the philosophical and religious meaning of life and of death. No matter what the religious background of the parents, it appears that most, if not all, seek support from religious sources. All religions speak to the unique dignity and worthiness of every human being and make the death of any person, particularly a child, an event of significance. Many bereaved parents will credit their strong religious convictions as the most important factor in the process of their grief resolution.

The final element in the grief support system, ceremony or ritual, provides the vehicle that brings the other elements together. Anthropologists have noted that all cultures throughout history have made use of a ritual to acknowledge and accept a major life event such as the death of someone loved. The ritual of a funeral is probably more important for the death of a child than any other type of death. The funeral provides the needed opportunity for the bereaved parents and others in the close family to be together. They are then surrounded by the love and concern of their friends and neighbors while being supported by the uplifting affirmations of their religion.

With all of its cultural variances and individual differences, this grief support system has worked well throughout the generations. In being aware of this system of support, promoting it, and tapping into it, those who are helping bereaved parents can ease the parents' sense of despair and isolation.

GENERAL SUGGESTIONS

Within the broad context of this grief support system, it is possible to make some general suggestions for the bereaved parents to follow. As these generalizations are given, it is important to remind the reader of the caveat that each person reacts differently and, for that reason, these suggestions should not be followed indiscriminately. The following are some of the most frequently asked questions about funeral arrangements with the answers that have proven to be beneficial to most bereaved parents.

How soon should the arrangements be made?

As mentioned earlier in this chapter, the parents should be encouraged to take their time, as much as 2 or 3 days, before final decisions are made. It is vital to remember that most things that are done or decided upon during this period cannot be undone later.

Should there be embalming?

Although in most instances embalming is not required by law, it is suggested that it be authorized to give the parents more time to make their decisions and to keep open all options, including viewing of their child's body.

Should the parents view the child?

It is almost unanimous among the experts and those parents who have experienced the loss of a child that viewing the body is important to accepting the reality and finality of the death. Visual confrontation is the first step and one of the most difficult in the grief process.

Where should the body be viewed?

In some circumstances viewing can take place at the hospital immediately following the death. It should be remembered, however, that often all of the immediate family cannot be present at the hospital when the death occurs. Therefore, most people have found it meaningful to view the body at the funeral home a day or two later, when they are not in the most acute state of shock, disbelief, and denial and all the family can be present to share the experience.

Should other family members and friends be allowed to view the body?

In most instances this is helpful and supportive for parents as well as other family members and friends. This does not necessarily imply an open casket funeral, as viewing can be done at the funeral home prior to the funeral.

Should there be a funeral?

Almost all parents who have lost a child attest to the importance and value of having a funeral. The funeral is the single event that brings together all elements of the grief support system.

Should the funeral be public or private?

Most parents have found that sharing the experience of the funeral with their friends has both short-term and long-term benefits. The short-term benefit is the comforting knowledge that people care and feel. The long-term benefit is the value of shared memories.

Where should the funeral be held?

Often the funeral is held at the funeral home. If the parents have a personal involvement with a church, it is appropriate to have the funeral there. It should be noted, however, that some parents found it difficult to return to that church later because they continued to visualize the casket. This factor should be considered before the place is decided upon. In some instances, the service is held at the grave.

These are just some of the general considerations that must be dealt with by most bereaved parents. But many circumstances will have unique and special considerations that can become factors during the funeral process.

SPECIAL CONSIDERATIONS

There are many variables that can influence what the parents decide to do after their child has died. Two of the most significant are the age of the child and the cause of death. There are some special considerations that can be followed by funeral directors and other professionals when the age or cause of death are important factors.

In discussing the age of the child at death as a variable affecting parental decisions following the death of their child, the tragedy of fetal or infant death should be addressed first. For many years, when a stillbirth or neonatal death occurred the parents were advised to carry out the final disposition as quickly and privately as possible. Often the mother was not even involved in the plans because of the mistaken assumption that it would be too painful. It has only been in recent years that books such as *Motherhood and Mourning* have drawn our attention to how poorly we as professionals have handled the neonatal death. The authors state:

> The birth that is anticipated with a sense of joy suddenly results in tragedy. The parents have little time to prepare themselves. Many

parents and relatives who take the responsibility for making arrangements are usually not aware of the options available to them. Sometimes, in the case of early miscarriage, the hospital will take responsibility for "disposal." The parents will be given the impression that this is not only the "usual," but perhaps the only, procedure. The hospital does not explain alternatives.

Sometimes a well-meaning relative, in an effort to reduce the expense of burial, will request that a funeral home pick up the infant and dispose of it in a "fitting" manner. Under these circumstances, parents never really know what becomes of their infant. Initially it may not seem important, but later this question can plague them.

Anytime a parent is excluded from decisions pertaining to funeral arrangements, problems can develop, if not immediately, then most certainly later. Therefore, as difficult as it may be, the mother and father should participate in the preparations for the disposition of their infant. It is very important that whoever takes the responsibility for final arrangements respect the wants and needs of the parents. Communication between both parents, the funeral director, and/or a hospital representative is of utmost importance, regardless of who ultimately makes the final arrangements. Excluding the parents, particularly the mother, for what is thought to save them further anguish, is not only unwise, but in the long run may cause resentment and bitter feelings. Even when the husband is involved, it is wise to consult with the mother. (Peppers & Knapp, 1980, p. 126)

Many of these thoughts can also be expressed when a child dies during the first 6 years. In these circumstances, it may be helpful to suggest even further involvement by the parents. In "Funerals: A Time for Grief and Growth" funeral directors Roy and Jane Nichols relate the following:

Consider Butchie, a two year old boy who drowned in a neighbor's pond. The body was taken to the nearest hospital and the nineteen and twenty-two year old parents sat in a stunned shock staring into a cup of coffee and watching smoke curl from a cigarette.

Almost twenty-four hours later, a neighbor stumbled into the situation and we were summoned. We were aware that a great deal of the time during that initial meeting with Butchie's parents, their minds drifted. They were not with it; they could not believe it; they wished to be somewhere else. Struck by the severity of their denial and numbness and armed with what dad's death had taught us, we simply said, "When you bring Butchie's clothing to the funeral home, you tell us whether or not you want to dress Butchie's body. Don't tell us now, think it over and tell us then."

Three hours later they came and Carol stated that they wanted to dress their son. We sat on the floor and talked for quite awhile preparing them for what they wanted to do. It would hurt. So let it hurt. Someday they would understand, then it would be okay. But not today.

> It took over two hours to dress Butchie. We stared, we swore, we cried, we talked, we apologized, we shared, we probed, we took time. Together, the four of us found our way through shock and disbelief, the beginning of emotional acceptance of what had happened.
>
> When friends came, Carol and Charles were quite at ease with themselves, they had unloaded tremendous surges of emotion and were ready to receive the affection, concern and support of their community. Shock, denial, and some hostility were behind them and their grief work was moving. (Nichols & Nichols, 1975, p. 90)

Options similar to this, such as the opportunity to hold the child or carry the casket to the grave, can be sensitively brought up to the parents. Yet it is extremely important that they not feel guilty if they choose not to participate in this manner.

When an older child dies, the involvement of the child's friends in the funeral becomes an option that can be presented. There used to be the erroneous assumption that seeing the child's friends might intensify the parents' pain of emptiness. On the contrary, there is evidence that suggests that involving them in the funeral, as well as seeing them frequently days and weeks after the funeral, helps the parents retain the memories of their child. This is the same concept that emphasizes the importance of mentioning the deceased child by name when speaking with the bereaved parents for long after the death has occurred.

The cause of death can also affect decisions made by parents following the death of their child. Conventional wisdom has been that the needs of the parents are different when the child has died as a result of a long-term illness as compared to when the death is sudden and unexpected. More recent literature indicates that the needs of the parents are not changed as much as once thought by the cause of death factor. Even though the parents of a child with a life-threatening illness may experience some anticipatory grief, their reaction to the death still will include the basic grief symptomatology. However, in this instance they may not need as much time to make decisions as when the death was unexpected. It becomes obvious that generalizations are not helpful in regard to this issue. Quite simply, the death of a child is painful, no matter what the cause.

How a person will feel cannot be anticipated. Some parents assume they can anticipate their decisions because they know the death of their child is imminent. An example may help to illustrate this point. The young parents of a 3-year-old girl who died of cystic fibrosis had discussed prior to the death the fact that they did not wish to view the body after the death. Arrangements were made to dispose of the body immediately, with a memorial service at their church 2 days later. A few minutes before the service the mother arrived at the funeral home requesting to see the body. Fortunately the death had occurred over the weekend and the body could not have been cremated until that afternoon. After viewing her daughter, the mother said that although she thought she had adjusted to the grief experience during the dying process, she could not face the fact that her daughter was really dead. She later indicated that the service had more meaning for her because she was fully aware that it related to her daughter's death, which she could have denied had she not seen the dead body. A firm decision a priori had to be rescinded because of feelings unanticipated at the time the decision was made.

NEEDS OF THE PARENTS

The age of the child and the cause of death are but two examples of the numerous variables that affect parental reactions and decisions. Generalizations have been avoided for obvious reasons. However, those who attempt to help the parents with their post-death decisions should be aware of their basic needs. These include the need for visual confrontation of the dead child to confirm the reality of the death; the need for an opportunity for emotional release; the need for an opportunity to receive social support; the need for an opportunity for religious support; and the need to finalize or close the relationship. A brief explanation of how the funeral should satisfy these parental needs may be helpful.

First, the funeral should help the parents and the family face the reality of what has happened. Death is real, final, and irreversible. It is natural to withdraw from a painful and traumatic experience, to avoid it, or to try to make believe it didn't happen. Most research has supported the premise that making the funeral arrangements, viewing the dead child, and participating in the funeral itself help to confirm the reality of what has happened.

Second, the period of the funeral should provide an appropriate setting and occasion for the direct expression of the strong emotions being felt, whether they be anger, guilt, hostility, or tears of grief. How much direct expression is enough depends partly on the individual and partly on the customs of that particular family. The important point is that the funeral becomes the accepted time and place for that emotional release. This is not to say that all emotions can or will be expressed at the funeral, but it does provide the beginning for the mourning process.

Third, the funeral should become the time in which the family is supported by the care and concern of friends and neighbors. There may be times during the funeral period when the family wants to be alone, but most times they will find the social support provided by a caring and sharing community to be a significant source of strength and comfort. Of course, it is hoped this same support would continue long after the funeral is over.

Fourth, the funeral should place the matter of life and death within a religious context of meaning. When the doctrine that life persists after death is ceremoniously presented to the bereaved in moments of high suggestibility, and when it coincides with the hopes and beliefs of the bereaved family, then the acceptability of this belief is enhanced and significant comfort is given to the family.

Fifth, the service should include a symbolic demonstration that the kind of relationship that existed between the parents and the dead child has now ended. For example, the funeral usually ends with a committal service at the place of final disposition. That painful finality of closing the relationship can make room for the recall of all memories that involve that child both in life and in death.

It would be erroneous to generalize that all parents surviving the death of a child need a funeral to resolve their grief. But it is even more erroneous to deny that for most people there is substantial meaning and value in the contemporary funeral experience. In *Twentieth Century Faith, Hope and Survival* (1972), Margaret Mead writes:

> The essence of ritual is the ability of the known form to reinvoke past emotion, to bind the individual to his own past experience, and to bring the members of the group together in a shared experience. . . . Ritual also gives people access to intensity of feelings at times when responsiveness is muted. (p. 127)

At a time when people need stabilizing behavior patterns more than ever to resolve their grief, it is ironic that there are efforts to minimize the ritual and context of this helpful response to death.

The funeral has been defined as an organized, purposeful, time-limited, flexible, group-centered response to death. For some persons, a memorial service, that is, a service without the body present, will satisfy most of the needs of the bereaved parents and other survivors. As Howard C. Raether (1981), former Executive Director of the National Funeral Directors Association, observed:

> The memorial service is less emotional, is not as time limited, and can be more economical to the extent that some of the services and facilities of the funeral director are not used. Yet without the presence of the body, there may be an evasion of therapeutic pain and a denial of the fact that life and death can occupy the same place at the same time. The presence of the body during the funeral ritual makes it easier for

people to vent their feelings and provides a climate for mourning and emotional catharsis. Somehow or other it is easier to approach the bereaved and discreetly help them get on the road back to the life that awaits them in the future. (pp. 144–145)

For the funeral directors and others who understand this process, the questions posed at the outset of this chapter will be substantially answered. They will realize that what they can do and say to help is based on their knowledge of different parents' reactions and their own experience in dealing with parental grief. They will be aware that bereaved parents will not know of all the available options unless they are brought up by the funeral director. They will know that the funeral director's most important function is to listen to what the parents are saying and feeling, to understand what the parents have gone through, to hear whether the parents agree on what is to be done, and to perceive the special needs that indicate particular things that can be done for those parents. Funeral directors who have read, learned, and listened well on the subject of parental loss have become a vital and positive influence during the grief resolution process for the parents. The recognition of this by the parents, as in the quote at the beginning of this chapter, becomes the reinforcement that gives the funeral director the emotional strength to fulfill the painful role of helping parents who have lost a child.

References

Mead, M. (1972). *Twentieth century faith, hope and survival.* New York: Harper & Row.

Nichols, R., & Nichols, J. (1975). Funerals: A time for grief and growth. In E. Kübler-Ross (Ed.), *Death: The final stage of growth.* Englewood Cliffs, NJ: Prentice-Hall.

Peppers, L. G., & Knapp, R. J. (1980). *Motherhood and mourning.* New York: Praeger.

Raether, H. C. (1981). The future may be now. In O. S. Margolis, H. C. Raether, A. H. Kutscher, J. B. Powers, I. B. Seeland, R. DeBellis, & D. J. Cherico (Eds.), *Acute grief: Counseling the bereaved.* New York: Columbia University Press.

Chapter 29

Advice to Professionals on Compassionate Involvement

Art Peterson

Art Peterson, a graduate of M.I.T., served as Executive Director for The Compassionate Friends on a volunteer basis from 1980 through 1983. He is a retired personnel administrator with experience in industrial management. Mr. Peterson has served on local and state school boards, a hospital board of managers, a zoning commission, and foundation boards. Mr. Peterson is a bereaved parent.

To our son, Tony.

———

When bereaved parents get together to share experiences or to discuss problems, some topics are sure to be on the agenda. Among these, one of the most common is the tale of the insensitive professional. The cast of characters does not change much from one discussion to another. The brusque doctor, the accusing police officer, the vanishing minister, the aggressive journalist—all appear in story after story. Is it accurate to say that many professionals cope badly with the death of children, or are parental expectations simply too high?

These are not accusations of malpractice or negligence. Those occur but are beyond the scope of this discussion. These alleged failures take place under circumstances that are apparently uncomplicated. A child is hit by a car, for example, is rushed to the hospital, lives for a few days, and finally dies despite all efforts to save her. If the doctor, the chaplain, the nurse, the funeral director, or any other of the professionals usually involved in a case like this did not perform as the parents would have wished, what might they have done differently?

I think the best way to answer this question is to study the behavior of those professionals who get good reviews. As you listen to some horror story about a member of the clergy who offered a few tired clichés and then beat a hasty retreat, somebody else will invariably tell of one who knew exactly what to say and do. The first few times you listen to an exchange like this, you tend to concentrate on the faults of the one who couldn't seem to handle an obvious responsibility. I think it more productive to direct our attention to the methods employed by the one who was successful.

Our own experience with this problem was limited. Tony died in an automobile accident that was uncomplicated by things like drunken driving, excessive speed, or other legal considerations, and the end came instantly. No waiting around the emergency room, no decisions about appropriate treatment, no probing reporters, no jury trial. During those hours and days while we were still stunned by the swiftness of our loss, we came into close contact with only two professionals, our priest and our funeral director. Both rose to the occasion. We could not have been in more competent hands or have asked for more understanding. Yet this was not a case of our stumbling on two experts in thanatology. This was the pastor of a rural church and a small-town mortician. What did they do that was so helpful? What did they understand that seems to have eluded so many of their peers? How did they learn that what we wanted and needed was their presence and their caring, not their advice?

Henri J. M. Nouwen, in *The Wounded Healer* (1979), discusses this. As his title suggests, he believes that it helps to "have been there" yourself, which is why one bereaved parent can be of so much comfort to another, but he does not insist that you must have experienced a pain identical to that of the sufferer. He writes that "it seems necessary to re-establish the basic principle that no one can help anyone without becoming involved, without entering with his whole person into the painful situation, without taking the risk of becoming hurt, wounded, or even destroyed in the process" (p. 72).

From what I've observed, the professionals who are most appreciated by bereaved parents, and probably by others in grief, are those who take the risk that Nouwen describes. It is hardly surprising that not all are willing to do so or that some appear to be unable to display such vulnerability. It is a lot to ask. It is particularly difficult for those who have been caring for the child physically, since they must deal with what they see as a personal failure to serve a patient adequately along with everything else. In addition, many professionals think it unwise to show a tender side. They have been taught and they believe that an air of detachment adds to their credibility within their profession as well as in the eyes of their clients. I disagree. In fact, the testimonials I've listened to indicate that the opposite may be true.

Do bereaved parents have unreasonable expectations of professionals? I believe we do, but the question is a complex one. To begin with, we almost all had an idealized picture of our family doctor, our pastor, our teachers, our counselors prior to our first encounter with a major loss. During this period, we assumed that a sick child, especially our sick child, could be rushed to a hospital and cured by our doctor. Our pastor, or at least some member of the local clergy, would not only know how to comfort us in times of sorrow but would have sound advice on the best way to recover. We believed and we wanted to believe that universities, seminaries, and other specialized institutions of higher education held the secret to turning out graduates with skills and powers far beyond those of ordinary mortals.

On the day that our child dies, we are abruptly and unceremoniously confronted with life as it is, not as we had imagined it. Along with having to cope with intense grief, anger, guilt, depression, or whatever, we found that we were alone. Those experts on whom we assumed we could depend could not help us. In our frustration, we even suspected that they were refusing to help us and this angered us. Very quickly, however, we learned that they were powerless to fix our shattered world, and this was even more devastating. We felt isolated, abandoned, and bitter. Wise professionals sense this and don't try to change what cannot be changed. Many accounts can be related about the doctor who sat with the parents, put his arms around them, and cried. The key element is being successful in convincing the bereaved parent that, for this professional, their child's death is the most terrible and most urgent problem in the world.

The deliberate concentration on the needs of one client to the apparent exclusion of everything else can be compared to the biblical account of the good shepherd and the lost sheep. Nouwen (1979) writes

> Personal concern makes it possible to experience that going after the "lost sheep" is really a service to those who were left alone. Many will put their trust in him who went all the way out of concern for just one of them. The remark "He really cares for us" is often illustrated by stories which show that forgetting the many for the one is a sign of true leadership. (p. 73)

What does the shepherd actually do for the sheep that was lost? He knows that a lecture on safety rules would be resented. He also knows that a technical and intellectual analysis of what happened would be wasted on this frightened animal. At the moment, what is called for is an explicit demonstration of concern and an open expression of love. Moreover, as Nouwen so wisely observed, the other sheep are watching the whole process, thinking about what would happen to them in a similar situation, and feeling reassured by what they see. So the good shepherd picks up the stray, holds it close, and postpones the lecture, possibly forever.

Even those professionals whose primary role is something other than that of a comforter can profit from understanding the mind of the bereaved parent. The reporter, for example, doesn't have to insist that a grieving mother describe her feelings at the moment she heard of the death of her child. It's just as easy to express concern and listen to what comes out voluntarily. There won't be any ambiguity about what she felt. Similarly, the investigating officer, when asking those very necessary questions about the accident, can often choose one time rather than another or select his words with care, and can certainly avoid appearing belligerent. Should he have reason to think that something illegal has occurred, it might even assist his inquiry if he kept his suspicions to himself. It would certainly be appreciated by the survivors.

In summary, then, the oft-heard criticisms of professionals by bereaved parents are in part based on the unrealistic expectations that existed prior to the child's death. When tragedy strikes, what happens next depends on specific circumstances, and no two situations are alike.

A familiar pattern, however, finds the bereaved parents stunned not only by the death itself but also by the destruction of those earlier expectations of friends and professionals. There is no expert to make the pain go away. It is at this time that the professional should spend time helping the parent find his own way and should, by her presence, indicate deep concern and love. Those who do this are respected. Those who attempt to perpetuate the myth of infallibility are not merely ignored; they are resented.

It seems reasonable to think that professionals from any discipline should be more comfortable in this reactive role. Being placed on a pedestal might be flattering on a short-term basis, but it has to be disconcerting when you know that a fall is inevitable. The Wizard of Oz was mighty impressive before Dorothy discovered that he was an ordinary man, but he was happier and more effective afterward.

Those of us who work with hundreds, perhaps thousands, of bereaved parents in small face-to-face discussion groups are very much aware of those doctors, nurses, ministers, funeral directors, counselors, and others in the professions who do outstanding, even heroic, work with those whose children have died. The fact that some of their fellow specialists misjudge or fail to comprehend the nature of our grief only makes their concern more appreciated and our admiration for them that much greater.

References

Nouwen, H. J. M. (1979). *The wounded healer.* New York: Image Books.

Section 6

Organizations

Chapter 30

The Compassionate Friends

Ronnie Peterson

Ronnie Peterson, a graduate of Radcliffe, has been a liaison between The Compassionate Friends and professionals of all disciplines from 1980 to 1985. She has been active in volunteer administration of social services, having headed a council of social agencies and a voluntary action center. Currently she is Chairman of the Mental Health Sub-Committee of the St. Lawrence County New York Community Service Board. She is a bereaved parent.

To our son, Tony

The Compassionate Friends (TCF) is a self-help group for parents who have experienced the death of a child. The primary method of help is providing sharing groups, but newsletters, lending libraries, guest speakers, and telephone friends are part of most chapter programs. Present at every meeting are parents who have survived and can model that it is possible to do so. There is no elaborate structure, no affiliation with any religion, and contributions are entirely voluntary.

Members are at all stages of recovery and shift among them. Some have a deep religious faith; some have lost theirs; many are adrift. Even a small chapter is apt to include some who are currently receiving professional help or who have had such help in the past, in addition to participating in TCF.

We recommend that all chapters have advisory boards of professionals from various disciplines and that the leaders turn to them for guidance whenever necessary. It is essential, of course, that those the chapter selects to serve on its advisory board believe in self-help and recognize that the process, like grieving itself, is slow and sometimes stumbling, but can usually be trusted to work itself out with a minimum of intervention.

The Compassionate Friends was founded in 1969 by Reverend Simon Stephens, an Anglican chaplain at the Coventry-Warwickshire Hospital in England, after he noticed that two sets of bereaved parents were of more comfort to each other than he or any other professional could be. Arnold and Paula Shamres brought him and TCF to the United States in 1972 after the death of their daughter, and there are now over 300 chapters in this country alone.

Our own son was killed in 1970 and we knew nothing of TCF until 1978, when we joined the new Buffalo, New York, chapter with the stated purpose of helping others. We had survived quite well, but remembered clearly how very difficult it had been even in our relatively simple situation: an exemplary child with whom we had had an excellent relationship, a really "accidental" death with no one seriously at fault, continuing support from family and friends, and a marriage with loving communication.

We discovered that we had had one great advantage: prior experience of tragedy. For many parents their child's death is the first really bad thing that has happened to them. We had already known the death of my parents in a flood and the suicide of my sister-in-law. These were hard lessons in real life. They made the headlines, and they had happened not to someone else, but to us.

In the self-help group, one of the first great learnings is this: I have not been singled out for this unspeakable affliction. There are all these others, and, as one gets to know them, they are fine people with beautiful children also. The absolute isolation that bereaved parents feel starts to break down into identification with the group. At some point, "Why me?" and "Why my child?" can begin to give way to "Why us?" and "Why all our children?"

MEETINGS

Meetings always start with the members introducing themselves by speaking briefly of their deceased children and the circumstances of those children's deaths. Those who cannot yet say the words need not speak. (Frequently they will say later the same evening, "I'm ready now" and tell their story.) Immediately the new member knows that these people *know*, unlike family and friends who seem to trivialize the death by likening it to the death of some other family member. These people know that losing a part of oneself, of one's future, is different from other losses. The inappropriate remarks, the "comforting" clichés of the uninformed, are repeated first ruefully, then often with rising humor about the ignorance betrayed. In the midst of the "How could they's" someone, blessedly, may say, "I remember when *I* said things like that." The door to understanding a neighbor's "uncaring" attitude begins to open.

Someone may have, without asking, dismantled our child's room "to spare us," and the impotence and guilty rage this aroused is remembered. Another has felt this way, too, and is still angry and hurt and feels no gratitude for the work involved. "Don't bother me with the good motives behind it, they had no *right!* So I would have cried all the way through it. What's wrong with that? I often feel better after crying." "Me, too."

It is, of course, the "me too's" that are the magic. Someone in the group will have felt "that way" too. And another part of the magic is that someone else won't have felt that way at all. We learn that there is no right way and no wrong way. Each has to find a way that works. We give no final answer; we give lots of answers. Pick one.

Sometimes drugs or alcohol are mentioned and there is real unanimity about the dangers involved—but no righteousness and no condemnation (except of the doctor who prescribes liberally and then disappears). The need for oblivion, for an even temporary sense of well-being, is too well understood and accepted.

The most important things that TCF offers are the endless capacity to listen with true empathy and the reassurance that one is not "going crazy." People come together with nothing else in common but their bereavement, and nothing else matters. We listen to each other's stories told over and over as each tries to convey the specialness of the lost child, to deal with the events surrounding the death itself, the bitterness and alienation that remain, the disappointment over anticipated support that does not materialize. Some doctors prescribe for our "nerves" and some clergy tell us that "it's God's will." Even our parents, our brothers and sisters, think that we should be over it. Our other children appear to be going on with their lives as though nothing had happened, or else they are in deep trouble and we have no idea what to do for them, or the strength to do it. We do not live up to the expectations of society; we are uncomfortable for friends and fellow-workers; we think that perhaps they are right and that we should be "putting it all behind us" and "getting on with our lives." We pretend, but we are frightened.

Attendance at TCF meetings brings us together with many other parents who feel the same way and with parents who have succeeded in resolving many of the problems. Each meeting includes a short presentation of cognitive knowledge about some aspect of grief and healing (a speaker, film, book review) and most chapters also have a lending library of books and tapes; but it is the sharing that brings parents back time after time. This is often the first group that they have felt comfortable with and may even be the first social contact since the death.

A wife may say that her husband won't talk to her about their child. (He may be sitting next to her when she says it!) Other wives present know all about that. But a husband in the group will counter that his wife would talk about nothing else, so that he didn't even want to come home at night. And yet another couple may say that they had not been able to resolve this, were growing farther and farther apart, and had gone to a counselor. Together they'd learned to reach compromises that worked for them. A woman will say that that is why she comes to TCF. She can talk about the child, and someone will listen. It takes the pressure off her husband. Everyone present has learned a little more about their mates and marriage.

We read terrible statistics about the marriages that break up after the death of a child and we are disturbed. TCF's constant counsel of patience with oneself and with others, as well as insights into marriages that seem to be holding, reinforces the idea that a relationship may be basically OK in spite of the fact that partners are not able to support each other while each is struggling to adapt to a crushing new reality.

All of us worry about our surviving children. We have trouble understanding their different styles of grieving. We ask for and receive a lot of advice about this. TCF family get-togethers have helped by putting our children in touch with each other. Some chapters have regular sibling programs.

In TCF we hear each other talk about how much it hurts, and all agree, and no one suggests any need to hurry it along or pretend that the pain is gone. There will be someone there to say that it isn't quite as bad as it was, that it does get a little better after a while. Another nods.

There are difficulties on the job (or at home) of being disorganized, unable to concentrate or reach decisions. Lots of company there. It feels safe to discuss fears, dreams, anything. Through it all, we listen and respond. We take each other very seriously. We recognize each other's needs as our own, and those a little farther along reach out to those coming up from behind. It feels very good to be able to help someone else, and we recognize it as a sign of our own progress.

Some of us stay on, listening, reading, listening, attending conferences, listening—and learning. We have seen a lot of pain and a lot of healing. We have received much more than we have given. The Compassionate Friends works.

FURTHER INFORMATION

For further information and a complimentary copy of the national newsletter, write to The Compassionate Friends, P.O. Box 1347, Oak Brook, IL 60521 or call (312) 323-5010.

Chapter 31
SHARE

Sister Jane Marie Lamb

Sister Jane Marie Lamb, a pediatric and maternity nurse with an M.A. in Health Ministry, has been involved in working with the bereaved since 1973. In 1977, she founded SHARE and has assisted in starting 140 SHARE groups in 40 states as well as in Germany and South Africa. She has worked with other support groups such as AMEND (Aiding Mothers Experiencing Newborn Death) and The Compassionate Friends and is an adjunct instructor to Southern Illinois University School of Medicine in the Departments of Humanities and Pediatrics. She has co-authored *Thumpy's Story* for children and is the executive producer of three video productions: *To Touch Today, Memories,* and *Alive Again.*

In our society, grief at the loss of a baby through miscarriage, stillbirth, ectopic pregnancy, or early infant death prior to dismissal from the hospital is not acceptable, especially after a week or two. The mother-child relationship has often been so brief—the mother may not even have held, coddled, fed, or embraced her baby—that other people do not see a reason for feeling a loss. The briefness of her contact with her baby, though, may increase the pain the mother feels at the child's death, rather than make her grief less.

Well-meaning relatives and medical personnel may try to protect the grieving mother by not talking about the baby, by making plans without including the mother (funeral arrangements, putting the baby's clothes and crib away, etc.), by not letting the mother see or hold the baby, by persuading her not to name the baby, and so on. People often intimate that it is abnormal to talk about the baby or even to have feelings about the baby. The mother's feelings may then be held inside and guarded. Time doesn't always heal these feelings because they are not released. The more time that lapses, the less acceptable it becomes to express these feelings.

The mother also needs to be assured that she is not in any way to blame for the loss of her baby and that she is not incompetent as a woman. She needs to be encouraged to care for herself physically, even though it may be very difficult to love herself now.

Fathers need the same support as mothers after the death of their baby. Although the father did not have morning sickness, feel the baby move, or go through the labor, he felt something for that life within the mother. As he supported the mother during labor, he also needs to support her during her grief after the delivery. Hospital staff can help support the father while he supports the mother by listening, sharing a cup of coffee, talking for a few minutes, and so on. If his anger and unhappiness can be brought out, he can be more relaxed and in touch with reality so he can better handle the mother's grief.

No parents should have to go through this grief alone. The mother and father experiencing the loss of their baby need as much, if not more, pampering, concern, affection, and attention to their needs as parents whose baby has survived. The staff at St. John's Hospital in Springfield, Illinois, felt the need to reach out to these parents. They established SHARE (Source of Help in Airing and Resolving Experiences) as a mutual-help group for parents grieving the loss of a baby through miscarriage, ectopic pregnancy, stillbirth, or early infant death prior to dismissal from the hospital. The basic reason for SHARE is the comfort and the mutual reassurance that parents who have lost their babies can offer to each other. The group offers support, friend-ship, understanding, and an open atmosphere.

HISTORY

The impetus to organize SHARE came from one determined, bereaved parent. From her recognized need and that of others, the idea grew. In October of 1977, a committee of people formed, including the grieving mother, social workers, a neonatologist, pastoral care persons, and nurses from the maternity, neonatal intensive care, and gynecology nursing areas. This committee discussed attachment, grief, and par-ents' needs and personal response to loss. SHARE grew out of these discussions, research, and experience with groups like AMEND, The Compassionate Friends, and Make Today Count. Once SHARE's goals were identified and plans for the group's meetings were established, hospital in-service training was held to familiarize appropriate person-nel with the SHARE concepts. Emphasis was placed on departments of the hospital where personnel would most likely have contact with the bereaved parents (sonography and X-ray, the laboratory, the business office, admitting, housekeeping, social service, pastoral care, dietary, and the emergency, operating, and recovery rooms) and staff who most needed to know about SHARE (all supervisory nursing staff and all obstetrics and gynecology medical staff).

By the end of 4 months, the groundwork was completed. Mothers who would benefit from such a group were contacted and their names placed on a potential mailing list. An explanatory, introductory letter was mailed to each of these parents inviting them to come to the first meeting in February of 1978. At first, morning meetings were held in the hospital. Some women indicated that their husbands would attend if evening meetings could be held, so evening meetings were added to provide for fathers in attendance. Their response was encouraging, and fathers have participated ever since. Today, there are over 140 SHARE groups in the U.S.A. and other countries.

SHARE was established as a model for hospital-based support systems. It is considered part of total patient care provided by staff during the time of antenatal (during pregnancy) and perinatal (at the time of birth) concerns, at the time of death, and during the postpartum hospitalization, as well as in the weeks and months of bereavement. The philosophy of SHARE is carried out in the response of personnel throughout the hospital. Hospital staff and the SHARE group provide assistance in decision making, planning meaningful rituals, and naming the baby. Keepsakes are provided, pictures taken, financial concerns addressed, and information provided on grief and mourning. Throughout the bereavement period, support is given on a one-to-one basis by staff and volunteer bereaved parents through the support group meetings, letters, phone calls, the newsletter, and educational materials. Individual needs are addressed as they surface. The enthusiasm of the hospital staff about the SHARE program has been phenomenal.

GOALS

The SHARE group developed at St. John's has these eight goals:

1. To show the Christian love and concern of St. John's Hospital and its personnel for parents experiencing loss of a newborn baby, stillbirth, miscarriage, or ectopic pregnancy
2. To recognize the need for expression of grief and related emotions, which society generally denies these parents
3. To further the hospital's philosophy of caring for the whole person and family beyond the hospital stay
4. To provide these parents with a situation in which they can share their feelings about their loss, and therein find acceptance—if not always meaning. It is also an opportunity to express the love they had for their baby in their compassion for others
5. To provide information about the various aspects of the grieving process through educational offerings and a lending library
6. To aid parents in the positive resolution of grief experienced at the death of their baby
7. To foster the physical and emotional health of the bereaved parents and, indirectly, of the siblings
8. To provide acquaintance with bereaved parents whose sorrow has softened and who have found fresh hope and strength for living

MEETINGS

SHARE is neither a therapy group, nor are the meetings "therapy" sessions. Yet healing is slowly and gently promoted as parents gain insight and understanding and have an opportunity to verbalize their feelings, attitudes, or experiences in group discussions. Through SHARE, parents learn that the intensity and longevity of their feelings are normal and that their problems and anxieties are shared by other bereaved parents.

Any bereaved parent or relative, regardless of length of time since the baby has died, may attend and benefit from the activities of the group without regard to age, creed, social status, sex, or financial condition. SHARE is nondenominational; what is important is the acceptance of the individual. When parents grieving the death of an older child come to a SHARE meeting, they are provided with support and are given the option of contact with other parents with similar experiences. SHARE would not turn any bereaved parents away without giving them support.

Members may bring support persons or someone who has provided transportation to the meetings. Care is taken to ensure that spectators or curiosity seekers do not offend participants. No formal membership or dues are required.

Some parents come only once, others come regularly. Still others continue with the group to provide support to the newly bereaved. A few parents have written a pamphlet to help other parents at the time of their baby's death. Other parents have been involved in producing videotapes on grief.

For some bereaved parents, it takes every ounce of courage to attend that first meeting. Therefore, the start of each meeting and the greeting of new members is very important. Professionals from the core group who planned the SHARE group and act as its facilitators arrive early to greet and get acquainted with parents. These core members establish a warm atmosphere and try to relate to the parents rather than to each other. Name tags with first names are used.

To promote participation and sharing, the group is seated around a table in a circle or square. Pencils and notepads are provided to parents to make notations on the speaker's presentation, to doodle to relieve tension, and to exchange members' addresses and telephone numbers. A sign-in sheet is used for future reference. A pot of coffee and tissues are provided.

One person introduces herself and sets the atmosphere. Each person then introduces herself in this manner: "My name is _____ , our baby boy/girl died (how long ago). He/she was (how old), or I was _____ weeks/months pregnant." The parent can offer any other details she may wish. If the parent becomes too emotional to continue, the group goes on and returns to her later.

When introductions are complete, eleven guidelines are shared with the group, giving them a sense of what to expect and assuring them of the mutual-help aspect of the group. The guidelines are very important in letting the members know that it is their meeting and to give a sense of direction and boundaries. The guidelines are:

1. Each of your experiences is unique and valid. No one is here to criticize or analyze.
2. Feel free to share or not share your feelings and experiences. We will not probe. If you have had a similar experience and care to talk about it, feel free to do so.
3. Notepads are available for you to write down any word or phrase that comes to mind. It is OK to write while others are talking; notes are for yourself, and you will not be asked to share them.
4. It is OK to cry—there are tissues available, and we ask that you be sensitive to your neighbor's needs. We ask your permission to cry too.
5. If you feel the need to leave, feel free to go. One of us will follow you out of the room to be sure that before you leave you are ready to drive.
6. Share your feelings about the meeting with your spouse—we do not want to create a communication gap, but rather increase communication.
7. The group time is not intended as a time for medical advice— if you have medical questions, we will respond to them after the general meeting.
8. Should you wish to share a bad experience you have had with a hospital, nurse, or doctor, feel free to relate the experience. We would ask that you not use the name in the discussion.
9. The tape recorder, if used, will be on for the presentation only.
10. After the short presentation, you may respond to what the speaker has said or open with anything you wish to bring up. We encourage you to respond to each other.
11. To respect the privacy of each parent, we will not discuss, except among SHARE members, the content of these meetings.

After the guidelines have been covered, a guest speaker gives a presentation. These presentations, or "heart talks," deal with painful aspects of grief and give parents a direction to move with their mourning. Once the presentation is completed, the parents relate experiences to each other. Any conversation directed to the facilitators is redirected back to parents within the group. Only when guidance is needed do facilitators become active participants. The parents should feel facilitator backing, but most of their support comes from relating to each other. The professionals assume a low-key role during the meetings, becoming more active outside the meeting or after the general session is over. Healing occurs as members help each other, and self-esteem is restored with the support of facilitators who enable parents to arrive at their own answers and solutions.

Informal visiting over coffee before and after the meeting is a significant part of the meetings. If the group has a library, books, pamphlets, and tapes may be checked out by members at this time.

ORGANIZING A SHARE GROUP

To give direction and prevent people from being misguided, a core group of professionals should organize SHARE, set the atmosphere, and direct the meetings when necessary. This core group, drawn from nurses, social workers, pastoral care staff, and physicians, should have sensitivity, good communication skills, dedication to the group, and a willingness to give freely of their time. Core group members could rotate attendance at meetings. As the group begins to form, it may be helpful to look at the organization of other mutual-help groups such as AMEND, Make Today Count, The Compassionate Friends, and so on.

The most direct way to involve parents is through personal contact. However, a small number of parents respond to newspaper articles. Articles keep the concept before the community's eyes, but cannot convey the concern and understanding that group members are able to convey.

It is helpful to use local newspapers and other media to announce a community information meeting on the formation of the SHARE group. The features editor of the local newspaper may be willing to print a sympathetic article on newborn loss, bereavement, and SHARE. This article could center around the grieving parents of the new group being formed. The date, place, and time of the meeting; names and phone numbers of the core group members; and an open invitation to bereaved parents and members of the helping professions to attend should be included.

Some parents who respond to the invitation will have been recently bereaved and will be looking for immediate help. Others, bereaved some time ago, will want to assist in forming the group. Some members of the helping professions will probably attend to learn about, and perhaps be involved with, the group. Initially, some groups may choose to gather a nucleus of bereaved parents and meet informally among themselves for a while. Later they may wish to expand as the group feels comfortable in doing so.

Once the SHARE group is established, parents are contacted during hospitalization. Then a letter is mailed 4 to 6 weeks after the loss of the baby when parents are more aware of their feelings and needs. The initial contact familiarizes parents with the support group and the newsletter. Parents are told that they are not isolated and alone, that they can share their feelings—by phone, a personal visit, or at a SHARE meeting—with other parents who are experiencing a similar loss.

St. John's keeps a file on parents who experience miscarriage, ectopic pregnancies, stillbirths, and deaths in the Neonatal Center. These parents are invited to SHARE meetings in a follow-up letter that includes a flier about the meetings and the most recent newsletter. Hospital staff, other SHARE members, professionals, and other people familiar with the group or its newsletter often make referrals, and the parents they refer also receive a letter of invitation.

The meeting place should be accessible with ample parking space and a pleasant atmosphere. Meetings may be held at community centers, the local YMCA, a church or a synagogue, or at the hospital. There may be concern about having parents return to the hospital—the place where their baby died—but simply by attending a meeting at the hospital, the parents can make a step forward in resolving their grief. If meetings are held in the hospital, they should be held in the same room each time and well away from maternity or gynecology units. Meetings should never be held at the same time as Lamaze classes.

A hospital-based SHARE group has definite advantages. First, parental grief can be dealt with in its early stages. Second, SHARE may make hospital staff more sensitive to these parents and subsequently create new hospital policies and procedures that will affect their care. Third, staff education and encouragement can lead to more comfortable and effective relationships in dealing with these parents.

A regular meeting time should be established, such as the first Friday of each month at 8:00 P.M. One morning meeting and one evening meeting each month are helpful to accommodate parents working different shifts. The group may, however, feel the need for more frequent meetings.

A permanent mailing address, convenient for the committee members, should be established. This may be a post office box number, church, public building, or other institution that would receive mail on behalf of SHARE. The home address of a committee member could be another possibility. A hospital address is particularly appropriate, since someone is apt to be available at all times.

Organizing members should have their phone numbers listed on the brochure, calling cards, and other materials used by the group.

Because people seem to phone more readily than write, a listing should be included in the phone directory if possible.

SHARE's main expenses are phone calls, correspondence, printed materials, and a newsletter. Since SHARE has no membership dues or fees, the main source of monies has been fund-raising. SHARE has also received donations from groups and individuals. Professionals often donate their time or provide their services as part of their job. St. John's Hospital has provided a meeting place and has given other support as well. Library books for the group are often donated by parents in the memory of babies. Members of the SHARE group take turns providing refreshments at the meetings.

PUBLICATIONS

Many publications are available at the SHARE office at St. John's. Some of these include:

Starting Your Own SHARE Group, a manual

The SHARE Newsletter, a bimonthly newsletter with resources, new developments relating to perinatal bereavement, and writings by bereaved parents (available to bereaved parents and other interested persons at no charge)

An updated list of perinatal loss support groups in the United States and in other countries

A listing of pamphlets and other printed materials relating to perinatal loss

Information on audio-visuals relating to perinatal loss

Most materials are available at a nominal charge.

FURTHER INFORMATION

For further information write to St. John's Hospital, 800 E. Carpenter, Springfield, IL 62769 or call (217) 544–6464 (ext. 5275).

Chapter 32

National Sudden Infant Death Syndrome Foundation

This chapter was written with information and assistance provided by Penny Williamson, Sc.D., the Executive Vice President of the National Sudden Infant Death Syndrome Foundation.

Every year, approximately 7,000 babies in the United States die from a little understood phenomenon called sudden infant death syndrome (SIDS), more commonly known as crib death. The National Sudden Infant Death Syndrome Foundation (NSIDSF) is a nonprofit organization whose volunteers help parents cope with the shock and grief of losing their baby to SIDS and sponsor research to prevent and eliminate this tragedy.

HISTORY

The E. Jedd Roe, Jr., family of Connecticut lost their son to SIDS in 1962. Their dismay at the small amount of research on crib death, despite the mystery surrounding the disease, as well as the failure of other people to understand their grief led them to organize the first NSIDSF group. Now NSIDSF is a national organization with volunteer representatives in every state. It is organized in over 80 chapters and has area contacts and/or parent groups in locations where chapters are not yet chartered. NSIDSF is governed by a national board of trustees and has a medical advisory board to ensure integrity of the medical and health reputation of the foundation.

GOALS

The National Sudden Infant Death Syndrome Foundation has three major goals: to provide service to families who have lost infants to SIDS as well as to community members involved in their care; to provide education to professionals and public awareness of SIDS in general; and to promote the support of major research efforts in this field. NSIDSF works toward prevention and eventual elimination of SIDS as a major cause of death for infants through public education and support.

SERVICES

To reach its goals, NSIDSF targets three groups: (1) families in crisis through loss of a child to SIDS or because they have a child who has been placed on a home monitor because of prolonged apnea (breathing problems), (2) professionals whose work leads them into contact with SIDS families and victims, including police, ambulance staff, hospital emergency personnel, funeral directors, and clergy and pastoral counselors, and (3) the general public. Services NSIDSF provides its target groups include family outreach programs, educational work, promotion of research, and consumer advocacy.

Volunteers from NSIDSF throughout the United States donate an average of 84,000 hours monthly. They serve as contacts for parents who have lost their child to SIDS and, as a result, find it helpful to deal with their grief with other parents who understand it because of their own experiences. Chapters provide support groups for grieving parents and/or one-to-one contacts. In their educational role, NSIDSF volunteers conduct seminars and workshops on SIDS for health professionals, emergency personnel, counselors, and interested members of the community.

NSIDSF's medical advisory board interprets new discoveries and controversial issues for the public, while the media services department at the national office distributes over 500,000 pamphlets, articles, and brochures annually. NSIDSF also funds professional research projects and provides fellowships for graduate students who wish to explore the SIDS problem through clinical or laboratory investigations.

In its campaign against SIDS, NSIDSF acts as a consumer advocate at the federal, state, and local levels for families of SIDS victims and potential victims. As a consumer advocate, NSIDSF has:

- Called attention to this leading cause of infant mortality
- Brought about disease acceptance in both lay and medical fields
- Won inclusion of SIDS in the International Classification of Diseases That Cause Death
- Increased research into preventive measures and the search for a cure
- Supported medical evaluation programs for infants in high-risk categories
- Lobbied for federal legislation for family assistance and research into the disease
- Designed and implemented a program among health professionals for treatment of families of SIDS victims

PUBLICATIONS

NSIDSF publishes a bimonthly newsletter, *The Leaflet,* and a monthly *Executive Report.* The newsletter is free to all SIDS parents and costs $16 per year for other subscriptions.

FURTHER INFORMATION

For further information, referral to your nearest chapter, or to receive a NSIDSF newsletter, write to the National SIDS Foundation, 8240 Professional Place, Suite 205, Landover, MD 20785 or call (301) 459–3388 (Maryland residents) or 1–800–221–SIDS (outside of Maryland).

Chapter 33

The Candlelighters Childhood Cancer Foundation

Minna Newman Nathanson

Minna Newman Nathanson is director of publications for the Candlelighters Childhood Cancer Foundation and a consultant on the psychosocial needs of families of children with chronic life-threatening and handicapping conditions. A former early childhood educator, she had a son who died of leukemia in 1974.

The Candlelighters Childhood Cancer Foundation is an international peer-support network of groups of parents of children who have or have had cancer. Some of the children are newly diagnosed, some are in remission, some are in relapse, some are in treatment, some are long-term survivors, and some have died.

HISTORY

One of the first Candlelighters groups was formed in 1970 when a group of parents lobbied for the National Cancer Act. These parents discovered that their contacts with each other became very important. They supported each other, sharing information, reactions, and feelings of frustration, fear, hope, and accomplishment. They shared social occasions without being thought heartless or unfeeling because they were smiling, laughing, and having a good time. They demonstrated to each other that they could handle with strength and grace the difficulties of living with their children's life-threatening cancer.

The Candlelighters Childhood Cancer Foundation now includes over 200 parent groups and contacts throughout the world. In addition to parents, medical and social service professionals also participate in the groups. The foundation helps new groups form, links existing groups, and provides communication services and printed materials.

GOALS

Believing "It is better to light one candle than to curse the darkness," Candlelighters groups share these goals:

- To link parent to parent, family to family, group to group
- To ease frustrations and fears through sharing of feelings and experiences
- To exchange information on research, treatment, medical institutions, and community resources
- To break down the social isolation of families of children with cancer
- To provide guidance in coping with childhood cancer's effects on the child, the parent, the siblings, and the family unit
- To identify patient and family needs so that medical and social support systems respond adequately
- To seek consistent research funding
- To be an emotional support system of "second families" for each other

Members of Candlelighters groups share the shock of diagnosis, the questions about treatment, the anxiety of waiting, the despair at relapse, the hope of remission, the uncertainty as treatment ends, the joy of cure, and the grief at death. They support one another in these times of need—at diagnosis, before surgery, during hospitalization, upon relapse, when treatment ends, when a child becomes an adult, as death approaches, or during bereavement.

SERVICES

Support

Local Candlelighter groups serve as informal forums where parents share feelings, experiences, and information on life in a family with a child who has cancer. Candlelighters self-help groups allow parents to exchange expertise in areas from caring for a sick child and working with the medical system, to dealing with other family members, friends, and the community and seeking a normal life after the death of a child.

Some groups have youth auxiliaries for young patients and their siblings. These youth groups permit the same kind of sharing of questions, fears, hopes, accomplishments, and happy and sad times.

Although members of the Candlelighters group may hear some difficult truths, they hear them from people who accept and understand their questions and fears—from "experts" who have had the same questions and fears and can offer guidance. Bereaved parents learn from other parents that they, too, will be able to survive the loss of their child. They come to rely on an understanding support network that will be there for their family after the child dies. Sharing and supporting each other in the group also gives parents and children strength through finding that sharing one's own difficult times can help others.

Community Outreach

Local Candlelighters groups reach out to the community in many ways. Part of the goal of community outreach is for Candlelighters groups to share with the community what they have learned as parents of children with a serious life-threatening disease. They work to identify patient and family needs and communicate these needs to medical and social work professionals so that these professionals can understand the needs and respond appropriately. They also seek consistent and sufficient research funding.

Local groups may present speakers, panels, or conferences on childhood cancer or run forums for teachers, nursing students, hospice volunteers, and medical students. Some groups maintain libraries, publish newsletters and handbooks of local resources, and have members who serve on community boards and advisory committees. Some groups sponsor 24-hour crisis lines, buddy systems, parent-to-parent contacts, and referrals to professional counseling.

PUBLICATIONS

The Candlelighters Childhood Cancer Foundation's publications include the *Quarterly Newsletter, Youth Newsletter, Progress Reports* journal, and the annotated *Bibliography and Resource Guide*. The foundation promotes quality educational materials and serves as a clearinghouse on pediatric/adolescent cancer and on state and federal programs. The foundation's newsletters are available at no charge. A nominal fee is charged for other publications.

FURTHER INFORMATION

For more information on the Candlelighters Childhood Cancer Foundation and/or the closest local group write to The Candlelighters Childhood Cancer Foundation, Suite 1011, 2025 Eye Street, N. W., Washington, DC 20006 or call (202) 659–5136. The Candlelighters Childhood Cancer Foundation's free services and publications are supported by the American Cancer Society and by tax-exempt donations.

Chapter 34

Mothers Against Drunk Driving

Janice Harris Lord

Janice Harris Lord, M.S.S.W., is the Director of Victim Services for Mothers Against Drunk Driving. She is a licensed and certified social worker who received her degree from the University of Texas at Arlington. Ms. Harris Lord works with MADD chapters on a daily basis to help victims with their grief and guide them through the often frustrating judicial process. She also provides training for other groups who want to learn more about being effective helpers to crime victims.

The event is sudden, the cause is senseless, and the pain is deep. Each year, drunk drivers kill and seriously injure thousands of Americans. The victims—those who are injured and the families and friends of those injured or killed—must live with the aftermath of that loss or injury for the rest of their lives. Their grieving is intense and further aggravated when the criminal justice system fails to adequately deal with the perpetrator.

HISTORY

Mothers Against Drunk Driving (MADD) was founded by Candy Lightner whose 13-year-old daughter was killed by a repeat offender drunk driver in Fair Oaks, California, in 1980. Her anguish and outrage led her and her supporters to wage an aggressive campaign against drunk driving, which resulted in California passing the toughest drunk driving laws in the country at that time. Since then, the organization has become a nationwide nonprofit organization with over half a million members and supporters and has established itself as the cornerstone of America's highway safety movement, serving as "the voice of the victims" of alcohol-related crashes. Today there are about 400 MADD chapters in the United States. Several other similar groups have also organized, following MADD's lead, including Students Against Driving Drunk, Truckers Against Drunk Driving, and Bartenders Against Drunk Driving.

Through an extensive chapter network of victims and their advocates, MADD has developed and expanded public awareness and community education programs to teach Americans that drunk driving is socially unacceptable and criminal. One of MADD's major successes was the formation of the National Commission Against Drunk Driving, which MADD urged President Reagan to establish in 1982. MADD also was instrumental in passage of the National Minimum Drinking Age Act of 1984, which mandates sanctions against states that fail to raise their minimum drinking age to 21. MADD's strength is its chapter leaders and members, whose energy, creativeness, and dedication have enabled MADD to increase awareness, improve the judicial process, educate the citizenry, and aid victims of drunk and otherwise impaired driving.

GOALS

The goal of MADD is twofold: to support victims, their families, and friends in the aftermath of a drunk driving offense, and to create in the public consciousness a conviction that drunk or impaired driving is both socially unacceptable and criminal, so as to change policy, law, and social behavior to reflect that conviction.

SERVICES

Victim Services

Victims of alcohol-related crashes who ask MADD for help in dealing with their pain are assigned a companion family and/or a victim advocate. The victim advocate, usually another victim, will be with the family immediately after the crash or as soon as possible. Subsequently, victims are provided with regular phone and personal contact by the companion families and the victim advocates to support them through their grieving and adjustment process and their criminal court case.

Many MADD chapters have support groups for victims. These groups, usually co-led by a victim and a professional, are not meant as individual or group psychotherapy but are held to enable victims to help one another. The groups provide a safe setting for expression of the potent feelings of grief, such as anger, guilt, and rage.

MADD also provides information about victim rights under state law. Advice on procedures for obtaining crash reports, autopsy reports, and the driving record of the offender, as well as sources of financial assistance available to victims, are provided by MADD. MADD also will advise the victim family regarding interviews with investigating officers, victim/witness personnel, prosecuting attorneys, and probation departments and will assist families in preparing a Victim Impact Statement. (A Victim Impact Statement is a statement made by the victim or the victim family about the impact of the crash on their lives. It is presented after conviction but before sentencing of the defendant. Traditionally, only the defendant has been allowed to present statements that influence sentencing.) Victim advocates or other MADD members will also accompany the family to court and maintain follow-up contact after adjudication is complete.

MADD has made a significant contribution to victims' rights in the courts and in state law. Since MADD's inception, the number of state compensation programs allowing alcohol-impaired crash victims to qualify increased to 20, and the number of states calling for some degree of mandatory restitution increased to 32. MADD also has joined coalitions with other victim advocacy groups to increase the number of states with statutory victims' rights to 31. Written Victim Impact Statements are now allowed in 34 states and 11 states now allow oral Victim Impact Statements to be presented in court prior to sentencing of the convicted offender. Eight states now statutorily allow victims in the courtroom during trial, with some exceptions.

Public Awareness

MADD's goal of educating the public on the price and pain of drunk driving, so as to change social behavior and provide harsher penalties for drunk drivers, is accomplished both through the many local chapters and through the national headquarters. Chapters distribute literature and carry out nationally planned programs as well as media campaigns. They also offer trained speakers to address civic and professional organizations, community groups, legislatures, public and private industries, schools, and other interested groups on the issues of drunk driving and highway safety. Through its central office, MADD provides information to national media and concerned citizens who seek information about drunk driving. MADD maintains a resource library, with current data covering such topics as state legislation, victims' rights, civil liability, and other highway safety issues. Hundreds of requests for information are answered yearly and brochures, letters, and pamphlets, with topics ranging from statistics describing the extent of the drunk driving problem and the impact on victims to new methods to curtail the problem, are distributed to individuals and organizations. MADD also offers bumper stickers, MADD buttons, and Blood Alcohol Concentration charts to ensure continued visibility of the drunk driving issue in the public eye.

During the years since its inception, MADD has sponsored various special projects to raise the public consciousness about the destructiveness of drunk driving. These projects include the National Poster and Essay Contest, Project Graduation (designed to reduce teenage alcohol-related fatalities and injuries, and the annual Candlelight Vigil, in which thousands of MADD members and supporters gather to pay tribute to those dead or injured as the result of drunk driving crashes.

In the legal arena, MADD works for the enactment of harsher penalties for drunk drivers. MADD educates professionals in the criminal justice system about the needs and rights of alcohol-related crash victims. Its chapters encourage strict enforcement of anti-impaired driving and automobile occupant protection measures and promote public education activities that inform citizens about the impact of such laws. Specific projects MADD has been instrumental in implementing include an ongoing court monitoring program, in which MADD members view courtroom proceedings, and a case-watching program which follows cases from the time they are filed to see if they are being handled properly. MADD has also been responsible for formation of many state and local task forces to seek solutions to the impaired driving crisis. The majority of states and hundreds of local governments now have such task forces.

Legislative projects MADD is working on include:

- Establishment of victim compensation funds in all 50 states, to provide government sources of compensation for financial losses and expenses of injured victims and their families
- Victims' bill of rights to ensure that alcohol-related crash victims (as well as other crime victims) have guaranteed rights within the criminal justice system
- The practice of administrative revocation of drivers' licenses, a procedure which suspends at the time of arrest the driving privileges of people caught driving with an illegal concentration of alcohol in their bodies
- License plate confiscation for repeat offenders
- Open container laws in states without such legislation, prohibiting drivers and passengers from consuming alcoholic beverages while in an automobile
- Dramshop legislation allowing crash victims and survivors to sue drinking establishments and private hosts who serve alcoholic beverages to intoxicated drivers
- Changing the definition of legally drunk from .10 percent or higher blood alcohol concentration level to .08 percent

ORGANIZING A MADD CHAPTER

People wishing to organize a MADD chapter must go through a formal application process. They must meet and talk with judges, prosecuting attorneys, police officers, state troopers or the highway patrol, and probation officers. Twenty-three questions about the issue of drunk driving must be answered, along with an additional dozen questions about the MADD organization itself. The purpose of this research effort is to assure that chapter organizers are aware of the situation in their communities and are knowledgeable spokespersons regarding the issues of drunk driving and MADD's goals as an organization. Twenty dues-paying members (victims do not pay dues) must be enlisted before the chapter may be chartered.

PUBLICATIONS

MADD publishes a national newsletter, a chapter newsletter, and numerous brochures as well as a videotape entitled *Only You Share My Pain.*

The national newsletter, which comes out quarterly, highlights current events and offers regular columns such as "Voice of the Victim," "Impaired Driving Update," and "Chapter Highlights." Brochures include *Your Grief: You're Not Going Crazy, Helping Children Cope With Death in the Family, Victims' Rights in Alcohol Impaired Crashes,* and *The Unique Grief of Parents.* The *Victim Information Pamphlet,* which offers an overview of the judicial process in drunk driving cases and the services MADD provides to victims, is also available. MADD and the American Trauma Society have recently co-published a brochure for hospital emergency rooms.

FURTHER INFORMATION

MADD welcomes inquiries regarding impaired driving issues and requests for informational materials. Please address inquiries to MADD, Attn: Inquiries Department, 669 Airport Freeway, Suite 310, Hurst, TX 76053 or call (817) 268–6233.

Chapter 35

Concerned United Birthparents, Inc.

This chapter was written with information and assistance provided by Carole Anderson, M.S.W., J.D., the President of Concerned United Birthparents, Inc.

Adoption is often viewed as a happy solution to the problem of an unwanted or unplanned pregnancy. The baby is provided with a good home, the adoptive parents are able to at last have a child to raise, and the birthmother, who often is young and single, will not have the problems of raising a child alone. That view of adoption overlooks the fact that adoption may not be a happy choice for the birthmother, or perhaps, due to family pressure, not the birthmother's choice at all. Concerned United Birthparents, Inc. (CUB) recognizes that the loss of a child to adoption may be as real, as devastating, and as permanent a loss as death. It recognizes that while life may go on for the birthmother, as it does for other bereaved parents, it will never be the same; that adoption-bereaved parents, like other parents who have lost a child, need to grieve their loss rather than pretend they feel no pain, and that birthparents need to be recognized as parents in order to deal with the feelings of anger, bitterness, and loss the adoption of their child causes. To that end, CUB was organized.

HISTORY

United Birthparents was founded in Massachusetts in 1976 when four birthmothers who met through adoption reform activities identified a need for mutual support among birthparents and a concomitant need to educate people about the effects of adoption and resulting separation on birthparents and other family members. Thus, CUB was organized as a mutual help organization intended to assist adoption-separated relatives (particularly parents), as well as to prevent unnecessary family separations by adoption and to humanize adoptions that are necessary. There are approximately 40 CUB groups today.

GOALS

Concerned United Birthparents believes that thoughts about the birth family profoundly influence family members even if the families are separated. CUB's members know firsthand the pain of separation experienced by birthparents, adopted children, other children who lose the opportunity to grow up with their siblings, and extended family members, and therefore CUB feels a strong obligation to support families threatened with unnecessary separation. CUB has a strong interest and concern in preventing teen pregnancy, in making available accurate and complete information about all alternatives and resources for people with unplanned pregnancies, and in providing support for families at risk of separation through adoption.

CUB is also concerned with how adoptions are handled. It views adoption as the blending of two families, and thus encourages changes in agency policies and in legislation in order to meet the needs of adopted children, adoptive parents, and birthparents. Honesty and openness are essential in adoption so that all parties can respect each other and appreciate the place that both adoptive and birthparents have in the child's life.

SERVICES

Concerned United Birthparents maintains a reunion registry to match adoption-separated relatives who both register. Members assist one another in searching for relatives, in preparing for what they may find, and in coping with the effects of separation, adoption, search, rejection, and reunion on their lives and those of their families. CUB branches hold support meetings and search workshops. Most branches also maintain libraries of adoption-related material for members, and provide speakers to community groups to educate people about adoption and family separation issues.

WHO PARTICIPATES

Birthparents are the primary constituency of CUB, but adult adoptees also make up a sizable proportion of the membership. Adoptive parents, adoption-separated brothers and sisters, professionals and others who support the goals of CUB are also members. However, to ensure that the organization retains its focus on birthparents, only birthparents may serve as national officers and directors and branch coordinators. Nonbirthparent members may participate in all other ways, including serving on committees and directing projects.

MEETINGS

While meetings vary among branches, all begin with reading a uniform opening statement that describes the organization and its purposes, typically followed by a brief business meeting. Members then share their experiences and their ideas for helping others cope with adoption-related problems they are facing. Guest speakers are often invited and special programs are common.

PUBLICATIONS

Concerned United Birthparents publishes a newsletter that concentrates on birthparent support issues. All members are entitled to receive

CUB's newsletter for a year. Renewal members also receive an additional publication designed to provide more information on group and organizational activities. A list of publications, pamphlets, and papers is available from CUB headquarters.

FURTHER INFORMATION

For further information send $1 and a self-addressed business-size envelope to CUB, Inc., Attn: J. Fenton, Machinists' Building, 2000 Walker, Des Moines, IA 50317 or call (515) 262–9120.

Chapter 36

The Samaritans/
Safe Place

Carolyn Benedict Drew

Carolyn Benedict Drew has been the Executive Director of The Samaritans for 7 years. She started the Safe Place in Rhode Island. Presently she is Vicechair of the State of Rhode Island Task Force for the Lt. Governor. She is an executive member representing the United States and Canada to Befrienders, an international organization for suicide prevention.

One person dies from suicide somewhere in the world every 80 seconds. That is 1,100 people a day and over 300,000 people a year. Safe Place is a self-help group for people who are grieving another person's suicide. Survivors of suicide victims are often left with feelings of guilt, fear, and anger, coupled with the tremendous pain of an untimely, often unexpected, and always shocking death. Safe Place, a subsidiary organization of Samaritans, Inc., which is a group of volunteers organized worldwide to prevent suicide, gives the survivor, whether family members, friends, or significant others, the opportunity to share, and perhaps lessen, the unique grief that follows a suicide.

HISTORY

The Samaritans, the parent organization of Safe Place, was founded in England in 1953 to befriend the suicidal, the despairing, and the lonely. Its growth since then has been phenomenal. There are now 175 Samaritans branches and 22,000 volunteers in Britain alone, and the suicide rate there has dropped 38% in 12 years. The Samaritans' international group, Befrienders International Samaritans Worldwide, had over 110 branches in 25 nations, from Brazil to Zimbabwe, 10 years after its inauguration in 1974. Safe Place, organized by Samaritans exclusively for survivors of suicide victims and based on a model developed by Thomas A. Welch in Somerville, Massachusetts, has had similar success. Its counseling and hot line services are now offered by 6 of the 14 Samaritans centers in the United States.

GOALS

While the primary purpose of Samaritans is to befriend the suicidal and thus prevent suicide, the goal of Safe Place is to help survivors through the emotional crisis following a suicide. Safe Place is:

- A group of caring people who have experienced and who are still experiencing the pain of suicide
- A place to talk, cry, and scream in confidence with people you can trust
- People helping people through mutual understanding and support
- An organization offering hope in tomorrow

SERVICES

Because suicide is still a major taboo in our society, the survivor rarely has an appropriate support system. Family and friends often refuse to listen to what the survivor needs to say. During a Safe Place meeting, the survivor has an opportunity to talk about the way his loved one died and his reactions to the death then and now. If the survivor found the suicide, he needs to verbally express the exact details. The painful, visual memories need to be discussed, and Safe Place offers a forum for that discussion.

It is a painful irony that many survivors feel suicidal following the suicide of a loved one. Safe Place volunteers discuss suicidal feelings with Safe Place members—the majority of whom feel suicidal at some time during the lengthy recovery—in a way that reduces the shame they are feeling.

MEETINGS

Each Safe Place meeting begins with an opening statement by the facilitator, who may or may not be a survivor of a suicide victim.

> Each of us comes here asking for time to speak, possibly for a safe place to cry—or to express thoughts or feelings that seem harsh, or cynical, or "unkind." If someone needs time to formulate thoughts or explore feelings please don't infringe on that space by giving advice, responding too quickly, or trying to answer unanswerable questions.
> Let's make an effort to discern what kind of support others want by listening carefully to what they say. The best support seems to come when you tell the group how it was and is for you. By sharing your experience you can help us. And please hold in confidence what we share here tonight. Uplifted by one another's caring, we believe that we can pick up the pieces ourselves, and live more richly because of the gift of compassionate hearts.

Members are then encouraged to openly discuss feelings or to remain silent, absorbing what others have to say, if they feel more comfortable with that role or are not yet ready to share their experiences. At the end of a meeting the following statement is read:

> We come here to be with people who understand our struggle and our hurt; they too have tears in their hands and pain in their hearts. This is a sacred place where we can explore our feelings, our loneliness, our shock, our anger, our guilt, our sadness or whatever is hurting us inside. This is a place where we can share our humanity and find strength and inspiration in each other. For all of us, life remains a mystery and we can only choose to trust and to love; we cannot choose to know, we cannot choose for others. Although we remain deeply wounded people, let us find comfort and healing in what we believe and in our ability to care for each other.

Safe Place meets twice a month. Members of Safe Place may come and go as they wish. There are no contracts or expectations. Some members come twice a month in the beginning, others come when a special event like a birthday, anniversary, or holiday is approaching. Some members return after a lapse of time to share their growth and to assure new members that living becomes easier, that with time the pain will lessen.

As one mother said a year after her son's suicide, "I only wish people would remember my son as how he lived, not how he died." Safe Place offers survivors a safe place to remember how a loved one lived and helps the survivor find a way to live through the pain.

FURTHER INFORMATION

To receive further information on Safe Place, please write to The Samaritans, 33 Chestnut Street, Providence, RI 02903 or call (401) 272–4044 or your nearest Samaritans Center.

Chapter 37

Child Find
of America, Inc.

Carolyn Zogg

Carolyn Zogg is the Associate Director of Child Find of America, Inc. A graduate of Syracuse University with a B.A. degree, Ms. Zogg is also a licensed lay reader in the Episcopal Diocese of New York.

Child Find is one of the oldest, private, nonprofit agencies that registers, searches for, and assists in the location of missing children across the nation. Because Child Find believes that a missing child is everyone's responsibility, it also seeks to increase awareness of the issue of missing children through public education.

HISTORY

Child Find was founded in 1980 by a searching parent. It located its first child in 1981 through a story and pictures in *Ladies Home Journal*. Since then, Child Find has assisted in the location of more than 1,400 children, or about 33% of the children registered with Child Find.

SERVICES

Child Find provides four major services:

1. Location services for families searching for their missing children
2. Educational programs for the general public
3. Counseling services for the families of missing children
4. Mediation services for parents in conflict over child custody

Location

Child Find registers stranger-abducted and parentally abducted children and runaways to age 18. Registration is accepted from parents with legal custody, court-ordered visitation rights, or documentation of a runaway's existence. There is no registration fee; a $10 one-time donation for reproduction of photographs is requested. Preregistration and referrals may be made by calling (914) 255-1848 Monday through Friday during business hours.

Information and photographs of missing children are compiled into the *Directory of Missing Children*. Because the majority of missing children will be in schools, the directory is distributed to public and private schools around the nation to aid school personnel in spotting the children. Twenty children included in the directory were located in 1985 through distribution to schools. Child Find plans to expand distribution of the directory to every U.S. law enforcement agency, hospital, and school. Photographs of registered children are also distributed daily to commercial businesses, who publicize them on television, in newspapers and magazines, and even on paper bags, milk cartons, and cereal boxes.

Child Find sponsors a toll-free hot line (1-800-I-AM-LOST) for calls from people who think they have spotted a missing child and from the abducted children themselves. Between June of 1984 and 1985, 26,000 calls identifying possible missing children were received on the hot line. The following 12 guidelines are helpful for people who think that they have spotted a missing child:

1. Try to find out the child's name. (Birth date is helpful too.)
2. Make careful note of the child's appearance, especially identifying marks, moles, pierced ears, scars, etc.
3. Remember the description of the person(s) the child was with.
4. Record the license plate number, the state, and the description of the car.
5. Try to learn what school the child is enrolled in and where it is located. If the child has just moved to the area, try to learn what school he/she came from and in what city and state it was located.
6. Try to learn the address of the child and how long he/she has been in the area.
7. Many abducted children have their hair dyed to alter their appearance. Look for this.
8. Abducted children are often withdrawn, shy, and nervous.
9. Abducted youngsters are usually accompanied by an adult and have few friends their own age.
10. Follow your instincts. If something seems unusual, follow through.
11. If a child asks for help, act immediately.
12. Contact the police if you are certain there is a suspicious situation.

These guidelines are offered solely as suggestions and are not to be thought of as proof positive or fact. Every case is unique and people should be cautious and mature when dealing with these issues.

Child Find's location department is staffed by professional law enforcement officers and criminal justice education graduates who actively search for missing children through networking on leads from the hot line with other agencies searching for children and law enforcement agencies.

Education

Child Find's public education program is aimed at increasing awareness on the issue of missing children, assisting in the location of missing children, helping to prevent abductions, and publicizing the issue of parental kidnapping to make parents and the public more aware of the trauma that results to the children involved. Part of the public education program is carried out by Friends of Child Find (FOCF), a nationwide organization of volunteers who work at the community level to publicize the issue of missing children and distribute prevention information to parents and children. Each chapter designs the programs that will best serve the needs of their community. FOCF also lobbies for legislation and publicizes abducted children.

Eight tips that Child Find recommends to parents to help prevent abductions follow:

1. Arrange for your child's school to contact you if your child has not arrived by 9:30 A.M., if possible. Do this for all age children.
2. Phone school if your child is to be absent from school before roll call or homeroom attendance is checked. Again, do this for all age children.
3. Notify the school principal if the child is to be picked up from school. *Never* allow a child to be transported without prior *written* notification by the parent to the school authorities specifying the name of the person who will pick up your child.
4. Screen and reference baby-sitters and daycare centers. *Always* check references.
5. See your child safely onto transportation or make reliable arrangements before the school year begins. Ditto coming home. Who is greeting your child at the end of the school day?
6. Do not display the child's name on schoolbags, T-shirts, or jewelry.
7. Practice phone dialing. For beginners (K–2 grades), teach them their full name, address, phone number *with* area code. Have them make actual phone calls for practice. And, teach them the Child Find number (1-800-I-AM-LOST) to call for help.
8. A stranger can be someone you know. Teach the child NOT TO SPEAK TO STRANGERS. Remember the wolf in grandmother's nightgown in the story *Little Red Riding Hood*. Teach the child to run away to safety. Children speak to children, not to adults.

Counseling

Informal counseling for searching parents has always been provided by the Child Find staff. A new, more formal, program to help parents deal with the stress of having a missing child and cope with their own lives while the child is missing has been started under the directorship of the mother of a missing child. This program is also aimed at helping children deal with the stress of a missing sibling.

Mediation

Child Find, in conjunction with the Council and the Institute for Mediation, sponsors a program to help parents resolve custody disputes. This program began in 1986 in Florida and will be expanded across the nation.

PUBLICATIONS

The *Child Find Bulletin* is a bimonthly newsletter containing information about successful locations of children, volunteer projects, and important news in the area of missing children. The newsletter is free to those who send their name and address and request to be put on the mailing list. *The Dispatch* is a bimonthly newsletter containing organizational information and volunteer news. It is free to all FOCF volunteers. *Color Me Safe* is a coloring book that teaches safety tips to avoid abduction. Five thousand copies were distributed in 1984–85. The cost is $2.50. The *Childfinder Kit* is a kit of awareness/prevention materials and registration forms. The cost is $10 plus postage and handling. The *Directory of Missing Children* contains over 825 photographs of missing children. The cost is $10 plus postage and handling. The directory is distributed free to schools.

FURTHER INFORMATION

For further information write to Child Find of America, Inc., P. O. Box 277, New Paltz, New York, NY 12561 or call (914) 255–1848. Donations are tax deductible.

Epilog

The end of this book I hope marks the beginning of the realization of the two major goals of this work. The first, and most important goal, specifically concerns the unique case of the bereaved parent, while the second, an outgrowth of the first, pertains to a general issue for the entire thanatological field.

The primary goal of this book has been twofold—to acquaint caregivers with the experience of parental loss of a child and to promote more appropriate clinical interventions and therapeutic support for these bereaved parents. More appropriate interventions and support will be based upon the establishment of more realistic expectations for parents' coping and a recognition of the unique issues that make current conceptualizations of mourning and criteria for pathological grief less applicable to bereaved parents.

The issue of parental loss of a child has come into increasingly sharp focus given the decrease in infant and child mortality, the increase in accidental death and suicide among children and adolescents, and the increased longevity of adults, which results in more parents living to witness the deaths of their adult children. Consequently, when dealing with bereaved parents, it is incumbent upon caregivers of all disciplines and upon concerned lay persons not only to have an understanding of grief and mourning in general, but specifically to:

1. Be able to manage their own personal anxieties about the loss of a child so that they do not interfere with appropriate support and treatment of bereaved parents.
2. Have a sufficient appreciation for and sensitivity to the unique issues and impacts of the death of a child on bereaved parents and their experiences of grief and adaptation over time.
3. Have an increased awareness that this type of loss is sufficiently dissimilar from other losses so that it cannot be evaluated in terms of traditional models of mourning and criteria for diagnosis of pathology.

537

4. Have the knowledge and skills necessary to offer therapeutic assistance to bereaved parents.
5. Know what self-help groups or professional resources to refer bereaved parents to and when to refer them.

These are stiff and demanding requisites but necessary ones if care-givers are to help parents cope with this unparalleled loss and the trauma it generates.

From the indepth examination of the issues involved in parental loss of a child has sprung a more general secondary goal of this book. The inexplicability of the loss of a child via traditional models, criteria, and conceptualizations of grief and mourning makes it abundantly clear that we *must* begin to discriminate among losses more carefully. We must revise and hone what we know about grief and mourning, most of which has derived from the analysis of conjugal bereavement, and make it more applicable to nonconjugal losses. Different types of loss will create different types of bereavement and, within similar types of loss, individuals will mourn differently depending upon a host of idiosyncratic psychological, social, and physiological factors. As profes-sionals, we must do more than pay mere lip service to the fact that there are differences among grief experiences. We must start to develop new models and must carefully design our therapeutic interventions to reflect awareness of this critical fact. To rigidly adhere to particular models which fail to account for the issues and dynamics of a given loss, to sustain expectations for grief that are inappropriate for a specific person, to intervene in an individual's mourning with strategies that are not carefully chosen for the particular griever will not help and can actually hurt the bereaved individual we seek to assist. The time has come for clinical thanatology to move from the general conceptualiza-tions to the specific and idiosyncratic. Our field and our patients/clients will be better because of it. In conclusion, I hope that the information in this volume will have a positive impact on bereaved parents, their caregivers, and the entire field of thanatology.

Index

Balance, family. *See* Equilibrium
Befrienders International Samaritans
    Worldwide. *See* Samaritans
Bereavement committees, 470
Bereavement, defined, 343
Bereavement models, limitations of, 24
Bereavement overload, 12, 64, 232. *See
    also* Mourning; Grief; Stress
Biological continuation, loss of, 32
Biological mother as appropriate term in
    adoption, 259
Birthmother as appropriate term in
    adoption, 259
Birth order as factor in grief, 323
Blame as related to guilt, 155
Blaming and grief, 420–421
Bondage to deceased, 63
Bonding, pre-birth, 77, 131, 176, 246,
    433

Caffeine. *See* Drugs
Cancer
    and anticipatory grief during relapse
        period, 193–194
    family feelings during remission of,
        193
    reactions to diagnosis of, 193
Candlelighters Childhood Cancer
    Foundation, 33, 514–516
Caregiver
    assistance of, in accommodating to
        loss, 396–400
    expressions to be avoided by, 92
    as facilitator:
        anticipatory grief, 91
        communication between bereaved
            spouses, 389
    feelings of helplessness in, 380–381
    goal of, in normal grief intervention,
        376
    and health professionals:
        grief facilitation strategies, 78
        interdisciplinary approach, 90–91
        post-death support for parents, 82
    in hospitals as needed presence, 92
    and medical professionals:
        caregivers' feelings about, 460
        parents' disillusionment with, 461
    protocol for, 90–93
    qualifications of, 342, 349
    role of:
        in abortion, 249–254
        with bereaved mothers, 311–312
        with family of missing child, 274–
            275

Caregiver, role of—*cont'd*
    in missing in action loss, 287–288
    after SIDS death, 176–177
    and suffering siblings, 87–88
    support for grief process, 391–396
    support for parents' emotional
        reinvestment, 400–402
    See also Medical professionals;
        Professionals; Therapeutic
        intervention
Cemetery, visits to, 319
Center for Prisoners of War Studies
    (CPWS), 279
Child Find of America, Inc., 532–535
Children
    attending sibling's funeral, 334
    and dying sibling, 333–334
    explaining death to, 328–329:
        effects of avoidance, 329
        effects of sympathetic approach,
            328
        religious approaches, 328–329
        simple and direct language, 329
        suggestions, 332
    family's influence on grief of, 330–
        332
    grief reactions of, 329
    guidelines for therapy for, 333–334
    lack of advocate for, in crisis situation,
        333
    See also Siblings
Children, dying
    pre-bereavement support for families
        of, 84–85
    See also Infant death; Neonatal death;
        Newborn death; SIDS death;
        Stillbirth
Child's room as shrine, 71
Chronic grief, 62, 226–227, 366, 407–
    408
    motives for, 408
Chronic illness, 73, 432
    and advantages of pre-death
        intervention, 195, 196–197
    and after-death intervention
        strategies, 196, 197–199
    anticipatory mourning for, 193
    involvement of family members in, 197
    and parental reactions to impending
        death, 194–195
    and role of counselor, 197
Clergy
    and funeral planning, 470
    and funeral sermons, 470
    grief for newborn discounted by, 148